# 2019
# 青岛统计年鉴
# QINGDAO STATISTICAL YEARBOOK

（总 第40期 VOL.40）

青 岛 市 统 计 局
国家统计局青岛调查队 编
QINGDAO MUNICIPAL STATISTICS BUREAU
NBS SURVEY OFFICE IN QINGDAO

中国统计出版社
China Statistics Press

**图书在版编目（CIP）数据**

青岛统计年鉴．2019 / 青岛市统计局，国家统计局青岛调查队编．-- 北京：中国统计出版社，2019.7
ISBN 978-7-5037-8827-7

Ⅰ．①青… Ⅱ．①青… ②国… Ⅲ．①统计资料－青岛－2019－年鉴 Ⅳ．①C832.523-54

中国版本图书馆 CIP 数据核字 (2019) 第 122109 号

**青岛统计年鉴 -2019**

作　　者 / 青岛市统计局　国家统计局青岛调查队
责任编辑 / 钟　钰
装帧设计 / 青岛双福文化传播有限公司
出版发行 / 中国统计出版社有限公司
地　　址 / 北京市丰台区西三环南路甲 6 号
邮政编码 / 100073
电　　话 / 邮购（010）63376909　书店（010）68783171
网　　址 / http://csp.stats.gov.cn
印　　刷 / 青岛任缘印刷包装有限公司
经　　销 / 新华书店
开　　本 / 890mm×1240mm　1/16
字　　数 / 1130 千字
印　　张 / 26.375
版　　别 / 2019 年 7 月第 1 版
版　　次 / 2019 年 7 月第 1 次印刷
定　　价 / 280.00 元

如有印装差错，由本社发行部调换。

## 全市生产总值构成（%）

Composition Of Gross Domestic Product（%）

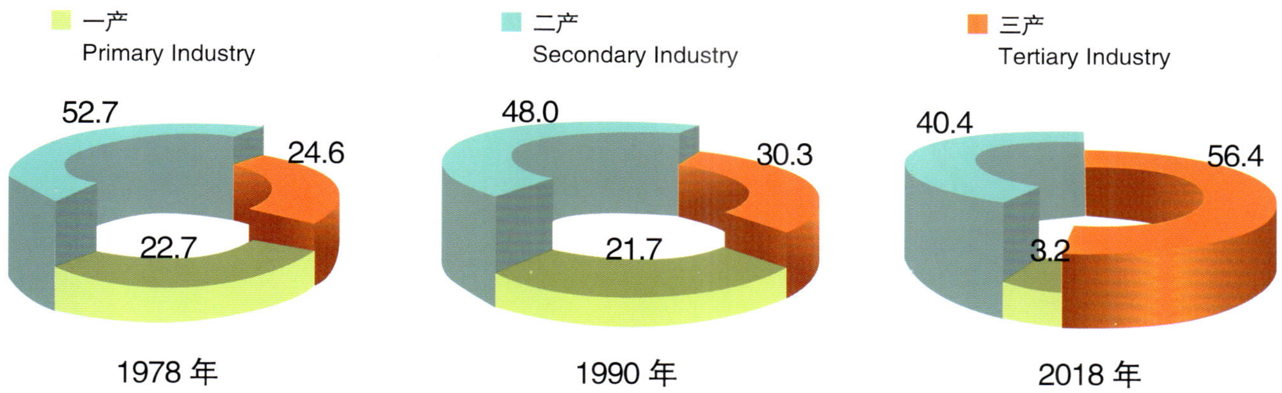


## 全市生产总值（亿元）

Gross Domestic Product（100 million yuan）

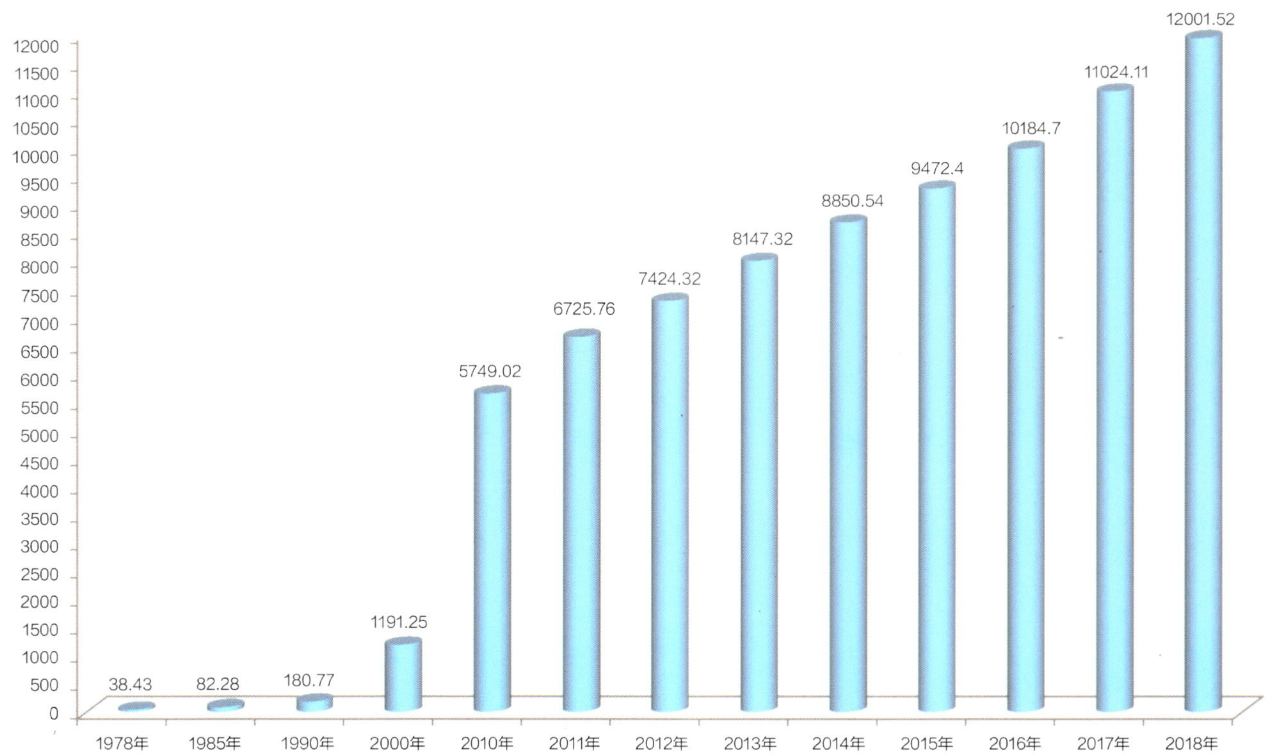

## 农林牧渔业总产值（亿元）

Gross Output Value Of Agriculture（100 million yuan）

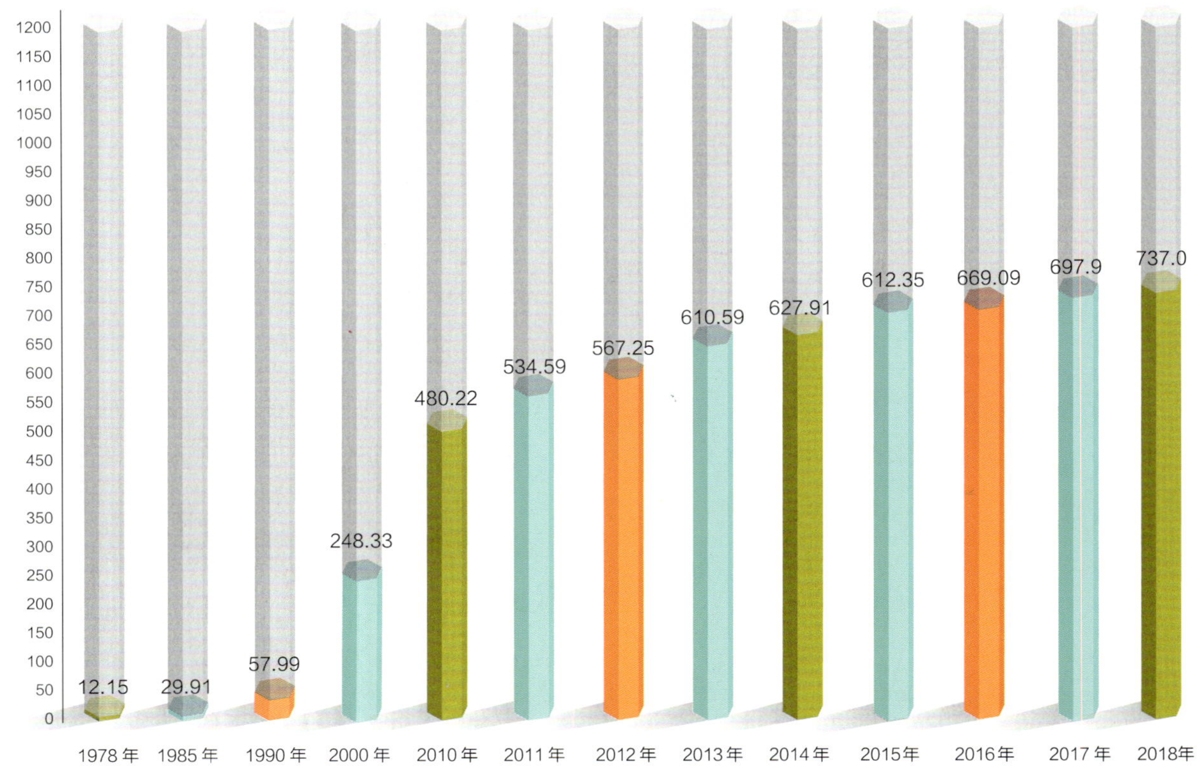


## 主要农产品产量（万吨）

Output Of Farm Products（10 000 tons）

## 工业总产值（亿元）

Gross Industrial Output Value（100 million yuan）

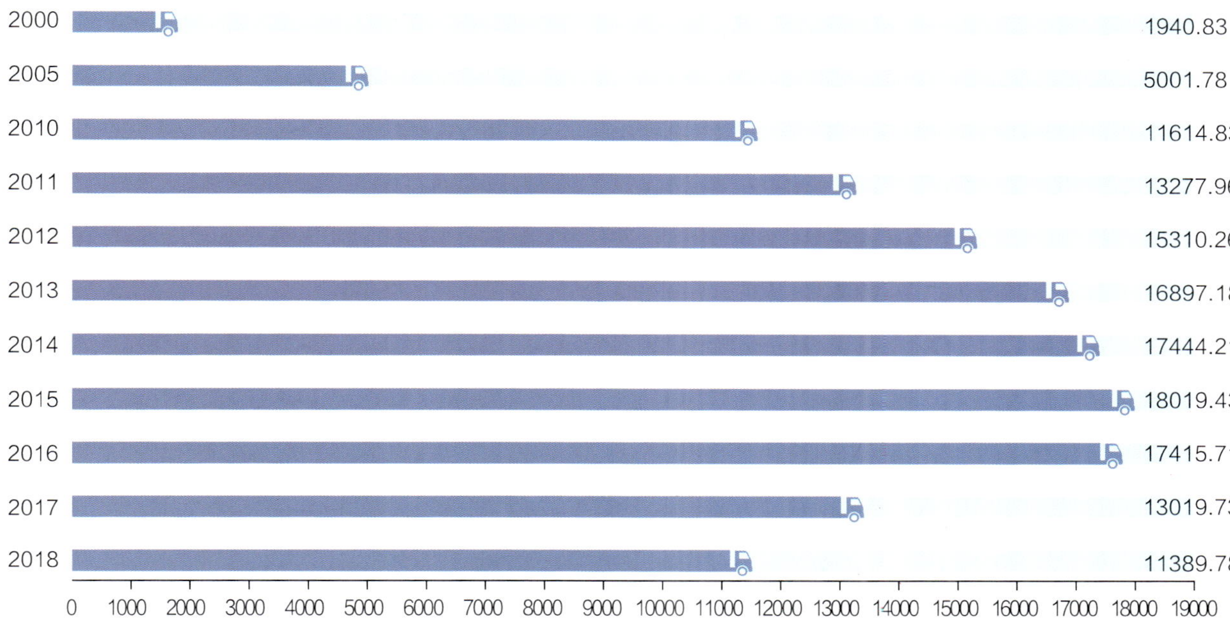


## 规模以上工业实现利润总额（亿元）

The Total Profits Made By The Industries Above The Designated Size（100 million yuan）

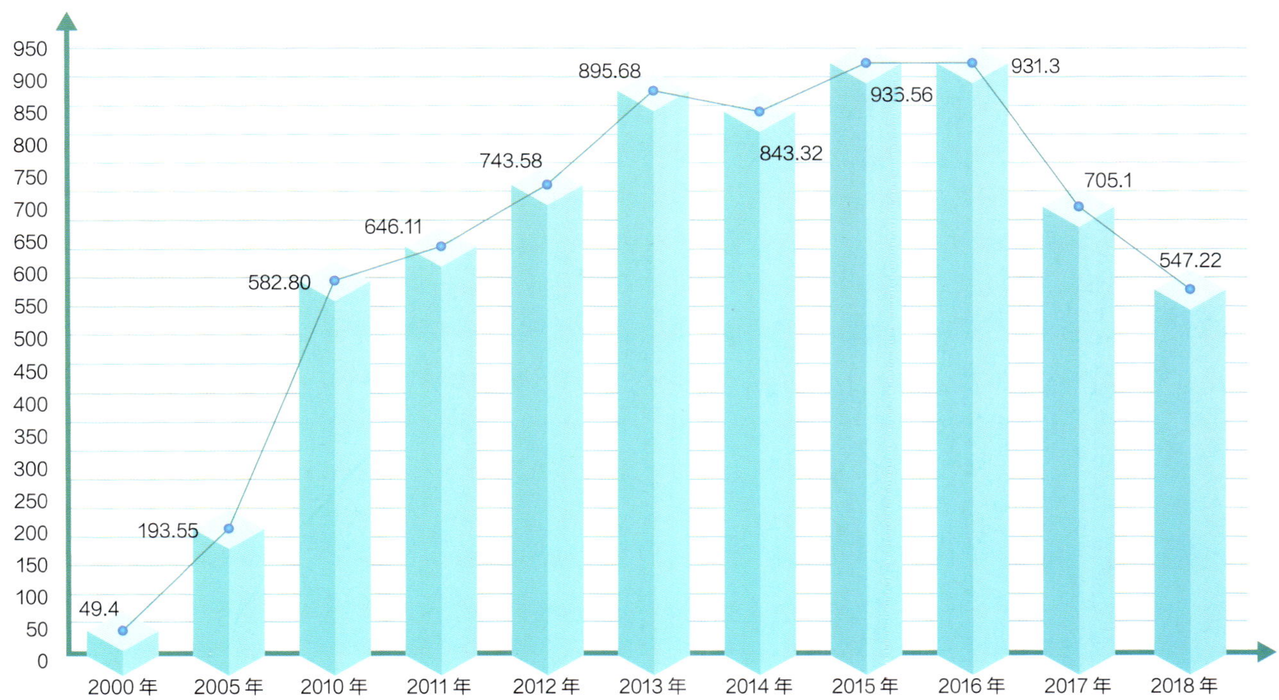

## 房地产开发投资（亿元）

Investrment In Real Estate Development（100 million yuan）

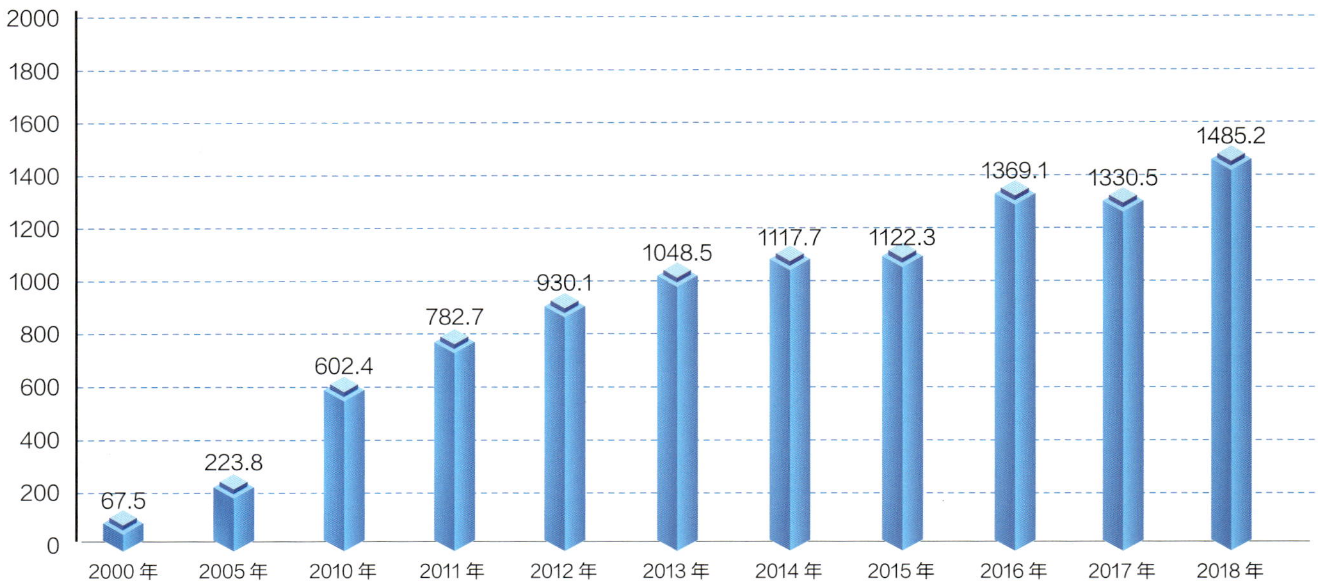


## 房屋销售面积（万平方米）

Floor Space Of Commercial Buildings Sold（10 000 sq.m）

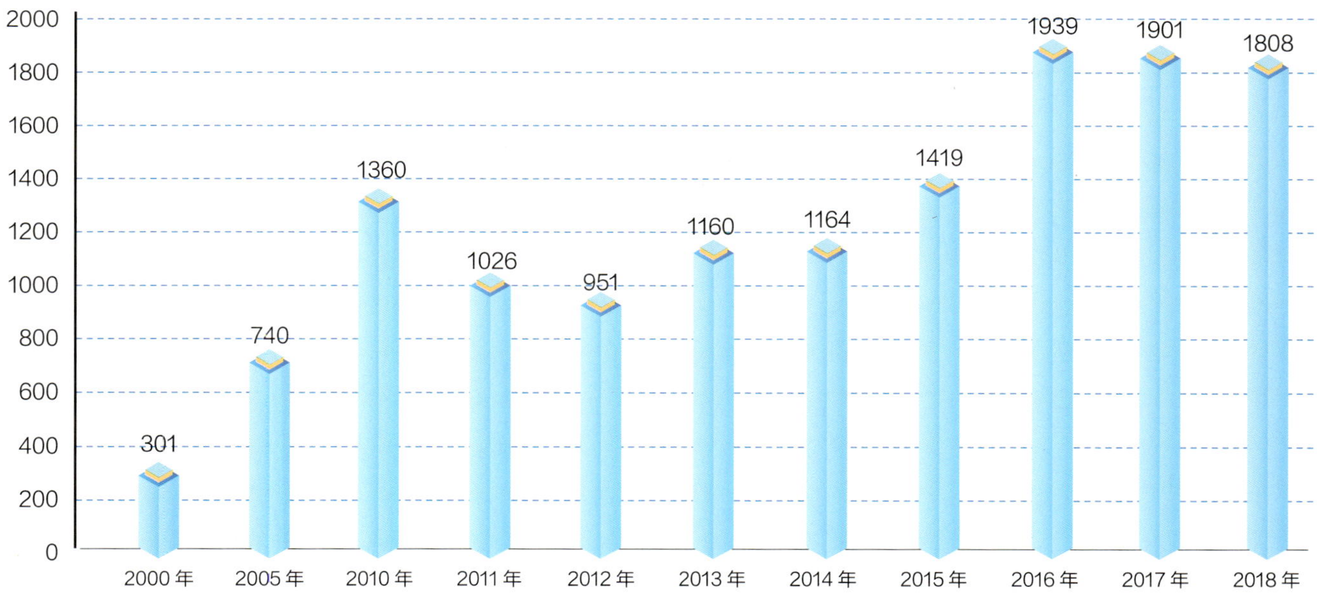

## 消费构成（%）（2018 年）

2018 Composition Of Consumption（%）

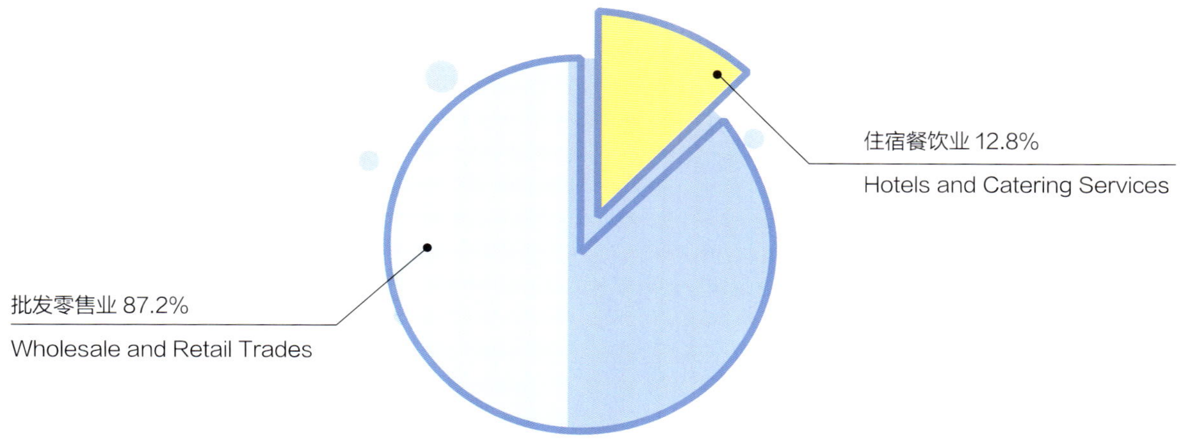


## 社会消费品零售总额（亿元）

Total Retail Sales Of Consumer Goods（100 million yuan）

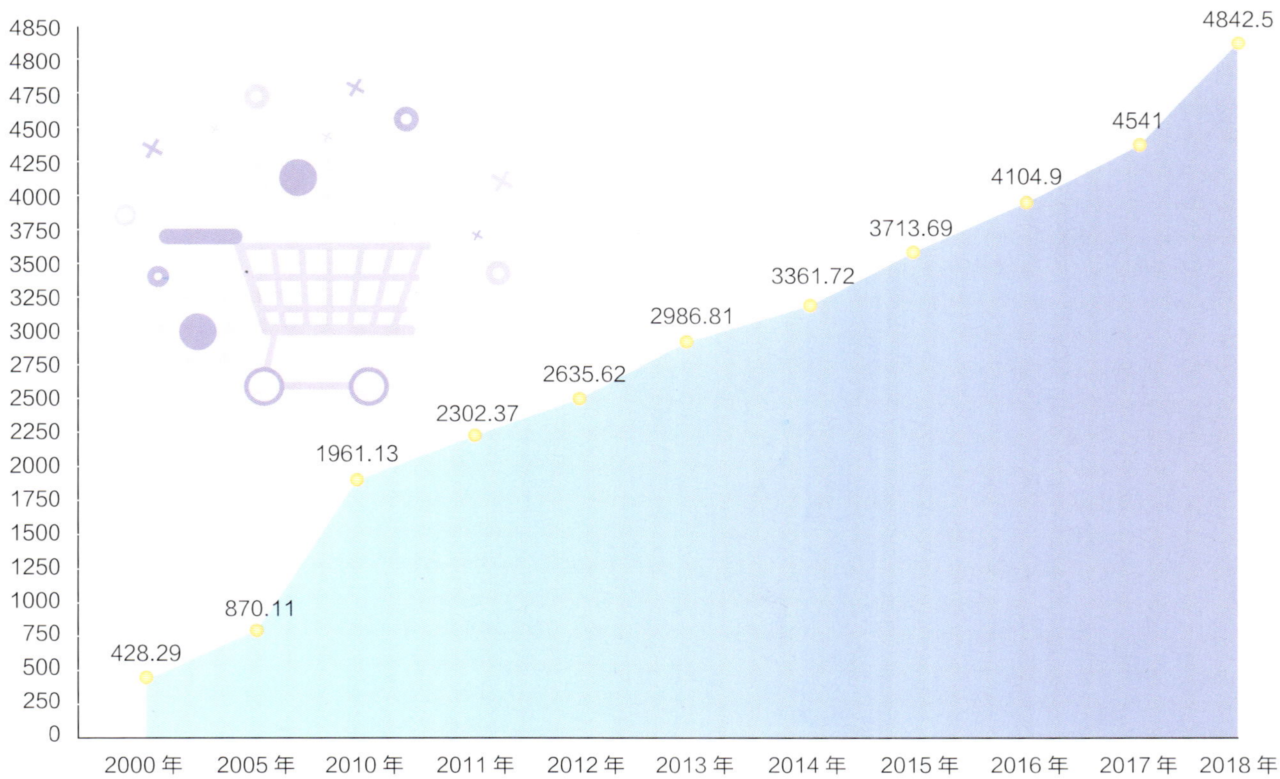

## 旅游总人数（万人次）

Number Of Tourists（10 000 person-times）

入境旅游人数

Number Of Oversea Visitor Arrivals

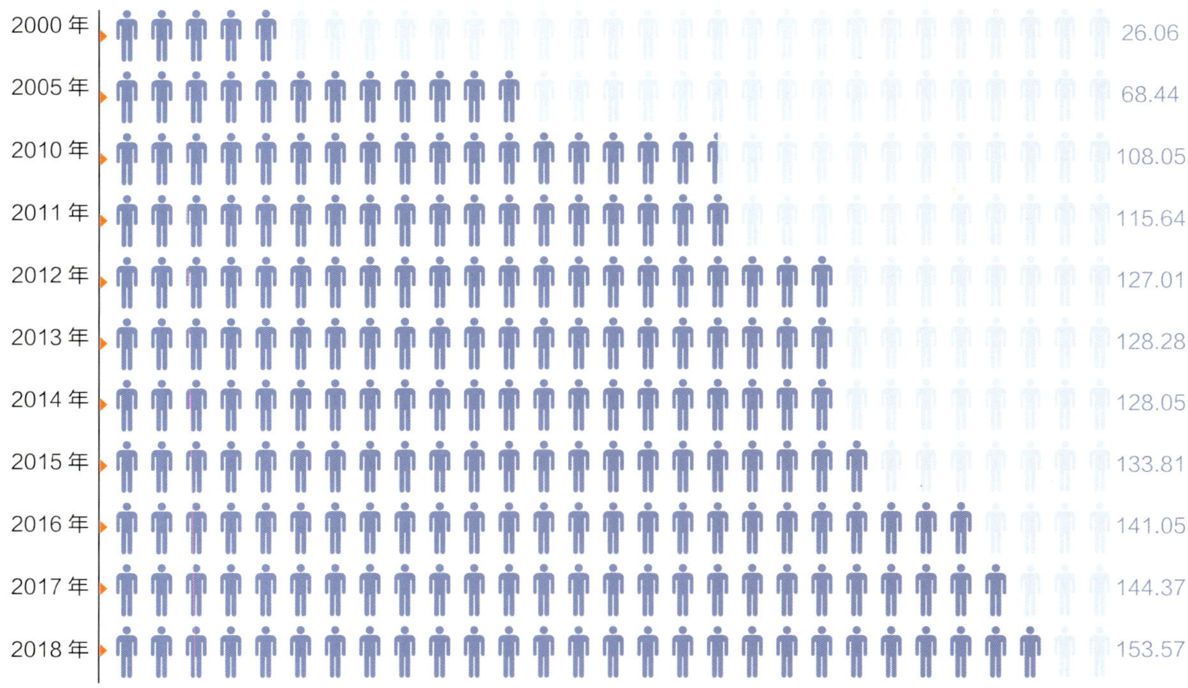


国内旅游人数

Number Of Domestic Tourists

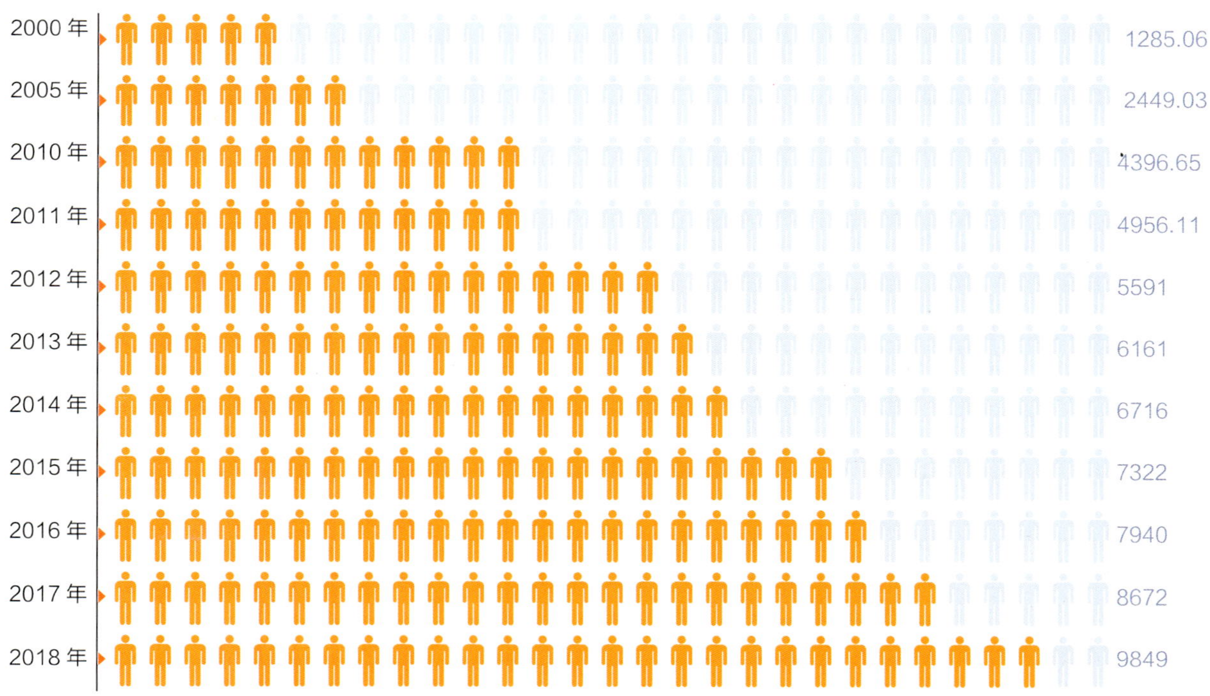

## 地方财政收入（亿元）

Revenue Of Local Government Finance（100 million yuan）

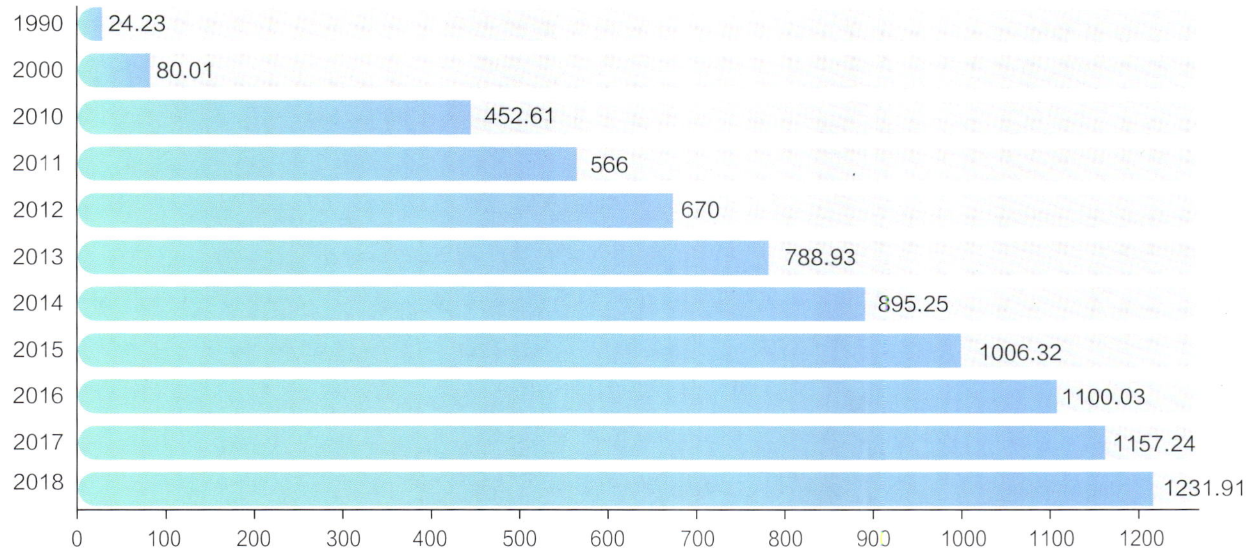


注：2002 年以后财政收入为一般预算收入数。

Note：Since 2002，revenue of government finance refers to general budgetary revenue.

## 金融机构年末人民币存贷款余额（亿元）

Year-end Savings Deposits And Loans Of Financial Institution（RMB）（100 million yuan）

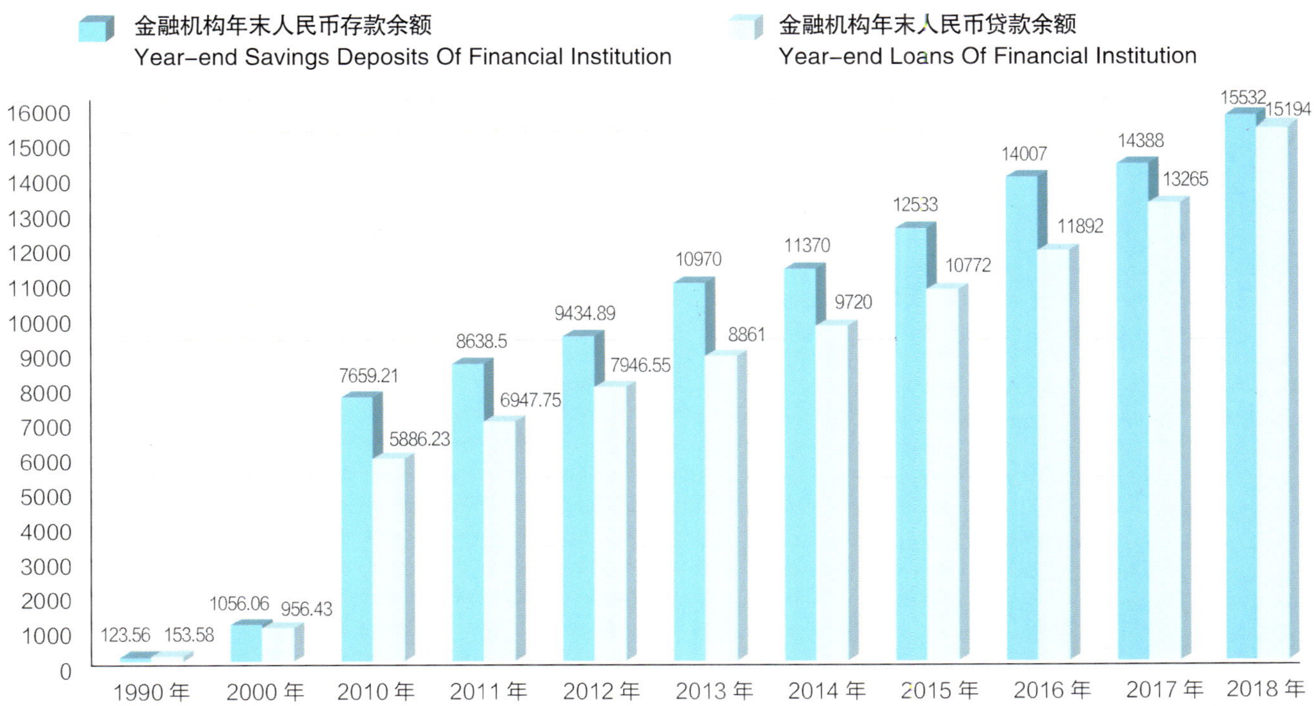

## 社会从业人数（万人）

Social Employment（10 000 persons）

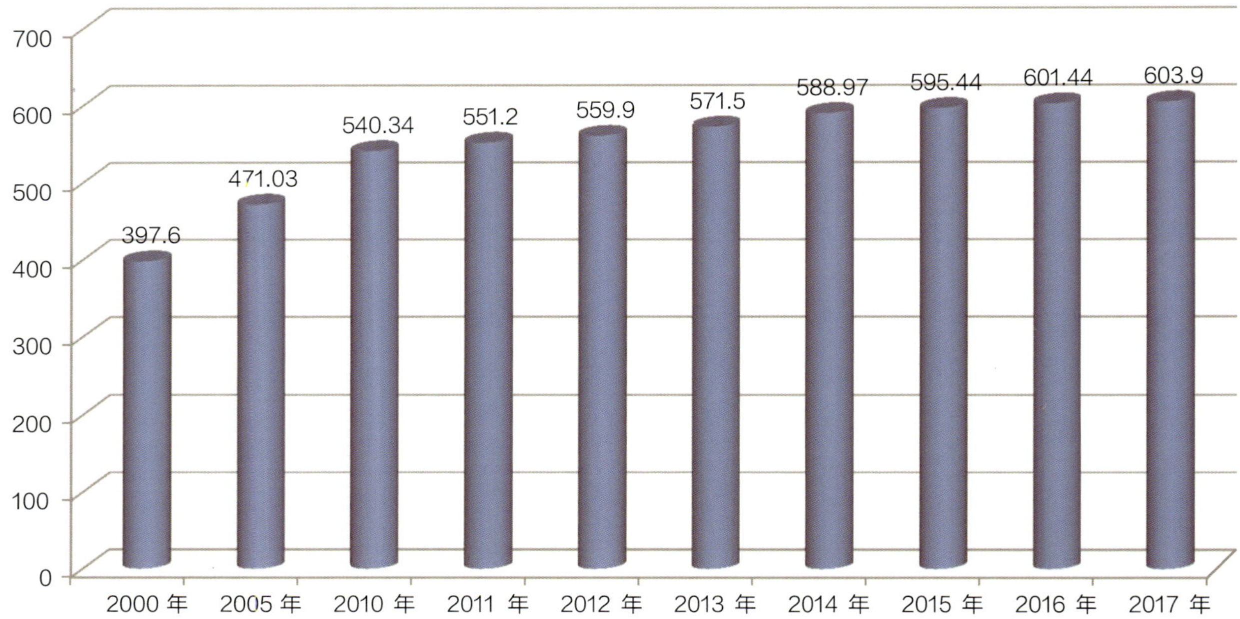


## 在岗职工平均工资（元）

Average Wage Of Employed Staff And Workers（yuan）

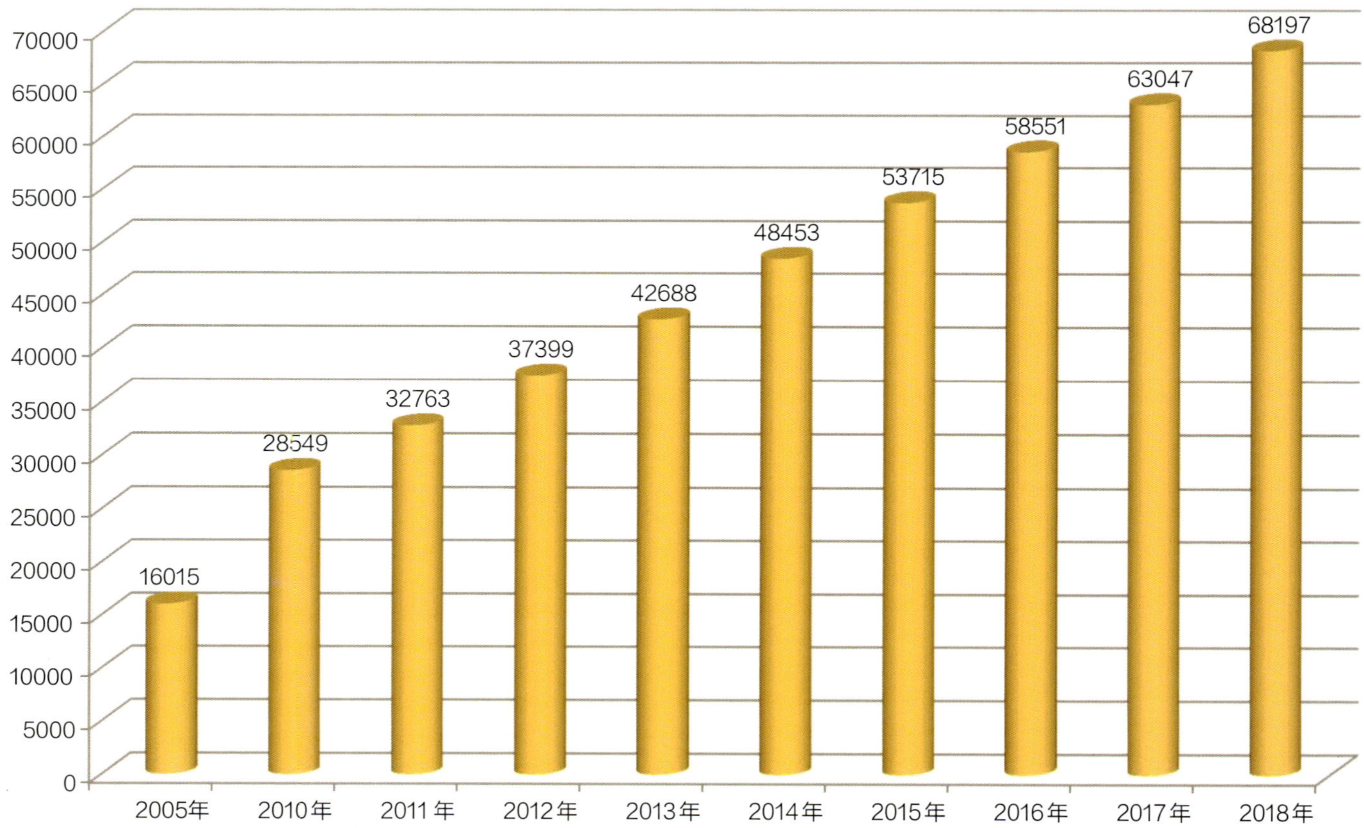

### 居民消费价格指数（上年=100）

Consumer Price Indices（preceding year = 100）

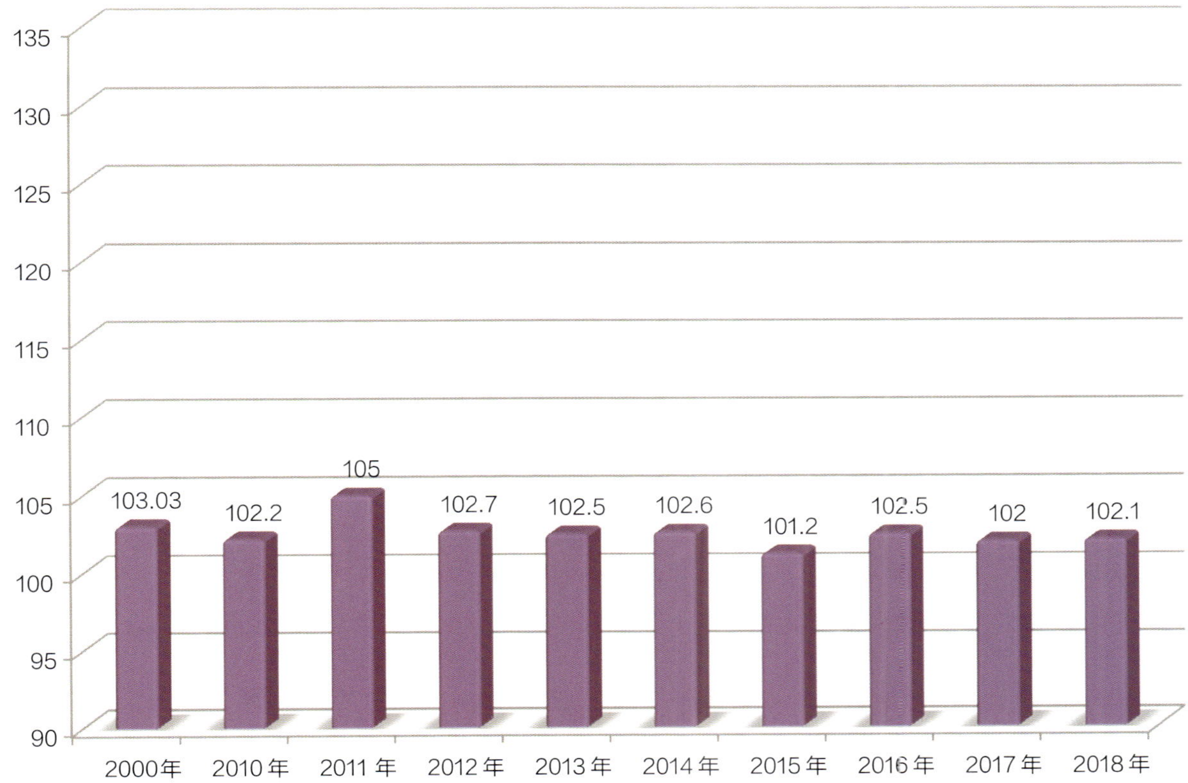


### 商品零售价格指数（上年=100）

Retail Price Indices（preceding year = 100）

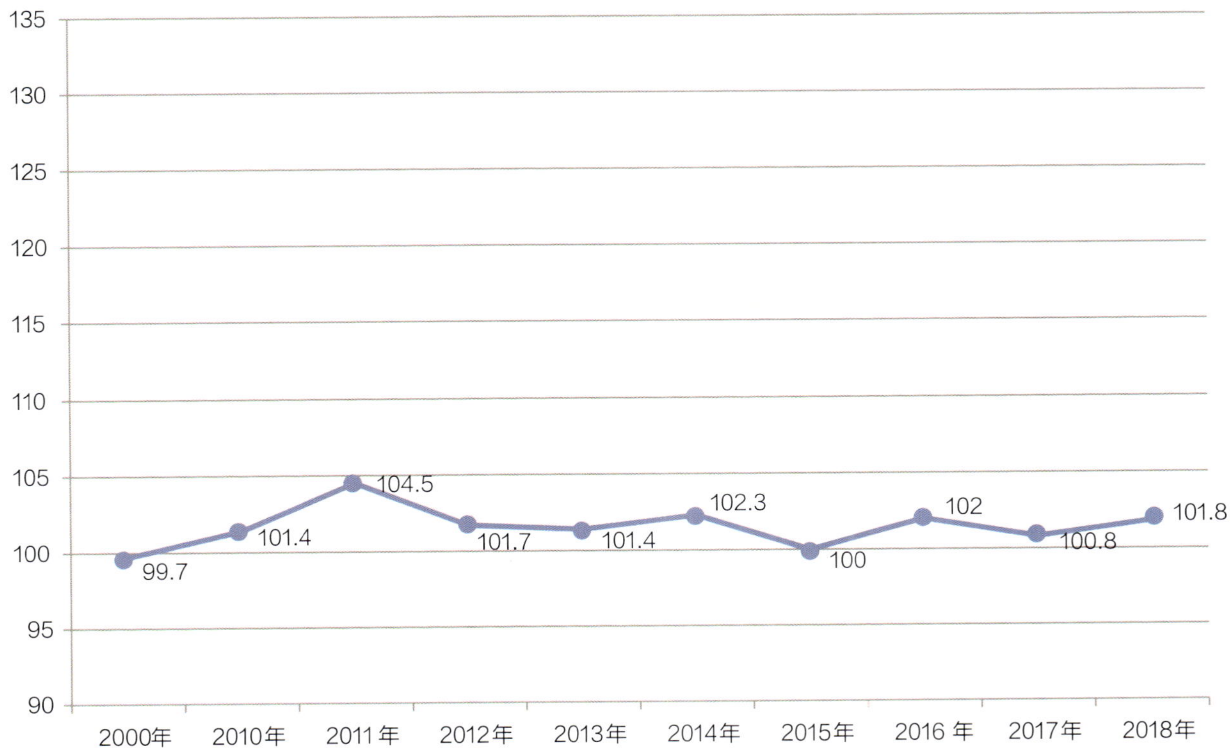

## 城市建成区面积（平方公里）

Developed Area Of the City（sq.km）

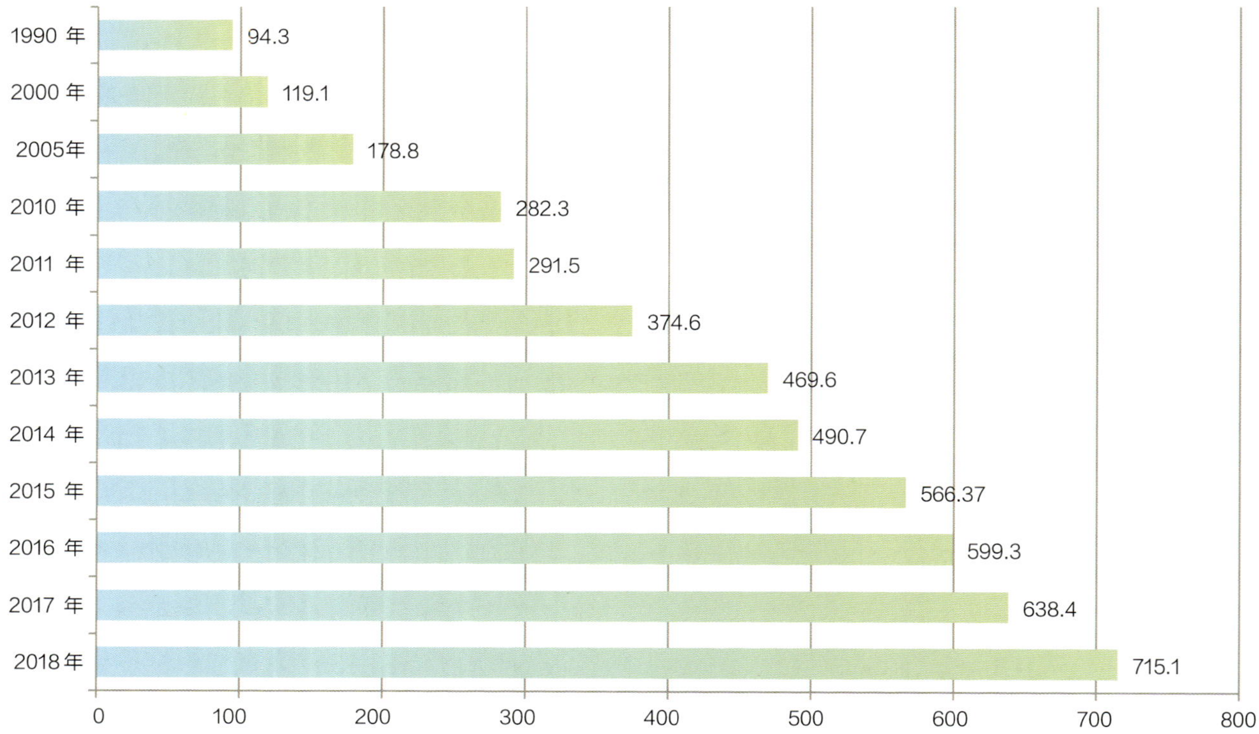


## 铺装道路面积（万平方米）

Area Of Roads（10 000 sq.m）

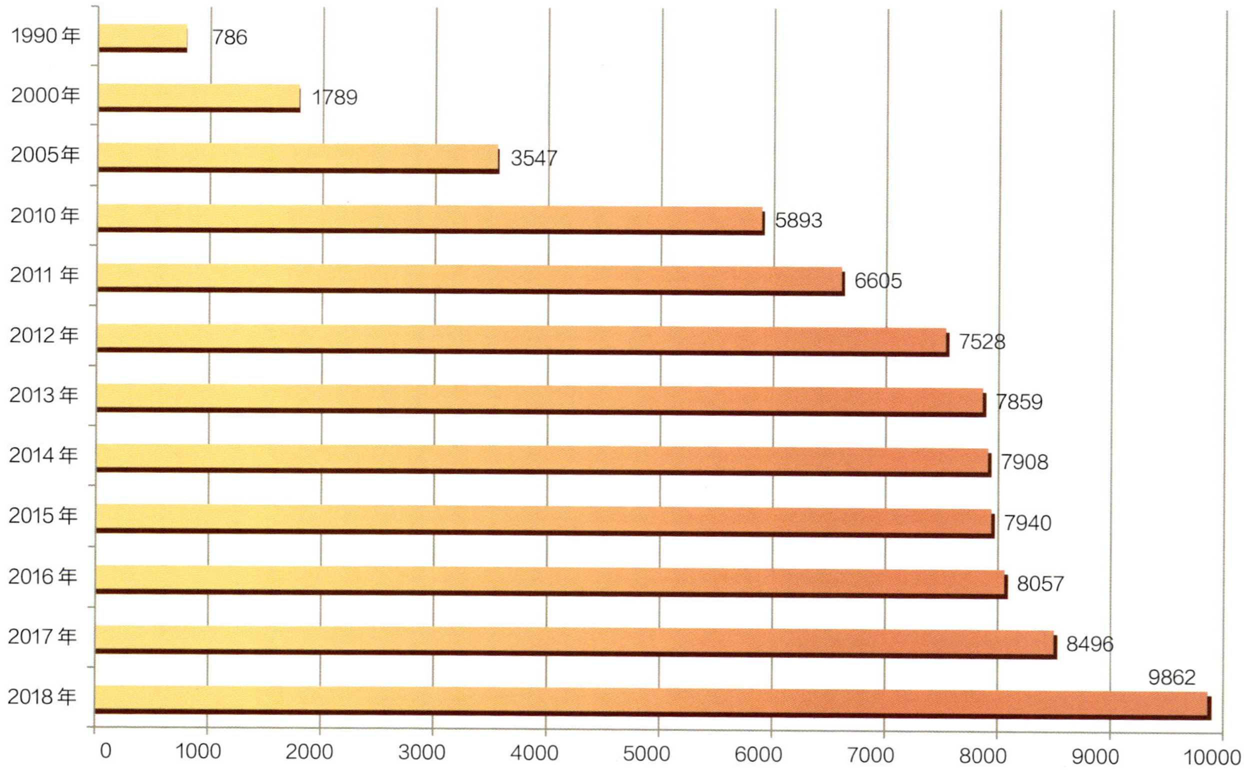

## 医疗卫生机构（个）

Health Care Institutions ( unit )

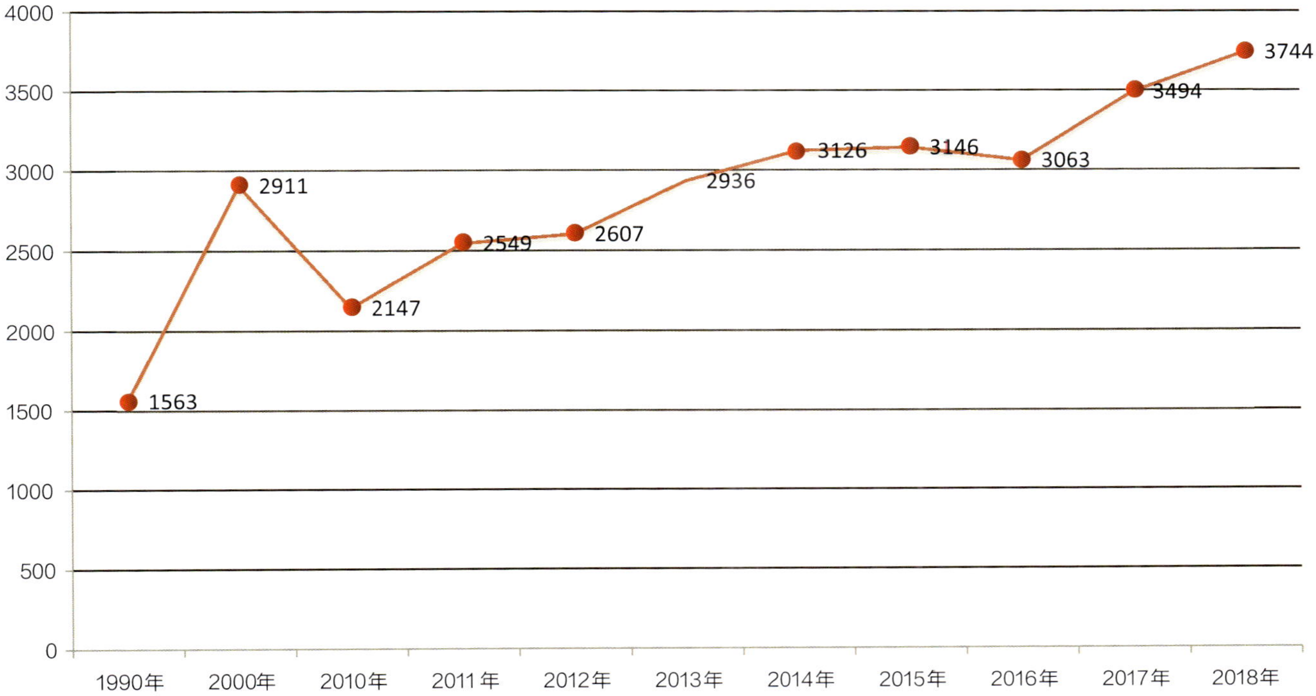


## 普通高校在校人数（万人）

Students Enrollment Of Regular Institutions Of Higher Education ( 10 000 persons )

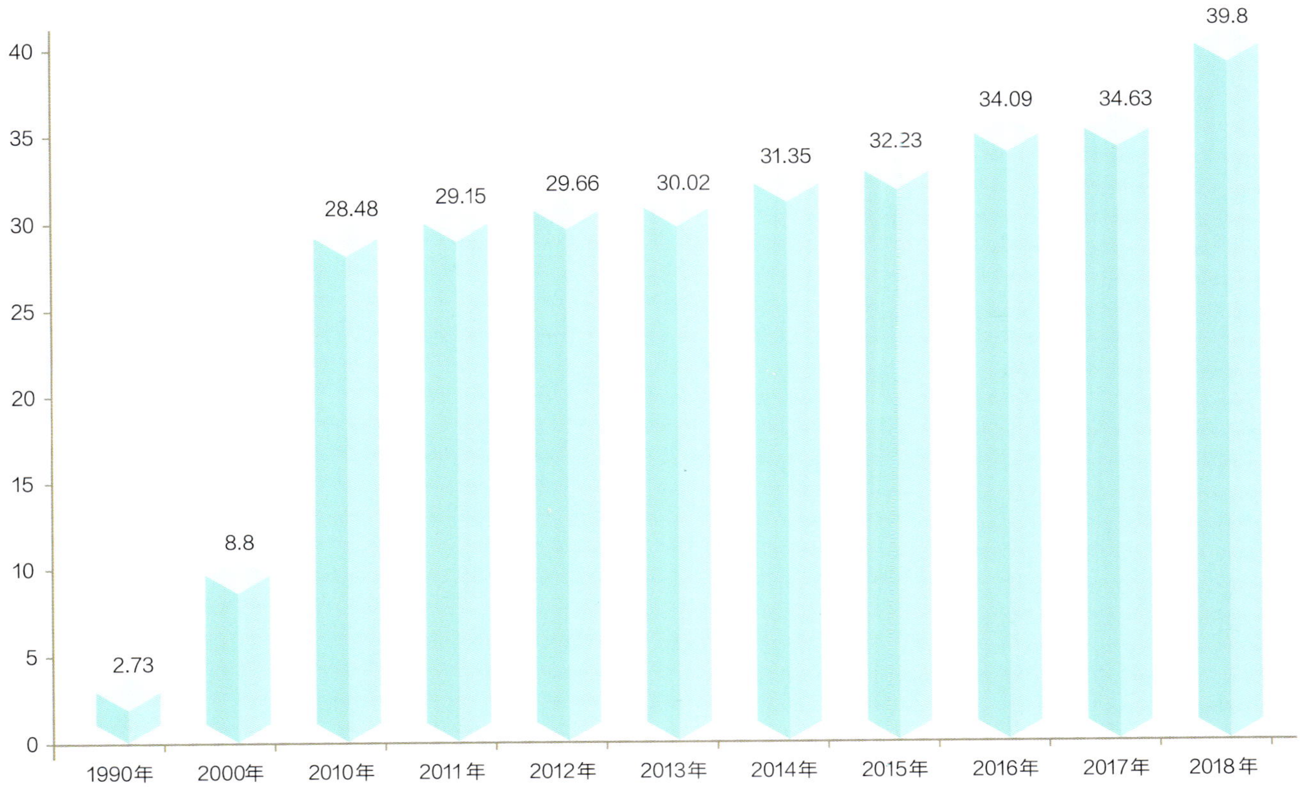

# 编辑委员会

# EDITORIAL BOARD

# 编者说明

一、《青岛统计年鉴 -2019》是一部全面反映青岛市国民经济和社会发展情况、信息高度密集的资料工具书。

二、《青岛统计年鉴 -2019》共包括发展成果图、统计公报、统计表、附录四大部分。

统计表部分收录了 2018 年青岛市经济和社会等各方面的统计数据，以及建国以来重要年份和改革开放以来的主要统计数据，包括：综合，人口，从业人员及职工工资，固定资产投资，对外经济贸易，城市建设、环境保护，能源消耗，财政金融和保险业，价格指数，人民生活，农业，工业，建筑业，运输、邮电，批发和零售业，住宿、餐饮业和旅游，教育、科技和文化，体育、卫生和民政、司法。

为方便读者正确地使用年鉴资料，各篇章前设有《简要说明》，概括介绍各篇主要内容和资料来源；篇末还附有《主要统计指标解释》。

三、本《年鉴》部分历史数据已根据经济普查和农业普查数据进行了调整，在此之前公布的数据凡与本年鉴数字不符的一律以本年鉴为准。

四、本年鉴中的符号说明：年鉴各表中的“空格”表示该项统计指标数据不足本表最小单位数、数据不详或无该项数据；"#" 表示其中的主要项。

五、《青岛统计年鉴》自公开出版以来，受到社会各界的关心和支持，对于年鉴的内容和编辑工作提出了许多宝贵的意见，对此我们深表谢意。限于我们的水平，欢迎读者继续对年鉴的不足之处给予批评和指正，帮助我们进一步改进年鉴编辑工作，以期更好地为广大读者服务。

《青岛统计年鉴》编委会

2019 年 7 月

# Editor's Note

Ⅰ. *Qingdao Statistical Yearbook 2019* is a very important reference book, which reflects various aspects of Qingdao's social and economic development and contains High-density information.

Ⅱ.The yearbook contains the following four parts: achievement graphs, statistic gazette, statistics and appendixes.

Statistics contains all kinds of data on Qingdao's social and economic development in 2018, and data in significant year or data since the beginning of reform and opening up, including: General Survey; Population; Employment and Wages; Investment in Fixed Assets; Foreign Trade; City Construction and Environment Protection; Consumption of Energy; Government Finance ,Financial Intermediation and Insurance; Price; People's Living Conditions; Agriculture; Industry; Construction; Transport, Postal and Telecommunication Services; Wholesale and Retail Trades; Hotels, Catering Services and Tourism; Education, Science and Culture; Sports, Public Health and Civil Affairs, Judicial Affairs; Enterprises Survey.

In brief introduction at the beginning of each chapter, main coverage, data sources and statistical coverage are concerned. Meanwhile explanatory notes on major statistical indicators have been attached for readers to use the data correctly.

Ⅲ. All of the data in the book are in accordance with new administrative division.

Some of the data have been adjusted on the basis of statistics of economic census and agriculture census . In any case the data of this book shall be deemed as the authentic ones.

Ⅳ. Marks in this book:

"(blank)" indicates that the figure is not large enough to be measured with the smallest unit in the table, the data is not available, or the data is not available;

"#" indicates the major items of the total.

Ⅴ. Previous editions of Qingdao Statistical Yearbook have won wide acclaim among the readers. In order to excel, we welcome all candid comments and criticism from our readers.

Editorial Board

JULY,2019

# 目　录
# CONTENTS



## 一、综　合
## Chapter 1.　GENERAL SURVEY

## 二、人　口
## Chapter 2.　POPULATION

## 三、从业人员及职工工资
## Chapter 3.　EMPLOYMENT AND WAGES



## 四、固定资产投资
## Chapter 4.　INVESTMENT IN FIXED ASSETS

## 五、对外经济贸易
## Chapter 5.　FOREIGN TRADE

## 六、城市建设、环境保护
## Chapter 6.　COTY CONSTRUCTION AND ENVIRONMENT PROTECTION

## 七、能源消耗
## Chapter 7.　CONSUMPTION OF ENERGY



## 八、财政、金融和保险业
## Chapter 8.　GOVERNMENT FINANCE FINACIAL INTERMEDIATION AND INSURANCE

## 九、价格指数
## Chapter 9.　PRICE INDEXES

# 十、人民生活

## Chapter 10.　PEOPLE SLIVING CONDITIONS

## 十一、农 业
## Chapter 11. AGRICULTURE

# 十二、工　业
# Chapter 12.　INDUSTRY

## 十三、建　筑　业
## Chapter 13.　CONSTRUCTION



## 十四、运输、邮电
## Chapter 14.　TRANSPORT，POSTAL AND TELECOMMUNICATION SERVICES

## 十五、批发和零售业
## Chapter 15.　WHOLESALE AND RETAIL TRADES

## 十六、住宿、餐饮业和旅游
## Chapter 16.　HOTELS，CATERING SERVICES AND TOURISM



## 十七、教育、科技和文化
## Chapter 17.　EDUCATION SCIENCE & TECHNOLOY AND CULTURE

## 十八、体育、卫生和民政、司法

## Chapter 18.　SPORTS，PUBLIC HEALTH ANDCIVIL AFFAIRS，JUDICIAL AFFAIRS

## 附　录

## APPENDIX

# 2018 年
# 青岛市国民经济和社会发展
# 统 计 公 报

青岛市统计局

国家统计局青岛调查队

（2019 年 3 月 19 日）

2018 年，全市坚持以习近平新时代中国特色社会主义思想为指导，深入贯彻习近平总书记视察山东、视察青岛重要讲话、重要指示批示精神，在市委、市政府坚强领导下，坚持稳中求进工作总基调，贯彻新发展理念，落实高质量发展要求，以新旧动能转换重大工程为引领，统筹推进稳增长、促改革、调结构、惠民生、防风险，经济社会保持持续健康发展。

## 一、综　合

初步核算，2018 年全市生产总值 12001.5 亿元，按可比价格计算，增长 7.4%。其中，第一产业增加值 386.9 亿元，增长 3.5%；第二产业增加值 4850.6 亿元，增长 7.3%；第三产业增加值 6764.0 亿元，增长 7.7%。三次产业比例为 3.2：40.4：56.4。人均 GDP 达到 128459 元。

图 1：2015-2018 年全市生产总值及增速

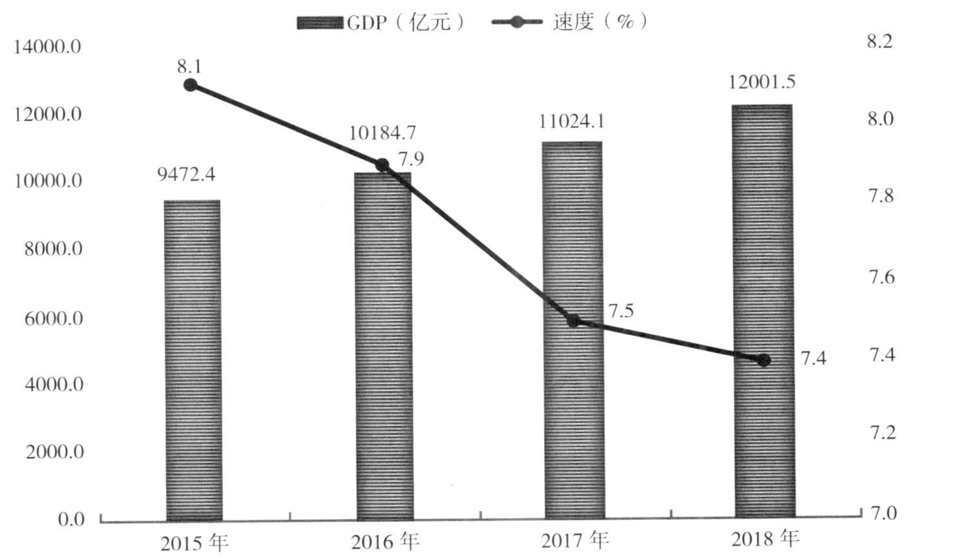


注：2015 年全市生产总值和增速为研发支出计入 GDP 核算修订后数据；2016 年 -2017 年为研发支出计入 GDP 核算并根据第三次农业普查修订后数据。

年末全市常住总人口 939.48 万人，增长 1.1%。其中，市区常住人口 635.25 万人，增长 1.6%。

表 1：2018 年全市及区市常住人口情况

| 区　市 | 年末数（万人） |
| --- | --- |
| 全　市 | 939.48 |
| 市南区 | 58.83 |
| 市北区 | 110.11 |
| 李沧区 | 57.74 |
| 崂山区 | 44.59 |
| 西海岸新区 | 157.73 |
| 城阳区 | 72.05 |
| 即墨区 | 123.83 |
| 胶州市 | 90.05 |
| 平度市 | 137.89 |
| 莱西市 | 76.29 |
| 红岛经济区 | 10.37 |

全年财政总收入 3705.5 亿元，增长 15.0%。一般公共预算收入 1231.9 亿元，增长 6.5%。其中，税收收入 905.9 亿元，增长 9.9%；增值税 327.9 亿元，增长 6.1%；企业所得税 152.4 亿元，增长 3.9%；个人所得税 48.8 亿元，增长 15.1%；城市维护建设税 57.7 亿元，增长 9.5%。一般公共预算支出 1561.2 亿元，增长 11.3%。其中，一般公共服务支出 162.7 亿元，增长 6.9%；教育支出 263.0 亿元，增长 3.6%；科学技术支出 45.1 亿元，增长 17.0%；社会保障和就业支出 156.1 亿元，增长 1.8%；城乡社区事务支出 332.0 亿元，增长 3.0%。全年税务系统组织税收收入（含海关代征）2409.0 亿元，增长 6.3%。其中，国内税收 1720.1 亿元，增长 8.0%。

图 2：2015-2018 年全市一般公共预算收入及增速

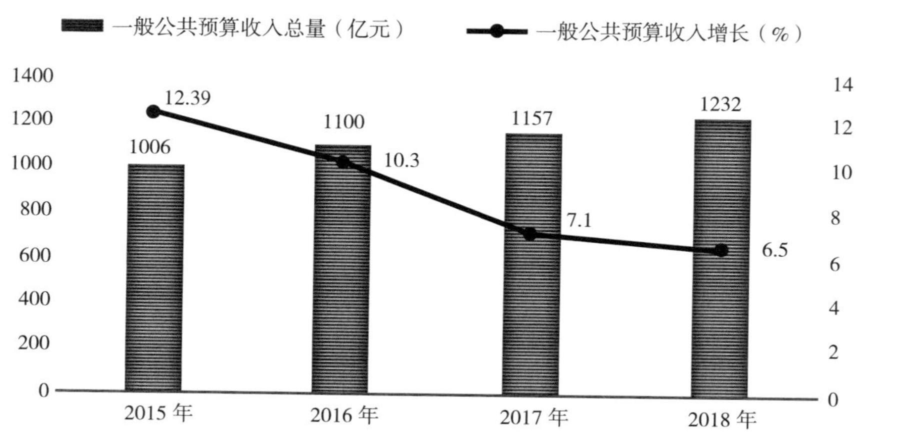

全年居民消费价格指数为 102.1，工业生产者出厂价格指数为 104.22，工业生产者购进价格指数为 105.22。12 月新建商品住宅销售同比价格指数为 113.3，二手住宅同比价格指数为 111.2。

表 2：2018 年全市居民消费价格指数

| 指标名称 | 全年（上年同期 =100） |
| --- | --- |
| 居民消费价格总指数 | 102.1 |
| 非食品价格指数 | 101.9 |
| 服务价格指数 | 101.6 |
| 消费品价格指数 | 102.4 |
| 一、食品烟酒 | 102.9 |
| 食品 | 103.1 |
| # 粮食 | 100.5 |
| 鲜菜 | 114.0 |
| 猪肉 | 92.4 |
| 鸡蛋 | 111.7 |
| 二、衣着 | 103.8 |
| 三、居住 | 100.9 |
| 四、生活用品及服务 | 101.3 |
| 五、交通和通信 | 100.8 |
| 六、教育文化和娱乐 | 103.1 |
| 七、医疗保健 | 102.4 |
| 八、其他用品和服务 | 101.3 |

重点领域改革取得新成效。争取国家、省改革试点任务 59 项。大力推进一流营商环境提升年行动，市级行政审批事项和权力事项分别精简 62.6% 和 55.3%，“一次办好”基本实现全覆盖，市级审批事项网上办理率达到 94%，市行政审批服务大厅全面实行“一窗受理”。户籍制度改革取得新成效，人才落户、居住落户、项目落户、积分落户更加便捷。全部完成 6015 个村集体资产清产核资任务，完成 5550 个村集体产权制度改革。

“三去一降一补”取得新进展。年末商品房待售面积 433.3 万平方米，下降 7.8%；其中，住宅待售面积 162.1 万平方米，下降 22.8%。全市规模以上工业企业每百元主营业务收入中的成本为 81.9 元，与上年持平。全面落实国家减税降费政策，全年为企业新增减负 147 亿元。农业投资增长 15.8%，教育投资增长 14.8%，基础设施投资增长 15.7%。

“三大攻坚战”稳步推进。全市银行不良贷款率降至 1.87%，较年初下降 0.07 个百分点。各级共安排财政扶贫资金

3.3亿元。实施动态调整机制，年末“脱贫享受政策”建档立卡贫困人口为29531人。新建产业扶贫项目111个，累计落地项目达800个，累计资产收益超过6000万元。主要污染物细颗粒物（PM2.5）、二氧化硫、二氧化氮年均值分别为34、10、31微克/立方米，与上年相比，PM2.5改善8.1%，二氧化硫改善28.6%，二氧化氮改善6.1%。

## 二、新动能

初步核算，全年实现海洋生产总值3327亿元，增长15.6%，海洋生产总值占GDP比重27.7%。其中，海洋第一产业增加值110亿元，增长5.1%；第二产业增加值1766亿元，增长18%；第三产业增加值1451亿元，增长13.7%。其中，滨海旅游业、海洋交通运输业、海洋设备制造业和涉海产品及材料制造业等4个支柱产业共实现增加值2025亿元，增长14.5%，占海洋经济比重60.9%。海洋新兴产业实现增加值366亿元，增长8.6%，占海洋经济比重11%。

“新经济”增加值3065.8亿元，占全市生产总值比重25.5%。“新产业”稳步发展，全年全市高技术产业实现增加值增长6.9%，占GDP比重为4.6%。其中，高技术制造业增加值增长3.3%，占GDP比重为2.0%；高技术服务业增加值增长10.0%，占GDP比重为2.5%。战略性新兴产业增加值增长6.2%，占GDP比重为8.1%。其中，战略性新兴产业工业增加值增长5.0%，占GDP比重为5.4%；战略性新兴产业服务业增加值增长8.6%，占GDP比重为2.7%。“新业态、新模式”显现活力，全市电子商务交易平台实现交易额1.0万亿元，限额以上批发和零售业单位网络零售额增长27.6%。“新技术”发展迅速，全市规模以上高技术服务业企业营业收入占规模以上服务业企业收入比重提升至22.8%。“新产品”产量增速较快，工业机器人2288套，增长59.4%；城市轨道车辆1538辆，增长20.5%；新能源汽车9.2万辆，增长14.4%。新动能投资拉动明显。装备制造业投资增长10.7%，战略新兴产业投资增长32.8%，高技术制造业投资增长59.0%，工业技改投资增长22.6%。

初步统计，全市共获得国家级科技奖励14项。其中，自然科学奖1项，技术发明奖1项，国际科学技术合作奖1项，科技进步奖11项。技术合同交易额155.8亿元，增长23.0%。涉海技术合同成交额18.2亿元，增长21.2%。全年有效发明专利26267件，增长20.5%。每万人有效发明专利拥有量28.5件，PCT国际专利申请1088件。国家知识产权示范企业10家，国家知识产权优势企业60家，国家技术创新示范企业14家。国家企业技术中心39家，高新技术企业总数达到3112家。杰华生物成为全省首家独角兽企业。研发力量加快聚集，国家重点实验室达到9家，省级以上企业技术中心达到193家，工程（技术）研究中心达到292家。

## 三、农　业

全年农业增加值410.6亿元，增长3.6%。其中，种植业增加值194.0亿元，增长3.0%；林业增加值2.3亿元，增长11.9%；牧业增加值76.1亿元，增长7.9%；渔业增加值114.5亿元，增长2.2%。

全年粮食播种面积48.1万公顷，蔬菜播种面积11.3万公顷，花生播种面积8.0万公顷。粮食总产量310.1万吨，增长4.4%；蔬菜及食用菌总产量644.4万吨，增长2.6%；花生总产量38.5万吨，增长0.3%；水果（含果用瓜）总产量109万吨，下降8.0%。现代农业园区987个，新增51个；认证“三品一标”（无公害农产品、绿色食品、有机农产品和农产品地理标志）产品1056个，其中国家地理标志保护产品51个。

全年新增造林13.5万亩，人工更新造林1.7万亩。

全年肉类总产量52.2万吨，增长3.0%；禽蛋产量18.2万吨，下降13.8%；奶类产量29.8万吨，增长10.3%。

全年水产品产量（不包括远洋捕捞）103.5万吨，增长1.6%。海、淡水养殖面积3.5万公顷，增长0.9%。远洋捕捞量14.5万吨，与上年持平。

农机总动力737.8万千瓦，增加9.9万千瓦。农作物生产综合机械化水平达到87.8%。农田有效灌溉面积33.1万公顷，其中节水灌溉面积18.8万公顷。

表 3：2018 年主要种植业产品产量及增速

| 指标 | 单位 | 产量 | 增长（%） |
| --- | --- | --- | --- |
| 粮食 | 万吨 | 310.1 | 4.4 |
| 夏粮 | 万吨 | 137.7 | 8.9 |
| 秋粮 | 万吨 | 172.4 | 1.1 |
| 油料 | 万吨 | 38.5 | 0.3 |
| 蔬菜及食用菌 | 万吨 | 644.4 | 2.6 |
| 水果 | 万吨 | 109 | -8.0 |
| 园林水果 | 万吨 | 71 | -5.1 |

## 四、工业与建筑业

全市全部工业增加值 4137.1 亿元，增长 6.9%。其中，规模以上工业增加值增长 6.8%。轻工业增加值增长 8.5%，重工业增加值增长 6%。分经济类型看，国有控股企业增加值增长 4.8%，集体企业增加值增长 2.8%，股份制企业增加值增长 7.0%，外商及港澳台商投资企业增加值增长 6.3%。分门类看，采矿业增加值下降 14.5%，制造业增加值增长 6.6%，电力、热力、燃气及水生产和供应业增加值增长 11.8%。全年规模以上工业企业产销率达到 99.9%。规模以上工业企业实现出口交货值增长 8.0%，比上年提高 3.2 个百分点。

表 4：2018 年规模以上工业主要产品产量及增速

| 产品名称 | 单位 | 产量 | 增长（%） |
| --- | --- | --- | --- |
| 彩色电视机 | 万台 | 1695.2 | -0.5 |
| 其中：智能电视 | 万台 | 1695.2 | -0.5 |
| 家用电冰箱 | 万台 | 886.6 | 3.3 |
| 家用洗衣机 | 万台 | 601.7 | -0.3 |
| 房间空气调节器 | 万台 | 1058.1 | 5.3 |
| 移动通信手持机 | 万台 | 2010.2 | -28.9 |
| 橡胶轮胎外胎 | 万条 | 6388.8 | 36.6 |
| 平板玻璃 | 万重量箱 | 561.5 | 0.7 |
| 粗钢 | 万吨 | 309.7 | 10.2 |
| 汽车 | 万辆 | 9.2 | 14.4 |
| 金属集装箱 | 万立方米 | 1385.5 | 18.6 |

规模以上工业利润增长 6%。其中，国有控股企业下降 6.9%，集体企业增长 33.3%，股份制企业增长 4.3%，外商及港澳台商投资企业增长 10.4%。

表 5：2018 年规模以上工业利润增速

| 指标 | 增长（%） |
|---|---|
| 规模以上工业利润 | 6 |
| 其中：国有控股 | -6.9 |
| 集体企业 | 33.3 |
| 股份制企业 | 4.3 |
| 外商及港澳台投资企业 | 10.4 |

全年资质内总承包专业承包建筑业企业 711 家，实现增加值 723.4 亿元，增长 10.5%；完成建筑业总产值 2309.3 亿元，增长 22.9%；签订合同额 4777.9 亿元，增长 18.0%；实现利税总额 105.6 亿元，增长 8.9%。

## 五、服务业

全市服务业增加值占全市生产总值比重为 56.4%，比上年提高 0.9 个百分点；对经济增长的贡献率为 55.6%。

表 6：2018 年全市服务业增加值情况

| 行 业 | 增加值（亿元） | 增长（%） | 比重（%） |
|---|---|---|---|
| 农林牧渔服务业 | 23.65 | 6.6 | 0.2 |
| 金属制品、机械和设备修理业 | 9.89 | 6.9 | 0.1 |
| 批发和零售业 | 1440.66 | 7.3 | 12 |
| 交通运输、仓储和邮政业 | 830.58 | 2.7 | 6.9 |
| 住宿和餐饮业 | 268.18 | 5.7 | 2.2 |
| 金融业 | 800.4 | 5.2 | 6.7 |
| 房地产业 | 672.46 | 1.2 | 5.6 |
| 其他服务业 | 2718.2 | 12.2 | 22.7 |
| #营利性服务业（主要包括电信、信居租文） | 1416.11 | 19.6 | 11.8 |
| #非营利性服务业 | 1302.09 | 4.8 | 10.9 |

全市规模以上服务业总体较快增长，实现营业收入 19577.3 亿元，增长 12.0%。生产性服务业中，商务服务业营业收入增长 29.5%，科技服务业营业收入增长 14.2%。生活性服务业中，影视节目制作营业收入增长 97.7%，电影和广播电视节目发行营业收入增长 12.7 倍，艺术表演场馆营业收入增长 15.8%，体育组织营业收入增长 32.0%。全市现代服务业实现增加值 3773.4 亿元，增长 9.2%，占全市 GDP 比重为 31.4%。

表 7：2018 年规模以上服务业营业收入情况

| 行 业 | 营业收入（亿元） | 增长（%） |
| --- | --- | --- |
| 规模以上服务业 | 19577.3 | 12.0 |
| 交通运输、仓储和邮政业 | 10067.8 | 9.0 |
| 信息传输、软件和信息技术服务业 | 3068.0 | 12.2 |
| 房地产业（不含房地产开发经营） | 312.8 | 10.8 |
| 租赁和商务服务业 | 3063.2 | 27.4 |
| 科学研究和技术服务业 | 1429.1 | 6.8 |
| 水利、环境和公共设施管理业 | 274.2 | −29.3 |
| 居民服务业、修理和其他服务业 | 225.4 | −4.2 |
| 教育 | 209.2 | 14.2 |
| 卫生和社会工作 | 185.5 | 13.1 |
| 文化、体育和娱乐业 | 742.1 | 27.1 |

交通运输、仓储和邮政业平稳发展。全年港口吞吐量 5.4 亿吨，增长 6.1%；外贸吞吐量 3.9 亿吨，增长 6.2%；集装箱吞吐量 1932 万标准箱，增长 5.5 %。年末拥有航线 192 条，增长 3.2%。其中，国内航线 160 条，国际航线 29 条，港澳台地区航线 3 条。全年航空旅客吞吐量达到 2454 万人次，增长 5.7%；航空货邮吞吐量 22 万吨，下降 3.2%。年末全市机动车保有量 282.6 万辆，增长 8.1%；其中，私人汽车 232.1 万辆，增长 9.4 %。全年地铁开行列车 33 万列次，总运营里程 915 万列公里，总客运量 15294 万人次。全年完成邮电业务总量 650.9 亿元，增长 105.2%。其中，邮政业务总量 82.9 亿元，增长 14.4%；电信业务总量 568 亿元，增长 132.1%。快递业务量 3.8 亿件，增长 23%。固定宽带互联网用户 398 万户，增长 7.9%。全市移动电话 1259 万户，其中 3G 和 4G 用户 1064 万户，增长 8.7%。

表 8：2018 年各种运输方式完成的运输量及增速

| 运输方式 | 单位 | 运输量 | 增长(%) |
| --- | --- | --- | --- |
| 客运周转量 | 亿人公里 | 182.49 | 6.4 |
| 铁路 | 亿人公里 | 105.36 | 8.7 |
| 公路 | 亿人公里 | 76.97 | 3.4 |
| 水运 | 亿人公里 | 0.16 | -27.2 |
| 货运周转量 | 亿吨公里 | 1647.12 | 9.3 |
| 铁路 | 亿吨公里 | 190.90 | 4.3 |
| 公路 | 亿吨公里 | 532.20 | 3.2 |
| 水运 | 亿吨公里 | 924.02 | 14.4 |

金融业健康发展。年末金融机构本外币存款余额 16121.3 亿元，比年初增加 992.3 亿元；人民币存款余额 15532.2 亿元，比年初增加 1144.4 亿元，其中，住户存款 5913.7 亿元，比年初增加 518.6 亿元。本外币贷款余额 16098 亿元，比年初增加 1692.9 亿元；人民币贷款余额 15194.2 亿元，比年初增加 1923.8 亿元。保险业实现保费收入 439.4 亿元，增长 10.8%。其中，产险公司实现保费收入 132.8 亿元，增长 20%；寿险公司实现保费收入 306.6 亿元，增长 7.2%。证券经营机构代理成交额 27268.1 亿元，下降 22.7%。年末私募基金机构 236 家，实缴管理基金规模 640.4 亿元，增长 30.9%。

旅游业快速发展。全市共接待国内外游客 1.0 亿人次，增长 15%；实现旅游消费总额 1867.1 亿元，增长 13.8%。接待入境游客 153.6 万人次，增长 6.4%；实现旅游消费 11.6 亿美元，增长 14%。接待国内游客 9848.9 万人次，增长 13.7%；实现旅游消费 1651 亿元，增长 13.8%。年末拥有 A 级旅游景区 122 处，其中，5A 级旅游景区 1 处，4A 级旅游景区 26 处，3A 级旅游景区 74 处。拥有星级酒店 99 个，其中，5 星级酒店 10 个，4 星级酒店 25 个，3 星级酒店 60 个。拥有旅行社 544 个，其中，经营出境旅游业务旅行社 59 个，经营入境和国内旅游业务旅行社 544 个。

## 六、固定资产投资

全市固定资产投资增长 7.9%。其中，第一产业投资增长 14.3%，第二产业投资增长 9.1%，第三产业投资增长 7.5%。亿元以上新开工项目（含房地产）702 个，较上年增加 1 个，完成投资 1737.5 亿元，下降 12.4%，占全市固定资产投资的比重为 33.2%。

全年房地产开发完成投资 1485.2 亿元，增长 11.6%。其中，住宅投资 1034.8 亿元，增长 11.8%。商品房销售面积 1808 万平方米，下降 4.9%。其中，住宅销售面积 1578.3 万平方米，下降 3.4%。

表 9：2018 年全市房地产开发投资、商品房销售面积及增速

| 分 类 | 房地产开发投资（亿元） | 增长（%） | 商品房销售面积（万平方米） | 增长（%） |
| --- | --- | --- | --- | --- |
| 总计 | 1485.2 | 11.6 | 1808 | -4.9 |
| 住宅 | 1034.8 | 11.8 | 1578.3 | -3.4 |
| 办公楼 | 98.5 | -12.5 | 76.7 | -21.6 |
| 商业营业用房 | 153.7 | -17.3 | 119.9 | -7.9 |
| 其他 | 198.2 | 85.7 | 33.1 | -14.6 |

全年保障性住房基本建成15540套，其中，公共租赁住房11212套，经济适用住房2225套，限价商品住房2103套。截至年末，全市正在享受租赁补贴家庭共7326户，全年发放租赁补贴4367万元。

## 七、国内贸易

全年实现社会消费品零售额4842.5亿元，增长10.0%。按经营地统计，城镇消费品零售额4026.9亿元，增长9.7%；乡村消费品零售额815.6亿元，增长11.4%。分行业看，批发和零售业实现零售额4221亿元，增长9.1%；住宿和餐饮业实现零售额621.5亿元，增长16.6%。

全年限额以上单位实现消费品零售额1644.2亿元，增长9.1%。其中，粮油、食品类零售额增长17.5%，烟酒类零售额增长27.0%，服装、鞋帽、针纺织品类零售额增长8.6%，化妆品类零售额增长4.8%，金银珠宝类零售额增长11.5%，日用品类零售额增长19.1%，家用电器和音响器材类零售额增长18.5%，中西药品类零售额增长25.1%，文化办公用品类零售额增长10.1%，建筑及装潢材料类零售额增长12.3%，石油及制品类零售额增长9.8%，汽车类零售额比上年下降0.1%。

## 八、对外经济

全市实现外贸货物进出口总额5321.3亿元，增长5.7%。其中，出口额3172.2亿元，增长4.7%；进口额2149.0亿元，增长7.3%。对"一带一路"沿线国家市场进出口总额2590.4亿元，增长4.2%。其中，出口1630.6亿元，增长1.9%；进口959.8亿元，增长8.4%。

全市服务进出口176.1亿美元，增长9.6%。其中，出口87.5亿美元，增长5.6%；进口88.6亿美元，增长13.8%。全市承接服务外包合同8652份，增长43.9%；合同额56.7亿美元，增长39.7%；执行额44.3亿美元，增长18.3%。其中，离岸服务外包合同7275份，增长53.9%；合同额45.8亿美元，增长43.3%；执行额36.1亿美元，增长18.9%。

青岛口岸对外贸易进出口总额12196.8亿元，增长9.7%。其中，出口额6738.5亿元，增长6.5%；进口额5458.3亿元，增长13.9%。

表10：2018年全市主要商品进出口情况

| 项目 | 进出口 | | 出口 | | 进口 | |
|---|---|---|---|---|---|---|
| | 金额（亿元） | 增长（%） | 金额（亿元） | 增长（%） | 金额（亿元） | 增长（%） |
| 纺织服装 | 511.2 | 6.5 | 482.0 | 7.7 | 29.2 | -9.8 |
| 农产品 | 797.7 | 11.8 | 387.3 | 8.4 | 410.4 | 15.2 |
| 机电产品 | 1786.8 | 1.6 | 1352.2 | 0.5 | 434.6 | 5.2 |
| 高新技术产品 | 525.2 | 5.1 | 316.1 | 5.1 | 209.1 | 5.1 |

表 11：2018 年对主要国家和地区货物进出口额及增速

| 国别（地区） | 出口额（万美元） | 增长（%） | 进口额（万美元） | 增长（%） |
| --- | --- | --- | --- | --- |
| 亚洲 | 119950 | 8.0 | 1280932 | 5.3 |
| 香港 | 522 | -48.6 | 11487 | 19.6 |
| 台湾 | 7943 | -22.2 | 118789 | 15.9 |
| 日本 | 15717 | -6.2 | 185504 | 3.8 |
| 韩国 | 28535 | 9.3 | 342617 | 12.8 |
| 东盟 | 31712 | -26.3 | 379222 | -14.9 |
| 南亚 | 4493 | -23.8 | 63178 | 23.0 |
| 中东 | 3895 | -62.2 | 60583 | -54.8 |
| 非洲 | 3850 | -31.2 | 47902 | 14.5 |
| 南非 | 13203 | -8.5 | 134631 | -12.8 |
| 欧洲 | 4057 | 76.5 | 38975 | 57.3 |
| 欧盟 | 3705 | 85.3 | 34467 | 60.0 |
| 英国 | 26720 | 341.4 | 135723 | 82.5 |
| 德国 | 26757 | 20.2 | 260346 | 44.9 |
| 法国 | 810 | -54.6 | 26943 | 25.6 |
| 意大利 | 47121 | 43.4 | 506724 | 29.5 |
| 独联体及东欧 | 26130 | 3.9 | 290470 | 19.7 |
| 俄罗斯 | 6219 | 30.5 | 60435 | 52.8 |
| 南美洲 | 7689 | 38.8 | 85797 | 26.0 |
| 巴西 | 2248 | -53.0 | 36255 | 9.5 |
| 北美洲 | 1312 | -42.1 | 21093 | -0.3 |
| 美国 | 18336 | 276.2 | 183367 | 52.4 |
| 加拿大 | 17761 | 292.7 | 174582 | 51.2 |
| 大洋洲 | 51717 | 51.4 | 531235 | -2.4 |
| 澳大利亚 | 44561 | 187.2 | 374326 | 53.2 |

注：本表非全口径。

2018 年，全市新批外商投资项目 956 个，增长 47.1%；合同外资 98.2 亿美元，增长 7.8%。全市实际使用外资 86.9 亿美元，增长 10%；按商务部 FDI（外商直接投资）统计口径，实际使用外资 58.0 亿美元，增长 4.1%。

全市企业对“一带一路”沿线国家和地区投资项目 22 个，协议投资额 2.0 亿美元，增长 8.9%；实际投资额 6.8 亿美元，增长 86.9%。

全市对外承包工程业务新承揽项目 107 个，新签合同额 49.3 亿美元，增长 11.9%；完成营业额 43.1 亿美元，增长 12.8%。对外劳务合作业务派出各类劳务人员 11820 人。

## 九、社会事业

年末全市共有各类大专院校（含民办高校）25 所，其中，普通高校 23 所。全年研究生招生 1.6 万人，在学研究生 4.5 万人，毕业生 1.1 万人（不含驻青科研院所研究生）。普通本专科招生 10.2 万人，在校生 35.3 万人，毕业生 9.4 万人。中等职业教育招生 2.6 万人，在校生 8.4 万人，毕业生 2.8 万人。普通高中招生 3.8 万人，在校生 11.7 万人，毕业生 3.8 万人。初中招生 8.6 万人，在校生 26.8 万人，毕业生 7.2 万人。普通小学招生 10.4 万人，在校生 57.0 万人，毕业生 8.6 万人。特殊教育招生 0.02 万人，在校生 0.2 万人，毕业生 0.02 万人。幼儿园在园幼儿 26.4 万人。

年末全市共有卫生机构（不含村卫生室）3745 处，其中，医院、卫生院 422 处，疾病预防控制中心 26 处，妇幼保健机构 12 处，门诊部（所）、诊所、卫生所、医务室 2917 处。年末各类卫生技术人员 8.4 万人，其中，医生 3.5 万人。全市拥有医疗床位 5.8 万张，其中，医院、卫生院床位 5.6 万张。

全市运动员在各项比赛中共获得金牌 353 枚，银牌 247 枚，铜牌 236 枚。重点体校 8 所，学员 1370 人；业余体校 10 所，学员 1846 人。

## 十、城市建设

年末全市常住人口城镇化率达到 73.67%，比上年提高 1.1 个百分点。城市平均每天供水量 129.7 万吨，增长 2.9%。城市全年实际用水量 4.1 亿吨，其中，生产用水和生活用水分别为 1.6 亿吨和 2.5 亿吨。

城市使用液化气、天然气的总户数达到 189.8 万户，全年供应液化气总量 2.7 万吨，供应天然气总量 10.7 亿立方米。城市气化率达到 100%。

全年新增供热面积 1060.4 万平方米，年末供热面积达到 2 亿平方米。

年末市区公共汽、电车线路 623 条，共有营运的公交汽、电车 8475 辆。市区共有巡游出租汽车 10867 辆。年末市区共有地铁线路 4 条，地铁年客运量 15294.12 万人次，日均客运量 41.9 万人次。

全市共有公共厕所 788 座，三类以上的 774 座，新增 202 座，改建 54 座。

年末城市下水道总长度 8128.1 公里。

## 十一、能源、环境和安全生产

初步统计，全年全市规模以上工业综合能源消费量 1489 万吨标准煤，增长 4.1%。其中，煤炭消费量 1360 万吨，下降 1.7%；原油消费量 1542 万吨，增长 1.2%；天然气消费量 10 亿立方米，增长 89.3%。全社会用电量 432 亿千瓦时，增长 7.7%。其中，工业用电量 238 亿千瓦时，增长 5.4%；城乡居民生活用电量 77 亿千瓦时，增长 2.2%。

全年全市能源生产量2834万吨标准煤，增长2.1%。其中，原油加工量1541万吨，增长1.2%；汽油生产量474万吨，增长3.9%；柴油生产量383万吨，下降6.2%；发电量192亿千瓦时，增长4.8%。新能源发电量17亿千瓦时，增长13.5%。其中，风力发电量增长12.6%，生物质发电量增长25.4%。新能源发电量占全市发电总量比重为9.1%，提高0.7个百分点。

全市年平均气温13.3℃，平均年降水量为722.7毫米。市区空气质量优良天数达307天，占全年的85%。近岸海域水质达到或好于二类海水水质标准的点位数占90.6%，与上年持平。市区区域环境噪声平均值56.9分贝，市区交通干线噪声平均值68.0分贝。

全市七个行业（领域）发生各类生产安全事故63起，死亡69人，分别下降42.2%和38.4%。亿元GDP生产安全事故死亡率0.006，十万工矿商贸企业就业人员生产安全事故死亡率0.72，道路交通事故万车死亡1.13人。

## 十二、人民生活和社会保障

全年全市居民人均可支配收入42019元，增长8.4%。按常住地分，城镇居民人均可支配收入50817元，增长7.7%；农村居民人均可支配收入20820元，增长7.5%。全市城乡居民收入比为2.44：1。全市居民人均消费支出27316元，增长8.3%，恩格尔系数为28.5%。按常住地分，城镇居民人均消费支出32890元，增长7.6%；农村居民人均消费支出13885元，增长7.4%。

表12：2018年城乡居民人均可支配收入构成情况

| 指标名称 | 全体居民 | | 城镇居民 | | 农村居民 | |
|---|---|---|---|---|---|---|
| | 绝对值（元） | 增长（%） | 绝对值（元） | 增长（%） | 绝对值（元） | 增长（%） |
| 可支配收入 | 42019 | 8.4 | 50817 | 7.7 | 20820 | 7.5 |
| 工资性收入 | 25303 | 7.6 | 30955 | 6.8 | 11684 | 7.4 |
| 经营净收入 | 8027 | 7.3 | 7836 | 7.4 | 8487 | 7.3 |
| 财产净收入 | 3475 | 12.8 | 4789 | 11.4 | 310 | 10.8 |
| 转移净收入 | 5214 | 11.3 | 7237 | 9.9 | 339 | 17.1 |

表 13：2018 年城乡居民人均消费支出情况

| 指标名称 | 全体居民 | | 城镇居民 | | 农村居民 | |
|---|---|---|---|---|---|---|
| | 绝对值（元） | 增长（%） | 绝对值（元） | 增长（%） | 绝对值（元） | 增长（%） |
| 消费支出 | 27316 | 8.3 | 32890 | 7.6 | 13885 | 7.4 |
| 食品烟酒 | 7787 | 4.0 | 9318 | 2.9 | 4098 | 5.9 |
| 衣着 | 2538 | 2.9 | 3168 | 1.7 | 1020 | 5.1 |
| 居住 | 6365 | 16.7 | 7751 | 17.3 | 3024 | 8.0 |
| 生活用品及服务 | 1837 | 5.1 | 2207 | 4.0 | 945 | 6.7 |
| 交通和通信 | 4084 | 8.8 | 4765 | 8.3 | 2445 | 8.1 |
| 教育文化娱乐 | 2571 | 9.5 | 3122 | 8.6 | 1245 | 10.3 |
| 医疗保健 | 1480 | 9.6 | 1764 | 8.6 | 794 | 10.6 |
| 其他用品和服务 | 654 | 4.6 | 795 | 3.4 | 314 | 6.9 |

表 14：2018 年每百户居民家庭主要耐用消费品拥有量

| 指标名称 | 单位 | 数　量 | | |
|---|---|---|---|---|
| | | 全体居民 | 城镇居民 | 农村居民 |
| 家用汽车 | 辆 | 56 | 62 | 43 |
| 摩托车 | 辆 | 28 | 15 | 61 |
| 电冰箱（柜） | 台 | 108 | 108 | 109 |
| 洗衣机 | 台 | 99 | 100 | 97 |
| 热水器 | 台 | 97 | 101 | 88 |
| 空调 | 台 | 112 | 120 | 93 |
| 彩色电视机 | 台 | 107 | 107 | 105 |
| 计算机 | 台 | 70 | 81 | 45 |
| 移动电话 | 部 | 230 | 228 | 232 |

据抽样调查，年末城镇居民人均现住房建筑面积 32.9 平方米，农村居民人均现住房建筑面积 35.9 平方米。

全年城镇新增就业 77.6 万人，增长 6.3%。其中，本市劳动者就业增长 4.8%，外来劳动者来青就业增长 8.1%。服务业吸纳就业 50.7 万人，增长 16.9%。民营经济吸纳就业 59.6 万人，增长 11.3%。

年末全市城镇居民最低生活保障人数达 20457 人，城镇居民最低生活保障资金 19923 万元；农村特困供养人员 4843 人，农村特困供养支出 7624.5 万元。

年末全市城镇职工基本养老保险参保缴费人数为 273.51 万人，参加失业保险人数为 223.69 万人，全年累计领取失业保险金的人数为 7.5 万人。全市城镇登记失业率为 2.94%，降低 0.18 个百分点。

注：

1、公报中统计数据均为初步统计数。

2、全市生产总值（GDP）及各产业增加值绝对数按现价计算，增长速度按可比价计算。根据《三次产业划分规定》（国统字〔2012〕108 号），农林牧渔业中的农林牧渔服务业，工业中的开采辅助活动以及金属制品、机械和设备修理业等三个行业划入第三产业。

3、常住人口包括：①住本户、户口在本乡镇街道的人（含户口在本户，外出不满半年的人）；②住本户半年以上，户口在外乡镇街道的人；③住本户不满半年，户口在外乡镇街道，离开户口登记地半年以上的人；④住本户，户口待定的人。

4、PCT（Patent Cooperation Treaty）是《专利合作条约》的英文缩写。PCT 国际专利是指我国专利申请人根据 PCT 规定，可以向中国专利局或向世界知识产权组织提交国际专利申请，是反映地区外向型经济发展水平和地区国际技术竞争能力的重要指标。

5、战略性新兴产业根据国家规划，现阶段主要包括节能环保、新一代信息技术、生物、高端装备制造、新能源、新材料、新能源汽车等七个产业领域。

6、规模以上工业企业为年主营业务收入 2000 万元及以上企业。限额以上贸易企业为批发业年主营业务收入在 2000 万元及以上、零售业 500 万元及以上、住宿和餐饮业 200 万元及以上的单位。固定资产投资项目统计的起点标准为计划总投资额 500 万元。规模以上服务业企业，一是指年营业收入 1000 万元及以上或年末从业人员 50 人及以上服务业法人单位。包括：交通运输、仓储和邮政业，信息传输、软件和信息技术服务业，租赁和商务服务业，科学研究和技术服务业，水利、环境和公共设施管理业，教育，卫生和社会工作；以及物业管理、房地产中介服务、自有房地产经营活动和其他房地产业等行业。二是指年营业收入 500 万元及以上或年末从业人员 50 人及以上服务业法人单位。包括：居民服务、修理和其他服务业，文化、体育和娱乐业。

7、各类生产安全事故起数、死亡人数统计范围包括生产经营性道路交通、水上交通、铁路交通、民航飞行、农业机械、渔业船舶和工矿商贸七个行业（领域）发生的事故，不再包括森林火灾、火灾事故和非生产经营性道路交通。

8、供水、用水、供气、供热、道路、厕所、下水道等有关数据不含即墨区。

9、资料来源：本公报中财政数据来自市财政局，人才、登记失业率、社会保障数据来自市人力资源和社会保障局，银行数据来自人民银行青岛市中心支行，证券数据来自青岛证监局，保险数据来自青岛银保监局，水产品数据来自市海洋发展局，林业数据来自市园林和林业局，农机等数据来自市农业农村局，灌溉面积数据来自市水务管理局，交通运输数据来自市交通运输局，邮政数据来自市邮政管理局，固定电话、宽带、移动电话等数据来自市通信管理局，建成区面积、供水、供气、供热、道路、下水道等数据来自市住房城乡建设局，进出口、外资、对外承包工程、对外劳务合作、跨境电商等数据来自市商务局，旅游数据来自市文化和旅游局，教育数据来自市教育局，科技、专利数据来自市科技局，体育数据来自市体育局，卫生数据来自市卫生健康委，环境数据来自市生态环境局，用电量数据来自青岛供电公司，气象数据来自市气象局，安全生产数据来自市应急局，扶贫数据来自市扶贫开发办，汽车保有量来自市公安局，粮食、居民收支、价格、城乡居民住房面积等数据来自国家统计局青岛调查队，其他数据来自市统计局。

# STATISTICS COMMUNIQUE QINGDAO'S ECONOMIC AND SOCIAL DEVELOPMENT IN THE YEAR OF 2018

Qingdao Statistics Bureau

NBS Qingdao Survey Office

(March 19，2019)

In 2018, the city takes Xi Jinping's new era of socialism with Chinese characteristics as the guide, in-depth implementation of General Secretary Xi Jinping's inspection of Shandong, inspection of Qingdao's important speech and important instructions, and under the strong leadership of the municipal government of the Communist Party of China , the overall tone of the work is maintained ， implement the requirements of high-quality development, take the lead in the transformation of new and old kinetic energy projects, and promote the steady growth, promote reform, adjust the structure, benefit the people's livelihood, prevent risks, and maintain sustained and healthy development in the economy and society.

## Ⅰ .General

According to the preliminary accounting,annual gross domestic product 1.20015 trill-on yuan in 2018,caleulated at the comparable price,with an increase of 7.4%.Therein,the 38.69 billion yuan of added value of the first industry increased by 3.5 percent.The value-added 485.06 billion yuan of the second industry increased by 7.3.The value-added 676.40 billion yuan of the tertiary industry increased by 7.7%.The proportion of three industries is 3.2:40.4:56.4. GDP per capita reached 128459 yuan.

Figure1：Qingdao GDP and Growth Rate from 2015 to 2018

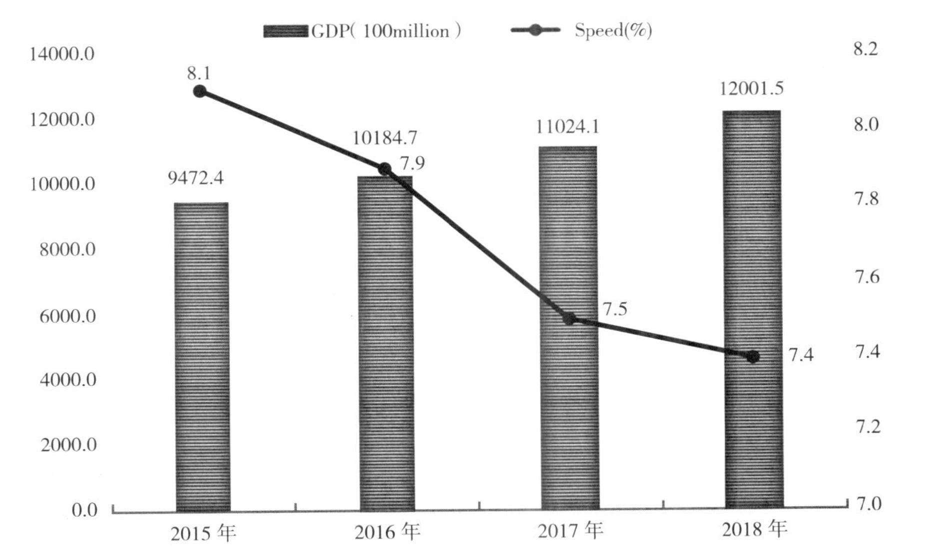


Note: The gross domestic product (GDP) and the growth rate in 2015 are the revised data of DGP input acounting for R & D expenditures

At the end of the year,the total population of the city is 939.48 million,with an inerease of 1.1%.Therein,the urban resident population is 635.25 million,with an increase of 1.6%.

Table 1: City resident population in 2018

| Region | Number of end–of–year ( 10 000 persons ) |
|---|---|
| Total | 939.48 |
| Shinan District | 58.83 |
| Shibei District | 110.11 |
| LIcang District | 57.74 |
| Laoshan District | 44.59 |
| West Coast New Area | 157.73 |
| Chengyang District | 72.05 |
| JImo District | 123.83 |
| Jiaozhou | 90.05 |
| Pingdu Laixi | 137.89 |
| Qingdao National High–tech | 76.29 |
| Industrial Development Zone | 10.37 |

The total annual financial income is 370.55 billion yuan,inereased by 15.0% .The general publie budget income 123.19 billion yuan rises by 6.5%. Therein the total price is RMB 3.9 billion Yuan,with an increase of 9.9%.The VAT accounting to 32.79 billion yuan increased by 6.1%.The enterprise income tax accounts to 15.24 billion yuan,with an increase of 3.9%.The individual income tax accounts to 4.88 billion yuan,increased by 15.1%.The urban maintenance and construction tax,accounting to 5.77 billion yuan,increased by9.5%.The 156.12 billion yuan of general public budget expenditures increased by 11.3%.Of these,general public service expenditure 16.27 billion yuan rises by 6.9%.Educational expenditure accounts to 26.30 billion yuan, with an increase of 3.6%.The4.51 billion yuan of scientific and technological expenditure inereased by 17.0%.The 15.61 billion yuan of social security and employment expenditure increased by 1.8%.The 33.20 billion yuan of urban and rural community affairs expenditure increased by 3.0%.The annual nation tax system organization revenue, including customs collected as an agency, accounts 240.90 billion yuan, increased by 6.3%。 Therein, the domestic tax revenue accounts to 172.01 billion yuan, increased by 8.0%.

Figure 2: General Public Budget Income and Speed–increasing in the City

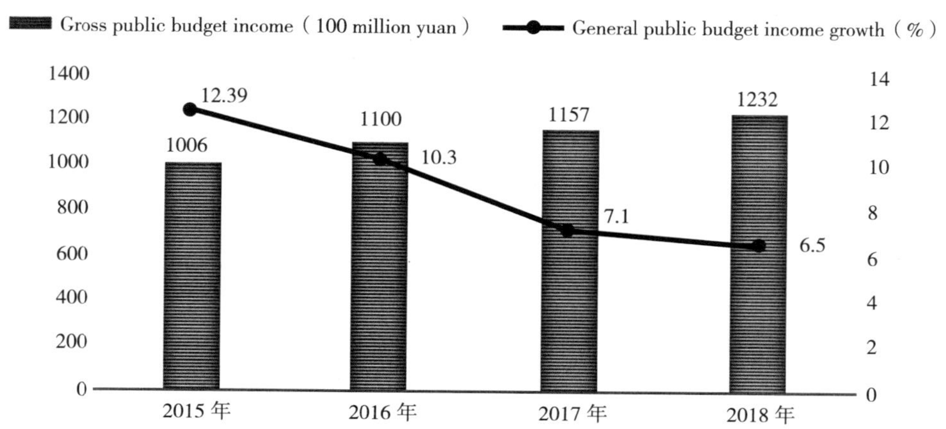

The annual consumer price index was 102.1, the industrial producer ex-factory price index was 104.22, and the industrial producer purchase price index was 105.22. The year-on-year price index for new commercial residential sales in December was 113.3, and the second-hand residential year-on-year price index was 111.2.

Table 2: Consumer Price Index of the City in 2018

| Name | Number of end-of-year(10 000 persons) |
|---|---|
| General Consumer Price Index | 102.1 |
| Non-Food Price Index | 101.9 |
| Service Price Index | 101.6 |
| Consumer Price Index | 102.4 |
| 1. Food, Tobacco and Liquor | 102.9 |
| Food | 103.1 |
| #Grain | 100.5 |
| Vegetables | 114.0 |
| Pork | 92.4 |
| Egg | 111.7 |
| 2. Clothing | 103.8 |
| 3. Residence | 100.9 |
| 4. Supplies and Services | 101.3 |
| 5. Transportation and Communication | 100.8 |
| 6. Education, Culture and Recreation | 103.1 |
| 7. Medical Care | 102.4 |
| 8. Others | 101.3 |

New achievements have been made in reforms in key areas. We will strive for 59 national and provincial reform pilot tasks. Vigorously promote the first-class business environment to improve the annual action, municipal administrative examination and approval matters and power matters were reduced by 62.6% and 55.3%, respectively, "one time to do a good job" to achieve full coverage, the city-level examination and approval matters online processing rate reached 94%, municipal administrative approval The service hall is fully implemented with "one window acceptance". The reform of the household registration system has achieved new results, and it has become more convenient for talents to settle down, settle in residences, settle projects, and settle in points. Completed the task of clearing assets and assets in 6015 village collective assets, and completed the reform of the collective property rights system of 5,550 villages.

"Three to one, one drop and one supplement" made new progress. At the end of the year, the saleable area of commercial housing was 4.333 million square meters, decreased 7.8%. Among them, the residential area for sale was 1.621 million square meters, decreased 22.8%. The cost per 100 yuan of main business income of industrial enterprises above designated size in the city was 81.9 yuan, which was the same as the previous year. Full implementation of the national tax reduction and fee reduction policy, the company's new annual burden reduction of 14.7 billion yuan. Agricultural investment increased by 15.8%, education investment increased by 14.8%, and infrastructure investment increased by 15.7%.

The "three major battles" have steadily advanced. The non-performing loan ratio of the city's banks fell to 1.87%, a decrease of 0.07 percentage points from the beginning of the year. A total of 330 million yuan of financial poverty alleviation funds were arranged at all levels. The implementation of the dynamic adjustment mechanism, the end of the year "Poverty Alleviation Policy" filed the number of poverty-stricken people in the card is 29,531 people. There were 111 new industrial poverty alleviation projects, with a total of 800 projects, and the accumulated asset income exceeded 60 million yuan. The annual average values of fine particulate matter (PM2.5), sulfur dioxide and nitrogen dioxide of main pollutants were 34, 10, 31 μg/m3 respectively. Compared with the previous year, PM2.5 improved by 8.1%, sulfur dioxide improved by 28.6%, and dioxide dioxide. Nitrogen improved by 6.1%.

## Ⅱ. New Kinetic Energy

According to the preliminary accounting, the annual gross domestic product ( GDP ) 332.7 billion yuan grew by 15.6, accounting for 27.7% of GDP. Among them, the added value of the marine primary industry was 11 billion yuan, increased by 5.1%.The value-added 176.6 billion yuan of the second industry increased by 18%. The value-added 145.1 billion yuan of the tertiary industry increased by 13.7%.Therein, the four pillar industries of coastal tourism, marine transportation, marine equipment manufacturing and sea-related products and materials manufacturing realized an added value of 202.5 billion yuan, increased by 14.5%, accounting for 60.9% of the marine economy. The marine emerging industry realized an added value of 36.6 billion yuan, increased by 8.6%, accounting for 11% of the marine economy.

The added value of the "new economy" was 306.58 billion yuan, accounting for 25.5% of the city's GDP. "New industry" is developing steadily, In the whole year, the city's high-tech industry realized an increase of 6.9% in value added., accounting for 4.6% of GDP. Therein the added value of high-tech manufacturing increased by 3.3%, accounting for 2.0% of GDP. Strategic emerging industry added value increased by 6.2%, accounting for 8.1% of GDP. Among them, Strategic emerging industry service industry added value increased by 8.6%, accounting for 2.7% of GDP. "New business, new model" shows vitality, The city's e-commerce transaction platform achieved a transaction volume of 1.0 trillion yuan, and the retail sales of wholesale and retail units above designated size increased by 27.6%. The "new technology" has developed rapidly. The operating income of high-tech service enterprises above designated size in the city has increased to 22.8% of the revenue of service enterprises above designated size. The output of "new products" increased rapidly, with 2,288 sets of industrial robots, an increase of 59.4%; 1,538 urban rail vehicles, an increase of 20.5%; and 92,000 new energy vehicles, an increase of 14.4%. New kinetic energy investment is driving. Investment in equipment manufacturing increased by 10.7%, investment in strategic emerging industries increased by 32.8%, investment in high-tech manufacturing increased by 59.0%, and investment in industrial technology reform increased by 22.6%.

According to preliminary statistics, the city has won 14 national science and technology awards. Among them, 1 natural science award, 1 technical invention award, 1 international science and technology cooperation award, and 11 scientific and technological progress awards. The technical contract transaction volume was 15.58 billion yuan, an increase of 23.0%. The turnover of sea-related technology contracts was 1.82 billion yuan, an increase of 21.2%. There were 26,267 effective invention patents in the whole year, an increase of 20.5%. The number of valid invention patents per 10,000 people is 28.5, and the number of PCT international patent applications is 1088. There are 10 national IPR demonstration enterprises, 60 national IPR superiority enterprises and 14 national technology innovation demonstration enterprises. There are 39 national enterprise technology centers, and the total number of high-tech enterprises has reached 3,112. Jiehua Bio became the first unicorn company in the province. The research and development forces accelerated, and the number of national key laboratories reached 9, the number of enterprise technology centers above the provincial level reached 193,and the number of engineering (technical) research centers reached 292.

## Ⅲ. Agriculture

The annual agricultural added value was 41.06 billion yuan, an increase of 3.6%.Therein, the added value for the planting industry amounted to 19.40 billion yuan, increased by 3.0%. The added value for forestry amounted to 230 million yuan, increased by

11.9%. The added value for the husbandry amounted to 7.61 billion yuan, increased by 7.9%. The added value for the fishing industry amounted to 11.45 billion, declined by 2.2 %.

The grain sowing area stands at 481,000 acres throughout the year. The vegetables sowing area stands at 113,000 acres. And peanuts sowing area stands at 80,000 acres. The total output of grain stands at 3,101,000 tons, increased by 4.4%. The total output of vegetables and edible fungi stands at 6,444,000 tons, increased by 2.6%. The total output of peanuts stands at 385,000 tons, increased by 0.3%. The total output of fruits (including the fruits-purpose melons) stands at 1,090,000 tons, declined by 8.0%. The modern agricultural parks amount to 987, increased by 51. Those certified with 'three products and one mark(pollution-free agricultural products, green food, organic agricultural products and agricultural products geographical indication) amounts to 1056, including 51 national geographic mark protected products.

Throughout the year, 135,000 mu of new trees are planted. 17,000 mu forests are refreshed.

The total meat output is 522,000 tons in the whole year, increased by 3.0%. The output of poultry eggs weighs 180,000 tons, increased by 13.8%. The output of diary stands at 298,000 tons, increased by 10.3%..

Annual aquatic product yield (excluding far ocean fishing) stands at 1.035 million tons, decreased by 1.6%. The ocean and fresh water cultivation area stands at 35,000 acres, decreased by 0.9%.The ocean fishing volume stands at 145,000 tons, Flat with the previous year.

The total power of agricultural machinery is 7.378 million kW, increasing by 300,000 kW. The mechanization level of crop production reached 87.8%.The effective irrigation area of the farmland stands at 331,000 hectares, of which the water-saving irrigation area stands at 188,000 hectares.

Table 3 : Production and Growth of Major Plantation Products in 2018

| Indicators | Unit | Yield | Growth（%） |
|---|---|---|---|
| Grain | 10 000 tons | 310.1 | 4.4 |
| Summer grain | 10 000 tons | 137.7 | 8.9 |
| Autumn grain | 10 000 tons | 172.4 | 1.1 |
| Oilseed | 10 000 tons | 38.5 | 0.3 |
| Vegetable and edible fungi | 10 000 tons | 644.4 | 2.6 |
| Fruit | 10 000 tons | 109 | -8.0 |
| Garden fruit | 10 000 tons | 71 | -5.1 |

## Ⅳ. Industry and Construction

The city's total industrial added value was 413.71 billion yuan, an increase of 6.9%.

Among them, the added value of industrial enterprises above designated size increased by 6.8%. The added value of light industry increased by 8.5%, and the added value of heavy industry increased by 6%.According to the economic types, state-controlled enterprises grew by 4.8 %. The collective enterprises grew by 2.8%. Shareholding enterprises grew by7.0%. The foreign and Hong Kong , Macao and Taiwan business investment enterprises grew by 6.3%. In terms of categories, the added value of the mining industry fell by 14.5%, the added value of the manufacturing industry increased by 6.6%, and the added value of the electricity, heat, gas and water production and supply industries increased by 11.8%. The production and sales rate of industrial enterprises above designated size reached 99.9%. The export delivery value of industrial enterprises above designated size increased by 8.0%, an increase of 3.2 percentage points over the previous year.

Table 4 :  The Output and Growth Rate of the Main Products of Industries above Designated Size in 2018

| Description | Unit | Output | Growth（%） |
|---|---|---|---|
| Color TV | 10 000 sets | 1695.2 | -0.5 |
| Of which: Smart TV | 10 000 sets | 1695.2 | -0.5 |
| Household refrigerators | 10 000 sets | 886.6 | 3.3 |
| Household washing machin | 10 000 sets | 601.7 | -0.3 |
| Room air conditioners | 10 000 sets | 1058.1 | 5.3 |
| Smart phone Beer | 10 000 sets | 2010.2 | -28.9 |
| Tire casing Sheet glass Raw steel | 10 000 kiloliters | 6388.8 | 36.6 |
| Automobile | 10 000 pieces | 561.5 | 0.7 |
| Motor train units | 10 000 tons | 309.7 | 10.2 |
| urban rail vehicle | 10 000 vehicle | 9.2 | 14.4 |
| Metal shipping containers | 10 000 $m^3$ | 1385.5 | 18.6 |

The above-scale industrial profits rises by 6%, therein, the state-owned holding enterprises fell by 6.9%, the collective enterprises increased by 33.3%, the shareholding enterprises increased by 4.3%, the foreign merchants and Hong Kong, Macao and Taiwan merchants decreased by 10.4%.

Table 5: Above-scale industrial profit growth in 2018

| Indicators | Growth(%) |
|---|---|
| Industrial profits above the scale | 6 |
| Of which : State-owned holding | -6.9 |
| Collective businesses | 33.3 |
| Shareholder businesses | 4.3 |
| Businesses invested by foreigner or by compatriots from Hong Kong , Macao and Taiwan | 10.4 |

In the whole year, there were 711 contracted construction enterprises in the general contracting industry, achieving an added value of 72.34 billion yuan, an increase of 10.5%; the total output value of the construction industry was 230.93 billion yuan, an increase of 22.9%; the contract value was 477.79 billion yuan, an increase of 18.0%; The total profit and tax was 10.56 billion yuan, an increase of 8.9%.

## V .service enterprises

The added value of the city's service enterprises accounted for 56.4% of the city's GDP, an increase of 0.9 percentage points over the previous year; the contribution rate to economic growth was 55.6%.

Table6: Added modern service enterprises rate of the whole city in 2018

| Industry Classification | Value Added ( 100 million yuan ) | Growth ( % ) | proportion ( % ) |
|---|---|---|---|
| Farming, Forestry, Animal Husbandry and Fishery Industry Construction | 23.65 | 6.6 | 0.2 |
| Metal products, machinery and equipment repair industry | 9.89 | 6.9 | 0.1 |
| Wholesale and Retail Sales | 1440.66 | 7.3 | 12 |
| Transport, Storage and Post | 830.58 | 2.7 | 6.9 |
| Accommodation and catering | 268.18 | 5.7 | 2.2 |
| Finance | 800.4 | 5.2 | 6.7 |
| Real Estate | 672.46 | 1.2 | 5.6 |
| Other Services | 2718.2 | 12.2 | 22.7 |
| #For-profit service enterprises (mainly including telecommunications, letter of residence and rent) | 1416.11 | 19.6 | 11.8 |
| #Non-profit service enterprises | 1302.09 | 4.8 | 10.9 |

The service enterprises above designated size in the city has grown rapidly, achieving an operating income of 1,957.73 billion yuan, an increase of 12.0%. In the producer service industry, the business service enterprises revenue increased by 29.5%, and the technology service industry revenue increased by 14.2%. In the life service enterprises, the revenue from film and television program production increased by 97.7%, the revenue from film and radio and television program distribution increased by 12.7 times, the revenue of art performance venues increased by 15.8%, and the income of sports organizations increased by 32.0%. The city's modern service enterprises realized an added value of 377.34 billion yuan, an increase of 9.2%, accounting for 31.4% of the city's GDP.

Table 7: Operating income of service industry above designated size in 2018

| Catgory | business revenue | Growth（%） |
|---|---|---|
| Catgory | 19577.3 | 12.0 |
| Service enterprises above designated size Transport， storage and postal service | 10067.8 | 9.0 |
| Information transmission ， software and information technology service | 3068.0 | 12.2 |
| Real estate（Excluding real estate development and management） | 312.8 | 10.8 |
| Leasing and business service | 3063.2 | 27.4 |
| Scientific research and technical service | 1429.1 | 6.8 |
| Management of water conservancy， environment and public facilities | 274.2 | −29.3 |
| Households ‘service ， repair and other services | 225.4 | −4.2 |
| Education | 209.2 | 14.2 |
| Health and social work | 185.5 | 13.1 |
| Culture， sports and entertainment | 742.1 | 27.1 |

The transportation, warehousing and postal industries are developing steadily. The port throughput for the year was 540 million tons, an increase of 6.1%; the foreign trade throughput was 390 million tons, an increase of 6.2%; the container throughput was 19.32 million TEUs, an increase of 5.5%. At the end of the year, there are 192 routes， increased by 3.2%。 Therein， At the end of the year, there are 160 domestic airlines, 29 international airlines and 3 airlines from Hong Kong, Macao and Taiwan, with an annual total aviation passenger throughput of 2454.1 million and an increase of 5.7%. The throughput of air cargo is 220000 tons, an decrease of 3.2%. In the whole year, the number of subway trains was 330,000, with a total operating mileage of 9.15 million kilometers and a total passenger volume of 152.94 million. The total 65.09 billion yuan of the total business completed in the whole year increased by 105.2%. Among them, the total postal service 8.29 billion yuan increased by 14.4%. The total 56.8 billion yuan of telecommunication services increased by 132.1%.Express business volume amounted to 380 million, increased by 23%.Fixed broadband Internet users amounted to 3.98 million households, with an increase of 7.9%. The city's mobile phone users amounted to 12.59 million households, of which 3G and 4G user 10.64 million households, increased by8.7%.

Table 8 : Volume and Growth Rate Completed by transportation in 2018

| Transportation | Unit | Traffic volume | Growth ( % ) |
|---|---|---|---|
| Passenger volume | 100 billion person-km | 182.49 | 6.4 |
| Railways | 100 billion person-km | 105.36 | 8.7 |
| Highways | 100 billion person-km | 76.97 | 3.4 |
| Waterways | 100 billion person-km | 0.16 | -27.2 |
| Cargo volumes | 100 billion ton-km | 1647.12 | 9.3 |
| Railways | 100 billion ton-km | 190.90 | 4.3 |
| Highways | 100 billion ton-km | 532.20 | 3.2 |
| Waterways | 100 billion ton-km | 924.02 | 14.4 |

The financial industry is developing healthily. The foreign currency deposit balance of financial institution at year end stands at 1,612.13 billion yuan, increased by 99.23 billion yuan than the beginning of the year. The RMB deposit balance stands at 1,553.22 billion yuan, increased by114.44 billion yuan than the beginning of the year. Therein, the residents savings amounts to 591.37 billion yuan, increased by 51.86billion yuan than the beginning of the year. The foreign currency loan balance stands at 1.6098 trillion yuan, increased by 169.29 billion yuan than the beginning of the year. The RMB loan balance stands at 1.51942 trillion yuan, increased by 1.9238 billion yuan than the beginning of the year. The insurance industry realized the30.66 billion yuan of premium income, increased by 7.2%.Among them, the insurance company realized the 13.28 billion yuan of premium income, increased by 20%. Life insurance company realized the30.66 billion yuan of premium income, with an increase of 7.2%. The securities company' s securities trading volume stands at 2.72681 trillion yuan, decrease by 22.7%. There are 236 private funds collection institutions at the end of the year. The scale of the management fund stands at 60.04 billion yuan, increased by 30.9%.

The tourism industry is developing rapidly. The total tourism consumption stands at186.71 billion yuan, increased by 13.8%. the total tourism consumption reached 186.71 billion yuan, an increase of 13.8%. Among them, 153.6 million inbound visitors are

received, with an increase of 6.4%.; the tourism consumption reached 1.16 billion US dollars, an increase of 14%. It received 98.489 million domestic tourists, an increase of 13.7%; the tourism consumption reached 165.1 billion yuan, an increase of 13.8%. At the end of the year, there are 123 scenic spots at level A, including 1 5A-level tourist scenic spots, 4 4A-level tourist scenic spots, and 3A-level tourist scenic spots. There are 99 star-rated hotels, of which 10 are 5-star hotels, 25 are 4-star hotels, and 60 are 3-star hotels. It has 544 travel agencies, including 59 outbound travel business travel agencies and 544 travel and domestic travel business travel agencies.

## Ⅵ .Fixed Investment

The city's fixed asset investment increased by 7.9%. Among them, the investment in the primary industry increased by 14.3%, the investment in the secondary industry increased by 9.1%, and the investment in the tertiary industry increased by 7.5%. More than 702 new projects (including real estate) of more than 100 million yuan were added, an increase of 1 from the previous year. The investment was 173.75 billion yuan, down 12.4%, accounting for 33.2% of the city's fixed asset investment.

An investment of 148.52 billion yuan has been accomplished for the real estate development, increased by 11.6%. Therein, the residential investment stands at 103.48 billion yuan, increased by 11.8%. The sales area of the Commodity House is 18.08 million square meters, decreased by 4.9%. Therein, residential sales area stands at 15.783 million square meters, decreased by 3.4%.

Table 9 : Real Estate Development Investment, Commodity Housing Sales Area and Speed Increase in 2018

| Category | Real Estate Development Investment ( 100 million yuan ) | Growth ( % ) | Sales Area of Commodity House ( 10 000 $m^2$ ) | Growth ( % ) |
|---|---|---|---|---|
| Total | 1485.2 | 11.6 | 1808 | -4.9 |
| Residential | 1034.8 | 11.8 | 1578.3 | -3.4 |
| Office building | 98.5 | -12.5 | 76.7 | -21.6 |
| Commercial operation house | 153.7 | -17.3 | 119.9 | -7.9 |
| Other | 198.2 | 85.7 | 33.1 | -14.6 |

Throughout the year, the guaranteed housing basically established stands at 15540 sets, including 11212 sets of public rental housing, 2103 sets of affordable housing and 2225 sets of commodity housing. By the end of the year, 7326 families are enjoying the

rental subsidy, and the rental subsidy 43.67 million yuan is distributed throughout the year.

## Ⅶ.Domestic Trade

484.25 billion yuan of retail sales of consumer goods is achieved in the whole year, with an increase of 10.0%. According to the statistics, the retail sales amount of consumer goods in town stands at 4026.9 billion yuan, with an increase of 9.7%. Retail sales of consumer goods in rural areas stands at 81.56 billion yuan, with an increase of 11.4%.According to the industry, retail sales of wholesale and retail sales amounted to 422.1 billion, with an increase of 9.1%.The retail sales of accommodation and catering industry realized 62.15 billion yuan, increased by 16.6%.

The retail sales of consumer goods above designated size reached 164.42 billion yuan, increased by 9.1%. The retail sales of tobacco and alcohol increased by 27.0%, and the retail sales of clothing, shoes, hats and needles increased by 8.6%. The retail sales of cosmetics increased by 4.8%, the retail sales of gold and silver jewellery increased by 11.5%, the retail sales of daily necessities increased by 19.1%, the retail sales of household appliances and audio equipment increased by 18.5%, and the retail sales of Chinese and Western medicines increased by 25.1%. Retail sales increased by 10.1%, retail sales of construction and decoration materials increased by 12.3%, retail sales of petroleum and products increased by 9.8%, and retail sales of automobiles decreased by 0.1% compared with the previous year.

## Ⅷ.Foreign Trabe

The total imports and exports sales throughout the city stands at 532.13yuan, increased by 5.7.Therein, the exports valued 317.22 billion yuan, increased by 4.7%. The imports valued 214.90 billion yuan, increased by 7.3%.The total imports and exports to the countries along the 'Belt and Road' stands at 259.04 billion yuan, increased by 4.2%. Therein, the exports stands at 163.06 billion, increased by 1.9%. The imports stands at 95.98 billion, increased by 8.4%.

The total of import and export of foreign trade in Qingdao port stands at 1.21968 trillion yuan, increased by 9.7%. Among them,the exports stands at 673.85 billion yuan, increased by 6.5%. The imports stands at545.83 billion yuan, increased by 13.9%.

Table10 : Import & Export of Main Commodities to/from Qingdao in 2018

| Category | Import & Export | | Export | | Import | |
|---|---|---|---|---|---|---|
| | Amount ( 100 million yuan ) | GrowthRate ( % ) | Amount ( 100 million yuan ) | GrowthRate ( % ) | Amount ( 100 million yuan ) | GrowthRate ( % ) |
| Textiles and garments | 511.2 | 6.5 | 482.0 | 7.7 | 29.2 | -9.8 |
| Agricultural products | 797.7 | 11.8 | 387.3 | 8.4 | 410.4 | 15.2 |
| Elextrical and mechanical | 1786.8 | 1.6 | 1352.2 | 0.5 | 434.6 | 5.2 |
| High-tech products | 525.2 | 5.1 | 316.1 | 5.1 | 209.1 | 5.1 |

Table 11 : Import and Export Volume and Growth Ratefrom /to Major Countries and Regions in 2018

| Country ( Region ) | ExportAmount ( 10 000dollars ) | Growth ( % ) | Import Amount ( 10 000dollars ) | Growth ( % ) |
|---|---|---|---|---|
| Asia | 119950 | 8.0 | 1280932 | 5.3 |
| Hong Kong | 522 | -48.6 | 11487 | 19.6 |
| Taiwan | 7943 | -22.2 | 118789 | 15.9 |
| Japan | 15717 | -6.2 | 185504 | 3.8 |
| Korea | 28535 | 9.3 | 342617 | 12.8 |
| ASEAN | 31712 | -26.3 | 379222 | -14.9 |
| South Asia | 4493 | -23.8 | 63178 | 23.0 |
| Middle East | 3895 | -62.2 | 60583 | -54.8 |
| Africa | 3850 | -31.2 | 47902 | 14.5 |
| South Africa | 13203 | -8.5 | 134631 | -12.8 |
| Europe | 4057 | 76.5 | 38975 | 57.3 |
| EU | 3705 | 85.3 | 34467 | 60.0 |
| U.K. | 26720 | 341.4 | 135723 | 82.5 |
| Germany France | 26757 | 20.2 | 260346 | 44.9 |
| France | 810 | -54.6 | 26943 | 25.6 |
| Italy | 47121 | 43.4 | 506724 | 29.5 |
| CIS and Eastern Europe | 26130 | 3.9 | 290470 | 19.7 |
| Russia | 6219 | 30.5 | 60435 | 52.8 |
| South America | 7689 | 38.8 | 85797 | 26.0 |
| Brazil | 2248 | -53.0 | 36255 | 9.5 |
| North America | 1312 | -42.1 | 21093 | -0.3 |
| U.S.A. | 18336 | 276.2 | 183367 | 52.4 |
| Canada | 17761 | 292.7 | 174582 | 51.2 |
| Oceania | 51717 | 51.4 | 531235 | -2.4 |
| Australia | 44561 | 187.2 | 374326 | 53.2 |

In 2018, the city approved 956 new foreign investment projects, an increase of 47.1%; contractual foreign investment was US$9.82 billion, an increase of 7.8%. The actual use of foreign capital in the city was 8.69 billion US dollars, an increase of 10%; according to the statistics of the Ministry of Commerce FDI (foreign direct investment), the actual use of foreign capital was 5.80 billion US dollars, an increase of 4.1%.

Throughout the year, there are 22 investment projects to the countries and regions along the 'Belt and Road', with an agreed investment amount of US dollars 2.0 billion, increased by8.9%; The actual investment amounted to 680 million US dollars, an increase of 86.9%.

Of the 107 newly contracted projects in the whole city, the new contract amount is 49.3 billion US dollars, an increase of 11.9%,In the city's foreign labor service cooperation service, 18,294 people are sent,

## Ⅸ .Society enterprise

At the end of the year, there are 25 colleges and universities (including private universities) within the city, including 23universities. 16,000 post-graduate student enrollment in the entire year, 45,000 on-duty postgraduates and 110,000 graduates ( excluding the p ostgraduates stationed in Qingdao Research Institute)102,000 students enrolled by the General Higher Education Institutes,353,000 students in school and 94,000 graduated.26,000 persons for vocational education enrollment , 84,000 for in-school students, and 28,000 graduated. 38,000 persons for senior high school enrollment , 117,000 for in-school students, and 38,000 graduated.86,000 persons

for junior high school enrollment , 268,000 for in-school students, and 7,2000 graduated.104,000 persons for general primary school enrollment , 570,000 for in-school students, and 86,000 graduated.20 persons for special education enrollment , 200 for in-school students, and 20 graduated. There are 264,000 kids in the kindergartens.

At the end of the year, there are 3745 healthcare institutes (excluding the clinics in villages), 422 hospitals and health centers, 26 disease prevention and control centers, 12 maternal and child health institutions, 2917 clinics and Medical Rooms. At the end of theyear, there are 84,000 various health technicians, among them, the doctors amounted to 35,000 persons. There are 58,000 of medical beds in the city, of which there are 56,000 beds in hospitals and health centers.

The city athletes won 353 gold medals, 247 silver medals and 236 bronze medals in the competitions. There are 2 key sports universities with 1370 students. The amateur sports schools amounted to 10, with 1846 students.

## Ⅹ .Urban construction

At the end of the year, the urbanization rate of the city's permanent residents reached 73.67%, increasing by 1.1 percentage points over the previous year. The daily water supply for the city is 129,700 tons, increased by 2.9%.The actual water consumption of the city is 410 million tons in the whole year, in which the production water and living water accounts to 160 million tons and 250 million tons, respectively.

The total household number of liquefied gas and natural gas in cities reaches1.898 million households, and the total amount of liquefied gas is 27000 tons in the whole year, and the total amount of natural gas is 107 million cubic meters. And the gasification rate of the city reaches 100 percent.

In the year, the heating area is 10.604 million square meters, and the heating area at the end of the year reaches 200 million square meters.

At the end of the year, there are 623 bus routes and tram lines. There are 8475 buses running in public. There are 10867 Taxis. At the end of the year, there are 4 metro lines, with 152.9412 million of annual passenger capacity and 419000 of daily average passenger capacity.

There are 788 public toilets in the city, 774 above Category III, 202 newly-added toilets and 54 alterations.

## Ⅺ .Energy, Environment and Work Safety

Preliminary statistics show that the total industrial comprehensive energy consumption of the whole city in the whole year is 14.89 million tons of standard coal, increasing by 4.1 percent. Of these, coal consumption is 13.60 million tons, down by 1.7%. The consumption of crude oil is 15.42 million tons, increased by 1.2%. The natural gas consumption is 1000 million cubic meters, with an increase of 89.3%.The total power consumption of the whole society is 43.2 billion KWh , with an increase of 7.7%. Among them, the industrial electrical consumption amounted to 23.8 billion kilowatt-hour, increased by 5.4%. The living consumption of urban and rural residents amounts to 7.7 billion kilowatt-hours, with an increase of 2.2%.

In the year, the city's energy production stands at 28.34 million tons of standard coal, increased by 2.1%. Among them, the processing capacity of crude oil is 15.41 million tons, with an increase of 1.2%. The production of gasoline is 4.74 million tons, with an increase of 3.9%. The production of diesel oil is 3.83 million tons and the drop of diesel oil is 6.2%. The power generating capacity is 19.2 billion kWh, increased by 4.8%.The output of new energy is 1.7 billion, increased by 13.5%. The wind power generation increased by 12.6, and the biomass power generation increased by 25.4%.The power generation of new energy accounts for 9.1% of the total power generation of the city, and increased by 0.7 percentage points.

The annual average temperature of the whole city is 13.3 ℃ , and the average annual precipitation is 722.7 millimeters. The city's air quality is 307 days, accounting for 85% of the year. In the whole city, the water with quality up to or better than that of Category II sea water accounts for 90.6%, which was the same as the previous year. The average value of environmental noise in urban area is 56.9 decibels, and the average noise of urban traffic trunk line is 68.0 decibels.

There are 63 production safety accidents in seven industries (domains) in the city, including 69 deaths, decreased by 42.2% and 38.4% respectively. The death rate of 100 million GDP production safety accident rate is 0.006. The death rate of the production

safety accident of the employment personnel of the trade and commerce enterprise is 0.72. The death toll of the road traffic accidents is 11300.

## Ⅻ .Living Conditions and Social Security

In the whole year, the per capita disposable income of the city residents stands at 42019 yuan, increased by 8.4%. Categorizing according to the permanent residential place, the per capita disposable income of urban residents stands at 50817 yuan, increased

by 7.7%. The per capita disposable income of rural residents stands at20820 yuan, increased by 7.5%. The income ratio of urban and rural residents in the city is 2.44:1.

The per capita consumption expenditure, which stands at 27,316 yuan, in the whole city

increased by 8.3 percent, and the Engel coefficient is 28.5 percent. Categorizing according to the permanent residential place, the per capita consumption expenditure of urban residents stands at 32,890 yuan, increased by 7.6%. the per capita consumption expenditure of rural residents stands at 13,885 yuan, increased by 7.4%.

Table 12 : Per Capita Disposable Income of Urban and Rural Residents in 2018

| | Residents | | Urban Residents | | Rural Residents | |
|---|---|---|---|---|---|---|
| Description of inducators | Absolute Value ( yuan ) | Growth Rate ( % ) | Absolute Value ( yuan ) | Growth Rate ( % ) | Absolute Value ( yuan ) | Growth Rate ( % ) |
| Disposable income | 42019 | 8.4 | 50817 | 7.7 | 20820 | 7.5 |
| Salary income | 25303 | 7.6 | 30955 | 6.8 | 11684 | 7.4 |
| Operating net income | 8027 | 7.3 | 7836 | 7.4 | 8487 | 7.3 |
| Propetry net income | 3475 | 12.8 | 4789 | 11.4 | 310 | 10.8 |
| Transfer net income | 5214 | 11.3 | 7237 | 9.9 | 339 | 17.1 |

Table 13 : Per Capita Disposable Expense of Urban and Rural Residents in 2018

| Description of inducators | Residents | | Urban Residents | | Rural Residents | |
|---|---|---|---|---|---|---|
| | Absolute Value ( yuan ) | Growth Rate ( % ) | Absolute Value ( yuan ) | Growth Rate ( % ) | Absolute Value ( yuan ) | Growth Rate ( % ) |
| Consumption expense | 27316 | 8.3 | 32890 | 7.6 | 13885 | 7.4 |
| tobacco and liquor | 7787 | 4.0 | 9318 | 2.9 | 4098 | 5.9 |
| Chothing | 2538 | 2.9 | 3168 | 1.7 | 1020 | 5.1 |
| Housing Living | 6365 | 16.7 | 7751 | 17.3 | 3024 | 8.0 |
| product and services | 1837 | 5.1 | 2207 | 4.0 | 945 | 6.7 |
| Transportation andcommunication | 4084 | 8.8 | 4765 | 8.3 | 2445 | 8.1 |
| Education, culture and entertainment | 2571 | 9.5 | 3122 | 8.6 | 1245 | 10.3 |
| Medical and health care | 1480 | 9.6 | 1764 | 8.6 | 794 | 10.6 |
| Other product and services | 654 | 4.6 | 795 | 3.4 | 314 | 6.9 |

Table 14: Amount of Major Consumer Durable Owned by every 100 Households in2018

| Description of inducators | Unit | Quantity | | |
|---|---|---|---|---|
| | | Residents | Urban Residents | Rural Residents |
| Household automobile | vehicle | 56 | 62 | 43 |
| Motorcycles | vehicle | 28 | 15 | 61 |
| Refrigerators | set | 108 | 108 | 109 |
| Washing machines | set | 99 | 100 | 97 |
| Water heaters | set | 97 | 101 | 88 |
| Air-conditioners | set | 112 | 120 | 93 |
| Color TV | set | 107 | 107 | 105 |
| Computers | set | 70 | 81 | 45 |
| Mobile telephones | set | 230 | 228 | 232 |

According to the sample survey, the per capita housing construction area of urban residents at the end of the year is 32.9 square meters, and the per capita housing construction area of rural residents is 35.9 square meters.

In the whole year, the newly-increased urban residents employment number stands at 776,000 person, increased by 6.3%.Therein, the employment of workers in the city increased by 4.8%, and the employment of foreign workers increased by 8.1%.The service sector absorbed an employment of 507,000 persons, with an increase of 16.9%.The private economy absorbed an employment of 596,000 persons, with an increase of 11.3%.

At the end of the year, the minimum life guarantee number of urban residents in the city reached 20, 457. The minimum living security fund for urban residents stands at 199.23 million yuan. There are a total of 4, 843 people in the rural five-guarantee support,and the rural five-guarantee support expenditure amounts to 76.245 million yuan.

At the end of the year, the number of insured persons in the basic old-age insurance for workers in the whole city is 2.7351 million.The number of unemployed insurance is 2.2369 million persons. The number of unemployed insurance contributions received in thewhole year is 75,000 persons. The urban registered unemployment rate in the whole city is 2.94%, which decreased by 0.18 percentage points.

Note :

1. Figures reported herein are preliminary statistics.

2. The absolute figures of gross domestic product (GDP) and added value of each industry are calculated according to the current price, and the growth rate is calculated according to the current price. According to "three industry division regulations" (Guo Tong Zi[2012] No. 108), three industries, such as agro-forestry, fishing services, industry, auxiliary activities in industry, metalwork, machinery and equipment repair, are classified into the tertiary industry.

3. The resident population includes: (1) the person who lives in the household and the household registration in the township of this Town (including the person whose household registration is in the household and who has been out for less than half a year). (2) the person who has lived in the household for more than half a year, the household

registration is in the street outside the township. (3) The household registration is in the street of the foreign township, and the person who has left the household registration for more than half a year. (4) who lives in the household and whose household registration is pending.

4. PCT is an English abbreviation for "Patent Cooperation Treaty". The PCT international patent refers to Chinese patent application person can submit international patent application to the China Patent Office or to the World Intellectual Property Organization according to the PCT regulations, and is an important index to reflect the development level of export-oriented economic development in the region and the competitiveness of international technology in the region.

5. The strategic emerging industry, according to the national planning, mainly includes seven industrial fields such as energy conservation, environmental protection, new generation of information technology, biology, high-end equipment manufacturing, new energy, new materials and new energy Automobile.

6. The industrial enterprises above the scale are the annual main business income 20 million yuan and the above enterprises. Trade enterprises above designated size are units with a main business income of 20 million yuan or more in the wholesale industry, 5 million yuan or more in the retail industry, and 2 million yuan and above in the accommodation and catering industry. The starting point standard of the fixed asset investment project statistics is the planned total investment 5 million yuan. For service enterprises above designated size, the first refers to service companies with an annual business income of 10 million yuan or more or 50 or more employees at the end of the year. including transport, storage and postal services, information transmission, software and information technology services, rental and business services, scientific research and technology services, water resources, environmental and public facilities management, education, health and social work. As well as property management, real estate brokerage services, self-owned real estate business activities and other real estate industry. Second, it refers to a service legal entity with an annual operating income of 5 million yuan or more or 50 or more employees at the end of the year. Including: resident services, repairs and other services, cultures, sports and recreation.

7. The statistics range of the number of production safety accidents and the number of deaths include the accidents that occur in the seven industries (areas) of production and business road traffic, water transportation, railway transportation, civil aviation flight, agricultural machinery, fishery ship and maritime trade and commerce, and

no longer includes forest fire, Real-time and non-production operational road traffic.

8. The area of built-up area, water supply, water use, gas supply, heat supply, roads, toilets, sewers and other relevant data excludes Jimo District for now.

9. Source: The financial data in this bulletin comes from the Municipal Finance Bureau. the talents, registered unemployment rate, and social security data come from the Municipal Human Resources and Social Security Bureau. the bank data comes from the Qingdao Central Branch of the People's Bank of China. the securities data comes from

the Qingdao Securities Regulatory Bureau. the insurance data comes from Qingdao Insurance Regulatory Bureau. aquatic product data from the Municipal Ocean and Fisheries Bureau. forestry data from the Municipal Forestry Bureau. " three products and one standard" , agricultural machinery and other data from the Municipal Agricultural

Commission. irrigated area data from the Municipal Water Resources Bureau. transportation data from the city traffic Transportation Committee. postal data from the Municipal Postal Administration. fixed telephone, broadband, mobile phone and other data from the Municipal Communications Administration. built-up area, water supply, gas supply, heating, roads, sewers and other data from the Municipal Urban and Rural Construction Committee. Export, foreign investment, foreign contracted projects, foreign labor cooperation, cross-border e-commerce and other data from the Municipal Bureau of Commerce. tourism data from the Municipal Tourism Development Committee. education data from the Municipal Education Bureau. technology, patent data from the Municipal Science and Technology Bureau. sports data from Municipal Sports Bureau. health data from the Municipal Health and Family Planning Commission. environmental data From the Municipal Environmental Protection Bureau. meteorological data from the Municipal Meteorological Bureau. safety production data from the Municipal Safety Supervision Bureau. poverty alleviation data from the Municipal Poverty Alleviation Cooperation Office. car ownership from the Municipal Public Security Bureau. household income and expenditure, prices, urban and rural residential housing area and other data from Qingdao Bureau of Investigation, National Bureau of Statistics. other data from the Municipal Bureau of Statistics.

# 综 合 1

GENERAL SURVEY

# 简 要 说 明

**一、本篇资料的主要内容**

本篇资料是对我市行政区划、气象情况、分行业法人单位数、各部门机构数和国民经济、社会发展的综合反映，主要包括行政区划、气象情况、分行业法人单位数、各部门机构数、国民经济主要比例关系、国民经济和社会发展主要指标占全国全省比重、国民经济和社会发展主要指标及其增长速度等资料。

**二、本篇资料的来源**

1、“行政区划”主要包括2018年底各区（市）街道办事处（乡镇）、社区居委会（村民委员会）区划资料，数据来源于市民政局。

2、“气象情况”包括分区市、市区分月气象资料，数据来源于市气象局。

3、“全市生产总值”来源于国民经济核算统计报表，由市统计局国民经济核算处整理提供。

4、国民经济和社会发展综合部分来源于本年鉴各篇章中的资料，由市统计局国民经济综合统计处加工整理。

# Brief Introduction

***I. Main Content***

Data in this chapter cover the main indicators on divisions of administrative areas, meteorology, corporate units, number of grass-roots units and national economy and social development, including divisions of administrative areas, meteorology, number of corporate units, number of grass-roots units, average daily social and economic activities, ratio, and percentage of main indicators of Qingdao to the whole nation and the whole province and growth rate of main indicators.

***II. Source of Data***

(1) Data on divisions of administrative areas are mainly including the information on sub-district offices (villages and towns) and community neighborhood committees (villagers residents' committees) at the end of 2018. The data are provided by Qingdao Municipal Bureau of Civil Affairs.

(2) Data on meteorology are provided by Qingdao Municipal Meteorological Bureau.

(3) Data on gross national product are prepared according to the data of national accounts and compiled by the Division of National Accounts of Qingdao Municipal Bureau of Statistics.

(4) Data on general survey of economy and society are based on those of different chapters and compiled by the Division of Comprehensive Statistics of Qingdao Municipal Bureau of Statistics.

# 1-1　行政区划（2018年底）
ADMINISTRATIVE DIVISION（END OF 2018）

单位：个（unit）

| 市区名称 | Region | 街道办事处 Subdistrict Offices | 社区居委会 Community Residents' Committees | 镇 Town | 村民委员会 Villagers' Committees |
|---|---|---|---|---|---|
| **全　市** | **Whole Municipality** | **104** | **1206** | **41** | **5445** |
| 市南区 | Shinan District | 14 | 50 | | |
| 市北区 | Shibei District | 30 | 137 | | |
| 李沧区 | Licang District | 11 | 116 | | |
| 崂山区 | Laoshan District | 5 | 162 | | |
| 黄岛区 | Huangdao District | 12 | 267 | 10 | 961 |
| 城阳区 | Chengyang District | 8 | 247 | | 1 |
| 即墨区 | Jimo District | 8 | 65 | 7 | 1028 |
| 胶州市 | Jiaozhou | 8 | 78 | 4 | 811 |
| 平度市 | Pingdu | 5 | 51 | 12 | 1783 |
| 莱西市 | Laixi | 3 | 33 | 8 | 861 |

# 1-2　气象情况(2018 年)
METEOROLOGY (2018)

| 市区名称 | Region | 平均气温(摄氏度) Average Temperature (℃) | 极端气温 Extreme Temperature (centigrade) | | 降水量(毫米/年) Precipitation (millimeter/year) | 日照时数(小时/年) Sunshine Hours (hour/year) | 平均气压(百帕) Average Atmospheric Pressure (100 pa) |
|---|---|---|---|---|---|---|---|
| | | | 最高(摄氏度) Maximum (℃) | 最低(摄氏度) Minimum (℃) | | | |
| 市　区 | Urban Area | 13.5 | 35.3 | -10.9 | 686.2 | 2083 | 1008.1 |
| 崂山区 | Laoshan District | 13.3 | 35.1 | -11.3 | 806.8 | 2370.5 | 1010.8 |
| 黄岛区 | Huangdao District | 13.6 | 35.3 | -11.8 | 705.9 | 2368.5 | 1016.2 |
| 即墨区 | Jimo District | 13.6 | 36.1 | -13.7 | 862.3 | 2403.4 | 1011.6 |
| 胶州市 | Jiaozhou | 13.5 | 35 | -11.9 | 741.9 | 2355.1 | 1007.2 |
| 平度市 | Pingdu | 13.3 | 36 | -15.3 | 642.1 | 2296.8 | 1009.9 |
| 莱西市 | Laixi | 12.5 | 36.8 | -14.6 | 613.7 | 2512.4 | 1008.2 |

注：以上为 7 个国家基准站或基本站
Note：These are 7 national reference or base stations.

# 1-3　市区分月气象情况(2018 年)
MONTHLY METEOROLOGY OF URBAN AREA (2018)

| 月　份 | Month | 平均气温(摄氏度) Average Temperature (℃) | 降水量(毫米) Precipitation (millimeter) | 日照时数(小时) Sunshine Hours (hour) |
|---|---|---|---|---|
| 一月 | Jan. | -0.6 | 5 | 134.4 |
| 二月 | Feb. | 1.4 | 0.8 | 152.6 |
| 三月 | Mar. | 6.7 | 45.1 | 177.3 |
| 四月 | Apr. | 11.9 | 36.9 | 197.7 |
| 五月 | May | 16.9 | 95.3 | 199.1 |
| 六月 | June | 21 | 116.7 | 172.4 |
| 七月 | July | 25.3 | 150.4 | 134.9 |
| 八月 | Aug. | 27.7 | 85.2 | 222.6 |
| 九月 | Sept. | 22.5 | 90.4 | 194.5 |
| 十月 | Oct. | 16.1 | 14.9 | 240.7 |
| 十一月 | Nov | 10.8 | 17.8 | 145.5 |
| 十二月 | Dec. | 2.2 | 27.7 | 111.3 |
| 全　年 | Annual Total | 13.5 | 686.2 | 2083 |

# 1-4　各部门机构数（2018 年底）
GRASS-ROOTS UNITS IN VARIOUS SECTORS（END OF 2018）

| 项目 | Item | 单位 | Unit | 机构数 Grass-roots Units |
|---|---|---|---|---|
| **农村基层单位** | **Rural Grass-roots Units** | | | |
| 镇政府 | Town Governments | 个 | unit | 43 |
| 乡村户数 | Number of Rural Households | 万户 | 10 000 households | 131.2 |
| **工业企业单位** | **Industrial Enterprises** | 个 | **unit** | **34240** |
| 规模以上工业 | Above Designated Size | 个 | unit | 3508 |
| #国有企业 | State-owned Enterprises | 个 | unit | 145 |
| 集体企业 | Collective-owned Enterprises | 个 | unit | 4 |
| 外商及港澳台商投资企业 | Enterprises with Funds from Hong Kong，Macao，Taiwan and Foreign Conutries | 个 | unit | 938 |
| 规模以下工业 | Above Designated Size | 个 | unit | 30732 |
| **交通运输业** | **Transportation** | | | |
| 铁路 | Railway | 个 | unit | |
| 公路 | Highway | 个 | unit | 214 |
| 水运 | Waterway | 个 | unit | 14 |
| **邮电业** | **Rostal and Telecommunication Services** | | | |
| 邮政局（所） | Post Offices | 处 | unit | 265 |
| 电信营业网点（自有） | Telecom business outlets | 个 | unit | 458 |
| **建筑业企业** | **Construction Enterprises** | 个 | **unit** | 711 |
| 国有企业 | State-owned Enterprises | 个 | unit | 19 |
| 集体企业 | Collective-owned Enterprises | 个 | unit | 8 |
| 其他 | Others | 个 | unit | 684 |
| **批发和零售业、住宿和餐饮业** | Wholesale & Retail Trades，Hotels and Catering Services | | | |
| 限额以上批发业 | Wholesale Trade above Designated Size | 个 | unit | 1338 |
| 限额以上零售业 | Retail Trade above Designated Size | 个 | unit | 725 |
| 限额以上住宿业 | Hotel above Designated Size | 个 | unit | 181 |
| 限额以上餐饮业 | Catering Service above Designated Size | 个 | unit | 187 |

## 1-4　续表
Continued

| 项目 | Item | 单位 | Unit | 机构数 Grass-roots Units |
| --- | --- | --- | --- | --- |
| **教育事业** | Education | | | |
| 普通高等学校 | Regular Institutions of Higher Education | 所 | unit | 25 |
| 中等专业学校 | Specialized Secondary Schools | 所 | unit | 6 |
| 普通中学 | Regular Secondary Schools | 所 | unit | 319 |
| 普通小学 | Regular Primary Schools | 所 | unit | 713 |
| 幼儿园 | Kindergartens | 所 | unit | 2241 |
| **科研机构** | Science and Technology Institutions | | | |
| 中央属 | Central Level | 个 | unit | 22 |
| 地方属 | Local | 个 | unit | 36 |
| **文化及相关产业** | Culture and Related Industry | | | |
| 公共图书馆 | Public Libraries | 个 | unit | 12 |
| 影剧院 | Cinemas | 个 | unit | 72 |
| **卫生事业** | Public Health | | | |
| #医院 | Hospitals | 个 | unit | 421 |
| **民政行政单位** | Civil Affairs Departments | | | |
| #社会福利事业 | Institutions of Social Welfare | 个 | unit | 228 |

# 1-5　按行业分法人单位数
NUMBER OF CORPORATE UNITS BY SECTOR

单位：个（unit）

| 行　业 | Sector | 2018 |
|---|---|---|
| 总　计 | Total | 358783 |
| 农、林、牧、渔业 | Agriculture Forestry Animal Husbandry and Fishery | 842 |
| 采矿业 | Mining | 158 |
| 制造业 | Nanufacturing | 60631 |
| 电力、热力、燃气及水生产和供应业 | Electricity, heat, gas, water production and supply industry | 539 |
| 建筑业 | Construction | 27156 |
| 批发和零售业 | Wholesale and Retail Trades | 123864 |
| 交通运输、仓储和邮政业 | Transport Storage and Post | 13726 |
| 住宿和餐饮业 | Hotels and Catering Services | 5934 |
| 信息传输、软件和信息技术服务业 | Information Transmission Computer Services and Software | 14934 |
| 金融业 | Financial Intermediation | 654 |
| 房地产业 | Real Estate | 10066 |
| 租赁和商务服务业 | Leasing and Business Services | 42405 |
| 科学研究和技术服务业 | Scientific Research and Technical Services | 21059 |
| 水利、环境和公共设施管理业 | Management of Water Conservancy Environment and Public Facilities | 2065 |
| 居民服务、修理和其他服务业 | Services to Households and Other Services | 7309 |
| 教育 | Education | 6612 |
| 卫生和社会工作 | Health Social Security and Social Welfare | 3157 |
| 文化、体育和娱乐业 | Culture Sports and Entertainment | 7027 |
| 公共管理、社会保障和社会组织 | Public Management and Social Organizations | 10645 |

注：国家经普办正在审核查询数据，表中为初步数。

Note: The National Economic Census Office is reviewing the inquiry data. The preliminary figures are in the table.

# 1-6 国民经济主要平均指标
AVERAGE INDICATORS ON NATIONAL ECONOMY

| 指　标 | Indicator | 单位 | Unit | 2000 年 | 2005 年 |
|---|---|---|---|---|---|
| 人口密度 | DEensity of Population | 人 / 平方公里 | person/sq.km | 664 | 695 |
| 每户年平均人口 | Average Household Size | 人 | person | 3.14 | 3.12 |
| 城镇非私营单位在岗职工年平均工资 | The Average Annual Wage of Staff and Workers in the Post in Non-Private Units in Towns and Cities | 元 | yuan | 10 072 | 19086 |
| 城市居民人均年可支配收入 | Annual Per Capita Net Income of Rural Households | 元 | yuan | 8 016 | 12920 |
| 农民人均年纯收入 | Annual Per Capita Net Income of Rural Households | 元 | yuan | 3 637 | 5806 |
| 每一播亩平均粮食产量 | Output of Grain Per Mu of Sowing Area | 千克 | kg | 411 | 421 |
| 每亩蔬菜平均产量 | Average Output of Vegetables Per Mu | 千克 | kg | 2 735 | 2985 |
| 每亩茶叶平均产量 | Average Output of tea Per Mu | 千克 | kg | 8.1 | 16.5 |
| 每亩花生平均产量 | Average Output of Peanut Per Mu | 千克 | kg | 298 | 327 |
| 每亩棉花平均产量 | Average Output of Cotton Per Mu | 千克 | kg | 83 | 74 |
| 每台拖拉机负担耕地面积 | Cultivated Area Ploughed by Per Tractor | 亩 / 台 | mu/unit | 56 | 39 |
| 每亩耕地施用化肥量（折纯） | Chemical Fertilizer Consumption Per Mu (convert to pure amount) | 千克 | kg | 45 | 52 |
| 每人平均消费品零售额 | Per Capita Retail Sales of Consumer Goods | 元 | yuan | 6077 | 11822 |
| 城市每天平均生活用水量 | Daily Residential Consumption of Water | 万吨 | 10 000 tons | 33.33 | 34.35 |
| 城市每人平均公园绿地面积 | Per Capita Public Green Areas | 平方米 | sq.m | 8.50 | 11.82 |
| 每万人拥有医疗床位 | Number of Hospital Beds Per 10000 Population | 张 | bed | 34.5 | 41.3 |
| 每万人拥有医生数 | Number of Doctors per 10000 Population | 人 | person | 21.0 | 20.3 |
| 每万人中高等学校学生数 | Students Enrollment of Institutions of Higher Education per 10000 Population | 人 | person | 65 | 324 |
| 每万人中中等学校学生数 | Students Enrollment of Secondary Schools per 10000 Population | 人 | person | 704 | 768 |
| 每万人中小学学生数 | Students Enrollment of primary Schools per 10000 Population | 人 | person | 757 | 648 |

注：1. 自 2015 年开始，全市城乡住户调查统一使用一体化改革后的数据，与原数据相比，城乡居民收支指标的调查范围和口径均存较大变化。原“城市居民人均可支配收入”调整为“城镇居民人均可支配收入”；原“农民人均纯收入”调整为“农村居民人均可支配收入”。
2.2008 年 -2017 年农作物数据为根据第三次农业普查结果核定修正后数据。

Note: 1.Since 2015, the urban and rural households investigation unified the data after the integrated reform, compared with the original data, the investigation scope and the caliber of urban and rural residents' income and expenditure indicators have changed greatly.
The original “ per capita disposable income of urban residents” is adjusted to be a “ per capita disposable income of urban residents” . The original “ per capita net income of farmers” is adjusted to “ per capita disposable income of rural residents” .
2.Crop data from 2008 to 2017 are revised based on the results of the third agricultural census.

| 2008年 | 2009年 | 2010年 | 2011年 | 2012年 | 2013年 | 2014年 | 2015年 | 2016年 | 2017年 | 2018年 |
|---|---|---|---|---|---|---|---|---|---|---|
| 715 | 676 | 677 | 679 | 682 | | | | | | |
| 3.13 | 3.12 | 3.10 | 3.09 | 3.09 | | | | | | |
| 29404 | 32507 | 37501 | 43077 | 49052 | 55363 | 62104 | 69465 | 76616 | 83539 | |
| 20464 | 22368 | 24998 | 28567 | 32145 | 35227 | 38294 | 40370 | 43598 | 47176 | 50817 |
| 8509 | 9249 | 10550 | 12370 | 13990 | 15731 | 17461 | 16730 | 17969 | 19364 | 20820 |
| 408 | 411 | 399 | 407 | 411 | 407 | 396 | 400 | 404 | 414 | 430 |
| 3551 | 3624 | 3689 | 3867 | 3887 | 3957 | 3963 | 3889 | 3760 | 3931 | 3796 |
| 39 | 38 | 44 | 47 | 51 | 49 | 52 | 57 | 74 | 75 | 80 |
| 316 | 315 | 306 | 316 | 326 | 314 | 305 | 287 | 294 | 319 | 321 |
| 70 | 71 | 62 | 74 | 81 | 81 | 89 | 86 | 82 | 85 | 110 |
| 36 | 35 | 32 | 31 | | | 38 | 38 | 37 | 36 | 36 |
| 50 | 48 | 47 | 47 | | | 37 | 36 | 36 | 36 | 35 |
| 19640 | 22699 | 25694 | 30043 | 34248 | 38606 | 43064 | 47423 | 51765 | 56452 | 59214 |
| 30.96 | 33.56 | 34.31 | 27.53 | 33.21 | 32.50 | 40.60 | 42.10 | 67.60 | 50.3 | 50.6 |
| 14.53 | 14.50 | 14.58 | 14.58 | 14.60 | 14.60 | 14.60 | 14.60 | 18.60 | 17.4 | 16.0 |
| 42.5 | 43.0 | 47.2 | 52.2 | 61.4 | 58.0 | 60.3 | 62.0 | 63.9 | 69.4 | 68.2 |
| 21.4 | 21.9 | 23.2 | 23.9 | 28.1 | 31.2 | 32.0 | 33.5 | 34.9 | 38.4 | 42.3 |
| 354 | 361 | 373 | 380 | 386 | 388 | 402 | 411.0 | 430.0 | 431.0 | 486.6 |
| 765 | 740 | 701 | 659 | 635 | 626 | 614 | 596.0 | 593.0 | 611.0 | 612.5 |
| 627 | 610 | 606 | 626 | 630 | 642 | 662 | 685.0 | 690.0 | 685.3 | 696.9 |

# 1-7　主要年份社会经济主要指标
MAJOR YEAR'S INDICATORS ON SOCIETY AND ECONOMY

| 指　标 | Indicator | 单位 | Unit | 2000 年 | 2005 年 |
|---|---|---|---|---|---|
| **人口** | **Population** | | | | |
| 总人口（年末） | Population at Year-end | 万人 | 10 000 persons | 706.65 | 740.91 |
| 男性人口 | Male | 万人 | 10 000 persons | 357.74 | 374.03 |
| 女性人口 | Female | 万人 | 10 000 persons | 348.91 | 366.87 |
| 市区人口 | Urban Area | 万人 | 10 000 persons | 234.60 | 265.43 |
| **就业** | **Employment** | | | | |
| 社会从业人员 | Employment | 万人 | 10 000 persons | 397.6 | 471.0 |
| # 单位从业人员 | Employed Persons in Units | 万人 | 10 000 persons | 118.3 | 224.3 |
| **经济总量** | **Gross Economic Amount** | | | | |
| 全市生产总值（当年价） | GDP（at current price） | 亿元 | 100 million yuan | 1191.25 | 2687.46 |
| 第一产业增加值 | Primary Industry | 亿元 | 100 million yuan | 140.85 | 178.33 |
| 第二产业增加值 | Secondary Industry | 亿元 | 100 million yuan | 555.21 | 1392.02 |
| 第三产业增加值 | Tertiary Industry | 亿元 | 100 million yuan | 495.19 | 1117.10 |
| 人均生产总值 | Per Capita GDP | 元 | yuan | 16009 | 33085 |
| 农林牧渔业总产值（当年价） | Gross Output Value of Farming，Forestry，Animal Husbandry and Fishery（at current price） | 亿元 | 100 million yuan | 248.33 | 320.51 |
| 工业总产值（当年价） | Gross Industrial Output Value（at current price） | 亿元 | 100 million yuan | 1940.83 | 5001.78 |

注：1. 单位从业人员 2004 年以前为职工人数（不含私营企业）。
2. 规模以上固定资产投资数据 2003 年以前为城镇以上统计范围。
3. 2002 年以前地方财政一般预算收支数据为地方财政收支口径。
4. 2008 年 -2017 年农林牧渔业总产值为根据第三次农业普查结果核定修正后数据。

Note: 1.Before 2004，the data of employed persons in units refers to the number of staff and workers（excluding private enterprises）.
2.Before 2003，the data of investment in fixed assets above designated size refers to urban investment.
3.Before 2002，the data of general budgetaty revenue and expenditure of local government finance refers to revenue and expenditure of local government finance.
4.Gross Output Value of Farming，Forestry，Animal Husbandry and Fishery from 2008 to 2017 is revised according to the results of the third agricultural census.

| 2008年 | 2009年 | 2010年 | 2011年 | 2012年 | 2013年 | 2014年 | 2015年 | 2016年 | 2017年 | 2018年 |
|---|---|---|---|---|---|---|---|---|---|---|
| | | | | | | | | | | |
| 761.56 | 762.92 | 763.64 | 766.36 | 769.56 | | | | | | |
| 382.46 | 382.35 | 381.92 | 382.69 | 383.82 | | | | | | |
| 379.10 | 380.56 | 381.72 | 383.67 | 385.74 | | | | | | |
| 276.25 | 275.47 | 275.50 | 277.09 | 279.57 | | | | | | |
| | | | | | | | | | | |
| 513.8 | 525.7 | 540.3 | 551.2 | 559.9 | 571.5 | 589.0 | 595.4 | 601.4 | 603.9 | |
| 254.1 | 260.5 | 269.4 | 275.9 | 283.2 | 293.7 | 303.0 | 309.2 | 315.6 | 321.4 | |
| | | | | | | | | | | |
| 4401.56 | 4853.87 | 5749.02 | 6725.76 | 7424.32 | 8147.32 | 8850.54 | 9472.40 | 10184.7 | 11024.11 | 12001.52 |
| 223.40 | 230.25 | 276.99 | 306.38 | 324.41 | 340.50 | 349.62 | 363.98 | 359.3 | 368.85 | 386.91 |
| 2234.83 | 2420.14 | 2823.43 | 3236.92 | 3496.46 | 3745.12 | 4014.99 | 4163.11 | 4309.65 | 4546.21 | 4850.59 |
| 1943.33 | 2203.48 | 2648.60 | 3182.46 | 3603.45 | 4061.70 | 4485.93 | 4940.31 | 5515.75 | 6109.05 | 6764.02 |
| 52266 | 57251 | 65827 | 76804 | 84063 | 91376 | 98283 | 104418 | 111302 | 119215 | 128459 |
| 399.5 | 407.1 | 480.2 | 534.6 | 567.3 | 610.6 | 627.9 | 612.4 | 669.1 | 697.9 | 737.0 |
| 8946.73 | 10255.62 | 11614.83 | 13277.96 | 15306.32 | 16897.18 | 17444.21 | 18019.43 | 17416.71 | 13019.73 | 11389.78 |

# 1-7 续表 1
Contiuned

| 指 标 | Indicator | 单位 | Unit | 2000 年 | 2005 年 |
|---|---|---|---|---|---|
| **财政** | **Government Finance** | | | | |
| 公共财政预算收入 | Public Budget Revenue | 亿元 | 100 million yuan | 80.01 | 176.34 |
| 公共财政预算支出 | Public Budget Expenditure | 亿元 | 100 million yuan | 87.87 | 203.06 |
| **规模以上固定资产投资额** | **Investment in Fixed Assets above Designated Size** | **亿元** | **100 million yuan** | **242.68** | **1403.30** |
| **社会消费品零售额** | **Total Retail Sales of Consumer Goods** | **亿元** | **100 million yuan** | **428.29** | **870.11** |
| **港口吞吐量** | **Volume of Freight Handled in Ports** | **万吨** | **10 000 tons** | **8661** | **18727** |
| **集装箱吞吐量** | **Volume of Containers Handled** | **万标箱** | **Ten Thousand TEUs** | **212.0** | **630.7** |
| **民航货物吞吐量** | **Volume of Freight and Mail Handled in Covil Aviation** | **万吨** | **10 000 tons** | **4.84** | **8.91** |
| **对外贸易** | **Foreign Trade** | | | | |
| 外贸进出口总额 | Imports and Exports（excluding central and provincial companies） | 亿美元 | 100 million USD | 108.31 | 304.55 |
| #出口总额 | Exports | 亿美元 | 100 million USD | 61.14 | 175.88 |
| **教育、卫生、文化** | **Education Public Health，Culture** | | | | |
| 小学在校学生数 | Students Enrollment in Primaty Schools | 万人 | 10 000 persons | 53.49 | 47.98 |
| 普通中学在校学生 | Students Enorllment in Regular Secorndary Schools | 万人 | 10 000 persons | 39.85 | 39.11 |

| 2008年 | 2009年 | 2010年 | 2011年 | 2012年 | 2013年 | 2014年 | 2015年 | 2016年 | 2017年 | 2018年 |
|---|---|---|---|---|---|---|---|---|---|---|
| 342.44 | 376.99 | 452.61 | 566.14 | 670.18 | 788.93 | 895.25 | 1006.26 | 1100.03 | 1157.24 | 1231.9 |
| 369.41 | 433.58 | 532.39 | 658.06 | 765.98 | 1014.23 | 1074.71 | 1222.87 | 1352.85 | 1403.03 | 1561.23 |
| **2019.01** | **2458.89** | **3022.48** | **3502.54** | **4153.91** | **5027.86** | **5766.03** | **6555.70** | **7454.70** | **7777.09** | |
| **1492.22** | **1730.22** | **1961.13** | **2302.37** | **2635.62** | **2986.81** | **3361.72** | **3713.69** | **4104.93** | **4541.01** | **4842.5** |
| **30029** | **31668** | **35012** | **37971** | **41465** | **45782** | **47701** | **49749** | **51463** | **51314** | **54250** |
| **1037.7** | **1027.7** | **1201** | **1302** | **1450** | **1552** | **1658** | **1743** | **1805** | **1831** | **1932** |
| **13.05** | **13.54** | **16.37** | **16.65** | **17.19** | **18.62** | **20.44** | **20.80** | **23.07** | **23.00** | **22** |
| 521.59 | 439.86 | 561.49 | 712.63 | 732.08 | 779.12 | 798.88 | 702.22 | 4350.67（亿元） | 5033.50（亿元） | 5321.26（亿元） |
| 314.62 | 269.22 | 333.51 | 400.56 | 408.20 | 419.86 | 457.77 | 453.50 | 2821.91（亿元） | 3031.81（亿元） | 3172.22（亿元） |
| 47.72 | 46.50 | 46.27 | 47.95 | 49.50 | 49.63 | 51.65 | 53.65 | 54.72 | 55.05 | 56.99 |
| 37.39 | 37.74 | 38.00 | 37.32 | 36.96 | 36.51 | 36.26 | 35.54 | 35.61 | 37.22 | 38.54 |

## 1-7 续表 2
Contiuned

| 指　标 | Indicator | 单位 | Unit | 2000 年 | 2005 年 |
|---|---|---|---|---|---|
| 高等学校在校学生 | Students Enrollment in Instutions of Higher Education | 万人 | 10 000 persons | 4.61 | 23.98 |
| 小学专任教师 | Full-time Teachers in Primary Schools | 万人 | 10 000 persons | 3.17 | 3.17 |
| 普通中学专任教师 | Full-time Teachers in Regular Secorndary Schools | 万人 | 10 000 persons | 2.63 | 2.97 |
| 医生总数 | Doctors | 万人 | 10 000 persons | 1.49 | 1.50 |
| 医院床位数 | Hospital Beds | 万张 | 10 000 beds | 2.01 | 2.86 |
| **人民生活** | People's Living Conditions | | | | |
| 就业人员工资总额 | Total wages of Employed Persons | 亿元 | 100 million yuan | 120.40 | 359.5 |
| 城市居民人均可支配收入 | Per Capita Disposable Income of Urban Households | 元 | yuan | 8 016 | 12920 |
| 农民人均纯收入 | Per Capita Net Income of Rural Households | 元 | yuan | 3 637 | 5806 |
| 城乡人民币储蓄存款余额 | Savings Deposit of Urban and Rural Households | 亿元 | 100 million yuan | 535.32 | 1343.10 |
| **物价指数** | **Price Indexes** | | | | |
| 商品零售价格指数（以 1950 年价格为 100） | Retail Price Indes（1950=100） | % | % | 520.5 | 495.0 |
| 居民消费价格指数（以 1950 年价格为 100） | Consumer Price Index（1950=100） | % | % | 711.9 | 753.1 |
| #食品价格指数（以 1950 年价格为 100） | Food Price Index（1950=100） | % | % | 800.1 | 871.8 |

注：1. 就业人员工资总额 2005 年前统计范围为全部职工不含私营企业，2015 年及以前为在岗职工工资总额；
2 2015 年"城乡人民币储蓄存款余额"改为"住户存款"。

Note: 1.The total wages of the Full-Time Employees on duty were before 2005. The statistics ranged from all employees to private enterprises, Total wages for staff and workers in 2015 and before.
2. In 2015，"balance of RMB deposits in urban and rural areas" changed to "household deposits."

| 2008年 | 2009年 | 2010年 | 2011年 | 2012年 | 2013年 | 2014年 | 2015年 | 2016年 | 2017年 | 2018年 |
|---|---|---|---|---|---|---|---|---|---|---|
| 26.93 | 27.52 | 28.49 | 29.15 | 29.66 | 30.02 | 31.35 | 32.23 | 34.09 | 34.62 | 39.8 |
| 3.24 | 3.22 | 3.2 | 3.16 | 3.17 | 3.28 | 3.22 | 3.45 | 3.42 | 3.47 | 3.69 |
| 2.99 | 3.06 | 3.08 | 3.14 | 3.20 | 3.18 | 3.2 | 3.29 | 3.39 | 3.47 | 3.6 |
| 1.63 | 1.67 | 1.77 | 1.83 | 2.16 | 2.41 | 2.5 | 2.63 | 2.76 | 3.09 | 3.46 |
| 2.99 | 3.05 | 3.34 | 3.56 | 4.12 | 3.97 | 4.3 | 4.51 | 4.73 | 4.63 | 5.08 |
| | | | | | | | | | | |
| 578.7 | 638.1 | 738.0 | 877.5 | 1044.3 | 1251.7 | 1456.0 | 1644.4 | 1852.7 | 2034.7 | 2251.7 |
| 20464 | 22368 | 24998 | 28567 | 32145 | 35227 | 38294 | 40370 | 43598 | 47176 | 50817 |
| 8509 | 9249 | 10550 | 12370 | 13990 | 15731 | 17461 | 16730 | 17969 | 19364 | 20820 |
| 2123.36 | 2527.88 | 2912.33 | 3198.51 | 3757.60 | 4141 | 4436 | 5024 | 5326 | 5394 | 5914 |
| | | | | | | | | | | |
| 526.6 | 519.2 | 526.5 | 550.2 | 559.6 | 567.4 | 580.5 | 580.5 | 592.1 | 596.8 | 607.6 |
| 831.4 | 835.6 | 854.0 | 896.7 | 920.9 | 943.9 | 968.4 | 980.0 | 1004.5 | 1024.6 | 1046.1 |
| 1105.3 | 1123.0 | 1194.9 | 1327.5 | 1384.6 | 1458.0 | 1522.2 | 1543.1 | 1625.5 | 1619.0 | 1669.2 |

# 1-8　国民经济主要结构指标

COMPOSITION INDICATORS ON NATIONAL ECONOMY

| 指　标 | Indicator | 2000 年 | 2005 年 | 2008 年 | 2009 年 |
|---|---|---|---|---|---|
| **社会从业人员** | **Employment** | | | | |
| 产业结构 | Industrial Composition | | | | |
| 第一产业 | Primary Industry | 36.4 | 22.2 | 19.9 | 20.1 |
| 第二产业 | Secondary Industry | 33.9 | 41.8 | 43.0 | 41.9 |
| 第三产业 | Tertiary Industry | 29.7 | 36.0 | 37.1 | 38.0 |
| **全市生产总值** | **GDP** | | | | |
| 产业结构 | Industrial Composition | | | | |
| 第一产业 | Primary Industry | 11.8 | 6.6 | 5.1 | 4.7 |
| 第二产业 | Secondary Industry | 46.6 | 51.8 | 50.8 | 49.9 |
| 第三产业 | Tertiary Industry | 41.6 | 41.6 | 44.1 | 45.4 |
| **农业** | **Agriculture** | | | | |
| 农林牧渔业产值结构 | Composition of Farming, Forestry, Animal Husbandry and Fishery | | | | |
| # 农业 | Farming | 45.0 | 39.5 | 43.2 | 43.5 |
| 林业 | Forestry | 0.8 | 0.8 | 0.6 | 0.5 |
| 牧业 | Animal Husbandry | 27.9 | 33.4 | 29.9 | 27.9 |
| 渔业 | Fishery | 26.4 | 26.3 | 22.7 | 24.1 |
| **工业** | **Industy** | | | | |
| 轻重工业产值结构 | Composition of Output Value of Light and Heavy Industry | | | | |
| 轻工业 | Light Industry | 64.1 | 49.4 | 42.3 | 41.7 |
| 重工业 | Heavy Industry | 35.9 | 50.6 | 57.7 | 58.3 |
| **固定资产投资** | **Investment in Fixed Assets** | | | | |
| 投资结构 | Composition of Investment | | | | |
| 生产性 | Productive | 54.0 | 65.4 | 61.6 | 56.3 |
| 非生产性 | Non-productive | 46.0 | 34.6 | 38.4 | 43.7 |

注：2008 年 -2017 年农业数据为根据第三次农业普查结果核定修正后数据。

Note: Agricultural data from 2008 to 2017 are revised according to the results of the third agricultural census.

| 2010 年 | 2011 年 | 2012 年 | 2013 年 | 2014 年 | 2015 年 | 2016 年 | 2017 年 | 2018 年 |
|---|---|---|---|---|---|---|---|---|
| | | | | | | | | |
| 19.5 | 19.2 | 18.8 | 18.8 | 18.4 | 18.1 | 17.8 | 16.9 | |
| 41.4 | 41.2 | 41.0 | 40.6 | 39.0 | 38.5 | 38.0 | 37.8 | |
| 39.1 | 39.6 | 40.2 | 40.6 | 42.6 | 43.3 | 44.2 | 45.3 | |
| | | | | | | | | |
| 4.8 | 4.6 | 4.4 | 4.2 | 3.9 | 3.8 | 3.5 | 3.4 | 3.2 |
| 49.1 | 48.1 | 47.1 | 46 | 45.4 | 44.0 | 42.3 | 41.2 | 40.4 |
| 46.1 | 47.3 | 48.5 | 49.8 | 50.7 | 52.2 | 54.2 | 55.4 | 56.4 |
| | | | | | | | | |
| 45.8 | 40.9 | 40.0 | 41.7 | 42.1 | 40.3 | 42.5 | 43.0 | 44.7 |
| 0.4 | 0.4 | 0.4 | 0.4 | 0.4 | 0.4 | 0.4 | 0.4 | 0.5 |
| 25.5 | 28.1 | 26.6 | 25.5 | 24.8 | 25.0 | 24.2 | 23.8 | 22.1 |
| 24.6 | 26.7 | 28.8 | 28.0 | 27.7 | 29.6 | 26.6 | 26.2 | 26.1 |
| | | | | | | | | |
| 38.7 | 38.3 | 39.5 | 39.5 | 38.8 | 39.5 | 39.4 | 37.6 | 34.3 |
| 61.3 | 61.7 | 60.5 | 60.5 | 61.2 | 60.5 | 60.6 | 62.4 | 65.7 |
| | | | | | | | | |
| 53.6 | 53.2 | 58.4 | 61.65 | 57.08 | 63.16 | 59.81 | 53.64 | |
| 46.4 | 46.8 | 41.6 | 38.35 | 42.92 | 36.84 | 40.19 | 46.36 | |

# 1-9　平均每天主要社会经济活动

SELECTED INDICATORS ON AVERAGE DAILY SOCLAL AND ECONOMIC ACTIVITIES

| 指　标 | Indicator | 单位 | Unit | 2000 年 | 2005 年 |
|---|---|---|---|---|---|
| 全市生产总值 | GDP | 万元 | 10 000 yuan | 32637 | 73629 |
| 工业总产值 | Gross Industrial Output Value | 万元 | 10 000 yuan | 53174 | 137035 |
| 农林牧渔业总产值 | Gross Output Value of Farming，Forestry，Animal Husbandry and Fishery | 万元 | 10 000 yuan | 6803 | 8781 |
| 主要工业产品产量 | Output of Major Industrial Products | | | | |
| 发电量 | Electricity | 万千瓦时 | 10 000 kW·h | 2489 | 2701 |
| 钢材 | Rolled-steel | 吨 | ton | 2558 | 9049 |
| 纱 | Yarn | 吨 | ton | 191 | 198 |
| 布 | Cloth | 万米 | 10 000 m | 114 | 141 |
| 家用电冰箱 | Refrigerator | 台 | unit | 8523 | 24899 |
| 彩色电视机 | Color TV set | 台 | unit | 10395 | 36282 |
| 社会消费品零售总额 | Total Retail Sales of Consumer Goods | 万元 | 10 000 yuan | 11734 | 23839 |
| 固定资产投资 | Investment in Fixed Assets above Designated Size | 万元 | 10 000 yuan | 6649 | 38446 |
| 外贸进出口总额 | Imports and Exports | 万美元 | 10 000 USB | 3707 | 9047 |
| 港口吞吐量 | Volume of Freight Handled in Ports | 万吨 | 10 000 tons | 23.73 | 51.31 |

注：1. 固定资产投资包括城镇、农村 500 万元以上投资项目。
2. 一年按照 365 天计算。
3. 2008 年 -2017 年农林牧渔业总产值为根据第三次农业普查结果核定修正后数据。

Note :1. Investment in fixed assets includes construction projects involving an urban or rural investment of 5，000，00 yuan and over.
2. A year is computed according to 365 days.
3. Gross Output Value of Farming，Forestry，Animal Husbandry and Fishery from 2008 to 2017 is revised according to the results of the third agricultural census.

| 2008 年 | 2009 年 | 2010 年 | 2011 年 | 2012 年 | 2013 年 | 2014 年 | 2015 年 | 2016 年 | 2017 年 | 2018 年 |
|---|---|---|---|---|---|---|---|---|---|---|
| 120591 | 132983 | 157507 | 184267 | 203406 | 223214 | 242481 | 259518 | 279033 | 302030 | 328809 |
| 245116 | 280976 | 318215 | 363780 | 419351 | 462936 | 477924 | 493683 | 477143 | 356705 | 312048 |
| 10945 | 11153 | 13157 | 14646 | 15541 | 16728 | 17203 | 16777 | 18331 | 19120 | 20192 |
| | | | | | | | | | | |
| 4509 | 4730 | 4984 | 4759 | 4787 | 4935 | 4885 | 4754 | 4805 | 4981 | 5271 |
| 9593 | 9579 | 9136 | 9101 | 7525 | 6312 | 5830 | 3853 | 5243 | 7996 | 8764 |
| 118 | 106 | 97 | 53 | 53 | 92 | 89 | 76 | 92 | 73 | 79 |
| 133 | 85 | 48 | 120 | 134 | 141 | 122 | 77 | 68 | 65 | 127 |
| 19813 | 22663 | 21951 | 19686 | 15754 | 14366 | 16714 | 23893 | 24170 | 22429 | 24290 |
| 22922 | 29170 | 30444 | 31622 | 39452 | 41426 | 46984 | 37704 | 57855 | 46658 | 46443 |
| 40883 | 47403 | 52130 | 63079 | 72209 | 81831 | 92102 | 101745 | 112464 | 124411 | 132670 |
| 55315 | 67367 | 82808 | 95960 | 113806 | 137751 | 157973 | 179608 | 204238 | 213071 | |
| 14695 | 12288 | 15633 | 19768 | 20057 | 21346 | 21887 | 19239 | 119196（万元） | 137904（万元） | 145787（万元） |
| 82.27 | 86.76 | 96 | 104 | 114 | 125 | 131 | 136 | 141 | 141 | 149 |

# 1-10　主要指标占全国全省比重（2018 年）

## PERCENTAGE OF MAIN INDICATORS TO CHINA AND SHANDONG（2018）

| 指　标 | Indicator | 单位 | Unit |
| --- | --- | --- | --- |
| 一、生产总值 | GDP | 亿元 | 100 million yuan |
| 第一产业 | Primary Industry | 亿元 | 100 million yuan |
| 第二产业 | Secondary Industry | 亿元 | 100 million yuan |
| 第三产业 | Tertiary Industry | 亿元 | 100 million yuan |
| 二、年末总人口（常住人口） | The Total Population（Resident Population）at the End of the Year | 万人 | 10 000 persons |
| 三、主要工业产品产量 | Output of Major Industrial Products | | |
| 发电量 | Electricity | 亿千瓦小时 | 100 million kW · h |
| 汽车 | Automobile | 万辆 | 10 000 vehicle |
| 房间空气调节器 | Air Conditioner | 万台 | 10 000 units |
| 家用电冰箱 | Refrigerator | 万台 | 10 000 units |
| 彩色电视机 | Color TV Set | 万台 | 10 000 units |
| 钢材 | Rolled-steel | 万吨 | 10 000 tons |
| 水泥 | Cement | 万吨 | 10 000 tons |
| 四、主要农产品产量 | Output of Major Farm Products | | |
| 粮食 | Grain | 万吨 | 10 000 tons |
| 油料 | Oil Plants | 万吨 | 10 000 tons |
| 肉类产量 | Meat | 万吨 | 10 000 tons |
| 水产品 | Aquatic Products | 万吨 | 10 000 tons |
| 五、房地产开发投资 | Investment In Real Estate Development | 亿元 | 100 million yuan |
| 六、货物进出口总额 | Imports and Exports | 亿元 | 100 million yuan |
| 其中：出口 | Export | 亿元 | 100 million yuan |
| 进口 | Import | 亿元 | 100 million yuan |
| 七、高等学校在校学生 | Students Enrollment of Institutions of Higher Education | 万人 | 10 000 persons |

注：1. 本表全国、全省均为公报数。
　　2. 青岛市主要工业产品产量数据为本地口径。

Note：1. The number of the country and province in the table are obtained from the statistical report.
　　2. The output of main industrial products of qingdao are at local calibre.

| 全国<br>China | 全省<br>Shandong | 青岛市<br>Qingdao | 青岛市占全国比重（%）<br>Qingdao/China | 青岛市占全省比重（%）<br>Qingdao/Shandong |
|---|---|---|---|---|
| 900309 | 76469.7 | 12001.52 | 1.33 | 15.69 |
| 64734 | 4950.5 | 386.91 | 0.60 | 7.82 |
| 366001 | 33641.7 | 4850.59 | 1.33 | 14.41 |
| 469575 | 37877.4 | 6764.02 | 1.44 | 17.86 |
| 139538 | 10047.24 | 939.48 | 0.67 | 9.35 |
| | | | | |
| 71118 | 5608.2 | 192.4 | 0.27 | 3.43 |
| 2782 | 136.3 | 9.24 | 0.33 | 6.78 |
| 20486 | 1060.8 | 1058.10 | 5.16 | 99.75 |
| 7993 | 888.4 | 886.58 | 11.09 | 99.80 |
| 18835 | 1695.2 | 1695.18 | 9.00 | 100.00 |
| 110552 | 9427.8 | 319.90 | 0.29 | 3.39 |
| 221000 | 12280.2 | 284.47 | 0.13 | 2.32 |
| | | | | |
| 65789 | 5319.5 | 310.1 | 0.47 | 5.83 |
| 3439 | 310.9 | 38.5 | 1.12 | 12.38 |
| 8517 | 849.3 | 52.2 | 0.61 | 6.15 |
| 6469 | 816.6 | 103.5 | 1.60 | 12.67 |
| 120264 | 7553 | 1485.2 | 1.23 | 19.66 |
| 305050 | 19302.5 | 5321.2 | 1.74 | 27.57 |
| 164177 | 10569.6 | 3172.2 | 1.93 | 30.01 |
| 140874 | 8732.9 | 2149 | 1.53 | 24.61 |
| 2831.1 | 204.1 | 39.8 | 1.41 | 19.50 |

# 1-11 主要年份全市生产总值（按当年价格计算）

MAJOR YEAR'S GROSS DOMESTIC PRODUCT (AT CURRENT PRICE)

单位：亿元（100 million yuan）

| 年份<br>Year | 全市生产总值<br>GDP | 第一产业<br>Primary Industry | 第二产业<br>Secondary Industry | #工　业<br>Industry | 第三产业<br>Tertiary Industry | 人均生产总值（元）<br>Per Capita GDP (yuan) |
|---|---|---|---|---|---|---|
| 1949 | 2.87 | 1.19 | 1.10 | | 0.58 | 71 |
| 1952 | 6.74 | 1.76 | 3.25 | 2.95 | 1.73 | 163 |
| 1957 | 10.82 | 2.00 | 5.76 | 5.39 | 3.06 | 239 |
| 1962 | 9.69 | 1.11 | 4.68 | 4.27 | 3.90 | 205 |
| 1965 | 15.50 | 1.80 | 8.96 | 8.48 | 4.74 | 325 |
| 1970 | 23.23 | 3.15 | 14.46 | 13.86 | 5.62 | 451 |
| 1975 | 29.07 | 6.93 | 15.39 | 14.67 | 6.75 | 522 |
| 1978 | 38.43 | 8.73 | 20.25 | 19.15 | 9.45 | 663 |
| 1980 | 48.65 | 10.19 | 26.27 | 24.28 | 12.19 | 819 |
| 1985 | 82.28 | 21.29 | 37.55 | 34.03 | 23.44 | 1311 |
| 1988 | 142.87 | 32.72 | 70.32 | 63.42 | 39.83 | 2199 |
| 1990 | 180.77 | 39.26 | 86.76 | 78.94 | 54.75 | 2714 |
| 1991 | 205.65 | 43.04 | 98.94 | 89.64 | 63.67 | 3053 |
| 1992 | 261.35 | 43.92 | 130.27 | 117.61 | 87.16 | 3856 |
| 1993 | 371.90 | 62.20 | 183.35 | 164.35 | 126.35 | 5455 |
| 1994 | 510.81 | 85.12 | 244.30 | 218.87 | 181.39 | 7436 |
| 1995 | 631.45 | 112.53 | 294.43 | 263.98 | 224.49 | 9089 |
| 1996 | 713.60 | 133.27 | 322.33 | 289.87 | 258.00 | 10130 |
| 1997 | 802.59 | 117.47 | 378.25 | 342.80 | 306.87 | 11235 |
| 1998 | 901.19 | 140.66 | 409.60 | 369.89 | 350.93 | 12443 |
| 1999 | 1018.97 | 138.19 | 468.67 | 424.15 | 412.11 | 13884 |
| 2000 | 1191.25 | 140.85 | 555.21 | 504.44 | 495.19 | 16009 |

## 1-11 续表 1
Continued

单位：亿元（100 million yuan）

| 年份<br>Year | 全市生产总值<br>GDP | 第一产业<br>Primary Industry | 第二产业<br>Secondary Industry | #工 业<br>Industry | 第三产业<br>Tertiary Industry | 人均生产总值（元）<br>Per Capita GDP（yuan） |
|---|---|---|---|---|---|---|
| 2001 | 1368.55 | 144.35 | 643.44 | 582.99 | 580.76 | 18128 |
| 2002 | 1583.51 | 147.21 | 758.33 | 686.55 | 677.97 | 20655 |
| 2003 | 1869.44 | 148.92 | 923.76 | 832.31 | 796.76 | 23986 |
| 2004 | 2270.16 | 163.49 | 1149.94 | 1032.50 | 956.73 | 28540 |
| 2005 | 2687.46 | 178.33 | 1392.02 | 1259.06 | 1117.10 | 33085 |
| 2006 | 3183.18 | 183.95 | 1666.96 | 1517.28 | 1332.28 | 38608 |
| 2007 | 3750.16 | 203.59 | 1934.52 | 1766.28 | 1612.05 | 44964 |
| 2008 | 4401.56 | 223.40 | 2234.83 | 2034.25 | 1943.33 | 52266 |
| 2009 | 4853.87 | 230.25 | 2420.14 | 2174.43 | 2203.48 | 57251 |
| **2010** | **5749.02** | **276.99** | **2823.43** | **2519.00** | **2648.60** | **65827** |
| 2011 | 6725.76 | 306.38 | 3236.92 | 2880.76 | 3182.46 | 76804 |
| 2012 | 7424.32 | 324.41 | 3496.46 | 3135.54 | 3603.45 | 84063 |
| 2013 | 8147.32 | 340.50 | 3745.12 | 3356.16 | 4061.70 | 91376 |
| 2014 | 8850.54 | 349.62 | 4014.99 | 3559.81 | 4485.93 | 98283 |
| 2015 | 9472.40 | 363.98 | 4168.11 | 3689.57 | 4940.31 | 104418 |
| 2016 | 10184.70 | 359.30 | 4309.65 | 3802.65 | 5515.75 | 111302 |
| 2017 | 11024.11 | 368.85 | 4546.21 | 3952.87 | 6109.05 | 119215 |
| 2018 | 12001.52 | 386.91 | 4850.59 | 4137.08 | 6764.02 | 128459 |

注：1. 人均生产总值按常住人口计算。
2. 自 2005 年起三次产业分类采用《国民经济行业分类》（GB/T4754-2002）标准，自 2013 年起，根据《国民经济行业分类》（GB/T4754－2011）和《三次产业划分规定》（国统字［2012］108 号），将农林牧渔业中的农林牧渔服务业以及工业中的开采辅助活动和金属制品、机械和设备修理业归入第三产业。
3. 全国第三次农业普查后，对历年 GDP 数据进行了修订（以下相关表同）。
4. 2018 年 GDP 数据为初步核算数（以下相关表同）。

Note：1. Per capita GDP are calculated at permanent population.
2. Three Industries are grouped by "Classification and Code of the Sectors of the National Economy"（GB/T4754-2002）since 2005，from 2013 on, According to the Industrial Classification for National Economic Activities（GB/4754-2011）and the Rules for Classification of Three Industries（NBS No.［2012］108），the service industries of Agriculture，Forestry，Animal Husbandry and Fishery and mining auxiliary activities and metal products，machinery and equipment repair industries in the Industry are classified into the tertiary industry.
3. According to the the Third Agricultural Census,the date of GDP over the years have been revised (The same applies to tables following) .
4. GDP data for 2018 are preliminary accounting figures(The same applies to tables following).

# 1-12 主要年份全市生产总值构成（以全市生产总值为 100）

COMPOSITION OF MAJOR YRAR'S GROSS DOMESTIC PRODUCT (GROSS DOMESTIC PRODUCT=100)

单位：%

| 年份 Year | 全市生产总值 GDP | 第一产业 Primary Industry | 第二产业 Secondary Industry | #工业 Industry | 第三产业 Tertiary Industry |
|---|---|---|---|---|---|
| 1952 | 100 | 26.1 | 48.2 | 43.8 | 25.7 |
| 1957 | 100 | 18.5 | 53.3 | 49.8 | 28.2 |
| 1962 | 100 | 11.4 | 48.3 | 44.1 | 40.3 |
| 1965 | 100 | 11.6 | 57.8 | 54.7 | 30.6 |
| 1970 | 100 | 13.6 | 62.2 | 59.7 | 24.2 |
| 1975 | 100 | 23.9 | 52.9 | 50.5 | 23.2 |
| 1978 | 100 | 22.7 | 52.7 | 49.8 | 24.6 |
| 1980 | 100 | 21.0 | 54.0 | 49.9 | 25.1 |
| 1985 | 100 | 25.9 | 45.6 | 41.4 | 28.5 |
| 1988 | 100 | 22.9 | 49.2 | 44.4 | 27.9 |
| 1990 | 100 | 21.7 | 48.0 | 43.7 | 30.3 |
| 1991 | 100 | 20.9 | 48.1 | 43.6 | 31.0 |
| 1992 | 100 | 16.8 | 49.8 | 45.0 | 33.4 |
| 1993 | 100 | 16.7 | 49.3 | 44.2 | 34.0 |
| 1994 | 100 | 16.7 | 47.8 | 42.8 | 35.5 |
| 1995 | 100 | 17.8 | 46.6 | 41.8 | 35.6 |
| 1996 | 100 | 18.7 | 45.2 | 40.6 | 36.2 |
| 1997 | 100 | 14.6 | 47.1 | 42.7 | 38.2 |
| 1998 | 100 | 15.6 | 45.5 | 41.0 | 38.9 |
| 1999 | 100 | 13.6 | 46.0 | 41.6 | 40.4 |
| 2000 | 100 | 11.8 | 46.6 | 42.3 | 41.6 |
| 2001 | 100 | 10.5 | 47.0 | 42.6 | 42.4 |
| 2002 | 100 | 9.3 | 47.9 | 43.4 | 42.8 |
| 2003 | 100 | 8.0 | 49.4 | 44.5 | 42.6 |
| 2004 | 100 | 7.2 | 50.7 | 45.5 | 42.1 |
| 2005 | 100 | 6.6 | 51.8 | 46.8 | 41.6 |
| 2006 | 100 | 5.8 | 52.4 | 47.7 | 41.8 |
| 2007 | 100 | 5.4 | 51.6 | 47.1 | 43.0 |
| 2008 | 100 | 5.1 | 50.8 | 46.2 | 44.1 |
| 2009 | 100 | 4.7 | 49.9 | 44.8 | 45.4 |
| 2010 | 100 | 4.8 | 49.1 | 43.8 | 46.1 |
| 2011 | 100 | 4.6 | 48.1 | 42.8 | 47.3 |
| 2012 | 100 | 4.4 | 47.1 | 42.2 | 48.5 |
| 2013 | 100 | 4.2 | 46.0 | 41.2 | 49.8 |
| 2014 | 100 | 3.9 | 45.4 | 40.2 | 50.7 |
| 2015 | 100 | 3.8 | 44.0 | 39.0 | 52.2 |
| 2016 | 100 | 3.5 | 42.3 | 37.3 | 54.2 |
| 2017 | 100 | 3.4 | 41.2 | 35.9 | 55.4 |
| 2018 | 100 | 3.2 | 40.4 | 34.5 | 56.4 |

# 1-13 主要年份全市生产总值增长速度（以上年为 100）

GROWTH RATE OF MAJOR YEAR'S GROSS DOMESTIC PRODUCT (PRECEDING YEAR=100)

单位：%

| 年份 Year | 全市生产总值 GDP | 第一产业 Primary Industry | 第二产业 Secondary Industry | 第三产业 Tertiary Industry | 人均生产总值（元）Per Capita GDP（yuan） |
|---|---|---|---|---|---|
| 1979 | 12.0 | 10.6 | 12.9 | 11.4 | 10.4 |
| 1980 | 10.4 | 4.3 | 13.1 | 10.3 | 9.4 |
| 1981 | -2.0 | -9.1 | -2.4 | 4.7 | -3.2 |
| 1982 | 4.1 | 5.5 | -0.2 | 11.9 | 2.6 |
| 1983 | 16.9 | 42.8 | 9.3 | 12.7 | 15.3 |
| 1984 | 13.0 | 18.9 | 11.5 | 10.3 | 12.0 |
| 1985 | 9.9 | 5.4 | 5.8 | 21.3 | 9.3 |
| 1986 | 9.2 | 2.6 | 12.1 | 10.0 | 8.3 |
| 1987 | 12.0 | 3.6 | 16.0 | 12.0 | 10.6 |
| 1988 | 13.8 | -0.3 | 21.5 | 11.2 | 12.1 |
| 1990 | 9.3 | 9.8 | 7.3 | 12.2 | 8.0 |
| 1991 | 10.6 | 9.9 | 11.0 | 10.5 | 9.4 |
| 1992 | 18.1 | 2.7 | 23.5 | 20.7 | 17.4 |
| 1993 | 22.4 | 20.5 | 21.1 | 25.6 | 21.7 |
| 1994 | 14.4 | 3.6 | 14.7 | 20.2 | 13.5 |
| 1995 | 12.0 | 10.9 | 12.1 | 12.4 | 10.8 |
| 1996 | 7.2 | 7.7 | 7.6 | 6.4 | 5.7 |
| 1997 | 11.5 | -10.6 | 16.8 | 14.6 | 9.9 |
| 1998 | 12.9 | 17.6 | 11.3 | 13.4 | 11.3 |
| 1999 | 13.9 | 4.1 | 15.5 | 15.3 | 12.4 |
| 2000 | 15.2 | 6.5 | 16.4 | 16.4 | 13.6 |
| 2001 | 13.7 | 2.3 | 16.3 | 14.2 | 12.1 |
| 2002 | 14.5 | 3.2 | 16.9 | 14.6 | 12.7 |

# 1-13 续表 1
Continued

单位：%

| 年份<br>Year | 全市生产总值<br>GDP | 第一产业<br>Primary Industry | 第二产业<br>Secondary Industry | 第三产业<br>Tertiary Industry | 人均生产总值（元）<br>Per Capita GDP (yuan) |
|---|---|---|---|---|---|
| 2003 | 16.3 | 2.5 | 20.1 | 14.9 | 14.4 |
| 2004 | 16.7 | 2.7 | 20.3 | 15.2 | 14.3 |
| 2005 | 16.6 | 0.4 | 19.6 | 15.7 | 14.1 |
| 2006 | 15.3 | 0.9 | 16.8 | 15.8 | 13.6 |
| 2007 | 15.5 | -2.6 | 15.3 | 18.3 | 14.2 |
| 2008 | 13.2 | 1.4 | 11.1 | 17.1 | 12.1 |
| 2009 | 12.2 | 3.0 | 12.8 | 12.5 | 11.4 |
| 2010 | 12.9 | 1.4 | 12.6 | 14.4 | 11.2 |
| 2011 | 11.8 | 5.0 | 11.9 | 12.5 | 11.5 |
| 2012 | 10.6 | 3.2 | 11.3 | 10.5 | 9.6 |
| 2013 | 10.0 | 2.0 | 10.1 | 10.6 | 9.0 |
| 2014 | 8.0 | 3.8 | 8.3 | 8.1 | 7.0 |
| 2015 | 8.1 | 3.2 | 7.3 | 9.3 | 7.3 |
| 2016 | 7.9 | 2.9 | 6.7 | 9.2 | 6.9 |
| 2017 | 7.5 | 3.2 | 6.8 | 8.4 | 6.4 |
| 2018 | 7.4 | 3.5 | 7.3 | 7.7 | 6.3 |
| 1978-2010 平均每年增长<br>1978-2010 Average Increase Rate | 12.4 | 5.3 | 13.1 | 13.9 | 11.0 |
| 1991-2010 平均每年增长<br>1991-2010 Average Increase Rate | 14.2 | 4.2 | 15.5 | 15.3 | 12.8 |
| 1996-2010 平均每年增长<br>1996-2010 Average Increase Rate | 13.8 | 2.5 | 15.2 | 14.5 | 13.0 |
| 2001-2010 平均每年增长<br>2001-2010 Average Increase Rate | 14.7 | 1.5 | 16.1 | 15.2 | 13.0 |
| 2006-2010 平均每年增长<br>2006-2010 Average Increase Rate | 13.8 | 0.8 | 13.7 | 15.6 | 12.5 |
| 2010-2015 平均每年增长<br>2010-2015 Average Increase Rate | 9.7 | 2.8 | 9.8 | 10.3 | 8.9 |

# 1-14 分市、区生产总值（2018 年）
GROSS DOMESTIC PRODUCT BY REGION（2018）

单位：亿元（100 million yuan）

| 市、区名称 | Region | 地区生产总值 GDP | 第一产业 Primary Industry | 第二产业 Secondary Industry | 第三产业 Tertiary Industry |
|---|---|---|---|---|---|
| 市南区 | Shinan District | 1203.37 | | 115.12 | 1088.25 |
| 市北区 | Shibei District | 832.20 | | 174.26 | 657.94 |
| 李沧区 | Licang District | 453.53 | | 132.96 | 320.57 |
| 崂山区 | Laoshan District | 697.00 | 8.32 | 314.58 | 374.10 |
| 黄岛区 | Huangdao District | 3387.72 | 73.70 | 1542.68 | 1771.34 |
| 城阳区 | Chengyang District | 1079.02 | 3.28 | 538.87 | 536.87 |
| 即墨区 | Jimo District | 1413.43 | 70.84 | 761.72 | 580.87 |
| 胶州市 | Jiaozhou | 1211.38 | 53.27 | 603.94 | 554.17 |
| 平度市 | Pingdu | 895.85 | 101.36 | 461.48 | 333.01 |
| 莱西市 | Laixi | 620.11 | 61.88 | 299.50 | 258.73 |
| 红岛经济区 | Qingdao National High-tech Industrial Development Zone | 107.36 | 14.27 | 49.24 | 43.85 |
| 保税港区 | Qingdao Free Trade Port Area of Chinat | 129.35 | | 35.52 | 93.83 |

# 1-15　按支出法计算的全市生产总值（2018年）

## GROSS DOMESTIC PRODUCT BY EXPENDITURE APPROACH（2018）

单位：亿元（100 million yuan）

| 项目 | Item | 2018年 | 2018年为2017年%<br>2018/2017（%） |
|---|---|---|---|
| **支出法计算的全市生产总值** | **Gross Domestic Product by Expenditure Approach** | **12001.52** | **107.4** |
| （一）最终消费 | Final Consumption Expenditures | 4570.93 | 109.1 |
| 1. 居民消费 | Household Consumption Expenditures | 3325.15 | 109.0 |
| 农村居民 | Rural Household | 554.72 | 108.6 |
| 城镇居民 | Urban Household | 2770.42 | 109.1 |
| 2. 政府消费 | Government Consumption Expenditures | 1245.78 | 109.4 |
| （二）资本形成总额 | Gross Capital Formation | 6998.65 | 105.3 |
| 1. 固定资产形成总额 | Gross Fixed Capital Formation | 6659.32 | 104.6 |
| 2. 存货增加 | Change in Inventories | 339.33 | 119.6 |
| （三）货物和服务净流出 | Net Exports of Goods and Services | 431.94 | 114.9 |

注：绝对额按当年价格计算，速度按可比价格计算。
Note：The absolute numbers are calculated at current price，their growth are calculated at constant price.

# 1-16　全市生产总值构成（2018 年）
COMPOSITION OF GROSS DOMESTIC PRODUCT（2018）

| 指标 | Indicator | 增加值（亿元）Added Value（10 000 million yuan） | 2018 年为 2017 年 % 2018/2017（%） |
|---|---|---|---|
| **地区生产总值** | **GDP** | **12001.52** | **107.4** |
| 农林牧渔业 | Farming，Forestry，Animal Husbandry and Fishery | 410.56 | 103.6 |
| #农林牧渔服务业 | Agriculture，Forestry，Animal Husbandry and Fishery Service Industry | 23.65 | 106.6 |
| 工业 | Industry | 4137.08 | 106.9 |
| #开采辅助活动 | #Mining Auxiliary Activities | | |
| #金属制品、机械和设备修理业 | #Metal Products，Machinery and Equipment Pepair Industries | 9.89 | 106.9 |
| 建筑业 | Construction | 723.40 | 110.5 |
| 批发和零售业 | Wholesale and Retail Trade | 1440.66 | 107.3 |
| 批发业 | Wholesale | 940.64 | 108.1 |
| 零售业 | Retail Trade | 500.02 | 105.9 |
| 交通运输、仓储和邮政业 | Transport，Storage and Post | 830.58 | 102.7 |
| 住宿和餐饮业 | Hotels and Catering Services | 268.18 | 105.7 |
| 住宿业 | Hotels | 44.89 | 104.4 |
| 餐饮业 | Catering Services | 223.29 | 106.0 |
| 金融业 | Financial Intermediation | 800.40 | 105.2 |
| 房地产业 | Real Estate | 672.46 | 101.2 |
| 房地产业（K 门类） | Real Extate | 443.75 | 99.2 |
| 自有房地产经营活动 | Self-Owned Real Estate Business Activities | 228.71 | 105.0 |
| 其他服务业 | Other Services | 2718.20 | 112.2 |
| 营利性服务业 | For-Profit Services | 1416.11 | 119.6 |
| 非营利性服务业 | Non-Profit Services | 1302.09 | 104.8 |
| 第一产业 | Primary Industry | 386.91 | 103.5 |
| 第二产业 | Secondary Industry | 4850.59 | 107.3 |
| 第三产业 | Tertiary Industry | 6764.02 | 107.7 |

# 主要统计指标解释

**国内生产总值（GDP）**　指按市场价格计算的一个国家（或地区）所有常住单位在一定时期内生产活动的最终成果。国内生产总值有三种表现形态，即价值形态、收入形态和产品形态。从价值形态看，它是所有常住单位在一定时期内生产的全部货物和服务价值超过同期中间投入的全部非固定资产货物和服务价值的差额，即所有常住单位的增加值之和；从收入形态看，它是所有常住单位在一定时期内创造并分配给常住单位和非常住单位的初次收入分配之和；从产品形态看，它是所有常住单位在一定时期内最终使用的货物和服务价值与货物和服务净出口价值之和。在实际核算中，国内生产总值有三种计算方法，即生产法、收入法和支出法。三种方法分别从不同的方面反映国内生产总值及其构成。对于一个地区来说，称为地区生产总值或地区 GDP。

**人均 GDP**　人均 GDP 是一定时期内 GDP 与同期人口平均数的比值。按照国际标准，人口平均数应该是同期平均常住人口。我国在核算制度中也规定，无论是国家还是地区，人口数都采用常住人口。国家统计局规定从 2004 年开始，过去采用户籍人口计算人均 GDP 的地区，作为过渡性措施，可在两年内同时计算两种口径的人均 GDP（数据后面必须注明是什么口径），两年后取消按户籍人口计算的人均 GDP。我市采用常住人口计算人均 GDP。

**三次产业**　是根据社会生产活动历史发展的顺序对产业结构的划分，产品直接取自自然界的部门称为第一产业，对初级产品进行再加工的部门称为第二产业，为生产和消费提供各种服务的部门称为第三产业。它是世界上通用的产业结构分类，但各国的划分不尽一致。我国的三次产业划分是：

第一产业：是指农业、林业、畜牧业、渔业和农林牧渔服务业。

第二产业：是指采矿业，制造业，电力、燃气及水的生产和供应业；建筑业。

第三产业：除第一、第二产业以外的其他行业。

**支出法国内生产总值**　是从最终使用角度反映一个国家（或地区）一定时期内生产活动最终成果的一种方法，包括最终消费支出，资本形成总额及货物和服务净出口三部分。对于地区，名称为“支出法地区生产总值”。

最终消费指常住单位为满足物质、文化和精神生活的需要，从本国经济领土和国外购买的货物和服务的支出；不包括非常住单位在本国经济领土内的消费支出。最终消费分为居民消费和政府消费。

**居民消费**　指常住住户在一定时期内对货物和服务的全部最终消费支出。居民消费支出除了直接以货币形式购买货物和服务的消费之外，还包括以其他方式获得的货物和服务的消费支出，即所谓的虚拟消费支出。居民虚拟消费支出包括以下几种类型：单位以实物报酬及实物转移的形式提供给劳动者的货物和服务；住户生产并由本住户消费了的货物和服务，其中的服务仅指住户的自有住房服务和付酬的家庭雇员提供的家庭和个人服务；金融机构提供的金融媒介服务。

**政府消费**　指政府部门为全社会提供公共服务的消费支出和免费或以较低价格向居民住户提供的货物和服务的净支出。前者等于政府服务的产出价值减去政府单位所获得的经营收入的价值；后者等于政府部门免费或以较低价格向居民住户提供的货物和服务的市场价值减去向住户收取的价值。

**资本形成总额**　指常住单位在一定时期内获得的减去处置的固定资产和存货的净额，包括固定资本形成总额和存货增加。

**固定资本形成总额**　指常住单位在一定时期内获得的固定资产减处置的固定资产的价值总额。固定资产是通过生产活动生产出来的，且使用年限在一年以上、单位价值在规定标准以上的资产，不包括自然资产。分有形固定资产形成总额和无形固定资产形成总额。有形固定资产形成总额包括一定时期内完成的建筑工程、安装工程和设备工器具购置（减处置）价值，以及土地改良、新增役、种、奶、毛、娱乐用牲畜和新增经济林木价值。无形固定资产形成总额包括矿藏的勘探、计算机软件等获得减处置。

**存货增加**　指常住单位在一定时期内存货实物量变动的市场价值，即期末价值减期初价值的差额，再扣除当期由于价格变动而产生的持有收益。存货增加可以是正值，也可以是负值；正值表示存货上升，负值表示存货下降。它包括生产单位购进的原材料、燃料和储备物资等存货，以及生产单位生产的产成品、在制品和半成品等存货。

**货物和服务净出口**　指货物和服务出口减货物和服务进口的差额。出口包括常住单位向非常住单位出售或无偿转让的各种货物和服务的价值；进口包括常住单位从非常住单位购买或无偿得到的各种货物和服务的价值。由于服务活动的提供与使用同时发生，一般把常住单位从国外得到的服务作为进口，非常住单位从本国得到的服务作为出口。货物的出口和进口都按离岸价格计算。

**气候**　指地球与大气之间长期能量交换与质量交换所形成的一种自然环境状态，它是多种因素综合作用的结果。气候既是人类生活和生产的环境要素之一，又是供给人类生活和生产的重要资源。气温、降水、湿度等气象要素的多年平均值是用来描述一个地区气候状况的主要参数，而各种气象要素某年、某月的平均值（或总量）则可以反映出该时期天气气候状况的重要特征。

**气温**　指空气的温度，我国一般以摄氏度（℃）为单位表示。气象观测的温度表是放在离地面约 1.5 米处通风良好的百叶箱里测量的，因此，通常说的气温指的是离地面 1.5 米处百叶箱中的温度。其统计计算方法为：月平均气温是将全月各日的平均气温相加，除以该月的天数而得。

**年平均气温**　是将 12 个月的月平均气温累加后除以 12 而得。

**降水量**　指从天空降落到地面的液态或固态（经融化后）水，未经蒸发、渗透、流失而在地面上积聚的深度。其统计计算方法为：月降水量是将全月各日的降水量累加而得。年降水量是将 12 个月的月降水量累加而得。

## Explanatory Notes on Main Statistical Indicators

**Gross Domestic Product（GDP）**　refers to the final products at market prices producted by all resident units in a country（or a region）during a certain period of time. Gross domestic product is expressed in three different persperctives，namely value，income，and products respectively. GDP in its value perspective refers to the total value of all goods and services produced by all resident units during a certain period of time，minus the total value of input of goods and services of the nature of non–fixed assets；in other words，it is the sum of the value–added of all resident units. GDP from the perspective of products refers to the value of all goods and services for final consumption by all resident units minus the net exports of goods and services during a given period of time. In the practice of national accounting，gross domestic product is calculated from three approaches，namely production approach，income approach and expenditure approach，which reflect gross domestic product and its composition from different angles. For a certain region，it refers region gross product or region GDP.

**Per Capita GDP**　refers to the ratio of GDP in a certain term and average population in the same term. According to the international standard，average population should be average permanent population in the same term. In the account regulation，population of both the country and the region should be permanent population. In the after two yers since 2004，per capita GDP can be calculated at two coverage.i.e. at permanent population and household registered population（the note of coverage should follow the data.）The per capita GDP calculated with household registered population will be abolished after two years. Per capita GDP of Qingdao is calculated at permanent population.

**Three Strata of Industries**　has been classfied according to the historical sequence of development. Primary industry refers to extraction of natural resources；secondary industry involves processing of primary products；and tertiary industry provides services of various kinds for production and consumption. The above classification is universal although it varies to some extent form country to country. In China economic activities are categorized into the following three strata of industry：

Primary industry refers to farming，forestry，animal husbandryand fishery and services in support of these industries.

Secondary industry refers to mining and quarrying, manufacturing, production and supply of electricity, water and gas, and construction.

Tertiary industry refers to all other economic activities not included in primary or secondary industries.

**GDP by Expenditure Approach** refers to the method of measuring the final results of production activities of a country (region) during a given period from the perspective of final use. It includes final consumption, total capital formation and net export of goods and services. It reflects use and composition of gross domestic product. For a certain region, it refers region gross product by expenditure approach.

**Final Consumption** refers to the total expenditure of resident units for purchases of goods and services from both the domestic economic territory and abroad to meet the needs of material, cultural and spiritual life. It does not include the expenditure of non-resident units on consumption in the economic territory of the country. The final consumption is broken down into household consumption and government consumption.

**Household Consumption** refers to the total expenditure of resident households on the final consumption of goods and services. In addition to the consumption of goods and services bought by the households directly with money, the household consumption also includes expenditure on goods and services obtained by the households in other ways, i.e. the so-called imputed consumption, which includes the following: (a) the goods and services provided to households by employers in the form of payment in kind and transfer in kind; (b) goods and services produced and consumed by the households themselves, in which the services refer to the owner-occupied housing and services offered by payed family employees; (c) financial intermediate services provided by financial institution.

**Government Consumption** refers to the consumption expenditure spent for the provision of public services provided by the government to the whole country and the net expenditure on the goods and services provided by the government to households free of charge or at reduced prices. The former equals to the output value of the government services minus the value of operating income obtained by the government departments. The latter equals to the market value of the goods and services provided by the government free of charge or at reduced prices to the households minus the value received by the government from the households.

**Gross Capital Formation** refers to the fixed assets acquired less disposal and the net value of inventory, thus including the gross fixed capital formation and charges in inventories.

**Gross Fixed Capital Formation** refers to the value of acquisitions less those disposals of fixed assets during a given period. Fixed assets are the assets produced through production activities with unit value above a specified amount and which could be used for over one year. Natural assets are not included. Gross fixed capital formation can be categorized into total tangible fixed capital formation and total intangible fixed capital formation. Total tangible fixed capital formation includes the value of the construction projects and installation projects completed and the equipment, apparatus and instruments purchased (less those disposed) as well as the value of land improved, the value of draught animals, breeding stock and animals for milk, for wool and for recreational purposes and the newly increased forest with economic value. Total intangible fixed capital formation includes the prospecting of minerals and the acquisition of computer software minus the disposal of them.

**Charges in Inventories** refers to the market value of the change in the physical volume of inventory of resident units during a given period, i.e. the difference between the values at the beginning and at the end of the period minus the gains due to the change in prices. The changes in inventories can have a positive or a negative value. A positive value indicates an increase in inventory while a negative value indicates a decrease in inventory. The inventory includes raw materials, fuels and reserve materials purchased by the production units as well as the inventory of finished products, semi-finished products and work-in-progress.

**Net Export of Goods and Services** refers to the exports of goods and services subtracting the imports of goods and services.

Exports include the value of various goods and services sold or gratuitously transferred by resident units to non-resident units. Imports include the value of various goods and services purchased or gratuitously acquired resident units from non-resident units. Because the provision of services and the use of them happen simultaneously, the acquisition of services by resident units from abroad is usually treated as import while the acquisition of services by non-resident units in this country is usually treated as export. The exports and imports of goods are calculated at FOB.

**Climate** refers to the natural environmental status formed by the long-term exchange of energy and mass between the earth and the air, and is the results of interaction of many factors. Climate is both one of the environment factors and the important resources for the living and production activities of the human being. The average values across several years of meteorological factors such as temperature, rainfall and humidity are used as important parameters to describe the climate of a region, while the average values ( or total values ) of a given year or month of meteorological factors reflect the key characteristics of climate for that period of time.

**Temperature** refers to the air temperature. China uses centigrade as the unit. The thermometry used for weather observation is put in a breezy shutter, which is 1.5 meters high from the ground. Therefore, the commonly used temperature refers to the temperature in the breezy shutter 1.5 meters away from the ground. The calculation method is as follows:

Monthly average temperature is the summation of average daily temperature of one month divided by the actual days of that particular month.

Annual average temperature is the summation of monthly average of a year divided by 12 months.

**Volume of Precipitation** refers to the deepness of liquid state or solid state ( thawed ) water falling from the sky to the ground that has not been evaporated, infiltrated or run off. The calculation method is as follows:

Monthly precipitation is the summation of daily precipitation of a month.

Annual precipitation is the summation of 12 months precipitation of a year.

# 人口 2

POPULATION

# 简要说明

## 一、本篇资料的主要内容

本篇资料主要反映了全市人口方面的基本情况，包括全市主要年份和区（市）的户数、人口数、人口密度、土地面积数据、人口出生率、死亡率、自然增长率、计划生育等数据。另外还对建国以来开展的六次人口普查主要数据进行了比较。

## 二、本篇资料的来源

本篇资料分别来源于国家开展的人口普查、人口抽样调查和市公安局的户籍登记资料，由市统计局人口和社会科技统计处整理提供。

# Brief Introduction

## *I. Main Content*

Data in this chapter show the basic condition of population, such as the basic condition of districts and county-level cities, household, population, density of population, birth rate, death rate, natural growth rate and family planning situation. Furthermore, relevant figures obtained from the six national population censuses have been compared.

## *II. Source of Data*

Data in this chapter are from national population censuses, national sample survey. Some are derived from household registration provided by Qingdao Municipal Bureau of Public Security. The data are compiled by the Division of Population and Science & Technology of Qingdao Municipal Bureau of Statistics.

# 2-1 主要年份全市户籍人口数
MAJOR YEAR'S TOTAL REGISTERED POPULATION

单位：人（person）

| 年份<br>Year | 总人口<br>Total Population | 按性别分 Grouped by Sex<br>男<br>Male | 按性别分 Grouped by Sex<br>女<br>Female | 平均人口<br>Average Population |
|---|---|---|---|---|
| 1949 | 4056550 | 1997293 | 2059257 | 4054431 |
| 1952 | 4233586 | 2125392 | 2108194 | 4203428 |
| 1957 | 4822756 | 2424729 | 2398027 | 4773862 |
| 1962 | 4627432 | 2319658 | 2307774 | 4578313 |
| 1965 | 4901670 | 2461629 | 2440041 | 4859712 |
| 1970 | 5391852 | 2720633 | 2671219 | 5337282 |
| 1975 | 5742206 | 2904347 | 2837859 | 5717456 |
| 1978 | 5853321 | 2959800 | 2893521 | 5841638 |
| 1980 | 5961129 | 3015357 | 2945772 | 5937187 |
| 1985 | 6267223 | 3185409 | 3081814 | 6253157 |
| 1988 | 6516920 | 3319534 | 3197386 | 6474541 |
| 1989 | 6571597 | 3348454 | 3223143 | 6544259 |
| 1990 | 6666482 | 3392253 | 3274229 | 6619040 |
| 1991 | 6709277 | 3411776 | 3297501 | 6687880 |
| 1992 | 6731072 | 3420886 | 3310186 | 6720175 |
| 1993 | 6753497 | 3431149 | 3322348 | 6742285 |
| 1994 | 6785291 | 3446019 | 3339272 | 6769394 |
| 1995 | 6846346 | 3476300 | 3370046 | 6815819 |
| 1996 | 6902677 | 3502600 | 3400077 | 6874512 |
| 1997 | 6954391 | 3527588 | 3426803 | 6928534 |
| 1998 | 6995666 | 3545403 | 3450263 | 6975029 |
| 1999 | 7029707 | 3561061 | 3468646 | 7012687 |
| 2000 | 7066481 | 3577367 | 3489114 | 7048094 |
| 2001 | 7104875 | 3595652 | 3509223 | 7085678 |
| 2002 | 7156537 | 3619778 | 3536759 | 7130706 |
| 2003 | 7206806 | 3644032 | 3562774 | 7181672 |
| 2004 | 7311228 | 3692991 | 3618237 | 7259017 |
| 2005 | 7409052 | 3740309 | 3668743 | 7360140 |
| 2006 | 7493812 | 3779891 | 3713921 | 7451432 |
| 2007 | 7579910 | 3816620 | 3763290 | 7536861 |
| 2008 | 7615647 | 3824665 | 3790982 | 7597779 |
| 2009 | 7629161 | 3823534 | 3805627 | 7622404 |
| 2010 | 7636392 | 3819240 | 3817152 | 7632777 |
| 2011 | 7663612 | 3826931 | 3836681 | 7650002 |
| 2012 | 7695585 | 3838205 | 3857380 | 7679599 |

注：截止出书前，未获得公安部门青岛市 2013 年 –2018 年户籍人口信息。
Note: Data come from the Qingdao Nunicipal Public Security Bureau, and the Data of 2013–2018 are absent.

## 2-2 主要年份全市户数、人口数、人口密度（户籍）

MAJOR YEAR 'S HOUSEHOLDS, POPULATION AND DENSITY OF POPULATION（WITH PERMANENT RESIDENCE）

| 年份 Year | 总户数（万户）Total Households（10000 households） | | 总人口（万人）Total Population（10000 persons） | | 平均每户人口（人）Average Persons Per Household（person） | | 人口密度（人/平方公里）Density of Population（person/sq.km） | |
|---|---|---|---|---|---|---|---|---|
| | 全市 Whole Municipality | 市区 Urban Area | 全市 Whole Municipality | 市区 Urban Area | 全市 Whole Municipality | 市区 Urban Area | 全市 Whole Municipality | 市区 Urban Area |
| 1949 | 90.64 | 21.68 | 405.66 | 103.69 | 4.48 | 4.78 | 381 | 941 |
| 1952 | 93.96 | 22.70 | 423.36 | 107.62 | 4.51 | 4.74 | 397 | 977 |
| 1957 | 102.56 | 27.41 | 482.28 | 134.76 | 4.70 | 4.92 | 453 | 1223 |
| 1962 | 106.11 | 29.29 | 462.74 | 137.86 | 4.36 | 4.71 | 434 | 1251 |
| 1965 | 105.31 | 29.64 | 490.17 | 146.74 | 4.65 | 4.95 | 460 | 1332 |
| 1970 | 113.07 | 32.14 | 539.19 | 150.81 | 4.77 | 4.69 | 506 | 1369 |
| 1975 | 123.18 | 36.56 | 574.22 | 161.13 | 4.66 | 4.41 | 539 | 1462 |
| 1978 | 131.27 | 40.08 | 585.33 | 168.00 | 4.46 | 4.19 | 549 | 1525 |
| 1980 | 138.44 | 43.03 | 596.11 | 175.27 | 4.31 | 4.07 | 560 | 1591 |
| 1985 | 157.06 | 53.43 | 626.72 | 190.87 | 3.99 | 3.57 | 588 | 1732 |
| 1988 | 169.72 | 58.95 | 651.69 | 201.38 | 3.84 | 3.42 | 612 | 1827 |
| 1989 | 177.47 | 61.57 | 657.16 | 203.63 | 3.70 | 3.31 | 617 | 1848 |
| 1990 | 186.79 | 63.94 | 666.65 | 205.78 | 3.57 | 3.22 | 626 | 1867 |
| 1991 | 192.46 | 67.15 | 670.93 | 207.22 | 3.49 | 3.09 | 630 | 1880 |
| 1992 | 199.08 | 68.94 | 673.11 | 209.28 | 3.38 | 3.04 | 632 | 1899 |
| 1993 | 201.36 | 70.13 | 675.35 | 212.06 | 3.35 | 3.02 | 634 | 1924 |
| 1994 | 204.05 | 71.24 | 678.53 | 214.97 | 3.33 | 3.02 | 637 | 1951 |
| 1995 | 208.13 | 72.53 | 684.63 | 218.38 | 3.29 | 3.01 | 643 | 1982 |
| 1996 | 212.40 | 75.11 | 690.27 | 223.86 | 3.25 | 2.98 | 648 | 2032 |
| 1997 | 215.12 | 76.39 | 695.44 | 227.22 | 3.23 | 2.97 | 653 | 2062 |
| 1998 | 218.59 | 77.90 | 699.57 | 229.58 | 3.20 | 2.95 | 657 | 2084 |
| 1999 | 222.61 | 79.27 | 702.97 | 231.94 | 3.16 | 2.93 | 660 | 2105 |
| 2000 | 224.73 | 80.46 | 706.65 | 234.60 | 3.14 | 2.92 | 664 | 2129 |
| 2001 | 227.43 | 81.41 | 710.49 | 237.60 | 3.12 | 2.92 | 667 | 2156 |
| 2002 | 229.67 | 82.85 | 715.65 | 241.74 | 3.12 | 2.92 | 672 | 2194 |
| 2003 | 232.26 | 84.15 | 720.68 | 246.77 | 3.10 | 2.93 | 677 | 2240 |
| 2004 | 235.29 | 86.93 | 731.12 | 258.40 | 3.11 | 2.97 | 686 | 2229 |
| 2005 | 237.35 | 87.99 | 740.91 | 265.43 | 3.12 | 3.02 | 695 | 2290 |
| 2006 | 239.33 | 89.12 | 749.38 | 271 | 3.13 | 3.04 | 703 | 2338 |
| 2007 | 241.55 | 90.21 | 757.99 | 275.55 | 3.14 | 3.05 | 711 | 2377 |
| 2008 | 243.18 | 91.22 | 761.56 | 276.25 | 3.13 | 3.03 | 715 | 2384 |
| 2009 | 244.74 | 92.15 | 762.92 | 275.47 | 3.12 | 2.99 | 676 | 1873 |
| 2010 | 246.11 | 93.30 | 763.64 | 275.50 | 3.10 | 2.95 | 677 | 1873 |
| 2011 | 247.94 | 94.69 | 766.36 | 277.09 | 3.09 | 2.93 | 679 | 1884 |
| 2012 | 249.27 | 95.87 | 769.56 | 279.57 | 3.09 | 2.92 | 682 | 1901 |

## 2-3　主要年份全市常住人口数
MAJOR YESR ' S TOTAL RESIDENT POPULATION

单位：万人（10 000 person）

| 年份<br>Year | 总人口<br>Total population |
|---|---|
| 2005 | 819.55 |
| 2006 | 829.42 |
| 2007 | 838.67 |
| 2008 | 845.61 |
| 2009 | 850.03 |
| 2010 | 871.51 |
| 2011 | 879.51 |
| 2012 | 886.85 |
| 2013 | 896.41 |
| 2014 | 904.62 |
| 2015 | 909.70 |
| 2016 | 920.40 |
| 2017 | 929.05 |
| 2018 | 939.48 |

## 2-4　青岛市常住人口
TOTAL RESIDENT POPULATION

单位：万人（10 000 person）

| 市、区名称 | Region | 2018 年 | 2017 年 | 2018 年比 2017 年 ±<br>2018/2017（±） |
|---|---|---|---|---|
| **全市** | **Whole Municipality** | **939.48** | **929.05** | **10.43** |
| 市南区 | Shinan District | 58.83 | 58.53 | 0.30 |
| 市北区 | Shibei District | 110.11 | 109.32 | 0.79 |
| 李沧区 | Licang District | 57.74 | 56.12 | 1.62 |
| 崂山区 | Laoshan District | 44.59 | 43.87 | 0.72 |
| 黄岛区 | Huangdao District | 157.73 | 153.92 | 3.81 |
| 城阳区 | Chengyang District | 72.05 | 70.93 | 1.12 |
| 即墨区 | Jimo District | 123.83 | 122.45 | 1.38 |
| 胶州市 | Jiaozhou | 90.05 | 89.33 | 0.72 |
| 平度市 | Pingdu | 137.89 | 138.05 | –0.16 |
| 莱西市 | Laixi | 76.29 | 76.42 | –0.13 |
| 红岛经济区 | Qingdao National High-tech Industrial Development Zone | 10.37 | 10.11 | 0.26 |

注：黄岛区含保税港区数据。
Note：The Huangdao District contains the data of the bonded harbor area.

# 2-5 主要年份常住人口城镇化率
THE URBANIZATION RATE OF THE MAIN YEAR PERMANENT RESIDENTS

单位：%（%）

| 年份<br>Year | 城镇化率<br>Urbanization rate |
|---|---|
| 2005 | 63.20 |
| 2006 | 63.59 |
| 2007 | 63.90 |
| 2008 | 64.31 |
| 2009 | 64.68 |
| 2010 | 65.81 |
| 2011 | 66.52 |
| 2012 | 67.14 |
| 2013 | 67.72 |
| 2014 | 68.41 |
| 2015 | 69.99 |
| 2016 | 71.53 |
| 2017 | 72.57 |
| 2018 | 73.67 |

注：城镇化率为城镇区域常住人口数量与全市常住总人口的比值。
Note: The urbanization rate is the ratio of the number of permanent urban residents to the total resident population of the city.

# 2-6　分市、区土地面积（2018年底）
LAND AREA（END OF 2018）

| 市、区名称 | Region | 土地面积（平方公里）Land Area（aq.km） |
|---|---|---|
| **全　市** | **Whole Municipality** | **11293.36** |
| 市南区 | Shinan District | 32.21 |
| 市北区 | Shibei District | 65.85 |
| 李沧区 | Licang District | 99.10 |
| 崂山区 | Laoshan District | 395.79 |
| 黄岛区 | Huangdao District | 2128.31 |
| 城阳区 | Chengyang District | 583.68 |
| 即墨区 | Jimo District | 1920.90 |
| 胶州市 | Jiaozhou | 1323.65 |
| 平度市 | Pingdu | 3175.65 |
| 莱西市 | Laixi | 1568.22 |

注：2017年度土地变更调查结果。
Note：Survey results of land quality change in 2017.

# 2-7 第一、二、三、四、五、六次人口普查主要数据
MAIN DATA FROM THE SIX NATIONAL POPULATION CENSUSES

| 项目 | Item | 第一次人口普查 1st National Population Census | 第二次人口普查 2nd National Population Census | 第三次人口普查 3rd National Population Census | 第四次人口普查 4th National Population Census | 第五次人口普查 5th National Population Census | 第六次人口普查 6th National Population Census |
|---|---|---|---|---|---|---|---|
| **一、总人口（万人）** | **Total Population （10000 persons）** | **91.68** | **138.34** | **422.76** | **666.40** | **749.42** | **871.51** |
| 按性别分 | By Sex | | | | | | |
| 男（万人） | Male（10000 persons） | 48.44 | 69.64 | 214.09 | 338.86 | 375.74 | 439.18 |
| 女（万人） | Female（10000 persons） | 43.24 | 68.71 | 208.67 | 327.54 | 373.68 | 432.33 |
| **二、总户数（万户）** | **Total Household （10000 Household）** | **19.27** | **28.01** | **101.41** | **186.61** | **241.62** | **296.64** |
| 家庭户（万户） | Family Household （10000 Household） | | | 101.09 | 185.56 | 232.70 | 282.43 |
| 平均家庭户规模（人） | Average Family Household Size（person） | | | 4.07 | 3.49 | 2.97 | 2.79 |
| **三、民　族** | **Ethnicity** | | | | | | |
| 民族个数（个） | Number of Fthnic groups （unit） | 14 | 16 | 25 | 41 | 51 | 53 |
| 汉族人口（万人） | Populaiton of Han （10000 persons） | 91.33 | 137.76 | 422.09 | 665.58 | 746.12 | 863.84 |
| 少数民族人口（万人） | Populaiton of Ethnic Minorities（10000 persons） | 0.36 | 0.58 | 0.67 | 0.82 | 3.30 | 7.67 |
| **四、各种文化程度人口** | **Popution with Various Education Attainments** | | | | | | |
| 大　学（万人） | College（10000 persons） | | 1.51 | 3.62 | 12.39 | 41.64 | 129.54 |
| 高　中（万人） | Senior Secondary School （10000 persons） | | 4.86 | 34.82 | 68.42 | 111.40 | 150.82 |
| 初　中（万人） | Junior Secondary School （10000 persons） | | 13.72 | 102.28 | 195.10 | 281.91 | 334.22 |
| 小　学（万人） | Premary School （10000 persons） | | 51.25 | 144.52 | 236.34 | 206.91 | 170.77 |

# 2-8　计划生育情况（1978-2018年）
FAMILY PLANNING SITUATION（1978-2018）

| 年份<br>Year | 已婚有生育能力的人数（人）<br>Married and Fertile Persons（person） | 节育人数（人）<br>Persons under Birth Control（person） | 节育率（%）<br>Contraceptive Prevalence Rate（%） | 四项手术人数（人）<br>Persons Performed Four-operation（person） | #放环人数<br>Persons Set Rings |
|---|---|---|---|---|---|
| 1978 | 694292 | 571077 | 82.25 | 125913 | 68475 |
| **1980** | **763226** | **673069** | **88.19** | **180979** | **70927** |
| 1985 | 1017649 | 929284 | 91.32 | 146742 | 67234 |
| **1990** | **1258232** | **1165216** | **92.61** | **149327** | **70964** |
| 1991 | 1319722 | 1219795 | 92.43 | 153970 | 77406 |
| 1992 | 1348503 | 1256271 | 93.16 | 90107 | 56226 |
| 1993 | 1380717 | 1271884 | 92.12 | 76783 | 45492 |
| 1994 | 1400425 | 1268378 | 90.57 | 73169 | 41482 |
| 1995 | 1427442 | 1285264 | 90.04 | 84099 | 52716 |
| 1996 | 1459465 | 1316516 | 90.21 | 84370 | 57648 |
| 1997 | 1482204 | 1340399 | 90.43 | 76579 | 55285 |
| 1998 | 1505499 | 1367648 | 90.84 | 74199 | 50526 |
| 1999 | 1523471 | 1378131 | 90.46 | 73663 | 44976 |
| **2000** | **1521331** | **1371447** | **90.15** | **74285** | **45999** |
| 2001 | 1514274 | 1360543 | 89.85 | 70205 | 43601 |
| 2002 | 1541855 | 1400145 | 90.81 | 50575 | 45453 |
| 2003 | 1518448 | 1354917 | 89.23 | 57458 | 47953 |
| 2004 | 1540706 | 1357703 | 88.04 | 52934 | 42859 |
| 2005 | 1590476 | 1417755 | 89.14 | 58097 | 49716 |
| 2006 | 1604665 | 1427785 | 88.98 | 51864 | 42457 |
| 2007 | 1595390 | 1426787 | 89.43 | 50074 | 41198 |
| 2008 | 1587344 | 1410426 | 88.85 | 120539 | 93291 |
| 2009 | 1623969 | 1418178 | 87.33 | 111084 | 100193 |
| **2010** | **1591103** | **1377726** | **86.59** | **78721** | **51794** |
| 2011 | 1581231 | 1355808 | 85.74 | 70823 | 48210 |
| 2012 | 1575996 | 1349572 | 85.63 | 62880 | 43021 |
| 2013 | 1527731 | 1293810 | 84.69 | 53252 | 30851 |
| 2014 | 1506274 | 1275142 | 84.66 | 34008 | 12827 |
| 2015 | 1475887 | 1226439 | 83.10 | 34879 | 9108 |
| 2016 | 1456953 | 1183221 | 81.21 | 36449 | 4474 |
| 2017 | 1439008 | 1188307 | 82.58 | 20905 | 4669 |
| 2018 | 1406047 | 1159775 | 82.48 | 17786 | 5097 |

# 2-9 分市、区计划生育情况（2018年）
FAMILY PLANNING SITUATION BY REGION (2018)

| 市、区名称 | Region | 计划生育率（%）Fertility Rate（%） | 计划内出生（人）Birth within the Plan（person） | | 计划外出生（人）Birth without the Plan（person） | | 多胎（人）Third Birth and Above（person） |
|---|---|---|---|---|---|---|---|
| | | | 一胎 First Birth | 二胎 Second Birth | 一胎 First Birth | 二胎 Second Birth | |
| **全市** | **Whole Municipality** | **98.29** | **35981** | **49652** | **194** | **1606** | **2666** |
| 市南区 | Shinan District | 99.55 | 2982 | 2055 | 7 | 113 | 73 |
| 市北区 | Shibei District | 99.76 | 4420 | 3662 | 1 | 57 | 90 |
| 李沧区 | Licang District | 99.55 | 2696 | 3046 | 4 | 42 | 58 |
| 崂山区 | Laoshan District | 99.87 | 1505 | 1638 | 1 | 27 | 33 |
| 黄岛区 | Huangdao District | 97.84 | 6532 | 9808 | 52 | 381 | 603 |
| 城阳区 | Chengyang District | 99.37 | 2777 | 4023 | 5 | 128 | 130 |
| 即墨区 | Jimo District | 98.43 | 4291 | 7509 | 8 | 151 | 394 |
| 胶州市 | Jiaozhou | 97.59 | 3169 | 5620 | 13 | 167 | 381 |
| 平度市 | Pingdu | 96.68 | 4975 | 8165 | 66 | 370 | 642 |
| 莱西市 | Laixi | 97.75 | 2634 | 4126 | 37 | 170 | 262 |

注：黄岛区含保税港区数据；城阳区含红岛经济区数据。
Note: The Huangdao area contains the data of the bonded harbor area.Chengyang District contains red is land economic zone data.

## 主要统计指标解释

**人口数** 指一定时点、一定地区范围内有生命的个人总和。

**出生率（又称粗出生率）** 指在一定时期内（通常为一年）一定地区的出生人数与同期内平均人数（或期中人数）之比，用千分率表示。本资料中的出生率指年出生率，其计算公式为：

$$出生率=\frac{年出生人数}{年平均人数}\times 1000‰$$

式中：出生人数指活产婴儿，即胎儿脱离母体时（不管怀孕月数），有过呼吸或其他生命现象。

**死亡率（又称粗死亡率）** 指在一定时期内（通常为一年）一定地区的死亡人数与同期内平均人数（或期中人数）之比，用千分率表示。本资料中的死亡率指年死亡率，其计算公式为：

$$死亡率=\frac{年死亡人数}{年平均人数}\times 1000‰$$

**人口自然增长率** 指在一定时期内（通常为一年）人口自然增加数（出生人数减死亡人数）与该时期内平均人数（或期中人数）之比，用千分率表示。计算公式为：

$$人口自然增长率=\frac{本年出生人数-本年死亡人数}{年平均人数}\times 1000‰$$

$$=人口出生率-人口死亡率$$

## Explanatory Notes on Main Statistical Indicators

**Total Population** refers to the total number of people alive at a certain point of time within a given area.

**Birth Rate（or Crude Birth Rate）** refers to the ratio of the number of births to the average population（or mid-period population）during a certain period of time（usually a year）, expressed in ‰. Birth rate in the chapter refers to annual birth rate. The following formula is used:

Birth Rate=（Number of Births/Average Number of Population）×1000‰

Number of births in the formula refers to live births, i.e. when a baby has breathed or showed any vital phenomena regardless of the length of pregnancy.

Annual average number of population is the average of the number of population at the beginning of the year and that at the end of the year. Sometimes it is substituted by the mid-year population.

**Death Rate（or Crude Death Rate）** refers to the ratio of the number of deaths to the average population（or mid-period population）during a certain period of time（usually a year）, expressed in ‰. Death rate in the chapter refers to annual death rate. The following formula is used:

Death Rate=（Number of Deaths/Annual Average Number of Population）×1000‰

**Natural Growth Rate of Population** refers to the ratio of natural increase in population（number of births minus number of deaths）in a certain period of time（usually a year）to the average population（or mid-period population）of the same period, expressed in ‰. The following formula is applied:

Natural Growth Rate of Population=［（Number of Births-Number of Deaths）/Average Number of Population］×1000‰

Natural Growth Rate of Population=Birth Rate-Death Rate

# 从业人员及职工工资 3

EMPLOYMENT AND WAGES

# 简要说明

## 一、本篇资料的主要内容

本篇资料主要反映了全市从业人员和职工工资方面的基本情况，主要包括全市社会从业人数及各区（市）单位从业人数、在岗职工工资总额和平均工资等方面的资料。

## 二、本篇资料的来源

单位从业人员和职工工资来源于劳动统计年报，全市从业人员根据劳动统计年报、农村年报和市工商行政管理局、市人力资源和社会保障局、市交通委相关资料测算。由市统计局人口和社会科技统计处整理提供。

# Brief Introduction

## *I. Main Content*

Data in this chapter show the basic conditions of Qingdao' s employment and wages, including the main data on labor statistics of employment, number of employment of the whole city and 12 district and county-level cities, total wage bill and average wage of staff and workers, etc.

## *II. Source of Data*

Data on employment and wages are prepared according to the annual reports of labor statistics.Data on social employment are measured according to the annual reports of labor statistics, countryside statistics and related information from Industry & Commerce Administration Bureau, Human Resources & Social Security Bureau and Transportation Commision.

Data in this chapter are compiled by the Division of Population and Science & Technology of Qingdao Municipal Bureau of Statistics.

# 3-1　社会就业人数（1978-2017 年）
SOCIAL EMPLOYMENT（1978-2017）

单位：万人（10 000 persons）

| 年份<br>Year | 合计<br>Total | 第一产业<br>Primary Industry | 第二产业<br>Secondary Industry | 第三产业<br>Tertiary Industry |
|---|---|---|---|---|
| 1978 | 256.70 | 157.40 | 65.60 | 33.70 |
| 1979 | 265.60 | 156.10 | 72.20 | 37.30 |
| **1980** | **270.10** | **153.60** | **82.10** | **43.20** |
| 1981 | 278.90 | 153.60 | 82.10 | 43.20 |
| 1982 | 282.70 | 151.10 | 86.20 | 45.40 |
| 1983 | 289.60 | 156.40 | 85.00 | 48.10 |
| 1984 | 304.20 | 149.20 | 97.70 | 57.40 |
| 1985 | 315.30 | 149.20 | 104.50 | 61.70 |
| 1986 | 326.40 | 149.60 | 112.10 | 64.60 |
| 1987 | 334.80 | 149.90 | 120.20 | 64.70 |
| 1988 | 336.50 | 147.60 | 123.20 | 65.70 |
| 1989 | 344.20 | 152.50 | 122.10 | 69.60 |
| **1990** | **352.80** | **156.50** | **123.30** | **73.10** |
| 1991 | 361.20 | 161.90 | 124.30 | 74.90 |
| 1992 | 370.30 | 161.70 | 127.80 | 80.80 |
| 1993 | 365.70 | 160.50 | 128.80 | 76.40 |
| 1994 | 367.60 | 157.10 | 129.40 | 81.20 |
| 1995 | 374.20 | 155.40 | 132.40 | 86.40 |
| 1996 | 381.50 | 152.20 | 137.10 | 92.20 |
| 1997 | 388.70 | 155.20 | 138.10 | 95.30 |
| 1998 | 393.10 | 154.80 | 138.60 | 99.70 |
| 1999 | 396.10 | 150.30 | 142.00 | 103.80 |
| **2000** | **397.60** | **144.70** | **134.91** | **117.99** |
| 2001 | 400.50 | 133.90 | 142.30 | 124.30 |
| 2002 | 413.31 | 121.38 | 153.85 | 138.08 |
| 2003 | 438.96 | 119.91 | 163.93 | 155.12 |
| 2004 | 458.81 | 113.98 | 180.63 | 164.20 |
| 2005 | 471.03 | 104.48 | 196.80 | 169.75 |
| 2006 | 490.10 | 102.97 | 209.83 | 177.30 |
| 2007 | 505.80 | 102.30 | 217.80 | 185.70 |
| 2008 | 513.80 | 102.40 | 220.80 | 190.60 |
| 2009 | 525.71 | 105.65 | 220.33 | 199.73 |
| **2010** | **540.34** | **105.16** | **223.85** | **211.33** |
| 2011 | 551.18 | 106.02 | 227.08 | 218.08 |
| 2012 | 559.88 | 104.95 | 229.79 | 225.14 |
| 2013 | 571.47 | 107.59 | 232.17 | 231.71 |
| 2014 | 588.97 | 108.45 | 229.91 | 250.61 |
| 2015 | 595.44 | 107.92 | 229.51 | 258.01 |
| 2016 | 601.44 | 107.30 | 228.44 | 265.70 |
| 2017 | 603.90 | 101.86 | 228.14 | 273.90 |

# 3-2 主要年份全市单位就业人员人数

MAJOR YEAR' S NUMBER OF EMPLOYED PERSONS IN ALL UNITS OF THE CITY

单位：万人（10 000 persons）

| 年份<br>Year | 合计<br>Total | #市区<br>Urban Area | #国有单位<br>State-owned Units | #集体单位<br>Collective-owned Units | 其他所有制单位<br>Other Ownership Units |
|---|---|---|---|---|---|
| 1949 | 14.8 | 13.4 | 9.3 | 5.5 | |
| 1952 | 23.4 | 20.1 | 18.3 | 5.1 | |
| 1957 | 29.7 | 24.5 | 24.1 | 5.6 | |
| 1962 | 32.3 | 26.8 | 24.5 | 7.8 | |
| 1965 | 36.7 | 30.6 | 26.8 | 9.9 | |
| 1970 | 45.6 | 37.4 | 32.2 | 13.4 | |
| 1975 | 53.4 | 43.5 | 38.0 | 15.4 | |
| 1978 | 70.7 | 54.5 | 49.2 | 21.5 | |
| 1980 | 79.2 | 61.5 | 55.0 | 24.2 | |
| 1985 | 88.8 | 66.7 | 59.8 | 28.9 | 0.1 |
| 1988 | 98.2 | 70.0 | 66.7 | 31.2 | 0.3 |
| 1990 | 103.2 | 70.6 | 69.5 | 32.9 | 0.8 |
| 1991 | 105.4 | 78.4 | 71.5 | 32.5 | 1.4 |
| 1992 | 108.2 | 80.4 | 73.6 | 32.8 | 1.8 |
| 1993 | 109.4 | 80.8 | 75.3 | 29.5 | 4.6 |
| 1994 | 110.1 | 80.2 | 72.4 | 28.3 | 9.4 |
| 1995 | 111.6 | 80.2 | 72.4 | 27.5 | 11.7 |
| 1996 | 118.4 | 81.1 | 71.6 | 26.0 | 20.8 |
| 1997 | 117.1 | 78.1 | 69.0 | 22.6 | 25.5 |
| 1998 | 116.2 | 75.6 | 64.2 | 19.0 | 33.0 |
| 1999 | 119.0 | 78.3 | 60.4 | 16.6 | 42.0 |
| 2000 | 118.3 | 76.6 | 57.6 | 14.2 | 46.5 |
| 2001 | 117.5 | 75.1 | 53.2 | 12.2 | 52.1 |
| 2002 | 119.1 | 75.2 | 49.5 | 10.3 | 59.3 |
| 2003 | 118.0 | 74.3 | 47.2 | 8.9 | 61.9 |
| 2004 | 207.1 | 111.1 | 43.7 | 18.0 | 145.4 |
| 2005 | 224.3 | 122.3 | 43.9 | 18.2 | 162.2 |
| 2006 | 243.2 | 133.7 | 41.7 | 16.2 | 185.3 |
| 2007 | 249.8 | 137.3 | 45.1 | 17.9 | 186.8 |
| 2008 | 254.1 | 140.9 | 44.4 | 15.4 | 194.3 |
| 2009 | 250.5 | 145.6 | 44.4 | 14.6 | 201.5 |
| 2010 | 269.4 | 151.1 | 44.6 | 15.1 | 209.7 |
| 2011 | 275.9 | 156.5 | 44.3 | 14.7 | 216.9 |
| 2012 | 283.2 | 162.1 | 44.0 | 13.8 | 225.4 |
| 2013 | 293.7 | 184.1 | 37.8 | 5.4 | 250.5 |
| 2014 | 303.0 | 191.4 | 36.7 | 4.9 | 261.4 |
| 2015 | 309.2 | 192.4 | 35.8 | 4.6 | 268.8 |
| 2016 | 315.6 | 196.4 | 35.5 | 4.7 | 275.4 |
| 2017 | 321.4 | 249.1 | 35.1 | 4.6 | 281.7 |
| 2018 | 330.4 | 258.3 | 34.7 | 2.0 | 293.7 |

注：1.2004 年以前为城镇单位职工人数 .
2.2013 年统计口径变化，国有单位、集体单位数据与上年不可比。

Note：1. Before 2004，the data refer to number of staff and workers in urban units.
2. Because of the adjustment about the statistics system，the data of State-owned Units and Collective-owned Units since 2013are not fully comparable with historical statistics.

# 3-3 全市单位国民经济各行业就业人员人数（2018 年）
NUMBER OF EMPLOYED PERSONS IN ALL UNITS OF THE CITY BY SECTOR（2018）

单位：万人（10 000 persons）

| | | 2018 年 | | 2017 年 | |
|---|---|---|---|---|---|
| | | 合计 Total | 女性 Female | 合计 Total | 女性 Female |
| 总计 | **Total** | 330.4 | 125.2 | 321.4 | 125.7 |
| 1. 农、林、牧、渔业 | Farming，Forestry，Animal Husbandry and Fishery | 1.2 | 0.4 | 1.2 | 0.5 |
| 2. 采 矿 业 | Mining | 0.1 | | 0.1 | |
| 3. 制 造 业 | Manufacturing | 133.4 | 48.4 | 139.4 | 52.9 |
| 4. 电力、热力、燃气及水生产和供应业 | The Electricity，Heat，Gas and Water Production and Supply Industry | 2.5 | 0.6 | 2.6 | 0.6 |
| 5. 建筑业 | Construction | 32.7 | 5.2 | 29.4 | 4.7 |
| 6. 批发和零售业 | Wholesale and Retail Trade | 53.0 | 24.4 | 48.8 | 23.7 |
| 7. 交通运输、仓储和邮政业 | Transport，Storage and Post | 15.5 | 4.9 | 12.8 | 4.1 |
| 8. 住宿和餐饮业 | Hotels and Catering Services | 7.0 | 3.6 | 6.9 | 3.6 |
| 9. 信息传输、软件和信息技术服务业 | Information Transmission Computer Services and Software | 4.7 | 1.8 | 4.2 | 1.6 |
| 10. 金融业 | Financial Intermediation | 6.4 | 3.6 | 6.4 | 3.5 |
| 11. 房地产业 | Real Estate | 8.8 | 3.4 | 8.1 | 3.0 |
| 12. 租赁和商务服务业 | Leasing and Business Services | 16.0 | 6.0 | 14.7 | 5.7 |
| 13. 科学研究和技术服务业 | Scientific Research and Technical Services | 7.5 | 2.5 | 6.7 | 2.1 |
| 14. 水利、环境和公共设施管理业 | Management of Water Conservancy，Environmentand Public Facilities | 3.7 | 1.2 | 3.3 | 1.0 |
| 15. 居民服务、修理和其他服务业 | Residents Service，RePair and Other Services | 2.7 | 1.3 | 2.6 | 1.0 |
| 16. 教育 | Education | 14.1 | 8.3 | 14.4 | 8.4 |
| 17. 卫生和社会工作 | Health and Social Welfare | 8.0 | 5.5 | 7.7 | 5.3 |
| 18. 文化、体育和娱乐业 | Culture，Sports and Entertainment | 1.8 | 0.9 | 1.9 | 0.8 |
| 19. 公共管理、社会保障和社会组织 | Public Management，Social Security and SocialOrganization | 11.3 | 3.2 | 10.2 | 3.2 |

# 3-4 全市单位分市、区国民经济各部门就业人员人数（2018年）

NUMBER OF EMPLOYED PERSONS IN ALL UNTTS OF THE CITY BY REGION AND SECTOR（2018）

| 市、区名称 | Region | 合计 Total | 农林牧渔业 Farming，Forestry，Animal Husbandryand Fishery | 采矿业 Mining | 制造业 Manufacturing | 电力热力燃气及水生产和供应业 The Electricity，Heat，Gas and Water Production and Supply Industry |
|---|---|---|---|---|---|---|
| **全市** | **Whole Municipality** | **330.4** | **1.2** | **0.1** | **133.4** | **2.5** |
| 市南区 | Shinan District | 39.9 | | | 3.1 | 0.3 |
| 市北区 | Shibei District | 27.2 | | | 2.7 | 0.5 |
| 李沧区 | Licang District | 16.4 | | | 3.9 | 0.1 |
| 崂山区 | Laoshan District | 24.1 | 0.1 | | 6.1 | 0.1 |
| 黄岛区 | Huangdao District | 72.5 | 0.3 | | 28.3 | 0.4 |
| 城阳区 | Chengyang District | 38.6 | 0.1 | | 25.8 | 0.1 |
| 即墨区 | Jimo District | 32.7 | 0.1 | | 20.5 | 0.4 |
| 胶州市 | Jiaozhou | 34.2 | 0.1 | | 18.5 | 0.4 |
| 平度市 | Pingdu | 16.1 | 0.2 | 0.1 | 9.4 | 0.1 |
| 莱西市 | Laixi | 21.8 | 0.3 | | 11.7 | 0.1 |
| 红岛经济区 | Qingdao National High-tech Industrial Development Zone | 3.7 | | | 1.7 | |
| 保税港区 | Qingdao Free Trade Port Area of China | 3.2 | | | 1.7 | |

单位：万人（10 000 persons）

| 建筑业<br>Construction | 批发和零售业<br>Wholesale and Retail Trade | 交通运输仓储和邮政业<br>Transport，Storage and Post | 住宿和餐饮业<br>Hotels and Catering Services | 信息传输软件和<br>信息技术服务业<br>Information Transmission<br>Computer Services and Software |
|---|---|---|---|---|
| **32.7** | **53.0** | **15.5** | **7.0** | **4.7** |
| 2.5 | 9.1 | 2.6 | 2.0 | 1.9 |
| 3.1 | 7.3 | 2.9 | 0.4 | 0.4 |
| 0.8 | 3.8 | 0.6 | 1.0 | 0.1 |
| 4.1 | 2.4 | 1.4 | 0.6 | 1.6 |
| 9.7 | 14.3 | 4.5 | 1.5 | 0.4 |
| 2.1 | 2.9 | 1.3 | 0.8 | 0.1 |
| 2.2 | 3.9 | 0.3 | 0.3 | |
| 2.6 | 5.9 | 0.8 | 0.1 | 0.1 |
| 0.8 | 0.9 | 0.1 | 0.2 | |
| 4.5 | 1.6 | 0.1 | | |
| 0.3 | 0.3 | 0.1 | 0.1 | 0.1 |
| | 0.6 | 0.8 | | |

# 3-4 续表
Continued

| 市、区名称 | Region | 金融业 Financial Intermediation | 房地产业 Real Estate | 租赁和商务服务业 Leasing and Business Services | 科学研究和技术服务业 Scientific Research and Technical Services | 水利环境和公共设施管理业 Management of Water Conservancy, Environment and Public Facilities |
|---|---|---|---|---|---|---|
| **全市** | **Whole Municipality** | **6.4** | **8.8** | **16.0** | **7.5** | **3.7** |
| 市南区 | Shinan District | 5.7 | 1.4 | 3.5 | 1.5 | 0.5 |
| 市北区 | Shibei District | | 1.2 | 2.4 | 0.8 | 0.3 |
| 李沧区 | Licang District | | 0.5 | 2.1 | 0.5 | 0.5 |
| 崂山区 | Laoshan District | 0.7 | 0.8 | 0.8 | 2.4 | 0.5 |
| 黄岛区 | Huangdao District | | 1.8 | 3.3 | 1.1 | 0.6 |
| 城阳区 | Chengyang District | | 0.7 | 1.4 | 0.5 | 0.5 |
| 即墨区 | Jimo District | | 0.6 | 0.3 | 0.1 | 0.3 |
| 胶州市 | Jiaozhou | | 0.8 | 1.3 | 0.2 | 0.1 |
| 平度市 | Pingdu | | 0.7 | 0.1 | | 0.2 |
| 莱西市 | Laixi | | 0.2 | 0.5 | | 0.2 |
| 红岛经济区 | Qingdao National High-tech Industrial Development Zone | | 0.1 | 0.3 | 0.4 | |
| 保税港区 | Qingdao Free Trade Port Area of China | | | | | |

单位：万人（10 000 persons）

| 居民服务修理和其他服务业 Services to Households and Other Services | 教育 Education | 卫生和社会工作 Health and Social Welfare | 文化体育和娱乐业 Culture，Sports and Entertainment | 公共管理社会保障和社会组织 Public Management, Social Security and Social Organization | 国际组织 International Organization |
|---|---|---|---|---|---|
| **2.7** | **14.1** | **8.0** | **1.8** | **11.3** | |
| 0.4 | 1.7 | 1.5 | 0.4 | 1.8 | |
| 0.5 | 1.7 | 1.7 | 0.4 | 0.9 | |
| 0.3 | 1.0 | 0.6 | 0.2 | 0.4 | |
| 0.1 | 1.0 | 0.3 | 0.4 | 0.7 | |
| 0.4 | 2.8 | 0.9 | 0.3 | 1.9 | |
| 0.2 | 1.0 | 0.4 | | 0.7 | |
| 0.2 | 1.3 | 0.9 | 0.1 | 1.2 | |
| 0.1 | 1.2 | 0.6 | | 1.4 | |
| 0.2 | 1.5 | 0.5 | | 1.1 | |
| 0.2 | 0.8 | 0.6 | | 1.0 | |
| 0.1 | 0.1 | | | 0.1 | |
| | | | | 0.1 | |

# 3-5 全市单位分市、区全部就业人员人数（2018年底）

NUMBER OF EMPLOYED PERSONS IN ALL UNITS OF THE CITY BY REGION（END OF 2018）

单位：万人（10 000 persons）

| 市、区名称 | Region | 年末人数 Year-end Population | 国有单位 State-owned Units | 集体单位 Collective-owned Units | 其他经济类型单位 Units in Other Types of Economy |
|---|---|---|---|---|---|
| **全市** | **Whole Municipality** | **330.4** | **34.7** | **2.0** | **293.7** |
| 市南区 | Shinan District | 39.9 | 7.2 | 0.3 | 32.4 |
| 市北区 | Shibei District | 27.2 | 4.4 | 0.2 | 22.6 |
| 李沧区 | Licang District | 16.4 | 1.8 | 0.1 | 14.5 |
| 崂山区 | Laoshan District | 24.1 | 2.2 | 0.1 | 21.8 |
| 黄岛区 | Huangdao District | 72.5 | 5.6 | 0.1 | 66.8 |
| 城阳区 | Chengyang District | 38.6 | 2.0 | 0.1 | 36.5 |
| 即墨区 | Jimo District | 32.7 | 2.6 | 0.6 | 29.5 |
| 胶州市 | Jiaozhou | 34.2 | 3.4 | 0.2 | 30.6 |
| 平度市 | Pingdu | 16.1 | 2.9 | 0.2 | 13.0 |
| 莱西市 | Laixi | 21.8 | 2.3 | 0.1 | 19.4 |
| 红岛经济区 | Qingdao National High-tech Industrial Development Zone | 3.7 | 0.2 | | 3.5 |
| 保税港区 | Qingdao Free Trade Port Area of China | 3.2 | 0.1 | | 3.1 |

# 3-6 全市就业人员工资总额、平均工资(1978-2018年)
TOTAL WAGES AND AVERAGE WAGE OF CITYWIDE FULL-TIME EMPLOYEES (1978-2018)

| 年份 Year | 工资总额(亿元) Total Wage Bill (100 million yuan) | | 平均工资(元) Avergae Wage (yuan) | |
|---|---|---|---|---|
| | 全社会单位 All Units | 其中:非私营单位 of which: Non-private Units | 全社会单位 All Units | 其中:非私营单位 of which: Non-private Units |
| 1978 | | 4.0 | | 584 |
| 1979 | | 4.8 | | 662 |
| 1980 | | 6.0 | | 782 |
| 1981 | | 6.3 | | 778 |
| 1982 | | 6.6 | | 785 |
| 1983 | | 6.9 | | 809 |
| 1984 | | 9.0 | | 1041 |
| 1985 | | 9.6 | | 1103 |
| 1986 | | 11.8 | | 1311 |
| 1987 | | 14.2 | | 1519 |
| 1988 | | 18.0 | | 1862 |
| 1989 | | 20.7 | | 2120 |
| 1990 | | 24.4 | | 2400 |
| 1991 | | 26.4 | | 2553 |
| 1992 | | 31.8 | | 2970 |
| 1993 | | 40.4 | | 3694 |
| 1994 | | 59.5 | | 5455 |
| 1995 | | 68.3 | | 6164 |
| 1996 | | 78.2 | | 6640 |
| 1997 | | 82.5 | | 7030 |
| 1998 | | 87.2 | | 7518 |
| 1999 | | 100.1 | | 8405 |
| 2000 | | 120.4 | | 10072 |
| 2001 | | 135.8 | | 11426 |
| 2002 | | 153.8 | | 12839 |
| 2003 | 225.6 | 160.3 | 12597 | 15335 |
| 2004 | 280.5 | 193.4 | 13932 | 17190 |
| 2005 | 359.5 | 242.8 | 16015 | 20022 |
| 2006 | 445.6 | 292.0 | 18574 | 23457 |
| 2007 | 518.1 | 338.6 | 21419 | 27083 |
| 2008 | 578.7 | 371.9 | 23296 | 30233 |
| 2009 | 638.1 | 393.2 | 25396 | 33258 |
| 2010 | 738.0 | 446.8 | 28549 | 37805 |
| 2011 | 877.5 | 522.0 | 32763 | 43077 |
| 2012 | 1044.3 | 613.1 | 37399 | 49052 |
| 2013 | 1251.7 | 785.7 | 42688 | 55363 |
| 2014 | 1456.0 | 890.5 | 48453 | 62104 |
| 2015 | 1644.4 | 993.0 | 53715 | 69465 |
| 2016 | 1852.7 | 1088.5 | 58551 | 75803 |
| 2017 | 2034.7 | 1193.6 | 63047 | 82177 |
| 2018 | 2251.7 | 1290.8 | 68197 | 89525 |

注:1.2003年以前为职工工资总额、平均工资。
2.2015年以前为在岗职工工资总额、平均工资。

Note: 1. The data before 2003 refer to the total wage bill and average wage of stall and workers.
2. It was the total salary and average salart of the on-spot staff before 2015.

# 3-7 全市就业人员工资总额、平均工资指数（1978-2018 年）
INDEXES OF TOTAL WAGES AND AVERAGE WAGE OF CITYWIDE FULL-TIME EMPLOYEES（1978-2018）

| 年份 Year | 工资总额指数 Total Wage Bill Indexed | | 平均工资指数 Avergae Wage Indexes | |
|---|---|---|---|---|
| | 全社会单位 All Units | 其中：非私营单位 of which： Non-private Units | 全社会单位 All Units | 其中：非私营单位 of which： Non-private Units |
| 1978 | | 120.80 | | 104.66 |
| 1979 | | 119.53 | | 113.36 |
| 1980 | | 123.95 | | 118.13 |
| 1981 | | 106.71 | | 99.49 |
| 1982 | | 103.80 | | 100.90 |
| 1983 | | 104.14 | | 103.06 |
| 1984 | | 130.64 | | 128.68 |
| 1985 | | 107.11 | | 105.96 |
| 1986 | | 123.22 | | 118.86 |
| 1987 | | 120.10 | | 115.87 |
| 1988 | | 126.48 | | 122.58 |
| 1989 | | 115.29 | | 113.86 |
| 1990 | | 117.66 | | 113.21 |
| 1991 | | 108.28 | | 106.38 |
| 1992 | | 120.26 | | 116.33 |
| 1993 | | 127.09 | | 124.38 |
| 1994 | | 147.46 | | 147.67 |
| 1995 | | 114.76 | | 113.00 |
| 1996 | | 114.54 | | 107.72 |
| 1997 | | 105.50 | | 105.87 |
| 1998 | | 105.64 | | 106.94 |
| 1999 | | 114.81 | | 111.80 |
| 2000 | | 120.29 | | 119.83 |
| 2001 | | 112.77 | | 113.44 |
| 2002 | | 113.31 | | 112.37 |
| 2003 | | 108.84 | | 110.30 |
| 2004 | 124.34 | 120.65 | 110.60 | 112.10 |
| 2005 | 128.16 | 125.54 | 114.95 | 116.47 |
| 2006 | 123.95 | 120.26 | 115.98 | 117.16 |
| 2007 | 116.27 | 115.96 | 115.32 | 115.46 |
| 2008 | 111.70 | 109.83 | 108.76 | 111.63 |
| 2009 | 110.26 | 105.73 | 109.01 | 110.01 |
| 2010 | 115.66 | 113.63 | 112.42 | 113.67 |
| 2011 | 118.90 | 116.83 | 114.76 | 113.95 |
| 2012 | 119.01 | 117.45 | 114.15 | 113.87 |
| 2013 | 119.86 | 128.15 | 114.14 | 112.87 |
| 2014 | 116.32 | 113.34 | 113.50 | 112.18 |
| 2015 | 112.94 | 111.51 | 110.86 | 111.85 |
| 2016 | 110.25 | 106.49 | 109.71 | 110.33 |
| 2017 | 109.82 | 109.66 | 107.68 | 108.41 |
| 2018 | 110.66 | 108.14 | 108.17 | 108.94 |

注：1.2004 年以前为职工工资总额、平均工资指数。
2.2015 年以前为在岗职工工资总额、平均工资。

Note：1. The data before 2004 refer to the indexes of total wage of stall and workers.
2. It was the total salary and average salart of the on-spot staff before 2015.

# 3-8 分行业就业人员平均工资（2018 年）

AVERAGE WAGE OF FULL-TIME EMPLOYEES BY INDUSTRY（2018）

| 行业 | Sector | 全部单位（元）All Units（yuan） | 非私营单位（元）Non-private Units（yuan） | 私营单位（元）Private Units（yuan） |
|---|---|---|---|---|
| **总计** | **Total** | **68197** | **89525** | **51976** |
| （一）农、林、牧、渔业 | Farming，Forestry，Animal Husbandry | 40922 | 62087 | 39405 |
| （二）采矿业 | Mining | 44739 | 47046 | 37115 |
| （三）制造业 | Manufacturing | 58455 | 72284 | 49538 |
| （四）电力、热力、燃气及水生产和供应业 | The Electricity，Heat，Gas and Water Production and Supply Industry | 77673 | 86461 | 54059 |
| （五）建筑业 | Construction | 62364 | 69447 | 55402 |
| （六）批发和零售业 | Wholesale and Retail Trade | 54037 | 67985 | 51360 |
| （七）交通运输、仓储和邮政业 | Transport，Storage and Post | 78289 | 89768 | 58625 |
| （八）住宿和餐饮业 | Hotels and Catering Services | 48320 | 57303 | 43217 |
| （九）信息传输、软件和信息技术服务业 | Information Transmission Computer Services and Software | 101179 | 118509 | 89056 |
| （十）金融业 | Financial Intermediation | 136656 | 145388 | 59844 |
| （十一）房地产业 | Real Estate | 73370 | 94910 | 51253 |
| （十二）租赁和商务服务业 | Leasing and Business Services | 58715 | 74057 | 55104 |
| （十三）科学研究和技术服务业 | Scientific Research and Technical Services | 90648 | 121088 | 64298 |
| （十四）水利、环境和公共设施管理业 | Management of Water Conservancy，Environment and Public Facilities | 55114 | 63390 | 45520 |
| （十五）居民服务、修理和其他服务业 | Residents Service，RePair and Other Services | 50081 | 80554 | 45581 |
| （十六）教育 | Education | 122615 | 125322 | 64242 |
| （十七）卫生和社会工作 | Health and Social Welfare | 111966 | 123463 | 50340 |
| （十八）文化、体育和娱乐业 | Culture，Sports and Entertainment | 87377 | 95094 | 71331 |
| （十九）公共管理、社会保障和社会组织 | Public Management，Social Security and Social Organization | 123726 | 123726 | |

# 3-9 分市、区就业人员工资总额（2018年）

## TOTAL WAGES OF FULL-TIME EMPLOYEES BY CITY OR DISTRICT (2018)

单位：亿元（100 million yuan）

| 市、区名称 | Region | 合计<br>Total | 国有单位<br>State-owned Units | 集体单位<br>Collective-owned Units | 其他所有制单位<br>Other Owership Units |
|---|---|---|---|---|---|
| **全市** | **Whole Municipality** | **2251.7** | **428.4** | **17.6** | **1805.7** |
| 市南区 | Shinan District | 362.1 | 104.7 | 2.8 | 254.6 |
| 市北区 | Shibei District | 205.7 | 59.6 | 0.9 | 145.2 |
| 李沧区 | Licang District | 104.2 | 20.9 | 0.7 | 82.6 |
| 崂山区 | Laoshan District | 210.3 | 28.9 | 0.4 | 181.0 |
| 黄岛区 | Huangdao District | 462.2 | 67.4 | 0.9 | 393.9 |
| 城阳区 | Chengyang District | 260.1 | 29.5 | 1.0 | 229.6 |
| 即墨区 | Jimo District | 189.4 | 27.9 | 7.4 | 154.1 |
| 胶州市 | Jiaozhou | 194.0 | 33.2 | 1.1 | 159.7 |
| 平度市 | Pingdu | 91.4 | 30.6 | 1.2 | 59.6 |
| 莱西市 | Laixi | 124.9 | 23.1 | 1.2 | 100.6 |
| 红岛经济区 | Qingdao National High-tech Industrial Development Zone | 22.9 | 1.5 | | 21.4 |
| 保税港区 | Qingdao Free Trade Port Area of China | 24.5 | 1.1 | | 23.4 |

# 3-10 分市、区就业人员平均工资(2018年)
## AVERAGE WAGE OF FULL-TIME EMPLOYEES BY CITY OR DISTRICT (2018)

单位：元/年(yuan/year)

| 市、区名称 | Region | 合计 Total | 国有单位 State-owned Units | 集体单位 Collective-owned Units | 其他所有制单位 Other Owership Units |
|---|---|---|---|---|---|
| **全市** | **Whole Municipality** | **68197** | **124324** | **89742** | **61704** |
| 市南区 | Shinan District | 91683 | 144682 | 92312 | 79670 |
| 市北区 | Shibei District | 75753 | 135006 | 52142 | 64335 |
| 李沧区 | Licang District | 63018 | 117940 | 59766 | 56380 |
| 崂山区 | Laoshan District | 87257 | 133996 | 66615 | 82713 |
| 黄岛区 | Huangdao District | 65009 | 121635 | 75620 | 60193 |
| 城阳区 | Chengyang District | 66960 | 145961 | 91191 | 62543 |
| 即墨区 | Jimo District | 57891 | 109670 | 116028 | 52175 |
| 胶州市 | Jiaozhou | 57052 | 99649 | 63991 | 52362 |
| 平度市 | Pingdu | 57422 | 105454 | 73840 | 46388 |
| 莱西市 | Laixi | 56595 | 101123 | 114543 | 51132 |
| 红岛经济区 | Qingdao National High-tech Industrial Development Zone | 60800 | 80292 | 96611 | 59744 |
| 保税港区 | Qingdao Free Trade Port Area of China | 73302 | 164597 | | 71493 |

# 主要统计指标解释

**单位从业人员** 指报告期末最后一日24时在本单位中工作，并取得工资或其他形式劳动报酬的人员数。该指标为时点指标，不包括最后一日当天及以前已经与单位解除劳动合同关系的人员，是在岗职工、劳务派遣人员及其他就业人员之和。就业人员不包括：

（1）离开本单位仍保留劳动关系，并定期领取生活费的人员；

（2）利用课余时间打工的学生及在本单位实习的各类在校学生；

（3）本单位因劳务外包而使用的人员。

**在岗职工** 指在本单位工作且与本单位签订劳动合同，并由单位支付各项工资和社会保险、住房公积金的人员，以及上述人员中由于学习、病伤、产假等原因暂未工作仍由单位支付工资的人员。在岗职工还包括：

（1）应订立劳动合同而未订立劳动合同人员（如使用的农村户籍人员）；

（2）处于试用期人员；

（3）编制外招用的人员；

（4）派往外单位工作，但工资仍由本单位发放的人员（如挂职锻炼、外派工作等情况）。

**工资总额** 指根据《关于工资总额组成的规定》（1990年1月1日国家统计局发布的一号令）进行修订，在报告期内（季度或年度）直接支付给本单位全部就业人员的劳动报酬总额。包括计时工资、计件工资、奖金、津贴和补贴、加班加点工资、特殊情况下支付的工资，是在岗职工工资总额、劳务派遣人员工资总额和其他就业人员工资总额之和。

工资总额是税前工资，包括单位从个人工资中直接为其代扣或代缴的房费、水费、电费、住房公积金和社会保险基金个人缴纳部分等。

工资总额不论是计入成本的还是不计入成本的，不论是以货币形式支付的还是以实物形式支付的，均应列入工资总额的计算范围。

**平均工资** 指单位就业人员在一定时期内平均每人所得的工资额。它表明一定时期工资收入的高低程度，是反映就业人员工资水平的主要指标。

# Explanatory Notes on Main Statistical Indicators

**Jobholders** refers to the number of employees who works in the institution or company and gets salary or other form of labor reward at 24：00 of the last day of the report period. This is a time-point indicator which is the total of on-spot staff，labor dispatched personnel and other employees，excluding persons that have released the employment contract with the institution or company on the last day or bedore. The following are not deemed as Jobholders：

（1）Persons that keep the employment relations and get regular living expenst after leaving the institution or company；

（2）Various students who work part time or as internship；

（3）Personnel that uses by the institution or company in labour outsourcing.

**On-spot staff** refers to the employees that works for and signs the employment contract with the institution or company，and relevant salary，social insurance and house funding are paid by the institution or company，and the persons of the previous employees that are not working but still gets salary from the institution or company due to the reason of learning，injury，maternity leave，etc. It also includes the following：

(1) Employees who shall sign the employment contract with institution or company but not signed (for example, employees of rural household registration).

(2) Employees that are still in probation period;

(3) Employees that are recruited outside the authorized size;

(4) Employees that are sent to other institution or company but the salaries are still paid by the institution or company (such as onsite training and labour dispatching).

**Total salary** refers to total payment for labour made directly to all jobholders of the institution or company within the report period (quarterly or annually) revised according to Regulations on Constitution of Total Salary, Order No. 1 released by National Bureau of Statistics on January 1, 1990, including hourly wage, piece wage, bonus, allowance and subsidy, overtime wage, and wages paid under special situations. It is also the total volume of on-spot staff, labour dispatching staff and other employment.

Total salary is the pre-tax salary, including the expenses of housing, water, power and the personal part of house funding and social insurance funds, which has been withheld and paid by the institution or company from personal salaries.

No matter it is credited into cost or not, no matter it is paid in currency or in kind, all total salary shall be categorized as total salary.

**Average salary** refers to the total salary per capita of employees of the institution or company within the certain period, which is the major indicator of the salary level of employees and the level of salary income of the certain salary.

# 固定资产投资 4

INVESTMENT IN FIXED ASSETS

# 简要说明

### 一、本篇资料的主要内容

本篇资料主要反映了全市固定资产投资及房地产开发方面的情况，主要包括固定资产投资的规模、结构、资金来源和房地产开发投资、施竣工及销售情况等方面的资料。

### 二、本篇资料的来源

本篇资料来源于固定资产投资及房地产开发投资统计年报，由市统计局固定资产投资统计处整理提供。

# Brief Introduction

### *I. Main Content*

Data in this chapter show the basic conditions of investment in fixed assets and real estate development of the whole city, mainly including the total investment in fixed assets, the structure of investment, the resources of investment and investment in real estate development, construction, completion, sales, etc.

### *II. Source of Data*

Data in this chapter are based on the annual report on investment in fixed assets and real estate development, and provided by the Division of Investment and Construction Statistics of Qingdao Municipal Bureau of Statistics.

# 4-1 主要年份固定资产投资
MAJOR YEAR'S INVESTMENT IN FIXED ASSETS

单位：万元（10 000 yuan）

| 年份 Year | 规模以上固定资产投资总额 Investment in Fixed Assets above Designated Size | 按用途分 Crouped by Use | | |
|---|---|---|---|---|
| | | 生产性投资 Productive Investment | 非生产性投资 Non-Productive Investment | # 住宅投资 Investment in Residential Buildings |
| 1949 | 16 | 12 | 4 | 3 |
| 1952 | 3097 | 1368 | 1729 | 1007 |
| 1957 | 5923 | 3947 | 1976 | 1151 |
| 1962 | 2747 | 2049 | 698 | 192 |
| 1965 | 5481 | 4155 | 1326 | 375 |
| 1970 | 6100 | 5813 | 287 | 154 |
| 1975 | 15839 | 13548 | 2381 | 1064 |
| 1978 | 29660 | 23499 | 6161 | 3203 |
| 1980 | 47499 | 33865 | 13634 | 9335 |
| 1985 | 107421 | 60643 | 73424 | 19058 |
| 1990 | 284576 | 210453 | 74123 | 38898 |
| 1991 | 349031 | 256633 | 92398 | 51898 |
| 1992 | 583068 | 420748 | 162320 | 83844 |
| 1993 | 953274 | 511684 | 441590 | 162419 |
| 1994 | 1329716 | 728532 | 601184 | 324094 |
| 1995 | 1648281 | 925194 | 723087 | 390206 |
| 1996 | 1610562 | 972398 | 638164 | 285412 |
| 1997 | 1611902 | 932207 | 679695 | 278951 |
| 1998 | 1909711 | 1125821 | 783890 | 316999 |
| 1999 | 2205891 | 1246328 | 959563 | 421151 |
| 2000 | 2426820 | 1311538 | 1115282 | 470963 |
| 2001 | 2934728 | 1487762 | 1446966 | 729181 |
| 2002 | 3683623 | 1962588 | 1721035 | 765030 |
| 2003 | 5475526 | 3023930 | 2451596 | 1038304 |
| 2004 | 9845646 | 6336279 | 3509367 | 1608738 |
| 2005 | 14032960 | 9172206 | 4860754 | 1841644 |
| 2006 | 14856894 | 9214578 | 5642316 | 2222733 |
| 2007 | 16353636 | 10231673 | 6121963 | 2720970 |
| 2008 | 20190098 | 12443179 | 7746919 | 3315538 |
| 2009 | 24588889 | 13852653 | 10736236 | 3831976 |
| 2010 | 30224785 | 16207885 | 14016900 | 5609189 |
| 2011 | 35025382 | 18622819 | 16402563 | 5707625 |
| 2012 | 41539146 | 24246803 | 17292343 | 6689114 |
| 2013 | 50278649 | 30996768 | 19281881 | 7220432 |
| 2014 | 57660308 | 32913906 | 24746402 | 7311090 |
| 2015 | 65556685 | 41402714 | 24153971 | 7569123 |
| 2016 | 74547006 | 44588200 | 29958806 | 9561782 |
| 2017 | 77770902 | 41719893 | 36051009 | 9255095 |

注：1. 规模以上固定资产投资数据 2003 年以前为城镇以上统计范围。
2. 因 2004 年以来数据有调整，故表中数据不可比。

Note： 1.The data of investment above designated size refer to investment above city and town level before 2003.
2.The data since 2004 are not comparable with other data because of the adjustment.

# 4-1 续表
Continued

单位：万元（10 000 yuan）

| 年份 Year | 按构成分 Gouped by Composition of Funds | | | 按资金来源分 Grouped by Sources of Funds | | | |
|---|---|---|---|---|---|---|---|
| | 建筑安装工程 Constrection and Installation | 设备工器具购置 Purchase of Equipment and Instruments | 其他费用 Others | 国家投资 State Investment | 国内贷款 Domestic Loans | 利用外资 Foreign Investment | 自筹及其他 Self-raising Fund and Others |
| 1949 | 11 | 3 | 2 | 16 | | | |
| 1952 | 2146 | 870 | 81 | 1512 | | | 1585 |
| 1957 | 2853 | 2773 | 297 | 3816 | | | 2107 |
| 1962 | 1631 | 984 | 132 | 2205 | | | 542 |
| 1965 | 3346 | 1859 | 276 | 4451 | | | 1030 |
| 1970 | 3136 | 2835 | 129 | 2721 | | | 3379 |
| 1975 | 7489 | 8133 | 217 | 9378 | 1362 | | 5099 |
| 1978 | 19968 | 9124 | 568 | 16828 | 1601 | | 11231 |
| 1980 | 30993 | 15541 | 965 | 10371 | 12925 | 1420 | 22783 |
| 1985 | 64665 | 35100 | 7656 | 17377 | 35888 | 1136 | 53020 |
| 1990 | 167731 | 91305 | 25540 | 24687 | 91895 | 23688 | 144306 |
| 1991 | 196212 | 108929 | 43890 | 22615 | 131676 | 38325 | 156415 |
| 1992 | 304060 | 208384 | 70624 | 22660 | 213217 | 89130 | 258061 |
| 1993 | 600011 | 225555 | 127708 | 23736 | 208672 | 94469 | 626397 |
| 1994 | 842809 | 272126 | 214781 | 26062 | 318334 | 221265 | 764055 |
| 1995 | 1020484 | 385934 | 241863 | 25683 | 379198 | 328124 | 915276 |
| 1996 | 929735 | 458284 | 222543 | 35639 | 444443 | 310722 | 819758 |
| 1997 | 875057 | 485122 | 251723 | 27928 | 297089 | 363789 | 923096 |
| 1998 | 1034500 | 574852 | 300359 | 67762 | 491812 | 170709 | 1179428 |
| 1999 | 1456473 | 459596 | 289822 | 128603 | 584120 | 145589 | 1347579 |
| 2000 | 1476397 | 652640 | 297783 | 75978 | 489697 | 164175 | 1806238 |
| 2001 | 1781235 | 744549 | 408944 | 93491 | 620562 | 217526 | 2157787 |
| 2002 | 2328492 | 796685 | 558446 | 78775 | 719677 | 411704 | 2831288 |
| 2003 | 3544790 | 1133333 | 797403 | 127861 | 989178 | 722644 | 4237643 |
| 2004 | 6413046 | 2312139 | 1120461 | 85549 | 1100297 | 1016145 | 8245272 |
| 2005 | 8949231 | 3141732 | 1941997 | 136632 | 1250343 | 1850921 | 11540604 |
| 2006 | 8818614 | 3668191 | 2370089 | 391315 | 2126523 | 1662897 | 11856506 |
| 2007 | 9981666 | 4171878 | 2200092 | 215649 | 2427031 | 1788056 | 13109824 |
| 2008 | 11795435 | 5907195 | 2487468 | 322484 | 3309471 | 1951468 | 15855082 |
| 2009 | 14911874 | 5869214 | 3807801 | 778090 | 4217265 | 1593287 | 21555685 |
| 2010 | 18725922 | 6362880 | 5135983 | 1305737 | 5881886 | 2135736 | 27898294 |
| 2011 | 22865421 | 7521441 | 4638520 | 1640702 | 5871709 | 1766278 | 33579182 |
| 2012 | 26080239 | 8601282 | 6857625 | 1324159 | 5484459 | 1561597 | 37356847 |
| 2013 | 33237368 | 9969777 | 7071504 | 1959340 | 8154829 | 1528585 | 49552883 |
| 2014 | 39006113 | 11640126 | 7014069 | 1404667 | 7452983 | 1181541 | 55024776 |
| 2015 | 42893643 | 15972153 | 6690889 | 2067396 | 7249574 | 1098178 | 62458544 |
| 2016 | 45915827 | 16425993 | 8789790 | 1788103 | 14203650 | 903773 | 66069945 |
| 2017 | 55647641 | 10977494 | 11145767 | 2257927 | 14569701 | 641216 | 65055089 |

# 4-2 主要年份固定资产投资构成（以投资总额为 100）

COMPOSITION OF MAJOR YEAR'S INVESTMENT IN FIXED ASSETS (TOTAL INVESTMENT=100)

| 年份 Year | 按用途分 Crouped by Use | | |
|---|---|---|---|
| | 生产性投资 Productive Investment | 非生产性投资 Non-Productive Investment | #住宅投资占非生产性比重 Percentage of Investment in Residential Buildings to Non-Productive Investment |
| 1949 | 75.00 | 25.00 | 75.00 |
| 1952 | 44.17 | 55.83 | 58.24 |
| 1957 | 66.64 | 33.36 | 58.25 |
| 1962 | 74.59 | 25.41 | 27.51 |
| 1965 | 75.81 | 24.19 | 28.28 |
| 1970 | 95.30 | 4.70 | 53.66 |
| 1975 | 84.97 | 15.03 | 44.69 |
| 1978 | 79.23 | 20.77 | 51.99 |
| 1980 | 71.30 | 28.70 | 68.47 |
| 1985 | 56.45 | 43.55 | 40.74 |
| 1990 | 73.95 | 26.05 | 52.50 |
| 1991 | 73.53 | 26.47 | 56.17 |
| 1992 | 72.16 | 27.84 | 51.65 |
| 1993 | 53.68 | 46.32 | 36.78 |
| 1994 | 54.79 | 45.21 | 53.91 |
| 1995 | 56.10 | 43.90 | 54.00 |
| 1996 | 60.40 | 39.60 | 44.70 |
| 1997 | 57.80 | 42.20 | 41.00 |
| 1998 | 59.00 | 41.00 | 16.60 |
| 1999 | 56.50 | 43.50 | 19.10 |
| 2000 | 54.00 | 46.00 | 19.40 |
| 2001 | 50.70 | 49.30 | 50.40 |
| 2002 | 53.30 | 46.70 | 44.50 |
| 2003 | 55.20 | 44.80 | 42.40 |
| 2004 | 64.40 | 35.60 | 45.80 |
| 2005 | 65.40 | 34.60 | 37.90 |
| 2006 | 62.00 | 38.00 | 39.40 |
| 2007 | 62.60 | 37.40 | 44.40 |
| 2008 | 61.60 | 38.40 | 42.80 |
| 2009 | 56.30 | 43.70 | 35.70 |
| 2010 | 53.62 | 46.38 | 40.02 |
| 2011 | 53.17 | 46.83 | 34.80 |
| 2012 | 58.37 | 41.63 | 38.68 |
| 2013 | 61.65 | 38.35 | 37.45 |
| 2014 | 57.08 | 42.92 | 29.54 |
| 2015 | 63.16 | 36.84 | 31.34 |
| 2016 | 59.81 | 40.19 | 31.92 |
| 2017 | 53.64 | 46.36 | 25.67 |

## 4-2 续表
Continued

| 年份<br>Year | 按构成分 Gouped by Composition of Funds | | | 按资金来源分 Grouped by Sources of Funds | | | |
|---|---|---|---|---|---|---|---|
| | 建筑安装工程<br>Constrection and Installaticn | 设备工器具购置<br>Purchase of Equipment and Instruments | 其他费用<br>Others | 国家投资<br>State Investment | 国内贷款<br>Domestic Loans | 利用外资<br>Foreign Investment | 自筹及其他<br>Self-raising Fund and Others |
| 1949 | 68.75 | 18.75 | 12.5 | 100 | | | |
| 1952 | 69.29 | 28.09 | 2.62 | 48.82 | | | 51.18 |
| 1957 | 48.17 | 46.82 | 5.01 | 64.43 | | | 35.57 |
| 1962 | 59.37 | 35.82 | 4.81 | 80.27 | | | 19.73 |
| 1965 | 61.05 | 33.92 | 5.03 | 81.21 | | | 18.79 |
| 1970 | 51.41 | 46.48 | 2.11 | 44.61 | | | 55.39 |
| 1975 | 47.28 | 51.35 | 1.37 | 59.21 | 8.60 | | 32.19 |
| 1978 | 67.32 | 30.76 | 1.92 | 56.74 | 5.40 | | 37.86 |
| 1980 | 65.25 | 32.72 | 2.03 | 21.83 | 27.21 | 2.99 | 47.97 |
| 1985 | 60.2 | 32.68 | 7.12 | 16.18 | 33.41 | 1.06 | 49.35 |
| 1990 | 58.94 | 32.08 | 8.98 | 8.68 | 32.29 | 8.32 | 50.71 |
| 1991 | 56.22 | 31.21 | 12.57 | 6.48 | 37.73 | 10.98 | 44.81 |
| 1992 | 52.15 | 35.74 | 12.11 | 3.89 | 36.56 | 15.29 | 44.26 |
| 1993 | 62.94 | 23.66 | 13.4 | 2.49 | 21.89 | 9.91 | 65.71 |
| 1994 | 63.38 | 20.46 | 16.16 | 1.96 | 23.94 | 16.64 | 57.46 |
| 1995 | 61.9 | 23.4 | 14.7 | 1.6 | 23.0 | 19.9 | 55.5 |
| 1996 | 57.7 | 28.5 | 13.8 | 2.2 | 27.6 | 19.3 | 50.9 |
| 1997 | 54.3 | 30.1 | 15.6 | 1.7 | 18.4 | 22.6 | 57.3 |
| 1998 | 54.2 | 20.8 | 15.7 | 3.5 | 25.8 | 8.9 | 61.8 |
| 1999 | 66.0 | 20.8 | 13.2 | 5.8 | 26.5 | 6.6 | 61.1 |
| 2000 | 60.8 | 26.9 | 12.3 | 3.1 | 20.2 | 6.8 | 74.4 |
| 2001 | 60.7 | 25.4 | 13.9 | 3.0 | 20.1 | 7.0 | 69.9 |
| 2002 | 63.2 | 21.6 | 15.2 | 1.9 | 17.8 | 10.2 | 70.1 |
| 2003 | 64.7 | 20.7 | 14.6 | 2.1 | 16.3 | 11.9 | 69.7 |
| 2004 | 65.1 | 23.5 | 11.4 | 0.8 | 10.6 | 9.7 | 78.9 |
| 2005 | 63.8 | 22.4 | 13.8 | 0.9 | 8.5 | 12.5 | 78.1 |
| 2006 | 59.4 | 24.7 | 15.9 | 2.4 | 13.3 | 10.4 | 73.9 |
| 2007 | 61.0 | 25.5 | 13.5 | 1.2 | 13.8 | 10.2 | 74.8 |
| 2008 | 58.4 | 29.3 | 12.3 | 1.5 | 15.4 | 9.1 | 74.0 |
| 2009 | 60.6 | 23.9 | 15.5 | 2.8 | 15.0 | 5.6 | 76.6 |
| 2010 | 62.0 | 21.0 | 17.0 | 3.5 | 15.8 | 5.7 | 75.0 |
| 2011 | 65.3 | 21.5 | 13.3 | 3.8 | 13.7 | 4.1 | 78.4 |
| 2012 | 62.8 | 20.7 | 16.5 | 2.9 | 12.0 | 3.4 | 81.7 |
| 2013 | 66.1 | 19.8 | 14.1 | 3.2 | 13.3 | 2.5 | 81.0 |
| 2014 | 67.6 | 20.2 | 12.2 | 2.2 | 11.5 | 1.8 | 84.6 |
| 2015 | 65.4 | 24.4 | 10.2 | 2.8 | 10.0 | 1.5 | 85.7 |
| 2016 | 61.6 | 22.0 | 11.8 | 2.2 | 17.1 | 1.1 | 79.6 |
| 2017 | 71.6 | 14.1 | 14.3 | 2.7 | 17.7 | 0.8 | 78.8 |
| 2018 | 68.8 | 7.8 | 23.4 | 2.9 | 15.2 | 0.4 | 81.5 |

## 4-3 按三次产业分规模以上固定资产投资增速（2018 年）
GROWTH RATE OF INVESTMENT IN FIXED ASSETS ABOVE DESIGNATED SIZE BY THREE STRATA OF INDUSTRY (2018)

单位：%（%）

| 指标 | Indicator | 2018 年 |
|---|---|---|
| **总　计** | **Total** | **7.9** |
| 第一产业 | Primary Industry | 14.3 |
| 第二产业 | Secondary Industry | 9.1 |
| # 工业 | Industry | 7.4 |
| 第三产业 | Tertiary Industry | 7.5 |

## 4-4 分市、区固定资产投资额增速（2018 年）
GROWTH RATE OF INVESTMENT IN FIXED ASSETS BY REGION (2018)

单位：%（%）

| 市、区名称 | Region | 规模以上固定资产投资额 Investment in Fixed Assets above Designated Size | # 房地产开发 Investment in Real Estate Development |
|---|---|---|---|
| **全市** | **Whole Municipality** | **7.9** | **11.6** |
| 市南区 | Shinan District | 16.0 | -63.8 |
| 市北区 | Shibei District | 3.6 | -13.6 |
| 李沧区 | Licang District | 15.8 | -38.3 |
| 崂山区 | Laoshan District | 15.6 | 20.6 |
| 黄岛区 | Huangdao District | 13.1 | 2.7 |
| 城阳区 | Chengyang District | 3.5 | 49.5 |
| 即墨区 | Jimo District | 9.9 | 5.8 |
| 胶州市 | Jiaozhou | 9.9 | 160.3 |
| 平度市 | Pingdu | 3.1 | 40.7 |
| 莱西市 | Laixi | 3.0 | 17.9 |
| 红岛经济区 | Qingdao National High-tech Industrial Development Zone | 15.9 | 90.7 |
| 保税港区 | Qingdao Free Trade Port Area of China | 10.4 | 17.6 |

# 4-5 规模以上固定资产投资增速（2018 年）
## INVESTMENT IN FIXED ASSETS ABOVE DESIGNATED SIZE（2018）

单位：%（%）

| 项目 | Item | 合计 Total | #房地产开发 Investment in Real Estate Development |
|---|---|---|---|
| **一、本年施工项目（个）** | **Projects Under Consruction This Year（unit）** | **2434** | |
| #本年新开工（个） | of which：Newly Started（unit） | 1409 | |
| **二、本年建成投产项目（个）** | Projects Completed and Put into Use This Year（unit） | 1395 | |
| **三、本年完成投资（%）** | **Investment Completed This Year（%）** | **7.9** | **11.6** |
| 1. 按构成分 | **Grouped by Composition** | | |
| #建筑安装工程 | Construction installation project | 25.1 | -7.5 |
| 设备工器具购置 | Purchase of Equipment and Instruments | -67.1 | -18.4 |
| 2. 按建设性质分 | Grouped by Type of Construction | | |
| #新建 | New Construction | 8.5 | |
| 扩建 | Expansion | -39.9 | |
| 改建和技术改造 | Reconstruction | 112.7 | |
| 3. 按国民经济行业分 | Grouped by Economic Sector | | |
| （1）农、林、牧、渔业 | Farming，Forestry，Animal Husbandry and Fishery | 15.8 | |
| 农业 | Farming | 25.1 | |
| 林业 | Forestry | 146.6 | |
| 畜牧业 | Animal Husbandry | -24.4 | |
| 渔业 | Fishery | 325.6 | |
| 农、林、牧、渔服务业 | Farming，Forestry，Animal Husbandry and Fishery Services | 38.6 | |
| （2）采矿业 | Mining | 1123.7 | |
| 煤炭开采和洗选业 | Mining and Washing of Coal | | |
| 石油和天然气开采业 | Extraction of Petroleum and Natural Gas | | |
| 黑色金属矿采选业 | Mining of Ferrous Metal Ores | | |
| 有色金属矿采选业 | Mining of Non-ferrous Metal Ores | 776.2 | |
| 非金属矿采选业 | Mining and Processing of Nonmetal Ores | | |
| 开采辅助活动 | Auxiliary Activities of Mining | | |
| 其他采矿业 | Mining of Other Ores | | |

# 4-5 续表 1
Continued

单位：%（%）

| 项目 | Item | 合计 Total | #房地产开发 Investment in Real Estate Development |
|---|---|---|---|
| （3）制造业 | Manufacturing | 9.9 | |
| 农副食品加工业 | Processing of Food from Agricultural Products | -8.5 | |
| 食品制造业 | Manufacture of Foods | 13.2 | |
| 酒、饮料和精制茶制造业 | Manufacture of Liquor, Beverage and Refind Tea | 275.5 | |
| 烟草制品业 | Manufacture of Tobacco | | |
| 纺织业 | Manufacture of Textile | -13.1 | |
| 纺织服装、服饰业 | Manufacture of Textile Wearing Apparel | -46.6 | |
| 皮革、毛皮、羽毛及其制品和制鞋业 | Manufacture of Leather, Fur, Feather & Its Products Footwear | -44.1 | |
| 木材加工和木、竹、藤、棕、草制品业 | Processing of Timbers, Manufacture of Wood, Bamboo, Rattan, Palm and Straw Products | 133.8 | |
| 家具制造业 | Manudacture of Furniture | 84.8 | |
| 造纸和纸制品业 | Manufacture of Paper and Paper Products | -3.9 | |
| 印刷和记录媒介复制业 | Printing, Reproduction of Recording Media | -28.8 | |
| 文教、工美、体育和娱乐用品制造业 | Manufacture of Articles for Culture, Arts & Crafts, Sports and Entertainment | 6.2 | |
| 石油加工、炼焦和核燃料加工业 | Processing of Petroleum, Coking, Processing of Nucleus Fuel | -96.0 | |
| 化学原料和化学制品制造业 | Manufacture of Chemical Raw Material and Chemical Products | 266.2 | |
| 医药制造业 | Manufacture of Medicines | -25.3 | |
| 化学纤维制造业 | Manufacture of Chemical Fiber | 63.2 | |
| 橡胶和塑料制品业 | Manufacture of Rubber and Plastic | -18.2 | |
| 非金属矿物制品业 | Manufacture of Non-metallic Mineral Products | 57.2 | |
| 黑色金属冶炼和压延加工业 | Smelting and Pressing of Ferrous Metals | -86.1 | |
| 有色金属冶炼和压延加工业 | Smelting and Pressing of Non-ferrous Metals | -18.6 | |
| 金属制品业 | Manufacture of Metal Products | 42.9 | |
| 通用设备制造业 | Manufacture of General Purpose Machinery | 38.1 | |
| 专用设备制造业 | Manufacture of Special Purpose Machinery | -11.7 | |
| 汽车制造业 | Manufacture of Vehicle | -14.5 | |
| 铁路、船舶、航空航天和其他运输设备制造业 | Manufacture of Transport Equipement for Railway, Shipping, Aerospace and other uses | 7.8 | |
| 电气机械和器材制造业 | Manufacture of Electrical Machinery & Equipment | 38.4 | |
| 计算机、通信和其他电子设备制造业 | Namufacture of Computer, Communication Equipment and Other Electronic Equipment | 30.7 | |
| 仪器仪表制造业 | Manufacture of Measuring Instrument | -40.7 | |
| 其他制造业 | Manufacture of Other Products | -77.4 | |
| 废弃资源综合利用业 | Recycling and Disposal of Waste Resources | 180.6 | |
| 金属制品、机械和设备修理业 | Maintenance of Metal Products, Machinery and Equipment | 238.4 | |

## 4-5 续表 2
Continued

单位：%（%）

| 项目 | Item | 合计 Total | #房地产开发 Investment in Real Estate Development |
|---|---|---|---|
| （4）电力、燃气及水的生产和供应业 | Production and Supply of Electricity Gas and Water | -27.0 | |
| 电力、热力的生产和供应业 | Production and Supply of Electric Power and Heat Power | -34.3 | |
| 燃气生产和供应业 | Production and Supply of Gas | -61.1 | |
| 水的生产和供应业 | Production and Supply of Water | 8.8 | |
| （5）建筑业 | Construction | 474.1 | |
| （6）交通运输、仓储及邮政业 | Transport Storage and Post | -18.7 | |
| 铁路运输业 | Railway Transport | -12.3 | |
| 道路运输业 | Road Transport | -11.3 | |
| 水上运输业 | Water Transport | -21.4 | |
| 航空运输业 | Air Transport | -66.8 | |
| 管道运输业 | Pipeline Transport | -13.7 | |
| 装卸搬运和运输代理业 | Handing，Corrying and Transportation Agent | -74.8 | |
| 仓储业 | Ware houses and Storage | 90.4 | |
| 邮政业 | Post | | |
| （7）信息传输、软件和信息技术服务业 | Information Transmission Computer Services and Software | -27.3 | |
| （8）批发和零售业 | Wholesale and Retail Trade | -62.3 | |
| （9）住宿和餐饮业 | Hotels and Catering Services | -21.7 | |
| （10）金融业 | Financial Intermediation | 1241.4 | |
| （11）房地产业 | Financial Intermediation | -12.2 | 11.6 |

# 4-5 续表 3
Continued

单位：%（%）

| 项目 | Item | 合计 Total | #房地产开发 Investment in Real Estate Development |
|---|---|---|---|
| （12）租赁和商务服务业 | Leasing and Business Services | 107.9 | |
| （13）科学研究和技术服务业 | Scientific Research，Technical Service and Geologic Prospecting | -5.8 | |
| （14）水利、环境和公共设施管理业 | Management of Water Conservancy，Environment and Pubic Facilities | 105.0 | |
| 水利管理业 | Management of Water Conservancy | 39.7 | |
| 环境管理业 | Environmental Management | 223.0 | |
| 公共设施管理业 | Management of Public Facilities | 110.2 | |
| （15）居民服务和其他服务业 | Services to Households and Other Services | -29.8 | |
| 居民服务业 | Serviced to Households | -48.9 | |
| 机动车、电子产品和日用产品修理业 | Maintenance of Vehicle，Electronic Products and Daily Articles | -26.3 | |
| 其他服务业 | Other Services | -17.0 | |
| （16）教育 | Educatilon | 14.3 | |
| （17）卫生和社会工作 | Health and Social Work | -28.0 | |
| 卫生 | Health | -27.1 | |
| （18）文化、体育和娱乐业 | Culture，Sports and Entertainment | -69.1 | |
| 新闻出版业 | Journalism and Publishing Activities | 134.8 | |
| 广播、电视、体育和音像业 | Broadcasting，Movies，Televisions and Audiovisual Activities | -96.7 | |
| 文化艺术业 | Cultural and Art Activities | -19.3 | |
| 体育 | Sports Activities | -82.7 | |
| 娱乐业 | Entertainment | -14.0 | |
| （19）公共管理、社会保障和社会组织 | Public Management，Social Security and Social Organzation | 0.5 | |
| 中国共产党机关 | Communist Party of China | -89.1 | |
| 国家机构 | Govenment Agencies | 1.9 | |
| 人民政协、民主党派 | People' s Political Consultatioe Conference，Democratic Party | | |
| 社会保障 | Social Security | | |
| 群众团体、社会团体和其他成员组织 | Non-Governmental Institutions，Social Organizations and Other Organizations | | |
| 基层群众自治组织 | Local People Self-government Organization | -0.9 | |
| （20）国际组织 | International Organization | | |

## 4-5 续表 4
Continued

单位：%（%）

| 项目 | Item | 合计 Total | # 房地产开发 Investment in Real Estate Development |
|---|---|---|---|
| **四、本年资金来源合计** | **Total Funds This Year** | **5.6** | **12.6** |
| 上年末结余资金 | Balance of Last Year | 30.6 | 15.6 |
| 本年资金来源小计 | Sub-total Funds This Year | 1.6 | 11.5 |
| 国家预算内资金 | State Budget | -16.6 | |
| 国内贷款 | Domestic Loans | -19.2 | -13.9 |
| 债券 | State Treasury Bond | | |
| 利用外资 | Foreign Investment | -41.6 | -80.7 |
| 自筹资金 | Self-raising Funds | 1.8 | -9.5 |
| 其他资金来源 | Others | 21.1 | 33.6 |

# 4-6 主要年份房地产开发投资
MAJOR YEAR'S INVESTMENT IN REAL ESTATE DEVELOPMENT

单位：万元、万平方米（10 000 yuan，10 000 sq.m）

| 年份<br>Year | 房地产开发投资额<br>Investment in Real Estate Development | 房屋施工面积<br>Floor Space Under Construction | 房屋竣工面积<br>Floor Space Completed | 房屋实际销售面积<br>Floor Space of Buildings Sold | 房屋实际销售额<br>Sale of Buildings |
|---|---|---|---|---|---|
| 1995 | 562861 | 1008 | 240 | 103 | 185384 |
| 1996 | 455765 | 748 | 203 | 80 | 125150 |
| 1997 | 426570 | 675 | 237 | 113 | 216311 |
| 1998 | 438059 | 742 | 259 | 178 | 351805 |
| 1999 | 629717 | 900 | 474 | 240 | 430123 |
| 2000 | 675142 | 1047 | 352 | 301 | 550401 |
| 2001 | 925153 | 1374 | 532 | 406 | 802364 |
| 2002 | 1036476 | 1417 | 537 | 427 | 933031 |
| 2003 | 1277969 | 1765 | 552 | 469 | 1121885 |
| 2004 | 1626965 | 2101 | 635 | 516 | 1530964 |
| 2005 | 2238370 | 2363 | 811 | 740 | 2666738 |
| 2006 | 2683631 | 2751 | 654 | 719 | 3054907 |
| 2007 | 3223547 | 3224 | 641 | 833 | 4333566 |
| 2008 | 3805652 | 3773 | 672 | 770 | 3924175 |
| 2009 | 4594829 | 4310 | 814 | 1262 | 7036744 |
| 2010 | 6024387 | 5058 | 1020 | 1360 | 8952942 |
| 2011 | 7827193 | 5693 | 925 | 1026 | 7702379 |
| 2012 | 9301099 | 6474 | 1212 | 951 | 7660684 |
| 2013 | 10485229 | 7073 | 957 | 1160 | 9786176 |
| 2014 | 11177297 | 8171 | 1136 | 1164 | 9708984 |
| 2015 | 11223458 | 8971 | 1523 | 1419 | 12628568 |
| 2016 | 13691425 | 9101 | 1426 | 1939 | 17899532 |
| 2017 | 13305432 | 9533 | 1487 | 1901 | 19992012 |
| 2018 | 14852089 | 10390 | 1625 | 1808 | 22824618 |

## 4-7 房地产开发投资情况（2018年）
INVESTMENT IN REAL ESTATE DEVELOPMENT (2018)

单位：万元（10 000 yuan）

| 指标名称 | Indicator | 合计 Total | 按经济类型分 Grouped by Economic Types | | |
|---|---|---|---|---|---|
| | | | 国有经济 State-owned | 集体经济 Collective-owned | 其他经济 Others |
| **本年完成投资额** | **Investment Completed This Year** | **14852089** | **705310** | **37535** | **14109244** |
| 1. 住宅 | Residential Buildings | 10348412 | 418191 | 24493 | 9905728 |
| 2. 办公楼 | Office Buildings | 984710 | 94846 | | 889864 |
| 3. 商业营业用房 | Houses for Business Use | 1536861 | 94621 | 824 | 1441416 |
| 4. 其他 | Others | 1982106 | 97652 | 12218 | 1872236 |

## 4-7 续表
Continued

单位：万元（10 000 yuan）

| 指标名称 | Indicator | 按资质等级分 Grouped by Qualification Criteria | | | | | |
|---|---|---|---|---|---|---|---|
| | | 一级 First Grade | 二级 Second Grade | 三级 Third Grade | 四级 Fourth Grade | 暂定 Provistonal | 其他 Others |
| **本年完成投资额** | **Investment Completed This Year** | **351255** | **767378** | **338783** | **237751** | **10000875** | **3156047** |
| 1. 住宅 | Residential Buildings | 136358 | 595640 | 260740 | 149377 | 7150803 | 2055494 |
| 2. 办公楼 | Office Buildings | 57923 | 3731 | 10507 | 19525 | 595499 | 297525 |
| 3. 商业营业用房 | Houses for Business Use | 73991 | 24776 | 48632 | 51378 | 1075779 | 262305 |
| 4. 其他 | Others | 82983 | 143231 | 18904 | 17471 | 1178794 | 540723 |

## 4-8 房地产施工、竣工面积及竣工价值（2018 年）
FLOOR SPACE UNDER CONSTRUCTION AND COMPLETED AND COMPLETED VALUE OF REAL ESTATE（2018）

单位：万平方米（10 000 sq.m）

| 施工、竣工房屋面积及竣工价值 | Indicator | 施工面积 Floor Space Under Construction | #新开工 Newly Started | 竣工房屋 Floor Space Completed | 竣工房屋价值（万元）Completed Value（10 000 yuan） |
|---|---|---|---|---|---|
| **房屋建筑面积总计** | **Floor Space of Buildings** | **10390** | **2803** | **1625** | **4609219** |
| 住宅 | Residential Buildings | 6832 | 1848 | 1079 | 2861438 |
| 办公楼 | Office Buildings | 670 | 131 | 126 | 432764 |
| 商业营业用房 | Houses for Business Use | 1046 | 272 | 170 | 560814 |
| 其他 | Others | 1842 | 552 | 250 | 754103 |

## 4-9 商品房屋销售情况（2018 年）
BASIC STATISTICS ON SALES OF COMMERCIALIZED BUILBINGS（2018）

单位：万平方米（10 000 sq.m）

| 商品房屋销售情况 | Sales and Rental of Commercialized Buildings | 实际销售 Actual Sales | 实际销售额（万元）Actual Sales Volume（10 000 yuan） | 待售面积 Area for Sale |
|---|---|---|---|---|
| **房屋面积总计** | **Floor Space of Buildings** | **1808** | **22824618** | **433** |
| 住宅 | Residential Buildings | 1578 | 19529067 | 162 |
| 办公楼 | Office Buildings | 77 | 1123363 | 91 |
| 商业营业用房 | Houses for Business Use | 120 | 1781244 | 152 |
| 其他 | Others | 33 | 390944 | 28 |

# 主要统计指标解释

**固定资产投资** 是以货币形式表现的在一定时期内建造和购置固定资产的工作量以及与此有关的费用的总称。

**房地产开发投资** 指各种登记注册类型的房地产开发法人单位统一开发的住宅、厂房、仓库、饭店、宾馆、度假村、写字楼、办公楼等房屋建筑物，配套的服务设施，土地开发工程（如道路、给水、排水、供电、供热、通讯、平整场地等基础设施工程）和土地购置的投资；不包括单纯的土地开发和交易活动。

**固定资产投资的资金来源** 根据固定资产投资的资金来源不同，分为国家预算资金、国内贷款、利用外资、自筹资金和其他资金。

**固定资产投资** 按建设性质分建设项目的性质一般分为新建、扩建、改建和技术改造、单纯建造生活设施、迁建、恢复、单纯购置。

**固定资产投资** 按构成分固定资产投资活动按其工作内容和实现方式分为建筑安装工程，设备、工具、器具购置，其他费用三个部分。

**新增生产能力（或工程效益）** 指建成投产项目或工程新增生产能力（或工程效益）的名称。

**房屋施工面积** 是指报告期内施工的全部房屋建筑面积。包括本期新开工的面积和上期开工跨入本期继续施工的房屋面积，以及上期已停缓建在本期恢复施工的房屋面积。本期竣工和本期施工后又停缓建的房屋，其建筑面积仍计入本期房屋施工面积中。

**房屋竣工面积** 是指在报告期内房屋建筑按照设计要求全部完工，达到住人和使用条件，经验收鉴定合格（或达到竣工验收标准），正式移交使用单位的各栋房屋建筑面积的总和。

**本年新增固定资产** 指在报告期已经完成建造和购置过程，并已交付生产或使用单位的固定资产的价值，包括已经建成投入生产或交付使用的工程投资和达到固定资产标准的设备、工具、器具的投资及有关应摊入的费用。

# Explanatory Notes on Main Statistical Indicators

**Fixed investment** is a generic term of quantity of work from building and acquiring of fixed assets over a period of time and any relevant expenses incurred thereby in the form of currency.

**Real estate development investment** means investments in all kinds of registered housing & building, including residences, plants, warehouses, restaurants, hotels, resorts, office buildings and administrative buildings which are developed uniformly by real estate development corporation, supporting sevice facilities and land development projects (such as road, water supply & drainage, power supply, heat supply, telecommunication and ground leveling and other infrastructure projects) and land acquisition; excludes simple land development and transaction activities.

**Source of funds for fixed-asset investment** can be divided into national budget funds, domestic loans, utilization of foreign capital, self-raised funds and other funds in accordance with the different sources.

**Construction items of fixed-asset investment** can be divided into new construction, extension, reconstruction, technical reform, simply-constructed living facilities, relocation, restoration and simple acquisition by property of construction.

**Fixed-asset investment** activities can be divided into three parts, namely construction and installation project, acquisition of\ equipement, tools and appliances and other expenses by working content and method of achieving.

**New productive capacity (or project benefit)** means the completed projects or new productive capacity (or projevt benefit) of projects.

**Construction area** neans total areas of all buildings which are under construction in the ruport period, including the area which is newly constructed in this period and the areas of buildings which commence in the last period and carry forward to this period for continuing construction. and the areas of buildings which stop constructing in the last period and resume to be constructed in this period. The areas of the buildings which are completed in this period and stop constructing after this period' s construction are still reckoned in floor space under construction in this period.

**Completed ares** means the wum total of areas of housings & buildings which are completed according to design requirements in the report period, reach conditions of living and using and are transferred to building users formally after checked and accepted (or reach the standards of completion and acceptance).

**New fixed assets in this year** means the value of fixed assets which are completed and acquired in the report period and delivered for production or use, including investment in constructions which are put into production or service, investment in equipment, tools and appliances which reach the standards of fixed asset, and the expenses which should be added into fixed assets.

# 对外经济贸易 5

FOREIGN TRADE

# 简要说明

## 一、本篇资料的主要内容

本篇资料主要反映了全市外经外贸和外资企业的基本情况，主要包括外贸进出口、利用外资、对外投资与经济合作等方面的资料。

## 二、本篇资料的来源

1、口岸进出口数据来源于青岛市海关。

2、进出口、利用外资等资料、对外投资与经济合作来源于市商务局。

本篇资料由市统计局外经贸易统计处整理提供。

# Brief Introduction

## *I. Main Content*

Data in this chapter show the basic conditions of foreign trade and foreign-funded enterprises, mainly including imports and exports, utilization of foreign capitals, production and operation condition of foreign-funded enterprises, etc.

## *II. Source of Data*

1.Data on imports and exports of Qingdao port are provided by Office of Qingdao Port Administration.

2.Data on imports & exports and utilization of foreign capitals are provided by Qingdao Municipal Commerce Bureau.

3.Data on production and operation condition of foreign-funded enterprises are based on the National Union Annual Inspection of foreign-funded enterprises.

Data in this chapter are prepared and compiled by the Division of Trade and External Economic Relations Statistics of Qingdao Municipal Bureau of Statistics.

# 5-1 青岛口岸进出口总额(1985-2018年)

TOTAL VALUE OF IMPORTS AND EXPORTS OF QINGDAO PORT (1985-2018)

单位：万美元(10 000 USD)、万元(10 000 yuan)

| 年份 Year | 青岛口岸进出口总额 Total Value of Imports and Exports Oing dao Port | 出口 Exports | 进口 Imports |
|---|---|---|---|
| 1985 | 414448 | 234652 | 179796 |
| 1986 | 382840 | 191926 | 190914 |
| 1987 | 445090 | 259458 | 185632 |
| 1988 | 474516 | 259176 | 215340 |
| 1989 | 506152 | 268397 | 237755 |
| 1990 | 477117 | 304011 | 173106 |
| 1991 | 519273 | 332949 | 186324 |
| 1992 | 581495 | 350163 | 231332 |
| 1993 | 678013 | 360297 | 317716 |
| 1994 | 888574 | 510760 | 377814 |
| 1995 | 1307508 | 705245 | 602263 |
| 1996 | 1391323 | 760566 | 629757 |
| 1997 | 1542284 | 936142 | 609142 |
| 1998 | 1463718 | 933392 | 530326 |
| 1999 | 1696514 | 1063768 | 632746 |
| 2000 | 2520420 | 1423266 | 1097154 |
| 2001 | 2797085 | 1636888 | 1160197 |
| 2002 | 3128048 | 1889612 | 1238436 |
| 2003 | 4088096 | 2366046 | 1722050 |
| 2004 | 5677570 | 3197697 | 2479873 |
| 2005 | 6932944 | 3959947 | 2972997 |
| 2006 | 8019198 | 4495731 | 3523467 |
| 2007 | 9257099 | 5263539 | 3993560 |
| 2008 | 11558079 | 5953501 | 5604578 |
| 2009 | 9049699 | 4694832 | 4354867 |
| 2010 | 11912702 | 5988254 | 5924448 |
| 2011 | 15095088 | 7294226 | 7800862 |
| 2012 | 14888716 | 7120813 | 7767903 |
| 2013 | 15662732 | 7696141 | 7966591 |
| 2014 | 16489966 | 8736358 | 7753608 |
| 2015 | 14448349 | 8776286 | 5672063 |
| 2016 | 94927180 | 56513317 | 38413863 |
| 2017 | 111024375 | 63298062 | 47726314 |
| 2018 | 121968146 | 67385279 | 54582867 |

注：2016年起，统计单位为人民币万元。

Note : Statistic unit is RMB ten thousand Yuan as from 2016.

# 5-2 进出口总额（1988-2018 年）
TOTAL VALUE OF IMPORTS AND EXPORTS（1988-2018）

单位：万美元（10 000 USD）、万元（10 000 yuan）

| 年份<br>Year | 进出口总额（含中央、省驻青公司）<br>Total Value of Imports and Exports<br>（including central and provincial companies） | 出口<br>Exports | 进口<br>Imports | 进出口总额（不含中央、省驻青公司）<br>Total Value of Imports and Exports<br>（including central and provincial companies） | 出口<br>Exports | 进口<br>Imports |
|---|---|---|---|---|---|---|
| 1988 | | | | 28097 | 21731 | 6366 |
| 1989 | | | | 39327 | 27797 | 11530 |
| 1990 | | | | 41649 | 33529 | 8120 |
| 1991 | | | | 54624 | 44746 | 9878 |
| 1992 | | | | 88600 | 66291 | 22309 |
| 1993 | 517643 | 346288 | 171355 | 139048 | 100201 | 38847 |
| 1994 | 633213 | 434102 | 199111 | 234978 | 164135 | 70843 |
| 1995 | 858560 | 536386 | 322174 | 376372 | 245072 | 131300 |
| 1996 | 863521 | 516317 | 347204 | 461950 | 287123 | 174827 |
| 1997 | 916269 | 579261 | 377008 | 521967 | 338535 | 183432 |
| 1998 | 882042 | 573020 | 309022 | 595826 | 382657 | 213169 |
| 1999 | 1009885 | 631072 | 378813 | 775565 | 446260 | 329305 |
| 2000 | 1353222 | 826891 | 526331 | 1083133 | 611426 | 471707 |
| 2001 | 1541564 | 950160 | 591404 | 1235781 | 712024 | 523757 |
| 2002 | 1692567 | 1057141 | 635426 | 1409598 | 850420 | 559178 |
| 2003 | 2065912 | 1239199 | 826713 | 1784556 | 1035528 | 749028 |
| 2004 | 2698781 | 1578167 | 1120614 | 2433188 | 1391171 | 1042017 |
| 2005 | 3302230 | 1942242 | 1359988 | 3045542 | 1758834 | 1286708 |
| 2006 | 3911543 | 2346552 | 1564991 | 3655737 | 2164541 | 1491196 |
| 2007 | 4572534 | 2831004 | 1741530 | 4360499 | 2677596 | 1682903 |
| 2008 | 5363659 | 3262476 | 2101183 | 5215886 | 3146246 | 2069640 |
| 2009 | 4485115 | 2729865 | 1755250 | 4398639 | 2692197 | 1706442 |
| 2010 | 5705963 | 3391560 | 2314403 | 5614928 | 3335141 | 2279787 |
| 2011 | 7215217 | 4061309 | 3153908 | 7126310 | 4005572 | 3120738 |
| 2012 | | | | 7320781 | 4081968 | 3238813 |
| 2013 | | | | 7791217 | 4198605 | 3592612 |
| 2014 | | | | 7988833 | 4577696 | 3411137 |
| 2015 | | | | 7022243 | 4535015 | 2487228 |
| 2016 | | | | 43506659 | 28219059 | 15287600 |
| 2017 | | | | 50334973 | 30318103 | 20016870 |
| 2018 | | | | 53212551 | 31722209 | 21490342 |

注：1、2012 年起，中央、省驻青公司外贸统计划归青岛，取消含中央、省驻青公司统计口径；
2、2016 年起，统计单位为人民币万元。

Note：1. Since 2012，the statistical calibre including central and provincoal companies has been cancled.
2. Statistic unit is RMB ten thousand Yuan as from 2016.

# 5-3　分国别外贸出口总额

TOTAL VALUE OF EXPORTS BY COUNTRIES OR REGIONS

单位：万美元（10 000 USD）

| 国别（地区） | Country（Region） | 2018 年 | 2018 年比 2017 年 ±%<br>2018/2017（=%） | 占比 % |
|---|---|---|---|---|
| 亚洲 | Aioa | 2083063 | 9.8 | 43.5 |
| 香港 | Hong Kong | 191991 | 9.2 | 4.0 |
| 日本 | Japan | 562514 | 6.6 | 11.7 |
| 韩国 | Korea | 444012 | 7.6 | 9.3 |
| 东盟 | ASEAN | 463450 | 24.0 | 9.7 |
| 非洲 | Africa | 192717 | 14.1 | 4.0 |
| 南非 | South Africa | 45146 | 12.9 | 0.9 |
| 欧洲 | Europe | 1019206 | -3.3 | 21.3 |
| 欧盟 | EU | 881451 | 7.2 | 18.4 |
| 南美洲 | South America | 317302 | 7.9 | 6.6 |
| 北美洲 | North America | 1045878 | 13.7 | 21.8 |
| 美国 | United States | 930533 | 12.3 | 19.4 |
| 大洋洲 | Oceanica | 135684 | 10.8 | 2.8 |
| 澳大利亚 | Australia | 113291 | 11.3 | 2.4 |

# 5-4 外贸出口商品分类
EXPORT COMMODITIES BY CATEGORY

单位：万元（10 000 yuan）

| 项目 | Item | 2018年 | 2018年比2017±%<br>2018/2017（±%） | 占比% |
|---|---|---|---|---|
| **合计** | **Total** | **31722209** | **4.7** | **100.0** |
| 按企业性质划分 | By Enterprises Nature | | | |
| 国有企业 | State-owned Enterprises | 2794782 | -25.3 | 8.8 |
| 外商投资企业 | Foreign Funded Enterprises | 10116044 | 2.0 | 31.9 |
| 其他企业 | Other Enerprises | 18811383 | 13.0 | 59.3 |
| #集体企业 | #Collective-owned Enterprises | 897020 | -9.1 | 2.8 |
| 私营企业 | Private Enterprises | 17903042 | 14.4 | 56.5 |
| 按贸易方式划分 | By Customs Regime | | | |
| 一般贸易 | Ordinary Trade | 21953506 | 13.2 | 69.2 |
| 加工贸易 | Processing Trade | 8927337 | -8.4 | 28.2 |
| 其他贸易 | Others | 841366 | -28.1 | 2.6 |
| 按大类商品划分 | By Category of Commodities | | | |
| 纺织服装 | Textile Garments | 4820050 | 7.7 | 15.2 |
| 农产品 | Agricultural Products | 3872661 | 8.4 | 12.2 |
| 机电产品 | Mechanical and Electrical Products | 13522213 | 0.5 | 42.7 |
| 高新技术产品 | High-tech Products | 3160605 | 5.1 | 10.0 |

# 5-5 外贸进口商品分类
IMPORT COMMODITIES BY CATEGORY

单位：万元（10 000 yuan）

| 项目 | Item | 2018 年 | 2018 年比 2017 ± %<br>2018/2017（±%） | 占比 % |
|---|---|---|---|---|
| **合计** | **Total** | **21490342** | **7.3** | **100.0** |
| 按企业性质划分 | By Enterprises Nature | | | |
| 国有企业 | State-owned Enterprises | 4959960 | 7.5 | 23.1 |
| 外商投资企业 | Foreign Funded Enterprises | 6199653 | 12.0 | 28.8 |
| 其他企业 | Other Enerprises | 10330728 | 4.6 | 48.1 |
| # 集体企业 | #Collective-owned Enterprises | 215374 | 21.8 | 1.0 |
| 私营企业 | Private Enterprises | 10043400 | 4.3 | 46.7 |
| 按贸易方式划分 | By Customs Regime | | | |
| 一般贸易 | Ordinary Trade | 11282609 | 3.8 | 52.5 |
| 加工贸易 | Processing Trade | 3205228 | 1.8 | 14.9 |
| 其他贸易 | Others | 7002505 | 16.4 | 32.6 |
| 按大类商品划分 | By Category of Commodities | | | |
| 纺织服装 | Textile Garments | 292168 | -9.8 | 1.4 |
| 农产品 | Agricultural Products | 4104093 | 15.2 | 19.1 |
| 机电产品 | Mechanical and Electrical Products | 4345845 | 5.2 | 20.2 |
| 高新技术产品 | High-tech Products | 2091472 | 5.1 | 9.7 |

# 5-6 二十大出口商品出口情况

INFORMATION ON THE EXPORTATION OF TOP 20 PRODUCTS

单位：万美元（10 000 USD）

| 商品名称 | Name | 2018 年 | 2018 年比 2017 年 ±%<br>2018/2017（±%） | 占比 % |
|---|---|---|---|---|
| **合计** | **Total** | **4176922** | **6.6** | **100.0** |
| 机械设备 | Machinery and Equipment | 661917 | -9.0 | 15.8 |
| 电器及电子类产品 | Electric Appliance and Electronic Products | 571322 | 4.6 | 13.7 |
| 服装 | Garments | 463888 | 7.9 | 11.1 |
| 计算机与通信技术 | Computer and Communication Technology | 377063 | 4.8 | 9.0 |
| 运输工具 | Transport Tools | 434924 | 21.6 | 10.4 |
| 纺织品 | Textile Products | 266174 | 15.4 | 6.4 |
| 金属制品 | Metal Products | 240227 | 10.5 | 5.8 |
| 轮胎 | Tyre | 156194 | 11.0 | 3.7 |
| 电话机 | Telephone Sets | 160903 | 23.0 | 3.9 |
| 水海产品 | Aquatic and Seawater Products | 131601 | 4.7 | 3.2 |
| 蔬菜 | Vegetables | 120818 | 4.3 | 2.9 |
| 家具及其零件 | Furniture | 103243 | 2.4 | 2.5 |
| 钢材 | Rolled Steel | 134897 | 35.1 | 3.2 |
| 鞋类 | Shoes | 97556 | 10.0 | 2.3 |
| 塑料制品 | Plastic Articles | 82790 | 10.7 | 2.0 |
| 箱包 | Luggage and Bags | 59857 | -13.5 | 1.4 |
| 汽车零件 | Parts of Motor Vehicles | 72722 | 26.7 | 1.7 |
| 空调 | Air Conditioner | 40728 | -13.6 | 1.0 |
| 游戏机 | Game Console | 30 | 3.8 | |
| 铁合金 | Ferroalloy | 71 | | |

# 5-7 二十大进口商品进口情况

## INFORMATION ON THE IMPORTATION OF TOP 20 PRODUCTS

单位：万美元（10 000 USD）

| 商品名称 | Name | 2018 年 | 2018 年比 2017 年 ±%<br>2018/2017（±%） | 占比 % |
|---|---|---|---|---|
| **合计** | **Total** | **1902558** | **3.2** | **100.0** |
| 铁矿砂 | Machinery and Equipment | 321376 | -4.8 | 16.9 |
| 电器及电子产品 | Electric Appliance and Electronic Products | 240801 | -4.6 | 12.7 |
| 机械设备 | Machinery and Equipment | 198619 | 15.2 | 10.4 |
| 粮食 | Grain | 137134 | -10.9 | 7.2 |
| 合成橡胶 | Synthetic Rubber | 112878 | -13.3 | 5.9 |
| 天然橡胶 | Natural Rubber | 79625 | -37.8 | 4.2 |
| 仪器仪表 | Instruments and Meters | 136277 | 19.5 | 7.2 |
| 集成电路 | Integrated Circuits | 102051 | -2.6 | 5.4 |
| 塑料原料 | Plastic Raw Materials | 121952 | 25.7 | 6.4 |
| 冻鱼 | Frozen Fish | 110891 | 21.9 | 5.8 |
| 液晶显示板 | Liquid Crystal DIsplay | 61774 | 17.7 | 3.2 |
| 棉花 | Cotton | 80907 | 62.8 | 4.3 |
| 纺织品 | Textile Products | 40863 | -8.1 | 2.1 |
| 运输工具 | Means of Conveyance | 52784 | 25.7 | 2.8 |
| 钢材 | Rolled Steel | 41070 | 6.4 | 2.2 |
| 塑料制品 | Plastic Articles | 10644 | 0.9 | 0.6 |
| 铝锭及铝材 | Aluminum Ingots and Aluminum Products | 8621 | -2.7 | 0.5 |
| 成品油 | Refined Petroleum Products | 37449 | 377.1 | 2.0 |
| 氧化铝 | Alumina | | | |
| 钻石 | Diamonds | 3960 | 24.0 | 0.2 |

# 5-8 利用外资情况（2000-2018 年）
UTILIZATION OF FOREIGN CAPITAL（2000-2018）

| 项目 | Item | 单位 | Unit | 2000 年 | 2005 年 |
|---|---|---|---|---|---|
| **批准企业（项目）个数** | **Number of Enterprises（Projects）Approved** | **个** | **unit** | **1132** | **2530** |
| 一、外商直接投资 | Foreign Direct Investments | 个 | unit | 1128 | 2530 |
| 中外合资企业 | Sino-foreign Joint Ventures | 个 | unit | 303 | 274 |
| 中外合作企业 | Sino-foreign Cooperative Enterprises | 个 | unit | 57 | 18 |
| 外商独资企业 | Foreign-owned Enterprises | 个 | unit | 76 | 2236 |
| 其它 | Others | 个 | unit | 1 | 2 |
| 二、外商其他投资 | Other Foreign Investments | 个 | unit | 4 | |
| **合同外资金额** | **Total Amount of Contracted Foreign Investment** | **万美元** | **10000 USD** | **269081** | **954486** |
| 一、外商直接投资 | Foreign Direct Investments | 万美元 | 10000 USD | 266221 | 954486 |
| 中外合资企业 | Sino-foreign Joint Ventures | 万美元 | 10000 USD | 69889 | 112777 |
| 中外合作企业 | Sino-foreign Cooperative Enterprises | 万美元 | 10000 USD | 26835 | 17588 |
| 外商独资企业 | Foreign-owned Enterprises | 万美元 | 10000 USD | 169370 | 813485 |
| 其它 | Others | 万美元 | 10000 USD | 127 | 10636 |
| 二、外商其他投资 | Other Foreign Investments | 万美元 | 10000 USD | 2860 | |
| **实际利用外资金额** | **Total Amount of Foreign Investment Actually Utilized** | **万美元** | **10000 USD** | **128171** | **365625** |
| 一、外商直接投资 | Foreign Direct Investments | 万美元 | 10000 USD | 126132 | 365625 |
| 中外合资企业 | Sino-foreign Joint Ventures | 万美元 | 10000 USD | 39224 | 77636 |
| 中外合作企业 | Sino-foreign Cooperative Enterprises | 万美元 | 10000 USD | 3886 | 5654 |
| 外商独资企业 | Foreign-owned Enterprises | 万美元 | 10000 USD | 82992 | 280130 |
| 其它 | Others | 万美元 | 10000 USD | 30 | 2205 |
| 二、外商其他投资 | Other Foreign Investments | 万美元 | 10000 USD | 2039 | |

单位：万美元（10 000 USD）

| 2008年 | 2009年 | 2010年 | 2011年 | 2012年 | 2013年 | 2014年 | 2015年 | 2016年 | 2017年 | 2018年 |
|---|---|---|---|---|---|---|---|---|---|---|
| **640** | **647** | **731** | **707** | **553** | **645** | **619** | **763** | **680** | **650** | **956** |
| 640 | 647 | 731 | 707 | 553 | 645 | 619 | 763 | 680 | 650 | 956 |
| 99 | 99 | 153 | 158 | 113 | 165 | 140 | 162 | 154 | 188 | 294 |
| 4 | 2 | 4 | 4 | 2 | 2 | 1 | 2 |  | 1 | 8 |
| 537 | 545 | 574 | 544 | 438 | 478 | 475 | 597 | 523 | 457 | 653 |
|  | 1 |  | 1 |  |  | 3 | 2 | 3 | 4 | 1 |
|  |  |  |  |  |  |  |  |  |  |  |
| **304505** | **271504** | **475723** | **528501** | **600231** | **758063** | **638637** | **827357** | **769101** | **909629** | **980231** |
| 304505 | 271504 | 475723 | 528501 | 600231 | 758063 | 638637 | 827357 | 769101 | 909629 | 980231 |
| 81796 | 61734 | 124148 | 142535 | 102252 | 191172 | 126878 | 116013 | 207933 | 246280 | 195336 |
| 367 | 4531 | 9179 | 15173 | 122 | 4765 | -849 | 1731 | 28 | 327 | 34333 |
| 221759 | 204187 | 341977 | 369425 | 490764 | 562208 | 506271 | 706172 | 554073 | 655377 | 756426 |
| 583 | 1052 | 419 | 1368 | 7093 | -82 | 6337 | 3441 | 7067 | 7645 | -5864 |
|  |  |  |  |  |  |  |  |  |  |  |
| **264295** | **186397** | **284281** | **363350** | **460027** | **552227** | **608100** | **669062** | **700273** | **773500** | **869257** |
| 264295 | 186397 | 284281 | 363350 | 460027 | 552227 | 608100 | 669062 | 700273 | 773500 | 869257 |
| 43810 | 46856 | 84920 | 100699 | 169469 | 159424 | 172180 | 135671 | 171051 | 195189 | 191040 |
| 2945 | 3971 | 3567 | 2759 | 6262 | 2355 | 128 | 1570 | 251 | 220 | 19032 |
| 217540 | 135026 | 194500 | 255763 | 275579 | 390210 | 435102 | 531544 | 520052 | 569461 | 658368 |
|  | 544 | 1294 | 4129 | 8717 | 238 | 690 | 277 | 8918 | 8325 | 817 |

# 5-9 当年外商直接投资项目数和投资额（2018年）

NUMBER OF PROJECTS AND TOTAL AMOUNT OF FOREIGN DIRECT INVESTMENT（2018）

单位：万美元（10 000 USD）

| 项目 | Item | 批准企业项目数（个）Number of Projects Approved（unit） | 合同外资金额（万美元）Total Amount of Contracted Foreign Investment（10000 USD） | 实际利用外资金额（万美元）Total Amount of Foreign Investment Aetually Utilized（10000 USD） |
|---|---|---|---|---|
| **外商直接投资** | **Foreign Direct Investments** | | | |
| **一、按投资方式分** | **Grouped by Investment Form** | | | |
| #中外合资企业 | Sino-foreign Joint Ventures | 294 | 195336 | 191040 |
| 中外合作企业 | Sino-foreign Cooperative Enterprises | 8 | 34333 | 19032 |
| 外商独资企业 | Foreign-owned Enterprises | 653 | 756426 | 658368 |
| **二、按主要行业分** | **Grouped by Sector** | | | |
| #农、林、牧、渔业 | Farming，Foresty，Animal Hus-bandry and Fishery | 12 | 724 | 5499 |
| 制造业 | Manufacturing | 248 | 302982 | 318301 |
| 电力、燃气及水的生产和供应业 | Production and Supply of Electricity，Gas and Water | | 3446 | 5385 |
| 建筑业 | Construction | 12 | 16405 | 13278 |
| 信息传输、计算机服务和软件业 | Information transmission，computer services and software industry | 15 | 21870 | 20393 |
| 批发和零售业 | Wholesale and Retail Trades | 307 | 83170 | 130478 |
| 房地产业 | Real estate industry | 39 | 147112 | 237697 |
| 租赁和商务服务业 | Leasing and Business Services | 75 | 80238 | 54226 |
| 科学研究、技术服务和地质勘查业 | Scientific Research，Technical Service and Geological Survey | 60 | 108114 | 23167 |
| **三、按主要国别（地区）分** | **Grouped by Countries（Regions）** | | | |
| #香港 | Hong Kong | 254 | 701315 | 529004 |
| 韩国 | Korea | 356 | 115816 | 103323 |
| 美国 | United States | 53 | 19396 | 20035 |
| 日本 | Japan | 36 | 7615 | 26664 |
| 德国 | Germany | 27 | 22266 | 26593 |
| 澳大利亚 | Australia | 13 | 9020 | 13028 |
| 新加坡 | Singapore | 22 | 6947 | 26142 |

## 5-10 对外投资与经济合作
OUTBOUND INVESTMENT AND INTERNATIONAL ECONOMIC COOPERATION

| 名称 | Name | 单位 | Unit | 2018 年 | 2018 年比 2017 年 ±% 2018/2017（±%） |
|---|---|---|---|---|---|
| 对外投资项目数 | Number of Outbound Investment Projects | 个 | unit | 95 | -39.1 |
| 对外投资中方投资额 | The Amount of Investment by Chinese Sides in Outbound Investment | 万美元 | 10000 USD | 504818.28 | -21.5 |
| 对外承包工程新签合同额 | The Amount of New Contracts for Foreign Contracted Projects | 万美元 | 10000 USD | 493108 | 11.9 |
| 对外承包工程完成营业额 | The Completed Turnover of Foreign Contracted Projects | 万美元 | 10000 USD | 431244 | 12.8 |
| 对外劳务合作 | Number of Persons Sent Overseas for International Labor Srevice Cooperation | 人 | Person | 11820 | -35.4 |

## 5-11 对外投资分国别（地区）情况表（2018 年）
INFORMATION ON OUTBOUND INVESTMENT BY COUNTRY/REGION FOR（2018）

| 国别（地区） | Country（Region） | 项目数量（个） Number of Projects（unit） | 2018 年比 2017 年 ±% 2018/2017（±%） | 中方投资额（万美元） Amount of Investment by Chinese Sides（10000 USD） | 2018 年比 2017 年 ±% 2018/2017（±%） |
|---|---|---|---|---|---|
| **总计** | **Total** | 95 | -39.1 | 504818 | -21.5 |
| 亚洲 | Asia | 48 | -44.8 | 201888 | -8.8 |
| 韩国 | Korea | 13 | | 71562 | 382.3 |
| 中国香港 | Hong Kong，China | 12 | -52 | 117693 | 497 |
| 越南 | Vietnam | 8 | -38.5 | 4852 | -74.93 |
| 乌兹别克斯坦 | Uzbekistan | 3 | | 145 | |
| 泰国 | Thailand | 2 | | 1011 | -85.1 |
| 柬埔寨 | Cambodia | 2 | -50 | 1160 | -91.2 |
| 巴基斯坦 | Pakistan | 1 | | 20000 | 16428.9 |
| 老挝 | Laos | 1 | | 40 | -99.7 |
| 马来西亚 | Malaysia | 1 | -80 | -7250 | -109.8 |
| 日本 | Japan | 1 | -88.9 | -6379 | -151.6 |
| 缅甸 | Myanmar | 1 | | 950 | 90 |

# 5-11 对外投资分国别（地区）情况表（2018 年）

INFORMATION ON OUTBOUND INVESTMENT BY COUNTRY/REGION FOR（2018）

| 国别（地区） | Country（Region） | 项目数量（个）Number of Projects（unit） | 2018 年比 2017 年 ± % 2018/2017（± %） | 中方投资额（万美元）Amount of Investment by Chinese Sides（10000 USD） | 2018 年比 2017 年 ± % 2018/2017（± %） |
|---|---|---|---|---|---|
| 哈萨克斯坦 | Kazakhstan | 1 | | 26 | |
| 新加坡 | Singapore | 1 | -83.3 | 896 | -83.4 |
| 印度 | India | 1 | -50 | 30 | -99.2 |
| 欧洲 | Europe | 7 | -30 | 63603 | 313.9 |
| 英国 | U.K. | 2 | -33.3 | 150 | -97.7 |
| 荷兰 | Holland | 2 | | 1512 | 7460.4 |
| 德国 | Germany | 1 | -80 | 12 | -99.6 |
| 葡萄牙 | Portugal | 1 | | 351 | |
| 意大利 | Italy | 1 | | 61139 | |
| 俄罗斯联邦 | Russian | 增资 | -100 | 440 | -92.9 |
| 拉丁美洲 | Latin America | 6 | | 13465 | -95.5 |
| 英属维尔京群岛 | British Virgin Islands | 2 | | 12750 | 99.1 |
| 墨西哥 | Mexico | 2 | | 540 | |
| 阿根廷 | Argentina | 1 | | 23 | |
| 玻利维亚 | Bolivia | 1 | | 3 | |
| 巴拿马 | Panama | 增资 | | 150 | |
| 北美洲 | North America | 18 | -51.3 | 202549 | 176.1 |
| 美国 | United States | 14 | -57.6 | 92335 | 106.4 |
| 加拿大 | Canada | 4 | | 100378 | 250.6 |
| 百慕大群岛 | Bermuda | 增资 | | 9837 | |
| 大洋洲 | Oceanica | 7 | 16.7 | 29455 | 1478.7 |
| 澳大利亚 | Australia | 7 | 40 | 28911 | 2087.3 |
| 新西兰 | New Zealand | 增资 | -100 | 544 | |

# 主要统计指标解释

**批准企业（项目）个数** 是指外商直接投资中批准设立的外商投资企业个数、批准的合作开发项目个数。

合同外资金额是指批准外商投资企业的合同、章程中规定的外国投资者认缴的出资额和企业投资总额内的应由外方投资者以自己的境外自有资金直接向企业提供的贷款。包括新批准企业合同外资和原有企业的增资减资，增资减资不对企业（项目）个数进行调整。

**实际使用外资金额** 是指合同外资金额的实际执行金额。

外商直接投资是指外国企业和经济组织或个人（包括华侨、港澳台胞以及我国在境外注册的企业）按我国有关政策、法规，用现汇、实物、技术等在我国境内开办外商独资企业、与我国境内的企业或经济组织共同举办中外合资经营企业、合作经营企业或合作开发资源的投资（包括外商投资收益的再投资）以及经政府有关部门批准的项目投资总额内，企业从境外借入的资金。

**外商其它投资** 是指除外商直接投资以外其他方式吸收的外资。

**进出口总额** 指实际进出我国国境的货物总金额。包括对外贸易实际进出口货物，来料加工装配进出口货物，国家间、联合国及国际组织无偿援助物资和赠送品，华侨、港澳台同胞和外籍华人捐赠品，租赁期满归承租人所有的租赁货物，进料加工进出口货物，边境地方贸易及边境地区小额贸易进出口货物（边民互市贸易除外），中外合资企业、中外合作经营企业、外商独资经营企业进出口货物和公用物品，到、离岸价格在规定限额以上的进出口货样和广告品（无商业价值、无使用价值和免费提供出口的除外），从保税仓库提取在中国境内销售的进口货物，以及其他进出口货物。

# Explanatory Notes on Main Statistical Indicators

**Enterprises（Projects）Permitted** refers to number of foreign invested enterprises and developed projects under cooperation through the permission.

**Contracted Foreign Investment** refers to expenditure promised by the foreign investor and loan stemed from broad innate fund of the foreign investor, according to the contract and regulation approved of enterprise invested by foreigner.

Actual Utilization of Foreign Investmentrefers to actual usage of contracted foreign investment, including cash, investment in kind and incorporeal agreed by the both sides as part of the investment, such as services and technology.

**Foreign Direct Investmen** trefers to the investments by foreign enterprises and economic organizations or individuals（including overseas Chinese, compatriots from Hong dong, Macao and Taiwan, and Chinese enterprises registered abroad）, following the relevant policies and laws of China, for the establishment of ventures and cooperative enterprises or cooperative exploration of resources with enterprises or economic organizations in China, It includes the reinvestment of the foreign entrepreneurs with the profits gained from the investment and the funds that enterprises borrow from aboard in the total investment of projects which are approved by the relevant department of the government.

**Other Investment by Foreign Entrepreneurs** refers to all forms of utilization of foreign capitals other than foreign direct investment.

**Total Imports and Exports** refers to the real value of commodities imported into and exported from the boundary of China. They include the actual imports and exports through foreign trade, imported and exported goods under the processing and assembling trades and materials, supplies and gifts as aid given gratis between governments and by the United Nations and other international organizations, and contributions donated by overseas Chinese, compatriots in Hong Kong and Macao and Chinese with foreign citizenship, leasing commodities owned by tenant at the expiration of leasing period, the imported and exported commodities processed with imported materials, commodities trading in border areas (excluding mutual exchange goods), the imported and exported commodities and articles for public use of the Sino-foreign joint ventures, cooperative enterprises and ventures exclusively with foreign own investment. Also included are import or export of samples and advertising goods for whose CIF or FOB value are beyond the permitted ceiling (excluding goods of no trading or use value and free commodities for export), imported goods sold in China from bonded warehouses and other imported or exported goods.

# 城市建设、环境保护 6

COTY CONSTRUCTION AND
ENVIRONMENT PROTECTION

# 简要说明

**一、本篇资料的主要内容**

本篇资料主要反映了全市城市基础设施基本情况，包括市政设施、供水、供电、公共交通、园林绿化、燃气供热、城市环卫、环境保护及工业“三废”排放情况等方面的资料。

**二、本篇资料的来源**

1、本篇资料中市政设施、供水、公共交通、园林绿化、燃气供热、城市环卫相关资料来源于市建设委员会的城市建设统计年报，由市统计局固定资产投资统计处整理提供。

2、本篇资料中供电资料来源于青岛供电公司，由市统计局能源统计处整理提供。

3、本篇资料中环境保护、环境质量及工业“三废”排放情况来源于市环境保护局，由市统计局能源统计处整理提供。

# Brief Introduction

***I. Main Content***

Data in this chapter show the basic conditions of public facilities of the whole city, including urban construction and infrastructure, water supply, electricity supply, public communications, urban greenery, gas and heating, urban sanitation, environmental protection and discharge conditions of industrial waste water, waste gas and solid waste, etc.

***II. Source of Data***

(1) Data on conditions of urban construction and infrastructure, water supply, public communications, urban greenery, gas and heating, urban sanitation are based on the annual report of city construction provided by Qingdao Municipal Construction Commission, and compiled by the Division of Investment and Construction Statistics of Qingdao Municipal Bureau of Statistics.

(2) Data on electricity supply are provided by Qingdao Power Corporation, and compiled by the Division of Energy Statistics of Qingdao Municipal Bureau of Statistics.

(3) Data on environmental protection, environmental conditions and discharge conditions of industrial waste water, waste gas and solid waste are provided by Qingdao Municipal Bureau of Environmental Protection, and compiled by the Division of Energy Statistics of Qingdao Municipal Bureau of Statistics.

# 6-1 主要年份城市建设和公用事业
MAJOR YEAR'S CITY CONSTRUCTION AND PUBLIC UTILITIES

| 年份<br>Year | 建成区面积<br>（平方公里）<br>Developed Areas<br>（sq.km） | 年末道路长度<br>（公里）<br>Length of Roads at<br>Year-end（km） | 年末道路面积<br>（万平方米）<br>Area of Roads at<br>Year-end（10 000 sq.m） | 公共汽车、电车线路网长度<br>（公里）<br>Network Length of Bus and<br>Trolley Bus（km） |
|---|---|---|---|---|
| 1949 | 27 | 243 | 206 | 26.4 |
| 1952 | 29 | 245 | 213 | 124.4 |
| 1957 | 36 | 248 | 217 | 232.3 |
| 1962 | 55 | 266 | 235 | 252.8 |
| 1965 | 57 | 266 | 235 | 308.1 |
| 1970 | 59 | 374 | 346 | 358.5 |
| 1975 | 63 | 392 | 355 | 389.3 |
| 1978 | 66 | 408 | 368 | 422.1 |
| 1980 | 72 | 408 | 377 | 474.1 |
| 1985 | 79 | 462 | 464 | 611.3 |
| 1990 | 94.3 | 667 | 786 | 777 |
| 1991 | 94.7 | 673 | 826 | 922 |
| 1992 | 95.4 | 683 | 840 | 988 |
| 1993 | 99.9 | 764 | 944 | 1094 |
| 1994 | 103.9 | 811 | 985 | 1372 |
| 1995 | 106 | 936 | 1177 | 1101 |
| 1996 | 110 | 991 | 1339 | 1211 |
| 1997 | 112 | 1047 | 1436 | 1492 |
| 1998 | 114 | 1106 | 1436 | 1859 |
| 1999 | 116 | 1171 | 1698 | 2339 |
| 2000 | 119.1 | 1192 | 1789 | 2711 |
| 2001 | 123 | 1248 | 2169 | 2521 |
| 2002 | 133 | 1426 | 2594 | 896 |
| 2003 | 145.9 | 1595 | 2816 | 973 |
| 2004 | 154.8 | 1755 | 3254 | 1185 |
| 2005 | 178.8 | 1862 | 3547 | 1159 |
| 2006 | 227.5 | 3160 | 5218 | 1362 |
| 2007 | 250.7 | 3288 | 5411 | 1480 |
| 2008 | 267.1 | 3318 | 5596 | 1470 |
| 2009 | 272.9 | 3402 | 5763 | 1216 |
| 2010 | 282.3 | 3409 | 5893 | 1383 |
| 2011 | 291.5 | 3705 | 6605 | 1719 |
| 2012 | 374.6 | 4281 | 7528 | 1978 |
| 2013 | 469.6 | 4334 | 7859 | 2002 |
| 2014 | 490.7 | 4393 | 7908 | 2023 |
| 2015 | 566.4 | 4375 | 7940 | 2106 |
| 2016 | 599.3 | 4484 | 8057 | 2116 |
| 2017 | 638.4 | 4865 | 8496 | 2220 |
| 2018 | 715.1 | 5770 | 9862 | 2400 |

## 6-1 续表 1
Continued

| 年份 Year | 自来水供水管道长度（公里）Length of Tap Water Pipelines (km) | 全年供水总量（万立方米）Annual Volume of Tap Water Supply (10 000 cu.m) | #全年售水量（万立方米）Annual Volume of Tap Water Sale (10 000 cu.m) | #居民家庭用水 of which: Consumption for Residential Use | 用水普及率（%）Coverage Rate of Population with Access to Tap Water (%) | 排水管道长度（公里）Length of Sewage Pipes (km) | 全年用电量（亿千瓦时）Annual Volume of Electricity Supply (100 million kW·h) | #居民生活用电 of which: Consumption for Residential Use |
|---|---|---|---|---|---|---|---|---|
| 1949 | 308 | 721 | 456 | 331 | 89 | 200 | 0.88 | 0.14 |
| 1952 | 341 | 778 | 612 | 310 | 90 | 227 | 1.85 | 0.14 |
| 1957 | 412 | 1392 | 1296 | 606 | 93 | 273 | 2.61 | 0.26 |
| 1962 | 483 | 2700 | 2512 | 937 | 98 | 290 | 3.77 | 0.57 |
| 1965 | 500 | 3220 | 2979 | 929 | 98 | 295 | 5.92 | 0.68 |
| 1970 | 521 | 4503 | 4106 | 1085 | 99 | 350 | 9.83 | 1.02 |
| 1975 | 564 | 6726 | 6302 | 1950 | 99 | 361 | 12.41 | 1.43 |
| 1978 | 572 | 5334 | 4975 | 1314 | 99 | 382 | 16.34 | 1.62 |
| 1980 | 588 | 8224 | 7874 | 2577 | 99 | 394 | 21.48 | 2.78 |
| 1985 | 685 | 7557 | 7038 | 2628 | 99.9 | 505 | 26.39 | 2.87 |
| 1990 | 873 | 11896 | 10211 | 4270 | 96.9 | 645 | 41.08 | 4.32 |
| 1991 | 908 | 13865 | 11760 | 4990 | 96.6 | 649 | 44.51 | 5.34 |
| 1992 | 1035 | 16385 | 13070 | 5931 | 96.5 | 672 | 51.78 | 6.84 |
| 1993 | 1123 | 16137 | 14027 | 6124 | 99.1 | 734 | 55.02 | 7.66 |
| 1994 | 1124 | 17367 | 14716 | 6405 | 100 | 811 | 60.74 | 8.78 |
| 1995 | 1046 | 22513 | 15810 | 7050 | 100 | 990 | 67.23 | 10.16 |
| 1996 | 1182 | 23277 | 16566 | 7731 | 100 | 1051 | 72.87 | 12.23 |
| 1997 | 1266 | 24130 | 17215 | 8787 | 100 | 1167 | 77.82 | 13.73 |
| 1998 | 1390 | 23845 | 17271 | 9115 | 100 | 1210 | 79.65 | 14.28 |
| 1999 | 1471 | 23849 | 18558 | 10032 | 100 | 1301 | 88.12 | 15.31 |
| 2000 | 1524 | 25414 | 20642 | 11405 | 100 | 1460 | 106.80 | 16 |
| 2001 | 1665 | 22225 | 18556 | 10555 | 100 | 1539 | 116.10 | 17.62 |
| 2002 | 1781 | 27662 | 21684 | 10129 | 100 | 1641 | 131.44 | 18.31 |
| 2003 | 2060 | 27594 | 21483 | 10142 | 100 | 1884 | 147.68 | 19.88 |
| 2004 | 2566 | 30877 | 23864 | 11695 | 100 | 2002 | 167.95 | 23.63 |
| 2005 | 2876 | 33265 | 25874 | 12536 | 100 | 2309 | 193.81 | 33.76 |
| 2006 | 3984 | 30524 | 25572 | 10682 | 100 | 3994 | 215.35 | 34.87 |
| 2007 | 4187 | 31533 | 26454 | 11408 | 100 | 4079 | 236.42 | 37.40 |
| 2008 | 4642 | 32675 | 27396 | 11301 | 100 | 4229 | 250.07 | 40.31 |
| 2009 | 4767 | 33490 | 28274 | 12250 | 100 | 4555 | 259.42 | 43.29 |
| 2010 | 4926 | 34909 | 29617 | 12524 | 100 | 4708 | 292.97 | 49.50 |
| 2011 | 5121 | 34109 | 28837 | 10049 | 100 | 5187 | 313.44 | 50.13 |
| 2012 | 5243 | 38945 | 33039 | 12121 | 100 | 6814 | 318.36 | 51.64 |
| 2013 | 5522 | 38331 | 32418 | 11851 | 100 | 6536 | 339.27 | 57.52 |
| 2014 | 6177 | 46649 | 40612 | 14834 | 100 | 6840 | 337.82 | 59.95 |
| 2015 | 6142 | 46203 | 40202 | 15381 | 100 | 6993 | 342.29 | 64.71 |
| 2016 | 6132 | 43033 | 36748 | 14430 | 100 | 7146 | 367.26 | 69.52 |
| 2017 | 6498 | 45991 | 38963 | 17439 | 100 | 7367 | 401.06 | 74.84 |
| 2018 | 7531 | 53235 | 43298 | 18473 | 100 | 8854 | 431.82 | 77.39 |

# 6-1 续表 2
Continued

| 年份<br>Year | 公共汽车、电车营运车辆（辆）<br>Number of Bus and Trolley Bus under Operation（unit） | 全年客运量（万人次）<br>Annual Passenger Traffic（10 000 person-times） | 出租汽车（辆）<br>Number of Taxi（unit） | 使用液化气、煤气、天然气人数（万人）<br>Population with Access to Gas（10 000 persons） | 液化气<br>Liquefied Petroleum | 煤气<br>Coal Gas | 天然气<br>Natural Gas | 液化气供气量（吨）<br>Volume of Liquefied Petroleum Supply（ton） |
|---|---|---|---|---|---|---|---|---|
| 1949 | 32 | 298 | | | | | | |
| 1952 | 76 | 932 | | | | | | |
| 1957 | 112 | 4110 | | | | | | |
| 1962 | 127 | 4747 | | | | | | |
| 1965 | 173 | 6092 | | | | | | |
| **1970** | **224** | **13002** | | | | | | |
| 1975 | 324 | 14426 | | 2 | 2 | | | 184.9 |
| 1978 | 409 | 27351 | | 17 | 17 | | | 3246 |
| **1980** | **485** | **38981** | **48** | **24** | **24** | | | **4345** |
| 1985 | 621 | 48852 | 219 | 42.1 | 42.1 | | | 10619 |
| **1990** | **801** | **63495** | **832** | **75.0** | **57.4** | **17.6** | | **17512** |
| 1991 | 1372 | 67552 | 1070 | 76.2 | 57.4 | 18.8 | | 17963 |
| 1992 | 1470 | 73529 | 1828 | 82.8 | 62.0 | 20.8 | | 19565 |
| 1993 | 1875 | 72427 | 4874 | 88.4 | 64.6 | 23.8 | | 22224 |
| 1994 | 1850 | 78231 | 5806 | 103.6 | 77.4 | 26.2 | | 24684 |
| 1995 | 1891 | 71867 | 5887 | 116.2 | 82.9 | 33.3 | | 32443 |
| 1996 | 2012 | 49077 | 6660 | 126.0 | 88.0 | 38.0 | | 4065 |
| 1997 | 2148 | 55642 | 6861 | 133.6 | 92.9 | 40.7 | | 38717 |
| 1998 | 2184 | 51042 | 7469 | 146.8 | 97.8 | 49.0 | | 45381 |
| 1999 | 2470 | 55414 | 7839 | 154.9 | 98.3 | 56.6 | | 40537 |
| **2000** | **3141** | **59879** | **7933** | **164.1** | **93.3** | **70.8** | | **46951** |
| 2001 | 3453 | 60167 | 8110 | 168.8 | 87.5 | 81.3 | | 45295 |
| 2002 | 3681 | 61713 | 8376 | 224.2 | 133.8 | 90.4 | | 60123 |
| 2003 | 3648 | 58792 | 8109 | 246.7 | 138.3 | 93.1 | 15.3 | 67803 |
| 2004 | 3848 | 66463 | 8144 | 258.4 | 140.6 | 78.8 | 39.0 | 58548 |
| 2005 | 4039 | 68776 | 8121 | 265.0 | 132.6 | 45.7 | 86.7 | 78000 |
| 2006 | 4167 | 73726 | 8146 | 271.0 | 112.5 | 49.5 | 109.0 | 97343 |
| 2007 | 4524 | 78702 | 8221 | 275.6 | 104.1 | 12.1 | 159.4 | 79715 |
| 2008 | 4701 | 82460 | 9241 | 276.3 | 91.9 | 10.5 | 173.9 | 81987 |
| 2009 | 4288 | 81768 | 9316 | 276.1 | 59.8 | 12.3 | 204.0 | 96721 |
| **2010** | **4664** | **85251** | **9539** | **276.3** | **36.7** | **12.6** | **227.0** | **80073** |
| 2011 | 5419 | 89614 | 9683 | 277.1 | 25.8 | 12.6 | 238.7 | 79812 |
| 2012 | 5640 | 97922 | 9693 | 313.7 | 36.7 | 13.1 | 263.9 | 54341 |
| 2013 | 6179 | 101108 | 9826 | 318.9 | 33.0 | 0.0 | 285.9 | 41302 |
| 2014 | 6515 | 105592 | 9720 | 325.4 | 33.0 | 0.0 | 292.4 | 39255 |
| 2015 | 6748 | 102402 | 10033 | 338.3 | 28.9 | 0.0 | 309.4 | 35255 |
| 2016 | 7210 | 99596 | 10048 | 441.6 | 29.0 | 0.0 | 412.6 | 32291 |
| 2017 | 7420 | 104898 | 10875 | 445.8 | 26.2 | 0.0 | 419.6 | 28309 |
| 2018 | 7795 | 104782 | 10867 | 512.7 | 29.9 | 0.0 | 482.8 | 30427 |

注：1990 年以前公共营运车辆不包括系统外及个体。

Note：Vehicles not belonging to system and individual vehicles are not contained in public operating vehicles before 1990.

# 6-1 续表 3
Continued

| 年份 Year | 煤气供气量（万立方米）Volume of Coal Gas Supply (10 000 cu.m) | 天然气供气量（万立方米）Volume of Natural Gas Supply (10 000 cu.m) | 燃气普及率(%) Coverage Rate of Population with Access to Gas (%) | 绿地面积（公顷）Area of Green Areas (Hectate) | 公园绿地面积（公顷）Park Green Areas (hectare) | 人均公园绿地面积(平方米) Per Capita Park Green Areas (sq.m) | 建成区绿化覆盖率(%) Green Coverage Rate of Developed Areas (%) | 公园(个) Number of Parks and Zoos (unit) | 公园面积（公顷）Area of Parks and zoos (hectare) |
|---|---|---|---|---|---|---|---|---|---|
| 1949 | | | | 133 | 42 | 0.7 | 4.9 | 3 | 43 |
| 1952 | | | | 134 | 43 | 0.7 | 4.4 | 4 | 45 |
| 1957 | | | | 245 | 132 | 1.7 | 6.9 | 10 | 122 |
| 1962 | | | | 771 | 184 | 2.2 | 14.0 | 12 | 174 |
| 1965 | | | | 777 | 184 | 2.1 | 13.7 | 12 | 174 |
| 1970 | | | | 772 | 184 | 2.1 | 13.0 | 6 | 117 |
| 1975 | | | 2.3 | 465 | 162 | 1.8 | 7.6 | 5 | 134 |
| 1978 | | | 18.6 | 469 | 162 | 1.7 | 7.6 | 6 | 165 |
| 1980 | | | 24.5 | 625 | 206 | 2.1 | 10.4 | 6 | 152 |
| 1985 | | | 36.3 | 1072 | 255 | 2.3 | 17.3 | 7 | 153 |
| 1990 | 3073 | | 56.2 | 2120 | 492 | 3.7 | 22.8 | 26 | 404 |
| 1991 | 3439 | | 56.5 | 2318 | 500 | 3.7 | 24.4 | 28 | 443 |
| 1992 | 3824 | | 60.0 | 2471 | 515 | 3.7 | 25.9 | 28 | 417 |
| 1993 | 4215 | | 63.1 | 2488 | 543 | 3.9 | 26.5 | 31 | 453 |
| 1994 | 4116 | | 63.1 | 2866 | 572 | 4.0 | 27.9 | 31 | 463 |
| 1995 | 4734 | | 79.2 | 4547 | 771 | 5.3 | 30.1 | 33 | 675 |
| 1996 | 5447 | | 83.9 | 4679 | 836 | 5.6 | 30.4 | 33 | 675 |
| 1997 | 5920 | | 87.3 | 4717 | 924 | 6.0 | 31.3 | 34 | 730 |
| 1998 | 5959 | | 92.5 | 6812 | 1047 | 6.6 | 35.0 | 35 | 775 |
| 1999 | 7319 | | 96.0 | 7007 | 1186 | 7.4 | 35.9 | 36 | 791 |
| 2000 | 9567 | | 98.0 | 7439 | 1423 | 8.5 | 37.0 | 37 | 790 |
| 2001 | 11814 | | 99.0 | 7688 | 1588 | 9.3 | 37.5 | 39 | 832 |
| 2002 | 13500 | | 99.5 | 7967 | 1791 | 8.1 | 36.4 | 43 | 926 |
| 2003 | 14826 | 1181 | 100 | 8829 | 2305 | 9.3 | 37.5 | 45 | 1034 |
| 2004 | 15503 | 2710 | 100 | 10047 | 2842 | 11.0 | 38.0 | 48 | 1421 |
| 2005 | 16573 | 7456 | 100 | 11137 | 3132 | 11.8 | 38.8 | 47 | 1110 |
| 2006 | 9821 | 13876 | 100 | 11756 | 3198 | 11.8 | 39.2 | 47 | 1188 |
| 2007 | 9516 | 18103 | 100 | 15369 | 3661 | 13.3 | 37.8 | 73 | 1268 |
| 2008 | 8691 | 21780 | 100 | 15630 | 4014 | 14.5 | 41.5 | 77 | 1815 |
| 2009 | 7523 | 26948 | 100 | 16003 | 4003 | 14.5 | 43.4 | 71 | 1897 |
| 2010 | 9153 | 35681 | 100 | 16619 | 4027 | 14.6 | 43.38 | 72 | 1917 |
| 2011 | 9137 | 46147 | 100 | 18013 | 4041 | 14.6 | 44.69 | 74 | 1931 |
| 2012 | 8148 | 68397 | 100 | 21471 | 4573 | 14.6 | 44.7 | 78 | 2112 |
| 2013 | 0 | 70918 | 100 | 28007 | 4649 | 14.6 | 44.7 | 87 | 2698 |
| 2014 | 0 | 74823 | 100 | 28805 | 4741 | 14.6 | 44.7 | 91 | 2988 |
| 2015 | 0 | 70311 | 100 | 29117 | 4802 | 14.6 | 44.7 | 87 | 3163 |
| 2016 | 0 | 70586 | 100 | 34851 | 8194 | 18.6 | 38.6 | 151 | 4460 |
| 2017 | 0 | 91572 | 100 | 36209 | 7763 | 17.4 | 39.1 | 175 | 4727 |
| 2018 | 0 | 120089 | 100 | 39229 | 8587 | 16 | 39 | 191 | 5767 |

注：1. 自 2002 年起人均公共绿地面积按辖区内全部人口计算。
2. 2005 年以前所用园林绿地面积；公共绿地面积；人均公共绿地面积；公园、动物园个数；公园、动物园面积指标分别改为现在的绿地面积；公共绿地面积；人均公园绿地面积；公园个数；公园面积。
3. 由于城阳区绿化指标进行了调整，部分绿地属性发生变化。导致 2017 年公园绿地面积及人均公园绿地面积的数据小于 2016 年。

Note：1. Per capita public green areas is calculated at total population in the area under jurisdiction since 2002.
2. Before 2005，the corresponding indicators of greenbelt atea，public greenbelt area，public greenbelt area，ber capita public greenbelt area，coverage rate of green，number of parks and zoos，area of parks and zoos.
3. As the green index of Chengyang District has been adjusted, some green space properties have changed. As a result, the data of park green area and per capita park green area in 2017 are smaller than 2016.

# 6-2 全年供电（2018 年）
ANNUAL ELECTRICITY SUPPLY（2018）

| 全年供电项目 | Item | 单位 | Unit | 2018 年 |
|---|---|---|---|---|
| 发电设备总容量 | Total Capacity of Generation Equipment | 万千瓦 | 10 000 kW | 376.30 |
| #青岛电厂 | Qingdao Power Plant | 万千瓦 | 10 000 kW | 127.00 |
| 黄岛电厂 | Huangdao Power Plant | 万千瓦 | 10 000 kW | 156.50 |
| 全年发电量 | Annual Electricity Generation | 亿千瓦时 | 100 million kw·h | 181.70 |
| #青岛电厂 | Qingdao Power Plant | 亿千瓦时 | 100 million kw·h | 65.03 |
| 黄岛电厂 | Huangdao Power Plant | 亿千瓦时 | 100 million kw·h | 81.24 |
| 全年实际用电量 | Annual Electricity Consumption | 亿千瓦时 | 100 million kw·h | 431.82 |
| #工业 | Industrial Consumption | 亿千瓦时 | 100 million kw·h | 237.79 |
| 农业 | Agricultural Consumption | 亿千瓦时 | 100 million kw·h | 8.32 |
| 生活 | Residential Consumption | 亿千瓦时 | 100 million kw·h | 77.39 |
| 平均每日用电量 | Average Daily Consumption | 万千瓦时 | 100 million kw·h | 11831 |

## 6-3　分行业用电（2018 年）
ELECTRICTTY CONSUMPTION BY SECTOR（2018）

单位：万千瓦时（10 000 kW · h）

| 行业 | Sector | 2018 年 | 2018 年比 2017 年增长（%）Growth Rate in 2018 over 2017（%） |
|---|---|---|---|
| **全社会用电总计** | **Total Electricity Consumption** | **4318172** | **7.67** |
| 一、农、林、牧、渔业 | Tarming，Forestry，Animal Husbandryand Fishery | 83162 | 0.84 |
| 二、工业 | Industry | 2377894 | 5.39 |
| 三、建筑业 | Construction | 87095 | 9.82 |
| 四、交通运输、仓储和邮政业 | Transport，Storage and Post | 161244 | 15.71 |
| 五、信息传输、计算机服务和软件业 | Information Transmission，Computer Services and Software | 60337 | 11.44 |
| 六、商业、住宿和餐饮业 | Trade，Hotels and Catering Services | 234794 | 8.33 |
| 七、金融、房地产、商务及居民服务业 | Financial Intermediation，Real Estate and Business Services | 223995 | 31.02 |
| 八、公共事业及管理组织 | Public Management and Social Organization | 315778 | 24.28 |
| 九、城乡居民生活用电 | Household Consumption | 773874 | 2.21 |
| 城镇居民 | Urban Area | 484712 | -1.65 |
| 乡村居民 | Rural Area | 289161 | 9.40 |

# 6-4 城市供水
ANNUAL ELECTRICITY SUPPLY

| 项目 | Item | 单位 | Unit | 2018 年 |
|---|---|---|---|---|
| 自来水供水管道长度 | Length of Tap Water Pipelines | 公里 | km | 7462.96 |
| 综合生产能力 | Synthesis Producton Capacity | 万立方米 / 日 | 10 000 cu.m/day | 217.29 |
| 全年供水总量 | Annual Volume of Tap Water Supply | 万立方米 | 10 000 cu.m | 50113.64 |
| #售水量 | of which： Volume of Tap Water Supply | 万立方米 | 10 000 cu.m | 43297.84 |
| #生产运营用水 | of which： Consumption for Production Use | 万立方米 | 10 000 cu.m | 15544.6 |
| 公共服务用水 | Consumption for Public Services Use | 万立方米 | 10 000 cu.m | 9123.89 |
| 居民家庭用水 | Consumption for Residential Use | 万立方米 | 10 000 cu.m | 18472.66 |
| 其他用水 | Consumption for Other Uses | 万立方米 | 10 000 cu.m | 156.69 |
| 平均每日供水量 | Daily Volume of Tap Water Supply | 万立方米 | 10 000 cu.m | 137.3 |
| #生产用 | of which： Consumption for Production Use | 万立方米 | 10 000 cu.m | 42.6 |
| 生活用 | Consumption for Residential Use | 万立方米 | 10 000 cu.m | 50.6 |
| 用水户数 | Households with Access to Water | 户 | household | 1811462 |
| 用水人口 | Population with Access to water | 万人 | 10 000 persons | 510.82 |
| 工业用水量重复利用率 | Recycle Rate of water for Industrial Use | % | % | 89.99 |

# 6-5　城市公共交通
URBAN PUBLIC TRAFFIC

| 项目 | Itme | 单位 | Unit | 2018 年 |
|---|---|---|---|---|
| 公共汽车、电车线路网长度 | Network Length of Bus and Trolley Bus | 公里 | km | 2400 |
| 公共汽车、电车营运车辆 | Number of Bus and Trolley Bus under Operation | 辆 | unit | 7795 |
| #汽车 | Bus | 辆 | unit | 5192 |
| 电车 | Trolley Bus | 辆 | unit | 2603 |
| 公共汽车、电车全年客运量 | Annual Passenger Traffic of Bus and Trolley Bus | 万人次 | 10 000 person-times | 104782 |
| 公共汽车、电车平均每日客运量 | Daily Passenger Traffic of Bus and Trolley Bus | 万人 | 10 000 persons | 287 |
| 出租汽车数 | Number of Taxi | 辆 | unit | 10867 |
| 轮渡运营船数 | Number of Ferry Boat under Operation | 艘 | ship | 3 |
| 轮渡客运总量 | Passenger Traffic of Ferry Boat | 万人次 | 10 000 person-times | 19.2 |
| 轮渡平均每日客运量 | Daily Passenger Traffic of Ferry Boat | 万人 | 10 000 persons | 0.05 |

# 6-6 城市供气
URBAN GAS SUPPLY

| 项目 | Itme | 单位 | Unit | 2018 年 |
|---|---|---|---|---|
| 煤气供应总量 | Volume of Coal Gas Supply | 万立方米 | 10 000 cu.m | 0 |
| #家庭用量 | Household Consumption | 万立方米 | 10 000 cu.m | 0 |
| 煤气用气户数 | Households with Access to Coal Gas | 户 | household | 0 |
| #家庭用户 | Household Users | 户 | household | 0 |
| 液化石油气供应总量 | Volume of Liquefied Petroleum Supply | 吨 | ton | 30421 |
| #家庭用量 | Household Consumption | 吨 | ton | 17199 |
| 液化石油气用气户数 | Households with Access to Liquefied Petroleum | 户 | household | 129217 |
| #家庭用户 | Household Users | 户 | household | 125783 |
| 天然气供应总量 | Volume of Natural Gas Supply | 万立方米 | 10 000 cu.m | 120089 |
| #家庭用量 | Household Consumption | 万立方米 | 10 000 cu.m | 28343 |
| 天然气用气户数 | Households with Access to Natural Gas | 户 | household | 1974645 |
| #家庭用户 | Household Users | 户 | household | 1961323 |
| 燃气普及率 | Coverage Rate of Population with Access to Gas | % | % | 100 |

# 6-7　城市环境卫生
URBAN ENVIRONMENTAL SANITATION

| 项目 | Itme | 单位 | Unit | 2018 年 |
|---|---|---|---|---|
| 市容环卫专用车辆总数 | Number of Special Vehicles for Environmental Sanitation | 辆 | unit | 6194 |
| 生活垃圾清运量 | Volume of Garbage Disposal | 万吨 | 10 000 ton | 268 |
| 生活垃圾无害化处理厂（场）数 | Number of Bio-safety Disposal Plant of Garbage | 座 | unit | 5 |
| 生活垃圾无害化处理能力 | Bio-safety Disposal Capacity of Garbage | 吨 / 日 | ton/dan | 6800 |
| 生活垃圾无害化处理量 | Bio-safety Disposal Volume of Garbage | 万吨 | 10 000 ton | 268 |
| 道路清扫保洁面积 | Area under Cleaning Program | 万平方米 | 10 000 sq.m | 8146.7 |
| #机械化 | of which： Mechanization | 万平方米 | 10 000 sq.m | 4525 |
| 公共厕所 | Public Toilets | 个 | unit | 849 |

## 6-8　城市道路、下水道及绿化
URBAN ROAD，SEWAGE AND GREEN

| 项目 | Itme | 单位 | Unit | 2018 年 |
|---|---|---|---|---|
| **道路** | **Road** | | | |
| 年末道路长度 | Length of Roads at Year-end | 公里 | km | 5770 |
| 年末道路面积 | Area of Roads at Year-end | 万平方米 | 10 000 sq.m | 9862 |
| #人行道面积 | of which： Area of Pavements | 万平方米 | 10 000 sq.m | 2230 |
| 排水管道长度 | Length of Sewage Pipes | 公里 | km | 8854 |
| **园林绿化** | **Greening** | | | |
| 绿化覆盖面积 | Area of Green Coverage Areas | 公顷 | hectare | 41914.27 |
| 绿地面积 | Area of Green Areas | 公顷 | hectare | 39228.68 |
| 公园绿地面积 | Area of Park Green Areas | 公顷 | hectare | 8587.16 |
| 公园数 | Number of Parks and Zoos | 个 | unit | 191 |
| 公园面积 | Area of Parks and Zoos | 公顷 | hectare | 5766.75 |
| 城市每人平均公园绿地面积 | Per Capita Park Green Area | 平方米 | sq.m | 16.3 |
| 建成区绿化覆盖率 | Green Coverage Rate of Developed Areas | % | % | 39.2 |

## 6-9 环境保护基本情况
BASIC CONDITIONS OF ENVIRONMENTAL PROTECTION

| 项目 | Itme | 单位 | Unit | 2018 年 | 2017 年 | 2018 年比 2017 年增（+）减（-）% 2018 Compared to 2017（+/-） |
|---|---|---|---|---|---|---|
| 二氧化硫排放总量 | Sulphur Dioxide Emission | 吨 | ton | 14631.39 | 15540.54 | -5.85 |
| 氮氧化物排放总量 | Discharge Amount of Nitrogenoxides | 吨 | ton | 16095.77 | 16673.86 | -3.47 |
| 烟（粉）尘排放总量 | Soot（Dust）Emission | 吨 | ton | 12773.77 | 15404.52 | -17.08 |
| 工业固体废物排放总量 | Industrial Solid Wastes Discharged | 吨 | ton | 0 | 0 | 0.00 |
| 化学需氧量排放总量 | Discharge Amount of Chemical Oxygen Demand | 吨 | ton | 25889.04 | 27615.18 | -6.25 |
| 氨氮排放总量 | Discharge Amount of Ammonia and Nitrogen | 吨 | ton | 2468.11 | 2796.91 | -11.76 |
| 废水排放总量 | Waste Water Discharged | 万吨 | 10 000 tons | 58722.15 | 53421.38 | 9.92 |

## 6-10 环境质量状况
ENVIRONMENT CONDITION

| 项目 | Itme | 单位 | Unit | 2018 年 | 2017 年 | 2018 年比 2017 年增（+）减（-）% 2018 Compared to 2017（+/-） |
|---|---|---|---|---|---|---|
| 一、二类海水水质点位比例 | Point Location Proportion of Sea Water Quality of Category 2 | % | % | 90.6 | 90.6 | 0.00 |
| 市区区域环境噪声平均等效声级 | The Average Equivalent Sound Level of the Urban Regional Environmental Noise | 分贝（A） | db（A） | 56.9 | 57.3 | -0.70 |
| 市区道路交通噪声平均等效声级 | The Average Equivalent Sound Level of the Urban Road Traffic Noise | 分贝（A） | db（A） | 68 | 68.7 | -1.02 |

# 6-11 工业“三废”排放情况
DISCHARGE CONDITIONS OF INDUSTRIAL WASTE WSTER，WASTE GAS AND SOLID WASTE

| 项目 | Itme | 单位 | Unit | 2018年 | 2017年 | 2018年比2017年增（+）减（-）% 2018 Compared to 2017（+/-） |
|---|---|---|---|---|---|---|
| 工业废水排放总量 | Industrial Waste Water Discharged | 万吨 | 10 000 tons | 5527 | 5613.22 | -1.54 |
| 废水治理设施数 | Number of Facilities for Treatment of Wsate water | 套 | set | 365 | 391 | -6.65 |
| 废水治理设施处理能力 | Capacity of Facilities for Treatment of Waste Water | 万吨/日 | 10 000 tons/day | 38.08 | 40.02 | -4.85 |
| 进入城市污水处理厂量 | Volume Handled by Sewage Treatment Plant | 万吨 | 10 000 tons | 5030.47 | 5195.84 | -3.18 |
| 化学需氧量排放量 | Discharge Amount of Chemical Oxygen Demand | 吨 | ton | 1620.28 | 2184.05 | -25.81 |
| 氨氮排放量 | Discharge Amount of Ammonia and Nitrogen | 吨 | ton | 75.99 | 115.17 | -34.02 |
| 工业废气排放总量 | Industrial Waste Air Discharged | 万标立方米 | 10 000 cu.m | 35367746 | 28818474 | 22.73 |
| 废气治理设施数 | Number of Facilities for Treatment of Waste Air | 套 | set | 2071 | 1704 | 21.54 |
| 其中：脱硫设施数 | of which：Desulphurization Facilities | 套 | set | 268 | 270 | -0.74 |
| 废气治理设施处理能力 | Capacity of Facilities for Treatment of Waste Air | 万标立方米/时 | 10 000 cu.m/hr | 11986 | 10377.1 | 15.50 |
| 二氧化硫去除量 | Sulphur Dioxide Removed | 吨 | ton | 215570.67 | 225677.97 | -4.48 |
| 二氧化硫排放量 | Sulphur Dioxide Emission | 吨 | ton | 4227.39 | 5136.54 | -17.70 |
| 烟（粉）尘排放量 | Soot（Dust）Emission | 吨 | ton | 4613.88 | 7244.52 | -36.31 |
| 工业固体废物产生量 | Industrial Solid Wastes Producted | 万吨 | 10 000 tons | 793.36 | 769.55 | 3.09 |
| 其中：危险废物 | of which：Hazardous Wastes | 吨 | ton | 147026 | 114589 | 28.31 |
| 工业固体废物综合利用量 | Industrial Solid Wastes Comprehensive Utilized | 万吨 | 10 000 tons | 734.36 | 707.17 | 3.84 |
| 工业固体废物排放量 | Industrial Solid Wastes Discharged | 万吨 | 10 000 tons | 0 | 0 | 0.00 |
| 其中：危险废物 | of whick：Hazardous Wastes | 吨 | ton | 0 | 0 | 0.00 |
| 污染治理项目完成投资 | Investment in Treatment Projects of Pollution | 万元 | 10 000 yuan | 41191.94 | 61194.7 | -32.69 |
| 污染治理项目数 | Number of Treatment Projects of Pollution | 个 | item | 31 | 62 | -50.00 |
| 当年竣工治理项目数 | Number of Completed Treatment Projects in the Year | 个 | item | 25 | 48 | -47.92 |

# 主要统计指标解释

**供水综合生产能力** 指按供水设施取水、净化、送水、出厂输水干管等环节设计能力计算的综合生产能力。

**年末供水管道长度** 指从送水泵至用户水表之间所有管道的长度。不包括新安装尚未使用的管道。

用水普及率指城市用水人口数与城市人口总数的比率。计算公式：

$$用水普及率=\frac{城市用水人口数}{城市人口总数}\times 100\%$$

**全年供水总量** 指报告期供水企业（单位）供出的全部水量。包括有效供水量和漏损水量。

**全年供气总量** 指全年燃气企业（单位）向用户供应的燃气数量。包括销售量和损失量。

**用气普及率** 指报告期末使用燃气的城市人口数与城市人口总数的比率。计算公式为：

$$用气普及率=\frac{城市用气人口数}{城市人口总数}\times 100\%$$

**年末道路长度** 指年末道路长度和与道路相通的广场、桥梁、隧道的长度，按车行道中心线计算。在统计时只统计路面宽度在3.5米（含3.5米）以上的各种铺装道路，包括开放型工业区和住宅区道路在内。

**工业废气排放量** 指报告期内企业厂区内燃料燃烧和生产工艺过程中产生的各种排入大气的含有污染物的气体的总量，以标准状态（273K，101325Pa）计算。

**工业废水排放量** 指经过企业厂区所有排放口排到企业外部的工业废水量。包括生产废水、外排的直接冷却水、超标排放的矿井地下水和与工业废水混排的厂区生活污水，不包括外排的间接冷却水（清污不分流的间接冷却水应计算在内）。

**工业废水排放达标量** 指各项指标都达到国家或地方排放标准的外排工业废水量，包括未经处理外排达标的和经过处理后外排达标的和两部分。国家排放标准见GB8978–88。

**工业固体废物产生量** 指企业在生产过程中产生的固体状、半固体状和高浓度液体状废弃物的总量，包括危险废物、冶炼废渣、粉煤灰、炉渣、煤矸渣、尾矿、放射性废物和其他废物等；不包括矿山开采的剥离废石和掘进废石（煤矸石和呈酸性或碱性的废石除外）酸性或碱性废石是指采掘的废石其流经水、雨淋水的pH值小于4或pH值大于10.5者。

**工业粉尘排放量** 指企业在生产工艺过程中排放的能在空气中悬浮一定时间的固体颗粒物排放量。如钢铁企业的耐火材料粉尘、焦化企业的筛焦系统粉尘、烧结机的粉尘、石灰窑的粉尘、建材企业的水泥粉尘等。不包括电厂排入大气的烟尘。

**化学需氧量（COD）** 测量有机和无机物质化学分解所消耗氧的质量浓度的水污染指数。

# Explanatory Notes on Main Statistical Indicators

**Production Capacity of Water Supply** refers to the designed comprehensive production capacity of water facilities, covering the 4 links of water collection, purification, conveyance, and outflow through trunk pipelines.

**Length of Water Supply Pipelines at the Year–end** refers to the total length of all the pipelines between the water pumps and the user water meters, excluding pipelines newly installed but not used yet.

**Coverage Rate of Urban Population with Access to Tap Water** refers to the ratio of the urban population with access to tap water to the total urban population. The formula is:

Coverage rate of urban population with access to tap water= ( Urban population with access to tap water ) / ( Urban population ) × 100%

**Annual Volume of Water Supply** refers to the total volume of water supplied by water-works ( units ) during the reference period, including both the effective water supply and loss during the water supply.

**Annual Volume of Gas Supply** refers to the total volume of gas provided to users by gas-producing enterprises ( units ) in a year, including the volume sold and the volume lost.

**Coverage Rate of Urban Population with Access to Gas** refers to the ratio of the urban population with access to gas to the total urban population at the end of the reference period.The formula is:

Coverage rate of urban population with access to gas= ( Urban population with access to gas/Urban population ) × 100%

**Length of Paved Roads at the Year-end** refers to the length of roads with paved surface including squares bridges and tunnels connected with roads by the end of the year.Length of the roads is measured by the central lines for vehicles for paved roads with a width of 3.5 meters and over, including roads in open-ended factory compounds and residential quarters.

**Industrial Waste Air Emission** refers to discharge into atmosphere of waste air containing pollutants generated from fuel burning and production process in enterprises within a given period of time.It is calculated at standard status ( 273K, 101325Pa ) .

**Waste Water Discharged by Industry** refers to the volume of waste water discharged by industrial enterprises through all their outlets, including waste water from production process, directly cooled water, groundwater from mining wells which does not meet discharge standards and sewage from households mixed with waste water produced by industrial activities, but excluding indirectly cooled water discharged ( It should be included if the discharge is not separated with waste water ) .

**Industrial Waste Water Meeting Discharge Standards** refers to volume of industrial waste water discharge which, with or without treatment, reaches national or local standards with regard to all pollutants.National Discharge standards see GB8978-88.

**Industrial Solid Wastes Produced** refers to total volume of solid, semi-solid and high concentration liquid residues produced by industrial enterprises from production process in a given period of time, including hazardous wastes, slag, coal ash, gangue, tailings, radioactive residues and other wastes, but excluding stones stripped or dug out in mining ( gangue and acid or alkaline stones not included ) .A stone is acid or alkaline depending on the pH value of the water below 4 or above 10.5 when the stone is in, or soaked by, the water.

**Industrial Dust Emission** refers to volume of dust emitted by production process of enterprises and suspended in the air for a given period of time, including dust from refractory material of iron and steel works, dust from coke-screening systems and sintering machines of coke plants, dust from lime kilns and dust from cement production in building material enterprises, but excluding soot and dust emitted from power plants.

**Chemical Oxygen Demand ( COD )** refers to index of water pollution measuring the mass concentration of oxygen consumed by the chemical breakdown of organic and inorganic matter.

# 能源消耗 7

# CONSUMPTION OF ENERGY

# 简要说明

**一、本篇资料的主要内容**

本篇资料主要反映了全市规模以上工业主要能源消费与库存情况，主要包括规模以上工业主要能源消费与库存、规模以上工业主要能源分行业消费量、重点耗能工业企业能源加工转换、规模以上工业主要能源工业消费量等方面的资料。

**二、本篇资料的来源**

本篇资料来源于规模以上工业能源统计年报，由市统计局能源统计处整理提供。

# Brief Introduction

***I. Main Content***

Data in this chapter show the consumption and stock of major energy of industry above designated size, including consumption and stock of major energy of industry above designated size, major energy consumption of industry above designated size grouped by sector, energy conversion of major energy-consuming industrial enterprises and major energy consumption of industry above designated size, etc.

***II. Source of Data***

Data in this chapter are based on the annual report of energy consumed by industrial enterprises above designated size. The data are provided by the Division of Energy Statistics of Qingdao Municipal Bureau of Statistics.

# 7-1 规模以上工业主要能源消费与库存（2018 年）
CONSUMPTION AND STOCK OF MAJOR ENERGY OF INDUSTRY ABOVE DESIGNATED SIZE（2018）

| 名称 | Name | 计算单位 | Unit | 年初库存 Stock at Year-beginning | 本年消费 Consumption in the Year | #工业 Industry | 非工业 Non-industry | 年末库存 Stock at Year-end |
|---|---|---|---|---|---|---|---|---|
| 原　煤 | Raw Coal | 吨 | ton | 1604467.69 | 11437971.31 | 11401665.54 | 36305.77 | 1683068.85 |
| 焦　炭 | Coke | 吨 | ton | 295.00 | 1491996.00 | 1491996.00 | | 76180.00 |
| 焦炉煤气 | Coking Gas | 万立方米 | 10 000 cu.m | | 36141.20 | 36141.20 | | |
| 高炉煤气 | Blast Furnace Gas | 万立方米 | 10 000 cu.m | | 158161.70 | 158161.70 | | |
| 原　油 | Grude Oil | 吨 | ton | 391907.36 | 15422450.59 | 15422419.39 | 31.20 | 418902.36 |
| 汽　油 | Petrol | 吨 | ton | 184.35 | 35328.55 | 21858.80 | 13469.75 | 59.41 |
| 煤　油 | Kerosene | 吨 | ton | | 638.92 | 480.94 | 157.98 | |
| 柴　油 | Diesel Oil | 吨 | ton | 1660.73 | 62561.97 | 47021.70 | 15540.27 | 2654.71 |
| 燃料油 | Fuel Oil | 吨 | ton | 8458.97 | 89822.04 | 89651.16 | 170.88 | 9224.79 |
| 液化石油气 | Liquefied Petroler Gas | 吨 | ton | 44.75 | 99389.59 | 99362.94 | 26.65 | |
| 炼厂干气 | Refinery Dry Gas | 吨 | ton | | 446466.00 | 446466.00 | | |
| 热　力 | Heat | 百万千焦 | million kJ | | 18097873.17 | 17615671.95 | 482201.22 | |
| 电　力 | Electricity | 万千瓦时 | 10 000kW·h | | 1819017.44 | 1800302.87 | 18714.57 | |

补充资料：2018 年综合能源消费量 1492.19 万吨标准煤。
Note：In 2018，comprehensive energy consumption is 1492.19 million rons SCE.

## 7-2 规模以上工业主要能源分行业消费量（2018年）

MAJOR ENERGY CONSUMPTION OF INDUSTRY ABOVE DESIGNATED SIZE BY SECTOR (2018)

| 名称 | Name | 原煤（吨） Raw Coal（ton） | 焦炭（吨） Coke（ton） | 焦炉煤气（万立方米） Coking Gas（10 000 cu.m） | 原油（吨） Crude Oil（ton） | 汽油（吨） Petrol（ton） |
|---|---|---|---|---|---|---|
| **总　计** | **Total** | **11437971** | **1491996** | **36141** | **15422451** | **35329** |
| 采掘业 | Mining | 20 | | | | 1 |
| 制造业 | Manufacturing | 1435674 | 1491996 | 4949 | 15422451 | 34167 |
| 电力煤气及水生产供应业 | Production and Supply of Electricity，Gas and Water | 10002277 | | 31192 | | 1160 |

## 7-2 续表

Continued

| 名称 | Name | 煤油（吨） Kerosene（ton） | 柴油（吨） Diesel Oil（ton） | 燃料油（吨） Fuel Oil（ton） | 液化石油气（吨） Liquefied Petroleum Gsa（ton） | 热力（百万千焦） Heat（millon kJ） | 电力（万千瓦时） Electricity（10 000kW·h） |
|---|---|---|---|---|---|---|---|
| **总　计** | **Total** | **639** | **62562** | **89822** | **99390** | **18097873** | **1819017** |
| 采掘业 | Mining | | 272 | | | | 1660 |
| 制造业 | Manufacturing | 639 | 60235 | 88777 | 99389 | 17343697 | 1607106 |
| 电力煤气及水生产供应业 | Production and Supply of Electricity，Gas and Water | | 2055 | 1045 | 1 | 754176 | 210252 |

# 7-3 重点耗能工业企业能源加工转换（2018 年）

## ENERGY CONVERSION OF MAJOR ENERGY-CONSUMING INDUSTRIAL ENTERPRISES（2018）

| 名称 | Name | 单位 | Unit | 能源消费合计 Total Energy Constumption | #加工转换投入 Conversion Input | 火电 Thermal Power | 供热 Leating | 炼油 Petrolume Refining | 制气 Gas Production | 能源加工转换产出 Conversion Output of Energy |
|---|---|---|---|---|---|---|---|---|---|---|
| 原 煤 | Raw Coal | 吨 | ton | 10680529.47 | 10128200.95 | 5937193.23 | 4191007.72 | | | |
| 洗精煤 | Dressing Coal | 吨 | ton | 2129966.00 | 2129966.00 | | | | | |
| 煤制品 | Coal Products | 吨 | ton | 13512.37 | 13512.37 | | 13512.37 | | | |
| 焦 炭 | Coke | 吨 | ton | 1490948.00 | | | | | | 1532645.00 |
| 其他焦化产品 | Other Coking Products | 吨 | ton | 51407.97 | | | | | | 77013.00 |
| 焦炉煤气 | Coking Gas | 万立方米 | 10 000 cn.m | 31192.20 | 31192.20 | 29745.00 | 1447.20 | | | 36675.40 |
| 高炉煤气 | Blast Furnace GAS | 万立方米 | 10 000 cn.m | 148855.40 | 148855.40 | 141583.90 | 7271.50 | | | |
| 原 油 | Raw Oil | 吨 | ton | 15422347.01 | 15407527.01 | | | 15407527.01 | | |
| 汽 油 | Petrol | 吨 | ton | 61.55 | | | | | | 4739129.00 |
| 煤 油 | Kerosene | 吨 | ton | | | | | | | 1885917.00 |
| 柴 油 | Diesel Oil | 吨 | ton | 1644.32 | 180.00 | 180.00 | | | | 3828611.46 |
| 燃料油 | Fule Oil | 吨 | ton | 30344.00 | 30259.00 | 777.00 | 103.00 | 29379.00 | | 217949.00 |
| 液化石油气 | Liquefied Petroleum Gas | 吨 | ton | | | | | | | 1124441.00 |
| 炼厂干气 | Refinery Dry Gas | 吨 | ton | 446466.00 | 8260.00 | 826.00 | 7434.00 | | | 446466.00 |
| 其他石油制品 | Other Petroleum Products | 吨 | ton | 773305.44 | 332657.00 | | | 332657.00 | | 1235872.50 |
| 热 力 | Heat | 百万千焦 | million kJ | 1372551.00 | | | | | | 77971831.92 |
| 电 力 | Electricity | 万千瓦时 | 10 000kW·h | 499415.20 | | | | | | 1817014.92 |
| 其他燃料 | Other Fuel | 吨标准煤 | ton SCE | | | | | | | |
| **能源合计** | **Total** | **吨标准煤** | **ton SCE** | **37219514.30** | **33364047.39** | **5482675.02** | **3442332.14** | **22415572.53** | | **28336630.86** |

# 7-4 规模以上工业主要能源工业消费量（2018 年）
MAJOR ENERGY CONSUMPTION OF INDUSTRY ABOVE DESIGNATED SIZE（2018）

| 行业 | Sector |
|---|---|
| 总　　计 | **Total** |
| 煤炭开采和洗选业 | Mining and Washing of Coal |
| 石油和天然气开采业 | Extraction of Petroleum and Natural Gas |
| 黑色金属矿采选业 | Mining of Ferrous Metal Ores |
| 有色金属矿采选业 | Mining of Non-ferrous Metal Ores |
| 非金属矿采选业 | Mining and Processing of Nonmetal Ores |
| 开采辅助活动 | Auxiliary Activities of Mining |
| 其他采矿业 | Mining of Other Ores |
| 农副食品加工业 | Processing of Food from Agricultural Products |
| 食品制造业 | Manufacture of Foods |
| 酒、饮料和精制茶制造业 | Manufacture of Liquor，Beverage and Refind Tea |
| 烟草制品业 | Manufacture of Tobacco |
| 纺织业 | Manufacture of Textile |
| 纺织服装、服饰业 | Manufacture of Textil Wearing Apparel |
| 皮革、毛皮、羽毛及其制品和制鞋业 | Manufacture of Leather，Fur，Feathre&Its Products Footwear |
| 木材加工和木、竹、藤、棕、草制品业 | Processing of Timbers，Manufacture of Wood，Bamboo，Rattan，Palm and Straw Products |
| 家具制造业 | Manufacture of Furniture |
| 造纸和纸制品业 | Manufacture of Paper and Paper Products |
| 印刷和记录媒介复制业 | Printing，Reproduction of Recording Media |
| 文教、工美、体育和娱乐用品制造业 | Manufacture of Articles for Culture，Arts& Crafts，Sports and Entertainment |
| 石油加工、炼焦和核燃料加工业 | Processing of Petroleum，Coking，Processing of Nucleus Fuel |
| 化学原料和化学制品制造业 | Manufacture of Chemical Raw Material and Chemical Products |
| 医药制造业 | Manufacture of Medicines |
| 化学纤维制造业 | Manufacture of Chemical Fiber |
| 橡胶和塑料制品业 | Manufacture of Rubber and Plastic |
| 非金属矿物制品业 | Manufacture of Non-metallic Mineral Products |
| 黑色金属冶炼和压延加工业 | Smelting and Pressing of Ferrous Metals |
| 有色金属冶炼和压延加工业 | Smelting and Pressing of Non-ferrous Metals |
| 金属制品业 | Manufacture of Metal Products |
| 通用设备制造业 | Manufacture of General Purpose Machinery |
| 专用设备制造业 | Manufacture of Special Purpose Machinery |
| 汽车制造业 | Manufacture of Vehicle |
| 铁路、船舶、航空航天和其他运输设备制造业 | Manufacture of Transport Equipment for Railway，Shipping，Aerospace and other uses |
| 电气机械和器材制造业 | Manufacture of Electrical Machinery &Equipment |
| 计算机、通信和其他电子设备制造业 | Manufacture of Computer，Communication Equipment and Other Electronic Equipmen |
| 仪器仪表制造业 | Manufacture of Measuring Imstrument |
| 其他制造业 | Manufacture of Other Products |
| 废弃资源综合利用业 | Recycling and Disposal of Waste Resources |
| 金属制品、机械和设备修理业 | Manufacture of Metal Products，Machinery and Equipment |
| 电力、热力生产和供应业 | Production and Supply of Electric Power and Heat Power |
| 燃气生产和供应业 | Production and Supply of Gas |
| 水的生产和供应业 | Production and Supply of Water |

| 原煤<br>（吨）<br>Raw Coal<br>（ton） | 洗精煤<br>（吨）<br>Dressing Coal<br>（ton） | 其他洗煤<br>（吨）<br>Other Dressing Coal<br>（ton） | 煤制品<br>（吨）<br>Coal Products<br>（ton） | 焦炭<br>（吨）<br>Coke<br>（ton） |
|---:|---:|---:|---:|---:|
| **11437971** | **2129966** | **40361** | **14811** | **1491996** |
| 20 | | | | |
| 33217 | | 278 | 302 | |
| 1392 | | | | |
| 15589 | | | | |
| 8865 | | | 6 | |
| 5785 | | 1006 | | |
| 5203 | | | | |
| 247 | | | 19 | |
| 75459 | | | 379 | |
| 3789 | | | | |
| 6976 | | | | |
| 10688 | | | | |
| 383030 | | 39077 | | |
| 50 | | | 562 | |
| 113054 | | | | |
| 204099 | | | | |
| 551328 | 2129966 | | | 1490948 |
| 1140 | | | | |
| 4481 | | | | 747 |
| 3943 | | | | 230 |
| 2030 | | | 14 | |
| 1078 | | | | 71 |
| 972 | | | | |
| 1642 | | | 16 | |
| 1616 | | | | |
| 9999992 | | | 13512 | |
| 2285 | | | | |

# 7-4 续表 1
Continued

| 行业 | Sector |
|---|---|
| 总　　计 | **Total** |
| 煤炭开采和洗选业 | Mining and Washing of Coal |
| 石油和天然气开采业 | Extraction of Petroleum and Natural Gas |
| 黑色金属矿采选业 | Mining of Ferrous Metal Ores |
| 有色金属矿采选业 | Mining of Non-ferrous Metal Ores |
| 非金属矿采选业 | Mining and Processing of Nonmetal Ores |
| 开采辅助活动 | Auxiliary Activities of Mining |
| 其他采矿业 | Mining of Other Ores |
| 农副食品加工业 | Processing of Food from Agricultural Products |
| 食品制造业 | Manufacture of Foods |
| 酒、饮料和精制茶制造业 | Manufacture of Liquor, Beverage and Refind Tea |
| 烟草制品业 | Manufacture of Tobacco |
| 纺织业 | Manufacture of Textile |
| 纺织服装、服饰业 | Manufacture of Textil Wearing Apparel |
| 皮革、毛皮、羽毛及其制品和制鞋业 | Manufacture of Leather, Fur, Feathre&Its Products Footwear |
| 木材加工和木、竹、藤、棕、草制品业 | Processing of Timbers, Manufacture of Wood, Bamboo, Rattan, Palm and Straw Products |
| 家具制造业 | Manufacture of Furniture |
| 造纸和纸制品业 | Manufacture of Paper and Paper Products |
| 印刷和记录媒介复制业 | Printing, Reproduction of Recording Media |
| 文教、工美、体育和娱乐用品制造业 | Manufacture of Articles for Culture, Arts& Crafts, Sports and Entertainment |
| 石油加工、炼焦和核燃料加工业 | Processing of Petroleum, Coking, Processing of Nucleus Fuel |
| 化学原料和化学制品制造业 | Manufacture of Chemical Raw Material and Chemical Products |
| 医药制造业 | Manufacture of Medicines |
| 化学纤维制造业 | Manufacture of Chemical Fiber |
| 橡胶和塑料制品业 | Manufacture of Rubber and Plastic |
| 非金属矿物制品业 | Manufacture of Non-metallic Mineral Products |
| 黑色金属冶炼和压延加工业 | Smelting and Pressing of Ferrous Metals |
| 有色金属冶炼和压延加工业 | Smelting and Pressing of Non-ferrous Metals |
| 金属制品业 | Manufacture of Metal Products |
| 通用设备制造业 | Manufacture of General Purpose Machinery |
| 专用设备制造业 | Manufacture of Special Purpose Machinery |
| 汽车制造业 | Manufacture of Vehicle |
| 铁路、船舶、航空航天和其他运输设备制造业 | Manufacture of Transport Equipment for Railway, Shipping, Aerospace and other uses |
| 电气机械和器材制造业 | Manufacture of Electrical Machinery &Equipment |
| 计算机、通信和其他电子设备制造业 | Manufacture of Computer, Communication Equipment and Other Electronic Equipmen |
| 仪器仪表制造业 | Manufacture of Measuring Imstrument |
| 其他制造业 | Manufacture of Other Products |
| 废弃资源综合利用业 | Recycling and Disposal of Waste Resources |
| 金属制品、机械和设备修理业 | Manufacture of Metal Products, Machinery and Equipment |
| 电力、热力生产和供应业 | Production and Supply of Electric Power and Heat Power |
| 燃气生产和供应业 | Production and Supply of Gas |
| 水的生产和供应业 | Production and Supply of Water |

| 焦炉煤气（万立方米）Coking Gas（10 000 cu.m） | 高炉煤气（万立方米）Blast Furnace GAS（10 000 cu.m） | 原油（吨）Crude Oil（ton） | 汽油（吨）Petrol（ton） | 煤油（吨）Kerosene（ton） |
|---|---|---|---|---|
| **36141** | **158162** | **15422451** | **35329** | **639** |
| | | | | |
| | | | | |
| | | | | |
| | | | | |
| | | | 1 | |
| | | | | |
| | | | | |
| | | | 3411 | 316 |
| | | | 669 | |
| | | | 270 | 23 |
| | | | | |
| | | | 493 | |
| | | | 1575 | |
| | | | 823 | |
| | | | 54 | |
| | | | 153 | |
| | | | 354 | |
| | | | 1304 | 25 |
| | | | 1579 | 23 |
| | | 15422347 | 151 | |
| | | | 1452 | |
| | | | 815 | |
| | | | | |
| | | 1 | 2472 | |
| 4949 | 9306 | 61 | 1710 | |
| | | | 99 | |
| | | | 111 | |
| | | 15 | 2311 | 8 |
| | | | 3517 | 70 |
| | | | 2141 | |
| | | 19 | 4285 | 51 |
| | | | 982 | 123 |
| | | | 1890 | |
| | | | 1038 | |
| | | | 362 | |
| | | | 104 | |
| | | | | |
| | | | 41 | |
| 31192 | 148855 | | 278 | |
| | | | 321 | |
| | | | 562 | |

## 7-4 续表 2
Continued

| 行业 | Sector |
| --- | --- |
| 总　计 | **Total** |
| 煤炭开采和洗选业 | Mining and Washing of Coal |
| 石油和天然气开采业 | Extraction of Petroleum and Natural Gas |
| 黑色金属矿采选业 | Mining of Ferrous Metal Ores |
| 有色金属矿采选业 | Mining of Non-ferrous Metal Ores |
| 非金属矿采选业 | Mining and Processing of Nonmetal Ores |
| 开采辅助活动 | Auxiliary Activities of Mining |
| 其他采矿业 | Mining of Other Ores |
| 农副食品加工业 | Processing of Food from Agricultural Products |
| 食品制造业 | Manufacture of Foods |
| 酒、饮料和精制茶制造业 | Manufacture of Liquor, Beverage and Refind Tea |
| 烟草制品业 | Manufacture of Tobacco |
| 纺织业 | Manufacture of Textile |
| 纺织服装、服饰业 | Manufacture of Textil Wearing Apparel |
| 皮革、毛皮、羽毛及其制品和制鞋业 | Manufacture of Leather, Fur, Feathre&Its Products Footwear |
| 木材加工和木、竹、藤、棕、草制品业 | Processing of Timbers, Manufacture of Wood, Bamboo, Rattan, Palm and Straw Products |
| 家具制造业 | Manufacture of Furniture |
| 造纸和纸制品业 | Manufacture of Paper and Paper Products |
| 印刷和记录媒介复制业 | Printing, Reproduction of Recording Media |
| 文教、工美、体育和娱乐用品制造业 | Manufacture of Articles for Culture, Arts& Crafts, Sports and Entertainment |
| 石油加工、炼焦和核燃料加工业 | Processing of Petroleum, Coking, Processing of Nucleus Fuel |
| 化学原料和化学制品制造业 | Manufacture of Chemical Raw Material and Chemical Products |
| 医药制造业 | Manufacture of Medicines |
| 化学纤维制造业 | Manufacture of Chemical Fiber |
| 橡胶和塑料制品业 | Manufacture of Rubber and Plastic |
| 非金属矿物制品业 | Manufacture of Non-metallic Mineral Products |
| 黑色金属冶炼和压延加工业 | Smelting and Pressing of Ferrous Metals |
| 有色金属冶炼和压延加工业 | Smelting and Pressing of Non-ferrous Metals |
| 金属制品业 | Manufacture of Metal Products |
| 通用设备制造业 | Manufacture of General Purpose Machinery |
| 专用设备制造业 | Manufacture of Special Purpose Machinery |
| 汽车制造业 | Manufacture of Vehicle |
| 铁路、船舶、航空航天和其他运输设备制造业 | Manufacture of Transport Equipment for Railway, Shipping, Aerospace and other uses |
| 电气机械和器材制造业 | Manufacture of Electrical Machinery &Equipment |
| 计算机、通信和其他电子设备制造业 | Manufacture of Computer, Communication Equipment and Other Electronic Equipmen |
| 仪器仪表制造业 | Manufacture of Measuring Imstrument |
| 其他制造业 | Manufacture of Other Products |
| 废弃资源综合利用业 | Recycling and Disposal of Waste Resources |
| 金属制品、机械和设备修理业 | Manufacture of Metal Products, Machinery and Equipment |
| 电力、热力生产和供应业 | Production and Supply of Electric Power and Heat Power |
| 燃气生产和供应业 | Production and Supply of Gas |
| 水的生产和供应业 | Production and Supply of Water |

| 柴油<br>（吨）<br>Diesel Oil<br>（ton） | 燃料油<br>（吨）<br>Fule Oil<br>（ton） | 液化石油气<br>（吨）<br>Liquefied Petroleum Gas<br>（ton） | 炼厂干气<br>（吨）<br>Refinery Dry Gas<br>（ton） |
|---|---|---|---|
| **62562** | **89822** | **99390** | **446466** |
| | | | |
| | | | |
| | | | |
| | | | |
| 272 | | | |
| | | | |
| | | | |
| 3793 | 788 | 343 | |
| 848 | | | |
| 856 | | 252 | |
| | | | |
| 298 | | 9 | |
| 2159 | | | |
| 358 | 136 | | |
| 44 | | | |
| 389 | | | |
| 1099 | | | |
| 1220 | 231 | | |
| 934 | 12 | | |
| 119 | 29379 | | 446466 |
| 2338 | 703 | 97090 | |
| 432 | | | |
| | | | |
| 2083 | 1620 | 988 | |
| 23618 | 55434 | 19 | |
| 859 | | 22 | |
| 511 | | | |
| 1972 | 39 | 371 | |
| 3833 | 7 | 37 | |
| 1416 | | | |
| 1911 | | 47 | |
| 6193 | 430 | 41 | |
| 1230 | | 152 | |
| 1154 | | 19 | |
| 423 | | | |
| 118 | | | |
| | | | |
| 27 | | | |
| 1658 | 1045 | 1 | |
| 27 | | | |
| 370 | | | |

# 7-4 续表 3
Continued

| 行业 | Sector |
|---|---|
| 总　计 | **Total** |
| 煤炭开采和洗选业 | Mining and Washing of Coal |
| 石油和天然气开采业 | Extraction of Petroleum and Natural Gas |
| 黑色金属矿采选业 | Mining of Ferrous Metal Ores |
| 有色金属矿采选业 | Mining of Non-ferrous Metal Ores |
| 非金属矿采选业 | Mining and Processing of Nonmetal Ores |
| 开采辅助活动 | Auxiliary Activities of Mining |
| 其他采矿业 | Mining of Other Ores |
| 农副食品加工业 | Processing of Food from Agricultural Products |
| 食品制造业 | Manufacture of Foods |
| 酒、饮料和精制茶制造业 | Manufacture of Liquor, Beverage and Refind Tea |
| 烟草制品业 | Manufacture of Tobacco |
| 纺织业 | Manufacture of Textile |
| 纺织服装、服饰业 | Manufacture of Textil Wearing Apparel |
| 皮革、毛皮、羽毛及其制品和制鞋业 | Manufacture of Leather, Fur, Feathre&Its Products Footwear |
| 木材加工和木、竹、藤、棕、草制品业 | Processing of Timbers, Manufacture of Wood, Bamboo, Rattan, Palm and Straw Products |
| 家具制造业 | Manufacture of Furniture |
| 造纸和纸制品业 | Manufacture of Paper and Paper Products |
| 印刷和记录媒介复制业 | Printing, Reproduction of Recording Media |
| 文教、工美、体育和娱乐用品制造业 | Manufacture of Articles for Culture, Arts& Crafts, Sports and Entertainment |
| 石油加工、炼焦和核燃料加工业 | Processing of Petroleum, Coking, Processing of Nucleus Fuel |
| 化学原料和化学制品制造业 | Manufacture of Chemical Raw Material and Chemical Products |
| 医药制造业 | Manufacture of Medicines |
| 化学纤维制造业 | Manufacture of Chemical Fiber |
| 橡胶和塑料制品业 | Manufacture of Rubber and Plastic |
| 非金属矿物制品业 | Manufacture of Non-metallic Mineral Products |
| 黑色金属冶炼和压延加工业 | Smelting and Pressing of Ferrous Metals |
| 有色金属冶炼和压延加工业 | Smelting and Pressing of Non-ferrous Metals |
| 金属制品业 | Manufacture of Metal Products |
| 通用设备制造业 | Manufacture of General Purpose Machinery |
| 专用设备制造业 | Manufacture of Special Purpose Machinery |
| 汽车制造业 | Manufacture of Vehicle |
| 铁路、船舶、航空航天和其他运输设备制造业 | Manufacture of Transport Equipment for Railway, Shipping, Aerospace and other uses |
| 电气机械和器材制造业 | Manufacture of Electrical Machinery &Equipment |
| 计算机、通信和其他电子设备制造业 | Manufacture of Computer, Communication Equipment and Other Electronic Equipmen |
| 仪器仪表制造业 | Manufacture of Measuring Imstrument |
| 其他制造业 | Manufacture of Other Products |
| 废弃资源综合利用业 | Recycling and Disposal of Waste Resources |
| 金属制品、机械和设备修理业 | Manufacture of Metal Products, Machinery and Equipment |
| 电力、热力生产和供应业 | Production and Supply of Electric Power and Heat Power |
| 燃气生产和供应业 | Production and Supply of Gas |
| 水的生产和供应业 | Production and Supply of Water |

| 其他油制品 (吨) Other Petroleum Products (ton) | 热力 (百万千焦) Heat (million kJ) | 电力 (万千瓦时) Electricity (10 000kW · h) | 其他燃料 (吨标准煤) Other Fuel (ton SCE) |
|---|---|---|---|
| **774635** | **18097873** | **1819017** | **3805** |
| | | | |
| | | | |
| | | | |
| | | | |
| | | 1660 | |
| | | | |
| | | | |
| 2 | 1917701 | 93999 | 621 |
| | 266708 | 23973 | 75 |
| | 2203876 | 20587 | |
| | | | |
| | 1292481 | 20040 | 327 |
| | 1813260 | 28245 | |
| | 98705 | 11605 | 210 |
| | | 2962 | |
| | 1337 | 6742 | |
| | 881000 | 14926 | |
| | 14464 | 14185 | |
| | 43358 | 28333 | 964 |
| 715249 | 5241 | 130045 | |
| 59257 | 3787193 | 203155 | |
| | 517661 | 14493 | |
| | 4656 | 3760 | |
| | 1276995 | 147137 | |
| | 39459 | 96326 | |
| | 343085 | 213760 | |
| | 50276 | 20713 | |
| 12 | 59123 | 83085 | |
| | 68569 | 71300 | 442 |
| | 17331 | 32152 | 181 |
| | 711015 | 110959 | |
| 115 | 957547 | 70771 | 839 |
| | 606240 | 78008 | 146 |
| | 366415 | 56969 | |
| | | 4807 | |
| | | 1946 | |
| | | 166 | |
| | | 1956 | |
| | 754176 | 176282 | |
| | | 9540 | |
| | | 24430 | |

# 主要统计指标解释

**工业企业能源消费量** 工业企业能源消费包括工业企业在生产过程中作为燃料、动力、原料、辅助材料使用的能源以及工艺用能、非生产用能；作为能源加工转换企业，还要包括能源加工转换的投入量。工业企业能源消费量具体包括：

（1）用于本企业产品生产、工业性作业和其他生产性活动的能源。

（2）用于技术更新改造措施、新技术研究和新产品试制以及科学试验等方面的能源。

（3）用于经营维修、建筑及设备大修理、机电设备和交通运输工具等方面的能源。

（4）用于劳动保护的能源。

（5）其他非生产消费的能源。

不包括：

（1）由仓库发到车间，但在报告期最后一天没有消费的能源。这部分能源应在办理假退料手续后计入库存量。

（2）拨到外单位，委托外单位加工用的能源。

（3）调出本单位或借给外单位的能源。

**工业生产能源消费** 是指工业企业为进行工业生产活动所使用的能源。主要包括：

1. 用于本企业产品生产、工业性作业的能源，包括用作原料、材料、燃料、动力：作为能源加工转换企业，还包括用作加工转换的能源。

2. 产品生产过程中作为辅助材料使用的能源。

3. 生产工艺过程使用的能源。

4. 新技术研究、新产品试制、科学试验使用的能源。

5. 为了工业生产活动而在进行的各种修理过程中使用的能源。

6. 生产区内的劳动保护用能等。

# Explanatory Notes on Main Statistical Indicators

**Energy Consumption of Industrial Enterprises** include energy in the production process as fuel, power, raw materials, supplementary materials, and for use of technology and non-production. As energy processing and conversion enterprises, also include energy processing and conversion of inputs. These specifically include: （1）Energy for the enterprise product, industrial production operations and other activities.（2）Energy for technical upgrading measures and new technology research and new product production and scientific experiments.（3）Energy for operation maintenance, construction and equipment overhaul, electrical and mechanical equipment and transport, and other aspects.（4）Energy for the protection of labor.（5）Energy for Other non-production and consumption. And these exclude: （1）Energy from the warehouse to the workshop, but out of consumption on the last day of the reporting period. This part of the energy should leave retreat materials handling procedures included stock.（2）Energy transferred to other units, entrusted with the processing.（3）Energy transferred out of the unit or loans to other units.

**Energy Consumption for Industrial Production** refers to energy for industrial enterprises in industrial production activities. These mainly include: 1.Energy for the enterprise products, industrial operations, including energy as raw materials, materials, fuels, and power. As energy processing and conversion enterprises, also include energy for processing and conversion. 2. Energy as supplementary material in product process. 3. Energy used in production process. 4. Energy for new technologies, new product production, and scientific experiment. 5. Energy in process of repairing for industrial production activities. 6. Energy for labor protection in production areas and so on.

# 财政、金融和保险业 8

## GOVERNMENT FINANCE FINACIAL INTERMEDIATION AND INSURANCE

# 简要说明

## 一、本篇资料的主要内容

本篇资料主要反映了全市财政收支、金融和保险方面的情况，主要包括财政收入、财政支出、金融机构存贷款、保险业务开展等方面的资料。

## 二、本篇资料的来源

1、财政部分的资料来源于市财政局。

2、金融方面的资料来源于中国人民银行青岛市中心支行。

3、保险方面的资料来源于中国保险监督管理委员会青岛监管局。

本篇资料由市统计局国民经济核算处整理提供。

# Brief Introduction

## *I. Main Content*

Data in this chapter show the conditions of local government budgetary finance, banking and insurance, and securities, including government revenue and expenditure, deposits and loans of financial institutions and statistics on insurance companies.

## *II. Source of Data*

(1) Data on local government finance are provided by Qingdao Municipal Finance Bureau.

(2) Data on banking are provided by Qingdao Branch of the People' s Bank of China.

(3) Data on insurance are provide by China Insurance Regulatory Commission of Qingdao Bureau.

Data in this chapter are prepared and compiled by the Division of National Accounts of Qingdao Municipal Bureau of Statistics.

# 8-1 主要年份地方财政收支

MAJOR YEAR'S REVENUE AND EXPENDRRURE OF LOCAL GOVERNMENT FINANCE

单位：万元（10 000 yuan）

| 年份<br>Year | 财政收入<br>Revenue of<br>Government Finance | 财政支出<br>Expenditure of<br>Government Finance |
|---|---|---|
| 1949 | 1527 | 306 |
| 1952 | 19809 | 2226 |
| 1957 | 29875 | 3556 |
| 1962 | 32869 | 4327 |
| 1965 | 47682 | 6280 |
| 1970 | 95778 | 7825 |
| 1975 | 90220 | 11966 |
| 1978 | 130749 | 19427 |
| 1980 | 124835 | 20064 |
| 1985 | 165155 | 41996 |
| 1988 | 201206 | 93931 |
| 1990 | 242303 | 133875 |
| 1991 | 259377 | 137716 |
| 1992 | 275589 | 155696 |
| 1993 | 182348 | 211938 |
| 1994 | 227490 | 277331 |
| 1995 | 294771 | 376982 |
| 1996 | 379674 | 469569 |
| 1997 | 476804 | 564787 |
| 1998 | 580434 | 678575 |
| 1999 | 680089 | 740937 |
| 2000 | 800120 | 878702 |
| 2001 | 987080 | 1097848 |
| 2002 | 1006616 | 1243880 |
| 2003 | 1201398 | 1471747 |
| 2004 | 1305136 | 1646214 |
| 2005 | 1763412 | 2030622 |
| 2006 | 2257663 | 2367875 |
| 2007 | 2925798 | 3211777 |
| 2008 | 3424359 | 3694111 |
| 2009 | 3769896 | 4335754 |
| 2010 | 4526138 | 5323888 |
| 2011 | 5661400 | 6580605 |
| 2012 | 6701820 | 7659801 |
| 2013 | 7889313 | 10142273 |
| 2014 | 8952450 | 10747138 |
| 2015 | 10063220 | 12228664 |
| 2016 | 11000303 | 13528516 |
| 2017 | 11572389 | 14030252 |
| 2018 | 12319138 | 15597764 |

注：1. 1993 年以后实行新制度，财政收入数与历年不可比。
2. 2002 年以后，财政收入、支出为一般预算数。

Note：1. Since 1993, new regulations have been adopted in calculating revenue of government finance, the figutrs are not comparable with those over the years.
2. Since 2002, revenue of government finance and expenditure of government finance refer to general budgetary revenue and expenditure.

# 8-2 分市、区公共财政预算收入（2018年）
PULBIC FINANCE BUDGET REVENUE BY CITY AND DISTRICL（2018）

单位：万元（10 000 yuan）

| 市、区名称 | Region | 一般公共预算收入 Public Finance Bodget Revenue | #增值税 Value-added Tax | #营业税 Business Tax | #企业所得税 Enterprise Income Tax |
|---|---|---|---|---|---|
| **全　市** | **Whole Municipality** | **12319138** | **3278946** | **3713** | **1523764** |
| 市南区 | Shiman District | 921789 | 312727 | 1117 | 165931 |
| 市北区 | Shiben District | 1101239 | 320692 | 986 | 149746 |
| 李沧区 | Licang District | 1001717 | 191628 | 2077 | 65718 |
| 崂山区 | Laoshan District | 1532191 | 398735 | -4376 | 294115 |
| 黄岛区 | Huangdao District | 2498092 | 759811 | 287 | 367296 |
| 保税港区 | Qingdao Free Trade Port Area of Chinat | 128520 | 43889 | 6 | 42778 |
| 城阳区 | Chengyang District | 1125417 | 437273 | 26 | 140757 |
| 即墨区 | Jimo District | 1111918 | 270077 | 749 | 72135 |
| 胶州市 | Jiaozhou | 1003788 | 241928 | 1327 | 60461 |
| 平度市 | Pingdu | 560180 | 133525 | 869 | 31456 |
| 莱西市 | Laixi | 493777 | 81315 | 608 | 26529 |
| 红岛经济区 | Qingdao National High-tech Industrial Development Zone | 318152 | 87346 | 37 | 39375 |
| 市本级 | Municipal Level | 522358 | | | 67467 |

# 8-2 续表
Continued

单位：万元（10 000 yuan）

| 市、区名称 | Region | #个人所得税<br>Personal Income Tax | #城市维护建设税<br>Urban Maintenance and Development Tax | #基金预算收入<br>Funds Budgetary Revenue |
|---|---|---|---|---|
| **全　市** | **Whole Municipality** | **487635** | **576986** | **8855214** |
| 市南区 | Shiman District | 118780 | 43490 | |
| 市北区 | Shiben District | 50378 | 59369 | |
| 李沧区 | Licang District | 19962 | 38829 | |
| 崂山区 | Laoshan District | 90020 | 102369 | 743328 |
| 黄岛区 | Huangdao District | 84842 | 137234 | 1720353 |
| 保税港区 | Qingdao Free Trade Port Area of Chinat | 5380 | 6338 | 4849 |
| 城阳区 | Chengyang District | 37812 | 61782 | 925418 |
| 即墨区 | Jimo District | 22005 | 39316 | 828113 |
| 胶州市 | Jiaozhou | 18903 | 38907 | 989641 |
| 平度市 | Pingdu | 14125 | 20904 | 282606 |
| 莱西市 | Laixi | 13911 | 13853 | 29216 |
| 红岛经济区 | Qingdao National High-tech Industrial Development Zone | 11517 | 14595 | 1131694 |
| 市本级 | Municipal Level | | | 2199996 |

# 8-3 分市、区公共财政预算支出（2018年）
PUBLIC FINANCE BUDGET REVENUE BY CITY AND DISTRICT（2018）

单位：万元（10 000 yuan）

| 市、区名称 | Region | 一般公共预算支出 Pubic Finance Budget Revenue | #一般公共服务支出 General Public Services | #公共安全 Public Securty | #教育 Education | #科学技术 Science and Technology | #文化体育与传媒 Culture, Sport and Media |
|---|---|---|---|---|---|---|---|
| **全　市** | **Whole Municipality** | **15597764** | **1626828** | **1083753** | **2630041** | **451472** | **240026** |
| 市南区 | Shiman District | 614559 | 74049 | 34241 | 108140 | 5793 | 2461 |
| 市北区 | Shiben District | 753358 | 127340 | 30049 | 189206 | 17016 | 6533 |
| 李沧区 | Licang District | 869924 | 46414 | 20776 | 142081 | 131791 | 7904 |
| 崂山区 | Laoshan District | 987755 | 82625 | 45375 | 128072 | 99244 | 6877 |
| 黄岛区 | Huangdao District | 2149197 | 307976 | 102626 | 507568 | 23724 | 17769 |
| 保税港区 | Qingdao Free Trade Port Area of Chinat | 67940 | 19746 | 1202 | 104 | 4874 | 72 |
| 城阳区 | Chengyang District | 736420 | 85269 | 35665 | 216158 | 22233 | 3841 |
| 即墨区 | Jimo District | 1687264 | 140956 | 46749 | 294528 | 14409 | 21976 |
| 胶州市 | Jiaozhou | 1169575 | 138150 | 66503 | 257362 | 19761 | 12861 |
| 平度市 | Pingdu | 995209 | 98809 | 39746 | 284225 | 6003 | 8249 |
| 莱西市 | Laixi | 767102 | 82346 | 26486 | 106439 | 1249 | 4652 |
| 红岛经济区 | Qingdao National High-tech Industrial Development Zone | 286695 | 25795 | 4750 | 40376 | 35128 | 10569 |
| 市本级 | Municipal Level | 4512766 | 397353 | 629585 | 355782 | 70247 | 136262 |

# 8-3 续表
Continued

单位：万元（10 000 yuan）

| 市、区名称 | Region | #社会保障和就业 Social Security and Empooyment | #医疗卫生 Health Care | #节能环保 Environment Protection | #城乡社区事务 Urban and Rural Community Affairs | #农林水事务 Affairs of Agiculture Forest and Irrigatior | #基金预算支出 Funds Budgetary Expenditure |
|---|---|---|---|---|---|---|---|
| **全　市** | **Whole Municipality** | **1561217** | **1023535** | **248344** | **3320256** | **686776** | **9255764** |
| 市南区 | Shiman District | 71534 | 33614 | 6006 | 209040 | 108 | 38572 |
| 市北区 | Shiben District | 96793 | 48452 | 5934 | 198480 | 46 | 212935 |
| 李沧区 | Licang District | 79010 | 31910 | 69362 | 313492 | 2945 | 158026 |
| 崂山区 | Laoshan District | 39791 | 54547 | 31661 | 326577 | 63928 | 519549 |
| 黄岛区 | Huangdao District | 222410 | 151131 | 37973 | 382317 | 109079 | 1847380 |
| 保税港区 | Qingdao Free Trade Port Area of Chinat | 2942 | 83 | 1 | 27560 | | 9805 |
| 城阳区 | Chengyang District | 42436 | 49074 | 5144 | 223874 | 22211 | 1058540 |
| 即墨区 | Jimo District | 135735 | 103633 | 15785 | 344622 | 84837 | 1010711 |
| 胶州市 | Jiaozhou | 97946 | 89141 | 28996 | 257308 | 106962 | 1085727 |
| 平度市 | Pingdu | 175529 | 125398 | 12834 | 72631 | 123910 | 256028 |
| 莱西市 | Laixi | 147533 | 74350 | 12526 | 62688 | 76407 | 32778 |
| 红岛经济区 | Qingdao National High-tech Industrial Development Zone | 16803 | 9370 | 835 | 37135 | 3215 | 978863 |
| 市本级 | Municipal Level | 432755 | 252832 | 21287 | 864532 | 93128 | 2046850 |

# 8-4 主要年份金融系统人民币存贷款（年末余额）

## MAJOR YEAR'S DEPOSITS AND LOANS OF FINANCIAL INSTITUTIONS (YEAR-END BALANCE)

单位：万元（10 000 yuan）

| 年份 Year | 存款合计 Total Deposits | #企业存款 Deposits by Enterprises | #储蓄存款 Savings Deposits | 贷款合计 Total Loans |
|---|---|---|---|---|
| 1949 | 693 | 239 | 28 | 278 |
| 1952 | 9093 | 4308 | 1838 | 3322 |
| 1957 | 10372 | 3359 | 4037 | 30690 |
| 1962 | 20040 | 8579 | 3279 | 73601 |
| 1965 | 27331 | 11830 | 6347 | 64555 |
| 1970 | 38264 | 13024 | 7576 | 126382 |
| 1975 | 60622 | 22568 | 15637 | 207006 |
| 1978 | 66523 | 21004 | 21455 | 297184 |
| 1980 | 120644 | 38105 | 38609 | 379666 |
| 1985 | 344760 | 99736 | 155604 | 452142 |
| 1990 | 1235562 | 321542 | 655895 | 1535751 |
| 1991 | 1553564 | 411417 | 824428 | 1871462 |
| 1992 | 2076667 | 612868 | 1044165 | 2352449 |
| 1993 | 2747294 | 835617 | 1372239 | 2940658 |
| 1994 | 3769019 | 1399110 | 1918734 | 3610564 |
| 1995 | 5324026 | 2030382 | 2687888 | 4777864 |
| 1996 | 6991289 | 2630958 | 3499219 | 5941281 |
| 1997 | 7385092 | 2885632 | 4060259 | 6508776 |
| 1998 | 8183471 | 3018063 | 4591012 | 7239231 |
| 1999 | 9160001 | 3454570 | 4978045 | 8945730 |
| 2000 | 10560624 | 4386316 | 5353215 | 9564293 |
| 2001 | 12323942 | 4955336 | 6187409 | 10798871 |
| 2002 | 15225733 | 5819655 | 7449408 | 13044792 |
| 2003 | 18920868 | 7027227 | 9084693 | 16783917 |
| 2004 | 22462592 | 7924690 | 10894941 | 18472613 |
| 2005 | 26975372 | 8226661 | 13431016 | 20394792 |
| 2006 | 32453583 | 10144296 | 15676197 | 25779442 |
| 2007 | 38915882 | 13213434 | 17020383 | 30970553 |
| 2008 | 47353803 | 14641948 | 21233637 | 37483209 |
| 2009 | 63019764 | 21001185 | 25278658 | 48735326 |
| 2010 | 76592065 | 27271963 | 29123256 | 58862263 |
| 2011 | 86384994 | 49189415 | 31985099 | 69477500 |
| 2012 | 94348924 | 50978985 | 37576007 | 79465532 |
| 2013 | 109695588 | 60367185 | 41405946 | 88607439 |
| 2014 | 113703085 | 60791933 | 44358964 | 97200532 |
| 2015 | 125330268 | 45526577 | 50235905 | 107718528 |
| 2016 | 140071344 | 50912759 | 53263262 | 118916821 |
| 2017 | 143877550 | 53835435 | 53941843 | 132647913 |
| 2018 | 155321863 | 57270448 | 59137089 | 151941934 |

注：本表数据来源于人民银行，自 2015 年起，人民银行报表指标变化，企业存款指标暂用非金融企业存款，储蓄存款指标暂用住户存款，口径与以前年度不一致。

Note: The data in this table comes from the People's Bank of China. Since 2015, the report index of the People's Bank of China has changed, the enterprise deposit index is temporarily used as the deposit of the enterprise, the savings deposit index is temporarily used for household deposit, The caliber is not consistent with the previous year.

# 8-5 金融系统人民币存贷款（年末余额）
## DEPOSITS AND LOANS OF FINANCIAL INSTITUTIONS（YEAR-END BALANCE）

单位：万元（10 000 yuan）

| 项目 | Item | 2018 年 | 比年初增减数 Incremental/Reductions Compared to the Beginning of the Year |
|---|---|---|---|
| 一、存款总计 | Total Deposits | 155321863 | 11444315 |
| 住户存款 | Household Deposits | 59137089 | 5186155 |
| 非金融企业存款 | Non-Financial Corporate Deposits | 57270448 | 3444106 |
| 广义政府存款 | General Government Deposits | 29329183 | 4414777 |
| 非银行业金融机构存款 | Non-Banking Financial Institutions' s Deposits | 9130588 | -1637887 |
| 二、贷款总计 | Total Loans | 151941934 | 19238288 |
| 住户贷款 | Household Loans | 47898973 | 7331502 |
| #短期贷款 | Short-Term Loans | 4421237 | 561679 |
| 中长期贷款 | Medium And Long-Term Loans | 43477736 | 6769823 |
| 非金融企业及机关团体贷款 | Non-Financial Enterprises And Institutions/ Organizations' Loans | 103704752 | 11922783 |
| #短期贷款 | Short-Term Loans | 34346742 | 2197999 |
| 中长期贷款 | Medium&Long-term Loans | 62846188 | 6646810 |
| 票据融资 | Notes Financing | 5525190 | 2690625 |
| 非银行业金融机构贷款 | Non-Banking Financial Institution' s Loans | 20112 | -193821 |

注：自 2015 年起，人民银行报表中指标发生变化，本表数据按照新指标提供。

Note: Since 2015, the indexes in the People' s Bank of China' s statements have changed, the data in the talbe are provided according to the new indexes.

# 8-6 国内保险业务（2000-2018 年）
DOMESTIC INSURANCE BUSINESS（2000-2018）

| 项目 | Item | 2000 年 | 2005 年 | 2006 年 | 2008 年 | 2009 年 |
|---|---|---|---|---|---|---|
| **风险保障金额** | **Total domestic insurance Value** | **38357485** | **91691581** | **119396881** | **276989344** | **293519697** |
| **国内业务收入** | **Domestic Business Income** | **220780** | **495701** | **605143** | **1027258** | **1153101** |
| 1. 保费收入 | Premium Income | 218714 | 495701 | 605143 | 1027258 | 1153101 |
| #财产险 | Propetry Insurance | 85161 | 159746 | 199213 | 280008 | 339314 |
| 农业险 | Agiculture Insurance | 18 | 12 | 19 | 3135 | 4066 |
| 人身险 | Personal Insurance | 133535 | 335943 | 405911 | 744115 | 809721 |
| **国内业务支出** | **Domestic Business Expenditure** | 94877 | 214148 | 252477 | 423743 | 476377 |
| 1 . 赔款支出 | Cham Expenditure | 62275 | 111385 | 131321 | 196318 | 219546 |
| #财产险 | Property Insurance | 58361 | 92700 | 115214 | 164415 | 188723 |
| 农业险 | Agriculture Insurance | 5 | 11 | 3 | 907 | 3452 |
| 人身险 | Personal Insurance | 3909 | 18674 | 16104 | 30996 | 27371 |
| 2 . 给付支出 | Mature Payment | 27955 | 32739 | 63144 | 132621 | 123056 |
| 3 . 退保 | Surrended | 4647 | 70024 | 58012 | 94804 | 133775 |

注：本表由青岛保监局提供，风险保障金额 2012 年之前为国内保险总值。

Note：This table was provided by the Qingdao Insurance Regulatory Bureau. The amount of risk protection before 2012 was the total value of domestic insurance.

单位：万元（10 000 yuan）

| 2010 年 | 2011 年 | 2012 年 | 2013 年 | 2014 年 | 2015 年 | 2016 年 | 2017 年 | 2018 年 |
|---|---|---|---|---|---|---|---|---|
| **309244255** | **380829634** | **447476690** | **491953749** | **611632799** | **836499657** | **1687559828** | **2232390824** | **2337365406** |
| **1538526** | **1457269** | **1602881** | **1789854** | **2031421** | **2441172** | **3359013** | **3967170** | **4393970** |
| 1538526 | 1457269 | 1602881 | 1789854 | 2031421 | 2441172 | 3359013 | 3967170 | 4393970 |
| 492190 | 556257 | 644269 | 744470 | 872805 | 920229 | 1046908 | 1062116 | 1269489 |
| 3261 | 3587 | 5046 | 6824 | 8395 | 12100 | 12734 | 15670 | 18043 |
| 1043075 | 897425 | 953566 | 1038560 | 1150220 | 1508843 | 2299371 | 2889384 | 3106438 |
| 497832 | 463751 | 592167 | 757404 | 1031415 | 1236281 | 1522375 | 1704218 | 1919252 |
| 279019 | 307564 | 360085 | 432494 | 492693 | 539320 | 681211 | 733493 | 917964 |
| 250966 | 286214 | 328877 | 392860 | 442168 | 492573 | 526586 | 554513 | 756987 |
| 2808 | 1087 | 1833 | 3820 | 5519 | 9724 | 16337 | 18232 | 10985 |
| 25245 | 20263 | 29375 | 35814 | 45006 | 37023 | 138288 | 160749 | 149992 |
| 109318 | 156188 | 154922 | 194592 | 274790 | 340786 | 455300 | 470266 | 493511 |
| 109496 | 69275 | 77159 | 130318 | 263932 | 356175 | 376777 | 500459 | 507777 |

# 主要统计指标解释

**财政收入**　指国家财政参与社会产品分配所取得的收入，是实现国家职能的财力保证。财政收入所包括的内容几经变化，目前主要包括：

（1）税收收入：包括增值税、营业税、企业所得税、个人所得税、资源税、城市维护建设税、房产税、印花税、城镇土地使用税、土地增值税、车船税、耕地占用税、契税、烟叶税、其他税收收入。

（2）非税收入：包括专项收入、行政事业性收费收入、罚没收入、国有资本经营收入、国有资源有偿使用收入、其他收入。

**财政支出**　国家财政将筹集起来的资金进行分配使用，以满足经济建设和各项事业的需要，主要包括：

（1）一般公共服务支出：反映政府提供一般公共服务的支出。

（2）公共安全：反映政府维护社会公共安全方面的支出，有关事务包括武装警察、公安、国家安全、检察、法院、司法行政、监狱、劳教、国家保密、缉私警察等。

（3）教育支出：反映政府教育事务支出。有关具体教育事务包括教育行政管理、学前教育、小学教育、初中教育、普通高中教育、普通高等教育、初等职业教育、中专教育、技校教育、职业高中教育、高等职业教育、广播电视教育、留学生教育、特殊教育、干部继续教育、教育机关服务等。

（4）科学技术：反映政府用于科学技术方面的支出。

（5）文化体育与传媒：反映政府在文化、文物、体育、广播电视、新闻出版等方面的支出。

（6）社会保障和就业：反映政府在社会保障与就业方面的支出。有关事项包括社会保障与就业管理事务、民政管理事务、财政对社会保险基金的补助、补充全国社会保障基金、行政事业单位离退休、企业改革补助、就业补助、抚恤、退役安置、社会福利、残疾人事业、城市居民最低生活保障、其他城镇社会救济、农村社会救济、自然灾害生活补助、红十字事务等。

（7）医疗卫生支出：反映政府医疗卫生方面的支出。具体包括医疗卫生管理事务支出、医疗服务支出、医疗保障支出、疾病预防控制支出、卫生监督支出、妇幼保健支出、农村卫生支出等。

（8）环境保护：反映政府环境保护支出。具体包括：环境保护管理事务支出、环境监测与监察支出、污染治理支出、自然生态保护支出、天然林保护工程支出、退耕还林支出、风沙荒漠治理支出、退牧还草支出、已垦草原退耕还草支出。

（9）城乡社区事务：反映政府城乡社区事务支出。具体包括：城乡社区管理事务支出、城乡社区规划与管理支出、城乡社区公共设施支出、城乡社区住宅支出、城乡社区环境卫生支出、建设市场管理与监督支出等。

（10）农林水事务：反映政府农林水事务方面的支出。具体包括农业、林业、水利、扶贫支出、农业综合开发支出等。

**存款**　指企业、机关、团体或居民根据资金必须收回的原则，把货币资金存入银行或其他信贷机构保管并取得一定利息的一种信用活动形式。根据存款对象或性质的不同可划分为企业存款、财政存款、机关团体存款、基本建设存款、储蓄存款、农村存款、委托存款、其他存款等科目。它是银行信贷资金的主要来源。

**贷款**　指银行或其他信贷机构根据资金必须归还的原则，按一定利率，为企业、个人等提供资金的一种信用活动形式。我国银行贷款分为短期贷款、中期流动资金贷款、中长期贷款、信托贷款、融资租赁、委托贷款、票据融资、各项垫款等。

**承保额**　又叫保险金额，指保险人承担赔偿或者给付保险金责任的最高限额。

**保费**　指投保人为取得保险人在约定范围内所承担赔偿责任而支付给保险人的费用。

# Explanatory Notes on Main Statistical Indicators

**Government Revenue**　refers to the revenue of the government finance by means of participating in the distribution of the social products, which is the financial resources for ensuring the government to function. The contents of government revenue have been changed several times. Now it includes the following main items:

(1) Various tax revenues, including value added tax, business tax, enterprise income tax, personal income tax, resources tax, fixed assets investment direction regulating tax, tax on city maintenance and construction, real estate tax, stamp tax, tax on use of urban land, land value added tax, vehicle and vessel tax, tax on occupancy of cultivated land, property tax, tobacco leaf tax, and other tax revenues.

(2) Non-tax Revenues including special revenues, revenues from Administrative and institutional fees, penalty and confiscatory revenues, revenues from state-owned capital operationg, revenues from paid use of state-owned resources, and other revenues.

**Government Expenditure** refers to the distribution and use of the funds the government finance has raised, so as to meet the needs of economic construction and various causes. It includes the following main items:

(1) Expenditure for general public services: It reflects the expenditure from the government for general public services.

(2) Expenditure on public security: It reflects the expenditure from the government towards safeguarding the public security, including the related affairs of armed police, public security, state security, procuratorial administration, law court, judicial administration, jail, reeducation through labor, state confidentiality, anti-smuggling Patrol, etc.

(2) Expenditure on education: It reflects the expenditure from the government on education, including the related affairs of educational administration management, preschool education, primary education, junior secondary educate, regular senior secondary educate, regular higher education, primary vocational education, specialized secondary educate, technical educate, vocational senior secondary educate, vocational higher education, radio and television education, foreign student educate, special education, cadre continuing education, education institution services, etc.

(4) Expenditure on science and technology: It reflects the expenditure from the government on science and technology.

(5) Expenditure on culture, sport and media: It reflects the expenditure from the government on culture, cultural relics, sport, radio and television, publication, etc.

(6) Expenditure on social security and employment: It reflects the expenditure from the government on social security and employment, including the related affairs of management of social security and employment, civil administration, subsidies to social insurance funds, supplement to national social security funds, retirees of government agencies and institutions, subsidies to enterprises reform, subsidies to employment, pension, settling down demobilized servicemen, social security, disabled person administration, minimum living allowance in urban area, other social relief in urban area, social relief in rural area, subsidies to natural disaster, Red Cross business, etc.

(7) Expenditure on health care: It reflects the expenditure from the government on health care, including expenditure on management of health care, medical services, medical security, disease control and prevention, public health supervision, rural health care, etc.

(8) Expenditure on environment protection: It reflects the expenditure from the government on environment protection, including expenditure on management of environment protection, environment monitoring and supervisory, pollution government, natural ecological protection, project of natural forest protection, returning farmland to forest, sandstorm and wilderness government, returning grazing land to grassland, returning cultivated grassland to grassland, etc.

(9) Expenditure on urban and rural community affairs: It reflects the expenditure from the government on urban and rural community affairs, including expenditure on management of urban and rural community affairs, plan and management of urban and rural community, public utility of urban and rural community, residential buildings of urban and rural community, environmental sanitation of urban and rural community, management and supervision of markets construction, etc.

(10) Expenditure on agriculture, forest and irrigation: It reflects the expenditure from the government on agriculture, forest and irrigation, including expenditure on agriculture, forest, irrigation, poverty alleviation, comprehensive development of agriculture, etc.

**Deposit** is a form of credit by which enterprises, institutions, organizations or households can put money into banks and other credit institutions for safekeeping and interest earning under the principle of free withdrawal. According to different depositors, deposits are divided into enterprise deposits, treasury deposits, deposits of government agencies and organizations, capital construction deposits, savings deposits, rural saving deposits, entrusted deposits and other deposits. Deposits are major sources of the credit funds of banks.

**Loan** is a form of credit by which banks and other credit institutions provide funds at certain interest rate to enterprises and individuals in the light of the principle of unconditional repayment. Loans from Chinese banks include circulating capital loans, fixed assets loans, loans to urban and rural individuals engaged in industrial and commercial business and agricultural loans.

**Amount Covered** which also is known as amount Insured, refers to the maximum that the insurant will get for the claim of the case insured.

**Premium** is the fee paid by the insurant to the insurer to obtain the obligation of compensation from the insurance within the agreed terms.

# 价格指数 9

PRICE INDEXES

# 简 要 说 明

**一、本篇资料的主要内容**

本篇资料主要包括工业生产者出厂、工业生产者购进、固定资产投资、房地产、居民消费、商品零售等价格指数。

**二、本篇资料的来源**

1、工业生产者出厂、工业生产者购进、固定资产投资、房地产价格指数分别来源于生产、房地产价格统计调查年报，由国家统计局青岛调查队生产生产价格调查处整理提供。

2、居民消费、商品零售价格指数来源于消费价格统计调查年报，由国家统计局青岛调查队消费价格调查处整理提供。

# Brief Introduction

***I. Main Content***

Data in this chapter mainly include producer price indices for manufactured goods, purchasing price indices for industrial producers, price indices of investment in fixed assets, real estate price indices, consumer price indices and retail price indices.

***II. Source of Data***

(1) Data on producer price indices for manufactured goods, purchasing price indices for industrial producers, price indices of investment in fixed assets, real estate price indices are based on annual report of price survey on production, investment, real estate, and provided by the Division of Production Price Survey of Survey Office of the National Bureau of Statistics in Qingdao.

(2) Data on consumer price indices and retail price indices are based on annual report of consumer price survey, and provided by the Division of Consumer Price Survey of Survey Office of the National Bureau of Statistics in Qingdao.

# 9-1 主要年份居民消费和商品零售价格指数

MAJOR YEAR'S CONSUMER AND RETAIL PRICE INDEXES

（上年价格 =100）  (perceding year=100)

| 年份<br>Year | 居民消费价格指数<br>Consumer Price Index | #食品类<br>Food | #衣着类<br>Clothing | #服务项目价格指数<br>Services Price Index | 商品零售价格指数<br>Retail Price Index |
|---|---|---|---|---|---|
| 1951 | 110.5 | 105.2 | 112.4 | | 110.5 |
| 1952 | 99.8 | 99.6 | 98.7 | | 99.8 |
| 1957 | 101.4 | 101.3 | 101.4 | 99.3 | 101.4 |
| 1962 | 102.6 | 102.0 | 100.2 | 99.9 | 102.6 |
| 1965 | 101.2 | 101.3 | 98.8 | 96.9 | 101.2 |
| 1970 | 98.9 | 99.7 | 100.0 | 99.5 | 98.9 |
| 1975 | 100.3 | 100.1 | 100.0 | 100.0 | 100.3 |
| 1978 | 100.5 | 100.2 | 99.8 | 100.0 | 100.5 |
| 1980 | 105.2 | 108.5 | 100.3 | 100.6 | 105.5 |
| 1985 | 110.4 | 115.2 | 102.3 | 102.7 | 110.9 |
| 1988 | 120.7 | 125.2 | 117.3 | 118.3 | 120.9 |
| **1990** | **104.5** | **103.4** | **103.4** | **118.8** | **103.6** |
| 1991 | 107.0 | 107.0 | 112.1 | 109.6 | 106.8 |
| 1992 | 111.4 | 115.1 | 108.6 | 119.9 | 110.8 |
| 1993 | 123.9 | 120.9 | 119.0 | 158.5 | 119.8 |
| 1994 | 126.9 | 135.2 | 130.1 | 117.9 | 122.8 |
| 1995 | 116.2 | 118.1 | 122.8 | 123.2 | 114.2 |
| 1996 | 112.6 | 110.1 | 104.3 | 130.4 | 106.0 |
| 1997 | 104.0 | 101.2 | 102.3 | 120.8 | 100.2 |
| 1998 | 100.0 | 93.7 | 94.5 | 136.2 | 94.9 |
| 1999 | 100.2 | 96.7 | 97.1 | 115.6 | 96.6 |
| **2000** | **103.3** | **100.0** | **108.3** | **112.0** | **99.7** |
| 2001 | 101.0 | 100.6 | 98.0 | 108.7 | 98.9 |
| 2002 | 98.9 | 97.8 | 100.2 | 101.0 | 99.5 |
| 2003 | 101.4 | 104.3 | 98.4 | 101.7 | 98.3 |
| 2004 | 102.1 | 104.0 | 103.6 | 104.7 | 99.0 |
| 2005 | 102.3 | 102.1 | 108.3 | 101.4 | 99.3 |
| 2006 | 100.9 | 101.7 | 99.4 | 100.8 | 99.7 |
| 2007 | 104.5 | 111.6 | 99.4 | 102.4 | 102.7 |
| 2008 | 104.7 | 111.7 | 103.9 | 99.8 | 103.9 |
| 2009 | 100.5 | 101.6 | 101.4 | 100.6 | 98.6 |
| **2010** | **102.2** | **106.4** | **101.0** | **100.4** | **101.4** |
| 2011 | 105.0 | 111.1 | 108.2 | 103.1 | 104.5 |
| 2012 | 102.7 | 104.3 | 106.3 | 102.1 | 101.7 |
| 2013 | 102.5 | 105.3 | 104.9 | 100.7 | 101.4 |
| 2014 | 102.6 | 104.4 | 103.2 | 101.9 | 102.3 |
| 2015 | 101.2 | 101.7 | 102.8 | 101.3 | 100.0 |
| 2016 | 102.5 | 105.0 | 100.3 | 101.8 | 102.0 |
| 2017 | 102.0 | 99.6 | 100.5 | 103.4 | 100.8 |
| 2018 | 102.1 | 103.1 | 103.8 | 101.6 | 101.8 |

注：1.2016 年起，食品类统计口径有变化，不包括“茶及饮料”和“在外餐饮”两项内容。
2.2016 年起，统计分类“服务项目价格指数”改为“服务价格指数”，增加“养老服务”和“金融服务”两项内容。

Note: 1. Statistical caliber of food category has changed since 2016.The two sections of Tea and Drinks and Catering Service are not included.
2. The statistical category of "Price Index of Service Item" has been revised to "Price Index of Service" as of 2016 with two additional sections of "Elderiy Care Service" and "Financial Service".

# 9-2 主要年份居民消费和商品零售价格指数（以 1950 年价格为 100）

## MAJOR YEAR'S CONSUMER AND RETAIL PRICE INDEXES（1950=100）

| 年份<br>Year | 居民消费价格指数<br>Consumer Price Index | #食品类<br>Food | #衣着类<br>Clothing | #服务项目价格指数<br>Services Price Index | 商品零售价格指数<br>Retail Price Index |
|---|---|---|---|---|---|
| 1951 | 110.5 | 105.2 | 112.4 | | 110.5 |
| 1952 | 110.3 | 104.8 | 110.9 | | 110.3 |
| 1957 | 119.5 | 120.7 | 115.3 | 91.6 | 119.5 |
| 1962 | 127.4 | 128.8 | 115.1 | 94.2 | 127.4 |
| 1965 | 133.3 | 138.7 | 108.4 | 81.5 | 133.3 |
| 1970 | 129.0 | 137.6 | 110.3 | 76.8 | 129.0 |
| 1975 | 128.8 | 138.2 | 110.0 | 75.7 | 128.8 |
| 1978 | 129.1 | 138.7 | 109.8 | 75.7 | 129.1 |
| 1980 | 137.6 | 154.1 | 109.3 | 76.1 | 138.1 |
| 1985 | 160.8 | 196.1 | 103.8 | 80.5 | 162.5 |
| 1988 | 223.8 | 295.2 | 133.2 | 100.8 | 227.6 |
| 1990 | 269.7 | 333.3 | 166.8 | 155.9 | 269.7 |
| 1991 | 288.6 | 356.7 | 187.0 | 170.9 | 288.1 |
| 1992 | 321.5 | 410.5 | 203.1 | 204.9 | 319.2 |
| 1993 | 398.3 | 496.3 | 241.7 | 324.8 | 382.4 |
| 1994 | 505.4 | 671.1 | 314.4 | 382.9 | 469.5 |
| 1995 | 587.3 | 792.5 | 386.1 | 471.8 | 536.2 |
| 1996 | 661.3 | 872.6 | 402.7 | 615.2 | 568.4 |
| 1997 | 687.8 | 883.0 | 412.0 | 743.1 | 569.5 |
| 1998 | 687.8 | 827.4 | 389.3 | 1012.1 | 540.5 |
| 1999 | 689.2 | 800.1 | 378.0 | 1170.0 | 522.1 |
| 2000 | 711.9 | 800.1 | 409.4 | 1310.4 | 520.5 |
| 2001 | 719.0 | 804.9 | 401.2 | 1424.4 | 514.8 |
| 2002 | 711.1 | 787.2 | 402.0 | 1438.7 | 512.2 |
| 2003 | 721.1 | 821.0 | 395.6 | 1463.1 | 503.5 |
| 2004 | 736.2 | 853.9 | 409.8 | 1531.9 | 498.5 |
| 2005 | 753.1 | 871.8 | 443.8 | 1553.4 | 495.0 |
| 2006 | 759.9 | 886.6 | 441.2 | 1565.8 | 493.5 |
| 2007 | 794.1 | 989.5 | 438.5 | 1603.4 | 506.8 |
| 2008 | 831.4 | 1105.3 | 455.6 | 1600.2 | 526.6 |
| 2009 | 835.6 | 1123.0 | 462.0 | 1609.8 | 519.2 |
| 2010 | 854.0 | 1194.9 | 466.6 | 1616.2 | 526.5 |
| 2011 | 896.7 | 1327.5 | 504.9 | 1666.3 | 550.2 |
| 2012 | 920.9 | 1384.6 | 536.7 | 1701.3 | 559.6 |
| 2013 | 943.9 | 1458.0 | 563.0 | 1713.2 | 567.4 |
| 2014 | 968.4 | 1522.2 | 581.0 | 1745.8 | 580.5 |
| 2015 | 980.0 | 1548.1 | 597.3 | 1768.5 | 580.5 |
| 2016 | 1004.5 | 1625.5 | 599.1 | 1800.3 | 592.1 |
| 2017 | 1024.6 | 1619.0 | 602.1 | 1861.5 | 596.8 |
| 2018 | 1046.1 | 1669.2 | 625.0 | 1891.3 | 607.6 |

注：1.2016 年起，食品类统计口径有变化，不包括“茶及饮料”和“在外餐饮”两项内容。
2.2016 年起，统计分类“服务项目价格指数”改为“服务价格指数”，增加“养老服务”和“金融服务”两项内容。

Note：1. Statistical caliber of food category has changed since 2016.The two sections of Tea and Drinks and Catering Service are not included.
2. The statistical category of "Price Index of Service Item" has been revised to "Price Index of Service" as of 2016 with two additional sections of "Elderiy Care Service" and "Financial Service".

# 9-3 主要年份生产投资价格指数
## MAJOR YEAR'S PRICE INDEXES FOR PRODUCTION AND INVESTMENT

（上年价格 =100） (perceding year=100)

| 年份 Year | 工业生产者出厂价格指数 Producer Price Indexes for Industrial Producers | 工业生产者购进价格指数 Purchasung Price Indexes for Industrial Producers | 房屋销售价格指数 Sales Price Indexes of Houses | 房屋租赁价格指数 Renting Price Indexes of Houses | 物业管理价格指数 Property Managerment Price Indexes | 固定资产投资价格指数 Price Indexes for Investment in Fixed Assets |
|---|---|---|---|---|---|---|
| 1990 | 104.33 | 108.64 | | | | |
| 1991 | 101.68 | 108.10 | | | | |
| 1992 | 105.46 | 107.13 | | | | |
| 1993 | 115.49 | 126.91 | | | | |
| 1994 | 121.62 | 120.30 | | | | |
| 1995 | 112.70 | 114.25 | | | | |
| 1996 | 103.81 | 103.25 | | | | |
| 1997 | 100.22 | 101.93 | | | | |
| 1998 | 94.96 | 92.77 | 100.1 | 94.0 | | |
| 1999 | 96.93 | 95.88 | 103.7 | 104.3 | | |
| 2000 | 101.89 | 106.81 | 102.3 | 95.8 | | |
| 2001 | 98.00 | 97.81 | 104.1 | 107.0 | | |
| 2002 | 97.37 | 96.78 | 107.6 | 94.4 | | |
| 2003 | 100.97 | 106.51 | 114.6 | 99.4 | | |
| 2004 | 102.92 | 113.62 | 115.2 | 98.6 | | 105.8 |
| 2005 | 101.39 | 106.52 | 110.9 | 103.3 | 100.2 | 103.1 |
| 2006 | 101.08 | 105.80 | 106.9 | 110.1 | 99.8 | 102.6 |
| 2007 | 101.50 | 106.69 | 106.5 | 108.3 | 100.4 | 104.1 |
| 2008 | 105.33 | 115.91 | 105.1 | 106.5 | 102.1 | 111.0 |
| 2009 | 95.78 | 90.35 | 100.3 | 103.5 | 100.4 | 94.6 |
| 2010 | 103.75 | 112.21 | | 103.0 | 100.5 | 104.9 |
| 2011 | 104.90 | 109.39 | | | | 107.0 |
| 2012 | 98.61 | 97.00 | | | | 100.0 |
| 2013 | 98.82 | 96.53 | | | | 100.1 |
| 2014 | 99.20 | 97.40 | | | | 99.9 |
| 2015 | 97.04 | 94.24 | | | | 97.1 |
| 2016 | 98.77 | 97.28 | | | | 99.8 |
| 2017 | 104.40 | 110.73 | | | | 107.3 |
| 2018 | 104.22 | 105.22 | | | | 106.6 |

注：2010 年之前工业生产者出厂价格为工业品出厂价格；工业生产者购进价格为主要原材料、燃料、动力购进价格。

Note: Producer's Prices at works were the prices of industrial products at words before 2010; Producer's purchasing price refers to the purchasing price of main raw materials, fuels and power.

# 9-4 工业生产者出厂价格指数
## PRODICER PRICE INDEXES FOR INDUSTRIAL PRODUCERS

（上年价格 =100）

| 类别 | Item | 2000 年 | 2005 年 | 2008 年 | 2009 年 |
|---|---|---|---|---|---|
| **总指数** | **General Index** | **101.89** | **101.39** | **105.33** | **95.78** |
| 其中：轻工业 | Light Industry | 98.50 | 99.78 | 102.93 | 97.21 |
| 重工业 | Heavy Industry | 105.62 | 104.32 | 109.17 | 93.45 |
| **其中：生产资料** | **Means of Production** | **105.03** | **103.24** | **108.76** | **94.25** |
| 采掘 | Excavation | 95.67 | 114.74 | 115.24 | 93.44 |
| 原料 | Raw Materials | 113.82 | 106.91 | 108.81 | 90.67 |
| 加工 | Processing | 97.58 | 101.45 | 108.59 | 95.34 |
| **生活资料** | **Means of Livelihood** | **98.25** | **99.13** | **101.72** | **97.45** |
| 食品 | Food | 96.59 | 98.80 | 108.42 | 98.21 |
| 衣着 | Clothing | 99.37 | 101.48 | 103.36 | 102.03 |
| 一般日用品 | Articles for Daily Use | 104.52 | 101.97 | 103.03 | 99.39 |
| 耐用消费品 | Articles for Daily Use | 97.70 | 97.43 | 97.13 | 94.52 |

(perceding year=100)

| 2010年 | 2011年 | 2012年 | 2013年 | 2014年 | 2015年 | 2016年 | 2017年 | 2018年 |
|---|---|---|---|---|---|---|---|---|
| **103.75** | **104.90** | **98.61** | **98.82** | **99.20** | **97.04** | **98.77** | **104.40** | **104.22** |
| 100.80 | 103.46 | 99.70 | 99.11 | 99.62 | 98.74 | 99.70 | 101.13 | 101.27 |
| 107.57 | 105.89 | 97.87 | 98.62 | 98.91 | 98.79 | 97.87 | 106.46 | 106.01 |
| **106.43** | **105.54** | **97.55** | **98.58** | **98.87** | **95.23** | **98.60** | **106.34** | **105.86** |
| 130.94 | 132.07 | 93.35 | 91.72 | 100.65 | 95.12 | | | |
| 115.24 | 111.52 | 99.05 | 99.26 | 98.87 | 88.59 | 93.92 | 112.92 | 114.50 |
| 103.50 | 103.49 | 97.20 | 98.50 | 98.84 | 97.06 | 99.60 | 104.96 | 103.95 |
| **99.61** | **103.82** | **100.42** | **99.21** | **99.76** | **100.07** | **99.12** | **100.69** | **100.95** |
| 105.06 | 109.71 | 99.91 | 95.34 | 98.34 | 102.53 | 102.59 | 100.55 | 100.55 |
| 101.56 | 107.44 | 102.03 | 102.74 | 100.34 | 100.39 | 100.93 | 101.54 | 100.14 |
| 99.96 | 108.02 | 101.64 | 101.42 | 101.01 | 99.59 | 100.12 | 101.63 | 101.54 |
| 93.23 | 94.34 | 98.79 | 98.41 | 99.65 | 98.26 | 94.58 | 99.78 | 101.32 |

# 9-5 工业生产者购进价格指数
PURCHASING PRICE INDEXES FOR INDUSTRIAL PRODUCERS

（上年价格 =100）

| 类别 | Item | 2000 年 | 2005 年 | 2008 年 | 2009 年 |
|---|---|---|---|---|---|
| **总指数** | **General Index** | **106.81** | **106.52** | **115.91** | **90.35** |
| 燃料、动力类 | fuel ang Power | 113.82 | 117.34 | 126.19 | 90.53 |
| 黑色金属材料类 | Ferrous Metals | 102.66 | 107.84 | 122.19 | 82.38 |
| #钢材 | Rolled-steel | 105.44 | 106.57 | 119.10 | 85.25 |
| 其他 | Others | 101.1 | 112.88 | 132.40 | 72.73 |
| 有色金属材料及电线类 | Nonferrous Metals and Electric Wire | 106.75 | 108.06 | 93.41 | 86.24 |
| 化工原料类 | Raw Chemical Materials | 106.9 | 112.47 | 123.00 | 87.66 |
| 木材及纸浆类 | Timber and Paper Pulp | 108.98 | 103.8 | 103.58 | 89.16 |
| 建筑材料及非金属矿类 | Building Materials and Nonmetals | 99.5 | 115.54 | 124.52 | 100.98 |
| 其他工业原材料及半成品 | Other Industrial Raw Materials and Semi-fin-ished Goods | 105.32 | 97.87 | 109.65 | 92.70 |
| 农副产品 | Agricultural Products | 92.73 | 101.55 | 117.68 | 88.60 |
| 纺织原料类 | Textile Materials | 104.03 | 98.15 | 101.44 | 98.69 |

（perceding year=100）

| 2010年 | 2011年 | 2012年 | 2013年 | 2014年 | 2015年 | 2016年 | 2017年 | 2018年 |
|---|---|---|---|---|---|---|---|---|
| **112.21** | **109.39** | **97.00** | **96.53** | **97.40** | **94.24** | **97.28** | **110.73** | **105.22** |
| 115.43 | 111.29 | 100.64 | 95.18 | 97.65 | 88.51 | 89.94 | 112.91 | 112.55 |
| 111.97 | 113.08 | 93.20 | 93.76 | 95.81 | 87.26 | 97.23 | 117.41 | 104.02 |
| 108.67 | 107.95 | 92.33 | 92.87 | 96.87 | 89.99 | 96.89 | 119.10 | 108.75 |
| 122.64 | 129.01 | 94.64 | 96.57 | 92.49 | 78.70 | 98.41 | 110.30 | 86.82 |
| 122.65 | 108.45 | 93.64 | 96.23 | 96.24 | 92.34 | 96.29 | 114.82 | 103.94 |
| 111.04 | 113.79 | 96.72 | 96.47 | 99.51 | 96.44 | 101.00 | 107.63 | 101.55 |
| 117.06 | 103.78 | 93.12 | 98.79 | 102.42 | 98.33 | 99.93 | 125.23 | 111.21 |
| 107.61 | 116.71 | 102.48 | 100.13 | 97.36 | 95.52 | 100.91 | 115.06 | 115.97 |
| 106.41 | 103.31 | 98.05 | 96.65 | 96.25 | 96.95 | 97.50 | 106.42 | 102.41 |
| 121.30 | 115.04 | 98.21 | 98.54 | 97.62 | 99.75 | 101.53 | 105.92 | 99.70 |
| 112.90 | 111.11 | 95.61 | 99.60 | 97.38 | 95.86 | 99.81 | 110.09 | 105.80 |

# 9-6 按工业行业分工业生产者出厂价格指数
PRODUCER PRICE INDEXES FOR INDUSTRIAL PRODUCERS BY SECTOR

（上年价格 =100）

| 行业 | Sector |
|---|---|
| **工业生产者出厂价格指数** | **Producer Price Indexes for Manufactured Manufactured Goods** |
| 黑色金属矿采选业 | Mining of Ferrous Metal Ores |
| 有色金属矿采选业 | ining of Non-ferrous Metal Ores |
| 非金属矿采选业 | Mining and Processing of Nonmetal Ores |
| 农副食品加工业 | Processing of Food from Agricultural Products |
| 食品制造业 | Manufacture of Foods |
| 酒、饮料和精制茶制造业 | Manufacturing Industry of Alcohol，Beverage and Refined Tea |
| 纺织业 | Manufacture of Textile |
| 纺织服装、服饰业 | Industry of Textile and Garment，and Apparel |
| 皮革、毛皮、羽毛及其制品和制鞋业 | Industry of Leather，Furs，Down and Related Products，and Shoes Making |
| 木材加工和木、竹、藤、棕、草制品业 | Processing of Timbers，Manufacture of Wood，Bamboo，Rattan，Palm，and Staw Products |
| 家具制造业 | Manufacture of Furniture |
| 造纸和纸制品业 | Manufacture of Paper and Paper Products |
| 印刷和记录媒介复制业 | Printing，Reproduction of Recording Media |
| 文教、工美、体育和娱乐用品制造业 | Industry of Culture and Education，Arts and Crafts，and Entertainment Products Manufacturing |
| 石油加工、炼焦和核燃料加工业 | Processing of Petroleum，Coking，Processing of Nucleus Fuel |
| 化学原料和化学制品制造业 | Manufacture of Chemical Raw Material and Chemical Products |
| 医药制造业 | Manufacture of Medicines |
| 化学纤维制造业 | Manufacture of Chemical Fiber |
| 橡胶和塑料制品业 | Industry of Rubber and Plastic Products |
| 非金属矿物制品业 | Manufacture of Non-metallic Mineral Products |
| 黑色金属冶炼和压延加工业 | Smelting and Pressing of Ferrous Metals |
| 有色金属冶炼和压延加工业 | Smelting and Pressing of Non-ferrous Metals |
| 金属制品业 | Manufacture of Metal Products |
| 通用设备制造业 | Manufacture of General Purpose Machinery |
| 专用设备制造业 | Manufacture of Special Purpose Machinery |
| 汽车制造业 | Vehicle Manufacturing Industry |
| 铁路、船舶、航空航天和其他运输设备制造业 | aufacturing Industry of Railroads. Vessels，Aerospace and Other Transporation Equipment |
| 电气机械和器材制造业 | Manufacture of Electrical Machinery&Equipment |
| 计算机、通信和其他电子设备制造业 | Computer. Communications and Other Electronic Equipment Manufacturing |
| 仪器仪表制造业 | Instruments Manufacturing Industry |
| 其他制造业 | Other Manufacturing Industry |
| 金属制品、机械和设备修理业 | Industry of Metal Products，and Repair of Machinery and Equipment |
| 电力、热力生产和供应业 | Production and Supply of Electric Power and Heat Power |
| 燃气生产和供应业 | Production and Supply of Gas |
| 水的生产和供应业 | Production and Supply of Water |

注：2012 年国民经济行业分类调整，本表中 2011 年— 2018 年数据采用新国民经济行业分类 GB/T4754-2011。

Note：Classification of national economic industries was adjusted in 2012. The new natinoal economic industries classification by GB/T4754-2011 applies to data from 2011 to 2018 in this table.

(perceding year=100)

| 2011年 | 2012年 | 2013年 | 2014年 | 2015年 | 2016年 | 2017年 | 2018年 |
|---|---|---|---|---|---|---|---|
| **104.90** | **98.61** | **98.82** | **99.20** | **97.04** | **98.77** | **104.40** | **104.22** |
| 104.33 | 99.93 | 100.00 | 99.86 | 100.00 | | | |
| 111.39 | 102.48 | 98.72 | 95.57 | 89.94 | | | |
| 145.13 | 89.33 | 87.06 | 102.14 | 94.85 | | | |
| 111.34 | 98.69 | 93.46 | 97.58 | 102.47 | 102.80 | 101.12 | 101.41 |
| 112.52 | 103.11 | 103.08 | 101.78 | 100.66 | 100.30 | 101.40 | 98.67 |
| 104.14 | 105.89 | 100.48 | 98.76 | 99.01 | 99.97 | 99.54 | 100.85 |
| 105.09 | 96.15 | 100.18 | 100.27 | 99.41 | 97.60 | 103.84 | 103.58 |
| 105.43 | 101.66 | 104.17 | 101.74 | 100.84 | 100.83 | 102.17 | 100.28 |
| 104.79 | 102.59 | 101.83 | 98.56 | 99.72 | 99.81 | 100.15 | 99.82 |
| 108.13 | 103.21 | 99.67 | 100.96 | 100.35 | | | |
| 101.11 | 102.00 | 100.02 | 100.00 | 99.91 | 93.46 | 98.72 | 100.48 |
| 105.71 | 95.59 | 96.13 | 101.96 | 99.78 | 99.58 | 115.83 | 104.86 |
| 110.06 | 107.10 | 108.65 | 96.97 | 95.96 | 93.45 | 101.11 | 102.77 |
| 100.61 | 101.47 | 100.47 | 100.00 | 99.96 | 99.88 | 101.90 | 100.54 |
| 114.95 | 104.26 | 99.49 | 97.38 | 76.03 | 91.60 | 114.48 | 121.44 |
| 114.60 | 89.61 | 98.04 | 99.70 | 96.53 | 95.20 | 119.17 | 113.72 |
| 107.33 | 95.05 | 105.08 | 127.56 | 100.73 | 104.83 | 101.06 | 100.95 |
| 123.72 | 92.56 | 95.65 | 96.69 | 90.31 | 89.56 | 117.03 | 98.53 |
| 114.68 | 99.67 | 95.40 | 95.50 | 94.93 | 97.60 | 100.62 | 100.10 |
| 108.19 | 98.39 | 99.82 | 100.91 | 101.62 | 99.08 | 114.14 | 120.19 |
| 111.00 | 86.47 | 93.52 | 94.45 | 83.44 | 99.13 | 117.16 | 108.23 |
| 108.26 | 89.14 | 93.87 | 94.43 | 87.95 | 95.29 | 125.17 | 102.35 |
| 99.79 | 99.82 | 104.14 | 96.62 | 96.59 | 103.64 | 106.15 | 105.34 |
| 101.39 | 100.07 | 103.87 | 101.02 | 100.37 | 98.78 | 103.45 | 104.80 |
| 101.69 | 101.26 | 99.99 | 99.81 | 99.72 | 98.36 | 100.00 | 101.23 |
| 99.27 | 98.97 | 98.59 | 102.49 | 101.04 | 101.46 | 100.93 | 99.83 |
| 99.17 | 99.66 | 97.65 | 100.96 | 100.03 | 99.29 | 100.16 | 99.79 |
| 103.10 | 98.40 | 98.82 | 99.24 | 98.61 | 98.96 | 102.82 | 102.36 |
| 84.65 | 95.43 | 94.31 | 98.88 | 96.31 | 90.16 | 102.17 | 100.06 |
| 102.01 | 98.72 | 98.01 | 98.43 | 97.05 | 100.00 | 100.09 | 100.15 |
| 95.16 | 98.52 | 99.94 | 100.12 | 99.89 | 100.87 | 104.20 | 105.84 |
| 102.17 | 98.43 | 88.75 | 91.69 | 90.21 | | | |
| 101.49 | 104.36 | 99.81 | 99.15 | 98.10 | 97.59 | 97.05 | 97.83 |
| 107.34 | 103.32 | 102.54 | 109.38 | 98.88 | 101.26 | 96.32 | 108.74 |
| 100.15 | 100.25 | 100.05 | 100.34 | 103.46 | 108.78 | 100.00 | 113.81 |

# 9-7 固定资产投资价格指数
PRICE INDEXES FOP INVESTMENT IN FIXED ASSETS

（上年价格 =100） (perceding year=100)

| 项目名称 | Item | 2005 | 2008 | 2009 | 2010 | 2011 | 2012 | 2013 | 2014 | 2015 | 2016 | 2017 | 2018 |
|---|---|---|---|---|---|---|---|---|---|---|---|---|---|
| **总计** | **Total** | **103.1** | **111.0** | **94.6** | **104.9** | **107.0** | **100.0** | **100.1** | **99.9** | **97.1** | **99.8** | **107.3** | **106.6** |
| 建筑安装、装饰工程 | Construction and Installation Project | 103.7 | 115.5 | 92.1 | 107.5 | 110.1 | 99.8 | 100.0 | 99.6 | 95.5 | 99.6 | 110.7 | 109.5 |
| 其中：人工费 | Of which： Labor Cost | 112.7 | 112.7 | 104.9 | 112.0 | 115.9 | 110.4 | 107.8 | 104.8 | 103.1 | 101.6 | 103.0 | 104.9 |
| 材料费 | Materials Expenses | 101.0 | 120.5 | 87.5 | 107.0 | 109.6 | 96.7 | 97.6 | 97.7 | 92 | 98.8 | 114.9 | 112.4 |
| 机械使用费 | Expenses on Machinery Use | 104.2 | 106.9 | 100.0 | 104.3 | 105.0 | 102.3 | 101.0 | 100.8 | 100.9 | 100.1 | 101.2 | 102.0 |
| 设备、工器具购置 | Purchase of Equipment，Tools and Instruments | 99.7 | 102.5 | 98.0 | 100.2 | 101.8 | 99.2 | 99.3 | 99.9 | 99.2 | 98.7 | 100.6 | 101.5 |
| 其他费用 | Others | 105.5 | 105.9 | 98.5 | 102.2 | 103.0 | 102.0 | 101.4 | 101.4 | 101.2 | 102.2 | 102.0 | 99.9 |

# 9-8 住宅销售价格指数（2018 年）
SALES PRICE INDEXES FOR RESIDENCE（2018）

（上年价格 =100） (perceding year=100)

| 项目 | Item | 2018 |
|---|---|---|
| **新建住宅销售价格指数** | **Sales Price Indexes for Newly Constucted Residence** | |
| 一月 | January | 103.6 |
| 二月 | February | 103.9 |
| 三月 | March | 103.3 |
| 四月 | April | 103.1 |
| 五月 | May | 104.8 |
| 六月 | June | 107.0 |
| 七月 | July | 108.8 |
| 八月 | August | 110.1 |
| 九月 | September | 110.4 |
| 十月 | October | 110.7 |
| 十一月 | November | 112.2 |
| 十二月 | December | 113.3 |
| **二手住宅销售价格指数** | **Sales Price Indexes for Secong-hand Residence** | |
| 一月 | January | 110.6 |
| 二月 | February | 108.0 |
| 三月 | March | 107.7 |
| 四月 | April | 107.7 |
| 五月 | May | 107.5 |
| 六月 | June | 107.2 |
| 七月 | July | 108.8 |
| 八月 | August | 110.4 |
| 九月 | September | 110.9 |
| 十月 | October | 111.4 |
| 十一月 | November | 111.9 |
| 十二月 | December | 111.2 |

# 9-9 居民消费价格分类指数（2018 年）
CONSUMER PRICE INDEXES BY CATEGORY（2018）

（上年价格 =100） (perceding year=100)

| 项目 | Item | 指数 Indexes |
|---|---|---|
| **居民消费价格总指数** | **Consumer Price Index** | **102.1** |
| 非食品烟酒价格指数 | Price index of non-food cigarettes and alcohol | 101.8 |
| 服务价格指数 | Price index of services | 101.6 |
| 鲜活食品价格指数 | Price index of fresh food | 105.3 |
| 消费品价格指数 | Consumer Goods Price Index | 102.4 |
| 扣除鲜菜鲜果价格指数 | Price Index Without Fersh Vegetables and Fresh Fruits | 101.8 |
| **一、食品烟酒** | **Food，cigarettes and liquor** | **102.9** |
| 1. 食品 | Food | 103.1 |
| （1）粮食 | Grain | 100.5 |
| （2）薯类 | Potatoes | 120.9 |
| （3）豆类 | Beans | 101.0 |
| （4）食用油 | Cooking Oil | 99.7 |
| （5）菜 | Vegetables | 112.9 |
| （6）畜肉类 | Livestock Products | 97.3 |
| （7）禽肉类 | Poultry Products | 106.5 |
| （8）水产品 | Aquatic Products | 104.5 |
| （9）蛋类 | Eggs | 111.4 |
| （10）奶类 | Dairy Products | 100.7 |
| （11）干鲜瓜果类 | Dried and Fresh Melons and Fruits | 102.1 |
| （12）糖果糕点类 | Candy and Pastry | 99.4 |
| （13）调味品 | Flavoring | 101.3 |
| （14）其他食品类 | Other foods | 100.3 |
| 2. 茶及饮料 | Tea and Beverages | 98.9 |
| 3. 烟酒 | Tobacco Liquor | 100.8 |
| 4. 在外餐饮 | Catering service | 103.5 |

注：2016 年起，居民消费价格调查目录进行了调整，新调查目录与国际标准更为接近。

Note：Since 2016，the consumption price investigation directory has been adjusted，and the new investigation directory is basically consistent with the household consumption expenditure catalogue.

## 9-9 续表
Continued

| 项目 | Item | 指数 Indexes |
|---|---|---|
| **二、衣着** | **Clothing** | **103.8** |
| 1. 服装 | Garments | 105.9 |
| 2. 服装材料 | Clothing material | 100.0 |
| 3. 其他衣着及配件 | Other clothing an accessories | 100.5 |
| 4. 衣着加工服务费 | Service charge of clothing processing | 100.4 |
| 5. 鞋类 | Shoes | 98.7 |
| **三、居住** | **Residence** | **100.9** |
| 1. 租赁房房租 | Rents | 100.6 |
| 2. 住房保养维修及管理 | Maintenance and management of house | 101.6 |
| 3. 水电燃料 | Water，Electricity and Fuels | 101.1 |
| 4. 自有住房 | Private Housing | 100.7 |
| **四、生活用品及服务** | **Article of daily use and service** | **101.3** |
| 1. 家具及室内装饰品 | Furniture and interior decoration | 103.2 |
| 2. 家用器具 | Home appliances | 99.4 |
| 3. 家用纺织品 | Home textile | 103.8 |
| 4. 家庭日用杂品 | Daiy Use Household Articles | 100.6 |
| 5. 个人护理用品 | Personal-care supply | 100.1 |
| 6. 家庭服务 | Household Services | 105.0 |
| **五、交通和通信** | **Transportation and Communication** | **100.8** |
| 1. 交通 | Transportation | 103.4 |
| 2. 通信 | Communication | 95.5 |
| **六、教育文化和娱乐** | **Education，culture and entertainment** | **103.1** |
| 1. 教育 | Education | 104.0 |
| 2. 文化娱乐 | Cultural | 102.3 |
| **七、医疗保健** | **Health Care** | **102.4** |
| 1. 药品及医疗器具 | Medicine and medical apparatus | 104.6 |
| 2. 医疗服务 | Medical service | 100.0 |
| **八、其他用品和服务** | **Other articles and services** | **101.3** |
| 1. 其他用品类 | Other articles | 97.3 |
| 2. 其他服务类 | Other services | 104.1 |

# 9-10 商品零售价格分类指数（2018 年）
RETAIL PRICE INDEXES BY CATEGORY (2018)

（上年 =100） (perceding year=100)

| 项目 | Item | 指数 Indexes |
|---|---|---|
| **商品零售价格总指数** | **Retail Price Indes** | **101.8** |
| **一、食品** | **Food** | **103.2** |
| 1. 粮食 | Grain | 100.5 |
| 2. 薯类 | Potatos | 120.9 |
| 3. 豆类 | Beans | 101.0 |
| 4. 食用油 | Edible oil | 99.7 |
| 5. 菜 | vegetables | 112.9 |
| 6. 畜肉类 | Stock rneat | 97.3 |
| 7. 禽肉类 | Poultiy meat | 106.5 |
| 8. 水产品 | Aquatic Products | 104.5 |
| 9. 蛋类 | Eggs | 111.4 |
| 10. 奶类 | Dairy | 100.7 |
| 11. 干鲜瓜果类 | Dried and Fresh Melon, and Fruits | 102.1 |
| 12. 糖果糕点类 | Sweets and cakes | 99.4 |
| 13. 调味品 | Flavoring | 101.3 |
| 14. 其他食品类 | Other food | 100.3 |
| 15. 在外餐饮 | Catering service | 103.5 |
| **二、饮料、烟酒** | **Beverages, Tobacco and Liquor** | **100.2** |
| 1. 茶及饮料 | Tea and Beverages | 98.9 |
| 2. 烟草 | Tobacco | 100.0 |
| 3. 酒类 | Liquor | 101.6 |
| **三、服装、鞋帽** | **Clothing** | **104.0** |
| 1. 服装 | Garments | 106.0 |
| 2. 鞋帽袜 | Footgear and Hats | 98.8 |
| 3. 其他衣着配件 | Other clothing and accessories | 100.6 |
| **四、纺织品** | **Textiles** | **104.3** |
| 1. 服装材料 | Clothing material | 100.0 |
| 2. 床上用品 | Blend Cloth | 104.9 |
| **五、家用电器及音像器材** | **Household Appliances, Music and Video Equipment** | **98.8** |
| 1. 家庭设备 | Household Facilities | 99.4 |
| 2. 文娱用耐用消费品 | Durable Consumer Goods for Cultural and Recreational Use and Services | 97.3 |
| 3. 专业音像器材 | Professional Audio and Video Equipment | 98.7 |

注：2016 年起，商品零售价格调查目录进行了微调。
Note: Contents of survey of retailing price of commodities have been finely adjusted as of 2017.

## 9-10 续表
Continued

| 项目 | Item | 指数 Indexes |
| --- | --- | --- |
| **六、文化办公用品** | **Culture and office Articles** | **100.7** |
| **七、日用品** | **Articles for Daily Use** | **100.4** |
| 1. 日用百货 | General Merchandise for Daily Use | 101.7 |
| 2. 厨具餐具茶具 | Kitchen ware，tableware，tea set | 99.4 |
| 3. 清洗用品 | Cleaning Products | 100.0 |
| 4. 其他日用品 | Other Articles for Daily Use | 99.8 |
| **八、体育娱乐用品** | **Sports and Recreation Articles** | **99.9** |
| 1. 体育户外用品 | Sports and outdoors | 99.7 |
| 2. 娱乐用品 | Recreation Articles | 100.0 |
| **九、交通、通信用品** | **Transportation and Communication Appliances** | **97.3** |
| 1. 交通运输机械 | Transportation Machines | 99.0 |
| 2. 通信器材 | Communication Equipment | 88.7 |
| **十、家具** | **Furniture** | **103.1** |
| **十一、化妆品** | **Cosmetics** | **100.2** |
| **十二、金银饰品** | **Gold，Silver and Jewelry** | **96.0** |
| **十三、中西药品及医疗保健用品** | **Traditional Chinese and Western Medicals and Health Care Articles** | **105.1** |
| 1. 医疗卫生器具 | Medical apparatus | 100.1 |
| 2. 中药 | Herbal medicine | 109.0 |
| 3. 西药 | Western Medicines | 104.7 |
| 4. 保健器具及用品 | Health Care Articles | 101.8 |
| **十四、书报杂志及电子出版物** | **Books，Newspapers，Magazines and Electronic Publications** | **102.5** |
| 1. 教材及参考书 | Teaching Material and Reference Books | 102.3 |
| 2. 书报杂志 | Books，Mewspapers and Magazines | 101.9 |
| 3. 计算机办公软件 | Computer office software | 106.2 |
| **十五、燃料** | **Fuels** | **109.7** |
| 1. 煤炭及制品 | Coal and Its Products | 107.6 |
| 2. 石油及制品 | Pertoleum and Its Products | 109.8 |
| **十六、建筑材料及五金电料** | **Building Materials and Hardware** | **100.7** |
| 1. 建筑装璜材料 | Building Decoration Materials | 99.4 |
| 2. 五金水暖 | Hardware | 104.2 |

# 主要统计指标解释

**居民消费价格指数**　是反映一定时期内城乡居民所购买的生活消费品价格和服务项目价格变动趋势和程度的相对数，是对城市居民消费价格指数和农村居民消费价格指数进行综合汇总计算的结果。该指数可以观察和分析消费品的零售价格和服务价格变动对城乡居民实际生活费支出的影响程度。

**商品零售价格指数**　是反映一定时期内城乡商品零售价格变动趋势和程度的相对数。商品零售价格的变动直接影响到城乡居民的生活支出和国家的财政收入，影响居民购买力和市场供需的平衡，影响到消费与积累的比例关系。因此，该指数可以从一个侧面对上述经济活动进行观察和分析。

**工业生产者出厂价格指数**　是反映一定时期内全部工业产品出厂价格总水平的变动趋势和程度的相对数，包括工业企业售给本企业以外所有单位的各种产品和直接售给居民用于生活消费的产品。该指数可以观察出厂价格变动对工业总产值及增加值的影响。

**工业生产者购进价格指数**　是反映工业企业作为生产投入，而从物资交易市场和能源、原材料生产企业购买原材料、燃料和动力产品时，所支付的价格水平变动趋势和程度的统计指标，是扣除工业企业物质消耗成本中的价格变动影响的重要依据。

**房地产价格指数**　是反映一定时期内房地产价格变动趋势和程度的相对数，包括新建住宅销售价格指数、二手住宅销售价格指数。

# Explanatory Notes on Main Statistical Indicators

**Consumer Price Indices**　reflect the trend and degree of changes in prices of consumer goods and services purchased by urban and rural households during a given period. They are obtained by combining the Urban Consumer Price Indices and the Rural Consumer Price Indices. The Indices enable the observation and analysis of the degree of impact of the changes in the prices of retailed goods and services on the actual living expenses of urban and rural residents.

**Retail Price Indices**　reflect the trend and degree of change in retail prices of commodities during a given period. The change in retail prices of commodities directly affect the living expenditure of urban and rural residents, government revenue, purchasing power of residents and the equilibrium of market supply and demand, and the ratio of consumption to accumulation. Therefore, the retail price indices are useful to analyze the changes of the above economic activities.

**Producer Price Indices for Industrial Producers**　reflect the trend and degree of changes in general ex-factory prices of all industrial products during a given period, including sales of industrial products by an industrial enterprise to all units outside the enterprise, as well as sales of consumer goods to residents. It can be used to analyze the impact of ex-factory prices on gross output value and value-added of the industrial sector.

**Purchasing Price Indices for Industrial Producers**　reflect changes in the level and degree of prices paid by industrial enterprises when they purchase production input such as raw materials, fuels and power from the market or from other energy or raw materials producing enterprises. These indices provide important basis for measuring the material consumption of industrial enterprises after removing influence of price changes.

**Price Indices for Real Estate** reflect the trend and degree of changes in prices of real estate during a given period, including sales price indices for newly constructed residential buildings and secondhand residential buildings.

# 人民生活 10

# PEOPLE'S LIVING CONDITIONS

# 简要说明

**一、本篇资料的主要内容**

本篇资料主要反映了全市居民的家庭收支、居住、家庭消费构成、耐用消费品拥有量等方面的情况。

**二、本篇资料的来源**

本篇资料中相关数据来源于居民收支调查年报，由国家统计局青岛调查队住户调查处整理提供。

# Brief Introduction

***I. Main Content***

This section mainly reflects the residents' household income and expenditure, housing, household consumption structure, quantity of durable consumer goods possessed and other information.

***II. Source of Data***

The relevant data in this material comes from the annual report of the residents' income and expenditure survey, which is provided by the Investigation Team of the Investigation Team of the National Bureau of Statistics.

# 10-1 城市居民收支（1978-2014 年）
INCOME AND EXPENDITURE DF URBAN RESIDENTS（1978-2014）

| 年份<br>Year | 城市居民人均可支配收入（元）<br>Aunual Per Capita Disposable Income of Urban Households（yuan） | 城市居民人均消费性支出（元）<br>Per Capita Consumption Expenditure of Urban Households（yuan） | 城市恩格尔系数（%）<br>Engel coefficient（%） |
|---|---|---|---|
| 1978 | 336 | 321 | |
| 1979 | 380 | 360 | |
| 1980 | 537 | 495 | |
| 1981 | 500 | 490 | 57.8 |
| 1982 | 528 | 484 | 61.6 |
| 1983 | 549 | 510 | 63.7 |
| 1984 | 665 | 580 | 62.8 |
| 1985 | 733 | 681 | 58.6 |
| 1986 | 882 | 806 | 59.2 |
| 1987 | 1089 | 996 | 58.1 |
| 1988 | 1225 | 1278 | 55.9 |
| 1989 | 1455 | 1439 | 57.8 |
| 1990 | 1624 | 1507 | 58.4 |
| 1991 | 1856 | 1767 | 57.4 |
| 1992 | 2138 | 1956 | 57.0 |
| 1993 | 2668 | 2445 | 51.8 |
| 1994 | 3880 | 3479 | 53.2 |
| 1995 | 5357 | 4606 | 52.5 |
| 1996 | 5602 | 5079 | 51.8 |
| 1997 | 6222 | 5525 | 48.2 |
| 1998 | 6554 | 5565 | 46.4 |
| 1999 | 7282 | 5981 | 44.5 |
| 2000 | 8016 | 6677 | 42.5 |
| 2001 | 8731 | 6849 | 41.9 |
| 2002 | 8721 | 7344 | 40.5 |
| 2003 | 10075 | 8056 | 39.3 |
| 2004 | 11089 | 9002 | 38.0 |
| 2005 | 12920 | 9883 | 37.6 |
| 2006 | 15328 | 11945 | 36.4 |
| 2007 | 17856 | 13376 | 37.0 |
| 2008 | 20464 | 14999 | 37.4 |
| 2009 | 22368 | 16080 | 38.5 |
| 2010 | 24998 | 17531 | 37.4 |
| 2011 | 28567 | 19297 | 37.5 |
| 2012 | 32145 | 20391 | 36.5 |
| 2013 | 35227 | 22060 | 36.5 |
| 2014 | 38294 | 24016 | 35.7 |

注：2002 年开始城市居民可支配收入为新计算口径。

Note：From 2002 on，disposable income of urban residents are counted by new gauges.

# 10-2 农村居民收支（1978-2014 年）
INCOME AND EXPENDITURE DF RURAL RESIDENTS（1978-2014）

| 年份 Year | 农民人均纯收入（元） Aunual Per Capita Net Income of Rural Households（yuan） | 农村居民人均生活消费支出（元） Per Capita Consumption Expenditure of Rural Households（yuan） | 农村恩格尔系数（%） Engel coefficient（%） |
|---|---|---|---|
| 1978 | 146 | 109 | 59.3 |
| 1979 | 153 | 129 | 58.4 |
| 1980 | 209 | 142 | 54.9 |
| 1981 | 218 | 163 | 44.3 |
| 1982 | 273 | 199 | 52.9 |
| 1983 | 399 | 277 | 52.8 |
| 1984 | 452 | 304 | 50.0 |
| 1985 | 567 | 376 | 47.8 |
| 1986 | 647 | 474 | 46.4 |
| 1987 | 730 | 462 | 42.9 |
| 1988 | 820 | 439 | 38.8 |
| 1989 | 876 | 510 | 38.9 |
| 1990 | 952 | 494 | 41.5 |
| 1991 | 1021 | 546 | 41.3 |
| 1992 | 1029 | 572 | 41.7 |
| 1993 | 1255 | 743 | 42.7 |
| 1994 | 1694 | 1384 | 54.5 |
| 1995 | 2225 | 1641 | 55.7 |
| 1996 | 2625 | 2173 | 50.5 |
| 1997 | 2599 | 2150 | 52.9 |
| 1998 | 3177 | 2119 | 49.5 |
| 1999 | 3415 | 2150 | 47.3 |
| 2000 | 3637 | 2380 | 43.2 |
| 2001 | 3901 | 2618 | 41.2 |
| 2002 | 4195 | 2820 | 38.9 |
| 2003 | 4530 | 2988 | 38.0 |
| 2004 | 5080 | 3353 | 38.7 |
| 2005 | 5806 | 3737 | 37.5 |
| 2006 | 6546 | 4203 | 36.6 |
| 2007 | 7477 | 4736 | 37.2 |
| 2008 | 8509 | 5303 | 37.7 |
| 2009 | 9249 | 5832 | 36.4 |
| 2010 | 10550 | 6662 | 35.5 |
| 2011 | 12370 | 7661 | 36.6 |
| 2012 | 13990 | 8653 | 36.2 |
| 2013 | 15731 | 9786 | 34.9 |
| 2014 | 17461 | 10808 | 33.8 |

## 10-3 城乡居民住房面积（1990-2014年）
HOUSING AREA OF URBAN AND RUREL RESIDENTS（1990-2014）

| 年份 Year | 城市居民人均现住房建筑面积（平方米） Per Capita Home Floor Area of Urban Residents（square meter） | 农村居民人均居住面积（平方米） Per Capita Housing Area of Rural Residents（square meter） |
|---|---|---|
| 1990 | 14.16 | 19.60 |
| 1995 | 17.12 | 23.03 |
| 2000 | 20.76 | 25.88 |
| 2001 | 21.86 | 26.59 |
| 2002 | 22.76 | 27.00 |
| 2003 | 23.73 | 27.00 |
| 2004 | 24.22 | 27.99 |
| 2005 | 22.96 | 29.54 |
| 2006 | 23.73 | 30.82 |
| 2007 | 23.72 | 30.95 |
| 2008 | 26.83 | 30.73 |
| 2009 | 26.71 | 31.39 |
| 2010 | 27.42 | 30.97 |
| 2011 | 27.67 | 31.73 |
| 2012 | 27.86 | 32.32 |
| 2013 | 29.12 | 33.50 |
| 2014 | 29.80 | 34.20 |

# 10-4 全体居民家庭基本情况（2015 年）
BASIC INFORMATION ON ALL HOUSEHOLDS (2015)

| 指标名称 | Name | 单位 | Unit | 2015 | 2014 | 2015 年比 2014 年增长（±%）2015/2014（±%） |
|---|---|---|---|---|---|---|
| **人均可支配收入** | **Per Capita Disposable Income** | **元** | **yuan** | **32885** | **30273** | **8.6** |
| （一）工资性收入 | Income from Wages and Salaries | 元 | yuan | 20068 | 18348 | 9.4 |
| （二）经营净收入 | Net Income from Household Operations | 元 | yuan | 6480 | 6035 | 7.4 |
| （三）财产净收入 | Income from Properties | 元 | yuan | 2522 | 2396 | 5.2 |
| （四）转移净收入 | Income from Transfers | 元 | yuan | 3815 | 3494 | 9.2 |
| **人均消费支出** | **Per Capita Consumption Expenditure** | **元** | **yuan** | **21326** | **19653** | **8.5** |
| （一）食品烟酒 | Food, Tobacco and Iquor | 元 | yuan | 6459 | 5970 | 8.2 |
| （二）衣着 | Cloth | 元 | yuan | 2096 | 1944 | 7.8 |
| （三）居住 | Residence | 元 | yuan | 4584 | 4316 | 6.2 |
| （四）生活用品及服务 | Household Facilities, Articles and Services | 元 | yuan | 1485 | 1374 | 8.1 |
| （五）交通通信 | Transportation and Communication | 元 | yuan | 3226 | 2905 | 11.0 |
| （六）教育文化娱乐 | Education, Cultural and Recreation Services | 元 | yuan | 1830 | 1654 | 10.6 |
| （七）医疗保健 | Health Care and Medical Services | 元 | yuan | 1115 | 1002 | 11.2 |
| （八）其他用品和服务 | Other Goods and Services | 元 | yuan | 531 | 488 | 8.8 |
| **城镇居民人均现住房建筑面积** | **Per Capita Building Space in Urban Areas** | **平方米** | **sq.m** | **31.5** | | |
| **农村居民人均现住房建筑面积** | **Per Capita Living Space in Rural Areas** | **平方米** | **sq.m** | **32.4** | | |

注：自 2015 年开始，全市城乡住户调查统一使用一体化改革后的数据，与原数据相比，城乡居民收支指标的调查范围和口径均存较大变化。原“城市居民人均可支配收入”调整为“城镇居民人均可支配收入”；原“农民人均纯收入”调整为“农村居民人均可支配收入”。2014 年数据也为新口径，与 2015 年年鉴数据不一致。2014 年农村居民住房为拥有面积，2015 年为现住房建筑面积。

Note: From 2015 on, the data used are statistics of the integrated survey of residents in urban and rural areas. Compared with previous data, there is a significant change in statistic coverage and gauge for indicators of urban and rural residents' income and expenditure. The 'per capita disposable income of residents in cities was changed to' per capita disposable income of urban residents'; the 'pe capita net income of farmers' was changed to 'per capita disposable income of rural residents. Data in 2014 are counted by new gauge and they are different from the data in last yrar's yearbook. As for the statistics of rural resident homes, the owned house area was taken in 2014, but in 2015, the construction area was counted.

# 10-5 全体居民家庭基本情况（2016 年）
BASIC INFORMATION ON ALL HOUSEHOLDS（2016）

| 指标名称 | Name | 单位 | Unit | 2016 | 2015 | 2016 年比 2015 年增长（±%）2016/2015（±%） |
|---|---|---|---|---|---|---|
| **人均可支配收入** | **Per Capita Disposable Income** | **元** | **yuan** | **35680** | **32885** | **8.5** |
| （一）工资性收入 | Income from Wages and Salaries | 元 | yuan | 21700 | 20068 | 8.1 |
| （二）经营净收入 | Net Income from Household Operations | 元 | yuan | 7011 | 6480 | 8.2 |
| （三）财产净收入 | Income from Properties | 元 | yuan | 2781 | 2522 | 10.3 |
| （四）转移净收入 | Income from Transfers | 元 | yuan | 4188 | 3815 | 9.8 |
| **人均消费支出** | **Per Capita Consumption Expenditure** | **元** | **yuan** | **23256** | **21326** | **9.0** |
| （一）食品烟酒 | Food，Tobacco and Iquor | 元 | yuan | 6983 | 6459 | 8.1 |
| （二）衣着 | Cloth | 元 | yuan | 2271 | 2096 | 8.4 |
| （三）居住 | Residence | 元 | yuan | 5018 | 4584 | 9.5 |
| （四）生活用品及服务 | Household Facilities，Articles and Services | 元 | yuan | 1607 | 1485 | 8.2 |
| （五）交通通信 | Transportation and Communication | 元 | yuan | 3479 | 3226 | 7.8 |
| （六）教育文化娱乐 | Education，Cultural and Recreation Services | 元 | yuan | 2075 | 1830 | 13.4 |
| （七）医疗保健 | Health Care and Medical Services | 元 | yuan | 1233 | 1115 | 10.6 |
| （八）其他用品和服务 | Other Goods and Services | 元 | yuan | 590 | 531 | 11.2 |
| **城镇居民人均现住房建筑面积** | **Per Capita Building Space in Urban Areas** | **平方米** | **sq.m** | **31.7** | **31.5** | **0.6** |
| **农村居民人均现住房建筑面积** | **Per Capita Living Space in Rural Areas** | **平方米** | **sq.m** | **33.2** | **32.4** | **2.5** |

# 10-6 全体居民家庭基本情况（2017 年）
BASIC INFORMATION ON ALL HOUSEHOLDS（2017）

| 指标名称 | Name | 单位 | Unit | 2017 | 2016 | 2017 年比 2016 年增长（±%）2017/2016（±%） |
|---|---|---|---|---|---|---|
| **人均可支配收入** | **Per Capita Disposable Income** | **元** | **yuan** | **38763** | **35680** | **8.6** |
| （一）工资性收入 | Income from Wages and Salaries | 元 | yuan | 23514 | 21700 | 8.4 |
| （二）经营净收入 | Net Income from Household Operations | 元 | yuan | 7485 | 7011 | 6.8 |
| （三）财产净收入 | Income from Properties | 元 | yuan | 3082 | 2781 | 10.8 |
| （四）转移净收入 | Income from Transfers | 元 | yuan | 4682 | 4188 | 11.8 |
| **人均消费支出** | **Per Capita Consumption Expenditure** | **元** | **yuan** | **25232** | **23256** | **8.5** |
| （一）食品烟酒 | Food，Tobacco and Iquor | 元 | yuan | 7489 | 6983 | 7.2 |
| （二）衣着 | Cloth | 元 | yuan | 2467 | 2271 | 8.6 |
| （三）居住 | Residence | 元 | yuan | 5454 | 5018 | 8.7 |
| （四）生活用品及服务 | Household Facilities，Articles and Services | 元 | yuan | 1747 | 1607 | 8.7 |
| （五）交通通信 | Transportation and Communication | 元 | yuan | 3753 | 3479 | 7.9 |
| （六）教育文化娱乐 | Education，Cultural and Recreation Services | 元 | yuan | 2347 | 2075 | 13.1 |
| （七）医疗保健 | Health Care and Medical Services | 元 | yuan | 1350 | 1233 | 9.5 |
| （八）其他用品和服务 | Other Goods and Services | 元 | yuan | 625 | 590 | 6.0 |
| **城镇居民人均现住房建筑面积** | **Per Capita Building Space in Urban Areas** | **平方米** | **sq.m** | **32.7** | **31.7** | **3.2** |
| **农村居民人均现住房建筑面积** | **Per Capita Living Space in Rural Areas** | **平方米** | **sq.m** | **34.8** | **33.2** | **4.8** |

# 10-7 全体居民家庭基本情况（2018 年）
BASIC INFORMATION ON ALL HOUSEHOLDS（2018）

| 指标名称 | Name | 单位 | Unit | 2018 | 2017 | 2018 年比 2017 年增长（±%）<br>2018/2017（±%） |
|---|---|---|---|---|---|---|
| **人均可支配收入** | **Per Capita Disposable Income** | **元** | **yuan** | **42019** | **38763** | **8.4** |
| （一）工资性收入 | Income from Wages and Salaries | 元 | yuan | 25303 | 23514 | 7.6 |
| （二）经营净收入 | Net Income from Household Operations | 元 | yuan | 8027 | 7485 | 7.3 |
| （三）财产净收入 | Income from Properties | 元 | yuan | 3475 | 3082 | 12.8 |
| （四）转移净收入 | Income from Transfers | 元 | yuan | 5214 | 4682 | 11.3 |
| **人均消费支出** | **Per Capita Consumption Expenditure** | **元** | **yuan** | **27316** | **25232** | **8.3** |
| （一）食品烟酒 | Food，Tobacco and Iquor | 元 | yuan | 7787 | 7489 | 4.0 |
| （二）衣着 | Cloth | 元 | yuan | 2538 | 2467 | 2.9 |
| （三）居住 | Residence | 元 | yuan | 6365 | 5454 | 16.7 |
| （四）生活用品及服务 | Household Facilities，Articles and Services | 元 | yuan | 1837 | 1747 | 5.1 |
| （五）交通通信 | Transportation and Communication | 元 | yuan | 4084 | 3753 | 8.8 |
| （六）教育文化娱乐 | Education，Cultural and Recreation Services | 元 | yuan | 2571 | 2347 | 9.5 |
| （七）医疗保健 | Health Care and Medical Services | 元 | yuan | 1480 | 1350 | 9.6 |
| （八）其他用品和服务 | Other Goods and Services | 元 | yuan | 654 | 625 | 4.6 |
| **城镇居民人均现住房建筑面积** | **Per Capita Building Space in Urban Areas** | **平方米** | **sq.m** | **32.9** | **32.7** | **0.8** |
| **农村居民人均现住房建筑面积** | **Per Capita Living Space in Rural Areas** | **平方米** | **sq.m** | **35.9** | **34.8** | **3.1** |

# 10-8 城镇居民家庭基本情况（2015 年）
BASIC CONDITIONS OF URBAN HOUSEHOLDS（2015）

| 指标名称 | Name | 单位 | Unit | 2015 | 2014 | 2015 年比 2014 年增长（±%）2015/2014（±%） |
|---|---|---|---|---|---|---|
| **人均可支配收入** | **Per Capita Disposable Income** | **元** | **yuan** | **40370** | **37346** | **8.1** |
| （一）工资性收入 | Income from Wages and Salaries | 元 | yuan | 25040 | 23034 | 8.7 |
| （二）经营净收入 | Net Income from Household Operations | 元 | yuan | 6277 | 5818 | 7.9 |
| （三）财产净收入 | Income from Properties | 元 | yuan | 3580 | 3436 | 4.2 |
| （四）转移净收入 | Income from Transfers | 元 | yuan | 5473 | 5058 | 8.2 |
| **人均消费支出** | **Per Capita Consumption Expenditure** | **元** | **yuan** | **26052** | **24122** | **8.0** |
| （一）食品烟酒 | Food，Tobacco and Iquor | 元 | yuan | 7856 | 7295 | 7.7 |
| （二）衣着 | Cloth | 元 | yuan | 2685 | 2497 | 7.5 |
| （三）居住 | Residence | 元 | yuan | 5607 | 5302 | 5.8 |
| （四）生活用品及服务 | Household Facilities，Articles and Services | 元 | yuan | 1819 | 1686 | 7.9 |
| （五）交通通信 | Transportation and Communication | 元 | yuan | 3810 | 3455 | 10.3 |
| （六）教育文化娱乐 | Education，Cultural and Recreation Services | 元 | yuan | 2264 | 2057 | 10.0 |
| （七）医疗保健 | Health Care and Medical Services | 元 | yuan | 1352 | 1227 | 10.2 |
| （八）其他用品和服务 | Other Goods and Services | 元 | yuan | 659 | 603 | 9.3 |

注：本表数据为新口径，2014 年数据与 2015 年年鉴数据不一致。

Note：The data in this sheet is in line with new statistic caliber，which leads to the inconsistency between the data of 2014 and of 2015.

# 10-9 城镇居民家庭基本情况（2016 年）
BASIC CONDITIONS OF URBAN HOUSEHOLDS（2016）

| 指标名称 | Name | 单位 | Unit | 2016 | 2015 | 2016 年比 2015 年增长（±%）<br>2016/2015（±%） |
|---|---|---|---|---|---|---|
| **人均可支配收入** | **Per Capita Disposable Income** | **元** | **yuan** | **43598** | **40370** | **8.0** |
| （一）工资性收入 | Income from Wages and Salaries | 元 | yuan | 26898 | 25040 | 7.4 |
| （二）经营净收入 | Net Income from Household Operations | 元 | yuan | 6846 | 6277 | 9.1 |
| （三）财产净收入 | Income from Properties | 元 | yuan | 3909 | 3580 | 9.2 |
| （四）转移净收入 | Income from Transfers | 元 | yuan | 5945 | 5473 | 8.6 |
| **人均消费支出** | **Per Capita Consumption Expenditure** | **元** | **yuan** | **28285** | **26052** | **8.6** |
| （一）食品烟酒 | Food，Tobacco and Iquor | 元 | yuan | 8473 | 7856 | 7.9 |
| （二）衣着 | Cloth | 元 | yuan | 2882 | 2685 | 7.4 |
| （三）居住 | Residence | 元 | yuan | 6105 | 5607 | 8.9 |
| （四）生活用品及服务 | Household Facilities，Articles and Services | 元 | yuan | 1962 | 1819 | 7.8 |
| （五）交通通信 | Transportation and Communication | 元 | yuan | 4039 | 3810 | 7.3 |
| （六）教育文化娱乐 | Education，Cultural and Recreation Services | 元 | yuan | 2553 | 2264 | 12.8 |
| （七）医疗保健 | Health Care and Medical Services | 元 | yuan | 1490 | 1352 | 10.2 |
| （八）其他用品和服务 | Other Goods and Services | 元 | yuan | 731 | 659 | 10.8 |

# 10-10 城镇居民家庭基本情况（2017年）
## BASIC CONDITIONS OF URBAN HOUSEHOLDS（2017）

| 指标名称 | Name | 单位 | Unit | 2017 | 2016 | 2017年比2016年增长（±%）<br>2017/2016（±%） |
|---|---|---|---|---|---|---|
| **人均可支配收入** | **Per Capita Disposable Income** | **元** | **yuan** | **47176** | **43598** | **8.2** |
| （一）工资性收入 | Income from Wages and Salaries | 元 | yuan | 28992 | 26898 | 7.8 |
| （二）经营净收入 | Net Income from Household Operations | 元 | yuan | 7299 | 6846 | 6.6 |
| （三）财产净收入 | Income from Properties | 元 | yuan | 4297 | 3909 | 9.9 |
| （四）转移净收入 | Income from Transfers | 元 | yuan | 6588 | 5945 | 10.8 |
| **人均消费支出** | **Per Capita Consumption Expenditure** | **元** | **yuan** | **30569** | **28285** | **8.1** |
| （一）食品烟酒 | Food，Tobacco and Iquor | 元 | yuan | 9059 | 8473 | 6.9 |
| （二）衣着 | Cloth | 元 | yuan | 3117 | 2882 | 8.1 |
| （三）居住 | Residence | 元 | yuan | 6605 | 6105 | 8.2 |
| （四）生活用品及服务 | Household Facilities，Articles and Services | 元 | yuan | 2121 | 1962 | 8.1 |
| （五）交通通信 | Transportation and Communication | 元 | yuan | 4399 | 4089 | 7.6 |
| （六）教育文化娱乐 | Education，Cultural and Recreation Services | 元 | yuan | 2875 | 2553 | 12.6 |
| （七）医疗保健 | Health Care and Medical Services | 元 | yuan | 1624 | 1490 | 9.0 |
| （八）其他用品和服务 | Other Goods and Services | 元 | yuan | 769 | 731 | 5.2 |

# 10-11 城镇居民家庭基本情况（2018 年）
BASIC CONDITIONS OF URBAN HOUSEHOLDS（2018）

| 指标名称 | Name | 单位 | Unit | 2018 | 2017 | 2018 年比 2017 年增长（±%）<br>2018/2017（±%） |
|---|---|---|---|---|---|---|
| **人均可支配收入** | **Per Capita Disposable Income** | 元 | **yuan** | **50817** | **47176** | **7.7** |
| （一）工资性收入 | Income from Wages and Salaries | 元 | yuan | 30955 | 28992 | 6.8 |
| （二）经营净收入 | Net Income from Household Operations | 元 | yuan | 7836 | 7299 | 7.4 |
| （三）财产净收入 | Income from Properties | 元 | yuan | 4789 | 4297 | 11.4 |
| （四）转移净收入 | Income from Transfers | 元 | yuan | 7237 | 6588 | 9.9 |
| **人均消费支出** | **Per Capita Consumption Expenditure** | 元 | **yuan** | **32890** | **30569** | **7.6** |
| （一）食品烟酒 | Food，Tobacco and Iquor | 元 | yuan | 9318 | 9059 | 2.9 |
| （二）衣着 | Cloth | 元 | yuan | 3168 | 3117 | 1.7 |
| （三）居住 | Residence | 元 | yuan | 7751 | 6605 | 17.3 |
| （四）生活用品及服务 | Household Facilities，Articles and Services | 元 | yuan | 2207 | 2121 | 4.0 |
| （五）交通通信 | Transportation and Communication | 元 | yuan | 4765 | 4399 | 8.3 |
| （六）教育文化娱乐 | Education，Cultural and Recreation Services | 元 | yuan | 3122 | 2875 | 8.6 |
| （七）医疗保健 | Health Care and Medical Services | 元 | yuan | 1764 | 1624 | 8.6 |
| （八）其他用品和服务 | Other Goods and Services | 元 | yuan | 795 | 769 | 3.4 |

# 10-12 农村居民家庭基本情况（2015 年）
BASIC CONDITIONS OF RURAL HOUSEHOLDS（2015）

| 指标名称 | Name | 单位 | Unit | 2015 | 2014 | 2015 年比 2014 年增长（±%）<br>2015/2014（±%） |
|---|---|---|---|---|---|---|
| **人均可支配收入** | **Per Capita Disposable Income** | **元** | **yuan** | **16730** | **15434** | **8.4** |
| （一）工资性收入 | Income from Wages and Salaries | 元 | yuan | 9337 | 8517 | 9.6 |
| （二）经营净收入 | Net Income from Household Operations | 元 | yuan | 6919 | 6489 | 6.6 |
| （三）财产净收入 | Income from Properties | 元 | yuan | 236 | 216 | 9.3 |
| （四）转移净收入 | Income from Transfers | 元 | yuan | 238 | 212 | 12.4 |
| **人均消费支出** | **Per Capita Consumption Expenditure** | **元** | **yuan** | **11127** | **10277** | **8.3** |
| （一）食品烟酒 | Food，Tobacco and Iquor | 元 | yuan | 3442 | 3188 | 8.0 |
| （二）衣着 | Cloth | 元 | yuan | 826 | 784 | 5.3 |
| （三）居住 | Residence | 元 | yuan | 2377 | 2248 | 5.8 |
| （四）生活用品及服务 | Household Facilities，Articles and Services | 元 | yuan | 765 | 720 | 6.2 |
| （五）交通通信 | Transportation and Communication | 元 | yuan | 1965 | 1751 | 12.2 |
| （六）教育文化娱乐 | Education，Cultural and Recreation Services | 元 | yuan | 895 | 809 | 10.6 |
| （七）医疗保健 | Health Care and Medical Services | 元 | yuan | 604 | 532 | 13.5 |
| （八）其他用品和服务 | Other Goods and Services | 元 | yuan | 253 | 245 | 3.3 |

注：本表数据为新口径，2014 年与去年年鉴数据不一致。

Note：The data in this sheet is in line with new statistic caliber，which leads to the inconsistency between the data of 2014 and of 2015.

# 10-13 农村居民家庭基本情况（2016年）
BASIC CONDITIONS OF RURAL HOUSEHOLDS（2015）

| 指标名称 | Name | 单位 | Unit | 2016 | 2015 | 2016年比2015年增长（±%）2016/2015（±%） |
|---|---|---|---|---|---|---|
| **人均可支配收入** | **Per Capita Disposable Income** | **元** | **yuan** | **17969** | **16730** | **7.4** |
| （一）工资性收入 | Income from Wages and Salaries | 元 | yuan | 10074 | 9337 | 7.9 |
| （二）经营净收入 | Net Income from Household Operations | 元 | yuan | 7381 | 6919 | 6.7 |
| （三）财产净收入 | Income from Properties | 元 | yuan | 256 | 236 | 8.6 |
| （四）转移净收入 | Income from Transfers | 元 | yuan | 258 | 238 | 8.2 |
| **人均消费支出** | **Per Capita Consumption Expenditure** | **元** | **yuan** | **12006** | **11127** | **7.9** |
| （一）食品烟酒 | Food，Tobacco and Iquor | 元 | yuan | 3651 | 3442 | 6.1 |
| （二）衣着 | Cloth | 元 | yuan | 905 | 826 | 9.5 |
| （三）居住 | Residence | 元 | yuan | 2586 | 2377 | 8.8 |
| （四）生活用品及服务 | Household Facilities，Articles and Services | 元 | yuan | 814 | 765 | 6.4 |
| （五）交通通信 | Transportation and Communication | 元 | yuan | 2113 | 1965 | 7.5 |
| （六）教育文化娱乐 | Education，Cultural and Recreation Services | 元 | yuan | 1004 | 895 | 12.2 |
| （七）医疗保健 | Health Care and Medical Services | 元 | yuan | 658 | 604 | 9.0 |
| （八）其他用品和服务 | Other Goods and Services | 元 | yuan | 275 | 253 | 8.8 |

# 10-14 农村居民家庭基本情况（2017 年）
## BASIC CONDITIONS OF RURAL HOUSEHOLDS（2017）

| 指标名称 | Name | 单位 | Unit | 2017 | 2016 | 2017 年比 2016 年增长（±%）<br>2017/2016（±%） |
|---|---|---|---|---|---|---|
| **人均可支配收入** | **Per Capita Disposable Income** | **元** | **yuan** | **19364** | **17969** | **7.8** |
| （一）工资性收入 | Income from Wages and Salaries | 元 | yuan | 10882 | 10074 | 8.0 |
| （二）经营净收入 | Net Income from Household Operations | 元 | yuan | 7913 | 7381 | 7.2 |
| （三）财产净收入 | Income from Properties | 元 | yuan | 280 | 256 | 9.0 |
| （四）转移净收入 | Income from Transfers | 元 | yuan | 289 | 258 | 12.2 |
| **人均消费支出** | **Per Capita Consumption Expenditure** | **元** | **yuan** | **12928** | **12006** | **7.7** |
| （一）食品烟酒 | Food，Tobacco and Iquor | 元 | yuan | 3869 | 3651 | 6.0 |
| （二）衣着 | Cloth | 元 | yuan | 971 | 905 | 7.3 |
| （三）居住 | Residence | 元 | yuan | 2801 | 2586 | 8.3 |
| （四）生活用品及服务 | Household Facilities，Articles and Services | 元 | yuan | 885 | 814 | 8.8 |
| （五）交通通信 | Transportation and Communication | 元 | yuan | 2262 | 2113 | 7.0 |
| （六）教育文化娱乐 | Education，Cultural and Recreation Services | 元 | yuan | 1129 | 1004 | 12.4 |
| （七）医疗保健 | Health Care and Medical Services | 元 | yuan | 717 | 658 | 9.0 |
| （八）其他用品和服务 | Other Goods and Services | 元 | yuan | 294 | 275 | 6.8 |

# 10-15 农村居民家庭基本情况（2018 年）
BASIC CONDITIONS OF RURAL HOUSEHOLDS（2018）

| 指标名称 | Name | 单位 | Unit | 2018 | 2017 | 2018 年比 2017 年增长（±%）<br>2018/2017（±%） |
|---|---|---|---|---|---|---|
| **人均可支配收入** | **Per Capita Disposable Income** | **元** | **yuan** | **20820** | **19364** | **7.5** |
| （一）工资性收入 | Income from Wages and Salaries | 元 | yuan | 11684 | 10882 | 7.4 |
| （二）经营净收入 | Net Income from Household Operations | 元 | yuan | 8487 | 7913 | 7.3 |
| （三）财产净收入 | Income from Properties | 元 | yuan | 310 | 280 | 10.8 |
| （四）转移净收入 | Income from Transfers | 元 | yuan | 339 | 289 | 17.1 |
| **人均消费支出** | **Per Capita Consumption Expenditure** | **元** | **yuan** | **13885** | **12928** | **7.4** |
| （一）食品烟酒 | Food，Tobacco and Iquor | 元 | yuan | 4098 | 3869 | 5.9 |
| （二）衣着 | Cloth | 元 | yuan | 1020 | 971 | 5.1 |
| （三）居住 | Residence | 元 | yuan | 3024 | 2801 | 8.0 |
| （四）生活用品及服务 | Household Facilities，Articles and Services | 元 | yuan | 945 | 885 | 6.7 |
| （五）交通通信 | Transportation and Communication | 元 | yuan | 2445 | 2262 | 8.1 |
| （六）教育文化娱乐 | Education，Cultural and Recreation Services | 元 | yuan | 1245 | 1129 | 10.3 |
| （七）医疗保健 | Health Care and Medical Services | 元 | yuan | 794 | 717 | 10.6 |
| （八）其他用品和服务 | Other Goods and Services | 元 | yuan | 314 | 294 | 6.9 |

# 10-16 全体居民家庭消费构成
HOUSEHOLDS CONSUMPTION STRUCTURE

| 项目 | Item | 2014年 | | 2015年 | | 2016年 | | 2017年 | | 2018年 | |
|---|---|---|---|---|---|---|---|---|---|---|---|
| | | 年人均支出金额（元） Per Capita Annual Expenditure（yuan） | 占消费支出的比重（%） Percentage to Consumption Expenditure（%） | 年人均支出金额（元） Per Capita Annual Expenditure（yuan） | 占消费支出的比重（%） Percentage to Consumption Expenditure（%） | 年人均支出金额（元） Per Capita Annual Expenditure（yuan） | 占消费支出的比重（%） Percentage to Consumption Expenditure（%） | 年人均支出金额（元） Per Capita Annual Expenditure（yuan） | 占消费支出的比重（%） Percentage to Consumption Expenditure（%） | 年人均支出金额（元） Per Capita Annual Expenditure（yuan） | 占消费支出的比重（%） Percentage to Consumption Expenditure（%） |
| **消费支出** | **Consumption Expenditure** | **19653** | **100** | **21326** | **100** | **23256** | **100** | **25232** | **100** | **27316** | **100.0** |
| （一）食品烟酒 | Food，Tobacco and Liquor | 5970 | 30.4 | 6459 | 30.3 | 6983 | 30.0 | 7489 | 29.7 | 7787 | 28.5 |
| （二）衣着 | Clothing | 1944 | 9.9 | 2096 | 9.8 | 2271 | 9.8 | 2467 | 9.8 | 2538 | 9.3 |
| （三）居住 | Residence a.r | 4316 | 21.9 | 4584 | 21.5 | 5018 | 21.6 | 5454 | 21.6 | 6365 | 23.3 |
| （四）生活用品及服务 | Household Facilities，Articles and Services | 1374 | 7.0 | 1485 | 7.0 | 1607 | 6.9 | 1747 | 6.9 | 1837 | 6.7 |
| （五）交通通信 | Transportation and Communication | 2905 | 14.8 | 3226 | 15.1 | 3479 | 15.0 | 3753 | 14.9 | 4084 | 15.0 |
| （六）教育文化娱乐 | Education. Cultural and Recreation Services | 1654 | 8.4 | 1830 | 8.6 | 2075 | 8.9 | 2347 | 9.3 | 2571 | 9.4 |
| （七）医疗保健 | Health Care and Medical Services | 1002 | 5.1 | 1115 | 5.2 | 1233 | 5.3 | 1350 | 5.4 | 1480 | 5.4 |
| （八）其他用品和服务 | Other Goods and Services | 488 | 2.5 | 531 | 2.5 | 590 | 2.5 | 625 | 2.4 | 654 | 2.4 |

# 10-17 城镇居民家庭消费构成
COMPOSITION OF URBAN HOUSEHOLDS CONSUMPTION

| 项目 | Item | 2014年 | | 2015年 | | 2016年 | | 2017年 | | 2018年 | |
|---|---|---|---|---|---|---|---|---|---|---|---|
| | | 年人均支出金额（元） Per Capita Annual Expenditure (yuan) | 占消费支出的比重（%） Percentage to Consumption Expenditure (%) | 年人均支出金额（元） Per Capita Annual Expenditure (yuan) | 占消费支出的比重（%） Percentage to Consumption Expenditure (%) | 年人均支出金额（元） Per Capita Annual Expenditure (yuan) | 占消费支出的比重（%） Percentage to Consumption Expenditure (%) | 年人均支出金额（元） Per Capita Annual Expenditure (yuan) | 占消费支出的比重（%） Percentage to Consumption Expenditure (%) | 年人均支出金额（元） Per Capita Annual Expenditure (yuan) | 占消费支出的比重（%） Percentage to Consumption Expenditure (%) |
| **消费支出** | **Consumption Expenditure** | **24122** | **100** | **26052** | **100** | **28285** | **100** | **30569** | **100** | **32890** | **100.0** |
| （一）食品烟酒 | Food, Tobacco and Liquor | 7295 | 30.2 | 7856 | 30.2 | 8473 | 30.0 | 9059 | 29.6 | 9318 | 28.3 |
| （二）衣着 | Clothing | 2497 | 10.4 | 2685 | 10.3 | 2882 | 10.2 | 3117 | 10.2 | 3168 | 9.6 |
| （三）居住 | Residence a.r | 5302 | 22.0 | 5607 | 21.5 | 6105 | 21.6 | 6605 | 21.6 | 7751 | 23.6 |
| （四）生活用品及服务 | Household Facilities, Articles and Services | 1686 | 7.0 | 1819 | 7.0 | 1962 | 6.9 | 2121 | 6.9 | 2207 | 6.7 |
| （五）交通通信 | Transportation and Communication | 3455 | 14.3 | 3810 | 14.6 | 4089 | 14.4 | 4399 | 14.4 | 4765 | 14.5 |
| （六）教育文化娱乐 | Education. Cultural and Recreation Services | 2057 | 8.5 | 2264 | 8.7 | 2553 | 9.0 | 2875 | 9.4 | 3122 | 9.5 |
| （七）医疗保健 | Health Care and Medical Services | 1227 | 5.1 | 1352 | 5.2 | 1490 | 5.3 | 1624 | 5.3 | 1764 | 5.4 |
| （八）其他用品和服务 | Other Goods and Services | 603 | 2.5 | 659 | 2.5 | 731 | 2.6 | 769 | 2.6 | 795 | 2.4 |

# 10-18 农村居民家庭消费构成
## COMPOSITION OF RURAL HOUSEHOLDS CONSUMPTION

| 项目 | Item | 2014年 | | 2015年 | | 2016年 | | 2017年 | | 2018年 | |
|---|---|---|---|---|---|---|---|---|---|---|---|
| | | 年人均支出金额（元） Per Capita Annual Expenditure (yuan) | 占消费支出的比重（%） Percentage to Consumption Expenditure (%) | 年人均支出金额（元） Per Capita Annual Expenditure (yuan) | 占消费支出的比重（%） Percentage to Consumption Expenditure (%) | 年人均支出金额（元） Per Capita Annual Expenditure (yuan) | 占消费支出的比重（%） Percentage to Consumption Expenditure (%) | 年人均支出金额（元） Per Capita Annual Expenditure (yuan) | 占消费支出的比重（%） Percentage to Consumption Expenditure (%) | 年人均支出金额（元） Per Capita Annual Expenditure (yuan) | 占消费支出的比重（%） Percentage to Consumption Expenditure (%) |
| **消费支出** | **Consumption Expenditure** | **10277** | **100** | **11127** | **100** | **12006** | **100** | **12928** | **100** | **13885** | **100.0** |
| （一）食品烟酒 | Food，Tobacco and Liquor | 3188 | 31.0 | 3442 | 30.9 | 3651 | 30.4 | 3869 | 29.9 | 4098 | 29.5 |
| （二）衣着 | Clothing | 784 | 7.6 | 826 | 7.4 | 905 | 7.5 | 971 | 7.5 | 1020 | 7.3 |
| （三）居住 | Residence a.r | 2248 | 21.9 | 2377 | 21.4 | 2586 | 21.5 | 2801 | 21.7 | 3024 | 21.8 |
| （四）生活用品及服务 | Household Facilities, Articles and Services | 720 | 7.0 | 765 | 6.9 | 814 | 6.8 | 885 | 6.8 | 945 | 6.8 |
| （五）交通通信 | Transportation and Communication | 1751 | 17.0 | 1965 | 17.7 | 2113 | 17.6 | 2262 | 17.5 | 2445 | 17.6 |
| （六）教育文化娱乐 | Education. Cultural and Recreation Services | 809 | 7.9 | 895 | 8.0 | 1004 | 8.4 | 1129 | 8.7 | 1245 | 9.0 |
| （七）医疗保健 | Health Care and Medical Services | 532 | 5.2 | 604 | 5.4 | 658 | 5.5 | 717 | 5.5 | 794 | 5.7 |
| （八）其他用品和服务 | Other Goods and Services | 245 | 2.4 | 253 | 2.3 | 275 | 2.3 | 294 | 2.4 | 314 | 2.3 |

# 10-19 城镇住户每百户家庭主要耐用品拥有量（1980-2018 年）
## OWNERSHIP OF MAJOR DURABLE CONSUMER GOODS PER 100 URBAN HOUSEHOLDS (1980-2018)

| 年份 Year | 家用电脑（台） Compuer (set) | 钢琴（架） Piano (set) | 空调器（台） Air Conditioner (set) | 热水器（台） Water Heater (unit) | 洗衣机（台） Washing Machine (set) | 电冰箱（台） Household Refrigerator (set) | 家用汽车（辆） Automobile (unit) | 彩色电视机（台） Color TV (set) | 移动电话（部） Call Phone (unit) | 照相机（架） Camera (set) |
|---|---|---|---|---|---|---|---|---|---|---|
| 1980 | | | | | | | | | | 2 |
| 1981 | | | | | 12 | | | 1 | | 2 |
| 1982 | | | | | 22 | | | 2 | | 4 |
| 1983 | | | | | 27 | 1 | | 6 | | 6 |
| 1984 | | | | | 30 | 2 | | 8 | | 8 |
| 1985 | | | | | 36 | 4 | | 18 | | 14 |
| 1986 | | | | | 40 | 5 | | 25 | | 15 |
| 1987 | | | | | 52 | 18 | | 34 | | 18 |
| 1988 | | | | | 61 | 33 | | 47 | | 21 |
| 1989 | | | | | 67 | 50 | | 59 | | 22 |
| 1990 | | | | | 66 | 62 | | 68 | | 26 |
| 1991 | | | | | 70 | 76 | | 82 | | 33 |
| 1992 | | 1 | 0 | 13 | 73 | 83 | | 81 | | 39 |
| 1993 | | 2 | 1 | 18 | 83 | 86 | | 88 | | 50 |
| 1994 | | 4 | 1 | 17 | 81 | 89 | | 92 | | 51 |
| 1995 | | 4 | 3 | 34 | 82 | 89 | | 100 | | 61 |
| 1996 | | 5 | 7 | 40 | 83 | 92 | | 105 | | 63 |
| 1997 | 1 | 5 | 9 | 47 | 83 | 93 | | 111 | 3 | 63 |
| 1998 | 8 | 5 | 17 | 53 | 83 | 92 | | 111 | 7 | 69 |
| 1999 | 11 | 4 | 22 | 61 | 83 | 94 | | 117 | 15 | 69 |
| 2000 | 19 | 2 | 25 | 66 | 83 | 94 | | 120 | 30 | 70 |
| 2001 | 20 | 2 | 24 | 66 | 84 | 93 | | 128 | 36 | 69 |
| 2002 | 32 | 2 | 38 | 75 | 89 | 93 | 1 | 123 | 80 | 73 |
| 2003 | 41 | 3 | 48 | 76 | 91 | 93 | 0 | 125 | 106 | 70 |
| 2004 | 46 | 3 | 55 | 79 | 93 | 93 | 2 | 124 | 128 | 68 |
| 2005 | 55 | 4 | 69 | 84 | 92 | 95 | 4 | 118 | 153 | 72 |
| 2006 | 71 | 8 | 89 | 88 | 97 | 99 | 6 | 125 | 187 | 82 |
| 2007 | 75 | 7 | 98 | 93 | 100 | 107 | 8 | 122 | 194 | 83 |
| 2008 | 75 | 5 | 94 | 90 | 95 | 103 | 13 | 116 | 191 | 67 |
| 2009 | 82 | 7 | 98 | 91 | 96 | 105 | 18 | 118 | 199 | 71 |
| 2010 | 86 | 8 | 99 | 91 | 97 | 107 | 20 | 119 | 208 | 71 |
| 2011 | 95 | 8 | 103 | 92 | 98 | 108 | 22 | 117 | 219 | 77 |
| 2012 | 101 | 9 | 104 | 93 | 98 | 108 | 29 | 115 | 231 | 79 |
| 2013 | 105 | 10 | 104 | 93 | 98 | 107 | 32 | 118 | 232 | 79 |
| 2014 | 105 | 10 | 104 | 98 | 99 | 105 | 34 | 109 | 235 | 79 |
| 2015 | 80 | 9 | 91 | 91 | 91 | 94 | 50 | 101 | 215 | 57 |
| 2016 | 86 | | 98 | 93 | 90 | 96 | 58 | 100 | 212 | 63 |
| 2017 | 80 | | 101 | 94 | 91 | 95 | 60 | 100 | 205 | |
| 2018 | 81 | | 120 | 101 | 100 | 108 | 62 | 107 | 228 | |

# 10-20 农村住户每百户家庭主要耐用品拥有量（1985-2018 年）
## OWNERSHIP OF MAJOR DURABLE CONSUMER GOODS PER 100 RURAL HOUSEHOLDS（1985-2018）

| 年份 Year | 家用电脑（台） Compuer（set） | 空调器（台） Air Conditioner（set） | 热水器（台） Water Heater（unit） | 自行车（辆） Bicycle（unit） | 洗衣机（台） Washing Machine（set） | 电冰箱（台） Household Refrigerator（set） | 彩色电视机（台） Color TV（set） | 移动电话（部） Call Phone（unit） | 照相机（架） Camera（set） | 家用汽车（辆） Automobile（unit） |
|---|---|---|---|---|---|---|---|---|---|---|
| 1985 | | | | 147 | 0.3 | | 3 | | 1 | |
| 1986 | | | | 165 | 1.1 | 0.3 | 4.5 | | 1 | |
| 1987 | | | | 148 | 2.4 | 0.5 | 7 | | 2 | |
| 1988 | | | | 154 | 2.4 | 1 | 9 | | 2 | |
| 1989 | | | | 170 | 3 | 1 | 12 | | 2 | |
| 1990 | | | | 164 | 4 | 2 | 13 | | 2 | |
| 1991 | | | | 173 | 5 | 4 | 16 | | 2 | |
| 1992 | | | | 178 | 5 | 7 | 20 | | 2 | |
| 1993 | | | | 203 | 7 | 14 | 26 | | 2 | |
| 1994 | | | | 204 | 9 | 21 | 35 | | 7 | |
| 1995 | | | | 203 | 16 | 28 | 43 | | 6 | |
| 1996 | | | | 198 | 13 | 33 | 46 | | 8 | |
| 1997 | | | | 191 | 15 | 36 | 56 | | 13 | |
| 1998 | | | | 184 | 17 | 39 | 63 | | 15 | |
| 1999 | | | | 185 | 20 | 42 | 74 | | 10 | |
| 2000 | | | | 165 | 28 | 47 | 86 | | 13 | |
| 2001 | | | | 153 | 28 | 53 | 92 | | 13 | |
| 2002 | | | | 152 | 36 | 58 | 98 | | 16 | |
| 2003 | 6 | 5 | 33 | 137 | 39 | 60 | 100 | 45 | 16 | 2 |
| 2004 | 8 | 8 | 39 | 142 | 48 | 68 | 105 | 68 | 21 | 2 |
| 2005 | 14 | 14 | 53 | 138 | 57 | 77 | 109 | 91 | 21 | 5 |
| 2006 | 17 | 15 | 54 | 116 | 63 | 87 | 112 | 114 | 14 | 7 |
| 2007 | 19 | 19 | 63 | 118 | 70 | 94 | 113 | 132 | 17 | 8 |
| 2008 | 25 | 23 | 68 | 124 | 76 | 97 | 114 | 148 | 19 | 9 |
| 2009 | 28 | 25 | 71 | 127 | 79 | 99 | 115 | 160 | 21 | 11 |
| 2010 | 34 | 30 | 75 | 128 | 82 | 102 | 117 | 170 | 21 | 12 |
| 2011 | 44 | 32 | 76 | 114 | 85 | 100 | 112 | 202 | 18 | 15 |
| 2012 | 55 | 37 | 85 | 119 | 91 | 102 | 114 | 216 | 21 | 16 |
| 2013 | 61 | 45 | 88 | 111 | 93 | 105 | 116 | 221 | 26 | 23 |
| 2014 | 61 | 49 | 85 | | 93 | 102 | 106 | 225 | 24 | 26 |
| 2015 | 46 | 54 | 86 | | 92 | 105 | 110 | 219 | 21 | 41 |
| 2016 | 56 | 70 | 89 | | 96 | 107 | 113 | 226 | 21 | 45 |
| 2017 | 52 | 78 | 90 | | 98 | 106 | 110 | 223 | | 48 |
| 2018 | 45 | 93 | 88 | | 97 | 109 | 105 | 232 | | 43 |

# 主要统计指标解释

**常住人员** 指住户成员中，经常在家居住、或者调查期内居住时间超过一半的人员，以及本住户供养的学生。

**可支配收入** 指调查户在调查期内获得的、可用于最终消费支出和储蓄的总和，即调查户可以用来自由支配的收入。可支配收入既包括现金，也包括实物收入。按照收入的来源，可支配收入包含四项，分别为：工资性收入、经营净收入、财产净收入和转移净收入。计算公式为：

可支配收入 = 工资性收入 + 经营净收入 + 财产净收入 + 转移净收入

居民人均可支配收入是按居民家庭常住人口计算的平均每人可支配收入

**消费支出** 指住户用于满足家庭日常生活消费需要的全部支出。根据用途不同，消费支出可划分为食品烟酒、衣着、居住、生活用品及服务、交通通信、教育文化娱乐、医疗保健、其他用品及服务八大类。根据来源不同，消费支出可划分为现金消费支出、实物消费支出（含自产自用、来自单位、来自政府和其他社会组织）。

# Explanatory Notes on Main Statistical Indicators

**Permanent resident** refers to residents that live usually in home or more than half of the survey period and students that are supported by them.

**Disposable income** refers to sum of all income earned within the survey period that can be used for deposit and expense on final consumption, which means the income that can be disposed freely by residents. The disposable income includes not only cash, but also income in kinds, which shall be categorized into four kinds according to source of incomes--salary income, net operating income, net property income, net transfer income. Computing formula is as follows:

Disposable income = salary income + net operating income + net property income + net transfer income

Disposable income per capita of residents is the average disposable income per person calculated based on the number of permanent residents of the family.

**Consumer spending** refers to all spending of residents to cover daily life consumption demands. According to different usages, the consumer spending shall be classified into eight categories: food, cigarettes and alcohol; clothing; housing; daily use articles and services; transportation & communication; education, culture & entertainment; medical and health care; other articles and services. According to sources, the consumer spending shall be classified as cash consumer spending, consumer spending in kinds (including self-produced, from the unit, from government and other social organization).

# 农　业 11

AGRICULTURE

# 简要说明

**一、本篇资料的主要内容**

本篇资料主要反映了全市农业生产和农村经济的基本情况，主要包括农林牧渔业总产值、中间消耗、增加值、农村劳动力、耕地、主要农产品产量、农业机械年末拥有量、农业机械化和电气化以及农田水利建设等方面的资料。

**二、本篇资料的来源**

1、本篇资料中耕地面积资料来源于市自然资源和规划局。

2、水产品产量等相关资料来源于市海洋发展局。

3、农业机械化等相关资料来源于市农村农业局。

4、农田水利灌溉等相关资料来源于市水务管理局。

5、植树造林等相关资料来源于市园林和林业局。

**三、说明**

本篇按照国家统计局规定，根据2016年第三次全国农业普查结果对2007年至2017年历史数据进行了核定和修正。

本篇资料由市统计局农村统计处、国家统计局青岛调查队农村调查处整理提供。

# Brief Introduction

***I. Main Content***

Data in this chapter show the basic conditions of agricultural production and rural economy, mainly including agricultural output, intermediate consumption, value added, rural labor force, cultivated land, output of main agricultural produces, agricultural machinery and electrification in rural areas and basic construction on irrigation and drainage.

***II. Source of Data***

(1) Data on area of cultivated land are provided by Qingdao Natural Resources and Planning Bureau.

(2) Data on output of aquatic products are provided by Qingdao Marine Development Bureau.

(3) Data on Agricultural machinery are provided by Qingdao Rural Agriculture Bureau.

(4) Data on farmland water conservancy are provided by Qingdao Water Administration Bureau.

(5) Data on forest planting are provided by Qingdao Landscape and Forestry Bureau.

***III. Explain***

This chapter is in accordance with the provisions of the State Statistical Bureau. According to the results of the third national agricultural census in 2016, the historical data from 2007 to 2017 were verified and revised.

Data in this chapter are compiled by the Division of Countryside Statistics of Qingdao Municipal Bureau of Statistics and Division of Rural Household Survey of Survey Office of the National Bureau of Statistics in Qingdao.

# 11-1 农村基本情况（2000-2018 年）
## BASIC STATISTICS ON RURAL AREA（2000-2018）

| 项目 | Item | 单位 | Unit | 2000 | 2005 | 2008 | 2009 | 2010 | 2011 | 2012 |
|---|---|---|---|---|---|---|---|---|---|---|
| **一、乡村户数人口、劳动力** | **Rural Households Population and Labor Force** | | | | | | | | | |
| 乡村户数 | Rural Households | 万户 | 10 000 households | 148 | 151 | 152 | 152 | 155 | 155 | 156 |
| 乡村人口 | Rural Population | 万人 | 10 000 persons | 483 | 479 | 480 | 485 | 487 | 489 | 491 |
| 乡村劳动力 | Rural Labor Force | 万人 | 10 000 persons | 255 | 258 | 271 | 275 | 276 | 277 | 277 |
| 男劳动力 | Male | 万人 | 10 000 persons | 137 | 138 | 144 | 146 | 147 | 147 | 146 |
| 女劳动力 | Female | 万人 | 10 000 persons | 118 | 120 | 126 | 129 | 129 | 131 | 130 |
| **二、年末实有耕地面积** | **Year-end Area of Cultivated Land** | **万公顷** | **10 000 hectares** | **48** | **42** | **42** | **42** | | | **53** |
| **三、农用机械总动力** | **Total Agricultural Machinery Power** | **万千瓦** | **10 000 kW** | **459** | **620** | **697** | **719** | **764** | **784** | **798** |
| 拖拉机 | Tractors | 台 | unit | 126981 | 163032 | 176156 | 180171 | 200208 | 202022 | 206290 |
| **四、农村用电量** | **Electricity Consumed in Rural Areas** | **万千瓦时** | **10 000 kW·h** | **189651** | **372645** | **424292** | **426306** | **426819** | **431646** | **426815** |
| **五、农用化肥施用量（折纯）** | **Consumption of Chemical Fertilizer（convert to pure amount）** | **万吨** | **10 000 tons** | **33** | **33** | **31** | **30** | **30** | **29** | **29** |
| **六、有效灌溉面积** | **Irrigated Area** | **万公顷** | **10 000 hectares** | **30** | **30** | **31** | **32** | **33** | **33** | **33** |

## 11-1 续表
Continued

| 项目 | Item | 单位 | Unit | 2013 | 2014 | 2015 | 2016 | 2017 | 2018 |
|---|---|---|---|---|---|---|---|---|---|
| **一、乡村户数人口、劳动力** | **Rural Households Population and Labor Force** | | | | | | | | |
| 乡村户数 | Rural Households | 万户 | 10 000 households | 155 | 157 | 155 | 155 | 140 | 131 |
| 乡村人口 | Rural Population | 万人 | 10 000 persons | 491 | 494 | 495 | 497 | 453 | 419 |
| 乡村劳动力 | Rural Labor Force | 万人 | 10 000 persons | 277 | 277 | 275 | 273 | 246 | 224 |
| 男劳动力 | Male | 万人 | 10 000 persons | 147 | 147 | 145 | 145 | 131 | 119 |
| 女劳动力 | Female | 万人 | 10 000 persons | 131 | 130 | 130 | 128 | 115 | 105 |
| **二、年末实有耕地面积** | **Year-end Area of Cultivated Land** | **万公顷** | **10 000 hectares** | **53** | **52** | **52** | **52** | **52** | **52** |
| **三、农用机械总动力** | **Total Agricultural Machinery Power** | **万千瓦** | **10 000 kW** | **809** | **827** | **854** | **698** | **728** | **738** |
| 拖拉机 | Tractors | 台 | unit | 206300 | 205065 | 207809 | 211689 | 214799 | 215668 |
| **四、农村用电量** | **Electricity Consumed in Rural Areas** | **万千瓦时** | **10 000 kW·h** | **359139** | **404380** | **401122** | **385434** | **382437** | **377858** |
| **五、农用化肥施用量（折纯）** | **Consumption of Chemical Fertilizer (convert to pure amount)** | **万吨** | **10 000 tons** | **29** | **29** | **28** | **28** | **28** | **27** |
| **六、有效灌溉面积** | **Irrigated Area** | **万公顷** | | **30** | **32** | **32** | **33** | **33** | **33** |

注：1. 农机机械总动力 2016 年为新统计口径，扣除农用运输汽车数据。
　　2. 乡村劳动力 2018 年为新统计口径。

Note：1.Data of total power of agricultural machinery of 2016 is based on the new statistic caliber，deducted by the data of agricultural vehicle.
　　2.Rural Labor Force of 2018 is based on the new statistic caliber.

# 11-2 农村劳动力（1985-2018 年）
RURAL LABOR FORCE（1985-2018）

单位：万人（10 000 persons）

| 年份 Year | 合计 Total | 农林牧渔业 Farming，Forestry，Animal Husbandry and Fishing | 工业 Industry | 建筑业 Construction |
|---|---|---|---|---|
| 1985 | 225.09 | 147.89 | 32.92 | 15.62 |
| 1988 | 238.93 | 146.00 | 44.46 | 17.51 |
| 1989 | 242.70 | 151.16 | 44.65 | 16.46 |
| 1990 | 247.29 | 155.20 | 44.48 | 16.17 |
| 1991 | 253.01 | 160.31 | 45.49 | 15.87 |
| 1992 | 258.23 | 160.04 | 47.00 | 17.25 |
| 1993 | 259.18 | 159.22 | 44.04 | 20.20 |
| 1994 | 258.34 | 155.74 | 43.70 | 21.52 |
| 1995 | 258.66 | 154.08 | 44.06 | 22.33 |
| 1996 | 256.34 | 151.10 | 43.08 | 21.80 |
| 1997 | 258.60 | 153.07 | 41.66 | 22.02 |
| 1998 | 258.50 | 152.79 | 40.79 | 21.68 |
| 1999 | 256.82 | 149.11 | 42.18 | 22.32 |
| 2000 | 254.62 | 143.59 | 42.76 | 22.99 |
| 2001 | 253.98 | 132.46 | 47.76 | 24.66 |
| 2002 | 254.08 | 119.98 | 53.66 | 26.52 |
| 2003 | 257.67 | 118.27 | 55.65 | 26.65 |
| 2004 | 258.91 | 112.05 | 60.32 | 28.36 |
| 2005 | 257.87 | 103.03 | 65.59 | 29.03 |
| 2006 | 264.70 | 102.28 | 71.46 | 28.16 |
| 2007 | 268.31 | 100.63 | 74.70 | 30.97 |
| 2008 | 270.71 | 100.90 | 74.82 | 30.87 |
| 2009 | 274.74 | 102.64 | 75.42 | 31.23 |
| 2010 | 276.04 | 102.45 | 76.32 | 32.10 |
| 2011 | 277.24 | 102.73 | 76.87 | 32.57 |
| 2012 | 276.97 | 102.24 | 76.82 | 32.36 |
| 2013 | 277.32 | 104.48 | 76.42 | 31.15 |
| 2014 | 276.90 | | | |
| 2015 | 274.77 | | | |
| 2016 | 273.43 | | | |
| 2017 | 245.92 | | | |
| 2018 | 223.54 | | | |

注：乡村劳动力 2018 年为新统计口径。

Note：Rural Labor Force of 2018 is based on the new statistic caliber.

# 11-2 续表
Continued

单位：万人（10 000persons）

| 年份<br>Year | 交通运输仓储和邮电业<br>Transport，Postal and Telecommunication Services | 批发零售贸易、餐饮业<br>Wholesale and Retail Trades and Catering Services | 金融保险业<br>Financial and Insurance | 其他劳动力<br>Other Labour Force |
|---|---|---|---|---|
| 1985 | 5.23 | 0.06 | 19.76 | 3.61 |
| 1988 | 5.89 | 0.09 | 20.40 | 4.58 |
| 1989 | 6.00 | 0.12 | 19.95 | 4.36 |
| 1990 | 6.11 | 0.12 | 20.71 | 4.50 |
| 1991 | 6.09 | 0.13 | 20.52 | 4.60 |
| 1992 | 7.02 | 0.16 | 21.74 | 5.02 |
| 1993 | 8.93 | 0.16 | 20.65 | 5.98 |
| 1994 | 6.48 | 10.10 | | 20.80 |
| 1995 | 7.11 | 10.71 | | 20.37 |
| 1996 | 7.33 | 11.78 | | 21.25 |
| 1997 | 7.62 | 12.40 | | 21.83 |
| 1998 | 8.02 | 13.32 | | 21.90 |
| 1999 | 8.19 | 14.03 | | 20.99 |
| 2000 | 8.39 | 16.10 | | 20.79 |
| 2001 | 9.02 | 17.80 | | 22.28 |
| 2002 | 10.00 | 20.07 | | 23.85 |
| 2003 | 9.96 | 20.60 | | 26.54 |
| 2004 | 10.20 | 24.08 | | 22.96 |
| 2005 | 10.70 | 25.88 | | 22.34 |
| 2006 | 11.66 | 25.31 | | 24.37 |
| 2007 | 11.61 | 27.61 | | 21.16 |
| 2008 | 11.06 | 28.76 | | 22.09 |
| 2009 | 11.40 | 29.03 | | 22.75 |
| 2010 | 11.78 | 28.85 | | 22.01 |
| 2011 | 11.89 | 29.34 | | 21.02 |
| 2012 | 11.96 | 29.56 | | 21.11 |
| 2013 | 11.92 | 29.48 | | 20.33 |
| 2014 | | | | |
| 2015 | | | | |
| 2016 | | | | |
| 2017 | | | | |
| 2018 | | | | |

# 11-3 分市、区乡村户数、人口、劳动力（2018年）
RURAL HOUSEHOLDS，POPULATION AND LABOR FORCE BY REGION（2018）

| 市、区名称 | Region | 乡村户数（万户）Rural Households（10 000 households） | 乡村人口（万人）Rural Population（10 000 persons） | 乡村劳动力（万人）Labour Force of Village（10 000 persons） | 男劳动力 Male Laborer | 女劳动力 Female Laborer | #种植业 Planting |
|---|---|---|---|---|---|---|---|
| **全市** | **Whole Municipality** | **131.23** | **419.07** | **223.54** | **118.53** | **105.02** | **74.27** |
| 崂山区 | Laoshan District | 4.51 | 13.37 | 7.57 | 4.02 | 3.55 | 1.85 |
| 黄岛区 | Huangdao District | 19.55 | 62.38 | 30.65 | 16.44 | 14.21 | 7.72 |
| 城阳区 | Chengyang District | 11.80 | 32.30 | 18.06 | 9.51 | 8.55 | 0.93 |
| 即墨区 | Jimo District | 23.70 | 78.42 | 41.51 | 22.08 | 19.44 | 13.81 |
| 胶州市 | Jiaozhou | 16.93 | 54.79 | 28.63 | 14.73 | 13.90 | 8.93 |
| 平度市 | Pingdu | 35.64 | 116.80 | 63.32 | 33.65 | 29.67 | 27.27 |
| 莱西市 | Laixi | 19.10 | 61.00 | 33.79 | 18.10 | 15.70 | 13.76 |

注：1. 城阳区含红岛经济区数据。
　　2. 乡村劳动力2018年为新统计口径。
Note：1.Chengyang District includes Hongdao Economic Zone.
　　2.Rural Labor Force of 2018 is based on the new statistic caliber.

# 11-4 主要年份农、林、牧、渔业总产值(按现价计算)

MAJOR YEAR'S GROSS OUTPUT VALUE OF FARMING, FORESTRY, ANINAL HUSBANDRY AND FISHERY (CURRENT PRICE)

单位：万元（10 000 yuan）

| 年份 Year | 农、林、牧、渔业总产值 Gross Output Value of Farming, Forestry, Animal Husbandry and Fishery | 农业产值 Farming | 林业产值 Forestry | 牧业产值 Animal Husbandry | 渔业产值 Fishery |
|---|---|---|---|---|---|
| 1949 | 16511 | 14755 | 325 | 1200 | 231 |
| 1952 | 24428 | 21353 | 479 | 1888 | 708 |
| 1957 | 26189 | 22717 | 644 | 2218 | 610 |
| 1962 | 15356 | 13257 | 230 | 1243 | 626 |
| 1965 | 25123 | 21488 | 854 | 2110 | 671 |
| 1970 | 44078 | 36889 | 1851 | 3817 | 1521 |
| 1975 | 93213 | 79208 | 2144 | 7923 | 3938 |
| 1978 | 121497 | 94397 | 3112 | 17293 | 6695 |
| 1980 | 149436 | 117547 | 2953 | 22215 | 6721 |
| 1985 | 299139 | 215729 | 8986 | 53894 | 20530 |
| 1987 | 378981 | 263066 | 5949 | 73271 | 36695 |
| 1989 | 463952 | 303679 | 19134 | 91885 | 49254 |
| 1990 | 579877 | 381287 | 13801 | 119208 | 65581 |
| 1991 | 664779 | 417111 | 12875 | 144909 | 89884 |
| 1992 | 703433 | 400471 | 15252 | 150942 | 136768 |
| 1993 | 989763 | 509601 | 20845 | 232143 | 227174 |
| 1994 | 1424074 | 763366 | 23101 | 356734 | 280873 |
| 1995 | 1923771 | 1021413 | 26765 | 503999 | 371594 |
| 1996 | 2317434 | 1145399 | 29100 | 692362 | 450573 |
| 1997 | 2047712 | 939922 | 24052 | 578443 | 505295 |
| 1998 | 2386303 | 1198043 | 16760 | 633735 | 537765 |
| 1999 | 2382320 | 1169596 | 17122 | 618020 | 577582 |
| 2000 | 2483256 | 1116397 | 19102 | 692782 | 654975 |
| 2001 | 2615228 | 1135816 | 20433 | 758313 | 700666 |
| 2002 | 2688532 | 1110671 | 23157 | 796007 | 758697 |
| 2003 | 2759692 | 1062576 | 36183 | 859915 | 801018 |
| 2004 | 2967389 | 1181009 | 32831 | 937494 | 816055 |
| 2005 | 3205057 | 1265695 | 25246 | 1070831 | 843285 |
| 2006 | 3396096 | 1360755 | 23546 | 1076254 | 855131 |
| 2007 | 3665342 | 1460800 | 20801 | 1143644 | 916648 |
| 2008 | 3995027 | 1723855 | 24356 | 1195857 | 907793 |
| 2009 | 4070777 | 1771982 | 22133 | 1133732 | 980995 |
| 2010 | 4802184 | 2197935 | 19090 | 1225222 | 1181911 |
| 2011 | 5345885 | 2188072 | 19049 | 1500469 | 1426786 |
| 2012 | 5672486 | 2270097 | 20221 | 1510234 | 1633469 |
| 2013 | 6105875 | 2547805 | 21875 | 1553621 | 1711549 |
| 2014 | 6279086 | 2644851 | 22266 | 1559709 | 1739234 |
| 2015 | 6123485 | 2469656 | 21789 | 1529587 | 1814625 |
| 2016 | 6690910 | 2844023 | 27741 | 1621935 | 1777293 |
| 2017 | 6978980 | 3003367 | 30891 | 1663278 | 1830324 |
| 2018 | 7369968 | 3290651 | 36575 | 1631422 | 1920519 |

注：2007 年 -2017 年数据为根据第三次农业普查结果核定修正后数据。

Note: The 2007-2017 data are the approved revised data based on the results of the third agricultural census.

# 11-5 分市、区农、林、牧、渔业总产值(2018年，现价)

GROSS OUTPUT VALUE OF FARMING，FORESTRY，ANIMAL HUSBANDYRY AND FISHERY BY REGION（2018，CURRENT PRICE）

单位：万元（10 000 yuan）

| 市、区名称 | Region | 农、林、牧、渔业总产值 Gross Output Value of Farming，Forestry，Animal Husbandry and Fishery | 农业 Farming | 林业 Forestry | 牧业 Animal Husbandry | 渔业 Fishery | 服务业 Services |
|---|---|---|---|---|---|---|---|
| **全市** | **Whole Municipality** | **7369968** | **3290651** | **36575** | **1631422** | **1920519** | **490802** |
| 崂山区 | Laoshan District | 163756 | 11635 | 782 | 0 | 130876 | 20463 |
| 黄岛区 | Huangdao District | 1386082 | 485918 | 5474 | 124343 | 681100 | 89247 |
| 城阳区 | Chengyang District | 63200 | 23542 | 997 | 17952 | 18534 | 2175 |
| 即墨区 | Jimo District | 1371472 | 440457 | 5753 | 233416 | 570913 | 120933 |
| 胶州市 | Jiaozhou | 1019778 | 435255 | 6430 | 232281 | 256085 | 89728 |
| 平度市 | Pingdu | 1886702 | 1239994 | 8135 | 538832 | 13178 | 86563 |
| 莱西市 | Laixi | 1232117 | 653337 | 8920 | 480315 | 11401 | 78143 |
| 红岛经济区 | Qingdao National High-tech Industrial Development Zone | 246861 | 513 | 85 | 4282 | 238432 | 3549 |

## 11-6 农、林、牧、渔业总产值、增加值（2018 年）
VALUE-ADDED OF FARMING, FORESTRY, ANIMAL, HUSBANDRY AND FISHERY (2018)

单位：万元（10 000 yuan）

| | | 总计 Total | 农业 Farming | 林业 Forestry | 牧业 Animal Husbandry | 渔业 Fishery | 服务业 Services |
|---|---|---|---|---|---|---|---|
| **总产值** | **Gross Output Value** | **7369969** | **3290650** | **36575** | **1631422** | **1920520** | **490801** |
| **中间消耗** | **Intermediate Expenditure** | 3264395 | 1351102 | 13734 | 870157 | 775086 | 254316 |
| 中间物质消耗 | Intermediate Expenditure of Matter | 2258032 | 965710 | 8948 | 660739 | 495110 | 127525 |
| 对非农生产部门的劳动支出 | Expenditure of Labour Services to Nonagricultural Production Development | 1006363 | 385392 | 4786 | 209418 | 279976 | 126791 |

## 11-7 分市、区农、林、牧、渔业增加值（2018 年）
VALUE-ADDED OF FARMING, FORESTRY, ANIMAL HUSBANDRY FISHERY BY REGION (2018)

单位：万元（10 000 yuan）

| 市、区名称 | Region | 增加值 Added Value | 农业 Farming | 林业 Forestry | 牧业 Animal Husbandry | 渔业 Fishery | 服务业 Services |
|---|---|---|---|---|---|---|---|
| **全市** | **Whole Municipality** | **4105574** | **1939549** | **22841** | **761265** | **1145434** | **236485** |
| 崂山区 | Laoshan District | 92828 | 7133 | 464 | | 75560 | 9672 |
| 黄岛区 | Huangdao District | 779542 | 267985 | 3522 | 60646 | 404897 | 42492 |
| 城阳区 | Chengyang District | 33707 | 12712 | 608 | 8487 | 10953 | 947 |
| 即墨区 | Jimo District | 767281 | 256183 | 3701 | 107611 | 340855 | 58931 |
| 胶州市 | Jiaozhou | 576299 | 260697 | 4199 | 109367 | 158407 | 43629 |
| 平度市 | Pingdu | 1055902 | 751700 | 4780 | 249316 | 7787 | 42319 |
| 莱西市 | Laixi | 655725 | 382834 | 5517 | 223858 | 6631 | 36886 |
| 红岛经济区 | Qingdao National High-tech Industrial Development Zone | 144290 | 306 | 50 | 1981 | 140344 | 1609 |

# 11-8 主要年份耕地面积与播种面积
MAJOR YEAR'S CULTIVATED AND SOWN AREA

单位：万公顷（10 000 hectares）

| 年份 Year | 年末实有耕地面积 Year-end Area of Cultivated Land | 农作物播种面积 Sown Area of Farm Crops | #粮食作物 Grain Crops | #经济作物 Economic Crops |
|---|---|---|---|---|
| 1949 | | 93.47 | 84.00 | 7.20 |
| 1952 | | 97.53 | 85.07 | 10.80 |
| 1957 | | 97.87 | 87.07 | 10.53 |
| 1962 | | 81.47 | 72.53 | 5.80 |
| 1965 | | 82.80 | 71.80 | 8.33 |
| 1970 | | 80.73 | 68.27 | 10.07 |
| 1975 | | 79.82 | 65.84 | 11.01 |
| 1978 | | 77.60 | 63.60 | 10.40 |
| 1980 | | 75.87 | 60.33 | 12.00 |
| 1985 | | 78.27 | 57.33 | 15.73 |
| 1987 | | 76.67 | 55.87 | 15.93 |
| 1989 | | 74.78 | 54.28 | 16.06 |
| 1990 | | 76.85 | 56.99 | 15.53 |
| 1991 | | 76.98 | 56.89 | 15.69 |
| 1992 | | 76.96 | 56.37 | 15.64 |
| 1993 | 56.90 | 77.75 | 56.22 | 15.71 |
| 1994 | | 76.61 | 54.08 | 16.20 |
| 1995 | | 76.54 | 53.71 | 15.65 |
| 1996 | 55.01 | 77.26 | 54.81 | 14.90 |
| 1997 | | 75.04 | 52.32 | 14.40 |
| 1998 | | 77.18 | 53.05 | 14.54 |
| 1999 | | 77.56 | 50.61 | 13.24 |
| 2000 | | 76.47 | 45.07 | 13.98 |
| 2001 | | 73.69 | 41.91 | 14.54 |
| 2002 | | 72.32 | 40.83 | 13.95 |
| 2003 | | 67.82 | 36.05 | 14.50 |
| 2004 | | 71.33 | 41.40 | 14.11 |
| 2005 | 42.10 | 75.02 | 49.93 | 11.89 |
| 2006 | 41.29 | 74.86 | 49.79 | 11.75 |
| 2007 | 41.31 | 64.13 | 39.16 | 24.98 |
| 2008 | 41.79 | 65.29 | 42.56 | 22.73 |
| 2009 | 41.87 | 63.72 | 42.01 | 21.72 |
| 2010 | | 64.10 | 42.65 | 21.45 |
| 2011 | | 64.53 | 43.84 | 20.70 |
| 2012 | 52.81 | 64.36 | 43.95 | 20.40 |
| 2013 | 52.55 | 66.16 | 45.69 | 20.48 |
| 2014 | 52.42 | 66.70 | 46.75 | 19.95 |
| 2015 | 52.22 | 67.10 | 47.93 | 19.17 |
| 2016 | 52 | 68.19 | 48.49 | 19.70 |
| 2017 | 51.86 | 67.32 | 47.79 | 19.54 |
| 2018 | 51.86 | 68.37 | 48.11 | 20.26 |

注：1.2009 年前本表数据由统计局提供。
2.2010 年起，耕地面积由国土部门提供，粮食作物面积由青岛调查队提供，经济作物面积由统计局提供。
3.2007 年 -2017 年农作物播种面积为根据第三次农业普查结果核定修正后数据。
4. 耕地面积数据由国土部门错年提供。

Note：1.Those of before 2009 were provided by the National Bureau of Statistics.
2. From 2010,data on area of cultivated land are provided by Ministry of Land and Resources, area of grain crops are provided by Nation Bureau of Statistics in Qingdao ,area of economic crops are provided by Nation Bureau of Statistics.
3. Sown Area of Farm Crops from 2007 to 2017 is revised according to the results of the third agricultural census.
4.Arable land data provided by the land department next year.

# 11-9 分市、区耕地面积（2018 年）
## AREA CULTIVATED LAND BY REGION（2018）

单位：公顷（hectares）

| 市、区名称 | Region | 年末耕地面积 Year-end Area of Cultivated Land | #旱田 Dry Farmland | 当年增加的耕地 Area of Culitivated Land Increased in the Year | #新开荒地 Wasteland Newly Opened up | 当年减少的耕地 Area of Culitivated Land Decreased in the Year |
|---|---|---|---|---|---|---|
| **全市** | **Whole Municipality** | 518620 | 273413 | 366 | | 943 |
| 崂山区 | Laoshan District | 898 | 866 | 0 | | 2 |
| 黄岛区 | Huangdao District | 74150 | 71820 | 1 | | 211 |
| 城阳区 | Chengyang District | 6682 | 5226 | 85 | | 89 |
| 即墨区 | Jimo District | 99463 | 86312 | 1 | | 182 |
| 胶州市 | Jiaozhou | 63764 | 23516 | 5 | | 268 |
| 平度市 | Pingdu | 184250 | 12616 | 153 | | 129 |
| 莱西市 | Laixi | 89378 | 73023 | 121 | | 63 |

注：城阳区含红岛经济区数据。

Note：Chengyang District includes Hongdao Economic Zone.

# 11-10 分市、区农作物播种面积（2018年）
## SOWN AREA OF FARM CROPS BY REGION (2018)

单位：万公顷（10 000 hectares）

| 市、区名称 | Region | 总播种面积 Total Sown Area | #粮食 Grain | #棉花 Cotton | #花生 Peanut | #烟叶 Tobacco | #蔬菜 Vegetable |
|---|---|---|---|---|---|---|---|
| **全市** | **Whole Municipality** | **68.37** | **48.11** | **0.06** | **8.00** | **0.03** | **11.32** |
| 崂山区 | Laoshan District | 0.05 | 0.01 | | 0.01 | | 0.03 |
| 黄岛区 | Huangdao District | 7.78 | 4.95 | | 1.93 | 0.02 | 0.81 |
| 城阳区 | Chengyang District | 0.31 | 0.19 | | 0.00 | | 0.11 |
| 即墨区 | Jimo District | 10.31 | 7.92 | | 1.37 | | 0.96 |
| 胶州市 | Jiaozhou | 9.07 | 6.29 | | 0.66 | 0.00 | 2.09 |
| 平度市 | Pingdu | 28.08 | 20.03 | 0.06 | 2.41 | 0.01 | 5.23 |
| 莱西市 | Laixi | 12.76 | 8.72 | | 1.63 | | 2.08 |

注：城阳区含红岛经济区数据。

Note: Chengyang District includes Hongdao Economic Zone.

# 11-11 分市、区部分农作物产量（2018年）
## OUTPUT OF FARM CROPS BY REGION (2018)

单位：吨（ton）

| 市、区名称 | Region | 粮食 Grain | 棉花 Cotton | 花生 Peanut | 烟叶 Tobacco | 蔬菜 Vegetable |
|---|---|---|---|---|---|---|
| **全市** | **Whole Municipality** | **3100964** | **977** | **384918** | **707** | **6443615** |
| 崂山区 | Laoshan District | 829 | | 262 | | 10845 |
| 黄岛区 | Huangdao District | 263545 | | 99290 | 569 | 601531 |
| 城阳区 | Chengyang District | 9629 | | 127 | | 42497 |
| 即墨区 | Jimo District | 448809 | | 59094 | | 564332 |
| 胶州市 | Jiaozhou | 368571 | | 28140 | 11 | 1071284 |
| 平度市 | Pingdu | 1450710 | 977 | 120207 | 126 | 2921519 |
| 莱西市 | Laixi | 558872 | | 77799 | | 1231606 |

注：城阳区含红岛经济区数据。

Note: Chengyang District includes Hongdao Economic Zone.

# 11-12 分市、区部分农作物播公顷单产量（2018年）
## OUTPUT OF FARM CROPS PER HECTARE BY REGION (2018)

单位：千克（kg）

| 市、区名称 | Region | 粮食 Grain | 棉花 Cotton | 花生 Peanut | 烟叶 Tobacco | 蔬菜 Vegetable |
|---|---|---|---|---|---|---|
| **全市** | **Whole Municipality** | **6446** | **1649** | **4809** | **2609** | **56942** |
| 崂山区 | Laoshan District | 7327 | | 3087 | | 32627 |
| 黄岛区 | Huangdao District | 5321 | | 5147 | 2688 | 74097 |
| 城阳区 | Chengyang District | 5139 | | 3289 | | 37769 |
| 即墨区 | Jimo District | 5668 | | 4326 | | 58883 |
| 胶州市 | Jiaozhou | 5862 | | 4272 | 3014 | 51303 |
| 平度市 | Pingdu | 7244 | 1649 | 4986 | 2277 | 55838 |
| 莱西市 | Laixi | 6406 | | 4785 | | 59214 |

注：城阳区含红岛经济区数据。

Note: Chengyang District includes Hongdao Economic Zone.

# 11-13 主要年份农作物总产量
MAJOR YEAR'S OUPTUT OF FARM CROPS

单位：吨（ton）

| 年份 Year | 粮食 Grain | #小麦 Wheat | #玉米 Corn | 棉花 Cotton | 花生 Peanut | 水果 Fruit | 蔬菜 Vegetable |
|---|---|---|---|---|---|---|---|
| 1949 | 723190 | 158815 | 25810 | 1280 | 71080 | 9955 | 356015 |
| 1952 | 967640 | 200380 | 58130 | 6025 | 115585 | 13468 | 284050 |
| 1957 | 921920 | 210690 | 141540 | 3520 | 90445 | 18869 | 625220 |
| 1962 | 628930 | 104340 | 53010 | 1280 | 35470 | 8366 | 524455 |
| 1965 | 917635 | 180610 | 135595 | 6090 | 88390 | 16034 | 465850 |
| 1970 | 1175985 | 243945 | 244530 | 16490 | 96280 | 33907 | 541145 |
| 1975 | 1899540 | 430135 | 420095 | 15390 | 98495 | 59206 | 693970 |
| 1978 | 1900850 | 514570 | 510635 | 8720 | 114370 | 82819 | 921140 |
| 1980 | 2164415 | 520045 | 819930 | 19630 | 160670 | 80840 | 996565 |
| 1985 | 2331060 | 961055 | 739455 | 19335 | 475270 | 200515 | 1253075 |
| 1987 | 2626029 | 996165 | 1030926 | 13819 | 394296 | 249655 | 1489250 |
| 1989 | 2654334 | 993406 | 1084441 | 14638 | 391782 | 288757 | 1664238 |
| 1990 | 2998246 | 1265157 | 1210687 | 17490 | 413636 | 292366 | 1786041 |
| 1991 | 3180893 | 1421143 | 1285043 | 25965 | 446880 | 294349 | 1837265 |
| 1992 | 2675641 | 1235755 | 981490 | 8160 | 321145 | 341415 | 2030327 |
| 1993 | 3164812 | 1463759 | 1248780 | 15344 | 419109 | 383368 | 2705349 |
| 1994 | 3106562 | 1392977 | 1252952 | 8326 | 494827 | 423024 | 3002318 |
| 1995 | 3291587 | 1480385 | 1365167 | 8177 | 510662 | 478685 | 3221507 |
| 1996 | 3390033 | 1513479 | 1466668 | 4001 | 486574 | 505711 | 3405056 |
| 1997 | 2523064 | 1584478 | 743199 | 2000 | 308233 | 438398 | 3333181 |
| 1998 | 3469821 | 1627261 | 1484182 | 4159 | 546786 | 529592 | 4036992 |
| 1999 | 3331124 | 1501182 | 1499775 | 3668 | 572941 | 606800 | 5459140 |
| 2000 | 2780481 | 1353445 | 1169649 | 2077 | 534174 | 651591 | 6649322 |
| 2001 | 2539257 | 1143679 | 1178851 | 3409 | 579441 | 675244 | 6250361 |
| 2002 | 2383802 | 1085936 | 1094731 | 3755 | 557714 | 579703 | 6847570 |
| 2003 | 2221697 | 931787 | 1117704 | 5324 | 568798 | 677361 | 7305618 |
| 2004 | 2650952 | 1301791 | 1202063 | 7216 | 580290 | 748516 | 6720886 |
| 2005 | 3150203 | 1535471 | 1478616 | 4042 | 503941 | 737300 | 5792110 |
| 2006 | 3039266 | 1548928 | 1372166 | 3954 | 471853 | 827755 | 6051239 |
| 2007 | 2319354 | 1118044 | 1106106 | 3546 | 495458 | 1366106 | 6180515 |
| 2008 | 2602592 | 1234264 | 1279002 | 3163 | 470424 | 1276385 | 6164760 |
| 2009 | 2590287 | 1276029 | 1228485 | 3213 | 467937 | 1294706 | 5743437 |
| 2010 | 2553744 | 1206593 | 1272970 | 2411 | 439872 | 1267226 | 5895190 |
| 2011 | 2678626 | 1213908 | 1386365 | 2375 | 441237 | 1262896 | 5948249 |
| 2012 | 2707295 | 1242299 | 1396704 | 2334 | 456372 | 1201836 | 5826702 |
| 2013 | 2791826 | 1295227 | 1432355 | 2057 | 440426 | 1217969 | 5906625 |
| 2014 | 2780244 | 1302282 | 1418469 | 1392 | 394461 | 1188690 | 6134061 |
| 2015 | 2878062 | 1332125 | 1497121 | 1279 | 342034 | 1189312 | 5988945 |
| 2016 | 2940668 | 1345273 | 1551200 | 408 | 365207 | 1207498 | 5915380 |
| 2017 | 2968896 | 1264073 | 1670338 | 420 | 383668 | 1187041 | 6277779 |
| 2018 | 3100964 | 1376646 | 1690817 | 977 | 384918 | 1092176 | 6443615 |

注：2007 年 -2017 年数据为根据第三次农业普查结果核定修正后数据。

Note: Agricultural data from 2007 to 2017 are revised according to the results of the third agricultural census.

## 11-13 续表 1
Continued

单位：吨（ton）

| 市、区名称 | Region | 蔬菜 Vegetable | #大白菜 Cabbage | #芹菜 Celery | #胡萝卜 Carrot | #马铃薯 Potato |
|---|---|---|---|---|---|---|
| **全市** | **Whole Municipality** | **6443615** | **1355475** | **172931** | **542514** | **1187282** |
| 崂山区 | Laoshan District | 10845 | 5276 | 45 | 74 | 2245 |
| 黄岛区 | Huangdao District | 601531 | 296779 | 24395 | 411 | 84415 |
| 城阳区 | Chengyang District | 42497 | 9710 | 1024 | | 2650 |
| 即墨区 | Jimo District | 564332 | 115802 | 14385 | 61384 | 80952 |
| 胶州市 | Jiaozhou | 1071284 | 260143 | 55922 | 5579 | 388271 |
| 平度市 | Pingdu | 2921519 | 463705 | 47768 | 236247 | 578943 |
| 莱西市 | Laixi | 1231606 | 204060 | 29392 | 238818 | 49806 |

注：1. 城阳区含红岛经济区数据。
　　2. 马铃薯作为蔬菜统计。

Note：1.Chengyang District includes Hongdao Economic Zone.
　　2. Statistics of potatoes as vegetables.

## 11-13 续表 2
Continued

单位：吨（ton）

| 市、区名称 | Region | #黄瓜 Cucumer | 西红柿 Tomato | #大葱 Green onion | #蒜头 Carlic | #食用菌 Edible fungi |
|---|---|---|---|---|---|---|
| **全市** | **Whole Municipality** | **408646** | **339822** | **745935** | **178025** | **82870** |
| 崂山区 | Laoshan District | 412 | 122 | 141 | 43 | |
| 黄岛区 | Huangdao District | 9220 | 39107 | 4172 | 1104 | 64714 |
| 城阳区 | Chengyang District | 8242 | 7535 | 780 | | 938 |
| 即墨区 | Jimo District | 51030 | 25547 | 55908 | 4850 | 13660 |
| 胶州市 | Jiaozhou | 22266 | 13408 | 53788 | 420 | 427 |
| 平度市 | Pingdu | 45760 | 78211 | 618353 | 162708 | 1602 |
| 莱西市 | Laixi | 271715 | 175893 | 12793 | 8900 | 1530 |

注：城阳区含红岛经济区数据。

Note：Chengyang District includes Hongdao Economic Zone.

## 11-14 分市、区猪、羊及家禽存养量（2018年）
HOGS、SHEEP、GOATS AND POULTRY IN STOCK BY REGION（2018）

单位：万头、万只（10 000 head）

| 市、区名称 | Region | 年末生猪存养量 Hoga in Stock (year-end) | #母猪 Sow | 牛 Cattle and Buffaloes | #奶牛 Cows | 年末羊存养量 Sheep and Goats in Stock (year-end) | 年末家禽存栏 Poultry stock at the eng of the year | #蛋鸡 Egg |
|---|---|---|---|---|---|---|---|---|
| **全市** | **Whole Municipality** | **170.1** | **18.3** | **16.2** | **8.8** | **21.1** | **5310.2** | **1289.2** |
| 崂山区 | Laoshan District | | | | | | | |
| 黄岛区 | Huangdao District | 30.7 | 2.9 | 1.0 | 0.1 | 4.2 | 530.0 | 178.4 |
| 城阳区 | Chengyang District | 0.8 | 0.1 | 0.2 | 0.2 | | 10.4 | 10.2 |
| 即墨区 | Jimo District | 24.0 | 2.6 | 1.9 | 1.2 | 1.8 | 811.5 | 350.3 |
| 胶州市 | Jiaozhou | 24.7 | 2.4 | 1.2 | 0.3 | 4.6 | 358.6 | 236.0 |
| 平度市 | Pingdu | 56.9 | 6.7 | 4.0 | 0.7 | 6.7 | 1604.1 | 240.4 |
| 莱西市 | Laixi | 32.5 | 3.7 | 7.9 | 6.3 | 3.7 | 1968.0 | 254.2 |
| 红岛经济区 | Qingdao National High-tech Industrial Development Zone | 0.5 | 0.0 | 0.0 | 0.0 | 0.0 | 27.6 | 19.6 |

## 11-15 分市、区肉、蛋、奶产量（2018年）
OUTPUT OF MEAT，EGGS AND MILK BY REGION（2018）

单位：万吨（10 000 tons）

| 市、区名称 | Region | 肉类产量 Output of Meat | #猪肉 Port | #禽肉 Poultry Meat | 禽蛋 Poultry Meat | 牛羊奶 Milk |
|---|---|---|---|---|---|---|
| **全市** | **Whole Municipality** | **52.2** | **22.5** | **27.8** | **18.2** | **29.8** |
| 崂山区 | Laoshan District | | | | | |
| 黄岛区 | Huangdao District | 7.2 | 4.0 | 2.5 | 2.5 | 1.1 |
| 城阳区 | Chengyang District | 0.1 | 0.1 | 0.0 | 0.1 | 0.5 |
| 即墨区 | Jimo District | 6.5 | 3.2 | 3.2 | 4.9 | 3.9 |
| 胶州市 | Jiaozhou | 4.7 | 3.5 | 0.9 | 3.3 | 1.7 |
| 平度市 | Pingdu | 16.8 | 7.4 | 8.9 | 3.5 | 2.6 |
| 莱西市 | Laixi | 16.8 | 4.2 | 12.2 | 3.6 | 19.9 |
| 红岛经济区 | Qingdao National High-tech Industrial Development Zone | 0.1 | 0.1 | 0.0 | 0.3 | 0.1 |

# 11-16 分市、区渔业养殖面积
## AQUACULTURE AREA BY REGION

单位：公顷（hectare）

| 市、区名称 | Region | 2018年 | | | 2017年 | | |
|---|---|---|---|---|---|---|---|
| | | 养殖面积 Aquaculture Area | #海水 Seawater | #淡水 Fresh Water | 养殖面积 Aquaculture Area | #海水 Seawater | #淡水 Fresh Water |
| **全市** | **Whole Municipality** | **35259** | **32344** | **2915** | **34941** | **32403** | **2538** |
| 崂山区 | Laoshan District | 1600 | 1600 | | 1600 | 1600 | |
| 黄岛区 | Huangdao District | 12076 | 11650 | 426 | 12124 | 11698 | 426 |
| 城阳区 | Chengyang District | 6728 | 6465 | 263 | 6871 | 6465 | 406 |
| 即墨区 | Jimo District | 11146 | 10878 | 268 | 10957 | 10889 | 68 |
| 胶州市 | Jiaozhou | 2276 | 1751 | 525 | 2059 | 1751 | 308 |
| 平度市 | Pingdu | 463 | | 463 | 365 | | 365 |
| 莱西市 | Laixi | 970 | | 970 | 966 | | 966 |

注：城阳区含红岛经济区数据。
Note: Chengyang District includes Hongdao Economic Zone.

# 11-17 分市、区水产品总产量（2018年）
## OUTPUT OF AQUATIC PRODUCTS BY REGION (2018)

单位：吨（ton）

| 市、区名称 | Region | 水产品总产量 Output of Aquatic Products | #养殖产量 Aquaculture Output | #捕捞产量 Catch | #鱼类 Fish | #甲壳类 Crust | #贝类 Shellfish | #藻类 Algae |
|---|---|---|---|---|---|---|---|---|
| **全市** | **Whole Municipality** | **1035135** | **833977** | **201158** | **151451** | **56083** | **748590** | **3630** |
| 崂山区 | Laoshan District | 60002 | 21102 | 38900 | 13200 | 6826 | 19922 | 1230 |
| 黄岛区 | Huangdao District | 350234 | 287655 | 62579 | 86584 | 17090 | 215045 | 2400 |
| 城阳区 | Chengyang District | 237444 | 214384 | 23060 | 8838 | 3152 | 213152 | |
| 即墨区 | Jimo District | 285057 | 234281 | 50776 | 12951 | 24407 | 233963 | |
| 胶州市 | Jiaozhou | 98492 | 72649 | 25843 | 26031 | 4552 | 66508 | |
| 平度市 | Pingdu | 1719 | 1719 | | 1668 | 48 | | |
| 莱西市 | Laixi | 2187 | 2187 | | 2179 | 8 | | |

注：城阳区含红岛经济区数据。
Note: Chengyang District includes Hongdao Economic Zone.

## 11-18 分市、区植树及造林面积（2018 年）

OUTPUT OF AQUATIC PRODUCTS BY REGION（2018）

| 市、区名称 | Region | 当年造林面积（公顷）Area of Afforestation in the Year( hectare ) | 育苗面积（公顷）Seeding Area ( hectare ) | 森林抚育作业面积（公顷）Forest Tending Area ( hectare ) | 零星（四旁）植树（万株）Surrounding Tree Planting ( 10 000trees ) |
|---|---|---|---|---|---|
| **全市** | **Whole Municipality** | **9018** | **11135** | **6714** | **536.2** |
| 崂山区 | Laoshan District | 80 | 120 | 1713 | 4.2 |
| 黄岛区 | Huangdao District | 1513 | 1862 | 667 | |
| 城阳区 | Chengyang District | 191 | 554 | 667 | 30.0 |
| 即墨区 | Jimo District | 1365 | 3480 | 1000 | 90.0 |
| 胶州市 | Jiaozhou | 1260 | 1790 | 667 | 17.0 |
| 平度市 | Pingdu | 1025 | 2539 | 1667 | 124.0 |
| 莱西市 | Laixi | 3584 | 790 | 333 | 271.0 |

注：城阳区含红岛经济区数据。

Note：Chengyang District includes Hongdao Economic Zone.

## 11-19 分市、区水果产量（2018 年）

AREA OF FORESTATION AND OUTPUT OF FRUITS BY REGION（2018）

单位：吨（ton）

| 市、区名称 | Region | 水果总产量 Output of Fruits ( ton ) | #园林水果 Garden Fruits | #瓜果类水果 Melon Fruits |
|---|---|---|---|---|
| **全市** | **Whole Municipality** | **1092176** | **712473** | **379703** |
| 崂山区 | Laoshan District | 7099 | 6983 | 116 |
| 黄岛区 | Huangdao District | 112683 | 86006 | 26676 |
| 城阳区 | Chengyang District | 17362 | 15677 | 1684 |
| 即墨区 | Jimo District | 40056 | 16627 | 23429 |
| 胶州市 | Jiaozhou | 56681 | 38418 | 18264 |
| 平度市 | Pingdu | 428202 | 260967 | 167235 |
| 莱西市 | Laixi | 430093 | 287794 | 142299 |

注：城阳区含红岛经济区数据。

Note：Chengyang District includes Hongdao Economic Zone.

## 11-19 续表
Continued

单位：吨（ton）

| 市、区名称 | Region | #苹果 Apple | #梨 Pear | #桃 Peach | #葡萄 Grape | #杏 Apricot | #山楂 Hawthorn | #西瓜 Watermelon | #甜瓜 Muskmelon |
|---|---|---|---|---|---|---|---|---|---|
| **全市** | **Whole Municipality** | **284595** | **96778** | **111206** | **146065** | **10422** | **2858** | **206979** | **117107** |
| 崂山区 | Laoshan District | 66 | 95 | 2172 | 8 | 1578 | 5 | | 11 |
| 黄岛区 | Huangdao District | 33686 | 4066 | 17932 | 4178 | 369 | 41 | 17030 | 1139 |
| 城阳区 | Chengyang District | 635 | 126 | 6109 | 5112 | 2888 | | | |
| 即墨区 | Jimo District | 4557 | 554 | 5930 | 3207 | 76 | 44 | 11356 | 5389 |
| 胶州市 | Jiaozhou | 14618 | 3639 | 9326 | 4320 | 5398 | 60 | 17091 | 214 |
| 平度市 | Pingdu | 96407 | 24198 | 43048 | 69095 | 113 | 814 | 140426 | 4702 |
| 莱西市 | Laixi | 134626 | 64102 | 26690 | 60146 | 1 | 1895 | 21075 | 105652 |

注：城阳区含红岛经济区数据。
Note: Chengyang District includes Hongdao Economic Zone.

## 11-20 分市、区果园、茶园面积和茶叶产量（2018年）
AREA OF ORCHARD AND TEA GARDEN AND PRODUCTION OF TES BY CTTY AND DISTRICT (2018)

单位：公顷（hectare），吨(ton)

| 市、区名称 | Region | 果园面积 Area of Orchards | #苹果园 Apple Orchard | #梨园 Pear Orchard | #葡萄园 Vineyand | #桃园 Peach Orchard | 茶园面积 Area of Tea Plantations | 茶叶产量 Cocoon yield |
|---|---|---|---|---|---|---|---|---|
| **全市** | **Whole Municipality** | **28184** | **8724** | **3072** | **4527** | **4836** | **3919** | **4430** |
| 崂山区 | Laoshan District | 644 | 3 | 4 | 1 | 80 | 1126 | 1261 |
| 黄岛区 | Huangdao District | 5489 | 1083 | 135 | 218 | 1333 | 2323 | 2577 |
| 城阳区 | Chengyang District | 837 | 32 | 6 | 170 | 247 | 65 | 99 |
| 即墨区 | Jimo District | 986 | 248 | 43 | 143 | 424 | 358 | 482 |
| 胶州市 | Jiaozhou | 1362 | 416 | 94 | 109 | 401 | 24 | 5 |
| 平度市 | Pingdu | 9972 | 3031 | 866 | 2079 | 1358 | 22 | 7 |
| 莱西市 | Laixi | 8895 | 3912 | 1924 | 1807 | 993 | 0 | 0 |

注：城阳区含红岛经济区数据。
Note: Chengyang District includes Hongdao Economic Zone.

# 11-21 主要年份主要农业机械拥有量
MAJOR YEAR'S OWNERSHIP OF AGRICULTURAL MACHINERY

| 年份 Year | 农业机械总动力（万千瓦）Total Agricultural Machinery Power (10 000kW) | 农用拖拉机 Agricultural Tractors | | 大、中型机引农具（万台）Large and Medium Towong Farm Machinery (10 000 sets) | 排灌机械 Draingage and Irrigation Machinery | |
|---|---|---|---|---|---|---|
| | | 混合台 set | 千瓦 kW | | 台 set | 万千瓦 10 000kW |
| 1949 | | | | | | |
| 1952 | | | | | | |
| 1957 | 0.22 | 59 | 2.2 | 0.01 | | |
| 1962 | 2.47 | 254 | 11.47 | 0.06 | | |
| 1965 | 3.49 | 296 | 13.2 | 0.08 | | |
| 1970 | 10.40 | 602 | 7963 | 0.07 | | |
| 1975 | 43.94 | 6447 | 103476 | 0.48 | | |
| 1978 | 75.45 | 15576 | 309287 | 1.02 | | |
| 1980 | 110.44 | 24278 | 502731 | 1.72 | | |
| 1985 | 174.76 | 33097 | 506217 | 1.71 | 67794 | 54.92 |
| 1990 | 253.52 | 55363 | 680903 | 2.03 | 105574 | 74.63 |
| 1991 | 250.58 | 57404 | 691332 | 2.20 | 134900 | 73.77 |
| 1992 | 253.94 | 57182 | 684182 | 2.28 | 124800 | 82.68 |
| 1993 | 261.24 | 56335 | 678161 | 2.34 | 144460 | 78.96 |
| 1994 | 278.41 | 58698 | 688886 | 2.39 | 147259 | 80.81 |
| 1995 | 289.23 | 56391 | 657025 | 2.28 | 138625 | 73.98 |
| 1996 | 303.57 | 59698 | 680447 | 2.32 | 148313 | 81.53 |
| 1997 | 326.72 | 66841 | 744424 | 2.42 | 155629 | 88.09 |
| 1998 | 364.21 | 87226 | 894985 | 2 | 156565 | 86.68 |
| 1999 | 411.44 | 105743 | 1075907 | 3 | 170875 | 96.20 |
| 2000 | 459.21 | 126981 | 1253210 | 3 | 182646 | 108.26 |
| 2001 | 496.27 | 141409 | 1394114 | 4 | 178437 | 104.18 |
| 2002 | 534.92 | 152920 | 1537544 | 5 | 182799 | 107.35 |
| 2003 | 560.94 | 160676 | 1666185 | 5 | 192930 | 109.44 |
| 2004 | 599 | 168061 | 1818276 | 5 | 192144 | 110 |
| 2005 | 620 | 163032 | 1757177 | 6 | 188689 | 112 |
| 2006 | 651 | 171155 | 1890402 | 6 | 192010 | 116 |
| 2007 | 680 | 173326 | 1958047 | 7 | 195050 | 118 |
| 2008 | 697 | 176156 | 2034453 | 8 | 208711 | 134 |
| 2009 | 719 | 180171 | 2266697 | 9 | 207648 | 134 |
| 2010 | 764 | 200208 | 2331867 | 10 | 190770 | 123 |
| 2011 | 784 | 202022 | 2649283 | 10 | 189834 | 127 |
| 2012 | 798 | 206290 | 2759004 | 10 | 190134 | 127 |
| 2013 | 809 | 206309 | 2968332 | 10 | 190433 | 127 |
| 2014 | 827 | 205065 | 2960438 | 10 | 190584 | 128 |
| 2015 | 854 | 207809 | 3176870 | 10 | 191152 | 128 |
| 2016 | 698 | 211689 | 3372681 | 10 | 191283 | 128 |
| 2017 | 728 | 214799 | 3550005 | 11 | 191417 | 128 |
| 2018 | 738 | 215668 | 3668505 | 0.8 | 232943 | |

注：大、中型机引农具 2018 年为新统计口径，只统计功率 58.8 千瓦以上机引农具。

Note: Large and medium type agricultural tools are the new statistical caliber in 2018, and only the statistical power is 58.8 kilowatts or more.

# 11-22 主要年份农业机械化用电量、化肥施用量
MAJOR YEAR'S MECHANIZATION, ELECTRICITY AND CHEMICAL FERTILIZER CONSUMPTION

| 年份 Year | 有效灌溉面积（公顷）Irrigated Area (hectare) | 配套机电井（眼）Number of Electromechanical Well (well) | 机耕面积（公顷）Area of Motorized Culitivation (hectare) | 机播面积（公顷）Area of Motorized Planting (hectare) | 机收面积（公顷）Area of Motorized Harvesing (hectare) | 农村用电量（万千瓦时）Electricity Consumption in Rural Area (10 000kW·h) | 化肥施用量（折纯万吨）Chemical Fertilizer Consumption (convert to 10 000tons) |
|---|---|---|---|---|---|---|---|
| 1949 | 8340 | | | | | | |
| 1952 | 14980 | | | | | | |
| 1957 | 59353 | | 12800 | 13 | | | 0.19 |
| 1962 | 55213 | 191 | 65680 | 927 | 927 | 55 | 0.10 |
| 1965 | 80000 | 125 | 11433 | 573 | 247 | 128 | 0.55 |
| 1970 | 147613 | 3947 | 143700 | 2527 | 133 | 1208 | 1.76 |
| 1975 | 233980 | 12820 | 248867 | 54507 | 953 | 2522 | 2.77 |
| 1978 | 276660 | 21017 | 329213 | 178533 | 15060 | 13975 | 3.64 |
| 1980 | 296606 | 22472 | 444800 | 187980 | 55333 | 20492 | 12.06 |
| 1985 | 302647 | 42925 | 366786 | 148433 | 56447 | 41524 | 11.66 |
| 1990 | 274680 | 56821 | 426680 | 220593 | 143133 | 67616 | 20.47 |
| 1991 | 281500 | 58987 | 431293 | 254266 | 192946 | 81200 | 22.53 |
| 1992 | 281610 | 62100 | 438533 | 270453 | 207780 | 88024 | 22.60 |
| 1993 | 284080 | 63954 | 439300 | 260287 | 225307 | 102501 | 28.04 |
| 1994 | 286750 | 64877 | 436820 | 262846 | 238593 | 121307 | 28.73 |
| 1995 | 287020 | 64651 | 435213 | 271707 | 250267 | 134284 | 31.45 |
| 1996 | 289320 | 65237 | 438947 | 280480 | 235933 | 143740 | 31.36 |
| 1997 | 292130 | 66783 | 442213 | 308267 | 266147 | 150971 | 28.99 |
| 1998 | 294120 | 64109 | 442920 | 359447 | 285513 | 153113 | 32.0 |
| 1999 | 294790 | 64734 | 440967 | 396180 | 286367 | 169337 | 32.6 |
| 2000 | 295190 | 65179 | 439980 | 346480 | 292787 | 189651 | 32.5 |
| 2001 | 296980 | 65547 | 436576 | 382870 | 265730 | 228069 | 31.7 |
| 2002 | 294310 | 65588 | 433660 | 364680 | 267690 | 256453 | 31.1 |
| 2003 | 292410 | 65406 | 415790 | 404980 | 256600 | 299425 | 31.9 |
| 2004 | 292520 | 65501 | 415220 | 454800 | 314680 | 330609 | 32.5 |
| 2005 | 296450 | 65303 | 409610 | 493240 | 367740 | 372644 | 33.0 |
| 2006 | 303070 | 65981 | 403980 | 493750 | 398700 | 413762 | 32.6 |
| 2007 | 305760 | 66400 | 400480 | 499590 | 429630 | 425715 | 33.9 |
| 2008 | 313920 | 66828 | 404080 | 517540 | 455120 | 424292 | 31.1 |
| 2009 | 322710 | 67027 | 404080 | 538220 | 481176 | 426306 | 30.2 |
| 2010 | 328960 | 67242 | 578726 | 558611 | 499248 | 426819 | 29.9 |
| 2011 | 331690 | 62104 | 600451 | 567947 | 547108 | 431646 | 29.4 |
| 2012 | 333850 | 62112 | 610382 | 627701 | 566653 | 426815 | 29.1 |
| 2013 | 302790 | 170008 | 410601 | 627701 | 566653 | 359138 | 29.1 |
| 2014 | 321670 | 169491 | 411355 | 590798 | 545360 | 404380 | 28.9 |
| 2015 | 323400 | 155074 | 417991 | 640022 | 600696 | 401122 | 28.5 |
| 2016 | 327600 | 135057 | 362912 | 561022 | 511000 | 385434 | 28.37 |
| 2017 | 329620 | 139342 | 360085 | 566264 | 516763 | 382437 | 27.83 |
| 2018 | 331240 | 136785 | 359238 | 578082 | 531733 | 377858 | 27.05 |

## 11-23 分市、区农业机械化和电气化（2018 年）
MECHANIZATION AND ELECTRIFICATION IN AGRICULTURE BY REGION (2018)

| 市、区名称 | Region | 农村用电量（万千瓦小时）Electricity Consumed in Rural Areas (10 000kW·h) | 机耕作业面积 Area of Motorized Cultivation(hectare) | 机播地面积 Area of Motorized Planting (hectare) | 机收面积 Area of Motorized Harvesting (hectare) |
|---|---|---|---|---|---|
| | | | 面积 Area（公顷）(hectare) | | |
| 全市 | **Whole Municipality** | **377858** | **359238** | **578082** | **531733** |
| 崂山区 | Laoshan District | 8773 | | | |
| 黄岛区 | Huangdao District | 56526 | 41291 | 66390 | 60497 |
| 城阳区 | Chengyang District | 45776 | 1929 | 2284 | 1915 |
| 即墨区 | Jimo District | 60459 | 48795 | 87811 | 83478 |
| 胶州市 | Jiaozhou | 99951 | 45638 | 74359 | 71289 |
| 平度市 | Pingdu | 71387 | 153445 | 238820 | 213569 |
| 莱西市 | Laixi | 34984 | 68139 | 108418 | 100985 |

注：城阳区含红岛经济区数据。
Note: Chengyang District includes Hongdao Economic Zone.

## 11-24 分市、区农用化肥施用量（2018 年）
CONSUMPTION OF CHEMICAL FERTILIZERS BY REGION (2018)

单位：折纯吨（ton converted to pure amount）

| 市、区名称 | Region | 农用化肥施用量 Consumption of Chemical Fertilizers | 氮肥 Nitrogenous Fertilizer | 磷肥 Phosphate Fertilizer | 钾肥 Potash Fertilizer | 复合肥 Compound Fertilizer | 附：平均每公顷耕地施用化肥量（折纯千克）Annotation: Consumption of Chemical Fertilizer Per Hectare (convert to pure volume) |
|---|---|---|---|---|---|---|---|
| 全市 | **Whole Municipality** | **270505** | **39773** | **10420** | **12197** | **208115** | **522** |
| 崂山区 | Laoshan District | 330 | 44 | 9 | 6 | 270 | 367 |
| 黄岛区 | Huangdao District | 30705 | 5494 | 2242 | 3541 | 19429 | 414 |
| 城阳区 | Chengyang District | 931 | 173 | 71 | 73 | 613 | 139 |
| 即墨区 | Jimo District | 36234 | 13216 | 2276 | 1099 | 19644 | 364 |
| 胶州市 | Jiaozhou | 35225 | 5737 | 847 | 3926 | 24715 | 552 |
| 平度市 | Pingdu | 118163 | 5162 | 1305 | 3077 | 108619 | 641 |
| 莱西市 | Laixi | 48918 | 9948 | 3670 | 476 | 34825 | 547 |

注：城阳区含红岛经济区数据。
Note: Chengyang District includes Hongdao Economic Zone.

# 11-25 分市、区农田水利（2018年）
FARMLAND WATER CONSERVANCY BY REGION (2018)

| 市、区名称 | Region | 有效灌溉面积（公顷）Irrigated Area (hectare) | 有效灌溉面积占耕地面积比重（%）Percentage of Irrigated Area to Area of Cultivated Land (%) | 机电井数（眼）Number of Electromechanical Well (well) |
|---|---|---|---|---|
| **全市** | **Whole Municipality** | **331240** | **63.9** | **136785** |
| 崂山区 | Laoshan District | 520 | 57.9 | 1307 |
| 黄岛区 | Huangdao District | 44990 | 60.7 | 10229 |
| 城阳区 | Chengyang District | 1990 | 29.8 | 1027 |
| 即墨区 | Jimo District | 59560 | 59.9 | 34297 |
| 胶州市 | Jiaozhou | 39710 | 62.3 | 17726 |
| 平度市 | Pingdu | 130590 | 70.9 | 45121 |
| 莱西市 | Laixi | 53880 | 60.3 | 27078 |

注：城阳区含红岛经济区数据。
Note: Chengyang District includes Hongdao Economic Zone.

# 11-26 分市、区主要农业机械拥有量（2018年）
OWNERSHIP OFMAJOR AGRICULTURAL MACHINERY BY REGION（2018）

| 市、区名称 | Region | 农业机械总动力（万千瓦）Agricultural Machinery Power（10 000kW） | 平均每公顷耕地拥有量（千瓦）Power Per Hectare of Cultivated Land（kW） | 大中型拖拉机 Large and Medium Tractors | | 小型拖拉机 Small Tractors | |
|---|---|---|---|---|---|---|---|
| | | | | 台 set | 千瓦 kW | 台 set | 千瓦 kW |
| **全市** | **Whole Municipality** | **738** | **14.2** | **43457** | **2172767** | **172211** | **1495738** |
| 崂山区 | Laoshan District | | | | | | |
| 黄岛区 | Huangdao District | 81 | 10.9 | 2658 | 126473 | 44740 | 282911 |
| 城阳区 | Chengyang District | 31 | 46.4 | 444 | 21893 | 1547 | 10193 |
| 即墨区 | Jimo District | 111 | 11.2 | 4223 | 231974 | 35273 | 325210 |
| 胶州市 | Jiaozhou | 108 | 16.9 | 4687 | 316822 | 20649 | 301865 |
| 平度市 | Pingdu | 274 | 14.9 | 24396 | 1151765 | 33723 | 320365 |
| 莱西市 | Laixi | 133 | 14.9 | 7049 | 323840 | 36279 | 255194 |

注：城阳区含红岛经济区数据。
Note：Chengyang District includes Hongdao Economic Zone.

# 11-26 续表
Continued

| 市、区名称 | Region | 种植机械（台）Planting Machinery（unit） | 机引犁（部）Towing Ploughs（unit） | 机引耙（部）Towing Rakes（unit） | 粮食加工机械（台）Grain Processing Machinery（unit） | 油料加工机械（部）Oill Processing Machinery（unit） | 棉花加工机械（部）Cotton Processing Machinery（unit） | 饲草料加工机械（台套）Forage Processing Machinery（unit） |
|---|---|---|---|---|---|---|---|---|
| **全市** | **Whole Municipality** | **966513** | **160392** | **32240** | **25683** | **9144** | **132** | **23093** |
| 崂山区 | Laoshan District | | | | | | | |
| 黄岛区 | Huangdao District | 71599 | 32920 | 109 | 1117 | 256 | | 3544 |
| 城阳区 | Chengyang District | 9639 | 1200 | 207 | 1605 | 520 | 17 | 338 |
| 即墨区 | Jimo District | 387432 | 19958 | 1680 | 3259 | 1472 | | 1481 |
| 胶州市 | Jiaozhou | 67138 | 15126 | 5242 | 3050 | 2125 | | 3589 |
| 平度市 | Pingdu | 255413 | 21850 | 16500 | 4372 | 1421 | 6 | 7538 |
| 莱西市 | Laixi | 175292 | 69338 | 8502 | 12280 | 3350 | 109 | 6603 |

注：城阳区含红岛经济区数据。
Note：Chengyang District includes Hongdao Economic Zone.

# 主要统计指标解释

**农业总产值**　是以货币表现的农、林、牧、渔业全部产品的总量，它反映一定时期内农业生产的总规模和总成果。

农、林、牧、渔业的统计范围是：

（1）农业包括农作物种植业和其他农业。

农作物种植业包括谷物、豆类、薯类、棉、油料、糖料、麻类、烟叶、蔬菜、药材、瓜类和其他农作物的种植，以及茶园、桑园、果园的生产经营。其他农业包括采集野生植物的果实、纤维、树胶、树脂、油料以及柴草、野生药材、菌类等及农民家庭兼营的商品性工业。

（2）林业包括林木的栽培（不包括茶园、桑园和果园的栽培、管理和收获等活动）、林产品的采集和村及村以下合作经济组织和农户的竹木采伐。

（3）牧业包括除渔业养殖以外的一切动物饲养和放牧，以及野生动物的捕猎和饲养。

（4）渔业包括水生动物和海藻类植物的养殖和捕捞。

**粮食产量**　指稻谷、小麦、玉米、高粱等谷物及薯类和豆类的全社会产量。包括国有经济经营的、集体统一经营的和农民家庭经营的粮食产量，还包括工矿企业办的农场和其他生产单位的产量。其产量计算方法，豆类按去豆荚后的干豆计算；薯类（不包括芋头、木薯和马铃薯）按5公斤鲜薯折1公斤粮食计算；马铃薯作为蔬菜统计；其他粮食一律按脱粒后的原粮计算。

**水产品产量**　指人工养殖的水产品和天然生长的水产品的捕捞量．包括海水的鱼类、虾蟹类、贝类和藻类以及内陆水域的鱼类、虾蟹类和贝类，不包括淡水生植物。

**猪、牛、羊肉产量**　指当年出栏并已屠宰、除去头蹄下水后带骨头肉（即胴体重）的重量。其统计范围为全社会。

**农用化肥施用量**　指本年内实际用于农业生产的化肥数量，包括氮肥、磷肥、钾肥和复合肥。化肥施用量要求按折纯量计算数量。折纯量是指把氮肥、磷肥、钾肥分别按含氮、含五氧化二磷、含氧化钾的百分之百成分进行折算后的数量。复合肥按其所含主要成分折算。

公式：折纯量 = 实物量 × 某种化肥有效成分含量的百分比

**农业机械总动力**　指用于农、林、牧、渔业生产的各种动力机械的动力总和。动力机械包括耕作、排灌、种植、植物保护、收获、农产品加工、运输、畜牧、渔业、农田水利等各种机械。不包括专门用于乡办工业、基本建设、非农业运输、科学试验和教学等非农业生产方面用的动力机械与作业机械的数量。

# Explanatory Notes on Main Statistical Indicators

**Gross Output Value of Agriculture**　refers to the total volume of products of farming, forestry, animal husbandry, and fishery expressed in the monetary terms.It reflects the overall scale and achievements of agricultural production during a given period of time.

The scope of statistics on farming, forestry, animal husbandry, and fishery are as follows:

Farming includes cultivation of farm crops and other agricultural activities.

Cultivation of farm crops include cultivation of grain crops, legume crops, tuber-crops, cotton, oil-bearing crops, sugar crops, and cultivation and management of tea plantations, mulberry fields and orchards.

Other agricultural activities include harvesting wild fruits, fiber, tree gum, resin, oil-bearing plants, firewood, wild medicinal herbs, fungus, and rural-household commodity industries.

Forestry refers to planting trees of various kinds (excluding tea plantations, mulberry fields and orchards), collection of forestry products and cutting and felling of bamboo and trees by villages and other cooperative organizations under village level.

Animal husbandry refers to raising and grazing of all kinds of farm animals except fishing and aquatic cultivating, and hunting and rising of wild animals.

Fishery refers to cultivation and catching of fish and other aquatic products and cultivation and collection of seaweed and other aquatic plants.

**Grain Output** refers to the total output of rice, wheat, corn, sorghum, millet and other miscellaneous grains as well as tubers and bean in the whole country including grains produced by states farms, collective unit, industrial enterprises and mines, output of beans refers to dry beans without pods, the output of tubers( excluding taros,cassava and potatoes )was converted into that of grain at the ratio 5: 1, i. e. 5 kilograms of fresh tubers was equivalent to 1 kilogram of grain. Statistics of potatoes as vegetables. Output of all other grains refers to husked grain.

**Output of Aquatic Products** refers to catches of both artificially cultured and naturally grown aquatic products, including fish, shrimps, crabs and shellfish in sea and inland water as well as seaweed. Freshwater plants are not included.

Output of Pork, Beef, and Muttonrefers to the meat of slaughtered hogs, cattle, sheep and goats with head, feet, and offal taken away. Data refers to the production of the whole country.

**Consumption of Chemical Fertilizers in Agriculture** refers to the quantity of chemical fertilizers applied in agriculture in the year, including nitrogenous fertilizer, phosphate fertilizer, potash fertilizer, and compound fertilizer. The consumption of chemical fertilizers is required in calculation to convert the gross weight into weight containing 100% effective component ( e.g. 100% nitrogen content in nitrogenous fertilizer, 100% phosphorous pent oxide contents in phosphate fertilizer, 100% potassium oxide contents in potash fertilizer ) . Compound fertilizer is converted with its major component. The formula is:

Volume of effective component= physical quantity x effective component of certain chemical fertilizer ( % )

**Total Power of Agriculture Machinery** Refers to the total mechanical power of machinery used in farming forestry animal husbandry and fishery, including machines used for ploughing, irrigation and drainage, crop growing, plant protection, harvesting, farm product processing, transport, stock breeding, fishery and water conservancy, Machinery employed for non agricultural purposes such as township industry, capital construction, non-agricultural transport, scientific experiments and for teaching is excluded.

# 工　业 12

INDUSTRY

# 简要说明

## 一、本篇资料的主要内容

本篇资料主要反映了全市工业生产和基本效益情况，主要包括工业企业单位数、历年工业总产值、规模以上工业、国有控股工业、国有工业、集体工业、外商投资和港澳台投资工业、大中型工业企业的主要经济指标、相关的财务分析指标和主要工业产品产量等方面的内容。

## 二、本篇资料的来源

1、本篇中规模以上工业资料来源于工业统计年报，由市统计局工业统计处整理提供。

2、规模以下工业资料产值与单位数均来源于抽样调查推算，工业单位数除普查年度外无分市（区）数据，由国家统计局青岛调查队工业与投资建筑业调查处整理提供。

# Brief Introduction

## *I. Main Content*

Data in this chapter show the basic condition of industrial production and benefit in Qingdao, mainly including the number of industrial enterprises, gross industrial output value and indices, the output of major industrial products and major economic and relevant financial indicators of industrial enterprises. Industrial enterprises include enterprises above designated size, state share-holding enterprises, state owned enterprises, collective owned enterprises, foreign funded enterprises, enterprises with funds from Hong Kong, Macao and Taiwan, large and medium sized enterprises.

## *II. Source of Data*

(1) Data on industry above designated size are based on the annual report of industrial statistics, and prepared by the Division of Industry Statistics of Qingdao Municipal Bureau of Statistics.

(2) Data on output value and unit number of industry below designated size are based on the sample survey, and there is no data on number of enterprises by region except census year. The Data are complied by the Division of Industry, Investment and Construction Survey of Survey Office of the National Bureau of Statistics in Qingdao.

# 12-1　规模以上工业企业单位数
NUMBER OF INDUSTRIAL ENTERPRISES ABOVE DESIGNATEO SIZE

单位：个（unit）

| 项　目 | Item | 1985 年 | 1990 年 | 1995 年 | 2000 年 | 2005 年 | 2006 年 |
|---|---|---|---|---|---|---|---|
| **总　计** | **Total** | **2411** | **2997** | **4987** | **1504** | **3697** | **4567** |
| **一、按隶属关系分** | **Grouped by Subordination** | | | | | | |
| 中央工业 | Central Indiustry | 24 | 16 | 102 | 18 | 26 | 17 |
| 地方工业 | Local Industry | 2361 | 2959 | 4821 | 1479 | 3634 | 4517 |
| **二、按经济类型分** | **Gronped by Economic Types** | | | | | | |
| 国有企业 | State-owned | 502 | 568 | 1084 | 179 | 76 | 74 |
| 集体企业 | Gollective-owned | 1907 | 2386 | 2731 | 226 | 87 | 72 |
| 其他经济类型企业 | Other Economic Types | 2 | 43 | 1172 | 1099 | 3534 | 4421 |
| # 外商及港澳台商投资企业 | Foreign Funded Enterprises and Enterprises with Funds from Hong Kong, Macao and Taiwan | | 35 | 1027 | 593 | 1658 | 1952 |
| **三、按轻重工业分** | **Grouped by Light and Heavy Industries** | | | | | | |
| 轻工业 | Light Industry | 1398 | 1730 | 2858 | 891 | 1942 | 2313 |
| 重工业 | Heavy Industry | 1013 | 1267 | 2129 | 613 | 1755 | 2254 |
| **四、按企业规模分** | **Grouped by Size of Enterprises** | | | | | | |
| 大型企业 | Large | 26 | 42 | 89 | 202 | 51 | 51 |
| 中型企业 | Medium | 80 | 168 | 216 | 229 | 441 | 469 |
| 小型企业 | Small | 2305 | 2787 | 4480 | 1073 | 3205 | 4047 |
| **五、按行业分** | **Grouped by sectors** | | | | | | |
| 黑色金属矿采选业 | Miring of Non-ferrous Metal Ores | | 4 | 6 | 1 | 2 | 5 |
| 有色金属矿采选业 | Mining of Non-ferrous Metal Ores | 2 | 7 | 9 | 7 | 5 | 5 |
| 非金属矿采选业 | Mining and Processing of Nometal Ores | 43 | 70 | 87 | 29 | 34 | 31 |
| 食品制造业 | Manufacture of Foods | 244 | 324 | 437 | 170 | 121 | 137 |
| # 粮食及饲料加工 | Processing of Gren and Feed | 62 | 57 | 60 | 27 | | |
| 饮料制造业 | Manufacture of Beverage | 31 | 44 | 74 | 23 | 29 | 28 |
| # 饮料酒 | Beverage Liquor | 20 | 28 | 27 | 19 | 20 | 25 |

注：1. 规模以上工业企业为年主营业务收入 2000 万元及以上的工业法人企业。
2. 2010 年以前为国有及年主营业务收入 500 万元以上的非国有工业企业。
3. 本表 1998 年以前为乡及乡以上工业企业单位数。
4. 2012 年行业分类按 2011 年发布的《国民经济行业分类》（GB/T4754-2011）重新划分。

Note: 1. Industrial enterprises above designated siza refers to industrial enterprises with revenue from pricipal business over 20 millinon yuan.
2. Before 2010, industrial enterprises above designated size refered to all the state-owned enterprises and non-state enterprises with revennie from principal business over 5 million yuan.
3. Before 1998, the number of industrial enterprises refer to those at and above county level.
4.The seetors are grouped by " Classification Code of the Sectors of the National Economy" (GB/T4754-2011) in 2012.

## 12-1 续表 1
Continued

单位：个（unit）

| 项 目 | Item | 2007 年 | 2008 年 | 2009 年 | 2010 年 | 2011 年 |
|---|---|---|---|---|---|---|
| **总 计** | **Total** | **5032** | **5628** | **5895** | **5674** | **4727** |
| **一、按隶属关系分** | **Grouped by Subordination** | | | | | |
| 中央工业 | Central Indiustry | 9 | 40 | 44 | 31 | 31 |
| 地方工业 | Local Industry | 4989 | 5560 | 5826 | 5618 | 4679 |
| **二、按经济类型分** | **Gronped by Economic Types** | | | | | |
| 国有企业 | State-owned | 63 | 65 | 163 | 61 | 147 |
| 集体企业 | Gollective-owned | 72 | 61 | 59 | 53 | 31 |
| 其他经济类型企业 | Other Economic Types | 4897 | 5502 | 5673 | 5560 | 4549 |
| # 外商及港澳台商投资企业 | Foreign Funded Enterprises and Enterprises with Funds from Hong Kong，Macao and Taiwan | 2091 | 2217 | 2244 | 2037 | 1618 |
| **三、按轻重工业分** | **Grouped by Light and Heavy Industries** | | | | | |
| 轻工业 | Light Industry | 2489 | 2704 | 2805 | 2635 | 2131 |
| 重工业 | Heavy Industry | 2543 | 2924 | 3090 | 3039 | 2596 |
| **四、按企业规模分** | **Grouped by Size of Enterprises** | | | | | |
| 大型企业 | Large | 53 | 48 | 50 | 52 | 50 |
| 中型企业 | Medium | 489 | 519 | 502 | 525 | 516 |
| 小型企业 | Small | 4490 | 5061 | 5343 | 5097 | 4161 |
| **五、按行业分** | **Grouped by sectors** | | | | | |
| 黑色金属矿采选业 | Miring of Non-ferrous Metal Ores | 7 | 23 | 22 | 12 | 12 |
| 有色金属矿采选业 | Mining of Non-ferrous Metal Ores | 5 | 6 | 6 | 4 | |
| 非金属矿采选业 | Mining and Processing of Nometal Ores | 33 | 30 | 26 | 26 | 23 |
| 食品制造业 | Manufacture of Foods | 156 | 158 | 174 | 167 | 127 |
| # 粮食及饲料加工 | Processing of Gren and Feed | | | | | |
| 饮料制造业 | Manufacture of Beverage | 33 | 40 | 42 | 42 | 36 |
| # 饮料酒 | Beverage Liquor | | | | | |

# 12-1 续表 2
Continued

单位：个（unit）

| 项 目 | Item | 1985年 | 1990年 | 1995年 | 2000年 | 2005年 | 2006年 |
|---|---|---|---|---|---|---|---|
| 烟草制品业 | Manufacture of Tobacco | 2 | 2 | 5 | 3 | 2 | 2 |
| 纺织业 | Manufacture of Textile | 169 | 225 | 330 | 132 | 300 | 327 |
| 纺织服装、鞋、帽制造业 | Manfacture of Testilee Wearing Apparel. Footware and Caps | 171 | 194 | 322 | 95 | 272 | 339 |
| 皮革、毛皮、羽毛(绒)及其制品业 | Manufacture of Leather, Fur, Feather and Related Products | 56 | 64 | 161 | 64 | 167 | 194 |
| 木材加工制品业 | Processing of Woon and Wood Prodncts | 71 | 89 | 116 | 19 | 40 | 53 |
| 家具制造业 | Manufacture of Furniture | 61 | 72 | 88 | 10 | 72 | 103 |
| 造纸及纸制品业 | Manufacture of Paper and Paper Producls | 66 | 74 | 110 | 56 | 102 | 128 |
| 印刷业和记录媒介的复制 | Printing, Reproduction of Recording Media | 61 | 81 | 215 | 23 | 44 | 59 |
| 文教体育用品制造业 | Manufacture of Articles For Culture, Education and Sport Activities | 31 | 27 | 93 | 48 | 89 | 91 |
| 石油、煤炭及其他燃料加工业 | Oil, coal and other fuel processing industries | 2 | 3 | 13 | 5 | 10 | 6 |
| 化学原料及制品 | Manufacture of Raw Chemical Materials and Chemical Products | 106 | 156 | 278 | 81 | 178 | 233 |
| 医药制造业 | Manufacture of Medicines | 16 | 14 | 39 | 20 | 30 | 46 |
| 化学纤维制造业 | Manufacure of Chemical Fibers | 2 | 4 | 26 | 15 | 14 | 13 |
| 橡胶制品业 | Manufacture of Rubber | 53 | 57 | 143 | 48 | 116 | 170 |
| 塑料制品业 | Manufacture of Plastics | 103 | 131 | 237 | 64 | 153 | 179 |
| 非金属矿物制品业 | Manufacture of Non-mettallic Mineral Products | 230 | 245 | 275 | 62 | 161 | 218 |
| 黑色金属压延加工业 | Smelting and Pressing of Ferrous Metals | 11 | 13 | 31 | 15 | 41 | 45 |
| 有色金属压延加工业 | Smelting and Pressing of Non-ferrous Metals | 6 | 8 | 19 | 9 | 28 | 40 |
| 金属制品业 | Manufacture of Metal Products | 161 | 186 | 372 | 88 | 186 | 250 |
| 通用设备制造业 | Manufacture of General Purpose Machinery | 320 | 398 | 320 | 94 | 299 | 397 |
| 交通运输制造业 | Manufacture of Electrical Machinery and Equipment | 104 | 114 | 358 | 52 | 151 | 194 |
| 电气机械及器材制造业 | Manufacture of Electrication Machinery and Equipment | 86 | 96 | 211 | 79 | 214 | 249 |
| 通信设备、计算机及其他电子设备制造业 | Manufacture of Communication Equipment, Computers and Other Eleetronic Equipment | 32 | 31 | 79 | 34 | 123 | 140 |
| 仪器仪表及文化、办公用机械制造业 | Manufacture of Measuring Instruments and Machinery for Cultural Activity and Office Work | 28 | 35 | 70 | 20 | 40 | 44 |
| 水的生产和供应业 | Production and Supply of Water | 8 | 12 | 12 | 8 | 10 | 10 |
| 电力、热力的生产和供应业 | Production and Supply of Electric Power and Heat Power | 10 | 16 | 20 | 17 | 27 | 32 |
| 燃气生产和供应业 | Production and Supply of Gas | 1 | 4 | 3 | 2 | 5 | 6 |
| 其他工业 | Other Industrial Sectors | 46 | 48 | 209 | 63 | 166 | 534 |

## 12-1 续表 3
Continued

单位：个（unit）

| 项　目 | Item | 2007 年 | 2008 年 | 2009 年 | 2010 年 | 2011 年 |
|---|---|---|---|---|---|---|
| 烟草制品业 | Manufacture of Tobacco | 2 | 2 | 2 | 1 | 1 |
| 纺织业 | Manufacture of Textile | 340 | 330 | 322 | 287 | 229 |
| 纺织服装、鞋、帽制造业 | Manfacture of Testilee Wearing Apparel. Footware and Caps | 362 | 418 | 434 | 392 | 295 |
| 皮革、毛皮、羽毛（绒）及其制品业 | Manufacture of Leather，Fur，Feather and Related Products | 197 | 209 | 210 | 211 | 160 |
| 木材加工制品业 | Processing of Woon and Wood Prodncts | 64 | 66 | 68 | 68 | 49 |
| 家具制造业 | Manufacture of Furniture | 119 | 130 | 133 | 117 | 97 |
| 造纸及纸制品业 | Manufacture of Paper and Paper Producls | 126 | 133 | 133 | 138 | 101 |
| 印刷业和记录媒介的复制 | Printing，Reproduction of Recording Media | 63 | 74 | 79 | 92 | 58 |
| 文教体育用品制造业 | Manufacture of Articles For Culture，Education and Sport Activities | 97 | 96 | 99 | 90 | 75 |
| 石油、煤炭及其他燃料加工业 | Oil, coal and other fuel processing industries | 7 | 7 | 9 | 8 | 7 |
| 化学原料及制品 | Manufacture of Raw Chemical Materials and Chemical Products | 261 | 276 | 275 | 262 | 231 |
| 医药制造业 | Manufacture of Medicines | 48 | 49 | 56 | 52 | 44 |
| 化学纤维制造业 | Manufacure of Chemical Fibers | 12 | 13 | 14 | 12 | 10 |
| 橡胶制品业 | Manufacture of Rubber | 183 | 211 | 214 | 196 | 187 |
| 塑料制品业 | Manufacture of Plastics | 199 | 227 | 234 | 233 | 169 |
| 非金属矿物制品业 | Manufacture of Non-mettallic Mineral Products | 259 | 311 | 320 | 327 | 303 |
| 黑色金属压延加工业 | Smelting and Pressing of Ferrous Metals | 39 | 24 | 27 | 31 | 29 |
| 有色金属压延加工业 | Smelting and Pressing of Non-ferrous Metals | 40 | 41 | 40 | 35 | 34 |
| 金属制品业 | Manufacture of Metal Products | 271 | 347 | 376 | 361 | 294 |
| 通用设备制造业 | Manufacture of General Purpose Machinery | 473 | 535 | 592 | 597 | 521 |
| 交通运输制造业 | Manufacture of Electrical Machinery and Equipment | 217 | 264 | 290 | 296 | 263 |
| 电气机械及器材制造业 | Manufacture of Electrication Machinery and Equipment | 274 | 303 | 300 | 281 | 230 |
| 通信设备、计算机及其他电子设备制造业 | Manufacture of Communication Equipment，Computers and Other Eleetronic Equipment | 152 | 163 | 168 | 167 | 124 |
| 仪器仪表及文化、办公用机械制造业 | Manufacture of Measuring Instruments and Machinery for Cultural Activity and Office Work | 47 | 47 | 55 | 54 | 39 |
| 水的生产和供应业 | Production and Supply of Water | 10 | 13 | 14 | 14 | 11 |
| 电力、热力的生产和供应业 | Production and Supply of Electric Power and Heat Power | 34 | 36 | 39 | 38 | 36 |
| 燃气生产和供应业 | Production and Supply of Gas | 7 | 13 | 13 | 14 | 11 |
| 其他工业 | Other Industrial Sectors | 895 | 1033 | 1109 | 1049 | 921 |

## 12-1 续表 4
Continued

单位：个（unit）

| 项目 | Item | 2012年 | 2013年 | 2014年 | 2015年 | 2016年 | 2017年 | 2018年 |
|---|---|---|---|---|---|---|---|---|
| **总计** | **Total** | **4817** | **4917** | **4790** | **4876** | **4431** | **3569** | **3508** |
| **一、按隶属关系分** | **Grouped by Subordination Relation** | | | | | | | |
| 中央工业 | Central Indiustry | 15 | 30 | 28 | 33 | 27 | 32 | 43 |
| 地方工业 | Local Industry | 4784 | 4871 | 4747 | 4831 | 4398 | 3532 | 3465 |
| **二、按经济类型分** | **Gronped by Economic Types** | | | | | | | |
| 国有企业 | State-owned | 144 | 140 | 132 | 141 | 128 | 131 | 145 |
| 集体企业 | Gollective-owned | 28 | 24 | 19 | 15 | 11 | 5 | 4 |
| 其他经济类型企业 | Other Economic Types | 4645 | 4753 | 4639 | 4720 | 4292 | 3433 | 3359 |
| #外商及港澳台商投资企业 | Foreign Funded Enterprises and Enterprises with Funds from Hong Kong，Macao and Taiwan | 1599 | 1551 | 1445 | 1361 | 1205 | 1037 | 938 |
| **三、按轻重工业分** | **Grouped by Light and Heavy Industries** | | | | | | | |
| 轻工业 | Light Industry | 2153 | 2190 | 2080 | 2095 | 1875 | 1522 | 1448 |
| 重工业 | Heavy Industry | 2664 | 2727 | 2710 | 2781 | 2556 | 2047 | 2060 |
| **四、按企业规模分** | **Grouped by Size of Enterprises** | | | | | | | |
| 大型企业 | Large | 98 | 97 | 91 | 89 | 85 | 78 | 76 |
| 中型企业 | Medium | 596 | 599 | 568 | 566 | 516 | 459 | 383 |
| 小型企业 | Small | 4123 | 4221 | 4131 | 4221 | 3830 | 3032 | 3049 |
| **五、按行业分** | **Grouped by sectors** | | | | | | | |
| 黑色金属采选业 | Mining of ferrous metal Ores | 10 | 11 | 8 | 7 | 1 | | 1 |
| 有色金属采选业 | Mining of non-ferrous Metal Ores | | | | | | | 1 |
| 非金属矿采选业 | Mining and processing of Nometal Ores | 14 | 13 | 7 | 6 | 5 | 2 | 1 |
| 农副食品加工业 | Processing of Food from Agricultural Products | 454 | 468 | 444 | 458 | 419 | 338 | 331 |
| 食品制造业 | Manufacture of Foods | 129 | 123 | 109 | 116 | 115 | 111 | 115 |
| 酒、饮料和精制茶制造业 | Manufacture of Liquor，Beverage and Refind Tea | 34 | 35 | 34 | 38 | 33 | 18 | 17 |

注：国家统计局根据《国民经济行业分类》(GB/T 4754-2017)，对《三次产业划分规定 (2012)》中行业类别进行了对应调整，其中“石油加工、炼焦和核燃料加工业”更名为“石油、煤炭及其他燃料加工业”，并将 2011 版《国民经济行业分类》4500 中部分内容和 4120 全部内容调到此类。

Note：According to the national economic industry classification (GB/ T 4754-2017), the National Bureau of Statistics carries out a corresponding adjustment to the three industries according to the classification of the national economy (GB/ T 4754-2017), in which the petroleum processing, coking and nuclear fuel processing industry is changed to petroleum, coal and other fuel processing industries, and the content of part of the content and 4120 of the 2011 edition of the national economy industry category 4500 are transferred to this category.

## 12-1 续表 5
Continued

单位：个（unit）

| 项 目 | Item | 2012 年 | 2013 年 | 2014 年 | 2015 年 | 2016 年 | 2017 年 | 2018 年 |
|---|---|---|---|---|---|---|---|---|
| 烟草制品业 | Manufacture of tobacco | 1 | 1 | 1 | 1 | 0 | 0 | 0 |
| 纺织业 | Manufacture of Textile | 181 | 175 | 146 | 133 | 111 | 91 | 93 |
| 纺织服装、服饰业 | Manufacture of Texitile Wearing Apparel | 312 | 283 | 249 | 244 | 206 | 152 | 144 |
| 皮革、毛皮、羽毛及其制品和制鞋业 | Manufacture of Leather, Fur, Feather & Its Products Footwear | 177 | 148 | 124 | 116 | 89 | 58 | 47 |
| 木材加工和木、竹、藤、棕、草制品业 | Processing of Timbers, Manufacture of Wood, Bamboo, Rattan, Palm and Straw Producls | 34 | 40 | 32 | 34 | 31 | 27 | 22 |
| 家具制造业 | Manufacture of Furniture | 103 | 107 | 96 | 98 | 88 | 65 | 64 |
| 造纸和纸制品业 | Manufacture of Paper and Paper Producls | 100 | 71 | 54 | 52 | 50 | 40 | 40 |
| 印刷和记录媒介复制业 | Printing, Reproduction of Recording Media | 80 | 121 | 150 | 156 | 137 | 110 | 101 |
| 文教、工美、体育和娱乐用品制造业 | Manufacture of Ariticles for Culture, Ars & Crafts, Sports and Entertaiment | 263 | 335 | 348 | 345 | 310 | 222 | 179 |
| 石油、煤炭及其他燃料加工业 | Oil, coal and other fuel processing industries | 8 | 8 | 9 | 9 | 9 | 9 | 8 |
| 化学原料和化学制品制造业 | Manufacture of Chemical Raw Material and Chemical Products | 224 | 240 | 246 | 249 | 223 | 176 | 171 |
| 医药制造业 | Manufacture of Medicines | 45 | 49 | 50 | 54 | 47 | 35 | 34 |
| 化学纤维制造业 | Manufacure of Chemical Fibers | 9 | 8 | 8 | 8 | 6 | 7 | 8 |
| 橡胶和塑料制品业 | Manufacture of Rubber and Plastic | 350 | 345 | 331 | 310 | 281 | 250 | 252 |
| 非金属矿物制品业 | Manufacture of Non-mettallic Mineral Products | 325 | 333 | 330 | 338 | 315 | 228 | 218 |
| 黑色金属冶炼和压延加工业 | Smelting and Pressing of Ferrous Metals | 105 | 93 | 87 | 83 | 73 | 27 | 30 |
| 有色金属冶炼和压延加工业 | Smelting and Pressing of Non-ferrous Metals | 37 | 36 | 38 | 39 | 30 | 23 | 24 |
| 金属制品业 | Manufacture of Metal Products | 399 | 389 | 380 | 388 | 348 | 289 | 278 |
| 通用设备制造业 | Manufacture of General Purpose Machinery | 362 | 382 | 395 | 402 | 383 | 301 | 316 |
| 专用设备制造业 | Manufacture of Special Purpose Machinery | 312 | 322 | 314 | 336 | 311 | 233 | 245 |
| 汽车制造业 | Manufacture of Vehicle | 136 | 141 | 145 | 158 | 154 | 156 | 168 |
| 铁路、船舶、航空航天和其他运输设备制造业 | Manufacture of Trarisport Epquipment for Railway, Shipping, Aerospace and other uses | 145 | 146 | 152 | 168 | 156 | 150 | 155 |
| 电气机械和器材制造业 | Manufacture of Electrical Machinery & Equipment | 202 | 212 | 217 | 226 | 211 | 184 | 186 |
| 计算机、通信和其他电子设备制造业 | Manufactuter of Computer, Communication Equipment and Other Electronic Equpment | 137 | 136 | 141 | 147 | 140 | 128 | 114 |
| 仪器仪表制造业 | Manufacture of Measuring Instument | 41 | 49 | 52 | 58 | 50 | 46 | 49 |
| 其他制造业 | Manufacture of Other Products | 18 | 17 | 13 | 15 | 16 | 10 | 11 |
| 废弃资源综合利用业 | Reeycling and Disposal of Waste Resources | 4 | 6 | 6 | 5 | 6 | 3 | 3 |
| 金属制品、机械和设备修理业 | Maintenance of Metal Products, Machinery and Equipment | 7 | 7 | 7 | 6 | 5 | 6 | 6 |
| 电力、热力生产和供应业 | Production and Supply of Electric Power and Heat Power | 36 | 39 | 40 | 43 | 42 | 43 | 44 |
| 燃气生产和供应业 | Production and Supply of Gas | 12 | 13 | 12 | 14 | 14 | 14 | 15 |
| 水的生产和供应业 | Production and Supply of water | 11 | 15 | 15 | 16 | 16 | 17 | 18 |

# 12-2 分市、区规模以上工业企业数（2018 年）
NUMBER OF ALL INDUSTRIAL ENTERPRISES BY REGION (2018)

单位：个（unit）

| 市、区名称 | Region | 规模以上 Above Designated | 按轻重工业分 Grouped by Light and Heavy Ind | | 按企业规模分 Grouped by Size of Enterprises | | |
|---|---|---|---|---|---|---|---|
| | | | 轻工业 Light Industry | 重工业 Heavy Industry | 大型企业 Large | 中型企业 Medium | 小型企业 Small |
| **全 市** | **Whole Municipality** | **3508** | **1448** | **2060** | **76** | **383** | **3049** |
| 市内三区 | Three Districts in Urban Area | 151 | 45 | 106 | 8 | 25 | 118 |
| 崂山区 | Laoshan District | 82 | 36 | 46 | 6 | 11 | 65 |
| 黄岛区 | Huangdao District | 731 | 214 | 517 | 20 | 97 | 614 |
| 城阳区 | Chengyang District | 474 | 191 | 283 | 11 | 52 | 411 |
| 即墨区 | Jimo District | 517 | 252 | 265 | 10 | 59 | 448 |
| 胶州市 | Jiaozhou | 737 | 334 | 403 | 5 | 59 | 673 |
| 平度市 | Pingdu | 381 | 169 | 212 | 4 | 33 | 344 |
| 莱西市 | Laixi | 279 | 160 | 119 | 6 | 23 | 250 |
| 红岛经济区 | Qingdao National High-tech Industrial Development Zone | 115 | 34 | 81 | 1 | 16 | 98 |
| 保税港区 | Qingdao Free Trade Port Area of China | 41 | 13 | 28 | 5 | 8 | 28 |

# 12-2 续表
Contiued

单位：个（unit）

| 市、区名称 | Region | 按经济类型分 Grouped by Economic Types | | | |
|---|---|---|---|---|---|
| | | 国有企业 State-owned | 集体企业 Gollective-wned | 其他经济 Others | #外资及港澳台商企业 Foreign Funded Entreprises and Enterprises with Funds from Kong Kong，Macao and Taiwan |
| **全 市** | **Whole Municipality** | **145** | **4** | **3359** | **938** |
| 市内三区 | Three Districts in Urban Area | 28 | 1 | 122 | 35 |
| 崂山区 | Laoshan District | 6 | | 76 | 23 |
| 黄岛区 | Huangdao District | 42 | | 689 | 179 |
| 城阳区 | Chengyang District | 13 | 1 | 460 | 169 |
| 即墨区 | Jimo District | 11 | | 506 | 138 |
| 胶州市 | Jiaozhou | 9 | | 728 | 161 |
| 平度市 | Pingdu | 19 | 2 | 360 | 91 |
| 莱西市 | Laixi | 5 | | 274 | 80 |
| 红岛经济区 | Qingdao National High-tech Industrial Development Zone | 12 | | 103 | 41 |
| 保税港区 | Qingdao Free Trade Port Area of China | | | 41 | 21 |

# 12-3 历年全部工业总产值
GROSS INDUSTRIAL OUTPUT VALUE OVER THE YEARS

单位：万元（10 000 yuan）

| 年 份<br>Year | 工业总产值<br>Gross Industrial Output Value | 轻工业产值<br>Light Industry | 重工业产值<br>Heavy Industry |
|---|---|---|---|
| 1949 | 21605 | 18494 | 3111 |
| 1950 | 34010 | 28720 | 5290 |
| 1951 | 53538 | 44600 | 8938 |
| 1952 | 84295 | 69258 | 15037 |
| 1953 | 115222 | 74716 | 40506 |
| 1954 | 126064 | 80604 | 45460 |
| 1955 | 118935 | 86956 | 31979 |
| 1956 | 144833 | 93809 | 51024 |
| 1957 | 142920 | 101202 | 41718 |
| 1958 | 217648 | 92407 | 125241 |
| 1959 | 282610 | 84376 | 198234 |
| 1960 | 291451 | 77043 | 214408 |
| 1962 | 120738 | 64233 | 56505 |
| 1963 | 139542 | 83630 | 55912 |
| 1964 | 177273 | 108884 | 68389 |
| 1965 | 215536 | 141765 | 73771 |
| 1966 | 252896 | 152304 | 100592 |
| 1967 | 287739 | 163627 | 124112 |
| 1968 | 299814 | 175791 | 123489 |
| 1969 | 296814 | 188860 | 107954 |
| 1970 | 345212 | 202903 | 142309 |

注：本表按当年价格计算，1995 年开始工业总产值按新规定计算。
Note：The data in this form are calculated at current price. Since 1995，new regulations have been adopted in calcnlating gross industrial output value.

## 12-3 续表 1
Continued

单位：万元（10 000 yuan）

| 年 份<br>Year | 工业总产值<br>Gross Industrial Output Value | 轻工业产值<br>Light Industry | 重工业产值<br>Heavy Industry |
|---|---|---|---|
| 1971 | 365770 | 216172 | 149598 |
| 1972 | 378266 | 230309 | 147957 |
| 1973 | 377943 | 245371 | 132572 |
| 1974 | 237219 | 154054 | 83165 |
| 1975 | 402541 | 261418 | 141123 |
| 1976 | 439793 | 278514 | 161279 |
| 1977 | 490669 | 296728 | 193941 |
| 1978 | 565503 | 336817 | 228686 |
| 1979 | 625227 | 379276 | 245951 |
| 1980 | 677690 | 442078 | 235612 |
| 1981 | 707434 | 479954 | 227480 |
| 1982 | 732705 | 474767 | 257938 |
| 1983 | 816793 | 513759 | 303034 |
| 1984 | 918364 | 569080 | 349284 |
| 1985 | 1113891 | 699524 | 414367 |
| 1986 | 1316230 | 833864 | 482366 |
| 1987 | 1703830 | 1065873 | 637957 |
| 1988 | 2481594 | 1451215 | 1030379 |
| 1989 | 3191643 | 1857019 | 1334624 |
| 1990 | 3571845 | 2057968 | 1513878 |

# 12-3 续表 2
Continued

单位：万元（10 000 yuan）

| 年 份 | Year | 工业总产值 Gross Industrial Output Value | 轻工业产值 Light Industry | 重工业产值 Heavy Industry |
|---|---|---|---|---|
| 1991 | 1991 | 3986427 | 2318257 | 1668170 |
| 1992 | 1992 | 4826834 | 2835728 | 1991106 |
| 1993 | 1993 | 5929236 | 3422107 | 2507129 |
| 1994 | 1994 | 8456974 | 4931262 | 3525712 |
| 1995 | 1995 | 9412635 | 5579637 | 3832998 |
| 1996 | 1996 | 11173672 | 6793007 | 4380665 |
| 1997 | 1997 | 13704735 | 8620710 | 5084025 |
| 1998 | 1998 | 15794106 | 10153634 | 5640472 |
| 1999 | 1999 | 16822436 | 10918827 | 5903609 |
| 2000 | 2000 | 19408338 | 12433214 | 6975124 |
| 2001 | 2001 | 22398464 | 14368582 | 8029882 |
| 2002 | 2002 | 25794324 | 14811106 | 10983218 |
| 2003 | 2003 | 31195595 | 17306539 | 13889056 |
| 2004 | 2004 | 39590783 | 21473202 | 18117581 |
| 2005 | 2005 | 50017829 | 24697792 | 25320037 |
| 2006 | 2006 | 59188120 | 28686826 | 30501294 |
| 2007 | 2007 | 74306364 | 33463071 | 40843293 |
| 2008 | 2008 | 89467300 | 37871227 | 51596073 |
| 2009 | 2009 | 102556155 | 42715781 | 59840374 |
| 2010 | 2010 | 116148345 | 44954630 | 71193715 |
| 2011 | 2011 | 132779629 | 50854938 | 81924691 |

## 12-3　续表 3
Continued

单位：万元（10 000 yuan）

| 年　份 | Year | 工业总产值 Gross Industrial Output Value | 轻工业产值 Light Industry | 重工业产值 Heavy Industry |
|---|---|---|---|---|
| 2012 | 2012 | 153102565 | 60516341 | 92546833 |
| 2013 | 2013 | 168971805 | 66799317 | 102172488 |
| 2014 | 2014 | 174442125 | 67683545 | 106758580 |
| 2015 | 2015 | 180194299 | 71176748 | 109017551 |
| 2016 | 2016 | 174157133 | 68552071 | 105605062 |
| 2017 | 2017 | 130197343 | 48954201 | 81243142 |
| 2018 | 2018 | 113897787 | 39054621 | 74843166 |
| “一五”时期合计 | “First Five-Year Plan” Peiod | 647974 | 437287 | 210687 |
| “二五”时期合计 | “Second Five-Year Plan” Peiod | 1077075 | 388406 | 688669 |
| 1963-1965 年合计 | 1963-1965 | 532351 | 334279 | 198072 |
| “三五”时期合计 | “Third Five-Year Plan” Peiod | 1481941 | 883485 | 598456 |
| “四五”时期合计 | “Fourth Five-Year Plan” Peiod | 1761739 | 1107324 | 654415 |
| “五五”时期合计 | “Fifth Five-Year Plan” Peiod | 2798882 | 1733413 | 1065469 |
| “六五”时期合计 | “Sixth Five-Year Plan” Peiod | 4289187 | 2737084 | 1552103 |
| “七五”时期合计 | “Seventh Five-Year Plan” Peiod | 12265142 | 7265939 | 4999204 |
| “八五”时期合计 | “Eighth Five-Year Plan” Peiod | 32612106 | 19087323 | 13524783 |
| “九五”时期合计 | “Ninth Five-Year Plan” Peiod | 76903287 | 48919392 | 27983895 |
| “十五”时期合计 | “Tenth Five-Year Plan” Peiod | 168996995 | 92657221 | 76339774 |
| “十一五”时期合计 | “Eleventh Five-Year Plan” Peiod | 175336465 | 73641456 | 101695009 |
| “十二五”时期合计 | “Twelveth Five-Year Plan” Peiod | 809490422 | 317030889 | 492420143 |

# 12-4　分市、区规模以上工业总产值（2018年）
GROSS INDUSTRIAL OUTPUT VALUE ABOVE DESIGNATED SFZE BY REGION（2018）

| 指标 | Indicator | 总　计<br>Total | 市内三区<br>Three Districts in Urban Area | 崂山区<br>Laoshan District | 黄岛区<br>Huangdao District |
|---|---|---|---|---|---|
| **总　　计** | **Total** | **96048610** | **6893905** | **5277439** | **38932632** |
| **按隶属关系分** | **Groped by Subordination** | | | | |
| 中央 | Centrality | 18295613 | 2106056 | 162509 | 7961919 |
| 县级及以下 | At and below the county level | 13037485 | 1412443 | 181488 | 6979832 |
| 其它 | Others | 64715512 | 3375406 | 4933441 | 23990881 |
| **按登记注册类型分** | **Grouped by Status of Registration** | | | | |
| 国有经济 | State-owned | 32973045 | 3516434 | 355601 | 17966417 |
| 集体经济 | Collecive-owned | 78599 | 2305 | | |
| 其他经济 | Others | 62996966 | 3375167 | 4921838 | 20966215 |
| #外资与港澳台企业 | Foreign Funded Enterprises and Enterprises with Funds fron Hong Kong，Macao and Taiwan | 24092865 | 1750726 | 763842 | 9339786 |
| **按轻重工业分** | **Grouped by Light and Heavy Industries** | | | | |
| 轻工业 | Light Industry | 32934284 | 2850483 | 3572441 | 12104305 |
| 重工业 | Heavy Industry | 63114325 | 4043422 | 1704998 | 26828327 |
| **按企业规模分** | **Grouped by Size of Enterprises** | | | | |
| 大型企业 | Large | 43857362 | 3121930 | 3938487 | 19313541 |
| 中型企业 | Medium | 25358975 | 2308370 | 581485 | 13075708 |
| 小型企业 | Small | 26832272 | 1463606 | 757467 | 6543383 |

单位：万元（10 000 yuan）

| 城阳区 Chengyang District | 即墨区 Jimo District | 胶州市 Jiaozhou | 平度市 Pingdu | 莱西市 Laixi | 红岛经济区 Qingdao National High-tech Industrial Development Zone | 保税港区 Qingdao Free Trade Port Area China |
|---|---|---|---|---|---|---|
| **12726134** | **10054580** | **7589934** | **6172057** | **4800416** | **2470580** | **1130934** |
| 4918626 | 2811187 | 6088 | 77632 | | 251596 | |
| 622979 | 1645990 | 31908 | 1733622 | 68767 | 360457 | |
| 7184529 | 5597404 | 7551938 | 4360803 | 4731649 | 1858527 | 1130934 |
| 5461724 | 2900694 | 132297 | 1836391 | 63114 | 740373 | |
| 52333 | | | 23962 | | | |
| 7212076 | 7153886 | 7457638 | 4311705 | 4737302 | 1730207 | 1130934 |
| 3074188 | 1675191 | 2440089 | 1570745 | 1593051 | 993867 | 891380 |
| 2281945 | 3614440 | 2668145 | 2330813 | 2871417 | 456086 | 184210 |
| 10444189 | 6440140 | 4921789 | 3841244 | 1928998 | 2014494 | 946724 |
| 6385829 | 4961923 | 1080572 | 1987532 | 2232149 | 241153 | 594247 |
| 2109033 | 1845278 | 2313001 | 1063409 | 862899 | 891632 | 308160 |
| 4231272 | 3247379 | 4196360 | 3121116 | 1705368 | 1337795 | 228527 |

## 12-4 续表
Continued

| 指标 | Indicator | 总　计 Total | 市内三区 Three Districts in Urban Area |
|---|---|---|---|
| **按行业分** | **Grouped by Industrial Sector** | **96048610** | **6893905** |
| 煤炭开采和洗选业 | Mining and Washing of Coal | | |
| 石油和天然气开采业 | Extraction of Petroleum and Natural Gas | | |
| 黑色金属矿采选业 | Mining of Ferrous Metal Ores | | |
| 有色金属矿采选业 | Mining of Non-ferrous Metal Ores | 12298 | |
| 非金属矿采选业 | Mining and Processing of Nometal Ores | 4395 | |
| 开采辅助活动 | Auxiliary Activities of Mining | | |
| 其他采矿业 | Mining of Other Ores | | |
| 农副食品加工业 | Processing of Food from Agricultural Products | 6763720 | 848287 |
| 食品制造业 | Manufacture of Foods | 2393024 | 57153 |
| 酒、饮料和精制茶制造业 | Manufacture of Liquor, Beverage and Refind Tea | 1619606 | 619041 |
| 烟草制品业 | Manufacture of Tobacco | | |
| 纺织业 | Manufacture of Textile | 874484 | 25467 |
| 纺织服装、服饰业 | Manufacture of Textile Wearing Apparel | 2300334 | 6609 |
| 皮革、毛皮、羽毛及其制品和制鞋业 | Processing of Leather, Fur, Feather & Its Products Footwear | 662706 | 9381 |
| 木材加工和木、竹、藤、棕、草制品业 | Processing of Timbers, Manufacture of Wood, Bamboo, Rattan, Palm and Straw Products | 118525 | |
| 家具制造业 | Manufacture of Furniture | 414226 | 18300 |
| 造纸和纸制品业 | Manufacture of Paper and Paper Products | 460542 | 5641 |
| 印刷和记录媒介复制业 | Printing, Reproduction of Recording Media | 859851 | 106617 |
| 文教、工美、体育和娱乐用品制造业 | Manufacture of Articles for Culture, Arts & Crafts, Sports and Entertainment | 1176298 | 44975 |
| 石油、煤炭及其他燃料加工业 | Oil, coal and other fuel processing industries | 7406847 | 1412239 |
| 化学原料和化学制品制造业 | Manufacture of Chemical Raw Material and Chemical Products | 4789079 | 130356 |
| 医药制造业 | Manufacture of Medicines | 1047219 | 23317 |
| 化学纤维制造业 | Manufacture of Chemical Fibers | 50643 | |
| 橡胶和塑料制品业 | Manufacture of Rubber and Plastic | 3990200 | 69274 |
| 非金属矿物制品业 | Manufacture of Non-mettallic Mineral Products | 2652062 | 191078 |
| 黑色金属冶炼和压延加工业 | Smelting and Pressing of Ferrous Metals | 2824713 | |
| 有色金属冶炼和压延加工业 | Smelting and Pressing of Nonferrous Metals | 606704 | |
| 金属制品业 | Manufacture of Metal Products | 3618624 | 25057 |
| 通用设备制造业 | Manufacture of General Purpose Machinery | 4391881 | 227471 |
| 专用设备制造业 | Manufacture of Special Purpose Machinery | 2796824 | 142341 |
| 汽车制造业 | Manufacture of Vehicle | 10008249 | 122242 |
| 铁路、船舶、航空航天和其他运输设备制造业 | Manufacture of Transport Equipment for Railway, Shipping, Aerospace and other uses | 7824563 | 528848 |
| 电气机械和器材制造业 | Manufacture of Electrical Machinery & Equipment | 15075296 | 1007553 |
| 计算机、通信和其他电子设备制造业 | Manufacture of Computer, Communication Equipment and Other Electronic Equipment | 8169914 | 409309 |
| 仪器仪表制造业 | Manufacture of Measuring Instrument | 838520 | 25417 |
| 其他制造业 | Manufacture of Other Products | 130145 | 18892 |
| 废弃资源综合利用业 | Recycling and Disposal of Waste Resources | 10287 | |
| 金属制品、机械和设备修理业 | Manufacture of Metal Products, Machinery and Equipment | 19641 | 4542 |
| 电力、热力生产和供应业 | Production and Supply of Electric Power and Heat Power | 1245197 | 503507 |
| 燃气生产和供应业 | Production and Supply of Gas | 651732 | 199774 |
| 水的生产和供应业 | Production and Supply of Water | 240264 | 111218 |

单位：万元（10 000 yuan）

| 崂山区 Laoshan District | 黄岛区 Huangdao District | 城阳区 Chengyang District | 即墨区 Jimo District | 胶州市 Jiaozhou | 平度市 Pingdu | 莱西市 Laixi | 红岛经济区 Qingdao National High-tech Industrial Development Zone | 保税港区 Qingdao Free Trade Port Area China |
|---|---|---|---|---|---|---|---|---|
| 5277439 | 38932632 | 12726134 | 10054580 | 7589934 | 6172057 | 4800416 | 2470580 | 1130934 |
| | | | | | | 12298 | | |
| | | | | | 4395 | | | |
| 40233 | 1301805 | 434971 | 400745 | 720598 | 1271723 | 1605519 | 124212 | 15628 |
| 70582 | 1077315 | 148621 | 134144 | 361484 | 68144 | 437913 | 37669 | |
| 263876 | 382282 | 1400 | 27196 | 2509 | 320736 | 2564 | | |
| 23961 | 54852 | 236835 | 100283 | 85896 | 115933 | 185020 | 10052 | 36187 |
| 12594 | 119009 | 168023 | 1678440 | 141878 | 86186 | 59382 | 28213 | |
| 7460 | 49925 | 17773 | 50730 | 210114 | 1401 | 315923 | | |
| | 51266 | 31327 | 11895 | 20643 | | | 3394 | |
| | 13250 | 106226 | 34277 | 185267 | 48238 | 2340 | 6330 | |
| 14700 | 147635 | 139409 | 9700 | 113011 | 28975 | 1473 | | |
| 8778 | 101766 | 164121 | 339331 | 63331 | 11647 | 14860 | 45450 | 3951 |
| 3945 | 120026 | 193988 | 206514 | 392933 | 133210 | 55522 | 3526 | 21659 |
| | 5530218 | 456668 | 7092 | 629 | | | | |
| 19538 | 2470153 | 466132 | 152725 | 424804 | 634350 | 230188 | 255047 | 5785 |
| 218203 | 468435 | 103792 | 33528 | 13411 | 20954 | 34174 | 131405 | |
| | 7736 | 19162 | 2926 | 5595 | | 15224 | | |
| 61702 | 1577577 | 443277 | 656996 | 280605 | 331036 | 385477 | 146009 | 38246 |
| 35457 | 1002749 | 255639 | 264056 | 281176 | 358741 | 210929 | 32148 | 20089 |
| | 2484440 | 157784 | 130479 | 6402 | 10956 | 34653 | | |
| | 88149 | 25989 | 25922 | 73762 | 355987 | | 36896 | |
| 15650 | 859050 | 621751 | 678110 | 1085345 | 166934 | 80651 | 45406 | 40672 |
| 25352 | 1036774 | 279756 | 421653 | 1608493 | 259675 | 74664 | 264492 | 193551 |
| 74886 | 1234781 | 597994 | 156325 | 274712 | 51671 | 39391 | 146210 | 78513 |
| 34940 | 4207526 | 787849 | 3317382 | 181353 | 226001 | 771824 | 251297 | 107837 |
| 192921 | 869575 | 5350110 | 80497 | 236292 | 116829 | 8263 | 441229 | |
| 3693994 | 8393802 | 410047 | 840153 | 488643 | 77051 | 60309 | 37547 | 66196 |
| 172090 | 4440514 | 888940 | 160583 | 62070 | 1286584 | 30779 | 249471 | 469574 |
| 250414 | 87931 | 79136 | 27223 | 158147 | 7625 | 21765 | 147814 | 33048 |
| 4465 | | 30859 | | 5175 | 70754 | | | |
| | | | | 1751 | 5592 | 2943 | | |
| | 10553 | | 4546 | | | | | |
| 27515 | 461990 | 38502 | 57707 | 17171 | 67673 | 56134 | 14997 | |
| | 205932 | 59681 | 35279 | 81043 | 23239 | 41735 | 5050 | |
| 4184 | 75618 | 10372 | 8143 | 5692 | 9820 | 8500 | 6717 | |

# 12-5 规模以上工业企业主要指标（2018 年）

MAN INDICATORS OFINDUSTRIAL ENTERPRISES ABOVE DESIGNATED SIXE（2018）

| 项目 | Indicator | 企业单位数（个）Number of Enterprises（Unit） |
|---|---|---|
| **总 计** | **Total** | **3508** |
| **按注册登记类型分** | **Grouped by Status of Registration** | |
| 国有及国有控股企业 | State–owned and State–holdinig Enterprises | 145 |
| 集体企业 | Gollective–owned Enterprises | 4 |
| 股份有限公司 | Share–holding Corporations Ltd | 103 |
| 外商投资企业 | Fereign Funded Enterprises | 751 |
| 港澳台商投资企业 | Invested by HongKong，Macao and Taiwan | 187 |
| **按轻重工业分** | **Grouped by Light and Heavy Industries** | |
| 轻工业 | Light Industry | 1448 |
| 重工业 | Heavy Industry | 2060 |
| **按企业规模分** | **Grouped by Size of Enterprises** | |
| 大型企业 | Large | 76 |
| 中型企业 | Medium | 383 |
| 小型企业 | Small | 3049 |
| **按所在地分** | **Grouped by Location** | |
| 市内三区 | Three Districts in Urban Area | 151 |
| 崂山区 | Laoshan District | 82 |
| 黄岛区 | Huangdao District | 731 |
| 城阳区 | Chengyang District | 474 |
| 即墨区 | Jimo District | 517 |
| 胶州市 | Jiaozhou | 737 |
| 平度市 | Pingdu | 381 |
| 莱西市 | Laixi | 279 |
| 红岛经济区 | Qingdao National High–tech Industrial Development Zone | 115 |
| 保税港区 | Qingdao Free Trade Port Area of China | 41 |
| **按行业分** | **Grouped by sector** | |
| 煤炭开采和洗选业 | Mining and Washing of Coal | |
| 石油和天然气开采业 | Extraction of Petroleum and Natural Gas | |
| 黑色金属矿采选业 | Mining of Ferrous Metal Ores | |
| 有色金属矿采选业 | Mining of Non–ferrous Metoul Ores | 1 |
| 非金属矿采选业 | Mining and Processing of Nometal Ores | 1 |
| 开采辅助活动 | Auxiliary Activities of Mining | |
| 其他采矿业 | Mining of Other Ores | |

单位：万元（10 000 yuan）

| 工业总产值<br>Gross Industrial Output Value | 资产合计<br>Total Assets | 流动资产年合计<br>Total Current Assets | 固定资产净值<br>Net Value of Fixed Assets |
|---|---|---|---|
| **96048610** | **128639538** | **78607024** | **23334538** |
| | | | |
| 32973045 | 42028433 | 27281061 | 8800214 |
| 78599 | 59050 | 38424 | 11735 |
| 20896522 | 46012470 | 27234709 | 3904589 |
| 19935021 | 23316927 | 16458795 | 4296015 |
| 4157844 | 4325408 | 2741677 | 1146110 |
| | | | |
| 32934284 | 50083387 | 27733925 | 6874143 |
| 63114325 | 78556151 | 50873099 | 16460396 |
| | | | |
| 43857362 | 72492349 | 45967165 | 8623051 |
| 25358975 | 24659089 | 14635748 | 6383878 |
| 26832272 | 31488100 | 18004111 | 8327609 |
| | | | |
| 6893905 | 10008662 | 5084233 | 2308825 |
| 5277439 | 11889495 | 6934242 | 1045610 |
| 38932632 | 52169793 | 32374618 | 8686548 |
| 12726134 | 15338963 | 11124619 | 2061443 |
| 10054580 | 11700272 | 7360097 | 2280735 |
| 7589934 | 10995580 | 5866366 | 3173744 |
| 6172057 | 6919282 | 3680384 | 1557441 |
| 4800416 | 4726725 | 3111261 | 1206571 |
| 2470580 | 4059158 | 2551313 | 781924 |
| 1130934 | 831610 | 519891 | 231699 |
| | | | |
| 12298 | 67057 | 2451 | 50918 |
| 4395 | 10223 | 6909 | 1361 |

## 12-5 续表 1
Continued

| 项目 | Indicator | 营业收入 Revenue from Principal Business |
|---|---|---|
| **总　计** | **Total** | **103439056** |
| **按注册登记类型分** | **Grouped by Status of Registration** | |
| 国有及国有控股企业 | State-owned and State-holdinig Enterprises | 35976282 |
| 集体企业 | Gollective-owned Enterprises | 85895 |
| 股份有限公司 | Share-holding Corporations Ltd | 23440589 |
| 外商投资企业 | Fereign Funded Enterprises | 21245635 |
| 港澳台商投资企业 | Invested by HongKong，Macao and Taiwan | 4736585 |
| **按轻重工业分** | **Grouped by Light and Heavy Industries** | |
| 轻工业 | Light Industry | 37245414 |
| 重工业 | Heavy Industry | 66193642 |
| **按企业规模分** | **Grouped by Size of Enterprises** | 0 |
| 大型企业 | Large | 49966203 |
| 中型企业 | Medium | 25504239 |
| 小型企业 | Small | 27968614 |
| **按所在地分** | **Grouped by Location** | |
| 市内三区 | Three Districts in Urban Area | 8718600 |
| 崂山区 | Laoshan District | 6272071 |
| 黄岛区 | Huangdao District | 41477166 |
| 城阳区 | Chengyang District | 13210425 |
| 即墨区 | Jimo District | 10588052 |
| 胶州市 | Jiaozhou | 7615308 |
| 平度市 | Pingdu | 6858600 |
| 莱西市 | Laixi | 4954742 |
| 红岛经济区 | Qingdao National High-tech Industrial Development Zone | 2574639 |
| 保税港区 | Qingdao Free Trade Port Area of China | 1169454 |
| **按行业分** | **Grouped by sector** | |
| 煤炭开采和洗选业 | Mining and Washing of Coal | |
| 石油和天然气开采业 | Extraction of Petroleum and Natural Gas | |
| 黑色金属矿采选业 | Mining of Ferrous Metal Ores | |
| 有色金属矿采选业 | Mining of Non-ferrous Metoul Ores | 12810 |
| 非金属矿采选业 | Mining and Processing of Nometal Ores | 5363 |
| 开采辅助活动 | Auxiliary Activities of Mining | |
| 其他采矿业 | Mining of Other Ores | |

单位：万元（10 000 yuan）

| 营业成本<br>Cost of Prinipal Business | 营业税金及附加<br>Taxes and Extra Charges on Principal Business | 利润总额<br>Total Profits | 全部从业人员年平均人数（人）<br>Annual Average Employed Persons（person） |
|---|---|---|---|
| **84897026** | **2014374** | **5472206** | **727998** |
| | | | |
| 29900096 | 1581325 | 1957865 | 115832 |
| 76721 | 525 | 3554 | 964 |
| 16757194 | 174020 | 1984935 | 84978 |
| 18033302 | 210958 | 1143635 | 193567 |
| 4068953 | 27422 | 188633 | 40668 |
| | | | |
| 29187541 | 288865 | 1810789 | 310516 |
| 55709485 | 1725509 | 3661417 | 417482 |
| | | | |
| 39938250 | 420207 | 3207973 | 242502 |
| 20854990 | 1414279 | 1154465 | 204079 |
| 24103786 | 179887 | 1109768 | 281417 |
| | | | |
| 7094501 | 435634 | 300250 | 36174 |
| 4226482 | 53420 | 568667 | 29665 |
| 33305141 | 1153114 | 2387984 | 185523 |
| 11106717 | 152662 | 738352 | 108231 |
| 9256939 | 59212 | 437134 | 112804 |
| 6537980 | 62337 | 386535 | 106205 |
| 5947041 | 53607 | 190415 | 60620 |
| 4395061 | 20866 | 217948 | 50136 |
| 2033892 | 19031 | 166053 | 22401 |
| 993273 | 4489 | 78867 | 16239 |
| | | | |
| 8209 | 647 | 327 | 219 |
| 3614 | 180 | 236 | 138 |

## 12-5 续表 2
Continued

| 项目 | Indicator | 企业单位数(个) Number of Enterprises (Unit) |
|---|---|---|
| 农副食品加工业 | Processing of Food from Agricultural Products | 331 |
| 食品制造业 | Manufacture of Foods | 115 |
| 酒、饮料和精制茶制造业 | Manufacture of Liquor, Beverage and Refind Tea | 17 |
| 烟草制品业 | Manufacture of Tobacco | |
| 纺织业 | Manufacture of Textile | 93 |
| 纺织服装、服饰业 | Manufacture of Texitile Wearing Apparel | 144 |
| 皮革、毛皮、羽毛及其制品和制鞋业 | Processing of Leather, Fur, Feather & Its Products Footwear | 47 |
| 木材加工和木、竹、藤、棕、草制品业 | Processing of Timbers, Manufacture of Wood, Bamboo, Rattan, Palm and Straw Products | 22 |
| 家具制造业 | Manufacture of Furniture | 64 |
| 造纸和纸制品业 | Manufacture of Paper and Paper Products | 40 |
| 印刷和记录媒介复制业 | Printing, Reproduction of Recording Media | 101 |
| 文教、工美、体育和娱乐用品制造业 | Manufacture of Articles for Culture, Arts & Crafts, Sports and Entertainment | 179 |
| 石油、煤炭及其他燃料加工业 | Oil, coal and other fuel processing industries | 8 |
| 化学原料和化学制品制造业 | Manufacture of Chemical Raw Material and Chemical Products | 171 |
| 医药制造业 | Manufacture of Medicines | 34 |
| 化学纤维制造业 | Manufacture of Chemical Fibers | 8 |
| 橡胶和塑料制品业 | Manufacture of Rubber and Plastic | 252 |
| 非金属矿物制品业 | Manufacture of Non-mettallic Mineral Products | 218 |
| 黑色金属冶炼和压延加工业 | Smelting and Pressing of Ferrous Metals | 30 |
| 有色金属冶炼和压延加工业 | Smelting and Pressing of Nonferrous Metals | 24 |
| 金属制品业 | Manufacture of Metal Products | 278 |
| 通用设备制造业 | Manufacture of General Purpose Machinery | 316 |
| 专用设备制造业 | Manufacture of Special Purpose Machinery | 245 |
| 汽车制造业 | Manufacture of Vehicle | 168 |
| 铁路、船舶、航空航天和其他运输设备制造业 | Manufacture of Transport Equipment for Railway, Shipping, Aerospace and other uses | 155 |
| 电气机械和器材制造业 | Manufacture of Electrical Machinery & Equipment | 186 |
| 计算机、通信和其他电子设备制造业 | Manufacture of Computer, Communication Equipment and Other Electronic Equipment | 114 |
| 仪器仪表制造业 | Manufacture of Measuring Instrument | 49 |
| 其他制造业 | Manufacture of Other Products | 11 |
| 废弃资源综合利用业 | Recycling and Disposal of Waste Resources | 3 |
| 金属制品、机械和设备修理业 | Manufacture of Metal Products, Machinery and Equipment | 6 |
| 电力、热力生产和供应业 | Production and Supply of Electric Power and Heat Power | 44 |
| 燃气生产和供应业 | Production and Supply of Gas | 15 |
| 水的生产和供应业 | Production and Supply of Water | 18 |

单位：万元（10 000 yuan）

| 工业总产值 Gross Industrial Output Value | 资产合计 Total Assets | 流动资产合计 Total Current Assets | 固定资产净值 Net Value of Fixed Assets |
|---|---|---|---|
| 6763720 | 4240506 | 2761683 | 1015009 |
| 2393024 | 3156057 | 1848791 | 718607 |
| 1619606 | 2807099 | 1212427 | 362699 |
| | | | |
| 874484 | 705756 | 488720 | 165930 |
| 2300334 | 1923312 | 1032906 | 467933 |
| 662706 | 521843 | 247719 | 222816 |
| 118525 | 127740 | 73870 | 36167 |
| 414226 | 457452 | 251217 | 137395 |
| 460542 | 371427 | 233008 | 105567 |
| 859851 | 779983 | 449480 | 250686 |
| 1176298 | 1153624 | 627029 | 349423 |
| 7406847 | 2977829 | 1933772 | 841356 |
| 4789079 | 6193540 | 3081663 | 1631150 |
| 1047219 | 1283683 | 740212 | 297820 |
| 50643 | 116562 | 36809 | 56780 |
| 3990200 | 5308413 | 2490199 | 1488952 |
| 2652062 | 3195185 | 2217490 | 698298 |
| 2824713 | 2509719 | 1233477 | 1184519 |
| 606704 | 535730 | 164834 | 240061 |
| 3618624 | 4171674 | 2428688 | 809639 |
| 4391881 | 6663964 | 4210520 | 1190500 |
| 2796824 | 4071620 | 2694739 | 683278 |
| 10008249 | 12909494 | 11087583 | 1255367 |
| 7824563 | 12164553 | 8722924 | 1869515 |
| 15075296 | 34724824 | 19485598 | 2642117 |
| 8169914 | 7413430 | 5750161 | 747246 |
| 838520 | 1274076 | 1004603 | 121535 |
| 130145 | 241088 | 200630 | 24794 |
| 10287 | 24217 | 9251 | 10997 |
| 19641 | 26521 | 8190 | 12078 |
| 1245197 | 3871872 | 1185855 | 2188398 |
| 651732 | 1304253 | 236884 | 917424 |
| 240264 | 1335214 | 446732 | 538206 |

## 12-5 续表 3
Continued

| 项目 | Indicator | 营业收入<br>Revenue from Principal Business |
|---|---|---|
| 农副食品加工业 | Processing of Food from Agricultural Products | 7674656 |
| 食品制造业 | Manufacture of Foods | 2139842 |
| 酒、饮料和精制茶制造业 | Manufacture of Liquor, Beverage and Refind Tea | 2371302 |
| 烟草制品业 | Manufacture of Tobacco | |
| 纺织业 | Manufacture of Textile | 928562 |
| 纺织服装、服饰业 | Manufacture of Textile Wearing Apparel | 2367809 |
| 皮革、毛皮、羽毛及其制品和制鞋业 | Processing of Leather, Fur, Feather & Its Products Footwear | 627305 |
| 木材加工和木、竹、藤、棕、草制品业 | Processing of Timbers, Manufacture of Wood, Bamboo, Rattan, Palm and Straw Products | 114446 |
| 家具制造业 | Manufacture of Furniture | 415958 |
| 造纸和纸制品业 | Manufacture of Paper and Paper Products | 434191 |
| 印刷和记录媒介复制业 | Printing, Reproduction of Recording Media | 908442 |
| 文教、工美、体育和娱乐用品制造业 | Manufacture of Articles for Culture, Arts & Crafts, Sports and Entertainment | 1168179 |
| 石油、煤炭及其他燃料加工业 | Oil, coal and other fuel processing industries | 7624113 |
| 化学原料和化学制品制造业 | Manufacture of Chemical Raw Material and Chemical Products | 5032020 |
| 医药制造业 | Manufacture of Medicines | 976336 |
| 化学纤维制造业 | Manufacture of Chemical Fibers | 50942 |
| 橡胶和塑料制品业 | Manufacture of Rubber and Plastic | 4069518 |
| 非金属矿物制品业 | Manufacture of Non-mettallic Mineral Products | 2445202 |
| 黑色金属冶炼和压延加工业 | Smelting and Pressing of Ferrous Metals | 3192791 |
| 有色金属冶炼和压延加工业 | Smelting and Pressing of Nonferrous Metals | 621703 |
| 金属制品业 | Manufacture of Metal Products | 3700194 |
| 通用设备制造业 | Manufacture of General Purpose Machinery | 4470508 |
| 专用设备制造业 | Manufacture of Special Purpose Machinery | 2752042 |
| 汽车制造业 | Manufacture of Vehicle | 10234396 |
| 铁路、船舶、航空航天和其他运输设备制造业 | Manufacture of Transport Equipment for Railway, Shipping, Aerospace and other uses | 7925571 |
| 电气机械和器材制造业 | Manufacture of Electrical Machinery & Equipment | 17956053 |
| 计算机、通信和其他电子设备制造业 | Manufacture of Computer, Communication Equipment and Other Electronic Equipment | 9838220 |
| 仪器仪表制造业 | Manufacture of Measuring Instrument | 872255 |
| 其他制造业 | Manufacture of Other Products | 148463 |
| 废弃资源综合利用业 | Recycling and Disposal of Waste Resources | 10119 |
| 金属制品、机械和设备修理业 | Manufacture of Metal Products, Machinery and Equipment | 19420 |
| 电力、热力生产和供应业 | Production and Supply of Electric Power and Heat Power | 1315545 |
| 燃气生产和供应业 | Production and Supply of Gas | 725965 |
| 水的生产和供应业 | Production and Supply of Water | 288820 |

单位：万元（10 000 yuan）

| 营业成本<br>Cost of Prinipal Business | 营业税金及附加<br>Taxes and Extra Charges on Principal Business | 利润总额<br>Total Profits | 全部从业人员年平均人数（人）<br>Annual Average Employed Persons（person） |
|---|---|---|---|
| 7175212 | 18717 | 61212 | 56912 |
| 1756042 | 15706 | 23005 | 17367 |
| 1887689 | 61834 | 106273 | 10216 |
| | | | |
| 844417 | 3865 | -3952 | 11691 |
| 2080163 | 21553 | 54808 | 57594 |
| 559385 | 5026 | 5244 | 21193 |
| 102969 | 792 | 6679 | 2446 |
| 355129 | 3727 | 11259 | 9950 |
| 393858 | 2850 | 8805 | 4404 |
| 776375 | 5489 | 32966 | 11405 |
| 1026088 | 9015 | 18006 | 25873 |
| 5694811 | 1297296 | 508530 | 2850 |
| 4300613 | 24693 | 241915 | 24265 |
| 483951 | 13756 | 171903 | 9551 |
| 41592 | 509 | -1818 | 586 |
| 3458551 | 24995 | 149307 | 43191 |
| 2063384 | 17993 | 149931 | 22864 |
| 2913693 | 13386 | 69835 | 8419 |
| 579032 | 3559 | 5851 | 2990 |
| 3280323 | 28639 | 255637 | 40343 |
| 3757249 | 28955 | 170922 | 50108 |
| 2218938 | 20100 | 130301 | 34150 |
| 9073265 | 91790 | 581911 | 49792 |
| 6559426 | 77753 | 559887 | 55025 |
| 12402164 | 129033 | 1432615 | 68028 |
| 8266807 | 55789 | 521150 | 54803 |
| 589442 | 7701 | 101193 | 9414 |
| 126757 | 1209 | 8215 | 3422 |
| 9564 | 156 | -468 | 189 |
| 15024 | 175 | 1408 | 439 |
| 1296033 | 11666 | -65923 | 11350 |
| 500633 | 3547 | 160150 | 2476 |
| 296625 | 12272 | -5113 | 4335 |

# 12-6 按行业分国有及国有控股工业企业主要指标（2018 年）
MAIN INDICATORS OF STATE-OWNED AND STATE-HOLDING INDUSTRIAL ENTERPRISES BY INDUSTRIAL SECTOR (2018)

| 项目 | Indicator | 企业单位数（个）Number of Enterprises（Unit） |
| --- | --- | --- |
| **总计** | **Total** | **145** |
| 煤炭开采和洗选业 | Mining and Washing of Coal | |
| 石油和天然气开采业 | Extraction of Petroleum and Natural Gas | |
| 黑色金属矿采选业 | Mining of Ferrous Metal Ores | |
| 有色金属矿采选业 | Mining of Non-ferrous Metal Ores | 1 |
| 非金属矿采选业 | Mining and Processing of Nometal Ores | 1 |
| 开采辅助活动 | Auxiliary Activities of Mining | |
| 其他采矿业 | Mining of Other Ores | |
| 农副食品加工业 | Processing of Food from Agricultural Products | 1 |
| 食品制造业 | Manufacture of Foods | 3 |
| 酒、饮料和精制茶制造业 | Manufacture of Liquor, Beverage and Refind Tea | 2 |
| 烟草制品业 | Manufacture of Tobacco | |
| 纺织业 | Manufacture of Textile | |
| 纺织服装、服饰业 | Manufacture of Textile Wearing Apparel | |
| 皮革、毛皮、羽毛及其制品和制鞋业 | Manufacture of Leather, Fur, Feather & Its Products Footwear | 1 |
| 木材加工和木、竹、藤、棕、草制品业 | Processing of Timbers, Manufacture of Wood, Bamboo, Rattan, Palm and Straw Products | 1 |
| 家具制造业 | Manufacture of Furniture | |
| 造纸和纸制品业 | Manufacture of Paper and Paper Products | 1 |
| 印刷和记录媒介复制业 | Printing, Reproduction of Recording Media | 1 |
| 文教、工美、体育和娱乐用品制造业 | Manufacture of Articles for Culture, Arts & Crafts, Sports and Entertainment | |
| 石油、煤炭及其他燃料加工业 | Oil, coal and other fuel processing industries | 3 |
| 化学原料和化学制品制造业 | Manufacture of Chemical Raw Material and Chemical Products | 10 |
| 医药制造业 | Manufacture of Medicines | 2 |
| 化学纤维制造业 | Manufacture of Chemical Fibers | |
| 橡胶和塑料制品业 | Manufacture of Rubber and Plastic | 6 |
| 非金属矿物制品业 | Manufacture of Non-mettallic Mineral Products | 10 |
| 黑色金属冶炼和压延加工业 | Smelting and Pressing of Ferrous Metals | 4 |
| 有色金属冶炼和压延加工业 | Smelting and Pressing of Non-ferrous Metals | 5 |
| 金属制品业 | Manufacture of Metal Products | 4 |
| 通用设备制造业 | Manufacture of General Purpose Machinery | 8 |
| 专用设备制造业 | Manufacture of Special Purpose Machinery | 5 |
| 汽车制造业 | Manufacture of Vehicle | 6 |
| 铁路、船舶、航空航天和其他运输设备制造业 | Manufacture of Transport Equipment for Railway, Shipping, Aerospace and other uses | 17 |
| 电气机械和器材制造业 | Manufacture of Electrical Machinery & Equipment | 5 |
| 计算机、通信和其他电子设备制造业 | Manufacture of Computer, Communication Equipment and Other Electronic Equipment | 3 |
| 仪器仪表制造业 | Manufacture of Measuring Instrument | 2 |
| 其他制造业 | Manufacture of Other Products | 1 |
| 废弃资源综合利用业 | Recycling and Disposal of Waste Resources | |
| 金属制品、机械和设备修理业 | Manufacture of Metal Products, Machinery and Equipment | 1 |
| 电力、热力生产和供应业 | Production and Supply of Electric Power and Heat Power | 23 |
| 燃气生产和供应业 | Production and Supply of Gas | 6 |
| 水的生产和供应业 | Production and Supply of Water | 12 |

单位：万元（10 000 yuan）

| 工业总产值<br>Gross Industrial Output Value | 资产合计<br>Total Assets | 流动资产合计<br>Total Current Assets | 固定资产净值<br>Net Value of Fixed Assets |
|---|---|---|---|
| **32973045** | **32973045** | **27281061** | **8800214** |
| 12298 | 67057 | 2451 | 50918 |
| 4395 | 10223 | 6909 | 1361 |
| 6086 | 6350 | 3238 | 2606 |
| 63008 | 87514 | 71264 | 3067 |
| 1038283 | 2293510 | 877507 | 223940 |
| 9381 | 14919 | 12083 | 1582 |
| 10911 | 22834 | 20748 | 1556 |
| 124288 | 62276 | 34758 | 15064 |
| 4960 | 11137 | 4891 | 5614 |
| 7232378 | 2847158 | 1870482 | 784804 |
| 1109007 | 1964108 | 605272 | 722959 |
| 265415 | 233159 | 138196 | 56415 |
| 546504 | 1549348 | 778706 | 394322 |
| 521436 | 359366 | 273148 | 49006 |
| 1891137 | 1800778 | 752939 | 1007910 |
| 119879 | 339538 | 47988 | 185767 |
| 19464 | 87068 | 33891 | 43162 |
| 225497 | 329635 | 223630 | 91716 |
| 168068 | 339521 | 174737 | 116118 |
| 5712097 | 8489024 | 7862306 | 405408 |
| 6317587 | 9877053 | 7127821 | 1461991 |
| 712176 | 1057699 | 709251 | 59362 |
| 5257778 | 5348439 | 4301947 | 319572 |
| 12850 | 17406 | 15588 | 502 |
| 14440 | 42870 | 36523 | 2882 |
| 4542 | 2747 | 2699 | 46 |
| 1036493 | 2728776 | 816685 | 1638534 |
| 341023 | 868103 | 121012 | 656541 |
| 191663 | 1170820 | 354393 | 497491 |

# 12-6 续表
Continued

| 项目 | Indicator | 营业收入<br>Revenue from Principal Business |
|---|---|---|
| **总计** | **Total** | **35976282** |
| 煤炭开采和洗选业 | Mining and Washing of Coal | |
| 石油和天然气开采业 | Extraction of Petroleum and Natural Gas | |
| 黑色金属矿采选业 | Mining of Ferrous Metal Ores | |
| 有色金属矿采选业 | Mining of Non-ferrous Metal Ores | 12810 |
| 非金属矿采选业 | Mining and Processing of Nometal Ores | 5363 |
| 开采辅助活动 | Auxiliary Activities of Mining | |
| 其他采矿业 | Mining of Other Ores | |
| 农副食品加工业 | Processing of Food from Agricultural Products | 7798 |
| 食品制造业 | Manufacture of Foods | 65301 |
| 酒、饮料和精制茶制造业 | Manufacture of Liquor, Beverage and Refind Tea | 1922370 |
| 烟草制品业 | Manufacture of Tobacco | |
| 纺织业 | Manufacture of Textile | |
| 纺织服装、服饰业 | Manufacture of Textile Wearing Apparel | |
| 皮革、毛皮、羽毛及其制品和制鞋业 | Manufacture of Leather, Fur, Feather & Its Products Footwear | 8634 |
| 木材加工和木、竹、藤、棕、草制品业 | Processing of Timbers, Manufacture of Wood, Bamboo, Rattan, Palm and Straw Products | 10091 |
| 家具制造业 | Manufacture of Furniture | |
| 造纸和纸制品业 | Manufacture of Paper and Paper Products | 103098 |
| 印刷和记录媒介复制业 | Printing, Reproduction of Recording Media | 4351 |
| 文教、工美、体育和娱乐用品制造业 | Manufacture of Articles for Culture, Arts & Crafts, Sports and Entertainment | |
| 石油、煤炭及其他燃料加工业 | Oil, coal and other fuel processing industries | 7433339 |
| 化学原料和化学制品制造业 | Manufacture of Chemical Raw Material and Chemical Products | 1073477 |
| 医药制造业 | Manufacture of Medicines | 238740 |
| 化学纤维制造业 | Manufacture of Chemical Fibers | |
| 橡胶和塑料制品业 | Manufacture of Rubber and Plastic | 542980 |
| 非金属矿物制品业 | Manufacture of Non-mettallic Mineral Products | 235788 |
| 黑色金属冶炼和压延加工业 | Smelting and Pressing of Ferrous Metals | 2033037 |
| 有色金属冶炼和压延加工业 | Smelting and Pressing of Non-ferrous Metals | 120983 |
| 金属制品业 | Manufacture of Metal Products | 19584 |
| 通用设备制造业 | Manufacture of General Purpose Machinery | 187513 |
| 专用设备制造业 | Manufacture of Special Purpose Machinery | 148195 |
| 汽车制造业 | Manufacture of Vehicle | 5927742 |
| 铁路、船舶、航空航天和其他运输设备制造业 | Manufacture of Transport Equipment for Railway, Shipping, Aerospace and other uses | 6249719 |
| 电气机械和器材制造业 | Manufacture of Electrical Machinery & Equipment | 1101055 |
| 计算机、通信和其他电子设备制造业 | Manufacture of Computer, Communication Equipment and Other Electronic Equipment | 6779254 |
| 仪器仪表制造业 | Manufacture of Measuring Instrument | 14557 |
| 其他制造业 | Manufacture of Other Products | 31559 |
| 废弃资源综合利用业 | Recycling and Disposal of Waste Resources | |
| 金属制品、机械和设备修理业 | Manufacture of Metal Products, Machinery and Equipment | 4542 |
| 电力、热力生产和供应业 | Production and Supply of Electric Power and Heat Power | 1076889 |
| 燃气生产和供应业 | Production and Supply of Gas | 377026 |
| 水的生产和供应业 | Production and Supply of Water | 240487 |

单位：万元（10 000 yuan）

| 营业成本<br>Cost of Prinipal Business | 营业税金及附加<br>Taxes and Extra Charges on Principal Business | 利润总额<br>Total Profits | 全部从业人员年平均人数（人）<br>Annual Average Employed Persons（person） |
|---|---|---|---|
| **29900096** | **1581325** | **1957865** | **115832** |
| | | | |
| 8209 | 647 | 327 | 219 |
| 3614 | 180 | 236 | 138 |
| | | | |
| 7604 | 39 | -144 | 57 |
| 47807 | 669 | 9554 | 756 |
| 1538507 | 53685 | 96327 | 6135 |
| | | | |
| 5451 | 148 | 287 | 165 |
| 9278 | 34 | 494 | 457 |
| | | | |
| 99333 | 540 | 74 | 950 |
| 3293 | 121 | 11 | 145 |
| | | | |
| 5524932 | 1295281 | 501076 | 2382 |
| 909460 | 4805 | 91423 | 3406 |
| 108176 | 2565 | 59931 | 1500 |
| | | | |
| 485298 | 3661 | -8507 | 6627 |
| 202689 | 1226 | 15569 | 1260 |
| 1839441 | 10742 | 39459 | 4230 |
| 98526 | 2522 | 2758 | 1272 |
| 16691 | 435 | 12 | 400 |
| 177424 | 1387 | -13722 | 2240 |
| 130026 | 783 | 16 | 1058 |
| 5267881 | 70259 | 343773 | 8652 |
| 5220340 | 59810 | 434379 | 30908 |
| 979320 | 5676 | 8153 | 6346 |
| 5586546 | 42325 | 342533 | 22346 |
| 11002 | 140 | 1091 | 166 |
| 29388 | 88 | 649 | 112 |
| | | | |
| 3904 | 23 | 178 | 42 |
| 1110837 | 8753 | -91863 | 8895 |
| 207780 | 3123 | 139346 | 1054 |
| 267343 | 11662 | -15555 | 3914 |

# 12-7　按行业分规模以上外商投资和港澳台商投资工业企业主要指标（2018年）

MAIN INDICATORS OF FOREIGN FUNEDE ENTERPRISES AND ENTERPRISES WITH FUNDS FROM HONG HONG，MACAO AND TAIWAN ABOVE DESIGNATED SIZE BY INDUSTRIAL SECTOR（2018）

| 项目 | Indicator | 企业单位数（个）Number of Enterprises（Unit） |
|---|---|---|
| **总计** | **Total** | **938** |
| 煤炭开采和洗选业 | Mining and Washing of Coal | |
| 石油和天然气开采业 | Extraction of Petroleum and Natural Gas | |
| 黑色金属矿采选业 | Mining of Ferrous Metal Ores | |
| 有色金属矿采选业 | Mining of Non-ferrous Metal Ores | |
| 非金属矿采选业 | Mining and Processing of Nometal Ores | |
| 开采辅助活动 | Auxiliary Activities of Mining | |
| 其他采矿业 | Mining of Other Ores | |
| 农副食品加工业 | Processing of Food from Agricultural Products | 98 |
| 食品制造业 | Manufacture of Foods | 39 |
| 酒、饮料和精制茶制造业 | Manufacture of Liquor，Beverage and Refind Tea | 8 |
| 烟草制品业 | Manufacture of Tobacco | |
| 纺织业 | Manufacture of Textile | 35 |
| 纺织服装、服饰业 | Manufacture of Textile Wearing Apparel | 62 |
| 皮革、毛皮、羽毛及其制品和制鞋业 | Manufacture of Leather，Fur，Feather & Its Products Footwear | 27 |
| 木材加工和木、竹、藤、棕、草制品业 | Processing of Timbers，Manufacture of Wood，Bamboo，Rattan，Palm and Straw Products | 5 |
| 家具制造业 | Manufacture of Furniture | 21 |
| 造纸和纸制品业 | Manufacture of Paper and Paper Products | 13 |
| 印刷和记录媒介复制业 | Printing，Reproduction of Recording Media | 26 |
| 文教、工美、体育和娱乐用品制造业 | Manufacture of Articles for Culture，Arts & Crafts，Sports and Entertainment | 57 |
| 石油、煤炭及其他燃料加工业 | Oil, coal and other fuel processing industries | 1 |
| 化学原料和化学制品制造业 | Manufacture of Chemical Raw Material and Chemical Products | 56 |
| 医药制造业 | Manufacture of Medicines | 6 |
| 化学纤维制造业 | Manufacture of Chemical Fibers | 3 |
| 橡胶和塑料制品业 | Manufacture of Rubber and Plastic | 54 |
| 非金属矿物制品业 | Manufacture of Non-mettallic Mineral Products | 36 |
| 黑色金属冶炼和压延加工业 | Smelting and Pressing of Ferrous Metals | 8 |
| 有色金属冶炼和压延加工业 | Smelting and Pressing of Non-ferrous Metals | 2 |
| 金属制品业 | Manufacture of Metal Products | 59 |
| 通用设备制造业 | Manufacture of General Purpose Machinery | 62 |
| 专用设备制造业 | Manufacture of Special Purpose Machinery | 43 |
| 汽车制造业 | Manufacture of Vehicle | 57 |
| 铁路、船舶、航空航天和其他运输设备制造业 | Manufacture of Transport Equipment for Railway，Shipping，Aerospace and other uses | 30 |
| 电气机械和器材制造业 | Manufacture of Electrical Machinery & Equipment | 43 |
| 计算机、通信和其他电子设备制造业 | Manufacture of Computer，Communication Equipment and Other Electronic Equipment | 54 |
| 仪器仪表制造业 | Manufacture of Measuring Instrument | 13 |
| 其他制造业 | Manufacture of Other Products | 5 |
| 废弃资源综合利用业 | Recycling and Disposal of Waste Resources | |
| 金属制品、机械和设备修理业 | Manufacture of Metal Products，Machinery and Equipment | 1 |
| 电力、热力生产和供应业 | Production and Supply of Electric Power and Heat Power | 4 |
| 燃气生产和供应业 | Production and Supply of Gas | 7 |
| 水的生产和供应业 | Production and Supply of Water | 3 |

单位：万元（10 000 yuan）

| 工业总产值<br>Gross Industrial Output Value | 资产合计<br>Total Assets | 流动资产合计<br>Total Current Assets | 固定资产净值<br>Net Value of Fixed Assets |
|---:|---:|---:|---:|
| **24092865** | **27642336** | **19200472** | **5442126** |
| 2176535 | 1707105 | 1292512 | 308419 |
| 1570361 | 1919797 | 1250215 | 431368 |
| 1184541 | 2446758 | 969369 | 278217 |
| 478805 | 364861 | 247938 | 99505 |
| 650510 | 582914 | 375573 | 137911 |
| 473560 | 232037 | 157718 | 60297 |
| 28558 | 35157 | 26534 | 7889 |
| 183671 | 196138 | 130569 | 53259 |
| 175872 | 160779 | 115408 | 38165 |
| 396696 | 414713 | 251096 | 124406 |
| 447802 | 470222 | 291349 | 137027 |
| 68377 | 30327 | 17959 | 7814 |
| 2114387 | 1889180 | 1071410 | 644777 |
| 176859 | 139820 | 80232 | 12238 |
| 31448 | 48768 | 28412 | 21759 |
| 935560 | 989811 | 495929 | 421041 |
| 475963 | 611717 | 362857 | 213079 |
| 389602 | 255770 | 185131 | 55707 |
| 50032 | 50440 | 35296 | 15299 |
| 1651556 | 1384669 | 941731 | 346924 |
| 1496323 | 1405849 | 924210 | 342102 |
| 634297 | 931859 | 637110 | 208854 |
| 4022309 | 7197708 | 6507805 | 545045 |
| 636189 | 955287 | 709909 | 163421 |
| 875948 | 686965 | 472688 | 158209 |
| 1942521 | 1313371 | 941643 | 272639 |
| 332494 | 341567 | 305802 | 19573 |
| 87398 | 173690 | 143583 | 19131 |
| 6290 | 2682 | 2612 | 50 |
| 34188 | 143303 | 43254 | 82225 |
| 334202 | 423121 | 145614 | 175917 |
| 30013 | 135956 | 39004 | 39862 |

## 12-7　续表
Continued

| 项目 | Indicator | 营业收入<br>Revenue from Principal Business |
|---|---|---|
| **总计** | **Total** | **25982220** |
| 煤炭开采和洗选业 | Mining and Washing of Coal | |
| 石油和天然气开采业 | Extraction of Petroleum and Natural Gas | |
| 黑色金属矿采选业 | Mining of Ferrous Metal Ores | |
| 有色金属矿采选业 | Mining of Non-ferrous Metal Ores | |
| 非金属矿采选业 | Mining and Processing of Nometal Ores | |
| 开采辅助活动 | Auxiliary Activities of Mining | |
| 其他采矿业 | Mining of Other Ores | |
| 农副食品加工业 | Processing of Food from Agricultural Products | 2660511 |
| 食品制造业 | Manufacture of Foods | 1399184 |
| 酒、饮料和精制茶制造业 | Manufacture of Liquor, Beverage and Refind Tea | 2140361 |
| 烟草制品业 | Manufacture of Tobacco | |
| 纺织业 | Manufacture of Textile | 516162 |
| 纺织服装、服饰业 | Manufacture of Textile Wearing Apparel | 668251 |
| 皮革、毛皮、羽毛及其制品和制鞋业 | Manufacture of Leather, Fur, Feather & Its Products Footwear | 471941 |
| 木材加工和木、竹、藤、棕、草制品业 | Processing of Timbers, Manufacture of Wood, Bamboo, Rattan, Palm and Straw Products | 26808 |
| 家具制造业 | Manufacture of Furniture | 176432 |
| 造纸和纸制品业 | Manufacture of Paper and Paper Products | 173936 |
| 印刷和记录媒介复制业 | Printing, Reproduction of Recording Media | 443396 |
| 文教、工美、体育和娱乐用品制造业 | Manufacture of Articles for Culture, Arts & Crafts, Sports and Entertainment | 452730 |
| 石油、煤炭及其他燃料加工业 | Oil, coal and other fuel processing industries | 68737 |
| 化学原料和化学制品制造业 | Manufacture of Chemical Raw Material and Chemical Products | 2300470 |
| 医药制造业 | Manufacture of Medicines | 163309 |
| 化学纤维制造业 | Manufacture of Chemical Fibers | 31157 |
| 橡胶和塑料制品业 | Manufacture of Rubber and Plastic | 947801 |
| 非金属矿物制品业 | Manufacture of Non-mettallic Mineral Products | 498319 |
| 黑色金属冶炼和压延加工业 | Smelting and Pressing of Ferrous Metals | 392840 |
| 有色金属冶炼和压延加工业 | Smelting and Pressing of Non-ferrous Metals | 50266 |
| 金属制品业 | Manufacture of Metal Products | 1674628 |
| 通用设备制造业 | Manufacture of General Purpose Machinery | 1555635 |
| 专用设备制造业 | Manufacture of Special Purpose Machinery | 639414 |
| 汽车制造业 | Manufacture of Vehicle | 4050052 |
| 铁路、船舶、航空航天和其他运输设备制造业 | Manufacture of Transport Equipment for Railway, Shipping, Aerospace and other uses | 710419 |
| 电气机械和器材制造业 | Manufacture of Electrical Machinery & Equipment | 828590 |
| 计算机、通信和其他电子设备制造业 | Manufacture of Computer, Communication Equipment and Other Electronic Equipment | 2085001 |
| 仪器仪表制造业 | Manufacture of Measuring Instrument | 342157 |
| 其他制造业 | Manufacture of Other Products | 88590 |
| 废弃资源综合利用业 | Recycling and Disposal of Waste Resources | |
| 金属制品、机械和设备修理业 | Manufacture of Metal Products, Machinery and Equipment | 6290 |
| 电力、热力生产和供应业 | Production and Supply of Electric Power and Heat Power | 35001 |
| 燃气生产和供应业 | Production and Supply of Gas | 353859 |
| 水的生产和供应业 | Production and Supply of Water | 29974 |

单位：万元（10 000 yuan）

| 营业成本<br>Cost of Prinipal Business | 营业税金及附加<br>Taxes and Extra Charges on Principal Business | 利润总额<br>Total Profits | 全部从业人员年平均人数（人）<br>Annual Average Employed Persons（person） |
|---|---|---|---|
| **22102255** | **238380** | **1332268** | **234235** |
| | | | |
| 2483635 | 6246 | 19141 | 20682 |
| 1154959 | 10601 | -33209 | 8702 |
| 1700456 | 55520 | 99489 | 7536 |
| | | | |
| 459422 | 2039 | 4860 | 5428 |
| 594004 | 5452 | 5189 | 18792 |
| 428875 | 3902 | 863 | 15337 |
| 23369 | 118 | 1069 | 740 |
| 145553 | 1704 | 7570 | 4651 |
| 156254 | 983 | 5570 | 1551 |
| 364615 | 3175 | 23082 | 5200 |
| 389672 | 3849 | 11088 | 11973 |
| 62327 | 254 | 1364 | 136 |
| 1994210 | 10315 | 62045 | 9062 |
| 94055 | 2709 | 22367 | 1175 |
| 24830 | 217 | -3261 | 268 |
| 783653 | 6069 | 50297 | 11646 |
| 408813 | 4559 | 34636 | 4651 |
| 374210 | 805 | 10699 | 1269 |
| 47690 | 163 | -1269 | 145 |
| 1509460 | 11077 | 178195 | 15546 |
| 1286915 | 8286 | 86751 | 16575 |
| 516801 | 3520 | 23009 | 6940 |
| 3363251 | 70865 | 351157 | 20472 |
| 556281 | 7866 | 60794 | 7154 |
| 709667 | 3421 | 44780 | 10462 |
| 1812082 | 9011 | 158029 | 20567 |
| 216707 | 3110 | 71400 | 2874 |
| 75649 | 888 | 3585 | 2793 |
| | | | |
| 3706 | 63 | 1019 | 127 |
| 22693 | 585 | 7099 | 312 |
| 319202 | 492 | 19458 | 1160 |
| 19242 | 519 | 5403 | 309 |

# 12-8 按行业分大中型工业企业主要指标(2018 年)
## MAIN INDICATORS OF LARGE AND MEDIUM-SIZED INDUSTRIAL ENTERPRISES BY INDUSTRIAL SECTOR (2019)

| 项目 | Indicator | 企业单位数(个) Number of Enterprises (Unit) |
|---|---|---|
| **总计** | **Total** | **459** |
| 煤炭开采和洗选业 | Mining and Washing of Coal | |
| 石油和天然气开采业 | Extraction of Petroleum and Natural Gas | |
| 黑色金属矿采选业 | Mining of Ferrous Metal Ores | |
| 有色金属矿采选业 | Mining of Non-ferrous Metal Ores | |
| 非金属矿采选业 | Mining and Processing of Nometal Ores | |
| 开采辅助活动 | Auxiliary Activities of Mining | |
| 其他采矿业 | Mining of Other Ores | |
| 农副食品加工业 | Processing of Food from Agricultural Products | 32 |
| 食品制造业 | Manufacture of Foods | 19 |
| 酒、饮料和精制茶制造业 | Manufacture of Liquor, Beverage and Refind Tea | 4 |
| 烟草制品业 | Manufacture of Tobacco | |
| 纺织业 | Manufacture of Textile | 7 |
| 纺织服装、服饰业 | Manufacture of Textile Wearing Apparel | 32 |
| 皮革、毛皮、羽毛及其制品和制鞋业 | Manufacture of Leather, Fur, Feather & Its Products Footwear | 13 |
| 木材加工和木、竹、藤、棕、草制品业 | Processing of Timbers, Manufacture of Wood, Bamboo, Rattan, Palm and Straw Products | 2 |
| 家具制造业 | Manufacture of Furniture | 8 |
| 造纸和纸制品业 | Manufacture of Paper and Paper Products | 1 |
| 印刷和记录媒介复制业 | Printing, Reproduction of Recording Media | 7 |
| 文教、工美、体育和娱乐用品制造业 | Manufacture of Articles for Culture, Arts & Crafts, Sports and Entertainment | 17 |
| 石油、煤炭及其他燃料加工业 | Oil, coal and other fuel processing industries | 3 |
| 化学原料和化学制品制造业 | Manufacture of Chemical Raw Material and Chemical Products | 18 |
| 医药制造业 | Manufacture of Medicines | 10 |
| 化学纤维制造业 | Manufacture of Chemical Fibers | |
| 橡胶和塑料制品业 | Manufacture of Rubber and Plastic | 25 |
| 非金属矿物制品业 | Manufacture of Non-mettallic Mineral Products | 16 |
| 黑色金属冶炼和压延加工业 | Smelting and Pressing of Ferrous Metals | 5 |
| 有色金属冶炼和压延加工业 | Smelting and Pressing of Non-ferrous Metals | 2 |
| 金属制品业 | Manufacture of Metal Products | 29 |
| 通用设备制造业 | Manufacture of General Purpose Machinery | 37 |
| 专用设备制造业 | Manufacture of Special Purpose Machinery | 23 |
| 汽车制造业 | Manufacture of Vehicle | 37 |
| 铁路、船舶、航空航天和其他运输设备制造业 | Manufacture of Transport Equipment for Railway, Shipping, Aerospace and other uses | 32 |
| 电气机械和器材制造业 | Manufacture of Electrical Machinery & Equipment | 31 |
| 计算机、通信和其他电子设备制造业 | Manufacture of Computer, Communication Equipment and Other Electronic Equipment | 26 |
| 仪器仪表制造业 | Manufacture of Measuring Instrument | 6 |
| 其他制造业 | Manufacture of Other Products | 1 |
| 废弃资源综合利用业 | Recycling and Disposal of Waste Resources | |
| 金属制品、机械和设备修理业 | Manufacture of Metal Products, Machinery and Equipment | |
| 电力、热力生产和供应业 | Production and Supply of Electric Power and Heat Power | 11 |
| 燃气生产和供应业 | Production and Supply of Gas | 2 |
| 水的生产和供应业 | Production and Supply of Water | 3 |

单位：万元（10 000 yuan）

| 工业总产值<br>Gross Industrial Output Value | 资产合计<br>Total Assets | 流动资产合计<br>Total Current Assets | 固定资产净值<br>Net Value of Fixed Assets |
|---|---|---|---|
| **69216338** | **97151438** | **60602913** | **15006929** |
| 2953132 | 1910761 | 1241876 | 468867 |
| 1545762 | 2234917 | 1361631 | 408545 |
| 1498188 | 2594251 | 1098266 | 287897 |
| 352424 | 213195 | 174224 | 27847 |
| 1759197 | 1354481 | 682090 | 331538 |
| 526353 | 255786 | 169261 | 63319 |
| 18187 | 29087 | 22159 | 2181 |
| 158046 | 171264 | 117299 | 45646 |
| 124288 | 62276 | 34758 | 15064 |
| 196071 | 157251 | 113289 | 40002 |
| 363909 | 344654 | 199503 | 95787 |
| 7232378 | 2847158 | 1870482 | 784804 |
| 2969413 | 3858657 | 1846949 | 1117444 |
| 883218 | 994248 | 595531 | 192583 |
| 2249375 | 3857330 | 1599260 | 1179538 |
| 878149 | 965338 | 688049 | 175618 |
| 1922189 | 2112626 | 963013 | 1083157 |
| 42659 | 221258 | 8239 | 133406 |
| 1774292 | 1493647 | 1026625 | 322447 |
| 2522728 | 4005134 | 2531412 | 552268 |
| 1326014 | 1410420 | 1096445 | 240432 |
| 8786414 | 11772188 | 10342009 | 983280 |
| 6913738 | 10794895 | 7764214 | 1611676 |
| 13616022 | 32572128 | 18160737 | 2224061 |
| 6847403 | 6348404 | 4983082 | 541088 |
| 485101 | 790823 | 668528 | 56768 |
| 70754 | 88028 | 59384 | 18191 |
| 895282 | 2400093 | 828978 | 1385985 |
| 199774 | 455110 | 109155 | 267667 |
| 105880 | 836032 | 246466 | 349825 |

# 12-8　续表
Continued

| 项目 | Indicator | 营业收入<br>Revenue from Principal Business |
|---|---|---|
| **总计** | **Total** | **75470442** |
| 煤炭开采和洗选业 | Mining and Washing of Coal | |
| 石油和天然气开采业 | Extraction of Petroleum and Natural Gas | |
| 黑色金属矿采选业 | Mining of Ferrous Metal Ores | |
| 有色金属矿采选业 | Mining of Non-ferrous Metal Ores | |
| 非金属矿采选业 | Mining and Processing of Nometal Ores | |
| 开采辅助活动 | Auxiliary Activities of Mining | |
| 其他采矿业 | Mining of Other Ores | |
| 农副食品加工业 | Processing of Food from Agricultural Products | 3603765 |
| 食品制造业 | Manufacture of Foods | 1329906 |
| 酒、饮料和精制茶制造业 | Manufacture of Liquor，Beverage and Refind Tea | 2216301 |
| 烟草制品业 | Manufacture of Tobacco | |
| 纺织业 | Manufacture of Textile | 336037 |
| 纺织服装、服饰业 | Manufacture of Textile Wearing Apparel | 1803238 |
| 皮革、毛皮、羽毛及其制品和制鞋业 | Manufacture of Leather，Fur，Feather & Its Products Footwear | 495194 |
| 木材加工和木、竹、藤、棕、草制品业 | Processing of Timbers，Manufacture of Wood，Bamboo，Rattan，Palm and Straw Products | 17498 |
| 家具制造业 | Manufacture of Furniture | 157752 |
| 造纸和纸制品业 | Manufacture of Paper and Paper Products | 103098 |
| 印刷和记录媒介复制业 | Printing，Reproduction of Recording Media | 201446 |
| 文教、工美、体育和娱乐用品制造业 | Manufacture of Articles for Culture，Arts & Crafts，Sports and Entertainment | 376233 |
| 石油、煤炭及其他燃料加工业 | Oil, coal and other fuel processing industries | 7433339 |
| 化学原料和化学制品制造业 | Manufacture of Chemical Raw Material and Chemical Products | 3069429 |
| 医药制造业 | Manufacture of Medicines | 811344 |
| 化学纤维制造业 | Manufacture of Chemical Fibers | |
| 橡胶和塑料制品业 | Manufacture of Rubber and Plastic | 2240952 |
| 非金属矿物制品业 | Manufacture of Non-mettallic Mineral Products | 628978 |
| 黑色金属冶炼和压延加工业 | Smelting and Pressing of Ferrous Metals | 2091672 |
| 有色金属冶炼和压延加工业 | Smelting and Pressing of Non-ferrous Metals | 43477 |
| 金属制品业 | Manufacture of Metal Products | 1793764 |
| 通用设备制造业 | Manufacture of General Purpose Machinery | 2575389 |
| 专用设备制造业 | Manufacture of Special Purpose Machinery | 1346653 |
| 汽车制造业 | Manufacture of Vehicle | 9018577 |
| 铁路、船舶、航空航天和其他运输设备制造业 | Manufacture of Transport Equipment for Railway，Shipping，Aerospace and other uses | 6909697 |
| 电气机械和器材制造业 | Manufacture of Electrical Machinery & Equipment | 16533556 |
| 计算机、通信和其他电子设备制造业 | Manufacture of Computer，Communication Equipment and Other Electronic Equipment | 8449405 |
| 仪器仪表制造业 | Manufacture of Measuring Instrument | 482968 |
| 其他制造业 | Manufacture of Other Products | 71114 |
| 废弃资源综合利用业 | Recycling and Disposal of Waste Resources | |
| 金属制品、机械和设备修理业 | Manufacture of Metal Products，Machinery and Equipment | |
| 电力、热力生产和供应业 | Production and Supply of Electric Power and Heat Power | 945232 |
| 燃气生产和供应业 | Production and Supply of Gas | 239876 |
| 水的生产和供应业 | Production and Supply of Water | 144555 |

单位：万元（10 000 yuan）

| 营业成本<br>Cost of Prinipal Business | 营业税金及附加<br>Taxes and Extra Charges on Principal Business | 利润总额<br>Total Profits | 全部从业人员年平均人数（人）<br>Annual Average Employed Persons（person） |
|---|---|---|---|
| **60793240** | **1834487** | **4362438** | **44658** |
| | | | |
| 3398260 | 6593 | 25180 | 3448 |
| 1083843 | 8690 | -19421 | 939 |
| 1777589 | 58437 | 102239 | 857 |
| | | | |
| 304711 | 707 | -763 | 345 |
| 1574265 | 17878 | 53071 | 4541 |
| 444225 | 4013 | 5044 | 1684 |
| 16447 | 117 | 506 | 101 |
| 128351 | 1666 | 7000 | 415 |
| 99333 | 540 | 74 | 95 |
| 159385 | 1606 | 13805 | 322 |
| 323216 | 3022 | 8338 | 869 |
| 5524932 | 1295281 | 501076 | 238 |
| 2658087 | 10874 | 156540 | 1129 |
| 379719 | 11966 | 160323 | 674 |
| | | | |
| 1839384 | 13521 | 106992 | 2362 |
| 518213 | 4354 | 45277 | 806 |
| 1854606 | 11621 | 56443 | 634 |
| 27665 | 1408 | 2288 | 120 |
| 1578695 | 14199 | 208502 | 1920 |
| 2196752 | 15276 | 94029 | 2291 |
| 1078770 | 7712 | 77820 | 1537 |
| 8031771 | 82673 | 544114 | 3500 |
| 5735813 | 67933 | 477315 | 4403 |
| 11226499 | 120859 | 1361529 | 5260 |
| 7089309 | 49834 | 414364 | 4284 |
| 332109 | 4475 | 52088 | 421 |
| 61963 | 653 | 1210 | 240 |
| | | | |
| 975648 | 8282 | -84253 | 823 |
| 191015 | 370 | 6027 | 116 |
| 182668 | 9928 | -14320 | 287 |

# 12-9　按行业分规模以上工业企业主要经济效益指标（2018 年）

## MAIN INDICATORS ON ECONOMIC BENEFIT OF INDUSTRIA ENTERPRISES ABOVE DESIGNATED SIZE BY INDOUSTRIAL SSECTOR（2018）

| 项目 | Indicator | 总资产贡献率(%) Ratio of Total Assets to Industrial Output Value (%) |
|---|---|---|
| **总计** | **Total** | **8.11** |
| 煤炭开采和洗选业 | Mining and Washing of Coal | |
| 石油和天然气开采业 | Extraction of Petroleum and Natural Gas | |
| 黑色金属矿采选业 | Mining of Ferrous Metal Ores | |
| 有色金属矿采选业 | Mining of Non-ferrous Metal Ores | 2.9 |
| 非金属矿采选业 | Mining and Processing of Nometal Ores | 8.49 |
| 开采辅助活动 | Auxiliary Activities of Mining | |
| 其他采矿业 | Mining of Other Ores | |
| 农副食品加工业 | Processing of Food from Agricultural Products | 4.02 |
| 食品制造业 | Manufacture of Foods | 3.07 |
| 酒、饮料和精制茶制造业 | Manufacture of Liquor，Beverage and Refind Tea | 8.98 |
| 烟草制品业 | Manufacture of Tobacco | |
| 纺织业 | Manufacture of Textile | 2.47 |
| 纺织服装、服饰业 | Manufacture of Textile Wearing Apparel | 8.39 |
| 皮革、毛皮、羽毛及其制品和制鞋业 | Manufacture of Leather，Fur，Feather & Its Products Footwear | 3.81 |
| 木材加工和木、竹、藤、棕、草制品业 | Processing of Timbers，Manufacture of Wood，Bamboo，Rattan，Palm and Straw Products | 6.79 |
| 家具制造业 | Manufacture of Furniture | 5.59 |
| 造纸和纸制品业 | Manufacture of Paper and Paper Products | 6.17 |
| 印刷和记录媒介复制业 | Printing，Reproduction of Recording Media | 8.26 |
| 文教、工美、体育和娱乐用品制造业 | Manufacture of Articles for Culture，Arts & Crafts，Sports and Entertainment | 4.05 |
| 石油、煤炭及其他燃料加工业 | Oil, coal and other fuel processing industries | 65.3 |
| 化学原料和化学制品制造业 | Manufacture of Chemical Raw Material and Chemical Products | 6.42 |
| 医药制造业 | Manufacture of Medicines | 20.43 |
| 化学纤维制造业 | Manufacture of Chemical Fibers | -0.07 |
| 橡胶和塑料制品业 | Manufacture of Rubber and Plastic | 5.41 |
| 非金属矿物制品业 | Manufacture of Non-mettallic Mineral Products | 7.94 |
| 黑色金属冶炼和压延加工业 | Smelting and Pressing of Ferrous Metals | 5.18 |
| 有色金属冶炼和压延加工业 | Smelting and Pressing of Non-ferrous Metals | 3.53 |
| 金属制品业 | Manufacture of Metal Products | 8.95 |
| 通用设备制造业 | Manufacture of General Purpose Machinery | 4.43 |
| 专用设备制造业 | Manufacture of Special Purpose Machinery | 5.74 |
| 汽车制造业 | Manufacture of Vehicle | 6.6 |
| 铁路、船舶、航空航天和其他运输设备制造业 | Manufacture of Transport Equipment for Railway，Shipping，Aerospace and other uses | 7.8 |
| 电气机械和器材制造业 | Manufacture of Electrical Machinery & Equipment | 6.34 |
| 计算机、通信和其他电子设备制造业 | Manufacture of Computer，Communication Equipment and Other Electronic Equipment | 12.83 |
| 仪器仪表制造业 | Manufacture of Measuring Instrument | 11.46 |
| 其他制造业 | Manufacture of Other Products | 7.14 |
| 废弃资源综合利用业 | Recycling and Disposal of Waste Resources | -0.1 |
| 金属制品、机械和设备修理业 | Manufacture of Metal Products，Machinery and Equipment | 9.22 |
| 电力、热力生产和供应业 | Production and Supply of Electric Power and Heat Power | -0.09 |
| 燃气生产和供应业 | Production and Supply of Gas | 15.15 |
| 水的生产和供应业 | Production and Supply of Water | 2.17 |

| 资产负债率 (%) Assets-Liability Ratio (%) | 流动资产周转次数(次/年) Number of Times of Annual of Turnover Current Assets (time/year) | 工业成本费用利润率 (%) Ratio of Profits to Industrial Costs (%) | 产品销售率 (%) Ratio of Sales to Output (%) |
|---|---|---|---|
| **61.53** | **1.32** | **5.62** | **100.18** |
| | | | |
| 50.97 | 5.23 | 2.75 | 100 |
| 80.22 | 0.78 | 4.89 | 88.39 |
| | | | |
| 65.3 | 2.78 | 0.81 | 98.86 |
| 62.68 | 1.16 | 1.12 | 95.86 |
| 41.89 | 1.96 | 4.58 | 161.07 |
| | | | |
| 73.27 | 1.9 | -0.43 | 99.03 |
| 52.53 | 2.29 | 2.38 | 99.24 |
| 60.87 | 2.53 | 0.85 | 94.57 |
| 50.6 | 1.55 | 6.03 | 99.97 |
| 61.09 | 1.66 | 2.8 | 98.18 |
| 61.79 | 1.86 | 2.07 | 98.01 |
| 58.7 | 2.02 | 3.78 | 98.42 |
| 51.92 | 1.86 | 1.58 | 99.83 |
| 55.13 | 3.94 | 8.74 | 99.62 |
| 52 | 1.63 | 5.05 | 98.35 |
| 32.81 | 1.32 | 21.33 | 96.46 |
| 56.05 | 1.38 | -3.62 | 98.63 |
| 59.26 | 1.63 | 3.8 | 99.34 |
| 60.56 | 1.1 | 6.53 | 99.33 |
| 71.72 | 2.59 | 2.24 | 99.95 |
| 69.19 | 3.77 | 0.95 | 100.16 |
| 48.33 | 1.52 | 7.11 | 99.72 |
| 53.47 | 1.06 | 3.97 | 98.21 |
| 54.89 | 1.02 | 4.99 | 97.99 |
| 66.57 | 0.92 | 6.03 | 98.97 |
| 62.99 | 0.91 | 7.45 | 101.6 |
| 68.98 | 0.92 | 8.53 | 96.54 |
| 51.34 | 1.71 | 5.52 | 103.73 |
| 60.1 | 0.87 | 13.39 | 101.73 |
| 61.19 | 0.74 | 5.86 | 99.73 |
| 48.37 | 1.09 | -4.49 | 98.88 |
| 24.65 | 2.37 | 7.89 | 98.77 |
| 75.03 | 1.11 | -4.64 | 97.76 |
| 43.27 | 3.06 | 27.57 | 99.86 |
| 65.91 | 0.65 | -1.49 | 99.34 |

# 12-10　按行业分国有控股工业企业主要经济效益指标（2018 年）

MAIN INDICATORS ON ECONOMIC BENEFIT OF STSTE-OWNED AND STATE-HOLDING INUSTRIAL ENTERPRISES BY INDUSTRIAL SECTOR（2018）

| 行业 | Indicator | 总资产贡献率(%) Ratio of Total Assets to Industrial Output Value (%) |
|---|---|---|
| **总计** | **Total** | **11.06** |
| 煤炭开采和洗选业 | Mining and Washing of Coal | |
| 石油和天然气开采业 | Extraction of Petroleum and Natural Gas | |
| 黑色金属矿采选业 | Mining of Ferrous Metal Ores | |
| 有色金属矿采选业 | Mining of Non-ferrous Metal Ores | 2.90 |
| 非金属矿采选业 | Mining and Processing of Nometal Ores | 8.49 |
| 开采辅助活动 | Auxiliary Activities of Mining | 0.00 |
| 其他采矿业 | Mining of Other Ores | 0.00 |
| 农副食品加工业 | Processing of Food from Agricultural Products | -1.38 |
| 食品制造业 | Manufacture of Foods | 14.83 |
| 酒、饮料和精制茶制造业 | Manufacture of Liquor, Beverage and Refind Tea | 9.31 |
| 烟草制品业 | Manufacture of Tobacco | |
| 纺织业 | Manufacture of Textile | |
| 纺织服装、服饰业 | Manufacture of Textile Wearing Apparel | |
| 皮革、毛皮、羽毛及其制品和制鞋业 | Manufacture of Leather, Fur, Feather & Its Products Footwear | |
| 木材加工和木、竹、藤、棕、草制品业 | Processing of Timbers, Manufacture of Wood, Bamboo, Rattan, Palm and Straw Products | 5.74 |
| 家具制造业 | Manufacture of Furniture | 0.84 |
| 造纸和纸制品业 | Manufacture of Paper and Paper Products | 3.17 |
| 印刷和记录媒介复制业 | Printing, Reproduction of Recording Media | 4.10 |
| 文教、工美、体育和娱乐用品制造业 | Manufacture of Articles for Culture, Arts & Crafts, Sports and Entertainment | |
| 石油、煤炭及其他燃料加工业 | Oil, coal and other fuel processing industries | 67.91 |
| 化学原料和化学制品制造业 | Manufacture of Chemical Raw Material and Chemical Products | 5.63 |
| 医药制造业 | Manufacture of Medicines | 32.80 |
| 化学纤维制造业 | Manufacture of Chemical Fibers | |
| 橡胶和塑料制品业 | Manufacture of Rubber and Plastic | 1.44 |
| 非金属矿物制品业 | Manufacture of Non-mettallic Mineral Products | 7.46 |
| 黑色金属冶炼和压延加工业 | Smelting and Pressing of Ferrous Metals | 4.90 |
| 有色金属冶炼和压延加工业 | Smelting and Pressing of Non-ferrous Metals | 2.94 |
| 金属制品业 | Manufacture of Metal Products | 2.40 |
| 通用设备制造业 | Manufacture of General Purpose Machinery | -2.23 |
| 专用设备制造业 | Manufacture of Special Purpose Machinery | 1.69 |
| 汽车制造业 | Manufacture of Vehicle | 5.98 |
| 铁路、船舶、航空航天和其他运输设备制造业 | Manufacture of Transport Equipment for Railway, Shipping, Aerospace and other uses | 7.45 |
| 电气机械和器材制造业 | Manufacture of Electrical Machinery & Equipment | 3.64 |
| 计算机、通信和其他电子设备制造业 | Manufacture of Computer, Communication Equipment and Other Electronic Equipment | 13.56 |
| 仪器仪表制造业 | Manufacture of Measuring Instrument | 9.49 |
| 其他制造业 | Manufacture of Other Products | 4.06 |
| 废弃资源综合利用业 | Recycling and Disposal of Waste Resources | |
| 金属制品、机械和设备修理业 | Manufacture of Metal Products, Machinery and Equipment | 12.66 |
| 电力、热力生产和供应业 | Production and Supply of Electric Power and Heat Power | -1.78 |
| 燃气生产和供应业 | Production and Supply of Gas | 19.69 |
| 水的生产和供应业 | Production and Supply of Water | 1.09 |

| 资产负债率 (%) Assets-Liability Ratio (%) | 流动资产周转次数(次/年) Number of Times of Annual of Turnover Current Assets (time/year) | 工业成本费用利润率 (%) Ratio of Profits to Industrial Costs (%) | 产品销售率 (%) Ratio of Sales to Output (%) |
|---|---|---|---|
| **62.46** | **1.32** | **5.91** | **103.55** |
| | | | |
| | | | |
| | | | |
| 50.97 | 5.23 | 2.75 | 100 |
| 80.22 | 0.78 | 4.89 | 88.39 |
| | | | |
| | | | |
| 98.54 | 2.41 | -1.83 | 100 |
| 31.94 | 0.92 | 17.31 | 93.23 |
| 35.02 | 2.19 | 5.09 | 194.21 |
| | | | |
| | | | |
| | | | |
| 57.72 | 0.71 | 3.50 | 100.11 |
| 87.26 | 0.49 | 5.16 | 100 |
| | | | |
| 61.91 | 2.97 | 0.07 | 96 |
| 10.38 | 0.89 | 0.26 | 87.72 |
| | | | |
| 55.37 | 3.97 | 8.89 | 99.62 |
| 56.51 | 1.77 | 9.24 | 93.76 |
| 24.09 | 1.73 | 31.97 | 101.49 |
| | | | |
| 78.96 | 0.70 | -1.49 | 99.9 |
| 71.92 | 0.86 | 7.07 | 100.17 |
| 80.22 | 2.70 | 1.99 | 99.02 |
| 74.15 | 2.52 | 2.37 | 95.44 |
| 72.28 | 0.58 | 0.06 | 100.29 |
| 56.64 | 0.84 | -7.05 | 79.67 |
| 79.28 | 0.85 | 0.01 | 85.73 |
| 67.11 | 0.75 | 6.23 | 100.85 |
| 65.04 | 0.88 | 7.26 | 101.29 |
| 65.60 | 1.55 | 0.75 | 101.35 |
| 51.16 | 1.58 | 5.22 | 105.23 |
| 58.42 | 0.93 | 8.27 | 100.83 |
| 75.43 | 0.86 | 2.09 | 100 |
| | | | |
| 81.50 | 1.68 | 4.10 | 100 |
| 81.15 | 1.32 | -7.66 | 97.48 |
| 30.58 | 3.12 | 57.36 | 99.9 |
| 67.40 | 0.68 | -5.08 | 99.74 |

# 12-11 按行业分规模以上外商及港澳台商投资工业企业主要经济效益指标（2018年）

## MAIN INDICATORS ON ECONOMIC BENEFIT OF FOREIGN FUNDED ENTERPRISES AND ENTERPRISES WITH FUNDS FROM HONG KONG，MACAO AND TAIWAN ABOVE DESIGNATED SIZE BY INDUSTRIAL SECTOR（2018）

| 行业 | Indicator | 总资产贡献率（%）<br>Ratio of Total Assets to Industrial Output Value（%） |
|---|---|---|
| **总计** | **Total** | **7.77** |
| 煤炭开采和洗选业 | Mining and Washing of Coal | |
| 石油和天然气开采业 | Extraction of Petroleum and Natural Gas | |
| 黑色金属矿采选业 | Mining of Ferrous Metal Ores | |
| 有色金属矿采选业 | Mining of Non-ferrous Metal Ores | |
| 非金属矿采选业 | Mining and Processing of Nometal Ores | |
| 开采辅助活动 | Auxiliary Activities of Mining | |
| 其他采矿业 | Mining of Other Ores | |
| 农副食品加工业 | Processing of Food from Agricultural Products | 3.32 |
| 食品制造业 | Manufacture of Foods | 0.88 |
| 酒、饮料和精制茶制造业 | Manufacture of Liquor，Beverage and Refind Tea | 9.38 |
| 烟草制品业 | Manufacture of Tobacco | |
| 纺织业 | Manufacture of Textile | 4.23 |
| 纺织服装、服饰业 | Manufacture of Textile Wearing Apparel | 3.03 |
| 皮革、毛皮、羽毛及其制品和制鞋业 | Manufacture of Leather，Fur，Feather & Its Products Footwear | 4.40 |
| 木材加工和木、竹、藤、棕、草制品业 | Processing of Timbers，Manufacture of Wood，Bamboo，Rattan，Palm and Straw Products | 2.64 |
| 家具制造业 | Manufacture of Furniture | 7.68 |
| 造纸和纸制品业 | Manufacture of Paper and Paper Products | 6.75 |
| 印刷和记录媒介复制业 | Printing，Reproduction of Recording Media | 9.50 |
| 文教、工美、体育和娱乐用品制造业 | Manufacture of Articles for Culture，Arts & Crafts，Sports and Entertainment | 4.35 |
| 石油、煤炭及其他燃料加工业 | Oil, coal and other fuel processing industries | 6.75 |
| 化学原料和化学制品制造业 | Manufacture of Chemical Raw Material and Chemical Products | 7.23 |
| 医药制造业 | Manufacture of Medicines | 29.55 |
| 化学纤维制造业 | Manufacture of Chemical Fibers | -4.39 |
| 橡胶和塑料制品业 | Manufacture of Rubber and Plastic | 7.71 |
| 非金属矿物制品业 | Manufacture of Non-mettallic Mineral Products | 9.09 |
| 黑色金属冶炼和压延加工业 | Smelting and Pressing of Ferrous Metals | 5.82 |
| 有色金属冶炼和压延加工业 | Smelting and Pressing of Non-ferrous Metals | -0.34 |
| 金属制品业 | Manufacture of Metal Products | 14.89 |
| 通用设备制造业 | Manufacture of General Purpose Machinery | 8.04 |
| 专用设备制造业 | Manufacture of Special Purpose Machinery | 4.62 |
| 汽车制造业 | Manufacture of Vehicle | 7.41 |
| 铁路、船舶、航空航天和其他运输设备制造业 | Manufacture of Transport Equipment for Railway，Shipping，Aerospace and other uses | 10.48 |
| 电气机械和器材制造业 | Manufacture of Electrical Machinery & Equipment | 9.08 |
| 计算机、通信和其他电子设备制造业 | Manufacture of Computer，Communication Equipment and Other Electronic Equipment | 13.65 |
| 仪器仪表制造业 | Manufacture of Measuring Instrument | 27.56 |
| 其他制造业 | Manufacture of Other Products | 5.59 |
| 废弃资源综合利用业 | Recycling and Disposal of Waste Resources | |
| 金属制品、机械和设备修理业 | Manufacture of Metal Products，Machinery and Equipment | 54.84 |
| 电力、热力生产和供应业 | Production and Supply of Electric Power and Heat Power | 8.32 |
| 燃气生产和供应业 | Production and Supply of Gas | 6.28 |
| 水的生产和供应业 | Production and Supply of Water | 6.74 |

| 资产负债率 (%) Assets-Liability Ratio (%) | 流动资产周转次数(次/年) Number of Times of Annual of Turnover Current Assets (time/year) | 工业成本费用利润率(%) Ratio of Profits to Industrial Costs (%) | 产品销售率(%) Ratio of Sales to Output (%) |
|---|---|---|---|
| **53.35** | **1.35** | **5.41** | **103.51** |
| | | | |
| 66.06 | 2.06 | 0.73 | 97.74 |
| 68.31 | 1.12 | -2.43 | 94.34 |
| 36.91 | 2.21 | 4.73 | 184.17 |
| | | | |
| 61.60 | 2.08 | 0.96 | 100.08 |
| 48.22 | 1.78 | 0.79 | 98.8 |
| 59.27 | 2.99 | 0.19 | 99.58 |
| 66.23 | 1.01 | 4.19 | 100 |
| 57.96 | 1.35 | 4.54 | 99.47 |
| 57.21 | 1.51 | 3.29 | 98.35 |
| 56.36 | 1.77 | 5.54 | 96.87 |
| 45.70 | 1.55 | 2.53 | 98.87 |
| 63.60 | 3.83 | 2.04 | 100 |
| 54.03 | 2.15 | 2.79 | 101.02 |
| 39.10 | 2.04 | 16.30 | 91.01 |
| 76.72 | 1.10 | -10.16 | 99.07 |
| 42.00 | 1.91 | 5.60 | 100.7 |
| 37.87 | 1.37 | 7.49 | 98.75 |
| 41.71 | 2.12 | 2.77 | 98.94 |
| 50.87 | 1.42 | -2.50 | 100 |
| 52.72 | 1.78 | 11.04 | 99.78 |
| 46.83 | 1.68 | 5.87 | 99.1 |
| 53.74 | 1.00 | 3.76 | 101.02 |
| 57.40 | 0.62 | 9.69 | 100.06 |
| 55.03 | 1.00 | 9.47 | 101.88 |
| 50.06 | 1.75 | 5.73 | 96.71 |
| 45.24 | 2.21 | 8.21 | 101.64 |
| 47.74 | 1.12 | 26.64 | 102.53 |
| 59.68 | 0.62 | 4.22 | 99.69 |
| | | | |
| 49.51 | 2.41 | 19.55 | 100 |
| 63.62 | 0.81 | 24.86 | 100 |
| 57.37 | 2.43 | 5.54 | 99.82 |
| 64.12 | 0.77 | 21.78 | 100 |

# 12-12 按行业分大中型工业企业主要经济效益指标（2018 年）

MAIN INDICATORS ON ECONOMIC BENEFIT OF LARGE AND MEDICM-SIZED INDUSTRIAL ENTERPRISES BY INDUSTRIAL SECTOR（2018）

| 行业 | Indicator | 总资产贡献率(%) Ratio of Total Assets to Industrial Output Value (%) |
|---|---|---|
| **总计** | **Total** | **8.67** |
| 煤炭开采和洗选业 | Mining and Washing of Coal | |
| 石油和天然气开采业 | Extraction of Petroleum and Natural Gas | |
| 黑色金属矿采选业 | Mining of Ferrous Metal Ores | |
| 有色金属矿采选业 | Mining of Non-ferrous Metal Ores | |
| 非金属矿采选业 | Mining and Processing of Nometal Ores | |
| 开采辅助活动 | Auxiliary Activities of Mining | |
| 其他采矿业 | Mining of Other Ores | |
| 农副食品加工业 | Processing of Food from Agricultural Products | 3.91 |
| 食品制造业 | Manufacture of Foods | 1.31 |
| 酒、饮料和精制茶制造业 | Manufacture of Liquor, Beverage and Refind Tea | 9.03 |
| 烟草制品业 | Manufacture of Tobacco | |
| 纺织业 | Manufacture of Textile | 2.05 |
| 纺织服装、服饰业 | Manufacture of Textile Wearing Apparel | 10.85 |
| 皮革、毛皮、羽毛及其制品和制鞋业 | Manufacture of Leather, Fur, Feather & Its Products Footwear | 5.97 |
| 木材加工和木、竹、藤、棕、草制品业 | Processing of Timbers, Manufacture of Wood, Bamboo, Rattan, Palm and Straw Products | 2.98 |
| 家具制造业 | Manufacture of Furniture | 8.97 |
| 造纸和纸制品业 | Manufacture of Paper and Paper Products | 3.17 |
| 印刷和记录媒介复制业 | Printing, Reproduction of Recording Media | 14.29 |
| 文教、工美、体育和娱乐用品制造业 | Manufacture of Articles for Culture, Arts & Crafts, Sports and Entertainment | 4.60 |
| 石油、煤炭及其他燃料加工业 | Oil, coal and other fuel processing industries | 67.91 |
| 化学原料和化学制品制造业 | Manufacture of Chemical Raw Material and Chemical Products | 6.46 |
| 医药制造业 | Manufacture of Medicines | 24.15 |
| 化学纤维制造业 | Manufacture of Chemical Fibers | |
| 橡胶和塑料制品业 | Manufacture of Rubber and Plastic | 4.98 |
| 非金属矿物制品业 | Manufacture of Non-mettallic Mineral Products | 7.09 |
| 黑色金属冶炼和压延加工业 | Smelting and Pressing of Ferrous Metals | 5.08 |
| 有色金属冶炼和压延加工业 | Smelting and Pressing of Non-ferrous Metals | 3.17 |
| 金属制品业 | Manufacture of Metal Products | 17.17 |
| 通用设备制造业 | Manufacture of General Purpose Machinery | 3.88 |
| 专用设备制造业 | Manufacture of Special Purpose Machinery | 8.94 |
| 汽车制造业 | Manufacture of Vehicle | 6.52 |
| 铁路、船舶、航空航天和其他运输设备制造业 | Manufacture of Transport Equipment for Railway, Shipping, Aerospace and other uses | 7.58 |
| 电气机械和器材制造业 | Manufacture of Electrical Machinery & Equipment | 6.36 |
| 计算机、通信和其他电子设备制造业 | Manufacture of Computer, Communication Equipment and Other Electronic Equipment | 12.93 |
| 仪器仪表制造业 | Manufacture of Measuring Instrument | 9.50 |
| 其他制造业 | Manufacture of Other Products | 3.74 |
| 废弃资源综合利用业 | Recycling and Disposal of Waste Resources | |
| 金属制品、机械和设备修理业 | Manufacture of Metal Products, Machinery and Equipment | |
| 电力、热力生产和供应业 | Production and Supply of Electric Power and Heat Power | -1.75 |
| 燃气生产和供应业 | Production and Supply of Gas | 3.37 |
| 水的生产和供应业 | Production and Supply of Water | 0.02 |

| 资产负债率 (%) Assets-Liability Ratio (%) | 流动资产周转次数(次/年) Number of Times of Annual of Turnover Current Assets (time/year) | 工业成本费用利润率 (%) Ratio of Profits to Industrial Costs (%) | 产品销售率 (%) Ratio of Sales to Output (%) |
|---|---|---|---|
| **63.74** | **1.25** | **6.18** | **100.65** |
| 62.09 | 2.90 | 0.70 | 99.22 |
| 68.57 | 0.98 | -1.51 | 93.88 |
| 41.02 | 2.02 | 4.70 | 165.46 |
| 77.16 | 1.93 | -0.23 | 98.77 |
| 51.37 | 2.64 | 3.05 | 99.55 |
| 65.12 | 2.93 | 1.04 | 93.31 |
| 80.26 | 0.79 | 2.99 | 100 |
| 70.57 | 1.34 | 4.69 | 99.9 |
| 61.91 | 2.97 | 0.07 | 96 |
| 54.66 | 1.78 | 7.42 | 100.32 |
| 39.91 | 1.89 | 2.30 | 101.48 |
| 55.37 | 3.97 | 8.89 | 99.62 |
| 52.78 | 1.66 | 5.35 | 98.31 |
| 28.93 | 1.36 | 24.57 | 95.72 |
| 60.27 | 1.40 | 4.99 | 99.09 |
| 64.32 | 0.91 | 7.82 | 99.4 |
| 74.24 | 2.17 | 2.78 | 100.06 |
| 60.20 | 5.28 | 5.54 | 100 |
| 49.55 | 1.75 | 12.24 | 101.51 |
| 54.28 | 1.02 | 3.77 | 97.37 |
| 68.48 | 1.23 | 6.15 | 97.12 |
| 67.07 | 0.87 | 6.41 | 99 |
| 64.59 | 0.89 | 7.24 | 101.69 |
| 70.17 | 0.91 | 8.81 | 96.65 |
| 50.30 | 1.70 | 5.08 | 104.48 |
| 72.68 | 0.72 | 12.48 | 100 |
| 82.71 | 1.20 | 1.74 | 99.62 |
| 80.78 | 1.14 | -7.97 | 97.36 |
| 63.68 | 2.20 | 2.49 | 100 |
| 58.50 | 0.59 | -7.01 | 99.53 |

# 12-13 主要年份主要工业产品产量
MAJOR YEAR 'S PRODUCTS OUTPUT OF INDUSTRY ABOVE DESIGNATED SIZE

| 年份<br>Year | 原盐<br>(万吨)<br>Salt<br>(10 000 tons) | 发电量<br>(亿千瓦小时)<br>Electricity<br>(100 million kW·h) | 饮料酒<br>(万吨)<br>Beverage Liquour<br>(10 000 tons) | #啤酒<br>Beer | 卷烟<br>(万箱)<br>Cigarettes<br>(10 000 cases) | 罐头<br>(吨)<br>Canned Food<br>(ton) | 化学纤维<br>(吨)<br>Chemical Fiber<br>(ton) | 纱<br>(吨)<br>Yarn<br>(ton) |
|---|---|---|---|---|---|---|---|---|
| 1949 | 15.16 | 1.21 | 0.18 | 0.12 | 2.36 | | | 27447 |
| 1952 | 35.08 | 2.11 | 0.37 | 0.18 | 12.27 | | | 59674 |
| 1957 | 44.34 | 2.92 | 0.96 | 0.58 | 23.41 | | | 50699 |
| 1962 | 38.60 | 3.86 | 1.58 | 0.79 | 16.59 | | 28 | 17939 |
| 1965 | 41.34 | 6.80 | 2.04 | 1.34 | 31.34 | | 205 | 68082 |
| 1970 | 29.96 | 10.57 | 3.39 | 2.55 | 42.16 | | 621 | 85591 |
| 1975 | 34.52 | 10.98 | 5.30 | 2.98 | 36.00 | | 357 | 79516 |
| 1978 | 60.68 | 13.63 | 6.25 | 3.75 | 44.00 | 4743 | 1413 | 85233 |
| 1980 | 41.19 | 12.50 | 8.49 | 4.84 | 48.79 | 3521 | 2116 | 83389 |
| 1985 | 47.34 | 26.97 | 13.76 | 10.05 | 51.81 | 6400 | 1747 | 91839 |
| 1988 | 53.28 | 29.35 | 26.61 | 15.58 | 57.01 | 27200 | 3393 | 107720 |
| 1990 | 35.70 | 40.22 | 29.18 | 19.61 | 61.94 | | 2900 | 100381 |
| 1991 | 31.39 | 54.60 | 36.75 | 27.38 | 56.19 | 130510 | 5200 | 96271 |
| 1992 | 46.24 | 58.63 | 44.59 | 37.01 | 59.37 | 3200 | 6000 | 99043 |
| 1993 | 48.88 | 59.39 | 54.74 | 45.92 | 63.46 | 1900 | 27100 | 91351 |
| 1994 | 53.02 | 59.62 | 60.00 | 50.92 | 69.20 | 2300 | 21400 | 86744 |
| 1995 | 50.84 | 64.69 | 60.85 | 54.16 | 70.96 | 4609 | 20973 | 79492 |
| 1996 | 41.39 | 83.02 | 61.79 | 54.40 | 73.04 | 1719 | 22945 | 66832 |
| 1997 | 34.11 | 95.12 | 66.64 | 56.06 | 88.32 | 554 | 26300 | 70402 |
| 1998 | 19.08 | 79.65 | 47.33 | 42.79 | 77.10 | | 23858 | 66504 |
| 1999 | 30.30 | 82.00 | 126.21 | 120.10 | 149.00 | 379 | 29967 | 56431 |
| 2000 | 41.83 | 90.84 | 211.47 | 206.50 | 148.10 | 225 | 65362 | 69561 |
| 2001 | 31.40 | 85.73 | 279.37 | 274.28 | 142.95 | 99 | 89989 | 72933 |
| 2002 | 42.50 | 89.70 | 323.20 | 320.60 | 138.10 | 11690 | 91394 | 70888 |
| 2003 | 36.85 | 87.69 | 353.90 | 351.80 | 148.00 | | 101752 | 65919 |
| 2004 | 34.36 | 89.01 | 393.30 | 390.60 | 147.10 | 10889 | 115187 | 71931 |
| 2005 | 10.00 | 98.63 | 439.70 | 435.20 | 150.70 | 10097 | 95887 | 72140 |
| 2006 | 15.30 | 124.54 | 101.60(本地) | 95.60(本地) | 95.16(本地) | 1668 | 72381 | 56128 |
| 2007 | 19.23 | 155.30 | 118.10(本地) | 112.50(本地) | 100.08(本地) | 1850 | 68746 | 47850 |
| 2008 | 15.90 | 164.58 | 132.07(本地) | 124.75(本地) | 100.02(本地) | 1510 | 51751 | 43102 |
| 2009 | 5.90 | 172.66 | 137.21(本地) | 127.12(本地) | 100.08(本地) | 4706 | 59852 | 38566 |
| 2010 | 11.25 | 181.93 | 144.66(本地) | 141.65(本地) | 102.55(本地) | 1092 | 68654 | 35278 |
| 2011 | | 173.69 | 164.04(本地) | 156.50(本地) | 104.51(本地) | 41204 | 38640 | 18556 |
| 2012 | | 174.72 | 174.03(本地) | 163.95(本地) | 106.03(本地) | 35026 | 32371 | 19404 |
| 2013 | 1.28 | 180.11 | 194.22(本地) | 185.17(本地) | 108.36(本地) | 30203 | 23647 | 33687 |
| 2014 | | 178.29 | 169.85(本地) | 164.59(本地) | 112.06(本地) | 23970 | 22053 | 32336 |
| 2015 | | 173.53 | 162.66(本地) | 157.83(本地) | 111.48(本地) | 36179 | 17419 | 27721 |
| 2016 | | 175.40 | 168.82(本地) | 164.27(本地) | | 53139 | 14839 | 33416 |
| 2017 | | 181.80 | 163.41(本地) | 159.97(本地) | | 85942 | 11565 | 26493 |
| 2018 | | 192.40 | 165.81(本地) | 162.44(本地) | | 43893 | 5545 | 28948 |

注：1998 年以前为乡及乡以上工业。
Note：Before 1998, the data refer to those at and above county level.

# 12-13　续表 1
Continued

| 年份<br>Year | 布<br>（万米）<br>Cloth<br>（10 000 m） | 印染布<br>（万米）<br>Printed Fabric<br>（10 000 m） | 机制纸及纸板（万吨）<br>Machine-made Paper and Paperboards<br>（10 000 tons） | 硫酸<br>（万吨）<br>Sulfuric Acid<br>（10 000 tons） | 烧碱<br>（万吨）<br>Caustic Soda<br>（10 000 tons） | 纯碱<br>（万吨）<br>Soda Ash<br>（10 000 tons） |
|---|---|---|---|---|---|---|
| 1949 | 10608 | 2947 | 0.98 | | 0.01 | |
| 1952 | 30069 | 13658 | 0.44 | | 0.17 | |
| 1957 | 27806 | 16053 | 1.54 | | 0.74 | |
| 1962 | 7444 | 7375 | 1.45 | 0.06 | 0.89 | |
| 1965 | 29538 | 13670 | 2.22 | | 1.66 | 5.32 |
| **1970** | **33660** | **21994** | **3.14** | **0.04** | **2.14** | **12.01** |
| 1975 | 31242 | 22828 | 3.10 | 0.53 | 2.36 | 9.15 |
| 1978 | 36877 | 25797 | 4.55 | 1.32 | 3.61 | 14.04 |
| **1980** | **34937** | **22900** | **5.25** | **4.11** | **4.33** | **18.18** |
| 1985 | 34998 | 17679 | 6.20 | 3.34 | 5.52 | 26.03 |
| 1988 | 35890 | 21213 | 7.42 | 4.88 | 6.62 | 31.12 |
| **1990** | **34066** | **21446** | **6.02** | **4.86** | **6.73** | **30.48** |
| 1991 | 34076 | 19999 | 5.99 | 5.62 | 5.99 | 29.50 |
| 1992 | 33682 | 21534 | 5.95 | 6.70 | 5.62 | 34.60 |
| 1993 | 35912 | 16606 | 8.84 | 6.96 | 6.07 | 40.43 |
| 1994 | 43241 | 16387 | 12.36 | 8.33 | 6.48 | 43.36 |
| 1995 | 41170 | 17864 | 11.06 | 9.69 | 7.90 | 43.20 |
| 1996 | 39023 | 16881 | 11.31 | 10.12 | 7.30 | 46.91 |
| 1997 | 43615 | 15722 | 7.78 | 10.16 | 8.45 | 50.55 |
| 1998 | 40440 | 9864 | 6.91 | 10.33 | 9.25 | 52.80 |
| 1999 | 39576 | 4340 | 7.77 | 12.56 | 8.96 | 53.70 |
| **2000** | **41783** | **3526** | **10.96** | **12.95** | **10.24** | **56.20** |
| 2001 | 40640 | 3402 | 23.05 | 13.03 | 11.44 | 58.47 |
| 2002 | 47609 | 5592 | 29.92 | 5.00 | 13.80 | 60.70 |
| 2003 | 35922 | 10131 | 31.76 | 4.50 | 13.53 | 62.50 |
| 2004 | 50111 | 7718 | 36.38 | 14.70 | 14.86 | 60.80 |
| 2005 | 51307 | 16027 | 31.95 | 14.80 | 16.10 | 62.50 |
| 2006 | 55093 | 20867 | 15.50 | 7.00 | 15.90 | 63.95 |
| 2007 | 44251 | 18708 | 24.04 | 9.22 | 14.91 | 71.02 |
| 2008 | 48399 | 58907 | 22.41 | 13.02 | 12.78 | 72.03 |
| 2009 | 31048 | 27998 | 34.59 | 1.40 | 12.24 | 68.21 |
| **2010** | **17457** | **29631** | **35.43** | **4.07** | **13.87** | **69.35** |
| 2011 | 49617 | 28449 | 32.28 | 5.06 | 13.20 | 70.07 |
| 2012 | 48987 | 32478 | 22.27 | 7.22 | 13.71 | 63.35 |
| 2013 | 51646 | 34381 | 17.95 | 4.32 | 11.06 | 61.66 |
| 2014 | 44593 | 33653 | 18.26 | | | 67.85 |
| 2015 | 28040 | 25458 | 18.29 | | | 68.95 |
| 2016 | 24973 | 28661 | 18.17 | | 11.33 | |
| 2017 | 23550 | 21530 | 17.39 | | 33.89 | |
| 2018 | 46737 | 22647 | 14.58 | | 35.36 | |

# 12-13 续表 2
Continued

| 年份<br>Year | 合成氨<br>(万吨)<br>Synthetic Ammonia<br>(10 000 tons) | 化学肥料<br>(万吨)<br>Chemical Fertilizer<br>(10 000 tons) | 化学农药<br>(吨)<br>Chemical Peticides<br>(ton) | 油漆<br>(吨)<br>Paint<br>(ton) | 染料<br>(吨)<br>Dye<br>(ton) |
|---|---|---|---|---|---|
| 1949 | | | | 30 | 599 |
| 1952 | | | | 480 | 2855 |
| 1957 | | | 1226 | 1247 | 4307 |
| 1962 | | 0.45 | 213 | 910 | 3560 |
| 1965 | | 1.42 | 2 | 4727 | 8667 |
| 1970 | 0.98 | 5.89 | 2313 | 6380 | 9347 |
| 1975 | 3.46 | 12.46 | 4439 | 7016 | 5967 |
| 1978 | 7.17 | 23.66 | 9714 | 8786 | 5877 |
| 1980 | 7.24 | 7.82 | 8333 | 14556 | 2159 |
| 1985 | 6.31 | 5.16 | 2000 | 26055 | 4448 |
| 1988 | 8.72 | 9.41 | 2400 | 28943 | 5527 |
| 1990 | 7.56 | 7.55 | 2500 | 29075 | 5119 |
| 1991 | 8.52 | 8.04 | 2800 | 33548 | 5263 |
| 1992 | 10.45 | 7.85 | 3400 | 35058 | 4821 |
| 1993 | 10.70 | 8.02 | 3600 | 33054 | 4550 |
| 1994 | 13.04 | 12.39 | 3600 | 29437 | 5097 |
| 1995 | 14.98 | 12.62 | 4934 | 37772 | 7185 |
| 1996 | 18.67 | 12.62 | 4976 | 26762 | 7668 |
| 1997 | 16.94 | 12.52 | 4600 | 19743 | 11189 |
| 1998 | 22.36 | 15.30 | 6755 | 17594 | 8274 |
| 1999 | 26.09 | 20.19 | 4480 | 3730 | 7866 |
| 2000 | 24.64 | 20.04 | 3758 | 693 | 9306 |
| 2001 | 35.53 | 28.07 | 3915 | 1349 | 9757 |
| 2002 | 20.30 | 9.80 | 4020 | 1701 | 9826 |
| 2003 | 21.55 | 9.70 | 2039 | 2106 | 10734 |
| 2004 | 30.30 | 19.60 | 5061 | 1955 | 3961 |
| 2005 | 33.80 | 22.10 | 6524 | 1687 | 13979 |
| 2006 | 33.30 | 21.30 | 12544 | | 26544 |
| 2007 | 28.22 | 25.70 | 16433 | 2957 | 28269 |
| 2008 | 17.93 | 21.51 | 12848 | 12105 | 18263 |
| 2009 | 17.71 | 21.23 | 49684 | | 24893 |
| 2010 | 16.84 | 14.10 | 16450 | | 41383 |
| 2011 | 10.78 | 9.26 | 23286 | | |
| 2012 | 7.71 | 6.98 | 28801 | | |
| 2013 | 6.48 | 5.10 | 27715 | | |
| 2014 | | | 27160 | | |
| 2015 | | | 36853 | | |
| 2016 | | 14.33 | 34993 | | |
| 2017 | | 7.38 | 18911 | | |
| 2018 | | 8.08 | 8507 | | |

# 12-13 续表 3
Continued

| 年份<br>Year | 化学原料药<br>（吨）<br>Chemical Medicines<br>（ton） | 水泥<br>（万吨）<br>Cement<br>（10 000 tons） | 平板玻璃<br>（万重量箱）<br>Plate Glass<br>（10 000 weight cases） | 耐火材料<br>（万吨）<br>Refractory Material<br>（10 000 tons） | 粗钢<br>（万吨）<br>Crude Steel<br>（10 000 tons） | 钢材<br>（万吨）<br>Rolled-steel<br>（10 000 tons） |
|---|---|---|---|---|---|---|
| 1949 | | | | | | 0.06 |
| 1952 | | | | 0.78 | 0.36 | 0.41 |
| 1957 | | | | 3.39 | 1.77 | 4.30 |
| 1962 | | 2.09 | | 2.41 | 4.59 | 2.94 |
| 1965 | | 6.59 | | 2.91 | 11.72 | 8.43 |
| 1970 | | 7.35 | 16.31 | 3.23 | 19.38 | 14.56 |
| 1975 | 55 | 20.93 | 19.44 | 4.88 | 21.25 | 20.01 |
| 1978 | 185 | 35.40 | 8.86 | 5.93 | 31.06 | 27.61 |
| 1980 | 123 | 44.66 | 70.13 | 5.38 | 37.14 | 32.82 |
| 1984 | 7228 | 70.27 | 91.25 | 7.98 | 37.81 | 32:43 |
| 1985 | 4222 | 82.70 | 77.00 | 4.35 | 37.51 | 32.68 |
| 1988 | 7655 | 141.00 | 108.81 | 4.56 | 50.17 | 38.26 |
| 1990 | 6913 | 139.48 | 83.13 | 3.91 | 54.55 | 38.04 |
| 1991 | 4754 | 165.66 | 96.90 | 3.71 | 56.96 | 39.02 |
| 1992 | 5743 | 191.50 | 120.00 | 3.86 | 63.75 | 50.09 |
| 1993 | 6566 | 221.30 | 148.71 | 3.55 | 61.75 | 44.88 |
| 1994 | 4238 | 246.50 | 145.12 | 3.06 | 60.82 | 46.95 |
| 1995 | 1993 | 213.82 | 426.40 | 3.88 | 67.27 | 49.60 |
| 1996 | 5505 | 181.45 | 423.60 | 3.54 | 72.02 | 50.60 |
| 1997 | 1693 | 208.04 | 570.85 | 2.45 | 75.71 | 51.06 |
| 1998 | 910 | 131.51 | 509.38 | 0.99 | 84.02 | 64.93 |
| 1999 | 1691 | 149.41 | 576.50 | 0.59 | 108.10 | 86.58 |
| 2000 | 2131 | 137.52 | 556.58 | 0.62 | 101.17 | 93.35 |
| 2001 | 2534 | 148.67 | 421.51 | 0.51 | 124.45 | 119.77 |
| 2002 | 2712 | 140.30 | 405.40 | 0.45 | 145.90 | 142.20 |
| 2003 | 3288 | 154.90 | 361.40 | 0.47 | 204.80 | 204.30 |
| 2004 | 4394 | 181.19 | 163.30 | 0.69 | 225.70 | 230.97 |
| 2005 | 4430 | 210.80 | 297.50 | 1.04 | 309.70 | 330.30 |
| 2006 | 32232 | 232.72 | 418.74 | 1.21 | 325.82 | 375.52 |
| 2007 | 14139 | 425.53 | 397.79 | 2.38 | 327.00 | 365.55 |
| 2008 | 17910 | 363.57 | 599.87 | 3.65 | 300.19 | 350.14 |
| 2009 | 19086 | 397.66 | 681.02 | 18.46 | 307.89 | 349.63 |
| 2010 | 26170 | 442.66 | 662.04 | 8.17 | 300.04 | 333.46 |
| 2011 | 29337 | 588.08 | 510.05 | 20.02 | 318.27 | 325.89 |
| 2012 | 49290 | 556.57 | 494.54 | 33.44 | 252.78 | 274.67 |
| 2013 | 49081 | 575.66 | 610.21 | 42.34 | 235.53 | 230.39 |
| 2014 | 50713 | 597.35 | 612.40 | 39.37 | 214.43 | 212.79 |
| 2015 | 45923 | 532.36 | 534.99 | 41.13 | 154.56 | 140.63 |
| 2016 | 2248 | 600.56 | 576.16 | 108.76 | 188.04 | 191.37 |
| 2017 | 2775 | 525.42 | 557.44 | 109.84 | 280.97 | 291.85 |
| 2018 | 1809 | 284.47 | 561.51 | 27.97 | 309.70 | 319.90 |

# 12-13 续表 4
Continued

| 年份<br>Year | 金属切削机床(台)<br>Metal-cutting Machine Tools<br>(unit) | 锻压机械(台)<br>Metal Forming Machinery<br>(unit) | 汽车(辆)<br>Motor Vehicles<br>(set) | 交流电动机(万千瓦)<br>AC Motors<br>(10 000 kW) |
|---|---|---|---|---|
| 1949 | | | | 0.02 |
| 1952 | 105 | | | 0.50 |
| 1957 | 76 | | | 3.61 |
| 1962 | 167 | 77 | | 3.85 |
| 1965 | 526 | 111 | 13 | 6.48 |
| 1970 | 2353 | 531 | 120 | 14.53 |
| 1975 | 3213 | 788 | 490 | 15.56 |
| 1978 | 2558 | 379 | 22 | 21.72 |
| 1980 | 595 | 444 | 1644 | 20.11 |
| 1985 | 900 | 607 | 4575 | 26.08 |
| 1988 | 1336 | 737 | 3722 | 39.60 |
| 1990 | 1049 | 440 | 2317 | 34.28 |
| 1991 | 869 | 764 | 1514 | 44.17 |
| 1992 | 1018 | 982 | 3287 | 61.08 |
| 1993 | 1532 | 919 | 4828 | 64.13 |
| 1994 | 1505 | 860 | 2793 | 37.71 |
| 1995 | 972 | 2563 | 5210 | 39.18 |
| 1996 | 1084 | 584 | 12247 | 22.65 |
| 1997 | 449 | 416 | 13020 | 20.74 |
| 1998 | 280 | | 15475 | 6.43 |
| 1999 | 251 | | 20038 | 11.10 |
| 2000 | 384 | | 30053 | 38.70 |
| 2001 | 472 | 2477 | 40658 | 42.72 |
| 2002 | 588 | | 70079 | 68.25 |
| 2003 | 990 | | 65612 | 95.63 |
| 2004 | 1287 | | 62572 | 96.13 |
| 2005 | 1347 | | 31055 | 63.50 |
| 2006 | 3636 | | 50278 | 702.02 |
| 2007 | 3392 | 1869 | 61016 | 119.23 |
| 2008 | 8381 | 1230 | 70161 | 96.89 |
| 2009 | 668 | | 458900 | 728.03 |
| 2010 | 1120 | | 566211 | 101.10 |
| 2011 | 1194 | | 488330 | 74.08 |
| 2012 | 1014 | | 574729 | 104.48 |
| 2013 | 2689 | | 708966 | 126.82 |
| 2014 | 2563 | | 770245 | 114.46 |
| 2015 | 618 | | 861250 | 104.30 |
| 2016 | 588 | | 816839 | 98.70 |
| 2017 | 610 | | 741455 | 202.79 |
| 2018 | 204 | | 92280 | 230.86 |

# 12-13　续表 5
Continued

| 年份<br>Year | 钢芯铝绞线（吨）<br>Steel-cored Aluminum Stranded Wire（ton） | 家用电冰箱（万台）<br>Home Refrigerators（10 000 sets） | 家用洗衣机（万台）<br>Home Washing Machines（10 000 sets） | 彩色电视机（万部）<br>Color TV Sets（10 000 sets） |
|---|---|---|---|---|
| 1949 | | | | |
| 1952 | | | | |
| 1957 | | | | |
| 1962 | | | | |
| 1965 | 250 | | | |
| 1970 | 34 | | | |
| 1975 | 188 | | | |
| 1978 | 684 | | | |
| 1980 | 1232 | | | |
| 1985 | 2327 | 1.66 | 0.48 | 6.60 |
| 1988 | 1571 | 15.22 | 42.38 | 17.00 |
| 1990 | 1880 | 27.41 | 45.86 | 18.50 |
| 1991 | 2463 | 31.51 | 45.70 | 22.27 |
| 1992 | 2248 | 54.84 | 46.31 | 28.07 |
| 1993 | 1144 | 50.48 | 56.59 | 36.08 |
| 1994 | 287 | 62.50 | 71.34 | 60.15 |
| 1995 | 1659 | 107.91 | 64.34 | 60.53 |
| 1996 | 2265 | 193.80 | 100.94 | 56.68 |
| 1997 | 2616 | 257.10 | 171.95 | 124.86 |
| 1998 | 1725 | 219.23 | 183.57 | 96.83 |
| 1999 | 2805 | 259.60 | 256.30 | 285.20 |
| 2000 | 4202 | 311.10 | 318.50 | 379.40 |
| 2001 | 4498 | 396.30 | 367.89 | 455.40 |
| 2002 | 5825 | 518.20 | 408.6 | 593.20 |
| 2003 | 4940 | 598.30 | 471.5 | 671.70 |
| 2004 | 6608 | 815.03 | 575.06 | 957.90 |
| 2005 | 116592 | 908.80 | 614.9 | 1324.30 |
| 2006 | 46974 | 1290.00 | 649.4 | 1205.60 |
| 2007 | 22564 | 1421.40 | 769.4 | 1243.10 |
| 2008 | 29507 | 723.19 | 407.54 | 836.66 |
| 2009 | | 827.21 | 488.72 | 1064.70 |
| 2010 | | 801.22 | 580.87 | 1111.19 |
| 2011 | | 718.54 | 604.55 | 1154.20 |
| 2012 | | 575.01 | 583.6 | 1439.98 |
| 2013 | | 524.35 | 606.65 | 1512.05 |
| 2014 | | 610.07 | 590.95 | 1714.93 |
| 2015 | | 872.09 | 595.11 | 1736.20 |
| 2016 | | 882.22 | 606.74 | 2111.71 |
| 2017 | | 818.65 | 603.4 | 1703.01 |
| 2018 | | 886.58 | 601.72 | 1695.18 |

# 12-14 规模以上工业主要产品产量
OUTPUT OF MAJOR INDUSTRIAL PRODUCTS OF INDUSTRY ABOVE DESIGNATED SIZE

| 产品名称 | Name | 计算单位 | Unit | 2018 年 | 2017 年 | 2018 年比 2017 年 (±%) 2018/2017 (±%) |
|---|---|---|---|---|---|---|
| **冶金工业产品** | **Products of Metallurgical Industry** | | | | | |
| 粗钢 | Crude Steel | 万吨 | 10 000 tons | 309.70 | 280.96 | 10.23 |
| 钢材 | Rolled-steel | 万吨 | 10 000 tons | 319.90 | 294.28 | 8.71 |
| 耐火材料制品 | Refractory Material | 万吨 | 10 000 tons | 27.97 | 27.59 | 1.39 |
| **电力工业产品** | **Products of Electricity Industry** | | | | | |
| 发电量 | Electricity | 亿千瓦小时 | 100 million kW · h | 192.4 | 183.6 | 4.79 |
| **化学工业产品** | **Products of Chemical Industry** | | | | | |
| 原油加工量 | Processing Amount of Crude Oill | 万吨 | 10 000 tons | 1540.75 | 1522.87 | 1.17 |
| 汽油 | Petrol | 万吨 | 10 000 tons | 473.91 | 456.07 | 3.91 |
| 柴油 | Diesel Oill | 万吨 | 10 000 tons | 382.86 | 408.08 | -6.18 |
| 燃料油 | Fuel Oil | 万吨 | 10 000 tons | 21.79 | 12.08 | 80.36 |
| 化学农药 | Chemical Pesticides | 万吨 | 10 000 tons | 0.85 | 2.11 | -59.59 |
| 塑料制品 | Plastic | 万吨 | 10 000 tons | 23.68 | 23.04 | 2.80 |
| 化学药品(原料) | Chemical Medicines ( Paw Materials ) | 万吨 | 10 000 tons | 0.18 | 0.15 | 22.99 |

## 12-14　续表 1
Continued

| 产品名称 | Name | 计算单位 | Unit | 2018 年 | 2017 年 | 2018 年比 2017 年 (±%) 2018/2017 (±%) |
|---|---|---|---|---|---|---|
| 橡胶轮胎外胎 | Tires | 万条 | 10 000 tires | 6388.78 | 4676.98 | 36.60 |
| **机械工业产品** | **Products of Machinery Industry** | | | | | |
| 工业锅炉 | Industrial Boiler | 蒸发量吨 | ton ( evaporation amunt ) | 10208.12 | 13772.67 | -25.88 |
| 交流电动机 | AC Motors | 万千瓦 | 10 000 kW | 230.86 | 202.79 | 13.84 |
| 金属切削机床 | Metal-cutting Machine | 台 | set | 204 | 188 | 8.51 |
| 汽车 | Motor Vehicles | 辆 | set | 92280 | 80669 | 14.39 |
| 改装汽车 | Refitted Motor Vehicles | 辆 | set | 20714 | 20982 | -1.28 |
| 民用钢质船舶 | Civil Steel Ships | 载重吨 | syn-ton | 88923 | 103207 | -13.84 |
| **电子产品** | **Electronic Products** | | | | | |
| 彩色电视机 | Color TV sets | 万台 | 10 000 sets | 1695.18 | 1703.01 | -0.46 |
| 电子元件 | Electronice | 万只 | 10 000 Units | 300433.49 | 345523.85 | -13.05 |
| **建材工业产品** | **Products of Construction Industry** | | | | | |
| 水泥 | Cement | 万吨 | 10 000 tons | 284.47 | 381.98 | -25.53 |
| 平板玻璃 | Plate Glass | 万重量箱 | 10 000 weight cases | 561.51 | 557.44 | 0.73 |

## 12-14　续表 2
Continued

| 产品名称 | Name | 计算单位 | Unit | 2018 年 | 2017 年 | 2018 年比 2017 年 (±%) 2018/2017 (±%) |
|---|---|---|---|---|---|---|
| **纺织工业产品** | **Products of Textile Industry** | | | | | |
| 纱 | Yarn | 吨 | ton | 28947.6 | 29403.88 | -1.55 |
| 布 | Cloth | 万米 | 10 000 m | 46737.31 | 49563.20 | -5.70 |
| 印染布 | Printed Fabric | 万米 | 10 000 m | 22646.85 | 19022.00 | 19.06 |
| 化学纤维 | Chemical Fibers | 吨 | ton | 5545.28 | 11617.76 | -52.27 |
| **轻工产品** | **Products of Light Industry** | | | | | |
| 机制纸及纸板 | Machine-made Paper and Paperboards | 万吨 | 10 000 tons | 14.58 | 17.32 | -15.85 |
| 家用洗衣机 | Home Washing Machines | 万台 | 10 000 sets | 601.72 | 603.40 | -0.28 |
| 糖果 | Sugar | 吨 | ton | 6550 | 11545 | -43.27 |
| 食用植物油 | Vegetable Oil | 万吨 | 10 000 tons | 45.94 | 38.42 | 19.55 |
| 饮料酒 | Beverage Liquor | 万千升 | 10 000 KL | 163.85 | 161.01 | 1.76 |
| # 白酒 | Wine | 万千升 | 10 000 KL | 2.09 | 1.97 | 6.13 |
| # 啤酒 | Beer | 万千升 | 10 000 KL | 160.52 | 158.07 | 1.55 |
| 塑料制品 | Plastic Products | 万吨 | 10 000 tons | 23.68 | 23.04 | 2.80 |
| 家具 | Furniture | 万件 | 10 000 articles | 257.66 | 422.32 | -38.99 |
| 家用电冰箱 | Home Refrigerators | 万台 | 10 000 sets | 886.58 | 857.89 | 3.34 |
| 皮革鞋靴 | Leather Shoes | 万双 | 10 000 pairs | 2006.43 | 2086.62 | -3.84 |
| 服装 | Chothing | 万件 | 10 000 articles | 48141.93 | 49412.83 | -2.57 |

# 12-15　规模以上工业主要产品生产能力
## OUTPUT OF MAJOR INDUSTRIAL PRODUCTS OF INDUSTRY ABOVE DESIGNATED SIZE

| 产品名称 | Name | 计算单位 | Unit | 2018年 生产能力 Production Capacity of 2018 | 2017年 生产能力 Production Capacity of 2017 |
|---|---|---|---|---|---|
| 发电设备容量总计 / 发电量 | Total Capacity of Generation Equipment | 万千瓦 / 万千瓦小时 | 10 000 kW/ 10 000 kW · h | 388 | 389 |
| 化学纤维 | Chemical Fiber | 吨 | ton | 15500 | 15450 |
| 棉纺锭 / 纺纱量 | Knitting Spindle | 锭 / 吨 | spindle/ton | 205016 | 205016 |
| 棉布织机 / 布 | Cotton Cloth Loom | 台 / 万米 | set/10 000 m | 2399 | 2401 |
| 焦炭 | Coke | 吨 | ton | 1600000 | 1600000 |
| 农用氮、磷、钾化学肥料总计（折纯） | Chemical Fertilizer | 吨 | ton | 80000 | 80000 |
| 水泥 | Cement | 吨 | ton | 6800000 | 6800000 |
| 平板玻璃 | Plate Glass | 重量箱 | weight cases | 6200000 | 6200000 |
| 生铁 | Pig Iron | 吨 | ton | 3227000 | 3227000 |
| 粗钢 | Crude Steel | 吨 | ton | 3125000 | 3125000 |
| 钢材 | Rolled-steel | 吨 | ton | 5146435 | 5125445 |
| 金属切削机床 | Metal-cutting Machine | 台 | set | 2995 | 2928 |
| 汽车 | Motor Vehicles | 辆 | set | 70000 | 68000 |
| 家用电冰箱 | Home Refrigerators | 台 | set | 10749793 | 11981493 |
| 房间空气调节器 | Air Conditioner | 台 | set | 14525970 | 10900000 |
| 移动通信手持机（手机） | Cell Phone | 台 | set | 25859000 | 33500000 |
| 彩色电视机 | Color TV Sets | 台 | set | 20700000 | 20700000 |

# 主要统计指标解释

**工业总产值** 是以货币表现的工业企业在一定时期内生产的已出售或可供出售工业产品总量，它是反映一定时间内工业生产的总规模和总水平。

**资产总计** 指企业拥有或控制的能以货币计量的经济资源，包括各种财产、债权和其他权利。资产按其流动性（即资产的变现能力和支付能力）划分为：流动资产、长期投资、固定资产、无形资产、递延资产和其他资产。

**负债合计** 指企业所承担的能以货币计量，将以资产或劳务偿付的债务，偿还形式包括货币、资产或提供劳务。负债一般按偿还期长短分为流动负债和长期负债。

**利润总额** 指企业生产经营活动的最终成果，是企业在一定时期内实现的盈亏相抵后的利润总额（亏损以“-”号表示），它等于营业利润加上补贴收入加上投资收益加上营业外净收入再加上以前年度损益调整。

# Explanatory Notes on Main Statistical Indicators

**Gross Industrial Output Value** is the total volume of final industrial products produced and industrial services provided during a given period. It reflects the total achievements and overall scale of industrial production during a given period.

**Total Assets** refer to all economic resources, in monetary terms, that is owned or controlled by enterprises, including properties, creditors equity and other economic rights of all forms. Classified by the degree of equitability, total assets include circulating assets, long-term investment, fixed assets, intangible assets and deferred assets, and other assets.

**Total Liabilities** refer to payable liabilities of enterprises that have to repay in terms of money, assets or labour services. In terms of payment, it can be divided into liquid liabilities and long-term liabilities.

**Total Profits** refer to the final achievements of production and operation of the enterprises, represented by the total profits after deducting losses (loss is expressed by the negative figure). It is the sum of profits from operation, income from subsidies, investment earnings, net income from activities other than operation, and adjustment of profits and losses of previous years.

# 建筑业 13

CONSTRUCTION

# 简 要 说 明

**一、本篇资料的主要内容**

本篇资料主要反映了全市建筑业基本情况，主要包括建筑业总产值、增加值、建筑企业生产指标、财务指标、重点建筑企业名单等方面的内容。

**二、本篇资料的来源**

本篇资料来源于建筑业统计年报，由市统计局固定资产投资统计处整理提供。

# Brief Introduction

***I. Main Content***

Data in this chapter show the basic conditions of construction of the whole city, mainly including the gross output value of construction, value added, major production and financial indicators and list of key enterprises of construction, etc.

***II. Source of Data***

Data in this chapter are based on the annual report of construction industry, and complied by the Division of Investment and Construction Statistics of Qingdao Municipal Bureau of Statistics.

# 13-1 建筑业企业生产情况（2018 年）
PRODUCTION SITUATION OF CONSTRUCTION ENTERPRISES（2018）

| 项目 | Item | 单位 | Unit | 合计 Total | #中央 of which: Central Enterprises | 国有企业 State-owned Enterprise | 集体企业 Collectiveowend Enterprise | 其他所有制企业 Other Ownership Enterprises |
|---|---|---|---|---|---|---|---|---|
| 施工企业单位数 | Number of Construction Enterpises | 个 | unit | 711 | 12 | 19 | 8 | 684 |
| 建筑业总产值 | Gross Output Value of Construction | 万元 | 1000yuan | 22617411 | 4758279 | 196626 | 7314 | 22413471 |
| #建筑工程 | of which: Construction | 万元 | 1000yuan | 20360384 | 4113263 | 155258 | 7277 | 20197849 |
| 安装工程 | Installation | 万元 | 1000yuan | 1814993 | 617342 | 17641 | 38 | 1797315 |
| 建筑业增加值 | Value Added of Construction | 万元 | 1000yuan | 7234000 | | | | |
| 全年竣工产值 | Output Value of Buildings Completed in the Year | 万元 | 1000yuan | 9037628 | 1100700 | 130671 | 26466 | 8880491 |
| 施工房屋面积 | Floor Spece of Buildings under Construction | 万平方米 | 1000sp.m | 15136 | 2907 | 12 | 20 | 15104 |
| #新开工 | of which: Newly Operating | 万平方米 | 1000sp.m | 5547 | 827 | 12 | 8 | 5527 |
| 竣工房屋面积 | Floor Space of Buildings Completed | 万平方米 | 1000sp.m | 3033 | 162 | 10 | 12 | 3011 |
| #住宅 | of which: Residential Buildings | 万平方米 | 1000sp.m | 1917 | 96 | 0 | 12 | 1905 |
| 计算建筑业劳动生产率平均人数 | Average Number of Persons for Caleulating the Labor Productivity | 人 | person | 576372 | 78991 | 3405 | 371 | 572596 |

# 13-2 建筑业企业财务状况（2018年）
## FINANCIAL SITUATION OF CONSTRUCTION ENTERPRISES（2018）

| 项目 | Item | 单位 | Unit | 合计 Total |
|---|---|---|---|---|
| 流动资产 | Circulating Funds | 万元 | 10000yuan | 21564526 |
| #存货 | of which：Inventory | 万元 | 10000yuan | 3412837 |
| 年末固定资产原价 | Original Value of Fixed Assets（year-end） | 万元 | 10000yuan | 2055214 |
| 本年固定资产折旧 | Depreciation of Fixed Assets in the Year | 万元 | 10000yuan | 126477 |
| 年末资产合计 | Total Assets（year-end） | 万元 | 10000yuan | 26069266 |
| 年末负债合计 | Total Liabilities（year-end） | 万元 | 10000yuan | 20142778 |
| 所有者权益合计 | Total Owners' Equity | 万元 | 10000yuan | 5926488 |
| #实收资本 | Paid-in Capitals | 万元 | 10000yuan | 5341314 |
| 主营业务收入 | Revenue from Principal Business | 万元 | 10000yuan | 22361816 |
| 主营业务成本 | Cost of Principal Business | 万元 | 10000yuan | 20768095 |
| 主营业务税金及附加 | Taxes and Extra Charges on Principal Business | 万元 | 10000yuan | 130363 |
| 管理费用 | Management Expenses | 万元 | 10000yuan | 684809 |
| 利润总额 | Total Profits | 万元 | 10000yuan | 552843 |
| 利税总额 | Total Pre-tax Profits | 万元 | 10000yuan | 1069277 |
| 年末应收工程款 | Account Receivable（year-end） | 万元 | 10000yuan | 7510128 |

| #中央<br>of which: Central Enterprises | 国有企业<br>State-owned Enterprise | 集体企业<br>Collectiveowend Enterprise | 其他所有制企业<br>Other Ownership Enterprises |
|---|---|---|---|
| 5848975 | 317799 | 5414 | 21241313 |
| 912009 | 8236 | 1769 | 3402832 |
| 760716 | 55042 | 4318 | 1995854 |
| 59570 | 1247 | 280 | 124950 |
| 7078410 | 374166 | 12932 | 25682168 |
| 6042307 | 268299 | 7592 | 19866888 |
| 1036103 | 105867 | 5341 | 5815280 |
| 519880 | 68404 | 5773 | 5267137 |
| 6300947 | 214932 | 19892 | 22126993 |
| 5897886 | 191485 | 17844 | 20558766 |
| 10314 | 1283 | 269 | 128811 |
| 204404 | 12278 | 1002 | 671529 |
| 134064 | 8198 | 510 | 544134 |
| 204095 | 15097 | 1391 | 1052789 |
| 1476694 | 174634 | 1891 | 7333604 |

# 13-3 建筑业企业主要经济效益指标（2018 年）
## MAIN INDICATORS ON ECONOMIC BENEFIT OF CONSTRUCTION ENTERPRISES (2018)

| 项目 | Item | 单位 | Unit | 合计 Total | #中央 of which: Central Enterprises | 国有企业 State-owned Enterprise | 集体企业 Collectiveowend Enterprise | 其他所有制企业 Other Ownership Enterprises |
|---|---|---|---|---|---|---|---|---|
| **建筑业劳动生产率** | **Labor Productivity of Construction** | | | | | | | |
| 按总产值计算 | In Terms of gross Output Value | 元／人 | yuan/person | 392170 | 502382 | 477463 | 297148 | 321194 |
| **竣工率** | **Rate of Buildings completd** | | | | | | | |
| 按产值计算 | In Terms of Gross output Value | % | % | 40.9 | 43.1 | 61.5 | 59.8 | 39.6 |
| 产值工资率 | Ratio of Wages to Gross Output Value | % | % | 12.8 | 11.1 | 15.7 | 24.9 | 12.8 |
| 资金利润率 | Ratio of Profit to Funds | % | % | 2.4 | 1.5 | 2.1 | 2.6 | 2.5 |
| 产值利润率 | Ratio of Profit to Gross Output Value | % | % | 2.8 | 3.2 | 4.5 | 5.3 | 2.7 |
| 流动比率 | Current Ratio | % | % | 117.9 | 104.8 | 113.1 | 101.2 | 117.3 |
| 资产负债率 | Assets-Liability Ratio | % | % | 77.2 | 85.3 | 71.7 | 58.7 | 75.1 |

# 13-4 建筑业增加值（2018年）
VALUE ADDED OF CONSTRUCTION (2018)

单位：亿元（100 million yuan）

| 市、区名称 | Region | 增加值 Vaiue Added |
|---|---|---|
| **全　市** | **Whole Municipality** | **723.4** |
| 市南区 | Shinan District | 65.6 |
| 市北区 | Shibei District | 88.1 |
| 李沧区 | Licang District | 16.8 |
| 崂山区 | Laoshan District | 104.8 |
| 黄岛区 | Huangdao District | 186.7 |
| 城阳区 | Chengyang District | 19.1 |
| 即墨区 | Jimo District | 84.4 |
| 胶州市 | Jiaozhou | 79.8 |
| 平度市 | Pingdu | 18.1 |
| 莱西市 | Laixi | 52.4 |
| 红岛经济区 | Qingdao National High-tech Industrial Development Zone | 7.6 |

注：黄岛区含保税港区数据。
Note: The Huangdao District contains the data of the bonded harbor area.

# 13-5 重点建筑企业一览表（2018 年）
LIST OF KEY CONSTRUCTION ENTERORISES（2018）

| 序号 Precedence | 企业单位名称 | Name | 所在地区 Location | 资质等级 Qualification Croteria |
|---|---|---|---|---|
| 1 | 青建集团股份公司 | Qingjian Group Co.，Ltd. | 市北区 Shibei District | A001 |
| 2 | 中青建安建设集团有限公司 | Zhongqing Jianan Construction Group Co.，Ltd. | 市南区 Shinan District | A001 |
| 3 | 荣华建设集团有限公司 | Ronghua Construction Group Co.，Ltd. | 莱西市 Laixi | A001 |
| 4 | 中建八局第四建设有限公司 | Fourth Construction of China Construction Eight Bureau Co.，Ltd. | 市南区 Shinan District | A001 |
| 5 | 中启胶建集团有限公司 | Zhongqi Rubber Construction Group Co.，Ltd. | 胶州市 Jiaozhou | A001 |
| 6 | 中铁十七局集团第一工程有限公司 | China Railway No.17 Bureau Group First Engineering Co.,Ltd | 黄岛区 Huangdao District | A003 |
| 7 | 中铁二十局集团第四工程有限公司 | Fourth Engineering of China Railway twenty Bureau Group Co.，Ltd. | 崂山区 Laoshan District | A103 |
| 8 | 中铁建工集团山东有限公司 | China Railway Construction Engineering Group Shandong Co.，Ltd. | 崂山区 Laoshan District | A301 |
| 9 | 东亚装饰股份有限公司 | East Asia Decoration Limited by Share Ltd. | 市南区 Shinan District | B103 |
| 10 | 青岛一建集团有限公司 | Qingdao Yi Jian Group Co.，Ltd. | 市北区 Shibei District | A001 |
| 11 | 青岛中建联合建设工程有限公司 | Qingdao Zhongjian United Construction Engineering Co.，Ltd. | 崂山区 Laoshan District | A101 |
| 12 | 中建筑港集团有限公司 | Zhongjian Zhu Gang Group Co.，Ltd. | 市北区 Shibei District | A104 |
| 13 | 青岛博海建设集团有限公司 | Qingdao Bohai Construction Group Co.，Ltd. | 市南区 Shinan District | A001 |
| 14 | 青岛海川建设集团有限公司 | Qingdao Hai Chuan Construction Group Co.，Ltd. | 市北区 Shibei District | A001 |
| 15 | 山东兴华建设集团有限公司 | Shandong Xinghua Construction Group Co.，Ltd. | 黄岛区 Huangdao District | A001 |
| 16 | 德才装饰股份有限公司 | Decai Decoration Limited by Share Ltd. | 崂山区 Laoshan District | B103 |
| 17 | 青岛海尔家居集成股份有限公司 | Qingdao Haier Integrated Limited by Share Ltd. | 胶州市 Jiaozhou | B103 |
| 18 | 青岛中嘉建设集团有限公司 | Qingdao Zhongjia Construction Group Co.，Ltd. | 市北区 Shibei District | A101 |
| 19 | 中铁二十五局集团第五工程有限公司 | Fifth Engineering Co.，Ltd. of China Railway twenty-five Bureau Group | 崂山区 Laoshan District | A110 |
| 20 | 山东莱钢建设有限公司 | Shandong Laiwu Iron and Steel Construction Co.，Ltd. | 市南区 Shinan District | A101 |
| 21 | 青岛亿联集团股份有限公司 | Qingdao Yilian Group Limited by Share Ltd. | 黄岛区 Huangdao District | A001 |
| 22 | 青建国际集团有限公司 | Qingjian International Group Limited | 市北区 Shibei District | A101 |
| 23 | 中铁十局集团青岛工程有限公司 | China Railway Ten Bureau Group Qingdao Engineering Co.，Ltd. | 市北区 Shibei District | A110 |
| 24 | 中交一航局第二工程有限公司 | Second Engineering Company Co.，Ltd. of China Communications Central Airlines | 市南区 Shinan District | A104 |
| 25 | 青岛即建建设集团有限公司 | Qingdao JiJian Construction Group Co.，Ltd. | 即墨区 Jimo District | A101 |
| 26 | 山东电力建设第三工程有限公司 | Third Engineering Co.，Ltd. of Shandong Electric Power Construction | 崂山区 Laoshan District | A006 |
| 27 | 青岛新华友建工集团股份有限公司 | Qingdao Xinhuayou Construction Engineering Group Limited by Share Ltd. | 崂山区 Laoshan District | A101 |
| 28 | 青岛温泉建设集团有限公司 | Qingdao Hot Spring Construction Group Co.，Ltd. | 即墨区 Jimo District | A101 |
| 29 | 山东荣泰建筑工程集团有限公司 | Shandong Rongtai Construction Engineering Group Co.，Ltd. | 黄岛区 Huangdao District | A001 |
| 30 | 青岛第一市政工程有限公司 | Qingdao First Municipal Engineering Co.，Ltd. | 市北区 Shibei District | A110 |
| 31 | 青岛恒生源集团建设有限公司 | Qingdao Hengshengyuan Group Construction Co.，Ltd. | 即墨区 Jimo District | A101 |
| 32 | 青岛城建集团有限公司 | Qingdao Urban Construction Group Co.，Ltd. | 市北区 Shibei District | A110 |
| 33 | 青岛海德工程集团股份有限公司 | Qingdao Hyde Road and Bridge Engineering Limited by Share Ltd. | 市南区 Shinan District | A210 |

## 13-5 续表 1
Continued

| 序号 Precedence | 企业单位名称 | Name | 所在地区 Location | 资质等级 Qualification Croteria |
|---|---|---|---|---|
| 34 | 青岛瑞源工程集团有限公司 | Qingdao Ruiyuan Engineering Group Co., Ltd. | 黄岛区 Huangdao District | A105 |
| 35 | 中国石油天然气第七建设有限公司 | China Petroleum and Natural Gas Seventh Construction Co., Ltd. | 崂山区 Laoshan District | A109 |
| 36 | 中石化第十建设有限公司 | Sinopec tenth Construction Company Limited | 黄岛区 Huangdao District | A109 |
| 37 | 青岛土木建工集团有限公司 | Qingdao Civil Engineering Group Co., Ltd. | 黄岛区 Huangdao District | A101 |
| 38 | 青岛建设集团有限公司 | Qingdao Construction Group Co., Ltd. | 市南区 Shinan District | A201 |
| 39 | 青岛福瀛建设集团有限公司 | Qingdao Fu ying Construction Group Co., Ltd. | 黄岛区 Huangdao District | A101 |
| 40 | 青岛颐金建筑装饰工程有限公司 | Qingdao Yijin Building Decoration Engineering Co., Ltd. | 市南区 Shinan District | B103 |
| 41 | 青岛登科市政工程有限公司 | Qingdao Dengke Municipal Engineering Co., Ltd. | 城阳区 Chengyang District | A110 |
| 42 | 青岛德泰建设工程有限公司 | Qingdao de Tai Construction Engineering Co., Ltd. | 黄岛区 Huangdao District | A101 |
| 43 | 山东国建工程集团有限公司 | Shandong State Construction Engineering Group Co., Ltd. | 崂山区 Laoshan District | A101 |
| 44 | 青岛胶城建设集团有限公司 | Qingdao Rubber City Construction Group Co., Ltd. | 胶州市 Jiaozhou | A101 |
| 45 | 青岛建工集团有限公司 | Qingdao Construction Engineering Group Co., Ltd. | 崂山区 Laoshan District | A102 |
| 46 | 青岛市政空间开发集团有限责任公司 | Qingdao Municipal Space Development Group Ltd | 市南区 Shinan District | A110 |
| 47 | 青岛营上建设集团有限公司 | Qingdao Yingshang Construction Group Co., Ltd. | 即墨区 Jimo District | A101 |
| 48 | 青岛鑫兴泰建筑工程有限公司 | Qingdao xinxingtai Construction Engineering Co., Ltd. | 城阳区 Chengyang District | A201 |
| 49 | 青岛市房屋建筑集团股份有限公司 | Qingdao Housing Construction Group Limited by Share Ltd. | 市北区 Shibei District | A101 |
| 50 | 山东天诚市政公路工程有限公司 | Shandong Tiancheng Municipal Highway Engineering Co., Ltd. | 崂山区 Laoshan District | A110 |
| 51 | 青岛安装建设股份有限公司 | Qingdao Installation and Construction Limited by Share Ltd. | 市北区 Shibei District | A112 |
| 52 | 青岛滨海建设集团有限公司 | Qingdao Binhai Construction Group Co., Ltd. | 黄岛区 Huangdao District | A101 |
| 53 | 青岛青房建安集团有限公司 | Qingdao Qingfang Jianan Group Co., Ltd. | 市南区 Shinan District | A101 |
| 54 | 青岛建祥建设集团有限公司 | Qingdao Jian Xiang Construction Group Co., Ltd. | 胶州市 Jiaozhou | A101 |
| 55 | 青岛平建建筑安装股份有限公司 | Qingdao Ping Jian Building and Installation Limited by Share Ltd. | 平度市 Pingdu | A101 |
| 56 | 青岛艺高城市建设工程有限公司 | Qingdao Yi Gao City Construction Engineering Co., Ltd. | 市北区 Shibei District | B237 |
| 57 | 青岛港务局港务工程公司 | Qingdao Port Bureau Port Engineering Company | 黄岛区 Huangdao District | A204 |
| 58 | 青岛公路建设集团有限公司 | Qingdao Highway Construction Group Co., Ltd. | 崂山区 Laoshan District | A102 |
| 59 | 青岛胶州湾建设集团有限公司 | Qingdao Jiaozhou Bay Construction Group Co., Ltd. | 胶州市 Jiaozhou | A101 |
| 60 | 青岛昶德建设集团有限公司 | Qingdao Changde Construction Group Co., Ltd. | 胶州市 Jiaozhou | A101 |
| 61 | 青岛营海建设（集团）有限公司 | Qingdao Ying hai Construction Group Co., Ltd. | 胶州市 Jiaozhou | A101 |
| 62 | 青岛新城发展建筑工程有限公司 | Qingdao New Town Development Engineering Co., Ltd. | 市北区 Shibei District | A101 |
| 63 | 青岛东捷建设工程有限公司 | Qingdao Dong jie Construction Engineering Co., Ltd. | 市北区 Shibei District | A101 |
| 64 | 青岛西海岸市政工程有限公司 | Qingdao West Coast municipal Group Municipal Engineering Company | 黄岛区 Huangdao District | A110 |
| 65 | 青岛环城建工集团有限公司 | Qingdao Ring City Construction Engineering Group Co., Ltd. | 黄岛区 Huangdao District | A101 |
| 66 | 青岛地矿岩土工程有限公司 | Qingdao Geotechnical Engineering Co., Ltd. | 市南区 Shinan District | B101 |

## 13-5 续表 2
Continued

| 序号 Precedence | 企业单位名称 | Name | 所在地区 Location | 资质等级 Qualification Croteria |
|---|---|---|---|---|
| 67 | 青岛东建建设有限公司 | Qingdao Dongjian Construction Co., Ltd. | 李沧区 Licang District | A201 |
| 68 | 青岛建设集团建兴工程有限公司 | Qingdao construction group LITE-ON Engineering Co., Ltd. | 红岛经济区 Qingdao National High-tech Industrial Development Zone | A101 |
| 69 | 青岛市崂山区古建建筑工程有限公司 | Qingdao Laoshan ancient building engineering Co., Ltd. | 崂山区 Laoshan District | A101 |
| 70 | 山东奥华建筑安装工程有限公司 | Shandong Ao Hua Construction and Installation Engineering Co., Ltd. | 市南区 Shinan District | A101 |
| 71 | 青岛建设装饰集团有限公司 | Qingdao Construction Decoration Group Co.,Ltd. | 市南区 Shinan District | B103 |
| 72 | 青岛万怡东方建设集团有限公司 | Qingdao Wan Yi Oriental Construction Group Co., Ltd. | 黄岛区 Huangdao District | A101 |
| 73 | 青岛柏高市政园林建设集团有限公司 | Qingdao BOGAO Municipal Garden Construction Group Co. Ltd | 市南区 Shinan District | A110 |
| 74 | 鲁建集团股份有限公司 | Lu Jian Group Limited by Share Ltd. | 崂山区 Laoshan District | A202 |
| 75 | 青岛通力建设集团有限公司 | Qingdao Tongli Construction Engineering Co.,Ltd. | 市南区 Shinan District | A101 |
| 76 | 山东省路通工程集团有限公司 | Shandong Lutong Engineering Group Co., Ltd. | 崂山区 Laoshan District | A102 |
| 77 | 青岛金沙滩建设集团有限公司 | Oingdao Jinshatan Construction Group Co., Ltd. | 黄岛区 Huangdao District | A101 |
| 78 | 青岛康太源建设集团有限公司 | Qingdao Kangtine Construciton Group.Lnc. | 李沧区 Licang District | A101 |
| 79 | 青岛九龙建设集团有限公司 | Qingdao Jiulong Construction Group Co., Ltd. | 胶州市 Jiaozhou | A101 |
| 80 | 青岛环海工程贸易发展有限公司 | Qingdao Huanhai Engineering & Trade Development Co., Ltd. | 市北区 Shibei District | A201 |
| 81 | 青岛三星工程有限公司 | Qingdao Sanxing Engineering Co., Ltd. | 城阳区 Chengyang District | A110 |
| 82 | 青岛鑫隆建设集团有限公司 | Qingdao Xinlong Construction Group Co., Ltd. | 黄岛区 Huangdao District | A101 |
| 83 | 青岛福海洋建设集团有限公司 | Qingdao Fu Ocean Construction Group Co., Ltd. | 胶州市 Jiaozhou | A201 |
| 84 | 青岛华联装饰工程有限公司 | Qingdao Hualian Decoration Engineering Co., Ltd. | 市北区 Shibei District | B203 |
| 85 | 青岛云柱电气有限公司 | Qingdao Yunzhu Electric Co., Ltd. | 城阳区 Chengyang District | A206 |
| 86 | 青岛四机建筑安装有限公司 | Qingdao Siji Construction Installation Co.,Ltd. | 市北区 Shibei District | A201 |
| 87 | 青岛市益水工程股份有限公司 | Qingdao Yishui Engineering Co.,Ltd. | 市南区 Shinan District | A210 |
| 88 | 青岛望城三宝建设有限公司 | Qingdao Wangcheng Sanbao Construction Co., Ltd. | 莱西市 Laixi | A101 |
| 89 | 青岛恒华机房设备工程有限公司 | Qingdao Heng Hua machine Room Equipment Engineering Co., Ltd. | 市南区 Shinan District | B123 |
| 90 | 青岛元昌盛房建集团有限公司 | Qingdao Yuanchangsheng Housing Construction Group Co., Ltd. | 胶州市 Jiaozhou | A201 |
| 91 | 青岛方圆达建设集团有限公司 | Qindao Fang Yuan Da Construction Group Co.,Ltd. | 李沧区 Licang District | A201 |
| 92 | 青岛嘉恒建设集团有限公司 | Qingdao Jiaheng Construction Group Co., Ltd. | 市南区 Shinan District | A101 |
| 93 | 青岛永鑫建筑工程有限公司 | Qingdao Yongxin Construction Engineering Co., Ltd. | 平度市 Pingdu | A201 |
| 94 | 青岛市黄岛区园林绿化工程有限公司 | Huangdao of Qingdao Landscaping Engineering Co., Ltd. | 黄岛区 Huangdao District | A310 |
| 95 | 青岛青城建工集团有限公司 | Qingdao Qingcheng Construction Group Co., Ltd. | 红岛经济区 Qingdao National High-tech Industrial Development Zone | A101 |
| 96 | 青岛施运机械施工有限责任公司 | Qingdao Construction Transportation Company | 市北区 Shibei District | B101 |
| 97 | 青岛恒源送变电工程有限公司 | Qingdao Hengyuan transmission and Transformation Engineering Co., Ltd. | 城阳区 Chengyang District | A201 |
| 98 | 青岛太行园林建设有限公司 | Qingdao Taihang Garden Construction Co., Ltd. | 黄岛区 Huangdao District | A310 |
| 99 | 青岛政益达实业有限公司 | Qingdao Zhengyida Industrial Co., Ltd. | 市北区 Shibei District | A210 |
| 100 | 青岛盛泽建设工程有限公司 | Qingdao Shengze Construction Engineering Co., Ltd. | 胶州市 Jiaozhou | A201 |

# 主要统计指标解释

**建筑业统计单位** 指从事房屋、构筑物建造和设备安装活动的法人企业。建筑业法人企业应具有建筑业资质并能够独立核算，同时其应具备以下条件：①依法成立，有自己的名称、组织机构和场所，能够承担民事责任；②独立拥有和使用资产，承担负债，有权与其他单位签订合同；③独立核算盈亏，能够编制资产负债表。

**建筑业总产值** 是以货币形式表现的建筑业企业在一定时期内生产的建筑业产品和提供的服务的总和。建筑业总产值包括：

（1）建筑工程产值：指列入建筑工程预算内的各种工程价值。

（2）安装工程产值：指设备安装工程价值，不包括被安装设备本身的价值。

（3）其他产值：建筑业总产值中除建筑工程、安装工程以外的产值。包括房屋构筑物修理产值、非标准设备制造产值、总包企业向分包企业收取的管理费以及不能明确划分的施工活动所完成的产值。

**建筑业增加值** 指建筑业企业在报告期内以货币形式表现的建筑业生产经营活动的最终成果。

**建筑业现价增加值** 按生产法和分配法（收入法）两种方法计算，以收入法的计算结果为准，即从收入的角度出发，根据生产要素在生产过程中应得的收入份额计算。具体计算方法：经济普查年度建筑业增加值按照《经济普查年度 GDP 核算方案》计算，非经济普查年度建筑业增加值按照《非经济普查年度 GDP 核算方案》计算。

# Explanatory Notes on Main Statistical Indicators

**Statistical Unit in Construction** refers to corporate enterprise engaged in the construction of buildings and structures and in the installation of equipment. A corporate construction enterprise should have qualification certificates with independent accounting system, and should meet the following 3 requirements: a) being set up in line with relevant legal basis, having its full name, organization and location, and capable of taking civil liabilities; b) independently possessing and using its assets and assuming its liabilities, and entitled to sign contracts with other institutions; and c) making independent accounts of its profits and losses, and capable of compiling its own balance sheet.

**Gross Output Value of Construction** refers to total of construction products and services, expressed in money terms, produced or rendered by construction and installation enterprises during a given period of time. It includes:

(1) Output value of construction projects, that is the value of projects covered by the project budgets;

(2) Output value of installation projects, that is the value of the installation of equipment, (excluding the value of the equipment to be installed);

(3) Output value of others, that is the output value of construction industry excluding that of construction projects and installation projects. It includes: output value of repair of buildings and structures; output value of non-standard equipment manufacturing; overhead expenses received by contracted enterprises to the sub-contracted enterprises and the completed output value of construction activities that have no clear definition.

# 运输、邮电 14

## TRANSPORT，POSTAL AND TELECOMMUNICATION SERVICES

# 简 要 说 明

**一、本篇资料的主要内容**

本篇资料主要反映了全市交通运输业和邮电业通讯业发展的基本情况，主要包括客货运输及港口吞吐量、民用汽车拥有量、独立核算运输邮电单位主要财务指标、邮电通讯基本情况、邮政行业发展情况、快递企业发展情况、电信行业基本情况、城市轨道交通发展情况等方面的内容。

**二、本篇资料的来源**

1、本篇资料中交通运输邮电资料来源于全市交通运输邮电业统计年报。

2、交通运输资料来源于青岛市交通运输委员会、青岛市港航局、青岛市运管局、青岛港（集团）有限公司、青岛国际机场集团有限公司、青岛地铁集团有限公司。

3、邮政业资料来源于青岛市邮政管理局、中国邮政集团公司青岛市分公司。

4、电信业资料来源于青岛市通信管理局、中国电信集团公司山东省青岛市电信分公司、中国电信股份有限公司青岛分公司、中国联合网络通信有限公司青岛市分公司、中国移动通信集团山东有限公司青岛分公司、中国铁通集团有限公司青岛分公司。

5、民用汽车拥有量资料来源于青岛市公安局交警支队车辆管理所。

本篇资料由市统计局服务业统计处整理提供。

# Brief Introduction

***I. Main Content***

Data in this chapter show the basic conditions of the development of transport, post and telecommunications in Shandong Province, mainly including the freight traffic and passenger traffic, cargo handled at port, possession of civil motor vehicles, major financial indices and basic conditions of transport, postal and telecommunication services, development of the postal services, express company development, development of urban rail transit.

***II. Source of Data***

(1) Data on transport are based on the annual report of transport.

(2) Data on transportation are provided by Qingdao Municipal Transportation Committee, Qingdao Port and Shipping Bureau , Qingdao Transportation Management Bureau, Qing Dao Port International Co.,Ltd, Qing Dao International Airport Group Co.,Ltd, Qingdao Metro Group Co.,Ltd.

(3) Data on postal and telecommunication are based on Qingdao Municipal Postal Administration, Qingdao Post Bureau.

(4) Data on business of telecommunication services Qingdao Communication Administration, China Telecom Group Corporation Qingdao Branch of Shandong Province, China Telecom Co., Ltd. Qingdao Branch, China United Network Communications Co., Ltd. Qingdao Branch, China Mobile Communications Group Shandong Co., Ltd. Qingdao Branch, China Tietong Group Co., Ltd. Qingdao Branch.

(5) Date on possession of civil motor vehicles are are provided by Qingdao Municipal Public Security Bureau Traffic Police Detachment Vehicle Management Office.

Data in this chapter are prepared and provide by the Division of Industry Statistics of Qingdao Municipal Bureau of Statistics.

# 14-1 主要年份客货运输及港口吞吐量
MAJOR YEAR'S PASSENGER & FREIGHT TRAFFIC AND HANDLING CAPACITY OF THE PORTS

| 年份 Year | 客运量（万人）Passenger Traffic (10000 persons) | | | | 货运量（万吨）Freight Traffic (10000 tons) | | | | 港口吞吐量（万吨）Cargo Handied at Ports (10000 tons) | 集装箱吞吐量（万标箱）Containers (10000 TEU) |
|---|---|---|---|---|---|---|---|---|---|---|
| | 铁路 Railways | 公路 Highways | 海运 Waterways | 航空 Civil Aviation | 铁路 Railways | 公路 Highways | 海运 Waterways | 航空 Civil Aviation | | |
| 1949 | 327 | 14 | 9 | | 386 | 162 | 22 | | 73 | |
| 1952 | 571 | 49 | 13 | | 447 | 399 | 44 | | 181 | |
| 1957 | 1054 | 149 | 13 | | 747 | 548 | 118 | | 269 | |
| 1962 | 3100 | 141 | 39 | | 909 | 524 | 97 | | 391 | |
| 1965 | 1424 | 230 | 19 | | 1257 | 690 | 158 | | 524 | |
| 1970 | 1329 | 373 | 20 | | 1856 | 736 | 232 | | 695 | |
| 1975 | 1803 | 159 | 30 | | 2325 | 817 | 282 | | 1542 | |
| 1978 | 1986 | 274 | 49 | | 2917 | 1561 | 528 | | 2081 | |
| 1980 | 1896 | 713 | 73 | | 2596 | 1642 | 941 | | 1779 | |
| 1985 | 2063 | 1894 | 86 | 1.0 | 3009 | 2303 | 919 | 0.03 | 2610 | |
| 1988 | 2083 | 3300 | 234 | 8.8 | 3418 | 6486 | 1160 | 0.04 | 3153 | |
| 1990 | 1488 | 3639 | 316 | 14.1 | 3741 | 6433 | 1556 | 0.20 | 3068 | |
| 1991 | 1453 | 4144 | 366 | 19.0 | 3774 | 6896 | 1789 | 0.31 | 3194 | |
| 1992 | 1488 | 4965 | 437 | 27.0 | 3899 | 6822 | 1981 | 0.45 | 3240 | |
| 1993 | 1499 | 6436 | 499 | 35.3 | 4044 | 7685 | 1910 | 0.64 | 3650 | |
| 1994 | 1564 | 6787 | | 47.0 | 4112 | 8336 | 1804 | | 4331 | |
| 1995 | 1480 | 9785 | | 66.6 | 4205 | 11788 | 2185 | | 5165 | |
| 1996 | 1230 | 10738 | | 79.9 | 4415 | 10749 | 474 | | 6056 | 81.1 |
| 1997 | 1308 | 11855 | | | 4466 | 11232 | 544 | | 6944 | 103.3 |
| 1998 | 1549 | 11754 | | | 4028 | 14311 | 1792 | 1.44 | 7044 | 121.3 |
| 1999 | 1674 | 12103 | | | 3919 | 14550 | 1926 | 1.96 | 7282 | 154.3 |
| 2000 | 1780 | 12145 | | 124.1 | 4256 | 17234 | 2998 | 2.30 | 8661 | 212.0 |
| 2001 | 1678 | 13686 | | 143.0 | 4778 | 20906 | 3432 | 2.40 | 10423 | 264.0 |
| 2002 | 1530 | 14516 | 777 | 163.7 | 5079 | 24480 | 2530 | 3.00 | 12252 | 341.0 |
| 2003 | 1366 | 13132 | 786 | 174.7 | 4929 | 27241 | 2773 | 3.60 | 14135 | 424.0 |
| 2004 | 1496 | 16420 | 862 | 241.9 | 5119 | 29937 | 3503 | 5.30 | 16303 | 514.0 |
| 2005 | 552 | 17212 | 972 | 280.9 | 2299 | 31009 | 4471 | 4.60 | 18727 | 630.7 |
| 2006 | 810 | 17752 | 999 | 320.2 | 2790 | 32047 | 4768 | 5.10 | 22438 | 770.0 |
| 2007 | 1101 | 18800 | 1080 | 733.8 | 2781 | 33336 | 4019 | 5.90 | 26507 | 946.6 |
| 2008 | 1278 | 19909 | 1055 | 755.8 | 3225 | 34172 | 5080 | 7.20 | 30029 | 1037.7 |
| 2009 | 1425 | 19612 | 1145 | 881.8 | 3772 | 16297 | 4332 | 7.19 | 31668 | 1027.6 |
| 2010 | 1537 | 20460 | 1302 | 1010.9 | 5031 | 17525 | 4407 | 8.44 | 35012 | 1201.0 |
| 2011 | 1693 | 21560 | 791 | 1074.8 | 5697 | 19208 | 4220 | 8.93 | 37971 | 1302.0 |
| 2012 | 1881 | 22724 | 414 | 1173.1 | 6126 | 21312 | 1791 | 9.06 | 41465 | 1450.0 |
| 2013 | 2056 | 23588 | 333 | 1572.4 | 6266 | 23270 | 1313 | 9.31 | 45782 | 1552.0 |
| 2014 | 2301 | 5588 | 324 | 1641.2 | 5564 | 19043 | 1434 | 10.22 | 47701 | 1658.0 |
| 2015 | 2421 | 5370 | 288 | 1820.2 | 5486 | 20073 | 1456 | 20.80 | 49749 | 1743.0 |
| 2016 | 2701 | 4532 | 225 | 2050.5 | 5569 | 20701 | 1685 | 23.07 | 51463 | 1805.0 |
| 2017 | 3179 | 4534 | 215 | 2321.1 | 6021 | 24716 | 1800 | 23.20 | 51314 | 1830.9 |
| 2018 | 3455 | 4602 | 161 | 2453.6 | 6280 | 27453 | 2502 | 22.45 | 54250 | 1931.5 |

注：从 2014 年公路客、货运量统计口径进行调整，与以前年度不可比。
Note: In 2014, the Ministry of Transportation made an adjustment to the statistical gauge for highway passenger and freight transportation and the data are not comparable directly.

# 14-2 民用车辆拥有量（2018 年底）

ROSSESSION OF CIVIL MOTOR VEHICLES（END OF 2018）

单位：辆（unit）

| 项目 | Item | 合计 Total | #个人 of which：Private Vehicles |
|---|---|---|---|
| | | 辆数 Number | 辆数 Number |
| **一、汽车** | **Automobile** | **2690558** | **2321113** |
| 1. 载客汽车 | Passenger Vehicles | 2426198 | 2176901 |
| 其中：轿车 | of which：Sedan | 1576286 | 1432953 |
| 2. 载货汽车 | Trucks | 248075 | 134205 |
| 3. 其他汽车 | Other Automobile | 16285 | 10007 |
| **二、电车** | **Tram** | **125** | **0** |
| **三、摩托车** | **Motorcycle** | **106356** | **104836** |
| **四、农用运输车** | **Agricultural Camion** | | |
| **五、挂车** | **Trailer Trucks** | **28610** | **273** |
| **六、其他类型车** | **Other Vehicles** | **142** | **2** |

补充资料：机动车驾驶员（3350694 人）Motor drivers（person）
其中：汽车驾驶员（3304193 人）of which：Automobile drivers（person）

## 14-3 客货运输及港口吞吐量（2018 年）
PASSENGER & FREIGHT TRAFFIC AND HANDLING CAPACITY OF THE PORTS (2018)

| 项目 | Item | 货运量（万吨）Freight Traffic (10 000 tons) | 货物周转量（亿吨公里）Freight Ton-kilometers (100million tons·km) | 客运量（万人）Passenger Traffic (10 000 persons) | 旅客周转量（亿人公里）Passenger-kilometers (100million persons-km) | 旅客吞吐量（万人）Volume of Passenger Handled (10000 persons) | 货物吞吐量（万吨）Volume of Freight Handled (10000 tons) | 集装箱（万标箱）Containers (10000 TEU) |
|---|---|---|---|---|---|---|---|---|
| **总计** | **Total** | **36235** | **1647.12** | **8218** | **182.49** | **2473** | **54272** | **1932** |
| 铁路 | Railways | 6280 | 190.90 | 3455 | 105.36 | | | |
| 公路 | Hilghways | 27453 | 532.20 | 161 | 0.16 | | | |
| 水运 | Waterways | 2502 | 924.02 | 4602 | 76.97 | | | |
| 机场 | Civil Aviation | | | | | 2454 | 22 | |
| 港口 | Ports | | | | | 19 | 54250 | 1932 |

## 14-4 规模以上运输邮电单位主要财务指标（2018 年）
MAJOR FINANCIAL INDICATORS OF TRANSPORTATION, POST AND TELECOMMUNICATION UNITS ABOVE DESIGNATED SCALE (2018)

单位：万元（10 000yuan）

| 项目 | Item | 营业收入 Revenue from principal Business | 营业成本 Cost of principal Business | 营业利润 Operating Profits | 营业税金及附加 Business taxes and surtax | 利润总额 Total Profits |
|---|---|---|---|---|---|---|
| **总计** | **Total** | **8739006** | **7740691** | **539461** | **34513** | **727935** |
| 道路运输业 | Road Transport | 1739578 | 1833292 | -70903 | 10541 | 82664 |
| 水上运输业 | Water Transport | 305332 | 227560 | 29216 | 5670 | 47375 |
| 航空运输业 | Air Transport | 385408 | 321742 | 39981 | 2182 | 42876 |
| 管道运输业 | Pipeline Transport | 24783 | 9291 | 13159 | 125 | 13590 |
| 多式联运和运输代理业 | Multimodal Transport and Transport Agent | 3824941 | 3574956 | 140759 | 5527 | 141518 |
| 装卸搬运和仓储业 | loading and unloading and storage | 900786 | 762783 | 45264 | 4628 | 55308 |
| 邮政业 | Post | 325276 | 283198 | 5870 | 1480 | 5497 |
| 电信、广播电视和卫星传输服务 | Telecommunticantions,Radia and Television and Satellite Transmission Services | 1232904 | 727869 | 336115 | 4359 | 339107 |

# 14-5 邮电通讯基本情况（2018年）
## BASIC CONDITIONS OF POSTAL AND TELECOMMUNICATION SERVICES（2018）

| 市、区名称 | Region | 邮电局（处）Post Office（unit） | #提供邮政全功能服务的 of which：Providing Omni-directional Services | 邮路总长度（公里）Length of Postal Routes（km） | 邮运汽车（辆）Vehicles for Postal Services（unit） | 信筒、信箱（个）Post Boxes（unit） |
|---|---|---|---|---|---|---|
| **全市** | **Whole Municipality** | **265** | **216** | **5974** | **391** | **663** |
| 市南区 | Shinan District | 19 | 10 | 1505 | 47 | 79 |
| 市北区 | Shibei District | 22 | 13 | 1743 | 54 | 92 |
| 李沧区 | Licang District | 9 | 4 | 71 | 20 | 31 |
| 崂山区 | Laoshan District | 7 | 4 | 56 | 15 | 25 |
| 黄岛区 | Huangdao District | 48 | 38 | 670 | 69 | 86 |
| 城阳区 | Chengyang District | 12 | 9 | 178 | 28 | 29 |
| 即墨区 | Jimo District | 36 | 34 | 522 | 48 | 75 |
| 胶州市 | Jiaozhou | 31 | 29 | 295 | 40 | 63 |
| 平度市 | Pingdu | 54 | 50 | 636 | 38 | 127 |
| 莱西市 | Laixi | 27 | 25 | 298 | 32 | 56 |

注：黄岛区含保税港区数据；城阳区含红岛经济区数据。

Note：The Huangdao District contains the data of the bonded harbor area，Chengyang District includes Hongdao Economic Zone.

# 14-6 邮政行业发展情况
## DEVELOPMENT OF THE POSTAL SERVICES

| 指标名称 | Name | 单位 | Unit | 2018年 | 2017年 |
|---|---|---|---|---|---|
| **一、邮政行业业务收入** | **Postal Services Business Income** | 亿元 | **100 million yuan** | **62.81** | **53.43** |
| 1、邮政寄递服务 | Postal Delivery Service | 亿元 | 100 million yuan | 3.05 | 2.88 |
| 2、快递业务 | Express Service | 亿元 | 100 million yuan | 50.22 | 41.33 |
| **二、邮政行业业务总量** | **Total Business Volume Of Postal Industry** | 亿元 | 100 million yuan | **82.87** | **72.46** |
| 1、邮政寄递服务 | Postal Delivery Service | 万件 | 10 000 articles | 17449 | 18243 |
| 其中：函件 | Number Of Letters | 万件 | 10 000 articles | 1612 | 1317 |
| 包裹 | Package | 万件 | 10 000 articles | 29 | 28 |
| 订销报纸累计数 | Cumulative number of newspapers ordered and sold | 万份 | 10 000 copies | 14566 | 15206 |
| 订销杂志累计数 | Cumulative number of magazines ordered and sold | 万份 | 10 000 copies | 629 | 677 |
| 汇兑 | Exchange | 万笔 | 10 000 sums | 11 | 17 |
| 2、快递业务 | Express Service | 万件 | 10 000 articles | 38323 | 31150 |
| 其中：同城 | Same City | 万件 | 10 000 articles | 10738 | 7700 |
| 异地 | Different Places | 万件 | 10 000 articles | 27016 | 22854 |
| 国际/港澳台 | International/Hong Kong, Macao And Taiwan | 万件 | 10 000 articles | 569 | 596 |

# 14-7 快递企业发展情况
## EXPRESS COMPANY DEVELOPMENT

| 指标名称 | Name | 单位 | Unit | 2018 年 | 2017 年 |
|---|---|---|---|---|---|
| **快递业务量** | **Express Business Volume** | **万件** | **10 000 articles** | **38323** | **31150** |
| 同城 | Same City | 万件 | 10 000 articles | 10738 | 7700 |
| 异地 | Different Places | 万件 | 10 000 articles | 27016 | 22854 |
| 国际及港澳台 | International/ Hong Kong, Macao And Taiwan | 万件 | 10 000 articles | 569 | 596 |
| **快递业务收入** | **Express Revenue** | **亿元** | **100 million yuan** | **50.22** | **41.33** |
| 同城 | Same City | 亿元 | 100 million yuan | 8.99 | 6.51 |
| 异地 | Different Places | 亿元 | 100 million yuan | 27.02 | 22.07 |
| 国际及港澳台 | International/ Hong Kong, Macao And Taiwan | 亿元 | 100 million yuan | 7.88 | 7.77 |
| 其他 | Others | 亿元 | 100 million yuan | 6.33 | 4.97 |

# 14-8 电信行业基本情况
## BASIC SITUATION OF TELECOM INDUSTRY

| 指标名称 | Name | 单位 | Unit | 2018 年 | 2017 年 |
|---|---|---|---|---|---|
| **一、电信业务总量（2015 年不变价）** | **TOTAL TELECOMMUNICATIONS BUSINESS** | **亿元** | **100 million yuan** | **568.01** | **260.72** |
| 其中：固定话音业务总量 | Total Fixed Voice Service | 亿元 | 100 million yuan | 1.84 | 2.41 |
| 固定数据及互联网业务总量 | Fixed Data And Total Internet Business | 亿元 | 100 million yuan | 16.26 | 14.36 |
| 移动话音业务总量 | Total Mobile Voice Service | 亿元 | 100 million yuan | 22.40 | 23.25 |
| 移动数据及互联网业务总量 | Total Mobile Data And Internet Services | 亿元 | 100 million yuan | 431.26 | 148.75 |
| 电信业务收入 | Telecommunications Revenue | 亿元 | 100 million yuan | 113.26 | 108.99 |
| **二、电信营业网点** | **Telecom Business Network** | **个** | **unit** | **482** | **495** |
| **三、固定电话交换机总容量（含农话）** | **Total Capacity Of Fixed Telephone Exchanges(Including Rural Fixed Telephone)** | **万门** | **10 000 line** | **339** | **299** |
| 固定电话年末用户 | Fixed Telephone Year-End User | 万户 | 10 000 households | 139 | 148 |
| 其中：新装电话 | Newly Installed Telephone | 万户 | 10 000 households | 7 | 12 |
| 城市电话用户 | Urban Telephone User | 万户 | 10 000 households | 105 | 111 |
| 乡村电话用户 | Village Phone User | 万户 | 10 000 households | 30 | 33 |
| 住宅电话年末用户 | Home Phone Year-End User | 万户 | 10 000 households | 54 | 58 |
| 城市电话用户 | Urban Telephone User | 万户 | 10 000 households | 38 | 41 |
| 乡村电话用户 | Village Phone User | 万户 | 10 000 households | 16 | 17 |
| **四、固定电话本地通话量** | **Fixed Telephone Local Call Volume** | **万分钟** | **10 000 minutes** | **109990** | **144430** |
| 长话电路 | Long Distance Circuit | 路 | line | 15665 | 15062 |
| 长途电话通话量 | Long Distance Call Volume | 万次 | 10 000 times | 618219 | 590271 |
| 长途电话通话时长 | Long-Distance Phone Call Duration | 万分钟 | 10 000 minutes | 16456 | 22348 |
| **五、互联网用户数** | **Number Of Internet Users** | **万户** | **10 000 households** | **1462** | **1311** |
| 固定宽带互联网用户数 | Number Of Fixed Broadband Internet Users | 万户 | 10 000 households | 398 | 369 |
| 移动互联网用户数 | Number Of Mobile Internet Users | 万户 | 10 000 households | 1064 | 941 |

## 14-8 续表
Continued

| 指标名称 | Name | 单位 | Unit | 2018 年 | 2017 年 |
|---|---|---|---|---|---|
| **六、互联网通信量** | **Internet Traffic** | | | | |
| 固定互联网宽带使用时长 | Fixed Internet Broadband Usage Time | 万分钟 | 10 000 minutes | 48342353 | 51871902 |
| 固定互联网宽带接入流量 | Fixed Internet Broadband Access Traffic | 万 G | 10 000 G | 517 | 867 |
| 移动互联网接入流量 | Mobile Internet Access Traffic | 万 G | 10 000 G | 25952 | 9731 |
| **七、光缆线路长度** | **Cable Line Length** | | | | |
| 长途光缆线路长度 | Long-Distance Cable Line Length | 公里 | km | 8068 | 7193 |
| 本地网中继光缆线路长度 | Line Length of Relay Optical Cable in Local Network | 公里 | km | 91564 | 75822 |
| 接入网光缆线路长度 | Optical Cable Line Length In Access Network | 公里 | km | 215744 | 173974 |
| **八、移动通信用户** | **Mobile Communication Users** | | | | |
| 移动电话交换机容量 | Mobile Phone Switch Capacity | 万户 | 10 000 households | 2930 | 2862 |
| 期末移动电话用户数 | nmber of mobile phone users at the end of the period | 万户 | 10 000 households | 1259 | 1223 |
| 其中：3G 移动电话用户 | 3G Mobile Phone Users | 万户 | 10 000 households | 132 | 120 |
| 其中：4G 移动电话用户 | 4G Mobile Phone Users | 万户 | 10 000 households | 932 | 821 |
| **九、移动电话通话量** | **Mobile Phone Call Volume** | | | | |
| 移动电话通话时长 | Mobile Phone Call Duration | 万分钟 | 10 000 minutes | 1402646 | 1441012 |
| **十、通信能力** | **Communication Ability** | | | | |
| 移动电话交换机容量 | Mobile Phone Switch Capacity | 万户 | 10 000 households | 2930 | 2862 |
| 移动电话基站数 | Number Of Mobile Phone Base Stations | 个 | unit | 53448 | 45041 |
| 其中：3G 移动电话基站数 | Number Of 3G Mobile Phone Base Stations | 个 | unit | 8295 | 9644 |
| 其中：4G 移动电话基站数 | Number Of 4G Mobile Phone Base Stations | 个 | unit | 30377 | 24005 |
| **十一、互联网通信能力** | **Internet Communication Capability** | | | | |
| 互联网宽带接入端口 | Internet Broadband Access Port | 个 | unit | 7263867 | 5610728 |

## 14-9 城市轨道交通发展情况
DEVELOPMENT OF URBAN RAIL TRANSIT

| 指标名称 | Name | 单位 | Unit | 2018 年 | 2017 年 |
|---|---|---|---|---|---|
| **客运量** | **Passenger Traffic** | **万人次** | **10 000 person-times** | **15294** | **6573** |
| 日均客运量 | **Average Daily Passenger** | 万人次 | 10 000 person-times | **42** | **18** |
| 旅客周转量 | **Passenger Turnover** | 万人公里 | **10 000 passenger-km** | **124411** | **58983** |
| 运营车数 | **Number Of Vehicles Operated** | 辆 | **unit** | **522** | **294** |
| 其中：地铁 | Subway | 辆 | unit | 522 | 294 |
| 轻轨 | Subway | 辆 | unit | | |
| 运营线路总数 | **Total Number Of Operating Lines** | 条 | **line** | **4** | **2** |
| 其中：新增运营线路 | New Operating Line | 条 | line | 2 | 1 |
| 其中：地铁 | Subway | 条 | line | 2 | 1 |
| 轻轨 | Light Rail | 条 | line | | |
| 运营线路总长度 | **Total Length Of Operating Line** | 公里 | **km** | **169** | **45** |
| 其中：新增运营线路长度 | New Operating Line Length | 公里 | km | 121 | 20 |
| 其中：地铁 | Subway | 公里 | km | 121 | 20 |
| 轻轨 | Light Rail | 公里 | km | | |
| 地铁站点总数 | **Total Number Of Subway Stations** | 个 | **unit** | **80** | **38** |
| 其中：换乘站点个数 | Number Of Transfer Stations | 个 | unit | 3 | 2 |
| 其中：新增站点个数 | Number Of New Sites | 个 | unit | 42 | 16 |
| 其中：新增换乘站点个数 | Increase The Number Of Transfer Stations | 个 | unit | 1 | 2 |
| 总开行次数 | **Total Number Of Trips** | 列次 | **train number** | **329849** | **119101** |
| 总运营里程 | **Total Operating Mileage** | 公里 | **km** | **9149612** | **2919273** |
| 列车准点率 | **Train On Time Rate** | % | % | **99.97** | **99.96** |

# 主要统计指标解释

**货（客）运量**　指在一定时期内，各运输部门实际运送的货物（旅客）数量。是反映运输业为国民经济和人民生活服务的数量指标，也是制定和检查运输生产计划，研究运输发展规模和速度的重要指标。货运按吨计算，客运按人计算。货物不论运输距离长短，货物类别，均按实际重量统计；旅客不论行程远近或票价多少，均按一人一次作为客运量统计。半价票、小孩票也按一人统计。

**货物（旅客）周转量**　指在一定时期内，由各种运输工具运送的货物（旅客）数量与其相应运输距离的乘积之总和，是反映运输业生产总成果的重要指标，也是编制和检查运输生产计划，计算运输效益、劳动生产率以及核算运输单位成本的主要基础资料。通常以吨公里和人公里为计算单位。计算货物周转量通常按发出站与到达站之间的最短距离，也就是计费距离计算。

**港口货物吞吐量**　指经水运进出沿海主要港区范围，并经过装卸的货物数量，包括邮件及办理托运手续的行李、包裹以及补给运输船舶的燃、物料和淡水。货物吞吐量按货物流向分为进口、出口吞吐量，按货物交流性质分为外贸货物吞吐量和国内贸易货物吞吐量。货物吞吐量的货类构成及其流向，是衡量港口生产能力大小的重要指标。

**邮政行业业务总量**　指以货币形式表现的邮政企业为社会提供各类邮政通信服务或其他服务的总数量。计算方法为各类邮政通信服务业务的实物量分别乘以相应的不变单价，求出各类业务的货币量后加总求得。该指标反映了一定时期邮政通信业务发展的总成果，是观察邮政通信业务发展变化总趋势的综合性指标。

**快递业务量**　指企业收寄的各类快递业务总数量，由受理用户委托的企业负责统计。包括国内同城快递业务量、国内异地快递业务量、港澳台快递业务量、国际快递业务量。

**电信业务总量**　指以货币形式表示的电信企业为社会提供的各类电信服务的总数量。包括固定话音业务总量、固定数据及互联网业务总量、固定增值及其他业务总量、移动话音业务总量、移动数据及互联网业务总量、移动增值及其他业务总量。

**长途光缆线路长度**　指长途光缆线路的实际长度。架空的光缆按实际杆路长度统计，埋设地下、水底的光缆按沟长统计。

**本地网中继光缆线路长度**　指本地网内各业务节点之间，从起点至终点所经由的光缆线路实际长度。架空光缆按实际杆路长度统计，埋设地下、水底的光缆按埋设光缆的沟长统计。

**移动电话基站数**　指为小区服务的无线收发信设备，处理基站与移动台之间的无线通信，在移动交换机与移动台之间起中继作用，监视无线传输质量的全套设备数。

**3G 移动电话基站数**　指报告期末本电信企业 3G 移动通信网络上实际使用的 NoFe-B 数量。包括 TF-SCFMA 基站、WCFMA 基站和 CFMA2000 基站。

**4G 移动电话基站数**　指报告期末本电信企业 4G 移动通信网络上实际使用的 Node-B 数量。包括 TD-LTE 基站和 FDD-LTE 基站。

**互联网宽带接入端口**　指用于接入互联网用户的各类实际安装运行的宽带接入端口的数量。

# Explanatory Notes on Main Statistical Indicators

**Freight ( Passenger ) Traffic** refers to the volume of freight ( passenger ) transported with various means. Freight transport is calculated in tons and passenger traffic is calculated in the number of persons. Despite the type of freight and traveling distance, the freight transport is calculated in the actual weight of the goods; and despite the traveling distance and ticket price, the passenger traffic is calculated by the principle that one person can be counted only once in one travel. The passengers who travel with a half price ticket or a child ticket is also calculated as one person. The freight ( passenger ) traffic provides a quantitative measure to show how the transport industry serves the national economy and people, and is also an important indicator for planning the transport industry and for studying the development scale and speed of the transport industry.

**Freight Ton-kilometers ( Passenger-kilometers )** refer to the sum of the products of the volume of transported cargo ( passengers ) multiplying by the transport distance. It is an important indicator to reflect the achievement of transportation industry. Normally, the shortest distance between the departure station and the destination station (i.e., the payable distance ) is the basis to calculate the freight ton-kilometers. This is an important indicator to show the total results of the transport industry, to prepare and examine the transport plan and to measure the efficiency, the labour productivity and the unit cost of transport.

**Volume of Freight Handled in Ports** refers to the volume of cargo passing in and out the harbor area of the major coastal ports and having been loaded and unloaded. The volume includes that of the postal matters, registered luggage and fuels, materials and fresh water as supplies of the ships. The volume of freight handled may be classified by direction of flow as freight for import and freight for export, or by nature of cargo as freight for domestic trade and freight for foreign trade. As an important indicator, the volume of freight handled by type of cargo and by main flow direction reflects the production capacity of ports.

**Business Volume of Post Services** refers to the total amount of post services or other services provided by the post departments for society. The calculation method is that the physical quantity of each type of postal communication service business is multiplied by the corresponding constant unit price, and the monetary quantity of each type of service is obtained and summed up. This indicator reflects the total results of the development of postal communication services in a certain period of time, and is a comprehensive indicator for observing the general trend of development and change of postal communication services.

**Business Volume of Express Services** refers to the total number of various types of express delivery services received and received by the enterprise, and the enterprises entrusted by the user are responsible for statistics. Including domestic city express business volume, domestic off-site express business volume, Hong Kong, Macao and Taiwan express business volume, international express business volume.

**Business Volume of Telecommunication Services** refers to the total number of telecommunication services provided by telecommunication enterprises in the form of money for the society. Including the total volume of fixed voice services, fixed data and total Internet services, fixed value-added and other services, total mobile voice services, total mobile data and Internet services, mobile value-added and other business.

**Long-Distance Cable Line Length** refers to the actual length of the long-distance cable line. The overhead optical cable is counted according to the actual length of the pole. The underground and underwater cables are counted according to the length of the trench.

**Local Network Trunk Cable Length** Refers to the actual length of the cable line between the service nodes in the local network and from the starting point to the destination. The overhead optical cable is counted according to the actual length of the pole. The underground and underwater optical cables are counted according to the length of the buried optical cable.

**Number of Mobile Phone Base Stations** refers to the wireless transceiver device serving the cell, handles the wireless communication between the base station and the mobile station, and acts as a relay between the mobile switch and the mobile station to monitor the total number of devices for wireless transmission quality.

**Number of 3G Mobile Phone Base Stations** refers to the number of NoFe–B actually used on the 3G mobile communication network of the telecommunications enterprise at the end of the reporting period. It includes TF–SCFMA base station, WCFMA base station, and CFMA2000 base station.

**Number of 4G Mobile Phone Base Stations** refers to the number of Node–B actually used on the 4G mobile communication network of the telecommunications enterprise at the end of the reporting period. It includes TD–LTE base station and FDD–LTE base station.

**Internet Broadband Access Port** refers to the number of broadband access ports that are actually installed and operated for accessing Internet users.

# 批发和零售业 15

## WHOLESALE AND RETAIL TRADES

# 简 要 说 明

**一、本篇资料的主要内容**

本篇资料主要反映了全市批发和零售业经营情况和效益情况，主要包括批发和零售业商品流转及财务情况、亿元以上商品交易市场、社会消费品零售总额等内容。

**二、本篇资料的来源**

本篇资料来源于批发和零售业统计年报和定期报表统计资料。由市统计局外经贸易统计处整理提供。

# Brief Introduction

***I. Main Content***

Data in this chapter show the development of wholesale and retail trade of the whole city, mainly including the circulation and financial indices of commodities in the wholesale and retail trade, commodity exchange markets over 100 million yuan, Total retail sales of consumer goods, etc.

***II. Source of Data***

Data in this chapter are based on annual report and regular reports of wholesale and retail trade.

Data in this chapter are prepared and compiled by the Division of Trade and External Economic Relations Statistics of Qingdao Municipal Bureau of Statistics.

# 15-1 社会消费品零售总额（1985-2018 年）

TOTAL RETAIL SALES OF CONSUMER GOODS（1985-2018）

单位：万元（10 000 yuan）

| 年份<br>Year | 消费品零售总额<br>Total Retail Sales of Consumer Goods | 批发零售业<br>Wholesale and Retail Trades | 住宿餐饮业<br>Hotels and Catering Services | 其他行业<br>Othres |
|---|---|---|---|---|
| 1985 | 307222 | 231477 | 16996 | 18753 |
| 1986 | 364091 | 269418 | 21384 | 27118 |
| 1987 | 432569 | 310658 | 23319 | 32617 |
| 1988 | 590538 | 434572 | 32304 | 45449 |
| 1989 | 619941 | 450812 | 34083 | 56303 |
| 1990 | 658264 | 484770 | 35568 | 67863 |
| 1991 | 760562 | 566767 | 43320 | 56812 |
| 1992 | 888411 | 666911 | 53045 | 67392 |
| 1993 | 1384533 | 1031794 | 80077 | 96759 |
| 1994 | 1880654 | 1352073 | 127313 | 202937 |
| 1995 | 2376776 | 1637349 | 186028 | 305947 |
| 1996 | 2708527 | 1873008 | 220322 | 321325 |
| 1997 | 3008981 | 2105728 | 241928 | 361248 |
| 1998 | 3368736 | 2322209 | 277696 | 411210 |
| 1999 | 3762754 | 2715635 | 315307 | 391388 |
| 2000 | 4282871 | 3116990 | 387944 | 403854 |
| 2001 | 4911735 | 3561731 | 507012 | 433851 |
| 2002 | 5574364 | 4162676 | 638358 | 402654 |
| 2003 | 6455113 | 5283584 | 849032 | 322497 |
| 2004 | 7475022 | 6266750 | 1017193 | 191079 |
| 2005 | 8701057 | 7304660 | 1176539 | 219858 |
| 2006 | 10163457 | 8458226 | 1443120 | 262111 |
| 2007 | 12162246 | 9995772 | 1837754 | 328720 |
| 2008 | 14922153 | 12995842 | 1554086 | 372225 |
| 2009 | 17302231 | 14232954 | 2549203 | 520074 |
| 2010 | 19611331 | 17151504 | 2459827 | |
| 2011 | 23023703 | 20153079 | 2870624 | |
| 2012 | 26356180 | 23043005 | 3313175 | |
| 2013 | 29868133 | 26142405 | 3725728 | |
| 2014 | 33617217 | 29435856 | 4181361 | |
| 2015 | 37136940 | 32459539 | 4677401 | |
| 2016 | 41049345 | 35840499 | 5208846 | |
| 2017 | 45410086 | 39669946 | 5740140 | |
| 2018 | 48424565 | 42209564 | 6215001 | |

注：1. 自 2003 年开始消费品零售总额不再包括制造业零售额和农民对非农居民的销售额分组。
2. 自 2005 年起，住宿业从其它行业调整到住宿餐饮业中。
3. 根据第二次经济普查结果，对 2005 年以来的历史数据进行了调整。

Note：1.Since 2003，retail sales of manufacturing and retail sales of rural residents to urban residents are excluded in total retail sales of consumer goods.
2.Since 2005，hotels is adjusted to hotels and catering services from the others.
3.Historical data since 2005 have been adjusted according to results of the Second China Economic Census.

# 15-2 分市、区社会消费品零售总额（2018 年）
TOTAL RETAIL SALES OF CONSUMER GOODS BY REGION（2018）

单位：万元（10 000 yuan）

| 市、区名称 | Region | 消费品零售总额<br>Total Retail Sales of Consumer Gddos | 按行业分 | |
|---|---|---|---|---|
| | | | 批发零售业<br>Wholesale and Retail Trades | 住宿餐饮业<br>Hotels and Catering Services |
| **全　市** | **Whole Municipality** | **48424565** | **42209564** | **6215001** |
| 市南区 | Shinan District | 6237329 | 5088017 | 1149312 |
| 市北区 | Shibei District | 7748227 | 6830252 | 917976 |
| 李沧区 | Licang District | 4629130 | 4172420 | 456710 |
| 崂山区 | Laoshan District | 2720213 | 2535450 | 184763 |
| 黄岛区 | Huangdao District | 6247883 | 5268752 | 979131 |
| 城阳区 | Chengyang District | 2758130 | 2410785 | 347346 |
| 即墨区 | Jimo District | 4981556 | 4504040 | 477516 |
| 胶州市 | Jiaozhou | 4877139 | 4232948 | 644191 |
| 平度市 | Pingdu | 4415180 | 3888430 | 526750 |
| 莱西市 | Laixi | 3429782 | 2932326 | 497456 |
| 红岛经济区 | Qingdao National Hightech Industrial Development Zone | 194745 | 166096 | 28648 |
| 保税港区 | Qingdao Free Trade Port Area of China | 185250 | 180048 | 5202 |

# 15-3 限额以上批发和零售业商品购销存总额（2018年）
TOTAL RETAIL SALES OF CONSUMER GOODS BY REGION （2018）

单位：万元（10 000 yuan）

| 项目 | Item | 商品销售总额 Total Sales Value | #批发总额 Wholesale Value | 零售总额 Retail Value | 库存总额 Stock |
|---|---|---|---|---|---|
| **总　计** | **Total** | **76342679.1** | **61087847.5** | **15254831.6** | **3801103.4** |
| 国有企业 | State-owned Enterprises | 96408.5 | 73158.0 | 23250.5 | 30739.9 |
| 集体企业 | Collective-owned Enterprises | 82616.1 | 77151.5 | 5464.6 | 654.2 |
| 其它企业 | Other Enterprises | 76163654.5 | 60937538.0 | 15226116.5 | 3769709.3 |
| 农、林、牧产品批发 | Wholesale of Farm Produce and Livestock Products | 1084294.8 | 1079890.4 | 4404.4 | 93370.3 |
| 食品、饮料及烟草制品批发 | Wholesale of Food, Beverages and Tobaccos | 4835490.1 | 4670466.9 | 165023.2 | 348306.0 |
| 纺织、服装及家庭用品批发 | Retail of Textiles, Garments and Daily Consumer Articles | 12795566.5 | 12449014.2 | 346552.3 | 279673.4 |
| 文化、体育用品及器材批发 | Wholesale of Culture, Sports Appliances and Equipments | 866029.1 | 836483.4 | 29545.7 | 73050.4 |
| 医药及医疗器材批发 | Wholesale of Medicines and Medical Appliances | 2036980.6 | 2032380.7 | 4599.9 | 176027.0 |
| 矿产品、建材及化工产品批发 | Wholesale of Machinery, Hardware and Electronic Equipment | 33066883.7 | 32910530.0 | 156353.7 | 931994.6 |
| 机械设备、五金产品及电子产品批发 | Wholesale of Machinery, Hardware and Electronic Equipment | 5090647.4 | 5008510.0 | 82137.4 | 317143.7 |
| 贸易经纪与代理 | Trade Broker and Agency | 200838.9 | 200838.9 | 0.0 | 5942.3 |
| 其它批发业 | Other Wholesale not Classified Elsewhere | 675459.6 | 675442.5 | 17.1 | 12198.9 |
| 综合零售 | Integrated Retail Trade | 3337941.6 | 308.5 | 3337633.1 | 232903.3 |
| 食品、饮料及烟草制品专门零售 | Retail of Food, Beverages and Tobaccos | 223381.5 | 21041.6 | 202339.9 | 25829.4 |
| 纺织、服装及日用品专门零售 | Retail of Textiles, Garments and Daily Consumer Articles | 1255013.2 | 253795.6 | 1001217.6 | 301935.9 |
| 文化、体育用品及器材专门零售 | Retail of Culture, Sports Appliances and Equipments | 281654.6 | 68185.4 | 213469.2 | 72567.6 |
| 医药及医疗器材专门零售 | Retail of Medicines and Medical Appliances | 770555.7 | 73987.1 | 696568.6 | 85511.9 |
| 汽车、摩托车、燃料及零配件专门零售 | Retail of Motor Vehicles, Motorcycles, Fuel and Parts | 5603640.3 | 367721.1 | 5235919.2 | 503740.5 |
| 家用电器及电子产品专门零售 | Retail of Household Electric Appliances and Electronic Products | 793738.9 | 72940.1 | 720798.8 | 73984.2 |
| 五金、家具及室内装饰材料专门零售 | Retail of Hardware, Furniture and Decoration Materials | 230022.5 | 129964.5 | 100058.0 | 13781.3 |
| 货摊、无店铺及其他零售业 | Non-shop and Other Retails | 3194540.1 | 236346.6 | 2958193.5 | 253142.7 |

# 15-4 限额以上批发和零售业商品分类销售额（2018 年）

SALES VALUE OF ENTERPRISES ABOVE DESIGNATED SIZE OF WHOLESALE AND RETAIL TRADES BY CATEGORY OF COMMODITIES（2018）

单位：万元（10 000 yuan）

| 项目 | Item | 销售总额 Total Sales Value | #批发总额 Wholesale Value | 零售总额 Retail Value |
|---|---|---|---|---|
| **销售总额** | **Total Sales Value** | **71119193.9** | **55846423.9** | **15272770** |
| 1. 粮油、食品类 | Grain & Oil and Food | 3783984 | 2192273.7 | 1591710.3 |
| 其中：粮油类 | Grain and Oil | 669575.8 | 495100.1 | 174475.7 |
| 肉禽蛋类 | Meat，Poultry and Eggs | 589878.3 | 379430.4 | 210447.9 |
| 水产品类 | Aquatic Products | 210369.6 | 145401.9 | 64967.7 |
| 蔬菜类 | Vegetable and Fruit | 206814.8 | 133619 | 73195.8 |
| 干鲜果品类 | Dried and Fresh Fruit | 627590.3 | 449122.3 | 178468 |
| 2. 饮料类 | Beverages | 258957.3 | 111817.1 | 147140.2 |
| 3. 烟酒类 | Tobacco and Liquor | 1866552.8 | 1552974.6 | 313578.2 |
| 4. 服装、鞋帽、针纺织品类 | Clothing，Shoes，Hats and Textiles | 3922632.7 | 2239862 | 1682770.7 |
| （1）服装类 | Clothing | 2031715.5 | 994685.1 | 1037030.4 |
| （2）鞋帽类 | Shoes and Hats | 745889.4 | 181242.7 | 564646.7 |
| （3）针纺织品类 | Knitwear and Textiles | 1145027.8 | 1063934.2 | 81093.6 |
| 5. 化妆品类 | Cosmetics | 317800.6 | 92467.5 | 225333.1 |
| 6. 金银珠宝类 | Gold，Silver and Jewellery | 533685.9 | 145144.8 | 388541.1 |
| 7. 日用品类 | Articles for Daily Use | 971334.7 | 314559.4 | 656775.3 |
| 其中：儿童玩具类 | Children toys | 28345.5 | 1514.8 | 26830.7 |
| 8. 五金、电料类 | Hardware and Electrical Materials | 351275.2 | 331523.8 | 19751.4 |
| 9. 体育、娱乐用品类 | Sports and Recreation Articles | 117429.9 | 18496.1 | 98933.8 |
| 其中：照相器材类 | Photographic Apparatus | 7961.6 | 0.3 | 7961.3 |
| 10. 书报杂志类 | Newspapers and Magazines | 167084 | 62802.9 | 104281.1 |
| 11. 电子出版物及音像制品类 | E-journals and Video Products | 6487.1 | 2049.7 | 4437.4 |
| 12. 家用电器和音像器材类 | Household Appliances and Video Appilances | 12481134.8 | 9648613.2 | 2832521.6 |
| 13. 中西药品类 | Traditional Chinese and Western Medicines | 2280243.1 | 1618977.2 | 661265.9 |
| 其中：西药类 | Western Medicines | 1858749.8 | 1379207.4 | 479542.4 |
| 中草药及中成药类 | Traditional Chinese Medicines | 204662.2 | 85904.2 | 118758 |
| 14. 文化办公用品类 | Cultural and Offices Appliances | 970275.5 | 561249.3 | 409026.2 |
| 其中：计算机及其配套产品 | Computer and Related Products | 430480.3 | 364463.3 | 66017 |
| 15. 家具类 | Furniture | 106811.7 | 10189.7 | 96622 |
| 16. 通讯器材类 | Communication Appliances | 738999.8 | 416209 | 322790.8 |
| 17. 煤炭及制品类 | Coal and Related Products | 3529013.2 | 3521048.8 | 7964.4 |
| 18. 木材及制品类 | Wood and Wooden Products | 617248.3 | 617248.3 | 0 |
| 19. 石油及制品类 | Petroleum and Related Products | 11343606.7 | 9557981.9 | 1785624.8 |
| 20. 化工材料及制品类 | Chemical Materials and Related Products | 5059435.6 | 5059435.6 | 0 |
| 其中：化肥类 | Fertilizers | 338366.1 | 338366.1 | 0 |
| 21. 金属材料类 | Metal Materials | 11886594.9 | 11886594.9 | 0 |
| 22. 建筑及装潢材料类 | Building and Decoration Materials | 513245.7 | 446892.3 | 66353.4 |
| 23. 机电产品及设备类 | Mechanical and El[illegible]ucts | 1735137 | 1688427.8 | 46709.2 |
| 其中：农机类 | Agricultural Mac[illegible]eries | 17291 | 17291 | 0 |
| 24. 汽车类 | Automobiles | 4744664.2 | 1068713.9 | 3675950.3 |
| 25. 种子饲料类 | Seeds and Feedstuff | 625634.2 | 625634.2 | 0 |
| 26. 棉麻类 | Cotton，Hemp | 441130.2 | 440930.3 | 199.9 |
| 27. 其他类 | Others | 1748794.8 | 1614305.9 | 134488.9 |

注：此表为定期报表数据。
Note：The data are from regular reports.

# 15-5 限额以上批发业财务状况（2018 年）

FINANCIAL POSITION OF ENTERPRISES ABOVE DESIGNATED SIZE OF WHOLESALE TRADE（2018）

单位：万元（10 000 yuan）

| 指标 | Indicator | 合计 Total | 国有经济 State-owned Enterprises | 集体经济 Collective-owned Enterprises | 外商及港澳台经济 Foreign Funded Enterprises and Enterprises with Funds from Hong Kong，Macao and Taiwan | 其它 Other Enterprises |
|---|---|---|---|---|---|---|
| **单位数** | **Number of Emterprises** | **1338** | **7** | **2** | **55** | **1274** |
| **年末资产负债** | **Year-end Assets-Liability** | | | | | |
| 资产总计 | Total Assets | 25029523 | 91205 | 44872 | 1742491 | 23150955 |
| 流动资产合计 | Sub-total of Current Assets | 22873778 | 68608 | 43511 | 1334069 | 21427590 |
| 负债合计 | Total Liabilities | 20993961 | 63876 | 39760 | 1238454 | 19651870 |
| 所有者权益合计 | Total Owners' Equities | 4035562 | 27329 | 5112 | 504037 | 3499085 |
| **损益及分配** | **Loss，Profits and Distributon** | | | | | |
| 主营业务收入 | Revenue from Principal Business | 53664627 | 71530 | 66485 | 2427113 | 51099499 |
| 主营业务成本 | Cost of Principal Business | 51179104 | 70082 | 60342 | 2276379 | 48772302 |
| 主营业务税金及附加 | Taxes and Extra Charges on Principal Business | 191702 | 40 | 98 | 3877 | 187688 |
| 营业利润 | Profits from Principal Business | 517305 | -1297 | -1583 | 68095 | 452090 |
| 其他业务利润 | Profits from other Business | 81444 | 1149 | 125 | 2456 | 77714 |
| 销售费用 | Operating Costs | 1096177 | 1287 | 892 | 40184 | 1053814 |
| 管理费用 | Management Expenses | 564044 | 3092 | 6887 | 29129 | 524937 |
| 财务费用 | Financial Expenses | 227726 | 964 | -4 | 18560 | 208206 |
| 利润总额 | Total Profits | 554044 | 792 | -1584 | 71905 | 482931 |
| **经济效益** | **Economic Benefit** | | | | | |
| 商品经营费用率 % | Ratio of Operating Costs to Revenue from Principal Business | 2.04 | 1.80 | 1.34 | 1.66 | 2.06 |
| 商品销售利润率 % | Ratio of Profit to Sales Revenue | 1.03 | 1.11 | -2.38 | 2.96 | 0.95 |

## 15-6 限额以上零售业财务状况（2018 年）
FINANCIAL POSITION OF ENTERPRISES ABOVE DESIGNATED SIZE OF RETAIL TRADE (2018)

单位：万元（10 000 yuan）

| 指标 | Indicator | 合计 Total | 国有经济 State-owned Enterprises | 集体经济 Collective-owned Enterprises | 外商及港澳台经济 Foreign Funded Enterprises and Enterprises with Funds from Hong Kong，Macao and Taiwan | 其它 Other Enterprises |
|---|---|---|---|---|---|---|
| **单位数** | **Number of Emterprises** | **725** | **5** | **2** | **40** | **678** |
| **年末资产负债** | **Year-end Assets-Liability** | | | | | |
| 资产总计 | Total Assets | 7222060 | 26359 | 2668 | 908207 | 6284825 |
| 流动资产合计 | Sub-total of Current Assets | 5012891 | 24153 | 2587 | 716855 | 4269296 |
| 负债合计 | Total Liabilities | 5667847 | 18514 | 1809 | 642365 | 5005160 |
| 所有者权益合计 | Total Owners' Equities | 1941127 | 7846 | 860 | 265842 | 1666579 |
| **损益及分配** | **Loss，Profits and Distributon** | | | | | |
| 主营业务收入 | Revenue from Principal Business | 13548768 | 19798 | 4846 | 1870188 | 11653936 |
| 主营业务成本 | Cost of Principal Business | 11980012 | 15587 | 4185 | 1535994 | 10424246 |
| 主营业务税金及附加 | Taxes and Extra Charges on Principal Business | 41045 | 74 | 14 | 10658 | 30298 |
| 营业利润 | Profits from Principal Business | 181965 | 2049 | 303 | 68763 | 110850 |
| 其他业务利润 | Profits from other Business | 152667 | 0 | 231 | 39228 | 113208 |
| 销售费用 | Operating Costs | 992239 | 167 | 82 | 192204 | 799786 |
| 管理费用 | Management Expenses | 421599 | 1960 | 259 | 103755 | 315626 |
| 财务费用 | Financial Expenses | 70396 | 98 | 3 | 2320 | 67974 |
| 利润总额 | Total Profits | 182252 | 2145 | 302 | 69444 | 110361 |
| **经济效益** | **Economic Benefit** | | | | | |
| 商品经营费用率 % | Ratio of Operating Costs to Revenue from Principal Business | 7.32 | 0.84 | 1.69 | 10.28 | 6.86 |
| 商品销售利润率 % | Ratio of Profit to Sales Revenue | 1.35 | 10.83 | 6.23 | 3.71 | 0.95 |

# 15-7 分市、区城乡亿元商品交易市场分布情况（2018年）
BASIC STATISTICS ON COMMODITY EXCHANGE MARKETS OF TRANSACTION VALUE OVER 100 NILLION YUAN BY REGION (2018)

| 市、区名称 | Region | 亿元商品交易市场数量（个） Number of Commodity Exchange Markets of Transaction Value over 100 Million Yuan (unit) | | | 亿元商品交易市场成交额（亿元） Turnover of Commodity Exchange Markets of Transaction Value over 100 Million yuan (100 million yuan) | | |
|---|---|---|---|---|---|---|---|
| | | 合计 Total | #综合市场 Integrated Markets | #专业市场 Special Markets | 合计 Total | #综合市场 Integrated Markets | #专业市场 Special Markets |
| **全　市** | **Whole Municipality** | **55** | **11** | **44** | **1250.8** | **464.8** | **786.0** |
| 市南区 | Shinan District | | | | | | |
| 市北区 | Shibei District | 7 | 1 | 6 | 79.4 | 47.0 | 32.4 |
| 李沧区 | Licang District | 6 | 1 | 5 | 46.9 | 14.8 | 32.1 |
| 崂山区 | Laoshan District | 2 | | 2 | 2.9 | | 2.9 |
| 黄岛区 | Huangdao District | 7 | 2 | 5 | 69.2 | 22.0 | 47.2 |
| 城阳区 | Chengyang District | 2 | 1 | 1 | 219.4 | 218.3 | 1.1 |
| 即墨区 | Jimo District | 10 | 1 | 9 | 611.2 | 137.2 | 474.0 |
| 胶州市 | Jiaozhou | 11 | 3 | 8 | 119.1 | 8.3 | 110.8 |
| 平度市 | Pingdu | 9 | 2 | 7 | 90.6 | 17.3 | 73.3 |
| 莱西市 | Laixi | | | | | | |
| 红岛经济区 | Qingdao National Hightech Industrial Development Zone | | | | | | |
| 保税港区 | Qingdao Free Trade Port Area of China | 1 | | 1 | 12.1 | | 12.1 |

# 主要统计指标解释

**社会消费品零售总额** 指各种经济类型的批发和零售业、住宿和餐饮业以及其他行业对城乡居民和社会集团的消费品零售额总和。该指标从2003年开始不再包括制造业零售额和农民对非农居民的零售额。

**商品购进总额** 指从本企业（单位）以外的单位和个人购进（包括从国外直接进口）作为转卖或加工后转卖的商品。这个指标反映批发零售贸易业从国内、国外市场上购进商品的总量。商品购进总额包括：（1）从工农业生产者购进的商品；（2）从出版社、报社的出版发行部门购进的图书、杂志和报纸；（3）从各种类型的批发零售贸易企业（单位）购进的商品；（4）从其他单位购进的商品，如从机关、团体、企业、单位购进的剩余物资，从餐饮业、服务业购进的商品，从海关、市场管理部门购进的缉私和没收的商品，向居民收购的废旧商品等；（5）从国（境）外直接进口的商品，但不包括企业（单位）为自身经营用和未通过买卖行为而收入的商品以及销售退回、商品损益等。

**商品销售总额** 指对本企业（单位）以外的单位和个人出售（包括对国（境）外直接出口）的商品。这个指标反映批发零售贸易业在国内市场上销售商品以及出口商品的总量。商品销售总额包括：（1）售给城乡居民和社会集团消费用的商品；（2）售给工业、农业、建筑业、运输邮电业、批发零售贸易业、餐饮业、服务业等作为生产、经营使用的商品；（3）售给批发零售贸易业作为转卖或加工后转卖的商品；（4）对国（境）外直接出口的商品。不包括：出售本企业（单位）自用的废旧包装用品，未通过买卖行为付出的商品，经本单位介绍，由买卖双方直接结算，本单位只收取手续费的业务，购货退出的商品以及商品损耗和损失等。

# Explanatory Notes on Main Statistical Indicators

**Total Retail Sales of Consumer Goods** refers to the sum of retail sales of consumer goods sold by all sectors of the national economy to urban and rural residents and social groups.Sectors of the national economy include wholesale and retail trade, accommodation and catering trade and others.Since 2003, retail sales of manufacture and retail sales of rural residents to urban residents are excluded in total retail sales.

**Total Purchases of Commodities** refer to the total value of purchases of commodities by the enterprises (establishments) from other establishments or individuals (including direct import from abroad) for the purpose of re-selling, either with or without further processing of the commodities purchased. This indicator is used to show the total value of purchases of commodities by wholesale and retail establishments from domestic and overseas markets. The total purchases include: (1) agricultural and industrial products purchased from producers; (2) books, magazines and newspapers purchased from distribution departments of the publishers; (3) commodities purchased from wholesale and retail establishments of different status of registration; (4) commodities purchased from other units, such as surplus materials purchased from government agencies, enterprises or institutions, commodities purchased from catering and service establishments, confiscated goods purchased from customs authorities or market management agencies, second-hand goods and wastes purchased from residents; and (5) commodities directly imported from abroad. Excluded are commodities purchased by enterprises (establishments) for use in their own business operation, commodities obtained without buying or selling procedures, rejected commodities, etc.

**Total Sales of Commodities** refer to value of commodities sold by the establishments to other establishments and individuals (including direct export). This indicator is used to show the total value of sales of commodities at domestic markets and export. The total sales include: (1) commodities sold to urban and rural residents and social groups for their consumption; (2) commodities sold to establishments in industry, agriculture, construction, transportation, post and telecommunications, wholesale and retail trades, hotels and catering services, and public utility for their production and operation; (3) commodities sold to wholesale and retail establishments for re-selling, with or without further processing; and (4) commodities for direct export to other countries. Excluded are selling of waste packaging materials used by the establishments (units) themselves, commodities transferred without buying or selling procedures, commission income from brokerage in transactions for which settlement is directly handled by buyers and sellers, rejected commodities in the purchase, loss in commodities, etc.

# 住宿、餐饮业和旅游 16

## HOTELS，CATERING SERVICES AND TOURISM

# 简要说明

## 一、本篇资料的主要内容

本篇资料主要反映了全市住宿和餐饮业的经营情况和效益情况以及旅游的基本情况，主要包括住宿和餐饮业经营情况和财务情况、涉外以及国内旅游基本情况等方面的内容。

## 二、本篇资料的来源

本篇资料中住宿和餐饮业经营情况和财务情况资料来源于住宿和餐饮业统计年报和定期报表统计资料；旅游资料来源于市旅游局。由市统计局外经贸易统计处整理提供。

# Brief Introduction

## *I. Main Content*

Data in this chapter show the development of wholesale and retail trade and tourism of the whole city, mainly including the circulation and financial indices of hotels and catering services, international and domestic tourism, etc.

## *II. Source of Data*

Data on hotels and catering services are based on annual report and regular reports of hotels and catering services. Data on international tourism are provided by Qingdao Tourism Bureau. The above data are prepared and compiled by the Division of Trade and External Economic Relations Statistics of Qingdao Municipal Bureau of Statistics.

# 16-1 限额以上住宿和餐饮业法人企业经营情况（2018年）
## BUSINESS CONDITIONS OF ENTERPRISES OF HOTELS AND CATERING SERVICES ABOVE DESIGNATED SIZE (2018)

单位：万元（10 000 yuan）

| 项目 | Item | 营业额 Turnover | #客房收入 Income from Guest Rooms | 餐费收入 Catering Income | 商品销售收入 Income from Commodity Sales | 其他收入 Other Income |
|---|---|---|---|---|---|---|
| 总　计 | **Total** | **1134264.3** | **288103.4** | **747476.5** | **22255.5** | **76428.9** |
| 一、住宿业 | **Hotels** | **522013.4** | **248898.4** | **194782.3** | **12528.9** | **65803.8** |
| 国有企业 | State-owned Enterprises | 76932.7 | 31876.7 | 34262.8 | 913.0 | 9880.2 |
| 集体企业 | Collective-owned Enterprises | | | | | |
| 其他企业 | Other Enterprises | 445080.7 | 217021.7 | 160519.5 | 11615.9 | 55923.6 |
| 独立门店 | Freestanding Stores | 453418.4 | 217839.5 | 181900.8 | 12356.4 | 41321.7 |
| 连锁总店 | General Chain Stores | | | | | |
| 连锁直营店 | Chain Store | 2081.2 | 1974.4 | 46.3 | 22.5 | 38.0 |
| 连锁加盟店 | Chain Store | 3974.1 | 3679.5 | 27.4 | 45.7 | 221.5 |
| 其他 | Others | 62539.7 | 25405.0 | 12807.8 | 104.3 | 24222.6 |
| 五星 | Five Star Class | 132615.8 | 60733.7 | 58312.5 | 1583.4 | 11986.2 |
| 四星 | Four Star class | 99476.3 | 43454.9 | 47584.0 | 911.5 | 7525.9 |
| 三星 | Three Star class | 46530.2 | 22493.1 | 19791.3 | 1096.8 | 3149.0 |
| 二星 | Two Star class | 1089.8 | 304.6 | 753.9 | 31.3 | 0.0 |
| 其他 | Others | 242301.3 | 121912.1 | 68340.6 | 8905.9 | 43142.7 |
| 二、餐饮业 | **Catering Services** | **612250.9** | **39205.0** | **552694.2** | **9726.6** | **10625.1** |
| 国有企业 | State-owned Enterprises | 10546.4 | 5821.8 | 4101.9 | 400.6 | 222.1 |
| 集体企业 | Collective-owned Enterprises | 3297.3 | 533.1 | 795.8 | 1931.1 | 37.3 |
| 其他企业 | Other Enterprises | 598407.2 | 32850.1 | 547796.5 | 7394.9 | 10365.7 |
| 独立门店 | Freestanding Stores | 241633.5 | 34189.8 | 191126.3 | 5735.2 | 10582.2 |
| 连锁总店 | General Chain Stores | 268364.2 | | 266313.3 | 2050.9 | |
| 连锁直营店 | Chain Store | 7714.5 | | 7684.6 | 29.9 | |
| 连锁加盟店 | Chain Store | 41755.2 | | 41755.2 | | |
| 其他 | Others | 52783.5 | 5015.2 | 45814.8 | 1910.6 | 42.9 |

# 16-2 限额以上住宿业财务状况（2018 年）
FINANCIAL SITUATION OF HOTELS ABOVE DESIGNATED SIZE（2018）

单位：万元（10 000 yuan）

| 指标 | Indicator | 合计 Total | 国有经济 State-owned Enterprises | 集体经济 Collective-owned Enterprises | 外商及港澳台经济 Foreign Funded Enterprises and Enterprises with Funds from Hong Kong，Macao and Taiwan | 其它 Other Enterprises |
|---|---|---|---|---|---|---|
| **单位数** | **Number of Emterprises** | **181** | **15** | | **11** | **155** |
| **年末资产负债** | **Year-end Assets-Liability** | | | | | |
| 资产总计 | Total Assets | 1270184 | 102633 | | 322699 | 844852 |
| 流动资产合计 | Sub-total of Current Assets | 481917 | 45066 | | 68056 | 368795 |
| 负债合计 | Total Liabilities | 956162 | 41343 | | 268130 | 646689 |
| 所有者权益合计 | Total Owners' Equities | 314021 | 61289 | | 54569 | 198163 |
| **损益及分配** | **Loss，Profits and Distributon** | | | | | |
| 主营业务收入 | Revenue from Principal Business | 483401 | 71926 | | 92986 | 318488 |
| 主营业务成本 | Cost of Principal Business | 171899 | 18147 | | 35359 | 118392 |
| 主营业务税金及附加 | Taxes and Extra Charges on Principal Business | 9199 | 948 | | 3135 | 5117 |
| 营业利润 | Profits from Principal Business | -6896 | 56 | | 607 | -7559 |
| 其他业务利润 | Profits from other Business | 4352 | 2386 | | 86 | 1880 |
| 销售费用 | Operating Costs | 144674 | 34287 | | 18074 | 92313 |
| 管理费用 | Management Expenses | 151291 | 20328 | | 36401 | 94563 |
| 财务费用 | Financial Expenses | 20651 | 95 | | 4451 | 16105 |
| 利润总额 | Total Profits | -5139 | 1064 | | 116 | -6318 |
| **其他** | **Others** | | | | | |
| 应付职工薪酬 | Total Wages Payble in This Year | 140147 | 30803 | | 27342 | 82001 |
| 主营业务利润率 | Profitability of Principal | -1.06 | 1.48 | | 0.12 | -1.98 |

# 16-3 限额以上餐饮业财务状况（2018 年）
FINANCIAL SITUATION OF CATERING SERVICES ABOVE DESIGNATED SIZE（2018）

单位：万元（10 000 yuan）

| 指标 | Indicator | 合计 Total | 国有经济 State-owned Enterprises | 集体经济 Collective-owned Enterprises | 外商及港澳台经济 Foreign Funded Enterprises and Enterprises with Funds from Hong Kong，Macao and Taiwan | 其它 Other Enterprises |
|---|---|---|---|---|---|---|
| **单位数** | **Number of Emterprises** | **187** | **6** | **2** | **18** | **161** |
| **年末资产负债** | **Year-end Assets-Liability** | | | | | |
| 资产总计 | Total Assets | 602422 | 15541 | 1030 | 145903 | 439948 |
| 流动资产合计 | Sub-total of Current Assets | 358413 | 10675 | 933 | 49122 | 297683 |
| 负债合计 | Total Liabilities | 498347 | 6325 | 993 | 109521 | 381508 |
| 所有者权益合计 | Total Owners' Equities | 104075 | 9216 | 37 | 36383 | 58440 |
| **损益及分配** | **Loss，Profits and Distributon** | | | | | |
| 主营业务收入 | Revenue from Principal Business | 572329 | 8995 | 3013 | 249664 | 310657 |
| 主营业务成本 | Cost of Principal Business | 288859 | 5594 | 2708 | 124323 | 156235 |
| 主营业务税金及附加 | Taxes and Extra Charges on Principal Business | 1619 | 97 | 7 | 284 | 1232 |
| 营业利润 | Profits from Principal Business | 29945 | -115 | 83 | 24930 | 5048 |
| 其他业务利润 | Profits from other Business | 965 | 5 | | 166 | 795 |
| 销售费用 | Operating Costs | 170827 | 1514 | 200 | 73708 | 95406 |
| 管理费用 | Management Expenses | 78972 | 2737 | 17 | 26770 | 49447 |
| 财务费用 | Financial Expenses | 5049 | -27 | -1 | 1478 | 3599 |
| 利润总额 | Total Profits | 29684 | -111 | 83 | 24845 | 4868 |
| **其他** | **Others** | | | | | |
| 应付职工薪酬 | Total Wages Payble in This Year | 128547 | 2824.0 | 362 | 46232 | 79128 |
| 主营业务利润率 | Profitability of Principal | 5.19 | -1.23 | 2.74 | 9.95 | 1.57 |

# 16-4 入境旅游人数（2000-2018 年）
NUMBER OF OVERSEA VISITOR ARRIVALS（2000-2018）

| 项目 | Item | 2000 年 | 2005 年 | 2008 年 | 2009 年 |
|---|---|---|---|---|---|
| **总计** | **Total** | **260592** | **684407** | **800455** | **1000670** |
| **一、外国人** | **Foreigner** | **177098** | **596177** | **697391** | **801424** |
| # 韩国 | Korea | 69878 | 295111 | 340648 | 363181 |
| 日本 | Japan | 67215 | 177121 | 210090 | 261553 |
| 美国 | United States | 10384 | 23284 | 28998 | 28745 |
| 俄罗斯 | Russia | 4820 | 12062 | 3774 | 9525 |
| 德国 | Germany | 3820 | 10646 | 11261 | 14735 |
| 新加坡 | Singapore | 6321 | 6060 | 10683 | 17453 |
| 英国 | United Kingdom | 2798 | 5744 | 10657 | 9103 |
| 加拿大 | Canada | 1865 | 4397 | 5467 | 7741 |
| 法国 | France | 2491 | 5166 | 6067 | 7030 |
| 意大利 | Italy | 1555 | 3963 | 3871 | 3747 |
| 澳大利亚 | Australia | 1817 | 4257 | 7940 | 6641 |
| 菲律宾 | Philippines | 7947 | 3459 | 2075 | 7800 |
| 泰国 | Thailand | 780 | 3261 | 2236 | 3685 |
| 印尼 | Indonesia | 1241 | 2349 | 1589 | 4221 |
| 新西兰 | New Zealand | 442 | 710 | 1161 | 2029 |
| **二、港澳和台湾同胞** | **Chinese Compatriots from Hong Kong，Macao and Taiwan** | **60367** | **88230** | **103064** | **199246** |

# 16-5 入境旅游收入（2000-2018 年）
EARNINGS FROM INTERNATIONAL TOURISM（2000-2018）

| 项目 | Item | 2000 年 | 2005 年 | 2008 年 | 2009 年 |
|---|---|---|---|---|---|
| **总计** | **Total** | **118164** | **340899** | **347645** | **377000** |
| 旅游购物 | Shopping | 20742 | 67047 | 66053 | 70763 |
| 住宿费 | Accommodation | 17443 | 37277 | 37198 | 41093 |
| 餐饮费 | Dining | 11223 | 33557 | 33374 | 36569 |
| 交通费 | Transportation | 35252 | 128112 | 9039 | 9877 |
| 邮电费 | Postal and Telecommunication | 5502 | 18394 | 17382 | 18812 |
| 文化娱乐费 | Culture and Entertainment | 6894 | 20240 | 20163 | 22394 |
| 游览 | Sightseeing | | | 18773 | 21037 |
| 其他 | Other Services | | 36272 | 145663 | 29745 |

单位：人次（person-time）

| 2010 年 | 2011 年 | 2012 年 | 2013 年 | 2014 年 | 2015 年 | 2016 年 | 2017 年 | 2018 年 |
|---|---|---|---|---|---|---|---|---|
| **1080511** | **1156391** | **1270113** | **1282814** | **1280526** | **1338098** | **1410494** | **1443715** | **1535733** |
| **826628** | **809043** | **877593** | **905415** | **951732** | **996191** | **1042213** | **1056800** | **1118860** |
| 382225 | 298096 | 338383 | 338191 | 366584 | 389832 | 68010 | 432430 | 451046 |
| 242082 | 216755 | 185613 | 146080 | 135179 | 140762 | 151832 | 164095 | 174147 |
| 35539 | 45842 | 48431 | 54178 | 57907 | 62771 | 68010 | 73905 | 79392 |
| 15793 | 15750 | 26432 | 26519 | 25356 | 28529 | 30534 | 32540 | 37053 |
| 21626 | 26178 | 26311 | 19014 | 21723 | 23425 | 25456 | 26636 | 28646 |
| 13444 | 16626 | 16316 | 16305 | 19975 | 21310 | 23713 | 25257 | 26060 |
| 17639 | 23955 | 28385 | 19496 | 22817 | 23812 | 26133 | 28006 | 28942 |
| 9279 | 12007 | 11678 | 9727 | 9483 | 10659 | 11592 | 12544 | 15473 |
| 11766 | 12019 | 15595 | 21422 | 17828 | 19388 | 21836 | 23507 | 25035 |
| 3867 | 7028 | 5622 | 5679 | 7705 | 8747 | 9234 | 10627 | 11559 |
| 8223 | 15465 | 16644 | 11149 | 15339 | 16798 | 18839 | 20304 | 21491 |
| 14140 | 14259 | 7546 | 18630 | 6668 | 7300 | 7891 | 8489 | 9837 |
| 2572 | 3271 | 2369 | 3692 | 4803 | 5331 | 5784 | 6628 | 7367 |
| 7863 | 8128 | 4571 | 10011 | 6568 | 5692 | 6220 | 7388 | 9816 |
| 1597 | 6265 | 6448 | 1452 | 2549 | 2872 | 3352 | 4230 | 7367 |
| **253883** | **347348** | **392520** | **377399** | **328794** | **342511** | **368281** | **386915** | **416873** |

单位：万元（10 000 yuan）

| 2010 年 | 2011 年 | 2012 年 | 2013 年 | 2014 年 | 2015 年 | 2016 年 | 2017 年 | 2018 年 |
|---|---|---|---|---|---|---|---|---|
| **399688** | **441171** | **519495** | **511158** | **503900** | **566742** | **656966** | **694103** | **798374** |
| 74104 | 80823 | 93872 | 94055 | 109246 | 122473 | 141970 | 129381 | 102192 |
| 43933 | 59823 | 59378 | 58577 | 62232 | 69879 | 81004 | 77184 | 150893 |
| 38747 | 40191 | 51378 | 51065 | 44041 | 49589 | 57483 | 68091 | 122950 |
| 145551 | 134425 | 170238 | 180945 | 160492 | 180791 | 209573 | 249113 | 273842 |
| 19081 | 16720 | 23014 | 22950 | 19400 | 21593 | 25031 | 33248 | 16766 |
| 24032 | 36132 | 32832 | 32103 | 33409 | 36271 | 42045 | 42201 | 62273 |
| 22978 | 51705 | 32832 | 32152 | 44192 | 49930 | 57879 | 40674 | 33532 |
| 31262 | 21353 | 55951 | 39311 | 30888 | 36216 | 41982 | 54211 | 35927 |

# 16-6 国内旅游人数及收入（2018 年）
NUMBER OF DOME STTC TOURISM INCOME（2018）

| 指标 | Indicator | 单位 | Unit | 2018 年 |
|---|---|---|---|---|
| 国内旅游人数 | Number of Domestic Toursts | 万人次 | 10000 person–times | 9848.94 |
| 1. 过夜旅游者人数 | Number of Overnight Tourists | 万人次 | 10000 person–times | 4855.06 |
| （1）旅游住宿设施国内旅游人数 | Domestic Tourists Staying Overnight at Hotels | 万人次 | 10000 person–times | 2135.26 |
| （2）住亲友家去景点的国内旅游人数 | Domestic Tourists Staying Overnight at Relatives and Friends' s Home | 万人次 | 10000 person–times | 2719.80 |
| 2. 不过夜旅游者（一日游人数） | Number of Same–day（One–day Sightseeing）Tourists | 万人次 | 10000 person–times | 4993.88 |
| 旅游景点接待一日游人数 | One–day Sightseeing Tourists Received by Tour Scenes | 万人次 | 10000 person–times | 4993.88 |
| （1）本地一日游人数 | Number of Local One–day Sightseeing Tourists | 万人次 | 10000 person–times | 2353.47 |
| （2）外地一日游人数 | Number of One–day Sightseeing Tourists from Outside Areas | 万人次 | 10000 person–times | 2640.41 |
| 国内旅游人均花费 | Per Capita Expenditure of Domestic Tourist | 元 | yuan | 1676.31 |
| 国内旅游收入 | Earings from Domestic Tourism | 亿元 | 100 million yuan | 1650.99 |
| 1. 接待过夜旅游者收入 | Earings from Overnight Tourists | 万元 | 10000 yuan | 14493800 |
| 2. 接待不过夜旅游者（一日游）收入 | Earings from Same–day（One–day Sightseeing）Tourists | 万元 | 10000 yuan | 2016100 |

# 主要统计指标解释

**住宿餐饮业营业额**　指住宿和餐饮业法人企业、产业活动单位在经营活动中因提供服务或销售商品等取得的收入，包括客房收入、餐费收入、商品销售收入和其他收入。客房收入指住宿和餐饮业法人企业、产业活动单位在经营活动中因提供住宿服务取得的客房收入。餐费收入指住宿和餐饮业法人企业、产业活动单位因为顾客提供就餐服务取得的收入，包括经烹饪、调制加工后出售的各种食品，如主食、炒菜、凉拌菜等的收入。商品销售收入指住宿和餐饮业法人企业、产业活动单位伴随服务而出售商品所取得的收入。其他收入指营业收入中除客房收入、餐费收入、商品销售收入以外的其他收入，包括娱乐、健身和商务服务等。

**国内旅游者**　是指不以谋求职业、获取报酬为目的，离开惯常居住环境，到国内其它地方从事参观、游览、度假等旅游活动（包括外出探亲、疗养、考察、参加会议和从事商务、科技、文化、教育、宗教活动过程中的旅游活动），出行距离超过 10 公里，出游时间超过 6 小时，但不超过 12 个月的我国大陆居民。

**入境旅游者**　指来我国参观、访问、旅行、探亲、访友、休养、考察、参加会议和从事经济、科技、文化、教育、体育、宗教等活动的外国人、华侨、港澳和台湾同胞的人数。不包括外国在我国的常驻机构，如领事馆、通讯社、企业办事处的工作人员；来我国常住的外国专家、留学生以及在岸逗留不过夜人员。

# Explanatory Notes on Main Statistical Indicators

**Business Revenue of Hotels and Catering Services**　refer to revenue received from providing services or selling commodities by corporate enterprises and establishments engaged in hotel and catering services，including income from hotel rooms，from catering services，from selling of commodities and from other services. Income from hotel rooms refers to income of corporate enterprises and establishments by providing lodging services. Income from catering services refers to income of corporate enterprises and establishments by providing catering services，including selling of cooked or prepared foods such as stable food，cooked dishes or cold dishes. Income from selling of commodities refers to income of corporate enterprises and establishments by selling commodities that accompany the services they provide. Income from other activities refers to income received other than income from hotel rooms，catering services or selling of commodities，such as income from providing recreation，fitness or business services.

**Domestic Tourists**　refers to residents in mainland China who are not for the purpose of seeking employment，remuneration，and leaving the usual living environment，elsewhere to engage in domestic visitors，sightseeing，vacation travel（including to go out to visit relatives，infirmary，observing，participate in the meeting and engage in business，science and technology，culture，education，religious activities in the course of tourism activities），trip distance of more than 10 km，trips longer than six hours，but not more than 12 months.

**Entrance Tourists**　refers to foreigners，overseas Chinese，Chinese compatriots from Hong Kong，Macao and Taiwan coming to China for sight-seeing，visits，tours，family reunions，vacations，study tours，conferences and other activities of a business，scientific and technological，cultural，educational and religious nature. It does not include representatives and employees of resident institutions of foreign countries in China such as embassies，consulates，news agencies and offices of foreign companies and organizations，nor does it include long-term foreign experts or students residing in China，or persons in transition without spending a night in China.

# 教育、科技和文化 17

EDUCATION SCIENCE & TECHNOLOY AND CULTURE

# 简 要 说 明

### 一、本篇资料的主要内容

本篇资料主要反映了全市教育、科技和文化事业基本情况。教育部分主要包括高等教育、中等教育、初等教育、成人教育、职业教育、幼儿园等方面的基本情况。科技部分主要包括科研机构、科学技术奖励、大中型工业企业技术开发情况。文化部分主要包括文化、文物、广播、电视、报纸杂志出版、图书出版等方面的发展状况。

### 二、本篇资料的来源

1、教育部分，技工学校的资料来源于市人力资源和社会保障局，其他资料来源于市教育局。

2、科技部分，科研机构及科技奖励资料来源于市科技局，大中型工业企业科技活动资料来源于市统计局统计调查年报。

3、文化部分，图书、杂志、报纸出版有关资料来源于青岛出版集团、海大出版社其他资料来源于市文化广电新闻出版局。

本篇资料由市统计局人口和社会科技统计处整理提供。

# Brief Introduction

### *I. Main Content*

Data in this chapter show the basic conditions of education, science & technology and culture. Data on education show the development of higher education, secondary education, primary education, adult education, vocational education and kindergartens. Data on science & technology show the basic conditions of science research institutions, scientific and technological achievements and prizes, scientific & technological activities of large and medium-size industrial enterprises. Data on culture show the basic conditions of arts, cultural relics, broadcasting, television and publication of newspapers, magazines and books.

### *II. Source of Data*

(1) In education component, data on the basic conditions of technical schools are provided by Qingdao Municipal Bureau of Human Resources and Social Security, and the other data on education are provided by Qingdao Municipal Bureau of Education.

(2) In science & technology component, data on science research institutions and scientific & technological achievements and prizes are provided by Qingdao Municipal Bureau of Science and Technology. Data on scientific and technological activities are from the annual report of scientific and technological activities, which is provided by Qingdao Municipal Bureau of Statistics.

(3) In culture component, data on publication of books, magazines and newspapers are provided by Qingdao Publishing Group and Ocean University Press. The other data are provided by Qingdao Municipal Bureau of Cluture, Broadcasting, Television, Press and Publication.

Data in this chapter are provided and compiled by the Division of Population and Science & Technology of Qingdao Municipal Bureau of Statistics.

# 17-1　各级各类学校基本情况（2018 年）
BASIC STATISTICS ON SCHOOLS BY LEVEL AND TYPE OF SCHOOL（2018）

| 项目 | Item | 学校数（所）Schools（unit） | 毕业生数（人）Graduates（person） | 招生数（人）New Students Enrollment(person) | 在校学生数（人）Students Enrollment(person) | 教职工数（人）Teachers and Staff（person） | #专任教师 of which：Full-time Teachers |
|---|---|---|---|---|---|---|---|
| 研究生 | Postgraduates | 8 | 11044 | 15679 | 41145 | 21935 | 8346 |
| 普通高等学校 | Regular Institutions of Higher Education | 25 | 105580 | 118247 | 397982 | 32628 | 21576 |
| 中等专业学校 | Specialized Secondary Schools | 6 | 10881 | 10390 | 31879 | 879 | 670 |
| 技工学校 | Technical Schools | 22 | 7054 | 9201 | 32110 | 2296 | 1737 |
| 职业学校 | Vocational Schools | 42 | 15801 | 15892 | 51440 | 7251 | 5994 |
| 普通中学 | Regular Secondary Schools | 319 | 110168 | 124356 | 385443 | 67526 | 36007 |
| 初中 | Junior Secondary Schools | 247 | 72370 | 86103 | 268336 | 25848 | 24007 |
| 高中 | Senior Secondary Schools | 72 | 37798 | 38253 | 117107 | 41678 | 12000 |
| 小学 | Primary Schools | 713 | 86070 | 103988 | 569923 | 35866 | 36890 |
| 特殊教育学校 | Special Education Schools | 13 | 235 | 292 | 1861 | 644 | 547 |
| 幼儿园 | Kindergartens | 2241 | 90149 | 90986 | 263890 | 32428 | 20957 |
| 成人高等学校 | Adult Institutions of Higher Education | 1 | 51281 | 45664 | 82721 | | |
| 成人中等学校 | Adult Institutions of Higher Education | 2 | 1021 | 9 | 974 | 36 | 28 |
| 成人初等学校 | Adult Primary Education Schools | | | | | | |

# 17-2 主要年份各级各类学校在校学生数
MAJOR YEAR'S STUDENTS ENROLLMENT OF SCHOOLS BY LEVEL AND TYPE OF SCHOOL

单位：人（person）

| 年份 Year | 普通高等学校 Pegular Institutions of Higher Education | 中等学校 Secondary Schools | 中等专业学校 Specialized Secondary Schools | 普通中学 Regular Secondary Schools | 职业中学 Vocational Schools | 技工学校 Technical Schools | 小学 Primary Schools |
|---|---|---|---|---|---|---|---|
| 1949 | 1 007 | 13 804 | 1 600 | 12 204 | | | 213 470 |
| 1952 | 2 761 | 27 951 | 3 770 | 24 181 | | | 413 286 |
| 1957 | 3 133 | 56 689 | 4 985 | 51 604 | 100 | | 482 397 |
| 1962 | 4 381 | 62 646 | 2 791 | 58 639 | 243 | 973 | 522 921 |
| 1965 | 2 987 | 99 605 | 9 405 | 88 187 | 1 490 | 523 | 788 485 |
| 1970 | 320 | 222 521 | 105 | 220 262 | 2 154 | | 728 433 |
| 1975 | 1 151 | 350 309 | 3 144 | 346 403 | | 762 | 928 153 |
| 1978 | 3 465 | 464 584 | 4 269 | 457 460 | 2 000 | 865 | 634 905 |
| 1980 | 6 783 | 325 935 | 5 195 | 318 193 | 1 344 | 1 203 | 816 970 |
| 1985 | 10 631 | 327 446 | 11 475 | 279 915 | 33 945 | 2 111 | 691 341 |
| 1988 | 14 408 | 352 576 | 11 819 | 306 943 | 28 933 | 4 881 | 629 212 |
| 1990 | 15 433 | 351 365 | 15 118 | 296 163 | 34 568 | 5 516 | 632 314 |
| 1991 | 15 491 | 353 410 | 14 618 | 298 568 | 34 421 | 5 803 | 612 772 |
| 1992 | 16 470 | 367 480 | 14 763 | 307 903 | 38 242 | 6 572 | 585 381 |
| 1993 | 23 858 | 383 043 | 16 877 | 318 179 | 40 743 | 7 244 | 583 585 |
| 1994 | 25 018 | 420 077 | 20 582 | 347 667 | 43 734 | 8 094 | 593 419 |
| 1995 | 24 908 | 450 212 | 23 744 | 372 335 | 46 044 | 8 089 | 595 891 |
| 1996 | 26 076 | 468 561 | 26 951 | 382 760 | 50 131 | 8 719 | 607 284 |
| 1997 | 27 434 | 463 619 | 28 543 | 362 305 | 61 640 | 11 131 | 626 749 |
| 1998 | 29 507 | 442 525 | 28 757 | 336 918 | 65 989 | 10 861 | 625 308 |
| 1999 | 33 681 | 459 520 | 26 955 | 352 238 | 70 236 | 10 091 | 583 594 |
| 2000 | 46 131 | 497 391 | 25 192 | 398 458 | 63 894 | 9 847 | 534 922 |
| 2001 | 60 728 | 542 400 | 25 358 | 443 693 | 62 003 | 11 346 | 499 147 |
| 2002 | 82 539 | 575 599 | 27 421 | 467 628 | 67 085 | 13 465 | 478 634 |
| 2003 | 168 439 | 586 704 | 28 948 | 461 435 | 75 221 | 21 100 | 467 560 |
| 2004 | 201 739 | 598 804 | 30 881 | 436 117 | 101 553 | 30 253 | 476 897 |
| 2005 | 239 761 | 569 230 | 33 522 | 391 148 | 106 400 | 38 160 | 479 781 |
| 2006 | 260 339 | 554 308 | 32 051 | 365 192 | 116 487 | 40 578 | 483 892 |
| 2007 | 264 917 | 558 527 | 28 011 | 360 410 | 130 156 | 39 950 | 484 775 |
| 2008 | 269 314 | 582 932 | 25 330 | 373 884 | 143 126 | 40 592 | 477 230 |
| 2009 | 275157 | 564476 | 22739 | 377427 | 127792 | 36518 | 465031 |
| 2010 | 284788 | 535079 | 24014 | 380025 | 98560 | 32480 | 462722 |
| 2011 | 291453 | 505051 | 25905 | 373226 | 74892 | 31028 | 479513 |
| 2012 | 296645 | 489103 | 27005 | 369580 | 65419 | 27099 | 484985 |
| 2013 | 300246 | 484025 | 28389 | 365110 | 61594 | 28932 | 496343 |
| 2014 | 313486 | 479260 | 28751 | 362599 | 58170 | 29740 | 516529 |
| 2015 | 322260 | 467231 | 33038 | 355401 | 48590 | 30202 | 536492 |
| 2016 | 340875 | 470333 | 32710 | 356107 | 50927 | 30589 | 547231 |
| 2017 | 346328 | 490796 | 32882 | 372196 | 52539 | 33179 | 550540 |
| 2018 | 397982 | 500872 | 31879 | 385443 | 51440 | 32110 | 569923 |

# 17-3　主要年份普通高等学校基本情况

MAJOR YEAR'S BASIC STATISTICS ON REGULAR INSTTUTIONS OF HIGHER EDUCATION

单位：人（person）

| 年份<br>Year | 学校数（所）<br>Schools<br>（unit） | 毕业生数<br>Graduates | 招生数<br>New Students<br>Enrollment | 在校学生数<br>Students<br>Enrollment | 教职工数<br>Teachers and<br>Staff | #专任教师<br>of which：<br>Full-time Teachers |
|---|---|---|---|---|---|---|
| 1949 | 1 | | 250 | 1 007 | 779 | 226 |
| 1952 | 2 | 262 | 565 | 2 761 | 12 530 | 308 |
| 1957 | 2 | 356 | 755 | 3 133 | 1 308 | 622 |
| 1962 | 5 | 647 | 653 | 4 381 | 1 866 | 749 |
| 1965 | 3 | 741 | 529 | 2 987 | 1 539 | 623 |
| 1970 | 2 | 684 | | 320 | 1 178 | 486 |
| 1975 | 2 | 460 | 473 | 1 151 | 1 353 | 582 |
| 1978 | 4 | 739 | 1 782 | 3 465 | 2 829 | 1 176 |
| 1980 | 6 | 431 | 1 717 | 6 783 | 4 182 | 1 606 |
| 1985 | 7 | 1 828 | 3 823 | 10 631 | 5 561 | 2 181 |
| 1988 | 7 | 3 496 | 4 687 | 14 408 | 6 875 | 2 499 |
| 1990 | 7 | 4 495 | 4 745 | 15 433 | 7 305 | 2 624 |
| 1991 | 7 | 4 880 | 4 954 | 15 491 | 7 282 | 2 489 |
| 1992 | 7 | 4 458 | 5 428 | 16 470 | 7 344 | 2 523 |
| 1993 | 7 | 3 140 | 9 449 | 23 858 | 7 366 | 2 520 |
| 1994 | 4 | 7 059 | 8 042 | 25 018 | 7 466 | 2 650 |
| 1995 | 4 | 7 828 | 7 978 | 24 908 | 7 545 | 2 682 |
| 1996 | 4 | 6 691 | 7 956 | 26 076 | 7 606 | 2 745 |
| 1997 | 4 | 7 091 | 8 503 | 27 434 | 7 790 | 2 813 |
| 1998 | 4 | 6 912 | 8 849 | 29 507 | 7 662 | 2 907 |
| 1999 | 4 | 7 202 | 11 584 | 33 681 | 7 662 | 2 928 |
| 2000 | 6 | 7 128 | 18 427 | 46 131 | 8 030 | 3 278 |
| 2001 | 6 | 8 991 | 22 787 | 60 728 | 8 706 | 4 058 |
| 2002 | 7 | 13 053 | 29 731 | 82 539 | 9 517 | 4 723 |
| 2003 | 25 | 25 747 | 61 975 | 168 439 | 18 911 | 10 293 |
| 2004 | 25 | 34 860 | 70 022 | 201 739 | 21 437 | 12 347 |
| 2005 | 25 | 46 114 | 79 725 | 239 761 | 23 078 | 13 894 |
| 2006 | 25 | 55 931 | 79 094 | 260 339 | 24 881 | 15 195 |
| 2007 | 25 | 68 354 | 78 728 | 264 917 | 25 956 | 16 005 |
| 2008 | 25 | 75 198 | 86 878 | 269 314 | 26 654 | 16 805 |
| 2009 | 25 | 69475 | 81025 | 275157 | 26983 | 16870 |
| 2010 | 25 | 70450 | 82220 | 284788 | 28145 | 16996 |
| 2011 | 22 | 79466 | 84434 | 291453 | 28151 | 17120 |
| 2012 | 22 | 79791 | 87981 | 296645 | 29445 | 18183 |
| 2013 | 22 | 78974 | 85707 | 300246 | 28958 | 18396 |
| 2014 | 22 | 77503 | 90127 | 313486 | 28944 | 18587 |
| 2015 | 24 | 79784 | 92251 | 322260 | 29620 | 19213 |
| 2016 | 26 | 86270 | 100525 | 340875 | 30390 | 20151 |
| 2017 | 25 | 95006 | 98983 | 346238 | 32013 | 21231 |
| 2018 | 25 | 105580 | 118247 | 397982 | 32628 | 21576 |

# 17-4 各类成人教育基本情况（2018 年）
BASIC STATISTICS ON ADULT EDUCATION（2018）

单位：人（person）

| 各类学校 | Schools by Type of School | 学校数（所） Schools（unit） | 毕业生数 Graduates | 招生数 New Students Enrollment | 在校学生数 Students Enrollment | 教职工数 Teachers and Staff | #专任教师 of which：Full-time Teachers |
|---|---|---|---|---|---|---|---|
| 总 计 | **Total** | | | | | | |
| 成人高等教育 | Adult Higher Education | 1 | 51281 | 45664 | 82721 | | |
| 广播电视大学 | Broadcasting and TV Universities | | | | | | |
| 职工、农民大学 | Universities of Vocational and Agricultural Education | | | | | | |
| 函授、夜大学 | Correspondence and Evening College Education | | | | | | |
| 管理干部学校 | Cadre Management Schools | | | | | | |
| 成人中等教育 | Adult Secondary Education | 2 | 1021 | 9 | 974 | 36 | 28 |
| 成人中等专业学校 | Adult Specialized Secondary Schools | 2 | 1021 | 9 | 974 | 36 | 28 |

# 17-5 分市、区普通中学情况（2018 年）

BASIC STATISTICS ON REGULAR SECONDARY SCHOOLS BY REGION (2018)

单位：人（person）

| 市、区名称 | Region | 普通高中 Regular Senior Secondary Schools | | | | 普通初中 Regular Junior Secondary Schools | | | |
|---|---|---|---|---|---|---|---|---|---|
| | | 学校数 Schools (unit) | 毕业生数 Graduates | 招生数 New Students Enrollment | 在校生数 Students Enrollment | 学校数 Schools (unit) | 毕业生数 Graduates | 招生数 New Students Enrollment | 在校生数 Students Enrollment |
| **全　市** | **Whole Municipality** | **72** | **37798** | **38253** | **117107** | **247** | **72370** | **86103** | **268336** |
| 市　直 | Municipal Level | 22 | 9153 | 9702 | 29711 | 3 | 2486 | 2614 | 7765 |
| 市南区 | Shinan District | 0 | 0 | | | 10 | 2315 | 2753 | 8146 |
| 市北区 | Shibei District | 1 | 0 | 180 | 331 | 25 | 5773 | 7109 | 20939 |
| 李沧区 | Licang District | 2 | 0 | 18 | 47 | 12 | 3177 | 4028 | 11640 |
| 崂山区 | Laoshan District | 2 | 0 | | | 10 | 1903 | 2319 | 7151 |
| 黄岛区 | Huangdao District | 11 | 6375 | 5745 | 18333 | 40 | 12149 | 14980 | 45726 |
| 城阳区 | Chengyang District | 6 | 2700 | 2712 | 8228 | 16 | 5275 | 7010 | 20643 |
| 即墨区 | Jimo District | 9 | 5382 | 5916 | 18233 | 30 | 11733 | 14268 | 41722 |
| 胶州市 | Jiaozhou | 7 | 4234 | 4424 | 13162 | 23 | 8920 | 10548 | 33610 |
| 平度市 | Pingdu | 7 | 6917 | 6245 | 18972 | 45 | 11634 | 12095 | 39115 |
| 莱西市 | Laixi | 4 | 3037 | 3240 | 10019 | 29 | 6371 | 7583 | 29539 |
| 红岛经济区 | Qingdao National High-tech Industrial Development Zone | 1 | 0 | 71 | 71 | 4 | 634 | 796 | 2340 |

注：黄岛区含保税港区数据。
Note: The Huangdao District contains the data of the bonded harbor area.

# 17-6　分市、区职业中学、小学情况（2018 年）
## BASIC STATISTICS ON VOCATIONAL SECONDARY SCHOOLS AND PRIMARY SCHOOLS BY REGION (2018)

单位：人（person）

| 市、区名称 | Region | 职业中学 Vocational Secondary Schools | | | | 小学 Primary School | | | |
|---|---|---|---|---|---|---|---|---|---|
| | | 学校数 Schools (unit) | 毕业生数 Graduates | 招生数 New Students Enrollment | 在校生数 Students Enrollment | 学校数 Schools (unit) | 毕业生数 Graduates | 招生数 New Students Enrollment | 在校生数 Students Enrollment |
| **全　市** | **Whole Municipality** | **50** | **27703** | **26291** | **84293** | **713** | **86070** | **103988** | **569923** |
| 市　直 | Municipal Level | 30 | 11206 | 9964 | 32734 | | 45 | 67 | 313 |
| 市南区 | Shinan District | | | | | 28 | 4488 | 5922 | 32529 |
| 市北区 | Shibei District | | | | | 68 | 7512 | 10965 | 59050 |
| 李沧区 | Licang District | | | | | 37 | 4329 | 7509 | 37250 |
| 崂山区 | Laoshan District | | | | | 27 | 2790 | 4474 | 24333 |
| 黄岛区 | Huangdao District | 10 | 5889 | 5840 | 18832 | 90 | 14941 | 19038 | 101670 |
| 城阳区 | Chengyang District | 3 | 2879 | 2736 | 8036 | 46 | 7320 | 12064 | 61620 |
| 即墨区 | Jimo District | 2 | 2041 | 1781 | 5944 | 169 | 14031 | 14032 | 83937 |
| 胶州市 | Jiaozhou | 1 | 2568 | 2153 | 7322 | 74 | 10151 | 10875 | 62449 |
| 平度市 | Pingdu | 1 | 1632 | 1228 | 4767 | 100 | 12151 | 11499 | 69058 |
| 莱西市 | Laixi | 3 | 1488 | 2589 | 6658 | 70 | 7547 | 6291 | 32238 |
| 红岛经济区 | Qingdao National High-tech Industrial Development Zone | | | | | 4 | 765 | 1252 | 5476 |

注：黄岛区含保税港区数据。
Note: The Huangdao District contains the data of the bonded harbor area.

# 17-7 分市、区中小学教职工情况（2018年）
## BASIC STATSTICS ON TEACHERS AND STAFF IN SECONDARY AND PRIMARY SCHOOLS BY REGION (2018)

单位：人（person）

| 市、区名称 | Region | 普通中学 Regular Secondary Schools | | 职业中学 Vocational Secondary Schools | | 小学 Primary School | |
|---|---|---|---|---|---|---|---|
| | | 教职工数 Teachers and Staff | #专任教师 of which: Full-time Teachers | 教职工数 Teachers and Staff | #专任教师 of which: Full-time Teachers | 教职工数 Teachers and Staff | #专任教师 of which: Full-time Teachers |
| **全　市** | **Whole Municipality** | **41678** | **38321** | **8166** | **6692** | **35866** | **34576** |
| 市　直 | Municipal Level | 4071 | 3325 | 3387 | 2549 | | |
| 市南区 | Shinan District | 1087 | 963 | | | 2104 | 2003 |
| 市北区 | Shibei District | 2451 | 2266 | | | 3565 | 3409 |
| 李沧区 | Licang District | 1400 | 1252 | | | 1994 | 1922 |
| 崂山区 | Laoshan District | 998 | 935 | | | 1606 | 1547 |
| 黄岛区 | Huangdao District | 6887 | 6384 | 1488 | 1305 | 6166 | 5982 |
| 城阳区 | Chengyang District | 3013 | 2750 | 661 | 581 | 3036 | 2867 |
| 即墨区 | Jimo District | 6529 | 6193 | 713 | 623 | 5467 | 5305 |
| 胶州市 | Jiaozhou | 4229 | 3869 | 632 | 504 | 3963 | 3883 |
| 平度市 | Pingdu | 6289 | 5929 | 651 | 625 | 5122 | 4938 |
| 莱西市 | Laixi | 4133 | 3887 | 634 | 505 | 2526 | 2405 |
| 红岛经济区 | Qingdao National High-tech Industrial Development Zone | 591 | 568 | | | 317 | 315 |

注：黄岛区含保税港区数据。
Note: The Huangdao District contains the data of the bonded harbor area.

# 17-8 分市、区幼儿园基本情况（2018年）
BASIC STATISTICS ON KINDERGARTENS BY REGION (2018)

单位：人（person）

| 市、区名称 | Region | 幼儿园（所）Kindergartens (unit) | 幼儿数 Children | 教职工数 Teachers and Staff | #专任教师 of which: Full-time Teachers |
|---|---|---|---|---|---|
| **全　市** | **Whole Municipality** | **2241** | **263890** | **32428** | **20957** |
| 市南区 | Shinan District | 65 | 14064 | 2361 | 1132 |
| 市北区 | Shibei District | 115 | 28029 | 3083 | 1956 |
| 李沧区 | Licang District | 57 | 20969 | 2687 | 1360 |
| 崂山区 | Laoshan District | 114 | 13941 | 2275 | 1374 |
| 黄岛区 | Huangdao District | 443 | 47474 | 6711 | 4158 |
| 城阳区 | Chengyang District | 151 | 25456 | 3637 | 2398 |
| 即墨区 | Jimo District | 361 | 35556 | 3791 | 2593 |
| 胶州市 | Jiaozhou | 355 | 29507 | 3285 | 2327 |
| 平度市 | Pingdu | 405 | 30533 | 2562 | 2053 |
| 莱西市 | Laixi | 146 | 15153 | 1583 | 1237 |
| 红岛经济区 | Qingdao National High-tech Industrial Development Zone | 29 | 3208 | 453 | 369 |

注：黄岛区含保税港区数据。
Note: The Huangdao District contains the data of the bonded harbor area.

# 17-9 科研机构基本情况（1978-2018 年）
BASIC STATISTICS ON SCIENTIFIC RESEARCH INSTITUTIONS（1978-2018）

| 年份<br>Year | 独立自然科研结构（个）<br>Independent Institutions of Natural Scientific Research（unit） | 独立自然科研结构中科技人员（个）<br>Personnel of Independent Institutions of Natural Scientific Research（person） | 完成科研项目（项）<br>Number of Scientific Research Projects Completed（item） | 取得科技成果（项）<br>Number of Achievements in S&T（item） |
|---|---|---|---|---|
| 1978 | 31 | 2701 | 306 | 306 |
| 1980 | | | 481 | 297 |
| 1982 | 41 | 2345 | 451 | 451 |
| 1983 | 48 | 3182 | 530 | 530 |
| 1984 | 53 | 3312 | 507 | 507 |
| 1985 | 52 | 3673 | 552 | 552 |
| 1986 | 63 | 3998 | 577 | 577 |
| 1988 | 101 | 5199 | 544 | 510 |
| 1990 | 141 | 6046 | 414 | 931 |
| 1991 | 72 | 5665 | 753 | 753 |
| 1992 | 71 | 5726 | 659 | 659 |
| 1993 | 69 | 5545 | 546 | 546 |
| 1994 | 69 | 5540 | 467 | 467 |
| 1995 | 59 | 5286 | 441 | 441 |
| 1996 | 58 | 4738 | 613 | 613 |
| 1997 | 54 | 4577 | 418 | 418 |
| 1998 | 52 | 4142 | 517 | 517 |
| 1999 | 58 | 3771 | 606 | 606 |
| 2000 | 54 | 3637 | 621 | 621 |
| 2001 | 50 | 3191 | 457 | 457 |
| 2002 | 52 | 3248 | 406 | 406 |
| 2003 | 53 | 3246 | 589 | 589 |
| 2004 | 50 | 3226 | 506 | 506 |
| 2005 | 50 | 3234 | 438 | 438 |
| 2006 | 50 | 3291 | 548 | 548 |
| 2007 | 50 | 3432 | 506 | 506 |
| 2008 | 42 | 3709 | 416 | 416 |
| 2009 | 43 | 3727 | 572 | 572 |
| 2010 | 44 | 4088 | 472 | 472 |
| 2011 | 47 | 4548 | 345 | 345 |
| 2012 | 48 | 4967 | 304 | 304 |
| 2013 | 48 | 6057 | 433 | 433 |
| 2014 | 50 | 5438 | 415 | 415 |
| 2015 | 54 | 6037 | 639 | 639 |
| 2016 | 57 | 5722 | 606 | 606 |
| 2017 | 57 | 6017 | 588 | 588 |
| 2018 | 58 | 6017 | 406 | 406 |

注：1991 年以后不包括民办科研机构。
Note：Since 1991，private institutions of scientific research are not included.

## 17-10 独立科学研究机构情况（2018 年）
BASIC STATISTICS ON INDEPENDENT INSHUTIONS OF SCIENTIFIC RESEARCH（2018）

| 项目 | Item | 计量单位 | Unit | 总计 Total | 中央属 Central | 地方属 Local |
|---|---|---|---|---|---|---|
| 机构数 | Number of Institutions | 个 | unit | 58 | 22 | 36 |
| 职工人数 | Staff and Workers | 人 | person | 8544 | 6470 | 2074 |
| 科技人员 | Personnel Engaged in S&T | 人 | person | 6107 | 4455 | 1652 |
| 经费收入 | Funding for S&T | 万元 | 10 000 yuan | 406021 | 291193.7 | 114827.3 |
| 经费支出 | Expenditures for S&T | 万元 | 10 000 yuan | 403589.4 | 305614.2 | 97975.2 |

## 17-11 科学技术奖励情况（2018 年）
AWARD STATISTICS ON SCIENCE AND TECHNOLOGY（2018）

| 项目 | Item | 单位 | Unit | 自然科学奖 Natural Science Prizes Awarded | 技术发明奖 Invention Prizes Awarded | 科技进步奖 Scientific and Technological Progress Prizes Awarded | 科学技术功勋奖 Scientific and Technolgical Credit Prizes Awarded | 国际科技合作奖 International S&T Cooperation Prizes Award | 最高奖 Highest Prizes Award |
|---|---|---|---|---|---|---|---|---|---|
| 国家级 | National Level | 项 | Item | 1 | 1 | 11 | | 1 | |
| 特等 | Special Grade | | | | | | | | |
| #一等 | First Prize | 项 | Item | | | 2 | | | |
| 二等 | Second Prize | 项 | Item | 1 | 1 | 9 | | | |
| 省级 | Provincial Level | 项 | Item | 6 | 7 | 52 | | | 1 |
| #一等 | First Prize | 项 | Item | 1 | 0 | 10 | | | |
| 二等 | Second Prize | 项 | Item | 5 | 5 | 27 | | | |
| 三等 | Third Prize | 项 | Item | | 2 | 15 | | | |
| 市级 | Municipal Level | 项 | Item | 11 | 5 | 129 | | 1 | 1 |
| #一等 | First Prize | 项 | Item | 2 | 0 | 14 | | | |
| 二等 | Second Prize | 项 | Item | 6 | 3 | 69 | | | |
| 三等 | Third Prize | 项 | Item | 3 | 2 | 46 | | | |

注：国际科技合作奖、最高奖不分等级。
Note：There is no grade in international scientific and technological cooperation prizes award and highest prizes award.

# 17-12 文化、文物事业机构、人员数（2018年）
NUMBER OF INSTITUTIONS AND PERSONNEL IN CUUTURE (2018)

| 项目 | Item | 文化机构数（个）Number of Cultural Institutions (unit) | | 文化人员数（人）Number of Cultural Personnel (Person) | |
|---|---|---|---|---|---|
| | | 2018年 | 2017年 | 2018年 | 2017年 |
| **一、艺术事业** | **Art** | | | | |
| 1.艺术表演团体 | Art Peformance Troupes | 9 | 8 | 830 | 575 |
| 2.艺术表演场所 | Art Centers | 10 | 10 | 201 | 197 |
| 3.艺术展览创作机构 | Art Creation Institutions | 5 | 5 | 28 | 33 |
| 4.艺术研究机构 | Art Research Institutions | | | | |
| 5.艺术展览机构 | Art Exhibition Institutions | | | | |
| 6.其他 | Others | 3 | 3 | 24 | 27 |
| **二、图书馆事业** | **Libraries** | | | | |
| 公共图书馆 | Publie Libraries | 12 | 12 | 279 | 275 |
| #县（区）级图书馆 | County Libraries | 11 | 11 | 170 | 175 |
| **三、群众文化事业** | **Nass Culture** | | | | |
| 1.群众艺术馆 | Nass Art Centers | | | | |
| 2.文化馆 | Cultural Palaces | 12 | 12 | 214 | 225 |
| 3.文化站 | Cultural Centers | 136 | 136 | 527 | 500 |
| 4.其他 | Others | | | | |

## 17-13 文化部门艺术剧团情况（2018年）
STATISTICS ON ART TROUPES OF CULTURAL DEPARTMENT (2018)

| 项目 | Item | 剧团数（个）Number of Troupes (unit) | 职工人数（人）Stalf and Workers (person) | 演出场次（场）Number of Performances (show) | 观众人数（万人次）Number of Spectators (10000 person-times) | 演出收入（万元）Income from Ticket Sales (10000 yuan) | #财政补贴（万元）Apporopriation Funds (10000 yuan) |
|---|---|---|---|---|---|---|---|
| **总　计** | **Total** | **8** | **574** | **1903** | **120.4** | **12717.0** | **10848.5** |
| **一、按隶属关系分** | **Grouped by Administrative Relationship** | | | | | | |
| 国营剧团 | State-run Troupes | 8 | 574 | 1903 | 120.4 | 12717.0 | 10848.5 |
| 集体经营剧团 | Collective-owned Troupes | | | | | | |
| **二、按剧种分** | **Grouped by Type of Drama** | | | | | | |
| 1. 话剧团 | Drama Troupes | 1 | 110 | 405 | 20.3 | 2450.9 | 2008.3 |
| 2. 歌舞团 | Song and Dance Troupes | | | | | | |
| 3. 戏曲剧团 | Local Opera Troupes | 6 | 371 | 1416 | 93.6 | 6332.2 | 5764.4 |
| #京剧 | of which: Beijing Opera | 1 | 87 | 116 | 5.5 | 1759.3 | 1661.7 |
| 4. 曲艺团 | Recitation and Ballad Troupes | | | | | | |
| 5. 文工团（艺术团） | Cultural and Performance Troupes | 1 | 93 | 82 | 6.5 | 3933.9 | 3075.8 |

## 17-14 图书馆、文化馆情况
STATISTICS ON LIBRARIES AND CULTURAL CENTERS

| 项目 | Item | 单位 | 2018年 | | 2017年 | |
|---|---|---|---|---|---|---|
| | | | 全市合计 Total | #市区 Urban Area | 全市合计 Total | #市区 Urban Area |
| **公共图书馆** | **Pubilc Libraries** | 个 | **12** | **9** | **12** | **9** |
| 工作人员 | Staff and Workers | 人 | 279 | 220 | 275 | 225 |
| 藏书册数 | Colicetion Books | 千册 | 7479 | 6540 | 6996 | 6108 |
| 阅览席位 | Seating Capacity of Reading Rooms | 张 | 5866 | 4609 | 6412 | 5351 |
| 读者人数 | Readers | 万人次 | 469.9 | 402.1 | 482.1 | 419.3 |
| **文化馆** | **Cultural Centers** | 个 | **12** | **9** | **12** | **9** |

# 主要统计指标解释

**普通高等学校** 指按照国家规定的设置标准和审批程序批准举办，通过国家统一招生考试，招收高中毕业生为主要培养对象，实施高等教育的全日制大学、独立设置的学院和高等专科学校、短期职业大学。

**成人高等学校** 指按照国家有关规定审批，招收通过全国成人高教统一招生考试的具有高中毕业或同等学历的在职从业人员，利用脱产、半脱产、业余或函授等多种形式对其实施高等学历教育，培养高等教育专科或本科毕业水平的专门人才，修业年限、课程设置和总学时数均按高等学历教育要求付诸实施的学校。包括广播电视大学、职工高等学校、农民高等学校、管理干部学院；教育学院、独立设置的函授学院等。

**科技活动人员** 指直接从事科技活动、以及专门从事科技活动管理和为科技活动提供直接服务，累计的实际工作时间占全年制度工作时间 10% 及以上的人员。

**文化事业机构** 指从事专业文化工作和为专业文化工作服务的独立建制的单独核算的单位。不包括这些单位另外举办独立核算的其他机构和各部门的业余文化组织。

# Explanatory Notes on Main Statistical Indicators

**Regular Institutions of Higher Education** refer to educational establishments set up according to the government evaluation and approval procedures, enrolling graduates from senior secondary schools and providing higher education courses and training for senior professionals. They include full-time universities, colleges, high professional schools, high professional vocational schools and others.

**Adult Institutions of Higher Education** refer to educational establishments, set up in line with relevant rules approved by the government, enrolling staff and workers with senior secondary school or equivalent education, and providing higher education courses in many forms of correspondence, spare time, or full time for adults. Professionals thus trained receive a qualification equivalent to graduates studying regular courses at regular universities, colleges and professional colleges. Institutions of higher learning for adults include schools of high education for staff and workers, schools of high education for peasants, colleges for management cadres, pedagogical colleges, independent correspondence colleges, Radio and TV universities and other educational establishments.

**Personnel Engaged in S&T Activities** refer to personnel directly engaged in S&T activities, in the management of S&T activities, and in providing direct service to S&T activities, who spend over 10% of the total working hours in a year in S&T activities.

**Cultural Institutions** refer to units, which have their own organizational system and independent accounting system and specialize in or serve cultural development. They exclude other establishments run by these cultural institutions and amateur cultural groups established by various departments.

# 18 体育、卫生和民政、司法

## SPORTS, PUBLIC HEALTH AND CIVIL AFFAIRS, JUDICIAL AFFAIRS

# 简要说明

## 一、本篇资料的主要内容

本篇资料反映了全市体育、卫生、民政、司法等社会事业的基本情况。体育部分主要包括主要年份运动员、教练员、裁判员发展人数、体育运动破纪录、获奖情况。卫生部分主要包括各类卫生机构及其人员、床位数。民政部分主要包括婚姻登记、社会救济、社会福利事业基本情况、殡葬服务情况。司法部分主要包括律师、公证、调解、社会治安基本情况。

## 二、本篇资料的来源

1、体育部分来源于市体育局。

2、卫生部分来源于市卫计委。

3、民政部分来源于市民政局。

4、司法部分，社会治安资料来源于市公安局，其他资料来源于市司法局。

本篇资料由市统计局人口和社会科技统计处整理提供。

# Brief Introduction

## *I. Main Content*

Data in this chapter show the basic conditions of sports, public health, civil affairs and judicial affairs. Data on sports are mainly including the number of athletes, coaches and referees, conditions of record and awards. Data on public health are mainly including the number of health institutions, personnel and beds. Data on civil affairs are mainly including the conditions of marriage registration, social relief, social welfare and funeral services. Data on judicial affairs are mainly including the conditions of lawyers, notarization, mediation and social order.

## *II. Source of Data*

(1) Data on sports are provided by Qingdao Municipal Bureau of Physical.

(2) Data on public health are provided by Qingdao Municipal Bureau of Health.

(3) Data on civil affairs are provided by Qingdao Municipal Bureau of Civil Affairs.

(4) In judicial affairs component, data on social order are provided by Qingdao Municipal Bureau of Public Security and the other data are provided by Qingdao Municipal Bureau of Justice.

Data in this chapter are provided and compiled by the Division of Population and Science & Technology of Qingdao Municipal Bureau of Statistics.

# 18-1 体育事业情况(2000-2018年)
STATISTICS ON SPORTS (2000-2018)

单位：人(person)

| 项目 | Item | 2000 | 2005 | 2007 | 2008 | 2009 | 2010 | 2011 | 2012 | 2013 | 2014 | 2015 | 2016 | 2017 | 2018 |
|---|---|---|---|---|---|---|---|---|---|---|---|---|---|---|---|
| **体育部门职工人数** | **Staff and Workers in Sports Commissions** | **849** | **834** | **772** | **1210** | **910** | **1015** | | | | **847** | **795** | **857** | **654** | **682** |
| #运动员 | Athletes | 90 | 87 | 55 | 452 | 512 | 287 | | | | 287 | 259 | | 284 | 1123 |
| 教练员 | Coaches | 174 | 235 | 211 | 173 | 106 | 170 | 136 | | | | | 120 | 133 | 134 |
| 重点体校 | Key Sports School | 126 | 117 | 249 | 109 | 97 | 115 | 129 | | | | | | 1061 | 1370 |
| 业余体校 | Sparetime Sports Schools | 142 | 223 | 145 | | 160 | | | | | | | | 1537 | 1846 |
| 体育专业队 | Professional Sports Teams | 135 | 132 | 121 | | 144 | 192 | 87 | 84 | 42 | 38 | 17 | 17 | 5 | 5 |
| 优秀运动员 | Exeellent Athletes | 90 | 87 | 55 | 71 | 72 | 146 | 57 | | | | | | | |
| 优秀运动队专职教练员 | Full-time Coaches of Excellennt Sports Teams | 18 | 23 | 47 | 106 | 92 | 97 | 54 | | | | 89 | 120 | | |
| **等级裁判员发展人数** | **Certified Referees** | **1114** | **275** | **781** | **205** | **292** | **212** | **510** | **558** | **512** | **514** | **490** | **167** | | **511** |
| #二级 | Second Grades | 451 | 275 | 781 | 181 | 252 | 169 | 510 | 484 | 463 | 514 | 490 | 116 | | 319 |
| 三级 | Third Grades | 616 | | | | | | | | | | | | | |
| **等级运动员发展人数** | **Certified Athletes** | **343** | **260** | **108** | **310** | **512** | **229** | **436** | **362** | **362** | **283** | **259** | | **176** | **327** |
| #二级 | Second Grades | 209 | 260 | 108 | 281 | 448 | 229 | 436 | 256 | 362 | 283 | 259 | | 176 | 290 |
| 三级 | Third Grades | 46 | | | | | | | | | | | | | |
| 少年级 | Juvenile | 88 | | | | | | | | | | | | | |

## 18-1 续表
Contiuned

单位：人（person）

| 项目 | Item | 单位 | Unit | 2000 | 2005 | 2007 | 2008 | 2009 | 2010 | 2011 | 2012 | 2013 | 2014 | 2015 | 2016 | 2017 | 2018 |
|---|---|---|---|---|---|---|---|---|---|---|---|---|---|---|---|---|---|
| **全年获得奖牌数** | **Number of Medals Won in the Year** | 枚 | **unit** | **347.5** | **669** | **481** | **494** | **602** | **754** | **829** | **746** | **659** | **576.5** | **596** | **729.5** | **3032** | **849** |
| #国家级金牌 | Golden Medals at National Level | 枚 | unit | 45 | 62 | 61 | 26 | 30 | 14 | 105 | 88 | 90 | 48 | 51 | 101 | 104 | 76 |
| 国家级银牌 | Silver Medals at National Level | 枚 | unit | 28 | 48 | 38 | 21 | 23 | 7 | 49 | 100 | 44 | 21 | 44 | 56 | 91 | 81 |
| 省级金牌 | Golden Medals at Provincial Level | 枚 | unit | 116.5 | 187 | 116 | 168 | 207 | 459 | 225 | 193 | 174.5 | 202.5 | 149 | 219.5 | 214.5 | 264 |
| 省级银牌 | Silver Medals at Provincial Level | 枚 | unit | 62 | 174 | 93 | 122 | 149 | 116 | 155 | 110 | 111.5 | 121.5 | 126 | 135 | 140 | 161 |
| **体育运动破全国记录** | **Records Broken the National Records** | | | | | | | | | | | | | | | | |
| 项目 | Number of Events | 项 | item | | 2 | 1 | | 1 | 1 | 2 | 1 | | | | | | 1 |
| 人数 | Number of Persons | 人 | person | | 2 | 1 | | 1 | 1 | 2 | 1 | | | | | | 1 |
| 次数 | Number of Times | 人次 | person-tims | | 4 | 1 | | 1 | 1 | 2 | 1 | | | | | | 1 |
| **体育运动破全省记录** | **Records Broken the Provincial Records** | | | | | | | | | | | | | | | | |
| 项目 | Number of Events | 项 | item | 7 | 3 | | 2 | | 1 | | | | | | | | |
| 人数 | Number of Persons | 人 | person | 7 | 1 | | 2 | | 1 | | | | | | | | |
| 次数 | Number of Times | 人次 | person-tims | 7 | 3 | | 2 | | 1 | | | | | | | | 15 |

# 18-2 主要年份卫生事业基本情况

MAJOR YEAR'S BASIC STATISTICS ON PUBLIC HEALTH

单位：人（person）

| 年份 Year | 卫生机构数（个）Health Institutions（unit） | #医院 of which: Hospitals | 医疗床位数（张）Beds in Health Institutions（bed） | #医院 of which: Hospitals | 卫生技术人员（个）Medical and Technical Personnel（person） | #医生 of which: Hospitals | 每千人口拥有医生数（人）Number of Doctors per 1000 Population（person） | 每千人口拥有床位数（张）Number of Hospital Beds per 1000 Population（bed） |
|---|---|---|---|---|---|---|---|---|
| 1949 | 80 | 26 | 1079 | 970 | 2637 | 1292 | 0.32 | 0.27 |
| 1952 | 260 | 34 | 2943 | 1691 | 3748 | 1559 | 0.37 | 0.70 |
| 1957 | 624 | 45 | 5163 | 2656 | 6941 | 2578 | 0.53 | 1.07 |
| 1962 | 849 | 149 | 7167 | 4526 | 8279 | 2972 | 0.64 | 1.55 |
| 1965 | 912 | 162 | 8428 | 5003 | 9051 | 3586 | 0.73 | 1.72 |
| 1970 | 712 | 170 | 8613 | 6603 | 9591 | 3761 | 0.70 | 1.60 |
| 1975 | 959 | 181 | 10902 | 9078 | 13558 | 4566 | 0.80 | 1.90 |
| 1978 | 1192 | 212 | 13084 | 10709 | 16921 | 5893 | 1.01 | 2.24 |
| 1980 | 1253 | 212 | 14170 | 11345 | 19265 | 6781 | 1.14 | 2.38 |
| 1985 | 1517 | 219 | 18469 | 13214 | 23413 | 9694 | 1.55 | 2.95 |
| 1990 | 1563 | 235 | 23541 | 16586 | 27932 | 13761 | 2.08 | 3.56 |
| 1991 | 1579 | 235 | 23727 | 16796 | 27772 | 13227 | 1.98 | 3.54 |
| 1992 | 1562 | 236 | 24765 | 17269 | 28305 | 13157 | 1.95 | 3.67 |
| 1993 | 1540 | 237 | 24885 | 17469 | 28705 | 13312 | 1.97 | 3.68 |
| 1994 | 1335 | 242 | 24732 | 17882 | 28938 | 13535 | 1.99 | 3.64 |
| 1995 | 1347 | 228 | 25282 | 18126 | 29816 | 13840 | 2.02 | 3.69 |
| 1996 | 2216 | 228 | 24334 | 18344 | 30048 | 13790 | 2.00 | 3.53 |
| 1997 | 2193 | 239 | 25201 | 19046 | 31121 | 14400 | 2.07 | 3.62 |
| 1998 | 2190 | 237 | 24887 | 19083 | 31623 | 14327 | 2.05 | 3.56 |
| 1999 | 2185 | 235 | 25481 | 19798 | 31965 | 14453 | 2.06 | 3.62 |
| 2000 | 2911 | 231 | 24392 | 20057 | 32160 | 14860 | 2.10 | 3.45 |
| 2001 | 3199 | 217 | 24755 | 20313 | 32765 | 15772 | 2.22 | 3.48 |
| 2002 | 3050 | 213 | 21370 | 20662 | 31469 | 13371 | 1.87 | 2.99 |
| 2003 | 3111 | 213 | 23980 | 21605 | 32337 | 13452 | 1.87 | 3.33 |
| 2004 | 2923 | 219 | 25432 | 23465 | 32937 | 13953 | 1.91 | 3.48 |
| 2005 | 2609 | 235 | 30627 | 28564 | 33942 | 15008 | 2.03 | 4.13 |
| 2006 | 2834 | 232 | 28724 | 26653 | 34360 | 15451 | 2.06 | 3.83 |
| 2007 | 2006 | 251 | 30062 | 28107 | 33807 | 15018 | 1.98 | 3.97 |
| 2008 | 1985 | 249 | 32350 | 29874 | 36574 | 16260 | 2.14 | 4.25 |
| 2009 | 2017 | 252 | 32803 | 30527 | 40217 | 16734 | 2.19 | 4.30 |
| 2010 | 2147 | 254 | 36066 | 33383 | 43285 | 17696 | 2.32 | 4.72 |
| 2011 | 2549 | 280 | 39980 | 35600 | 47347 | 18310 | 2.39 | 5.22 |
| 2012 | 2607 | 288 | 47254 | 41186 | 54488 | 21593 | 2.81 | 6.14 |
| 2013 | 2936 | 285 | 44876 | 39725 | 59961 | 24113 | 3.12 | 5.80 |
| 2014 | 3126 | 297 | 47081 | 42961 | 62738 | 24946 | 3.20 | 6.03 |
| 2015 | 3146 | 308 | 48601 | 45066 | 65264 | 26270 | 3.35 | 6.20 |
| 2016 | 7564 | 322 | 50649 | 47309 | 87733 | 27675 | 3.49 | 6.39 |
| 2017 | 7927 | 410 | 55798 | 46282 | 76146 | 30867 | 3.84 | 6.94 |
| 2018 | 8027 | 421 | 53154 | 50842 | 83975 | 34578 | 4.23 | 6.82 |

注：自 2016 年起，卫生机构及人员包含村卫生室。

Note: Health agency and personnel includes village clinic as of 2016.

# 18-3 各类卫生机构、床位、人员数（2018 年底）

NUMBER OF HEALTH INSTITUTIONS，BEDS AND EMPLOYED PERSONS（END OF 2018）

| 项　目 | Item | 机构数（个）Health Institutions（unit） | 床位数（张）Beds in Health Institutions（bed） | 人员数（人）Personnel（person） |
|---|---|---|---|---|
| 总　计 | | **8027** | **53154** | **102991** |
| 一、医院合计 | **Sub-total of Hospitals** | **421** | **50842** | **71213** |
| 1. 医院 | Hospitals | 318 | 45136 | 63621 |
| #综合医院 | General Hospitals | 179 | 27718 | 42017 |
| 中医医院 | Hospitals Specialized in Traditional Chinese Medicine | 35 | 6028 | 8012 |
| 中西医结合医院 | Hospitals of Combination of Chinese and Western Medicine | 6 | 762 | 932 |
| 专科医院 | Specialized Hospitals | 95 | 10433 | 12562 |
| #口腔医院 | Stomatological Hospitals | 8 | 140 | 653 |
| 眼科医院 | Ophthalmology Hospitals | 8 | 585 | 903 |
| 肿瘤医院 | Tumor Hospitals | 3 | 660 | 592 |
| 心血管病医院 | Cardiovascular Diseases Hospitals | 3 | 870 | 1080 |
| 精神病医院 | Mental Hospitals | 14 | 2434 | 1607 |
| 传染病医院 | Infectious Disease Hospitals | 2 | 490 | 516 |
| 皮肤病医院 | The Skin Disease Hospital | 1 | 40 | 50 |
| 骨科医院 | Orthopaedics Hospitals | 6 | 404 | 346 |
| 2. 卫生院 | Sanitation Stations | 103 | 5706 | 7592 |
| 二、社区卫生服务中心 | **Neighborhood Service Centers** | **72** | **616** | **3009** |
| 三、门诊部 | **Outpatient Service Stations** | **363** | | **5461** |
| 四、诊所 | **Clinics** | **2243** | | **8906** |
| 五、卫生所、医务室、护理站 | **Medical Houses Nursing Station** | **311** | | **914** |
| 六、社区卫生服务站 | **Neighorhood Service Stations** | **208** | **48** | **2840** |
| 七、急救中心 | **First Aid Centers** | **3** | | **178** |
| 八、采供血机构 | **Institutions of Blood Collection and Supply** | **1** | | **253** |
| 九、妇幼保健院（所、站） | **Maternity and Child Care Centers** | **12** | **524** | **1499** |
| 十、专科疾病防治院（所、站） | **Specialized Disease Prevention & Treatment Institutions** | **6** | **224** | **253** |
| 十一、疾病预防控制中心（防疫站） | **Centers for Disease Control and Prevention（Epidemic Prevention Stations）** | **26** | | **966** |
| 十二、卫生监督所 | **Sanitation Control Stations** | **11** | | **373** |
| 十三、卫生监督检验所（站） | **Sanitation Control and Test Stations** | | | |
| 十四、计划生育技术服务机构 | **Family Planning Service Institutions** | **23** | | **118** |
| 十五、临床检验中心（所、站） | **Clinical Laboratory Center** | **3** | | **202** |
| 十六、健康教育所（站、中心） | **Health Education Stations** | | | |
| 十七、其它卫生机构 | **Other Health Institutions** | **37** | | **304** |
| 十八、疗养院 | **Sanatoriums** | **4** | **900** | **432** |
| 十九、村卫生室 | **Village clinic** | **4283** | | **6070** |

| #卫生技术人员<br>Medical and Technical Personnel | #医生<br>Doctos | 注册护士<br>Registered Nurses | 药剂人员<br>Pharmacists | 检验人员<br>Laboratory Technicians |
|---|---|---|---|---|
| **83975** | **34578** | **38360** | **3988** | **2615** |
| **60286** | **21812** | **29944** | **3165** | **2050** |
| 53583 | 18999 | 27581 | 2660 | 1745 |
| 35891 | 12873 | 18595 | 1666 | 1114 |
| 6816 | 2515 | 3285 | 453 | 202 |
| 774 | 268 | 358 | 77 | 44 |
| 10035 | 3318 | 5314 | 456 | 383 |
| 502 | 269 | 216 | 6 | 4 |
| 621 | 197 | 350 | 20 | 18 |
| 517 | 172 | 304 | 17 | 13 |
| 830 | 299 | 431 | 45 | 29 |
| 1362 | 337 | 882 | 64 | 36 |
| 442 | 148 | 230 | 24 | 27 |
| 34 | 15 | 12 | 5 | 2 |
| 266 | 85 | 134 | 14 | 8 |
| 6703 | 2813 | 2363 | 505 | 305 |
| **2516** | **1098** | **974** | **223** | **92** |
| **4672** | **2317** | **1863** | **199** | **143** |
| **8763** | **5304** | **3324** | **102** | **9** |
| **892** | **536** | **332** | **11** | **3** |
| **2325** | **1134** | **876** | **196** | **49** |
| **112** | **45** | **62** | **1** | **3** |
| **183** | **51** | **79** | **0** | **52** |
| **1113** | **410** | **498** | **43** | **67** |
| **202** | **92** | **66** | **14** | **14** |
| **719** | **354** | **50** | **15** | **79** |
| **263** | | | | |
| **36** | **21** | **6** | | |
| **98** | **7** | **3** | | **42** |
| **223** | **106** | **65** | **5** | **4** |
| **272** | **112** | **97** | **14** | **8** |
| **1300** | **1179** | **121** | | |

# 18-4 分市、区各类卫生机构、床位、人员数（2018年底）

NUMBER OF HEALTH INSTITUTIONS，BEDS AND EMPLOYED PERSONS BY REGION（END OF 2018）

| 市、区名称 | Region | 机构数（个）Instiutions（unit） | 医院小计 Sub-total of Hospitals | #医院 Hospitals | #卫生院 Sanitation Staions |
|---|---|---|---|---|---|
| **全　市** | **Whole Municpality** | **8027** | **421** | **318** | **103** |
| 市南区 | Shinan District | 393 | 27 | 27 | |
| 市北区 | Shibei District | 758 | 79 | 79 | |
| 李沧区 | Licang District | 449 | 22 | 22 | |
| 崂山区 | Laoshan District | 423 | 20 | 18 | 2 |
| 黄岛区 | Huangdao District | 1317 | 60 | 44 | 16 |
| 城阳区 | Chengyang District | 729 | 28 | 23 | 5 |
| 即墨区 | Jimo District | 1034 | 50 | 29 | 21 |
| 胶州市 | Jiaozhou | 975 | 39 | 25 | 14 |
| 平度市 | Pingdu | 1130 | 55 | 26 | 29 |
| 莱西市 | Laixi | 819 | 41 | 25 | 16 |

注：黄岛区含保税港区数据；城阳区含红岛经济区数据。

Note：The Huangdao District contains the data of the bonded harbor area. Chengyang District contains red island economic zone data.

# 18-4 续表 1

Continued

| 市、区名称 | Region | 采供血机构 Institutions of Blood Collection and Supply | 妇幼保健院（所、站）Maternity and Child Care Centers | 专科疾病防治院（所、站）Specialized Disease Prevention & Treatment Institutions |
|---|---|---|---|---|
| **全　市** | **Whole Municpality** | **1** | **12** | **6** |
| 市南区 | Shinan District | 1 | 1 | 1 |
| 市北区 | Shibei District | | 2 | |
| 李沧区 | Licang District | | 1 | |
| 崂山区 | Laoshan District | | 1 | |
| 黄岛区 | Huangdao District | | 2 | 2 |
| 城阳区 | Chengyang District | | 1 | |
| 即墨区 | Jimo District | | 1 | 1 |
| 胶州市 | Jiaozhou | | 1 | |
| 平度市 | Pingdu | | 1 | 2 |
| 莱西市 | Laixi | | 1 | |

注：黄岛区含保税港区数据；城阳区含红岛经济区数据。

Note：The Huangdao District contains the data of the bonded harbor area. Chengyang District contains red island economic zone data.

| 社区卫生服务中心 Neighborhood Service Centers | 社区卫生服务站 Neighborhood Service Stations | 门诊部 Outpatient Service Stations | 诊所、卫生所、医务室、护理站 Clinics Medical Houses | 急救中心 First Aid Centers |
|---|---|---|---|---|
| 72 | 208 | 363 | 2554 | 3 |
| 11 | 30 | 37 | 275 | |
| 13 | 53 | 79 | 526 | 1 |
| 14 | 46 | 35 | 329 | |
| 3 | 30 | 26 | 196 | |
| 13 | 21 | 62 | 406 | 1 |
| 10 | 1 | 66 | 192 | 1 |
| 2 | 21 | 13 | 195 | |
| 4 | | 18 | 189 | |
| | | 26 | 196 | |
| 2 | 6 | 1 | 50 | |

| 疾病预防控制中心（防疫站） Centers for Disease Control and Prevention（Epidemic Prevention Stations） | 卫生监督所 Sanitation Control Stations | 村卫生室 Village health room | 计划生育技术服务机构 Family Planning Service Institutions |
|---|---|---|---|
| **26** | **11** | **4283** | **23** |
| 1 | 1 | | |
| 2 | 2 | | |
| 1 | 1 | | |
| 1 | 1 | 142 | |
| 7 | 1 | 742 | |
| 9 | 1 | 413 | 7 |
| 1 | 1 | 708 | 16 |
| 1 | 1 | 718 | |
| 1 | 1 | 846 | |
| 2 | 1 | 714 | |

## 18-4 续表 2
Continued

| 市、区名称 | Region | 健康教育所（站、中心）Health Education Station | 临床检验中心（站、所）Clinical Laboratory Center | 其他卫生机构 Other Health Institutions | 疗养院 Sanatoriums | 床位数（张）Beds in Health Institutions（bed） |
|---|---|---|---|---|---|---|
| **全　市** | **Whole Municipality** | | **3** | **37** | **4** | **53154** |
| 市南区 | Shinan District | | | 4 | 4 | 6424 |
| 市北区 | Shibei District | | 1 | | | 13932 |
| 李沧区 | Licang District | | | | | 3260 |
| 崂山区 | Laoshan District | | 2 | 1 | | 1374 |
| 黄岛区 | Huangdao District | | | | | 6898 |
| 城阳区 | Chengyang District | | | | | 3304 |
| 即墨区 | Jimo District | | | 25 | | 4896 |
| 胶州市 | Jiaozhou | | | 4 | | 5096 |
| 平度市 | Pingdu | | | 2 | | 5003 |
| 莱西市 | Laixi | | | 1 | | 2967 |

注：黄岛区含保税港区数据；城阳区含红岛经济区数据。
Note： The Huangdao District contains the data of the bonded harbor area. Chengyang District contains red island economic zone data.

## 18-4 续表 3
Continued

| 市、区名称 | Region | 专科疾病防治院（所、站）Specialized Disease Centers | 人员数（人）Personnel（person） | 卫生技术人员 Medical and Technical Personnel |
|---|---|---|---|---|
| **全　市** | **Whole Municipality** | | **102991** | **83975** |
| 市南区 | Shinan District | | 14598 | 11878 |
| 市北区 | Shibei District | | 24631 | 21528 |
| 李沧区 | Licang District | | 8109 | 7071 |
| 崂山区 | Laoshan District | | 4375 | 3320 |
| 黄岛区 | Huangdao District | | 12970 | 10511 |
| 城阳区 | Chengyang District | | 7639 | 6133 |
| 即墨区 | Jimo District | | 8710 | 6584 |
| 胶州市 | Jiaozhou | | 8220 | 6421 |
| 平度市 | Pingdu | | 7802 | 6037 |
| 莱西市 | Laixi | | 5937 | 4492 |

注：黄岛区含保税港区数据；城阳区含红岛经济区数据。
Note： The Huangdao District contains the data of the bonded harbor area. Chengyang District contains red island economic zone data.

| 医院小计 Sub-total of Hospitals | # 医院 Hospitals | # 卫生院 Sanitation Stations | 门诊部 Outpatient Service Stations | 妇幼保健院（所、站）Maternity and Child Care Centers |
|---|---|---|---|---|
| **421** | **318** | **103** | **363** | **12** |
| 27 | 27 | | 37 | 1 |
| 79 | 79 | | 79 | 2 |
| 22 | 22 | | 35 | 1 |
| 20 | 18 | 2 | 26 | 1 |
| 60 | 44 | 16 | 62 | 2 |
| 28 | 23 | 2 | 66 | 1 |
| 50 | 29 | 21 | 13 | 1 |
| 39 | 25 | 14 | 18 | 1 |
| 55 | 26 | 29 | 26 | 1 |
| 41 | 25 | 16 | 1 | 1 |

| 执业（助理）医师 Certified（Assistant）Doctors | 注册护士 Registered Nurses | 药剂人员 Pharmacists | 检验人员 Laboratory Technicians | 其他人员 Other Personnel |
|---|---|---|---|---|
| **34578** | **38360** | **3988** | **2615** | **3350** |
| 4624 | 5734 | 538 | 424 | 378 |
| 8945 | 9995 | 1021 | 631 | 748 |
| 3073 | 3302 | 327 | 183 | 103 |
| 1552 | 1330 | 140 | 125 | 136 |
| 4345 | 4864 | 484 | 306 | 358 |
| 2464 | 2724 | 314 | 200 | 355 |
| 2696 | 2823 | 373 | 207 | 371 |
| 2534 | 3014 | 291 | 190 | 293 |
| 2515 | 2650 | 280 | 192 | 302 |
| 1830 | 1924 | 220 | 157 | 306 |

## 18-5 收养性社会福利单位情况(2018 年)
BASIC STATICTICS ON SOCIAL WELFARE INSTITUTIONS (2018)

| 市、区名称 | Region | 单位数(个) Number of Institutions (unit) | 年末职工人数(人) Number of Staff and Workers at Year-end (person) | 年末床位数(张) Number of Beds at Year-end (bed) |
|---|---|---|---|---|
| **全　市** | **Whole Municpality** | **228** | **4682** | **38482** |
| 市本级 | Municipal Level | 8 | 689 | 2402 |
| 市南区 | Shinan District | 17 | 386 | 2813 |
| 市北区 | Shibei District | 58 | 1319 | 9784 |
| 李沧区 | Licang District | 34 | 698 | 3496 |
| 崂山区 | Laoshan District | 11 | 283 | 1782 |
| 黄岛区 | Huangdao District | 19 | 468 | 3118 |
| 城阳区 | Chengyang District | 16 | 178 | 3879 |
| 即墨区 | Jimo District | 20 | 134 | 3393 |
| 胶州市 | Jiaozhou | 8 | 91 | 2378 |
| 平度市 | Pingdu | 25 | 151 | 2557 |
| 莱西市 | Laixi | 12 | 185 | 2880 |

注：1. 年末在院人数仅包括老年人与残疾人服务机构。2. 黄岛区含保税港区数据；城阳区含红岛经济区数据。

Note： 1. At the end of the year, the number of people in hostitals includes the elderly and disabled service organizations only.
2. The Huangdao District contains the data of the bonded harbor area. Chengyang District contains red island economic zone data.

## 18-6 社会救济情况(2018 年)
BASIC STATISTICS ON SOCLAL RELIEF (2018)

| 市、区名称 | Region | 城镇居民最低生活保障人数(人) Number of Persons Receiving Minimun Living Allowance in Urban Area (Person) | 城镇居民最低生活保障家庭数(户) Number of Households Receiving Minimum Living Allowance in Urban Area (household) | 城镇低保资金计划支出(万元) Planned Expense of Funds for Minimum Living Allowance in Urban Area (10 000 yuan) |
|---|---|---|---|---|
| **全　市** | **Whole Municpality** | **20457** | **13638** | **19921.5** |
| 市南区 | Shinan District | 3305 | 2270 | 3359.1 |
| 市北区 | Shibei District | 12125 | 7904 | 11722.2 |
| 李沧区 | Licang District | 1922 | 1242 | 2009.9 |
| 崂山区 | Laoshan District | 109 | 64 | 106.9 |
| 黄岛区 | Huangdao District | 721 | 526 | 671 |
| 城阳区 | Chengyang District | 208 | 138 | 187.5 |
| 即墨区 | Jimo District | 927 | 660 | 855.3 |
| 胶州市 | Jiaozhou | 561 | 412 | 528.2 |
| 平度市 | Pingdu | 414 | 291 | 336 |
| 莱西市 | Laixi | 165 | 131 | 145.4 |

注：1. 全市农村低保资金计划支出中包含市本级数据。2. 黄岛区含保税港区数据；城阳区含红岛经济区数据。

Note： 1. The municipal level data shall be included in the expenditure of the rural low-insurance fund plan of the whole city.
2. The Huangdao District contains the data of the bonded harbor area. Chengyang District contains red island economic zone data.

| 年末在院人数（人）<br>Residences at Year-end<br>（person） | 老年人<br>Senior Citizens | 青壮年<br>Young and middle-aged | 少年儿童<br>Youth |
|---|---|---|---|
| **20614** | **19989** | **325** | **231** |
| 1715 | 1154 | 280 | 225 |
| 1289 | 1289 | | |
| 6620 | 6620 | | |
| 2702 | 2702 | | |
| 585 | 546 | 39 | |
| 1603 | 1597 | 6 | |
| 1918 | 1918 | | |
| 896 | 896 | | |
| 671 | 671 | | |
| 1409 | 1396 | | |
| 1206 | 1200 | | 6 |

| 农村居民最低生活保障人数（人）<br>Number of Persons Receiving Minimum living Allowance in Rural Area（person） | 农村居民最低生活保障家庭数（户）<br>Number of Households Receiving Minimum Living Allowance in Rural Area（household） | 农村低保资金计划支出<br>（万元）<br>Rural low-insurance fund plan expenditure<br>（10 000 yuan） |
|---|---|---|
| **77064** | **52421** | **51222.7** |
| | | |
| | | |
| | | |
| 1648 | 904 | 1357.6 |
| 12364 | 8449 | 9364 |
| 3098 | 2005 | 2390.9 |
| 17637 | 12151 | 14558.8 |
| 12225 | 8070 | 7276.5 |
| 21861 | 14673 | 12017 |
| 8231 | 6169 | 4257.9 |

# 18-7 分市、区婚姻登记情况(2018年)

BASIC STATISTICS ON MARRIAGE REGISTRATION BY REGION (2018)

| 市、区名称 | Region | 准予登记结婚 Registered Marriages | | |
|---|---|---|---|---|
| | | 合计(对) Total (couple) | 初婚(人) First Marriages (person) | 恢复结婚(对) Resumed Marriages (couple) |
| **全 市** | **Whole Municipality** | **56824** | **78993** | **120** |
| 市本级 | Municipal Level | 188 | 245 | 2 |
| 市南区 | Shinan District | 5318 | 7970 | 6 |
| 市北区 | Shibei District | 6717 | 8710 | 9 |
| 李沧区 | Licang District | 3034 | 4069 | 3 |
| 崂山区 | Laoshan District | 2679 | 4255 | 0 |
| 黄岛区 | Huangdao District | 9998 | 13522 | 0 |
| 城阳区 | Chengyang District | 4045 | 6009 | 0 |
| 即墨区 | Jimo District | 6699 | 9987 | 14 |
| 胶州市 | Jiaozhou | 5493 | 7302 | 1 |
| 平度市 | Pingdu | 8255 | 11097 | 85 |
| 莱西市 | Laixi | 4398 | 5827 | 0 |

注：黄岛区含保税港区数据；城阳区含红岛经济区数据。

Note: The Huangdao District contains the data of the bonded harbor area. Chengyang District contains red island economic zone data.

| 再婚（人）Remariages（person） | | 准予登记离婚（对）Registered Divorces（couple） | 涉外婚姻登记（对）Registered Marriages with Foreigner（couple） |
|---|---|---|---|
| 男 Male | 女 Female | | |
| **17212** | **17443** | **24085** | **51** |
| 67 | 64 | 51 | 51 |
| 1412 | 1254 | 2229 | |
| 2453 | 2271 | 3832 | |
| 1047 | 952 | 1572 | |
| 576 | 527 | 799 | |
| 3170 | 3304 | 4467 | |
| 1067 | 1014 | 1390 | |
| 1663 | 1748 | 2006 | |
| 1800 | 1884 | 2577 | |
| 2529 | 2884 | 3467 | |
| 1428 | 1541 | 1695 | |

# 18-8 律师、公证、调解、社会治安基本情况(2000-2018年)

BASIC STATISTICS ON LAW YERS, NOTARIZATION, MEDIATION AND SOCIAL ORDER (2000-2018)

| 项目 | Item | 单位 | Unit | 2000年 | 2005年 | 2008年 | 2009年 | 2010年 |
|---|---|---|---|---|---|---|---|---|
| **一、律师工作** | **Lawyers** | | | | | | | |
| 律师事务所 | Law Offices | 个 | Unit | 76 | 116 | 159 | 203 | 222 |
| 律师工作者 | Lawyers | 人 | person | 1439 | 1941 | 2915 | 3144 | 2487 |
| 专职 | Full-time Lawyers | 人 | person | 971 | 1542 | 1855 | 1934 | 2377 |
| 兼职(含特邀) | Part-time Lawyers | 人 | person | 150 | 73 | 90 | 86 | 94 |
| 请常年法律顾问单位 | Units with Permanent Legal Advisors | 个 | Unit | 2508 | 3564 | 4086 | 4457 | 4779 |
| 全年办理民事代理 | Agent of Civil Gases | 件 | case | 5571 | 11104 | 20547 | 29025 | 26935 |
| 刑事辩护 | Defender of Criminal Cases | 件 | case | 1755 | 3003 | 3655 | 3758 | 3964 |
| 非诉讼事件 | Agent of Non-litigious Legal Affairs | 件 | case | 5251 | 6501 | 5467 | 5897 | 4274 |
| 解答法律询问 | Agent of Legal Advisory Services | 件 | case | 58385 | 27880 | 31571 | 30123 | 21102 |
| 代写法律事务文书 | Agent of Legal Documents Written on Behalf of Clients | 件 | case | 9335 | 8595 | 9077 | 6015 | 6210 |
| **二、公证工作** | **Notarization** | | | | | | | |
| 公证处 | Notary Offices | 个 | Unit | 15 | 15 | 13 | 13 | 13 |
| 公证人员 | Notarial Personnel | 人 | person | 152 | 196 | 214 | 214 | 214 |
| 公证员 | Notaries | 人 | person | 106 | 112 | 117 | 118 | 117 |
| 办理公证文书 | Notarized Documents | 件 | case | 120849 | 105787 | 101766 | 97019 | 94077 |
| **三、人民调解** | **People's Mediation** | | | | | | | |
| 人民调解委员会 | People's Mediation Committees | 个 | Unit | 9750 | 11480 | 11223 | 9643 | 8014 |
| 调解人员 | Mediators | 人 | person | 34714 | 46735 | 33875 | 32675 | 27820 |
| 调解民间纠纷 | Civil Disputes Mediated | 件 | case | 18501 | 13658 | 12803 | 14660 | 20550 |
| **四、社会治安** | **Social Order** | | | | | | | |
| 交通事故发生次数 | Traffic Accidents | 次 | time | 15601 | 7051 | 3025 | 2570 | 2313 |
| 死亡人数 | Deaths | 人 | person | 1371 | 776 | 489 | 402 | 393 |
| 受伤人数 | Injuries | 人 | person | 8620 | 6639 | 3273 | 2943 | 2504 |
| 经济损失 | Losses | 万元 | 10000 yuan | 4815.70 | 2208.20 | 991.50 | 854.80 | 811.27 |
| 火灾发生次数 | Fire Accidents | 次 | time | 3088 | 1948 | 840 | 773 | 683 |
| 死亡人数 | Deaths | 人 | person | 10 | 3 | 16 | 5 | 9 |
| 受伤人数 | Injuries | 人 | person | 43 | 3 | 13 | | 4 |
| 经济损失 | Losses | 万元 | 10000 yuan | 1531.06 | 550.40 | 979.70 | 865.50 | 5566.11 |

| 2011年 | 2012年 | 2013年 | 2014年 | 2015年 | 2016年 | 2017年 | 2018年 |
|---|---|---|---|---|---|---|---|
| 247 | 266 | 285 | 322 | 337 | 355 | 371 | 394 |
| 2801 | 3130 | 3143 | 3637 | 3896 | 4260 | 4839 | 5451 |
| 2643 | 2944 | 2980 | 3443 | 3728 | 4134 | 4578 | 5179 |
| 105 | 107 | 93 | 110 | 112 | 123 | 127 | 129 |
| 5180 | 5228 | 5374 | 5647 | 6101 | 6294 | 6952 | |
| 27702 | 30586 | 31147 | 36317 | 39640 | 42216 | 47679 | 63277 |
| 4535 | 4935 | 4858 | 5370 | 5107 | 4560 | 4936 | 7490 |
| 3576 | 4251 | 4133 | 4833 | 4900 | 4624 | 5386 | 8486 |
| 42428 | 45388 | 53775 | 33717 | 34003 | 40884 | 55320 | |
| 6762 | 6388 | 7376 | 5961 | 6272 | 7326 | 7112 | |
| | | | | | | | |
| 13 | 13 | 13 | 13 | 12 | 12 | 12 | 12 |
| 221 | 225 | 244 | 249 | 242 | 250 | 264 | 265 |
| 119 | 118 | 113 | 119 | 129 | 125 | 127 | 125 |
| 88506 | 87703 | 99852 | 100553 | 96085 | 104423 | 105200 | 88619 |
| | | | | | | | |
| 8486 | 8426 | 8448 | 8027 | 7708 | 7861 | 7413 | 7366 |
| 28094 | 27421 | 27035 | 25646 | 25222 | 26318 | 23918 | 24761 |
| 22882 | 23999 | 19525 | 23737 | 23552 | 30084 | | 29989 |
| | | | | | | | |
| 2164 | 1951 | 1896 | 1857 | 1814 | 1759 | 1847 | 1825 |
| 374 | 343 | 333 | 321 | 313 | 308 | 324 | 319 |
| 2240 | 1913 | 1840 | 1796 | 1785 | 1770 | 1828 | 1814 |
| 861.05 | 652.10 | 609.80 | 561.80 | 509.1 | 506.6 | 528.7 | 573.8 |
| 369 | 366 | 742 | 1170 | 1001 | 1654 | 1458 | 1258 |
| 1 | 6 | 7 | 12 | 10 | 8 | 13 | 2 |
| 2 | 2 | 11 | 9 | 3 | 10 | 9 | 6 |
| 598.20 | 601.90 | 2348.10 | 1725.50 | 1491.0 | 1433.2 | 2739.7 | 2912 |

# 18-9　分区、市殡葬服务情况（2018 年）

BASIC STATISTICS ON FUNERAL SERVICES（2018）

| 区、市名称 | Region | 单位数（个）Number of Institutions（unit） | 年末职工人数（人）Number of Staff and Workers at Year-end（person） | 火化炉数（台）Number of Cremators（unit） | 处理遗体数（具）Number of Remains Cremated（body） |
|---|---|---|---|---|---|
| **全　市** | **Whole Municpality** | **7** | **176** | **51** | **64720** |
| 市本级 | Municipal Level | 1 | 47 | 14 | 13340 |
| 市南区 | Shinan District | | | | |
| 市北区 | Shibei District | | | | |
| 李沧区 | Licang District | | | | |
| 崂山区 | Laoshan District | | | | |
| 黄岛区 | Huangdao District | 1 | 18 | 7 | 9482 |
| 城阳区 | Chengyang District | 1 | 19 | 5 | 6738 |
| 即墨区 | Jimo District | 1 | 11 | 7 | 9964 |
| 胶州市 | Jiaozhou | 1 | 9 | 5 | 7017 |
| 平度市 | Pingdu | 1 | 18 | 7 | 11659 |
| 莱西市 | Laixi | 1 | 54 | 6 | 6520 |

注：黄岛区含保税港区数据；城阳区含红岛经济区数据。

Note： The Huangdao District contains the data of the bonded harbor area. Chengyang District contains red island economic zone data.

## 18-9 续表
Continued

| 区、市名称 | Region | 穴位数（个）Number of Graves (unit) | 本年销售穴位数 Number of Graves Saled in the Year | 安葬数（具）Number of Remains Buried (body) | 本年安葬数 Number of Remains Buried in the Year |
|---|---|---|---|---|---|
| **全　市** | **Whole Municipality** | **20118** | **125** | **4105** | **520** |
| 市本级 | Municipal Level | 20118 | 125 | 4105 | 520 |
| 市南区 | Shinan District | | | | |
| 市北区 | Shibei District | | | | |
| 李沧区 | Licang District | | | | |
| 崂山区 | Laoshan District | | | | |
| 黄岛区 | Huangdao District | | | | |
| 城阳区 | Chengyang District | | | | |
| 即墨区 | Jimo District | | | | |
| 胶州市 | Jiaozhou | | | | |
| 平度市 | Pingdu | | | | |
| 莱西市 | Laixi | | | | |

注：黄岛区含保税港区数据；城阳区含红岛经济区数据。
Note : The Huangdao District contains the data of the bonded harbor area. Chengyang District contains red island economic zone data.

# 主要统计指标解释

**卫生机构**　包括医疗机构、疾病预防控制中心（防疫站）、采供血机构、卫生监督及监测（检验）机构、医学科研和在职培训机构、健康教育所等。

**医疗机构**　包括医院、社区卫生服务中心（站）、疗养院、卫生院、门诊部、诊所（卫生所、医务室）、妇幼保健院（所、站）、专科疾病防治院（所、站）、急救中心（站）和临床检验中心。医疗机构分为非赢利性医疗机构和赢利性医疗机构。

**医院**　包括综合医院、中医医院、中西医结合医院、民族医院、各类专科医院和护理院。

**医生**　指在医疗、预防保健机构工作且取得《执业医师证书》的执业医师和执业助理医师。

**卫生技术人员**　指卫生事业机构中现任职务为卫生技术工作的人员。包括中医师、西医师、中西医结合高级医师、护师、中药师、西药师、检验师、其他技师、中医士、西医士、护士、助产士、中药剂士、西药剂士、检验士、其他技士、其他中医、护理员、中药剂员、西药剂员、检验员、其他初级卫生技术人员。

**社会福利事业单位**　指集中收养社会孤老、残、幼的机构，包括由民政部门管理的社会福利院、儿童福利院、精神病人福利院和城镇集体举办的福利院及农村集体举办的敬老院以及优抚医院和具有收养能力的社区服务中心等。

# Explanatory Notes on Main Statistical Indicators

**Health Care Institutions**　include：medical institutions，disease prevention and control centers（epidemic prevention stations），blood gathering and supplying institutions，health supervision and inspection（check up）institutions，medicinal scientific research and on-job training institutions，health education and so on.

**Medical Organizations**　include：hospitals，health service centers（stations）of communities，nursing homes，health centers，clinics，clinics（health stations and infirmaries），maternity and child care agencies（centers and stations），special disease prevention and curing agencies（centers and stations），first aid centers（stations）and clinical inspection centers.Medical organizations are grouped by two types：profit-making and non-profit-making medical organizations.

**Hospitals**　include：polyclinics，traditional Chinese medical hospitals，hospitals integrated with traditional Chinese therapeutics and western therapeutics，ethical hospitals，various specialties hospitals and nursing hospitals.

**Doctors**　refer to certified physicians and certified assistant physicians with certifications working in medical and health care and prevention agencies.

**Medical Technical Personnel**　refers to those medical workers employed institutions，including doctors of Chinese and Western medicine，senior doctors of integrated Chinese-Western medicine，head nurses，pharmacists of Chinese and Western medicine，laboratory specialists，other specialists，junior doctors of Chinese and Western medicine，nurses，midwives，druggists of Chinese and Western medicine，laboratory technicians，other technicians，other practitioners of Chinese medicine，nursing attendants，pharmacological workers of Chinese and Western medicine，laboratory workers，and other primary medical personnel.

**Social Welfare Institutionsr**　efer to institutions taking care of old people without children，handicapped people and orphans. They include social welfare institutions run by civil affairs departments，children welfare institutions，social welfare institutions for mental patients，collective-owned old people's homes in rural areas，convalescent homes and community service centers with the capacity of receiving those people.

# 附　录

APPENDIX

# 2018年省内各市主要经济指标对比情况

MAJOR ECONOMIC INDICATORS ON CTTIES OF THE PROVINCE（2018）

| 指标<br>Indicator | 单位<br>Unit | 山东省<br>Shandong | 青岛市<br>Qingdao | 济南市<br>JIman | 淄博市<br>Zibo | 枣庄市<br>Zaozhuang | 东营市<br>Dongying |
|---|---|---|---|---|---|---|---|
| 生产总值（GDP） | 亿元<br>（100 million yuan） | 76469.7 | 12001.5 | 7856.6 | 5068.4 | 2402.4 | 4152.5 |
| 比上年增长 YOY Growth | % | 6.4 | 7.4 | 7.4 | 6.1 | 4.3 | 4.5 |
| 规上工业增加值<br>YOY Growth of Industrial Added Value above Designated Size | % | 5.2 | 6.8 | 7.1 | 6.9 | 4.0 | 3.8 |
| 固定资产投资比上年增长<br>YOY Growth of Investment Fixed Assets | % | 4.1 | 7.9 | 9.6 | 6.6 | −19.8 | −10.0 |
| 货物进出口总额<br>Imports and Exports | 亿元<br>（100 million yuan） | 19302.5 | 5321.3 | 870.5 | 950.7 | 105.5 | 1627.2 |
| 比上年增长 YOY Growth | % | 7.7 | 5.7 | 13.7 | 35.9 | 5.4 | 20.2 |
| #货物出口 Exports | 亿元<br>（100 million yuan） | 10569.6 | 3172.2 | 564.7 | 416.8 | 98.5 | 368.2 |
| 比上年增长 YOY Growth | % | 6.1 | 4.7 | 11.1 | 12.0 | 11.8 | 10.3 |
| 货物进口 Imports | 亿元<br>（100 million yuan） | 8732.9 | 2149.0 | 305.7 | 533.9 | 7.0 | 1259.0 |
| 比上年增长 YOY Growth | % | 9.7 | 7.3 | 19.0 | 63.0 | −41.4 | 23.5 |
| 社会消费品零售总额<br>Total Retail Sales of Consumer Goods | 亿元<br>（100 million yuan） | – | 4842.5 | 4404.5 | – | 950.3 | 867.0 |
| 比上年增长 YOY Growth | % | 8.8 | 10.0 | 10.0 | 7.3 | 8.6 | 8.5 |
| 一般公共预算收入<br>General Public Budget Revenue | 亿元<br>（100 million yuan） | 6485.4 | 1231.9 | 752.8 | 385.2 | 146.7 | 244.6 |
| 比上年增长 YOY Growth | % | 6.3 | 6.5 | 11.2 | 6.5 | 1.0 | 5.0 |
| 全体居民人均可支配收入<br>Disposable income per capita of all residents | 元<br>yuan | 29205 | 42019 | 39944 | 34730 | 24334 | 37586 |
| 比上年增长 YOY Growth | % | 8.4 | 8.4 | 8.3 | 8.4 | 8.5 | 7.9 |
| 城镇居民人均可支配收入<br>Per Capita Disposable Income of Urban Households | 元<br>yuan | 39549 | 50817 | 50146 | 42277 | 32001 | 47912 |
| 比上年增长 YOY Growth | % | 7.5 | 7.7 | 7.5 | 7.3 | 6.9 | 7.0 |
| 农村居民人均可支配收入<br>Per Capital Net Income of Rural Households | 元<br>yuan | 16297 | 20820 | 17924 | 18273 | 15345 | 17485 |
| 比上年增长 YOY Growth | % | 7.8 | 7.5 | 8.0 | 7.8 | 8.3 | 7.6 |

注：山东省、淄博、济宁、威海未公布社会消费品零售总额数据。

Note：Shandong, Zibo, Jining and Weihai did not publish the total retail sales of consumer goods.

| 烟台市 Yantai | 潍坊市 Weifang | 济宁市 Jining | 泰安市 Taian | 威海市 Weihai | 日照市 Rizhao | 莱芜市 Laiwu | 临沂市 Linyi | 德州市 Dezhou | 聊城市 Liaocheng | 滨州市 Binzhou | 菏泽市 Heze |
|---|---|---|---|---|---|---|---|---|---|---|---|
| 7832.6 | 6156.8 | 4930.6 | 3651.5 | 3641.5 | 2202.2 | 1005.7 | 4717.8 | 3380.3 | 3152.2 | 2640.5 | 3078.8 |
| 6.4 | 6.5 | 5.8 | 5.7 | 6.7 | 7.3 | 7.2 | 7.3 | 6.7 | 5.4 | 1.5 | 7.9 |
| 6.8 | 5.6 | 6.1 | 5.5 | 6.0 | 8.4 | 8.3 | 8.7 | 7.3 | 2.8 | -2.3 | 7.2 |
| 6.0 | 4.4 | 7.1 | 5.8 | 7.5 | 6.3 | 7.2 | 7.8 | 7.3 | -4.3 | -16.8 | 8.0 |
| 3047.6 | 1623.4 | 423.8 | 157.5 | 1389.8 | 894.9 | 111.0 | 673.8 | 292.8 | 487.0 | 818.4 | 512.5 |
| -1.3 | 11.1 | 3.4 | 4.6 | -1.1 | -1.5 | 4.2 | 1.2 | 19.3 | 6.2 | 21.5 | 26.5 |
| 1767.0 | 1036.3 | 218.6 | 124.2 | 911.7 | 405.7 | 72.0 | 532.4 | 187.7 | 243.2 | 303.9 | 151.6 |
| 1.9 | 9.6 | -7.6 | 7.3 | 6.9 | 16.1 | 3.0 | 8.3 | 4.5 | 4.0 | 12.5 | -3.2 |
| 1280.6 | 587.1 | 205.2 | 33.2 | 478.1 | 489.2 | 39.0 | 141.5 | 105.1 | 243.8 | 514.5 | 360.9 |
| -5.4 | 13.9 | 18.4 | -4.4 | -13.5 | -12.5 | 6.4 | -18.8 | 59.6 | 8.3 | 27.6 | 45.2 |
| 3079.4 | 2702.7 | - | 1593.8 | - | 774.1 | 373.2 | 2482.2 | 1525.5 | 1334.4 | 993.7 | 1811.4 |
| 7.8 | 8.8 | 8.3 | 8.8 | 10.1 | 7.5 | 8.8 | 8.5 | 9.3 | 7.7 | 6.7 | 9.8 |
| 636.6 | 569.8 | 400.0 | 219.5 | 284.4 | 159.8 | 62.6 | 311.8 | 202.5 | 194.3 | 240.5 | 206.0 |
| 6.0 | 5.7 | 3.7 | 6.0 | 4.2 | 13.0 | 11.7 | 9.3 | 8.0 | 4.2 | 6.3 | 10.4 |
| 34901 | 30049 | 25902 | 27389 | 36626 | 25377 | 29254 | 25545 | 20761 | 19855 | 26371 | 18858 |
| 8.1 | 8.0 | 8.6 | 8.5 | 8.4 | 9.0 | 8.3 | 8.6 | 8.8 | 9.2 | 7.4 | 9.5 |
| 44875 | 39042 | 34796 | 35196 | 45896 | 33280 | 37401 | 35727 | 26562 | 27276 | 35049 | 26176 |
| 7.3 | 7.6 | 7.3 | 7.5 | 7.5 | 8.1 | 7.2 | 7.4 | 7.8 | 8.1 | 6.5 | 8.5 |
| 19425 | 18719 | 16055 | 16959 | 20423 | 15785 | 17468 | 13638 | 14564 | 13492 | 16061 | 12848 |
| 7.6 | 7.4 | 8.2 | 8.2 | 7.7 | 8.6 | 8.2 | 8.1 | 8.8 | 8.7 | 7.7 | 9.3 |

# 2018 年十五个副省级城市主要经济指标对比表

MAJOR ECONOMIC INDICATORS ON CTTIES UNDER PROVINCIAL LEVELS（2018）

| 指标<br>Indicator | 单位<br>Unit | 青岛<br>Qingdao | 沈阳<br>Shenyang | 大连<br>Dalian | 长春<br>Changchun | 哈尔滨<br>Harbin |
|---|---|---|---|---|---|---|
| 全市生产总值（GDP） | 亿元（100 million yuan） | 12001.5 | 6292.4 | 7668.5 | 7175.7 | 6300.5 |
| 比上年增长 YOY Growth | % | 7.4 | 5.4 | 6.5 | 7.2 | 5.1 |
| # 第一产业 Primary Industry | 亿元（100 million yuan） | 386.9 | 260.1 | 442.7 |  | 525.5 |
| 比上年增长 YOY Growth | % | 3.5 | 3.2 | 3.0 | 1.7 | -0.1 |
| 第二产业 Secondary Industry | 亿元（100 million yuan） | 4850.6 | 2376.6 | 3241.6 |  | 1689.3 |
| 比上年增长 YOY Growth | % | 7.3 | 5.7 | 11.9 | 7.3 | 2.7 |
| 第三产业 Tertiary Industry | 亿元（100 million yuan） | 6764.0 | 3655.7 | 3984.2 |  | 4085.7 |
| 比上年增长 YOY Growth | % | 7.7 | 5.4 | 2.9 | 7.8 | 7.5 |
| 三产占比 Three-yield ratio | % | 56.4 | 58.1 | 52.0 | 46.9 | 64.8 |
| 规上工业增加值 YOY Growth of Industrial Added Value above Designated size | % | 6.8 | 7.6 | 15.9 | 8.5 | 5.8 |
| 固定资产投资比上年增长 YOY Growth of Investment in Fixed Assets | % | 7.9 | 15.3 | 10.1 | 6.7 | -7.2 |
| 社会消费品零售总额 Total Retail Sales of Consumer Goods | 亿元（100 million yuan） | 4842.5 | 4051.2 | 3880.1 | 3003.6 | 4125.1 |
| 比上年增长 YOY Growth | % | 10.0 | 9.2 | 7.8 | 6.2 | 4.2 |
| 货物进出口总额 Imports and Exports | 亿元（100 million yuan） | 5321.2 | 984.3 | 4701.4 | 1054.6 | 209.7 |
| 比上年增长 YOY Growth | % | 5.7 | 13.5 | 13.9 | 10.7 | -8.0 |
| # 货物出口 Exports | 亿元（100 million yuan） | 3172.2 | 342.1 | 1889.6 | 152.5 | 103.5 |
| 比上年增长 YOY Growth | % | 4.7 | 7.7 | 8.5 | 17.5 | 5.2 |
| 货物进口 Imports | 亿元（100 million yuan） | 2149.0 | 642.1 | 2811.8 | 902.1 | 106.2 |
| 比上年增长 YOY Growth | % | 7.3 | 16.8 | 17.8 | 9.6 | -18.0 |
| 一般公共预算收入 General Public Budget Revenue | 亿元（100 million yuan） | 1231.9 | 720.6 | 704.0 | 478.0 | 384.4 |
| 比上年增长 YOY Growth | % | 6.5 | 10.0 | 7.0 | 6.2 | 4.4 |
| 城镇居民人均可支配收入 Per Capita Disposable Income of Urban Households | 元（yuan） | 50817 | 44054 | 43550 | 35332 | 37828 |
| 比上年增长 YOY Growth | % | 7.7 | 6.5 | 7.3 | 6.5 | 6.5 |
| 农村居民人均可支配收入 Per Capltal Net Income of Rural Households | 元（yuan） | 20820 | 16530 | 18103 | 14237 | 16934 |
| 比上年增长 YOY Growth | % | 7.5 | 6.9 | 7.3 | 6.0 | 9.0 |
| 居民消费价格指数 Consumer Price Index | % | 102.1 | 103.0 | 103.0 | 102.0 | 102.5 |

注：部分城市数据未公布。

Note：Some of the urban income data has not been finalized.

| 南京 Nanjing | 杭州 Hangzhou | 宁波 Mingbo | 厦门 Xiamen | 济南 Jinan | 武汉 Wuhan | 广州 Guangzhou | 深圳 Shenzhen | 成都 Chengdu | 西安 Xian |
|---|---|---|---|---|---|---|---|---|---|
| 12820.4 | 13509.0 | 10745.5 | 4791.4 | 7856.6 | 14847.3 | 22859.4 | 24222.0 | 15342.8 | 8349.9 |
| 8.0 | 6.7 | 7.0 | 7.7 | 7.4 | 8.0 | 6.2 | 7.6 | 8.0 | 8.2 |
| 273.4 | 306.0 | 306.0 | 24.4 | 272.4 | 362.0 | 223.4 | 22.1 | 522.6 | 258.8 |
| 0.6 | 1.8 | 2.2 | 2.6 | 2.5 | 2.9 | 2.5 | 3.9 | 3.6 | 3.3 |
| 4721.6 | 4572.0 | 5507.5 | 1980.2 | 2829.3 | 6377.8 | 6234.1 | 9962.0 | 6516.2 | 2925.6 |
| 6.5 | 5.8 | 6.2 | 8.1 | 7.8 | 5.7 | 5.4 | 9.3 | 7.0 | 8.5 |
| 7825.4 | 8632.0 | 4932.0 | 2786.9 | 4754.8 | 8107.5 | 16401.8 | 14237.9 | 8304.0 | 5165.4 |
| 9.1 | 7.5 | 8.1 | 7.5 | 7.5 | 10.1 | 6.6 | 6.4 | 9.0 | 8.3 |
| 61.0 | 63.9 | 45.9 | 58.2 | 60.5 | 54.6 | 71.8 | 58.8 | 54.1 | 61.9 |
| 7.8 | 6.3 | 6.3 | 8.8 | 7.1 | 5.7 | 5.5 | 9.5 | 8.5 | 9.4 |
| 9.4 | 10.8 | 3.6 | 10.1 | 9.6 | 10.6 | 8.2 | 20.6 | 10.0 | 8.5 |
| 5832.5 | 5715.0 | 4154.9 | 1542.4 | 4404.5 | 6843.9 | 9256.2 | 6168.9 | 6801.8 | 4658.7 |
| 8.4 | 9.0 | 8.1 | 6.6 | 10.0 | 10.5 | 7.6 | 7.6 | 10.0 | 9.6 |
| 4317.2 | 5245.3 | 8576.3 | 6002.1 | 825.0 | 2146.0 | 9810.2 | 29983.7 | 4983.2 | 3303.9 |
| 4.7 | 3.1 | 12.9 | 3.2 | 16.2 | 10.9 | 1.0 | 7.0 | 26.4 | 29.6 |
| 2500.7 | 3417.1 | 5550.6 | 3338.5 | 519.3 | 1272.7 | 5607.6 | 16274.7 | 2746.9 | 1957.5 |
| 7.9 | -1.0 | 11.4 | 2.6 | 14.6 | 10.0 | -3.2 | -1.6 | 33.0 | 26.1 |
| 1816.5 | 1828.2 | 3025.6 | 2663.5 | 305.7 | 873.3 | 4202.6 | 13709.1 | 2236.6 | 1346.4 |
| 0.6 | 11.8 | 15.7 | 4.0 | 19.0 | 12.2 | 7.1 | 19.4 | 19.2 | 35.0 |
| 1470.0 | 1825.1 | 1379.7 | 754.5 | 752.8 | 1528.7 | 1632.3 | 3538.4 | 1424.2 | 684.7 |
| 15.6 | 12.5 | 10.8 | 8.3 | 11.2 | 11.0 | 6.5 | 6.2 | 9.4 | 10.8 |
| 59308 | 61172 | 60134 | 54401 | 50146 | 47359 | 59982 |  | 42128 | 38729 |
| 8.7 | 8.7 | 8.0 | 8.8 | 7.5 | 9.1 | 8.3 |  | 8.2 | 8.1 |
| 25263 | 33193 | 33633 | 18842 | 17924 | 22652 | 26020 |  | 22135 | 13286 |
| 9.2 | 9.2 | 8.9 | 7.1 | 8.0 | 8.5 | 10.8 |  | 9.0 | 9.0 |
| 102.4 | 102.3 | 102.2 | 101.8 | 102.6 | 101.9 | 102.4 | 102.8 | 101.4 | 101.9 |

# 2018 年副省级城市之外部分城市主要经济指标情况

THE MAIN ECONOMIC INDICATORS OF SOME OTHER CITIES THAN THE SUB-PROVINCIAL CITY FOR（2018）

| 指标 Indicator | 单位 Unit | 北京 Beijing | 天津 Tianjin | 上海 Shanghai | 重庆 Chongqing | 苏州 Suzhou | 无锡 Wuxi |
|---|---|---|---|---|---|---|---|
| 全市生产总值（GDP） | 亿元（100 million yuan） | 30320.0 | 18809.6 | 32679.9 | 20363.2 | 18597.5 | 11438.6 |
| 同比增长 Year-on-year growth | % | 6.6 | 6.0 | 6.6 | 6.0 | 7.0 | 7.4 |
| #第一产业 Primary Industry | 亿元（100 million yuan） | 118.7 | 172.7 | 104.4 | 1378.3 | 214 | 125.1 |
| 同比增长 Year-on-year growth | % | -2.3 | 0.1 | -6.9 | 4.4 | -4.6 | -0.3 |
| 第二产业 Secondary Industry | 亿元（100 million yuan） | 5647.7 | 7609.8 | 9732.5 | 8328.8 | 8933.3 | 5464.0 |
| 同比增长 Year-on-year growth | % | 4.2 | 1.0 | 1.8 | 3.0 | 5.6 | 8.0 |
| 第三产业 Tertiary Industry | 亿元（100 million yuan） | 24553.6 | 11027.1 | 22843.0 | 10656.1 | 9450.2 | 5849.5 |
| 同比增长 Year-on-year growth | % | 7.3 | 5.9 | 8.7 | 6.0 | 7.0 | 7.1 |
| 第三产业增加值占 GDP 比重 Proportion taken by the added value in GDP for the Tertiary Industry | % | 81.0 | 58.6 | 69.9 | 52.3 | 50.8 | 51.1 |
| 规模以上工业增加值同比增长 YOY Growth of Industrial Added Value above Designated Size | % | 4.6 | 2.4 | 10.8 | 0.5 | 5.4 | 9.0 |
| 固定资产投资同比增长 YOY Growth of Investment in Fixed Assets | % | -9.9 | -5.6 | 5.2 | 7.0 | 4.5 | 5.8 |
| 社会消费品零售总额 Total Retail Sales of Consumer Goods | 亿元（100 million yuan） | 25405.9 |  | 12668.7 |  | 5746.9 | 3672.7 |
| 同比增长 Year-on-year growth | % | 7.4 | 1.7 | 7.9 | 8.7 | 7.4 | 9.0 |
| 进出口总额 Imports and Exports | 亿元（100 million yuan） | 27182.5 | 8077.0 | 34009.9 | 5222.6 | 23375.6 | 6161.8 |
| 同比增长 Year-on-year growth | % | 23.9 | 5.6 | 5.5 | 15.9 | 9.3 | 12.0 |
| #出口总额 Exports | 亿元（100 million yuan） | 4878.5 | 3207.2 | 13666.9 | 3395.3 | 13656.9 | 3743.7 |
| 同比增长 Year-on-year growth | % | 23.0 | 8.6 | 4.2 | 17.7 | 7.8 | 12.6 |
| 进口总额 Imports | 亿元（100 million yuan） | 22303.9 | 4869.9 | 20343.1 | 1827.3 | 9718.7 | 2418.2 |
| 同比增长 Year-on-year growth | % | 24.1 | 3.8 | 6.4 | 12.5 | 11.4 | 11.6 |
| 一般公共预算收入 General Public Budget Revenue | 亿元（100 million yuan） | 5785.9 | 2106.2 | 7108.2 | 2265.5 | 2120.0 | 1012.3 |
| 同比增长 Year-on-year growth | % | 6.5 | -8.8 | 7.0 | 0.6 | 11.1 | 8.8 |
| 期末金融机构本外币存款余额 The foreign currency deposit balance of financial institution at year end | 亿元（100 million yuan） | 157092.2 | 30983.2 | 121112.3 | 36887.3 | 30629.4 | 16056.8 |
| 同比增长 Year-on-year growth | % | 9.0 | 0.1 | 7.7 | 5.8 | 7.3 | 6.1 |
| 期末金融机构本外币贷款余额 The foreign currency loan balance of financial institution at year end | 亿元（100 million yuan） | 70483.7 | 34084.9 | 73272.4 | 32247.8 | 27308.3 | 12102.8 |
| 同比增长 Year-on-year growth | % | 1.3 | 7.9 | 9.1 | 13.3 | 9.3 | 7.8 |
| 居民消费价格指数 Consumer Price Index | % | 102.5 | 102.0 | 101.6 | 102.0 | 102.6 | 102.3 |

注：部分城市数据未公布。

Note：Some of the urban income data has not been finalized.

# 青岛西海岸新区统计指标表
QINGDAO WEST COAST NEW DISTRICT STATISTICAL INDICATOR TABLE

| 指　标 | Indicator | 单位 | Unit | 2014 | 2015 | 2016 | 2017 | 2018 |
|---|---|---|---|---|---|---|---|---|
| 年末常住人口 | Resident population at the end of the year | 万人 | 10 000 persons | 148.42 | 149.36 | 151.59 | 153.92 | 157.73 |
| 国民经济各部门就业人员人数 | Number of employed persons in various sectors of the national economy | 万人 | 10 000 persons | 55.6 | 61.2 | 63.2 | 69.3 | 75.8 |
| 公共财政预算收入 | Public Budget Revenue | 亿元 | 100 million yuan | 175.3 | 197.79 | 223.3 | 243.7 | 262.7 |
| 公共财政预算支出 | Public Budget Expenditure | 亿元 | 100 million yuan | 163.53 | 180.48 | 192.7 | 198.5 | 221.7 |
| 生产总值 | Total output value | 亿元 | 100 million yuan | 2404.74 | 2648.79 | 2942.08 | 3212.71 | 3517.07 |
| 第一产业 | Primary Industry | 亿元 | 100 million yuan | 60.24 | 61.7 | 63.26 | 67.45 | 73.7 |
| 第二产业 | Secondary Industry | 亿元 | 100 million yuan | 1219.53 | 1296.64 | 1366.60 | 1474.33 | 1578.20 |
| # 工业 | Industy | 亿元 | 100 million yuan | 1101.49 | 1170.27 | 1234.28 | 1315.48 | 1395.45 |
| 第三产业 | Tertiary Industry | 亿元 | 100 million yuan | 1124.97 | 1290.45 | 1512.22 | 1670.93 | 1865.17 |
| 生产总值增长速度 | Total output value growth rate | % | % | 9.8 | 12.2 | 12.3 | 11.0 | 9.8 |
| 生产总值构成 | Total output value composition | % | % | 100 | 100 | 100 | 100 | 100 |
| 第一产业 | Primary Industry | % | % | 2.5 | 2.3 | 2.2 | 2.1 | 2.1 |
| 第二产业 | Secondary Industry | % | % | 50.7 | 49.0 | 46.4 | 45.9 | 44.9 |
| # 工业 | Industy | % | % | 45.8 | 44.2 | 42.0 | 41.0 | 39.7 |
| 第三产业 | Tertiary Industry | % | % | 46.8 | 48.7 | 51.4 | 52.0 | 53.0 |
| 规模以上工业营业收入 | Above Designated Size | 亿元 | 100 million yuan | 4516.27 | 5203.69 | 4871.86 | 4452.76 | 4264.66 |
| 规模以上工业利润总额 | Total industrial profits above Designated Size | 亿元 | 100 million yuan | 196.12 | 254.43 | 287.42 | 289.22 | 246.69 |
| 房地产开发投资 | Investrment In Real Estate Development | 亿元 | 100 million yuan | 228.11 | 233.16 | 210.75 | 275.54 | 282.98 |
| 社会消费品零售总额 | Total Retail Sales Of Consumer Goods | 亿元 | 100 million yuan | 418.2 | 476.6 | 533.4 | 596.4 | 643.3 |
| 农林牧渔业总产值 | Gross Output Value of Farming, Forestry, Animal Husbandry and Fishery | 亿元 | 100 million yuan | 105.75 | 110.73 | 122.61 | 129.22 | 138.61 |
| 粮食产量 | Grain production | 吨 | ton | 252239 | 237170 | 249128 | 244014 | 263545 |
| 肉类产量 | Meat production | 吨 | ton | 69880 | 68906 | 67625 | 69928 | 72288 |
| 水产品总产量 | Output of Aquatic Products | 吨 | ton | 347712 | 349496 | 349496 | 366200 | 350234 |

注：2014 年 -2017 年农业数据为根据第三次农业普查结果核定修正后数据。

Note: Crop data from 2014 to 2017 are revised based on the results of the third agricultural census.

# 青岛改革开放以来主要指标数据

MAIN INDICATOR DATA SINCE QINGDAO'S REFORM AND OPENING UP

| 指　标 | Indicator | 单位 | Unit | 1978 年 |
|---|---|---|---|---|
| 全市生产总值 | GDP | 亿元 | 100 million yuan | 38.43 |
| 第一产业 | Primary Industry | 亿元 | 100 million yuan | 8.73 |
| 第二产业 | Secondary Industry | 亿元 | 100 million yuan | 20.25 |
| 第三产业 | Tertiary Industry | 亿元 | 100 million yuan | 9.45 |
| 人均生产总值 | Per Capita GDP | 元 | yuan | 663 |
| 一般公共预算收入 | General Public Budget Revenue | 亿元 | 100 million yuan | 13.07 |
| 一般公共预算支出 | General Public Budget Expenditures | 亿元 | 100 million yuan | 1.94 |
| 社会消费品零售总额 | Total Retail Sales of Consumer Goods | 亿元 | 100 million yuan | 10 |
| 外贸进出口总额 | Imports and Exports（excluding central and provincial companies） | 亿美元 | 100 million USD | – |
| #出口总额 | Exports | 亿美元 | 100 million USD | – |
| 实际利用外商直接投资 | Actual Use Of Foreign Direct Investment | 亿美元 | 100 million USD | – |
| 港口吞吐量 | Volume of Freight Handled in Ports | 万吨 | 10 000 tons | 2081 |
| 集装箱吞吐量 | Volume of Containers Handled | 万标箱 | Ten Thousand TEUs | – |
| 金融机构人民币存款余额 | Financial Institution's Rmb Deposit Balance | 亿元 | 100 million yuan | 6.65 |
| 金融机构人民币贷款余额 | Financial Institution's Rmb Loan Balance | 亿元 | 100 million yuan | 29.72 |
| 城镇非私营在岗职工平均工资 | Average Wage Of Non-Private Employees In Urban Areas | 元 | yuan | 584 |
| 城镇居民人均可支配收入 | Per Capita Disposable Income of Urban Households | 元 | yuan | 336 |
| 城镇居民人均消费支出 | Per Capita Consumption Expenditure Of Urban Residents | 元 | yuan | 321 |
| 农村居民人均可支配收入 | Per Capita Consumption Expenditure Of Rural Residents | 元 | yuan | 146 |
| 农村居民人均消费支出 | Per Capltal Net Income of Rural Households | 元 | yuan | 109 |

注：自 2015 年开始，全市城乡住户调查统一使用一体化改革后的数据，与原数据相比，城乡居民收支指标的调查范围和口径均存较大变化。故无法计算“平均每年增长（%）”一项。

Note: Since 2015, the urban and rural households investigation unified the data after the integrated reform, compared with the original data, the investigation scope and the caliber of urban and rural residents' income and expenditure indicators have changed greatly. Therefore, it is impossible to calculate the "average annual growth (%)".

| 1988 年 | 1998 年 | 2008 年 | 2018 年 | 平均每年增长（%）<br>Average Increase Rate（%） |
|---|---|---|---|---|
| 142.87 | 901.19 | 4401.56 | 12001.52 | 11.7 |
| 32.72 | 140.66 | 223.4 | 386.91 | 4.8 |
| 70.32 | 409.6 | 2234.83 | 4850.59 | 12.2 |
| 39.83 | 350.93 | 1943.33 | 6764.02 | 13.0 |
| 2199 | 12443 | 52266 | 128459 | 10.4 |
| 20.12 | 58.0 | 342.44 | 1231.90 | 12.0 |
| 9.39 | 67.9 | 369.41 | 1561.23 | 18.2 |
| 59.1 | 336.9 | 1492.2 | 4842.5 | 16.7 |
| 2.8 | 59.6 | 521.6 | 805 | 20.8 |
| 2.2 | 38.3 | 314.6 | 480 | 19.7 |
| 0.3 | 7.3 | 26.4 | 86.9 | 20.8 |
| 3153 | 7044 | 30029 | 54250 | 8.5 |
| 8.6 | 121.3 | 1037.7 | 1931.5 | 19.8 |
| 75.44 | 818.35 | 4735.38 | 15532.19 | 21.4 |
| 95.54 | 723.92 | 3748.32 | 15194.19 | 16.9 |
| 1862 | 7518 | 30233 | 90840 | 13.4 |
| 1225 | 6542 | 20034 | 50817 | – |
| 1278 | 5567 | 15055 | 32890 | – |
| 820 | 3144 | 7666 | 20820 | – |
| 439 | 2112 | 5083 | 13885 | – |

# 中国统计出版社有限公司最新图书简目

（仅供参考，以实际出版为准）

## 统计资料

| | | |
|---|---|---|
| 中国统计年鉴 | 中国统计摘要 | 中国第三产业统计年鉴 |
| 中国第三次全国农业普查综合资料 | 国际统计年鉴 | 金砖国家联合统计手册 |
| 中国-东盟国家统计手册 | 中国农村统计年鉴 | 中国县域统计年鉴 |
| 中国农产品价格调查年鉴 | 中国城市统计年鉴 | 中国价格统计年鉴 |
| 中国贸易外经统计年鉴 | 中国零售和餐饮连锁企业统计年鉴 | 中国商品交易市场统计年鉴 |
| 大中型批发零售和住宿餐饮企业统计年鉴 | 中国住户调查年鉴 | 中国工业统计年鉴 |
| 中国环境统计年鉴 | 中国能源统计年鉴 | 中国建筑业统计年鉴 |
| 中国房地产统计年鉴 | 中国固定资产投资统计年鉴 | 中国对外直接投资统计公报 |
| 中国人口和就业统计年鉴 | 中国劳动统计年鉴 | 中国社会统计年鉴 |
| 中国科技统计年鉴 | 中国高技术产业统计年鉴 | 全国企业创新调查年鉴 |
| 中国文化及相关产业统计年鉴 | 2018年时间利用调查资料 | 中国妇女儿童状况统计资料 |
| 中国基本单位统计年鉴 | 中国教育统计年鉴 | 中国教育经费统计年鉴 |
| 中国民族统计年鉴 | 中国残疾人事业统计年鉴 | 长江经济带发展统计年鉴 |

## 省级综合统计年鉴系列

北京 天津 河北 山西 内蒙古 辽宁 吉林 黑龙江 上海 江苏 浙江 安徽 福建 江西 山东 河南 湖北 湖南
广东 广西 海南 重庆 四川 贵州 云南 西藏 陕西 甘肃 青海 宁夏 新疆 新疆生产建设兵团

## 市(县)级综合统计年鉴系列

滨海新区 石家庄 唐山 邯郸 保定 沧州 邢台 廊坊 承德 衡水 秦皇岛 张家口 太原 大同 阳泉 长治 晋城
朔州 晋中 运城 忻州 临汾 吕梁 呼和浩特 鄂尔多斯 包头 沈阳 大连 长春 延吉 四平 白山 通化 哈尔滨
齐齐哈尔 黑龙江垦区 上海浦东新区 南京 无锡 徐州 常州 苏州 南通 连云港 淮安 盐城 扬州 镇江 泰州
宿迁 江阴 丹阳 海门 张家港 杭州 宁波 温州 嘉兴 湖州 绍兴 金华 衢州 舟山 台州 丽水 合肥 安庆 福州
厦门 宁德 漳州 龙岩 莆田 泉州 三明 南平 南昌 九江 上饶 新余 抚州 赣州 景德镇 济南 青岛 潍坊 枣庄
潍坊 聊城 郑州 洛阳 平顶山 三门峡 南阳 商丘 信阳 济源 汝州 武汉 十堰 荆州 宜昌 荆门 咸宁 黄冈
长沙 鹰潭 广州 深圳 惠州 东莞 汕尾 湛江 肇庆 南宁 柳州 桂林 贵港 梧州 来宾 河池 防城港 海口 三亚
儋州 成都 内江 贵阳 黔南 毕节 昆明 文山 德宏 西安 延安 安康 铜川 汉中 商洛 银川 兰州 庆阳 乌鲁木齐
昌吉 阿勒泰 兵团一师、二师、三师、四师、六师、七师、八师、十师、十三师、十四师

## 调查年鉴系列

天津 内蒙古 上海 河南 湖北 湖南 广东 广西 重庆 四川 云南 甘肃 宁夏 南宁 贵港 昆明

## 统计方法应用/实用手册

Python数据分析基础（第二版）　医用多元统计分析（第三版）　中华生物统计用表

中国国民经济核算体系（2016）基础知识　国民经济核算初级教程　医学统计学手册

全国统计专业技术资格考试系列考试用书：统计业务知识（第四版修订版）　统计业务知识学习指导与习题

全国统计专业技术资格考试系列考试用书：统计相关知识（第四版）　统计相关知识学习指导与习题

## 统计通俗读物/统计科普图书

领导干部统计知识问答　《防范和惩治统计造假、弄虚作假督察工作规定》辅导读本

统计新媒体运营指南　统计公文知识问答　理解国民账户　中国古代统计史简编

## 重点图书

新中国70年　第三次全国农业普查农作物面积遥感测量图集　中国第四次经济普查年鉴

新编英汉汉英统计大词典　中国国民经济核算体系2016　国民经济行业分类注释

挑大学选专业2019—考研择校指南　挑大学选专业2019—高考志愿填报指南　中华医学统计百科全书